MAGILL'S
SURVEY
OF
AMERICAN
LITERATURE

MAGILL'S SURVEY OF AMERICAN LITERATURE

Volume 1

Abbey–Cormier

Edited by

FRANK N. MAGILL

Marshall Cavendish Corporation
New York • London • Toronto • Sydney • Singapore

Published By
Marshall Cavendish Corporation
2415 Jerusalem Avenue
P.O. Box 587
North Bellmore, New York 11710
United States of America

∞ The paper used in these volumes conforms to the American National Standard for Permanence of Paper for Printed Library Materials, Z39.48-1984.

Library of Congress Cataloging-in-Publication Data
Magill's survey of American literature. Edited by Frank N. Magill.
    p. cm.
  Includes bibliographical references and index.
    1. American literature—Dictionaries. 2. American literature—Bio-bibliography. 3. Authors, American—Biography—Dictionaries. I. Magill, Frank Northen, 1907.
PS21.M34 1991
810.9′0003—dc20
ISBN 1-85435-437-X (set)   91-28113
ISBN 1-85435-438-8 (volume 1)   CIP

Second Printing

PRINTED IN THE UNITED STATES OF AMERICA

PUBLISHER'S NOTE

The six volumes of *Magill's Survey of American Literature* present 190 American writers from the seventeenth to the late twentieth centuries whose lives and work are significant in the literary world of our time. Articles in the set are arranged alphabetically by author. Highlighted ready-reference features guide the reader through each article, beginning with boxed introductory material and continuing with subheadings that aid the reader in retrieving information. Included in most of the essays is a photograph of the author being profiled.

Genres represented include long and short fiction, poetry, drama, and nonfiction. Writers included range from such renowned figures as Nathaniel Hawthorne, Edith Wharton, and Arthur Miller to writers whose work is so recent that its full impact has yet to be known, such as Ann Beattie and T. Coraghessan Boyle. Care has been taken to represent a wide variety of American experiences and voices. Native-American writers N. Scott Momaday and Louise Erdrich appear; African-American writers included range from Ralph Ellison to Amiri Baraka to Alice Walker. Maxine Hong Kingston writes of Chinese Americans, Jimmy Santiago Baca of Mexican Americans; Bharati Mukherjee writes of the Asian immigrant experience.

Also featured are writers who, although their works are widely read by younger readers, are often left out of literary surveys. Writers of young adult fiction include S. E. Hinton, Robert Cormier, and Paul Zindel. The world of science fiction is represented by such authors as Ray Bradbury, Ursula K. Le Guin, and Philip K. Dick. Writers of detective and Western fiction are also included. The humorous stories of Garrison Keillor as well as the horror novels of Stephen King are discussed.

Following the Magill reference tradition, each article begins with ready-reference top matter that presents the date and place of the author's birth and death. A separate boxed section then briefly encapsulates the writer's literary significance. The main text of the article begins with "Biography," a chronological overview of the author's life, with orientation toward his or her literary endeavors. In the "Analysis" section that follows, the author's style, themes, and literary characteristics are discussed; this section can be read independently as an overview of the author's work. Following the analysis are separate sections on individual works by the author. The ordering of these sections is first by genre, then chronological within the genre; each section is introduced by boxed information presenting the date of first publication and a capsule description of the work. The essay concludes with a brief "Summary" and a bibliography that directs the student to books and articles for further study.

Within the essays, literary works mentioned are accompanied by the date of first publication; dates given for plays represent the first major public performance of the work. When titles of foreign works appear in the text, the date of the original foreign publication is given, followed by the English translation title and the date of its first publication. A complete alphabetical list of authors profiled in the set appears at the end of each volume. To aid the reader further, a Glossary of literary terms that appear in the set can also be found at the end of each volume. At the end of volume 6 is an Author Index plus a Title Index that includes all works covered in separate sections within the articles.

We would like to acknowledge the work of the many fine academicians and other writers who contributed to this set. A list of their names and affiliations appears in the front matter of volume 1.

Photograph Credits

Courtesy of Alfred A. Knopf: *James Merrill*. Jules Allen, courtesy of St. Martin's Press: *Ntozake Shange.* Courtesy of American Literature, the Beinecke Rare Book and Manuscript Library, Yale University, and New Directions Publishing Corp.: *H.D.* AP/Wide World Photos: *Amiri Baraka, James M. Cain, Raymond Chandler, Don DeLillo, James T. Farrell, William Gaddis, Mary Gordon, Dashiell Hammett, Robert A. Heinlein, Garrison Keillor, William Kennedy, Jack Kerouac, Stephen King, Harper Lee, Edgar Lee Masters, Carson McCullers, N. Scott Momaday, Theodore Roethke, Neil Simon.* David Attie, courtesy of AP/Wide World Photos: *Lorraine Hansberry.* Jerry Bauer: *Robert Bly, Harold Brodkey, Louise Erdrich, Mary McCarthy, Bernard Malamud, Chaim Potok, Robert Stone.* Lawrence Benton, courtesy of New Directions Publishing Corp.: *Jimmy Santiago Baca.* Tom Berthiaume, courtesy of Farrar, Straus and Giroux: *John Berryman.* The Bettmann Archive: *Samuel R. Delaney, Wallace Stevens.* Hal Boucher, courtesy of Alfred A. Knopf: *Ross Macdonald.* Jane Bown, courtesy of Random House: *Gore Vidal.* Glenn Capers, 1984, courtesy of University of Arizona: *Leslie Marmon Silko.* Dan Carraco, courtesy of North Point Press: *Wendell Berry.* Margaret Chodos, courtesy of HarperCollins*Publishers*: *Ursula Le Guin.* Larry Colwell, courtesy of New Directions: *Henry Miller.* Mariana Cook, courtesy of G. P. Putnam's Sons: *Joseph Heller.* Nancy Crampton: 1981 *John Cheever, Philip Roth,* 1991 *Peter Matthiessen,* 1987 *Walker Percy,* 1988 *Larry Woiwode,* 1982 *Tom Wolfe.* Courtesy of Delacourt Press: *Robert Cormier.* Boris De Rachewiltz, courtesy of New Directions Publishing Corp.: *Ezra Pound.* Michael Dorris, courtesy of Harper & Row Perennial Library: *Louise Erdrich.* Christian Du Bois Larson, courtesy of The Swallow Press and Harcourt Brace & World: *Anaïs Nin.* Quintana Roo Dunne, courtesy of Simon & Schuster: *Joan Didion.* Marion Ettlinger: *Raymond Carver, John Irving, Thomas McGuane.* Copyright Estate of Walker Evans, courtesy of the estate of Walker Evans: *James Agee, Hart Crane.* Leonda Fiske: *Tillie Olsen.* Matthew Foley, courtesy of New Directions Publishing Corp.: *Robert Duncan.* Benjamin Ford, courtesy of Random House: *Ann Beattie.* Davis Freeman, Alfred A. Knopf: *John Updike.* Paul Fusco, courtesy of Magnum Photos, Inc.: *Ken Kesey.* Joel Gardner, courtesy of Alfred A. Knopf: *John Gardner.* Fay Godwin, courtesy of Farrar, Straus and Giroux: *Robert Lowell.* Courtesy of HarperCollins*Publishers*: *Annie Dillard.* Courtesy of the Harvard University Archives: *Henry Adams.* Michael Hendrickson, courtesy of E. P. Dutton, Inc.: *Edward Abbey.* George Holmes, courtesy of HarperCollins*Publishers*: *Allen Ginsberg.* Martha Holmes, courtesy of David Rothenberg Associates: *Sam Shepard.* Ken Howard, courtesy of Bantam Hardcover: 1984 *Louis L'Amour.* David Inhofe, courtesy of Ban-

PUBLISHER'S NOTE

tam, Doubleday, Dell: *S. E. Hinton*. Bruce Jackson, courtesy of New Directions Publishing Corp.: *Robert Creeley*. John Kings, courtesy of Random House: *James Michener*. Jill Krementz, courtesy of G. P. Putnam's Sons: *Kurt Vonnegut, Jr.* Judy Krementz, copyright Washington Post; reprinted with permission of the D.C. Public Library: *Nikki Giovanni*. Kimberly Dawson Kurnizki: *John Knowles, Gloria Naylor*. Brigitte Lacombe, courtesy of Grove Press: *David Mamet*. James Lerager, courtesy of St. Martin's Press: *Ishmael Reed*. Library of Congress: *Edward Albee, Louisa May Alcott, Nelson Algren, Sherwood Anderson, James Baldwin, Ambrose Bierce, Anne Bradstreet, Erskine Caldwell, Truman Capote, Willa Cather, James Fenimore Cooper, Stephen Crane, E. E. Cummings, Emily Dickinson, Theodore Dreiser, Paul Laurence Dunbar, Ralph Waldo Emerson, F. Scott Fitzgerald, Benjamin Franklin, Philip Freneau, Robert Frost, Ellen Glasgow, Bret Harte, Nathaniel Hawthorne, Lillian Hellman, William Dean Howells, Langston Hughes, Zora Neale Hurston, Washington Irving, Henry James, Robinson Jeffers, Sarah Orne Jewett, Sinclair Lewis, Jack London, Henry Wadsworth Longfellow, Norman Mailer, Herman Melville, Marianne Moore, Vladimir Nabokov, Frank Norris, John O'Hara, Edgar Allan Poe, Adrienne Rich, Conrad Richter, Charles Sandburg, Harriet Beecher Stowe, Henry David Thoreau, Mark Twain, Edith Wharton, Thornton Wilder, Thomas Wolfe, Richard Wright*. Christine Lyons: *Paul Zindel*. Joe McTyre, courtesy of Farrar, Straus and Giroux: *Flannery O'Connor*. Dorothy Marder, courtesy of Farrar, Straus and Giroux: *Grace Paley*. Lee Marmon, courtesy of Simon & Schuster: *Larry McMurtry*. Teturo Maruyama, courtesy of Little, Brown and Company: *John Barth*. Michael Montfort, 1990, courtesy of Black Sparrow Press: *Charles Bukowski*. Missouri Historical Society: *Kate Chopin*. Darrow Montgomery: *T. Coraghessan Boyle*. Richard O. Moore, courtesy of Harcourt Brace Jovanovich: *Eudora Welty*. Inge Morath, courtesy of Houghton Mifflin: *Louis Auchincloss*. Inge Morath/Magnum, courtesy of Grove Press: 1987 *Arthur Miller*. Jo Morris, courtesy of HarperCollins*Publishers*: *Wright Morris*. Maria Mulas, courtesy of Alfred A. Knopf: *Toni Morrison*. National Archives: *Ralph Ellison*. The National Portrait Gallery, Smithsonian Institution: *John Dos Passos, Walt Whitman*. Courtesy of New Directions Publishing Corp.: *Djuna Barnes, Nathanael West*. Copyright The Nobel Foundation, courtesy of The Nobel Foundation: *Saul Bellow, T. S. Eliot, William Faulkner, Ernest Hemingway, Eugene O'Neill, John Steinbeck*. Copyright Norman Seeff, courtesy of William Abrahams Books/Dutton : *Joyce Carol Oates*. Cherie Nutting, courtesy of Vintage International: *Paul Bowles*. Julius Ozick, courtesy of Alfred A. Knopf: *Cynthia Ozick*. Courtesy of the Philip K. Dick Society: *Philip K. Dick*. Courtesy of Jayne Anne Philips and Dutton/Seymour Lawrence: *Jayne Anne Philips*. Paul Porter, courtesy of Special Collections, University of Maryland at College Park Libraries: *Katherine Anne Porter*. Hugh Powers, courtesy of Alfred A. Knopf: *J. F. Powers*. Jonathan Price, courtesy of Vintage Contemporaries: *Charles Portis*. Jeff Reinking/Picture Group, courtesy of Harcurt Brace Jovanovich: *Alice Walker*. Jimm Roberts, courtesy of Little, Brown and Company: *Alison Lurie*. Franco Salmoiraghi, courtesy of Alfred A. Knopf: *Maxine Hong Kingston*. Margaret Sartor, courtesy of Atheneum: 1990 *Reynolds Price*. Sam Shaw, courtesy of New Directions Publishing Corp.: *Tennessee Williams*. Courtesy of Gary Snyder and North Point Press: *Gary Snyder*. Eric Stahlbert, 1955, courtesy of the Sophia Smith Collection, Smith College: *Sylvia Plath*. Constance Stuart Larrabee: *Richard Wilbur*. David Styles, courtesy of The Ecco Press: *Cormac McCarthy*. Courtesy of Glendon Swarthout: *Glendon Swarthout*. Arthur Tcholakian, courtesy of the D.C. Public Library: *William Saroyan*. Andrew Unangst, courtesy of G. P. Putnam's Sons: *Frank Herbert*. Courtesy of University of California Press, Berkeley: *Charles Olson*. Thomas Victor: *Elizabeth Bishop, Ray Bradbury, Bharati Mukherjee*. Fred Vuich, Henry Holt and Company: *John Edgar Wideman*. Diana Walker, courtesy of Alfred A. Knopf: *Anne Tyler*. Barbara Walz, courtesy of Random House: *E. L. Doctorow*. Copyright Washington Post; reprinted by permission of the D.C. Public Library: *John Ashbery, James Dickey, William Gibson, J. D. Salinger, Robert Penn Warren*. Erik Weber: *Richard Brautigan*. Irving Wellcome, courtesy of New Directions Publishing Corp.: *William Carlos Williams*. Bill Wittliff, courtesy of HarperCollins*Publishers*: *Donald Barthelme*. Photograph research done in part by Susan Hormuth, Visual Resource Consultant.

CONTRIBUTORS

Patrick Adcock
Henderson State University

Thomas P. Adler
Purdue University

Claudia Emerson Andrews
University of North Carolina—Greensboro

Terry L. Andrews
Rutgers University

Andrew J. Angyal
Elon College

Bryan Aubrey
Maharishi International University

Philip Auslander
Georgia Institute of Technology

James Baird
University of North Texas

Mary H. Barnes
Monmouth College

Dan Barnett
California State University, Chico

Melissa E. Barth
Appalachian State University

Alan Blackstock
University of New Mexico

Jo-Ellen Lipman Boon
Independent Scholar

Harold Branam
Temple University

Gerhard Brand
California State University, Los Angeles

J. R. Broadus
University of North Carolina

Keith H. Brower
Dickinson College

Alan Brown
Livingston University

Molly Brown
Stanford University

Carl Brucker
Arkansas Tech University

Jeffrey L. Buller
Georgia Southern University

Edmund J. Campion
University of Tennessee

Pamela Canal
Independent Scholar

Thomas Carmichael
University of Toronto

Warren J. Carson
University of South Carolina—Spartanburg

Thomas Cassidy
University of Wisconsin—Steven's Point

Leonard Casper
Boston College

Hal Charles
Eastern Kentucky University

C. L. Chua
California State University, Fresno

John J. Conlon
University of Massachusetts at Boston

Mary Virginia Davis
California State University, Sacramento

Frank Day
Clemson University

Bill Delaney
Independent Scholar

James E. Devlin
State University of New York College at Oneonta

Gweneth A. Dunleavy
University of Louisville

Bruce L. Edwards
Bowling Green State University

Clifford Edwards
Fort Hays State University

Robert P. Ellis
Worcester State College

Thomas L. Erskine
Salisbury State University

James Feast
New York University

John W. Fiero
University of Southwestern Louisiana

Edward Fiorelli
St. John's University, New York

Bruce E. Fleming
United States Naval Academy

Robert J. Forman
St. John's University, New York

Carol Franks
Portland State University

Robert L. Gale
University of Pittsburgh

Ann Davison Garbett
Averett College

Jill B. Gidmark
University of Minnesota

Charles Hackenberry
Pennsylvania State University Altoona Campus

Jay L. Halio
University of Delaware

Natalie Harper
Simon's Rock of Bard College

Sharon M. Harris
Temple University

Melanie Hawthorne
Texas A&M University

Terry Heller
Coe College

Joyce E. Henry
Ursinus College

Allen Hibbard
Middle Tennessee State University

Rebecca Stingley Hinton
Miami University

James L. Hodge
Bowdoin College

John R. Holmes
Franciscan University of Steubenville

Edward W. Huffstetler
Bridgewater College

David Huntley
Appalachian State University

Chandice M. Johnson, Jr.
North Dakota State University

Richard S. Keating
United States Air Force Academy

Richard Kelly
University of Tennessee

Paula D. Kopacz
Eastern Kentucky University

Leon Lewis
Appalachian State University

James L. Livingston
Northern Michigan University

Janet Lorenz
Independent Scholar

Reinhart Lutz
University of California, Santa Barbara

Janet McCann
Texas A&M University

Philip McDermott
Independent Scholar

Andrew Macdonald
Loyola University of New Orleans

Gina Macdonald
Loyola University of New Orleans

Edythe M. McGovern
West Los Angeles College

John L. McLean
Morehead State University

A. L. McLeod
Rider University

Marian B. McLeod
Trenton State College

Barry Mann
Independent Scholar

Charles E. May
California State University, Long Beach

Patrick Meanor
State University of New York at Oneonta

Kathleen Mills
Independent Scholar

Christian H. Moe
Southern Illinois University—Carbondale

CONTRIBUTORS

Robert A. Morace
Daemen College

Robert E. Morsberger
California State Polytechnic University, Pomona

Edwin Moses
Bloomsburg University

John M. Muste
Ohio State University

William Nelles
Northwestern State University

Terry Nienhuis
Western Carolina University

John G. Parks
Miami University

David B. Parsell
Lurwau University

Leslie Pearl
Independent Scholar

David Peck
California State University, Long Beach

Robert W. Peckham
Sacred Heart Major Seminary

William E. Pemberton
University of Wisconsin—La Crosse

Charles H. Pullen
Queen's, Ontario, Canada

John D. Raymer
Holy Cross College, Notre Dame

Jere Real
Lynchburg College

Peter J. Reed
University of Minnesota

Rosemary M. Canfield Reisman
Troy State University

Rodney P. Rice
United States Air Force Academy

James W. Robinson, Jr.
Chaminade University

Carl Rollyson
Baruch College, City University of New York

Paul Rosefeldt
University of New Orleans

Gabrielle Rowe
McKendree College

Susan Rusinko
Bloomsburg University

Judith Schnee
University of Massachusetts at Boston
Bentley College

Steven P. Schultz
Independent Scholar

Thomas C. Schunk
University of Wisconsin—Oshkosh

Kenneth Seib
University of Illinois

Barbara Kitt Seidman
Linfield College

R. Baird Shuman
University of Illinois at Urbana-Champaign

Marjorie Smelstor
University of Wisconsin—Eau Claire

Katherine Snipes
Eastern Washington University

Michael Sprinker
State University of New York—Stony Brook

Louise Stone
Bloomsburg University

Gerald H. Strauss
Bloomsburg University

James Sullivan
California State University, Los Angeles

David Sundstrand
Citrus College

Roy Arthur Swanson
University of Wisconsin—Milwaukee

Thomas J. Taylor
Independent Scholar

Terry Theodore
University of North Carolina at Wilmington

Eileen Tess Tyler
United States Naval Academy

George W. Van Devender
Hardin-Simmons University

Steven Weisenburger
University of Kentucky

CONTENTS

EDWARD ABBEY

Born: Home, Pennsylvania
January 29, 1927
Died: Tucson, Arizona
March 14, 1989

Principal Literary Achievement
Abbey is best known for his iconoclastic attacks on the forces of modern society that have encroached on the remaining wilderness areas in America, particularly the mountains and deserts of the Southwest.

Biography
Edward Abbey was at once intensely private and self-revelatory. The facts of his intellectual and professional life are accessible; his private life remains essentially private. He was born and educated in the Allegheny Mountains of Pennsylvania. In the summer of 1944, registration for the draft loomed large on the horizon for American males about to turn eighteen, so the seventeen-year-old Edward Abbey opted for a trip by thumb across the United States before being graduated from high school and swallowed up by the draft. He hitchhiked from Pennsylvania to Seattle, passing through Chicago and Yellowstone National Park. From Seattle, he traveled south through California as far as Bakersfield, then journeyed home by way of Barstow, California; Flagstaff, Arizona; and Albuquerque, New Mexico. He recounts this rite of passage into adulthood in "Hallelujah on the Bum" (1977), an essay filled with the warmth, wonder, and enthusiasm of youthful adventure. The vision of this Western land and its people marked Abbey in an inescapable way. Of his first sight of the Rocky Mountains, he wrote:

> On to Wyoming, where near Greybull I saw for the first time something I had dreamed of seeing for ten years. There on the western horizon, under a hot clear sky, sixty miles away, crowned with snow (in July), was a magical vision, a legend come true: the front range of the Rocky Mountains. An impossible beauty, like a boy's first sight of an undressed girl, the image of those mountains struck a fundamental chord in my imagination that has sounded ever since.

Perhaps nothing that Abbey has written so perfectly captures the intensity and passion of his love for the landscapes of the West. Thus, it is not surprising that the focus of his life and work has been on the preservation of this vision.

Soon after completing high school, Abbey was drafted into the Army. The years following his discharge found him yearning to return to the open spaces of the West. During this period he began to write, publishing his first novel, *Jonathan Troy*, in 1954. Like Abbey, the title character is caught between two worlds, the confining one of the East that he inhabits and the vision of the West, where personal freedom is only attainable in the open spaces of an untrammeled landscape. Troy's escape to the West reflects Abbey's own break with his roots upon moving to New Mexico, where he attended the state university, completing his B.A. in 1951. Abbey then won a Fulbright Scholarship to the University of Edinburgh to study philosophy. Upon returning to the United States, he made an unsuccessful attempt to undertake graduate studies at Yale University. By this time, it was too late; the die had been cast. Abbey was not meant to live and work in the East. He returned to the University of New Mexico to pursue his M.A. In 1956, he published his master's thesis, entitled "Anarchism and the Morality of Violence," and his second novel, *The Brave Cowboy: An Old Tale in a New Time*. Both works examine the nature and effects of violence. In his thesis, Abbey wrestles with the sticky question of when and to what degree violence is justified. In *The Brave Cowboy*, the anachronistic hero, Jack Burns, must cope with the forces of a bureaucratic brutality that employs violence to impose its will as a matter of course. These thematic concerns remain central to Abbey's work.

With the publication of *The Brave Cowboy*, Abbey gained critical and public recognition. The novel was well reviewed and made into a successful motion picture in 1962 under the title *Lonely Are the Brave*, starring Kirk Douglas as anachronistic hero Jack Burns. Unfortunately, Abbey sold his story outright for ten thousand dollars, so his financial gain was small indeed. Money problems continued to be a part of Abbey's life. He worked as a United States National Parks ranger and as a fire lookout for the forest service, and he did occasional stints as a college teacher. Although he could be considered a prolific writer, he was not to be widely read until the publication of *Desert Solitaire: A Season in the Wilderness* (1968), a collection of personal reflections that remains popular among students of nature, environmentalists, and lovers of the Western landscape.

As Abbey witnessed the encroachment of strip mining, development, and the beginning of what he termed "industrial tourism," his work took on a sense of desperation. In *Fire on the Mountain* (1962), the central character struggles against the forces of a faceless bureaucracy seeking to turn his ranch into a weapons test site. In the 1975 novel *The Monkey Wrench Gang*, the socially disenfranchised characters go on quixotic raids against the forces of development, burning billboards and plotting the destruction of the Glen Canyon Dam. In *Good News* (1980), set in the near future, ignorance and folly have prevailed; the landscape is blighted, and the government has become an expression of a darkly totalitarian state fueled by greed. The increasing rage and despair of the latter work is reflective of Abbey's own perception of the human condition. Despite his efforts to maintain a glimmer of hope, he reveals a misanthropic disgust with the "featherless biped" so intent on destroying his beloved West and the planet itself. As early as 1967, in the introduction to *Desert Solitaire*, he wrote that his work was an elegy to a lost land; he told the reader, "You're holding a tombstone in your hands."

Yet despite his pronouncements that the battle was already lost, he continued to write, to exhort his readers to action, and to be hopeful in the face of hopelessness. In his last major work, *The Fool's Progress* (1988), Abbey chronicles the adventures of a man suffering from a mortal ailment desperately trying to go home before dying. The main character, Henry Lightcap, reflects on the misadventures of his life. Retrospectively, one can see that the novel is thinly disguised autobiography written by a dying author trying to sum up his own efforts, to settle accounts before being overtaken by death. Abbey is nothing if not contradictory, for the book is both outrageously funny and painfully honest. It honors the love of life and makes one glad that Edward Abbey was here to make his readers think, to make them angry, and above all to be passionate in the defense of beauty.

It must be noted that, like it or not, Abbey has become a cult hero to radical environmental groups. It was a mantle that he himself never put on. He insisted on being an individual; above all, he despised "group-think." Yet his voice remains. One of his last works, published posthumously, is fittingly entitled *A Voice Crying in the Wilderness (Vox Clamantis in Deserto): Notes from a Secret Journal* (1990).

Analysis

It is tempting to see Edward Abbey as an itinerant preacher, with "love" tattooed on one hand and "hate" on the other. The dichotomy of his preferences appears to be crystal clear. Wilderness is good. Civilization, manifesting itself in the form of urban sprawl and industrialization, is bad. Stop the latter and preserve the former. Indeed, he has been dismissed as an "eco-crank," a leftover Luddite, and an anarchist, but this is to take the easy way out, for Abbey's voice challenges the common assumptions that modern society has come to accept complacently about the nature of progress and the idea of the "good life."

Abbey's first novel, *Jonathan Troy*, reveals the unhappy contrast between the decadent civilization of the East and the promising wilderness of the West. The title character encounters conflict and disappointment in his native Pennsylvania—squalor and hopelessness in the mining towns and barbarism in the backwoods. It is a place that suffers from rot, a rot he must escape by flight to the liberating landscape of the West, where there is room for the individual to be free.

The Brave Cowboy, Abbey's second novel, further develops the contrast between the landscape of the wilderness and the contamination of urban life established in *Jonathan Troy*. Jack Burns, the cowboy of the title, is one of Abbey's most memorable characters. He loves the freedom of his life as an itinerant herder, a life characterized by physical labor, personal freedom, and respect for the land, but he is a man out of step with his time. Abbey sends his hero riding into Duke City on horseback. Burns is a happy-go-lucky sort who hates fences, highways, and urban sprawl. When he comes to a fence, he cheerfully cuts it. When he comes to a highway, he and his horse have difficulty, but they manage to cross it. Burns lives by a personal code that has nothing to do with the constraints of modern civilization.

When Jack Burns comes into conflict with the law and is asked to produce his identification cards, he replies, "Don't have none. Don't need none. I already know who I am." To know Jack Burns is to like him, but he is doomed by his refusal to knuckle under to the forces of change. When he and his beloved little mare are run down on the highway by a truck carrying a load of bathroom fixtures, it is tragic but not unexpected. The message is clear. There is no room for a Jack Burns and the way of life he represents in urban, industrial society. The future belongs to the developers and bureaucrats who are the faceless representatives of modern repression.

The notion of government as an expression of the violent repression of the individual is more explicit in *Fire on the Mountain*. The United States government wants John Vogelin's ranch for a weapons testing site. Vogelin refuses to sell. He sees himself as a part of the land upon which he has lived his life. The conflict is intrinsically unequal, for it pits the collective power of government against the individual. Like Burns, Vogelin is doomed to perish in the defense of a lost cause, and like Burns he must resist the inevitable or lose his essential nature, the very core of his individuality.

The publication of *Desert Solitaire*, a series of reflective essays centered on Abbey's experiences as a park ranger at Arches National Monument, propelled Abbey into public attention and the center of controversy. Unconfined by the strictures of fiction, Abbey speaks in his own voice, and it is a voice that soars in lyrical praise of the land he loves and drips with contempt for the destructive forces of industrial and commercial development. For Abbey, the bringing of roads and automobiles into the wilderness means the beginning of its end and the onset of what he calls "industrial tourism."

The Monkey Wrench Gang might be considered a prescription for sedition, insurrection, and sabotage. It contains detailed descriptions of procedures for destroying earth-moving equipment and using explosives to destroy bridges. It counsels the destruction of private property in defense of the wilderness and the burning of billboards in the name of preserving beauty. His characters are fueled by rage against a society that would trade profit in the present against the future of the remaining wilderness; they believe their actions to be not only justified but also essential. Doc, Hayduke, Seldom Seen Smith, and Bonnie are fragments of Abbey that take action against an industrial society bent on destruction of the land. In *Desert Solitaire*, Abbey insisted that "wilderness is not a luxury but a necessity of the human spirit, and as vital to our lives as water and good bread."

In both his later fiction and nonfiction, Abbey's voice frequently becomes strident. The essays collected in *The Journey Home: Some Words in Defense of the American West* (1977) and *Abbey's Road* (1979) repeatedly lash out in furious anger or drop into despair. In *Good News*, set in a dark and grim future, both the land and the individual have fallen victim to the pervasive power of greed, the inevitable outcome when government becomes the tool of industrialism.

His last major work, *The Fool's Progress*, is transparently autobiographical, a darkly comic tale of a dying man wandering across the damaged landscape of America and the damaged landscape of his own life. The voice of Henry Holyoak Lightcap is one of comic despair. He is an irascible antihero who has an opinion about everything from French cuisine to feminism. Like his creator, for whom he speaks, Lightcap raises offensiveness to an art form. Nobody's cows are sacred. Nothing escapes his scathing observations, including himself. Lightcap's journey is filled with flashes of brilliance and a clarity of vision that is at once comical and deeply disturbing, for behind Lightcap's lament is a sense of loss, not so much for himself as for a United States that has lost its way—its land destroyed by rapacious development, its language debased by jargon, and its character dominated by loveless materialism. Yet despite the disquieting presence of impending death, Lightcap's life has been a joyous one, for he has fought the good fight, loved immoderately, and been loved in return. It remains to be seen whether *The Fool's Progress* will stand the test of time, but it surely lives up to the subtitle of its paperback edition: *An Honest Novel*.

DESERT SOLITAIRE

First published: 1969
Type of work: Essays

> Abbey's iconoclastic reflections on his experiences as a park ranger at Arches National Monument touch on everything from rattlesnakes to philosophy.

Desert Solitaire: A Season in the Wilderness is the work for which Edward Abbey is best known and by which he is most frequently defined. It contains his views on a variety of subjects, from the problems of the United States Park Service to an angry indictment of the evils of technology masquerading under the guise of progress. No voice is more eloquent in the praise of America's remaining wilderness nor more vitriolic in attacking those who would exploit and destroy it for profit.

In the introduction to *Desert Solitaire*, Abbey informs his readers that he has combined the experiences of three summers spent as a park ranger at Arches National Monument into one for the sake of narrative consistency. He writes that the first two summers were good but that the last summer was marred by the introduction of what he terms "industrial tourism." For Abbey, the tourist in the automobile (worse yet, in the huge recreational vehicle) spells the end of the wilderness spirit. Abbey's ambivalent stance toward the tourists, ostensibly fellow lovers of the outback, reflects the work's central dichotomy. Abbey's eloquent voice describes the beauty of the desert landscape, only to pause on the intrusion of industry and commerce into one of the last remaining wilderness areas in the United States.

The first sentence of *Desert Solitaire* declares, "This is the most beautiful place on earth." Although Abbey believes that the wilderness is as close as one can come to something sacred, his view is not simplistic. He sees wilderness as essential to the quality of human life. His quarrel is not with civilization itself but with civilization made manifest as industrial technology thrust on the physical and spiritual landscape of the human condition:

> A civilization which destroys what little remains of the wild, the spare, the original, is cutting itself off from its origins and betraying the principle of civilization itself.

Although Abbey is not a naturalist, *Desert Solitaire* is filled with the observations of the trained eye. He makes scientific observation serve the eloquence of his prose. The sureness of the scientific landscape lends validity to the thrust of his ideas. Nowhere in the book is the power of his prose or the sureness of his eye more apparent than in the chapter entitled "Down the River."

For Abbey, the construction of the Glen Canyon Dam was one of the great sins of American society. In a discussion of human failings, he suggests that "original sin, the true original sin, is the blind destruction for the sake of greed of this natural paradise which lies all around us—if only we were worthy of it." The rafting trip he and his friend Ralph Newcomb take down the Colorado River through Glen Canyon just before it is flooded under the waters of Lake Powell becomes a song of lamentation for a lost Eden. He intersperses the tale of their journey with excerpts from the journals of Major John Wesley Powell, who was the first white man to explore the Colorado River through Glen Canyon and the Grand Canyon. Despite the deprivation and hardships he experienced, Powell's journals are filled with wonder. Abbey's voice joins Powell's, as he too pauses on the untouched beauty of the place: the shimmering waterfalls, whose mists create rainbows across the red sandstone sides of the canyon, the changing sounds of the river on its journey to the Sea of Cortez, the shifting patterns of the sky, and the voices of the wildlife soon to be displaced by rising waters. The landscape of the canyon becomes a part of the landscape of the mind. As Abbey and Newcomb are swept past side canyons beckoning for exploration, they are aware that the canyons will remain unexplored—at least by them, their children, or their children's children.

Abbey and Newcomb camp at the mouth of the Escalante River, where it joins the Colorado. Newcomb remains behind to fish for catfish while the adventurous Abbey explores upstream. He wanders up the labyrinthine canyon past untouched cliff dwellings of the Anasazi, the ancient people who inhabited the land before the Navajo. He realizes that these too will be submerged under the flooding water of the Colorado. Moreover, Abbey points out that the waters of Lake Powell will irrigate no land, will grow no crops. Instead, the trapped water will produce power—power to make possible the continued urban sprawl of Phoenix and Albuquerque—and provide an aquatic playground for well-to-do suburbanites, whose noisy powerboats will drown out the cry of the red-tailed hawk, the calls of the killdeer and sandpiper.

When he returns down the canyon at nightfall to rejoin his fellow adventurer Newcomb, he is greeted by the smell of cooking catfish and the night sounds of the river. He reflects that this is all the paradise that is needed. The beauty of the place is heartbreaking, as is the tragedy of its imminent disappearance under mud and water. As Abbey and Newcomb approach the construction zone of the dam, a large sign that Abbey derisively dubs "first billboard erected in Glen Canyon" reminds them that government in the service of greed is willing to prosecute those who would trespass on the march of progress. The lyricism of Abbey's prose captures the mind and imagination; the force of his passion invites the reader to share his outrage. The temple has been profaned by the money changers, and one is invited to help drive them out.

Abbey's journey is spiritual as well as physical. He probes the boundaries of his beliefs. He searches for divinity among the rocks and canyons and finds it lacking. He muses that he suspects that the surface of reality is also its essence. Yet he resists the temptation to remake nature into a more comforting pattern. He refuses to succumb to the idea that human nature is special and separate from the natural environment, from the earth itself. Thus the desert, the wilderness, becomes a part of the temple of existence—an Edenic landscape and a part of that primeval source from which humans spring and to which they return. Abbey discovers the nature of his belief in his love of the land. He proclaims, "I am not an atheist, but an earthiest. Be true to the earth."

Near the confluence of the Green and Colorado rivers there is a labyrinthine landscape called the Maze. It held a particular place of affection in Abbey's heart, for he considered it one of the last places that was truly *terra incognita*—a place unmapped, untrodden by the foot of the casual tourist. Much like Abbey, it resists the domestication of being fully known, preserving its integrity and the mystery of its spirit; it is part of the voice that cries in the wilderness.

Summary

The most frequent criticisms of *Desert Solitaire* are that it is contradictory, inconsistent, excessive, and angry—charges which are largely true. Yet such criticism misses the point on two scores. Abbey's work reflects the complexities of the human condition, which is filled with contradiction, inconsistency, folly, and anger more often than not. Moreover, such criticism fails to see that Abbey's work is deliberately provocative. If he resorts to invective, he provokes response. When he reviles human behavior, it is to save humanity from itself. In the posthumously published volume *A Voice Crying in the Wilderness*, Abbey writes that "love implies anger. The man who is angered by nothing cares about nothing."

Bibliography

Hepworth, James, and Gregory McNamee, eds. *Resist Much, Obey Little: Some Notes on Edward Abbey*. Salt Lake City, Utah: Dream Garden Press, 1985.

Lyon, Thomas J. "The Nature Essay in the West." In *A Literary History of the American West*. Fort Worth: Texas Christian University Press, 1987.

McCann, Garth. *Edward Abbey*. Boise, Idaho: Boise State University Press, 1977.

Ronald, Ann. *The New West of Edward Abbey.* Albuquerque: University of New Mexico Press, 1982.

Standiford, Les. "Desert Places: An Exchange with Edward Abbey." *Western Review* 3 (Winter, 1966): 58-62.

Teale, Edwin Way. "Making the Wild Scene." *The New York Times Book Review,* January 28, 1968, p. 7.

David Sundstrand

HENRY ADAMS

Born: Boston, Massachusetts
February 16, 1838
Died: Washington, D.C.
March 26, 1918

Principal Literary Achievement

Adams' literary work, which is crowned by his internationally acclaimed autobiography, depicts the multiple challenges of the twentieth century against the backdrop of earlier ages.

Biography

Henry Brooks Adams, who dropped his middle name at age thirty-two, was born in Boston, Massachusetts, on February 16, 1838, the child of the writer and politician Charles Francis Adams and the homemaker Abigail Brooks Adams. The fourth of seven children, Henry came from an impressive New England family: He was grandson to John Quincy Adams, who was still alive during his childhood, and great grandson to John Adams; both men had been American presidents. This legacy of achievement bestowed a lifelong, influential sense of familial obligation on Adams at a very early age.

While young, Henry Adams, like his siblings, profited immensely from the liberal and intellectual atmosphere at home. By opening his huge library to him, his father gave Henry early access to works of literature and history; soon, the quiet and observant boy watched his father work and converse with his political friends. Adams entered Harvard College in 1854 and was graduated with a bachelor of arts degree in 1858. Looking back later, Adams did not think Harvard worthwhile; however, it gave him the intellectual background common to the elite of his time. The new *Harvard Magazine* also offered him an outlet for his first writing and awarded him with its editorship.

After graduation, Adams went to Europe, where, while writing for the *Boston Daily Courier* in 1860, he scored a minor coup with an interview of Italian rebel leader Giuseppe Garibaldi. After his move to Washington, D.C., in the fall of 1860, Adams matched his writing powers with his interest in politics. As private secretary to his father, a congressman, he combined access to information and journalistic skill in his work for the Bostonian *Daily Advertiser*. "The Great Secession Winter, 1860-1861," was his dramatic summary of the secession of the South.

The appointment of his father as minister to the English court in 1861 gave his son an inside view of global politics and a larger share of responsibility. Working for a while as an anonymous correspondent for *The New York Times*, Adams soon began to broaden the scope of his pen to move beyond politics to science, history, and economics. Combining a journalist's eye for the topical with a scholar's emphasis on knowledge and intellectual vigor, his articles soon attracted notice within the transatlantic intellectual community.

Adams' return to the United States in 1868 saw him becoming an important political journalist in Washington, where he wrote for reform and lambasted corruption. A few years later, however, he followed familial advice by accepting the professorship of medieval history at Harvard. From then on, his involvement in politics would remain indirect: Even though he continued to comment on current issues as outspoken writer and as editor of the *North American Review* from 1870 to 1876, he would never hold political office.

Adams married Miriam "Clover" Hooper in 1872. He resigned from Harvard in 1877 to go back to Washington to write *The Life of Albert Gallatin* (1879), the biography of President Thomas Jefferson's secretary of the treasury, whom Adams celebrated for his moral uprightness. Moving directly across from the White House in 1879, then relocating a few yards down the street in 1885, Henry Adams made his home the social center for an exclusive group of influential friends. Based there, he became an incessant traveler and would see the Far East, the South Seas, and the Caribbean; further, he undertook regular visits to Europe that, from 1899 to 1911, included annual summer stays in Paris.

His intimate knowledge of power politics made Henry Adams' first (anonymously published) satire, *Democracy: An American Novel*, an instant success in 1880. A second work, *Esther: A Novel*, followed in 1884, but Adams' prohibition of all advertisement made it virtually unknown to the public. The suicide of his wife, with whom he had had a loving marriage, on December 6, 1885, visibly shook Adams. The young Elizabeth Cameron, wife of an elderly senator, already had been a friend of the family; now, she and Adams grew closer. Throughout their ensuing years as friends, however, they, according to all sources, never took their intense relationship beyond a platonic level.

The final publication of Adams' great historical masterwork in nine volumes, the *History of the United States During the Administrations of Thomas Jefferson and James Madison*, occurred in 1889 and 1891; it was greeted with great critical acclaim and was widely popular. With the completion of this gigantic work, Adams embarked on a two-year journey to the South Seas and Europe, during which he must have finally decided to remain only friends with Elizabeth Cameron. Back in Washington in 1892, he completed a promised biography. In a manner that would become typical, he privately printed *Memoirs of Marau Taaroa, Last Queen of Tahiti* for his friends in 1893 (revised in 1901 and published in 1947).

A first visit to the cathedrals of Normandy in 1895 sparked the privately printed *Mont-Saint-Michel and Chartres* of 1904 (revised in 1912 and published in 1913);

Adams presents an imaginary "niece" with a grand tour of the architectural master-pieces of Norman France. In 1907, he printed for his friends *The Education of Henry Adams* (published in revised form in 1918). In this, his most famous work, the author struggles with the implied promise of his life and his apparent "failure" to live up to it; his autobiography has become one of the classic texts of American literature. His final work, *The Life of George Cabot Lodge* (1911), is a biography of a close friend. After a stroke in 1912, Adams recovered sufficiently to travel again in 1913. The outbreak of World War I found him in Paris, where he took leave of Elizabeth Cameron. Shortly after his eightieth birthday, he died in his sleep in his home in Washington on March 26, 1918.

Analysis

His familial heritage seemed to destine Henry Adams for a life in politics; how-ever, he discovered that the ideals of the past were no longer applicable to the reali-ties of a modern mass democracy in which alliance and obligation to a political party seemed to eclipse independent statesmanship. Unwilling to adapt, Adams turned from active participation in politics to a literary and scholarly career and became a brilliant, highly moral, and idealistic observer of the public life of the United States on the verge of entering the twentieth century. Adams' great interest in politics is never far from the forefront of his writing, and it comes as no surprise that his first piece of fiction, *Democracy: An American Novel*, tests the inner strength of his heroine, Madeleine Lee, to run the maze of power-obsessed Washington while try-ing to keep her morals intact and her ideals uncompromised. Adams had had ample opportunity to study his subject; his later autobiography, *The Education of Henry Adams*, is full of instances when he received a practical "education" in the corrupt means of contemporary power politics.

The crucial point that emerges in both fiction and autobiography is Adams' firm conviction (validated in principle by modern research) that the then-current system of partisan appointments led to an undignified run on offices with the onset of every new federal administration. With a keen eye on the abuses of the system, which Adams had observed with a wide-awake intelligence and well-trained moral sen-sitivity, and which he had lambasted directly in his earlier political writing, he suc-ceeded in making *Democracy: An American Novel* a powerful mirror of the ills of a system which had lost its earlier ideals in the quagmire of party politics.

Thus, the central question expressed directly in his first novel, and strongly im-plied in his autobiography, is whether a qualified person should compromise in or-der to achieve a position of power from which he or she may do some common good, or whether the risk of contaminating one's ideals is too high a price to pay. The fictional Madeleine Lee flees the arms of a corrupt senator who tempts her with power; the Henry Adams of his autobiography decides that "failure" to achieve political office is the only thing for which his idealistic and moral education has fitted him to suffer. The topic is again taken up in his 1895 reflection "Buddha and Brahma" (published in 1915), in which Adams' reworking of an Eastern legend privileges neither the active nor the contemplative life.

Critics have charged that much of Adams' disaffection with the American style of politicking was rooted in his unwillingness to compromise and his somewhat elitist tendency to remain aloof. His friend Justice Oliver Wendell Holmes once put it thus: "If the country had put him on a pedestal, I think Henry Adams with his gifts could have rendered distinguished public service. . . . He wanted it handed to him on a silver platter." Yet there is something of the power of the idealist in Adams' writing, and it is the finely honed ironic style and superb wit that accompany his observer point of view that give his works their unique voice. By keeping himself free to watch and analyze, Adams allowed his art to develop a sureness of touch, successfully conveying his critical opinions in a graceful and exciting manner—a style which would work equally well when he examined, for example, the topic of religion, as he did in his second novel, *Esther.*

Further, Adams' disgust at political corruption is not only the thematic concern of his literary work; it also looms large—indeed, it is the trademark—of his rich political and historical writing. Endowed with a brilliant analytical mind, and traveling widely from his dearly cultivated home base across from the White House, Adams was in a privileged position to see and analyze the dramatic shifts in power and culture that technology and industrialization brought following the Civil War, both in the United States and all over the globe.

Increasingly concerned with the breathtaking tempo with which these changes were happening wherever he placed his foot, be it the then-popular industrial "World" exhibitions, the Westernized islands of the South Seas, or the rapidly technologized Western Europe lying cheek by jowl with the inert giant of czarist Russia, Henry Adams began looking for a means of understanding and rationalizing what was happening. Toward the end of the century, he became convinced that the future would hold no more fixed truths or unifying ideas that could make sense of the increasingly fragmented "multiverse" he saw developing. For Adams, twentieth century multiplicity extended to all fields of human endeavor, ranging from science to economics to religion, and the centrifugal forces of unfettered progress threatened to tear apart what was left of historic systems.

Against this backdrop, a first visit to Norman France in 1895 offered Adams a vision of a time in history when spiritual unity was perfect and humanity lived in harmony with God and the cosmos. From his repeated travels to the abbeys and cathedrals of northern France, Adams created his *Mont-Saint-Michel and Chartres,* intended as a travel guide for his friends, but developed into an artistic statement offering an answer to the troubling present. Adams planned this work, which he subtitled "A Study in Thirteenth Century Unity," to stand alongside *The Education of Henry Adams,* which he gave the subtitle "A Study in Twentieth Century Multiplicity" to make obvious their close thematic relationship.

In these late works, Adams attached the different forces governing the thirteenth and twentieth centuries to the two central symbols of the Virgin Mary and the technological wonder of the dynamo; he also put the conflict into poetic form with his splendid "Prayer to the Virgin of Chartres" (published posthumously in 1920). In his autobiography, the dynamo epitomizes the accelerating dynamic of change in the Western world and finely dramatizes the author's frustrated apprehension of a process which threatens to sweep away history itself. The Virgin, in *Mont-Saint-Michel and Chartres*, becomes synonymous with Adams' lifelong longing for a center that will hold:

> She [the Virgin] never calls for sympathy by hysterical appeals to our feelings; she does not even altogether command, but rather accepts the voluntary, unquestioning, unhesitating, instinctive faith, love and devotion of mankind. She will accept ours, and we have not the heart to refuse it; we have not even the right, for we are her guests.

DEMOCRACY

First published: 1880
Type of work: Novel

Tempted to gain immense political power by marrying a ruthless and corrupt senator, the heroine decides for morality and rejects him.

Because of the sarcastic critique of his contemporary Washington which his first novel offered, Henry Adams decided to publish *Democracy: An American Novel* anonymously; he succeeded in keeping his secret to his death and continued to move in the society whose moral flaws and rampant corruption he had exposed with such incisiveness.

As the novel opens, the thirty-year-old Madeleine (Mrs. Lightfoot) Lee decides to go to Washington, D.C., to observe the play of power politics in an effort to overcome the sense of hollowness with which the death of her husband, the Southerner Lightfoot Lee, and her infant baby have filled her. Clearly modeled after both the author and his wife, Miriam "Clover" Adams, Madeleine Lee has independent means and great social charm, and she is inevitably drawn to "the action of primary forces," "the machinery of society, at work," thus echoing one of Henry Adams' personal longings. Further, the fact that Madeleine's arrival comes after a disappointing series of attempts to make herself and her inherited fortune useful to society is a fine play on the author's own, most burning obsessions; her frustrations with the products of higher education parallel the author's recent resignation from Harvard University in 1877; and she moves to a "newly hired house on Lafayette Square" opposite the White House, effectively next door to Adams' own. Most important, her sarcastic wit and ironic self-detachment from the political jungle she observes are the voice of Henry Adams himself.

In her endeavor to see "POWER" at work, Madeleine is aided by her distant relation, the forty-one-year-old Southern veteran turned lawyer John Carrington, who introduces her to the political powerhouse Senator Silas P. Ratcliffe, the "Prairie

Giant of Peonia." While her younger sister Sybil Ross helps to make her salon a success, a variety of minor characters are introduced, all typical of people wrapped up in the machinations at the Capitol.

The inauguration of a new president, a masterful composite caricature of President Ulysses S. Grant and the young Abraham Lincoln, sets in motion the game as everybody begins hustling for appointments and political power. After their initial sizzling meeting at a political dinner, Adams lets Ratcliffe, a fiftyish widower of considerable attraction, charm himself into Madeleine's confidence while she dreams of using power to reform this appallingly corrupt system. Asking her for political advice, Ratcliffe offers Madeleine a first draught of power; she still shies away from the responsibility that comes with it.

Carefully worming his way into the confidence of the bumbling new president, Ratcliffe is equally adept at enticing Madeleine, whom society begins to see as a potential occupant of the White House if she chooses the ambitious senator for a husband. In the Southerner Carrington, however, Adams has created a central conscience who is aided in his destruction of Ratcliffe's pretensions of morality by the accident of privileged knowledge of the latter's evil deeds.

During a carefully set excursion to the tomb of George Washington, who rather obviously stands for a better, moral America now betrayed by politicians, Carrington brings Ratcliffe to a first admission of having instrumented political fraud. The latter fires back, however, and sends Carrington on a distracting mission to Mexico. Yet Carrington's alliance with Sybil Ross thwarts Ratcliffe, whose proposal of marriage is delayed until the two sisters have a private heart-to-heart talk.

What began as a political satire now becomes a romantic drama as, critics have insisted, the characters develop a life of their own and draw the reader into their conflicts. Presented with final evidence of Ratcliffe's corruption, Madeleine Lee confronts him the morning after his proposal and is given the opportunity to reject soundly his Machiavellian belief that the end—the welfare of himself and his party, in which he subsumes that of the nation—justifies the dirty means he has employed. Rejected (and physically assaulted by a minor character), Ratcliffe receives a thorough dose of poetic justice and is left abandoned by the time of the epilogue, a letter of Sybil's to Carrington, in which she hints at possible success for his proposal to the purified heroine.

While the romantic plot of the novel is somewhat conventional and the rejection of Silas Ratcliffe comes as no surprise, Adams nevertheless delivers an interesting social satire. His well-drawn characters indeed come alive once their problems take center stage, and the political conflict moves toward a more universal clash between morals and ambition. Adams' contemporary critics rather liked the novel, which they compared to the fiction of Henry James and Anthony Trollope; it is still regarded as a minor achievement that can capture a modern reader interested in its central conflict.

MONT-SAINT-MICHEL AND CHARTRES

First published: 1913 (privately printed, 1904)
Type of work: Travel literature

Presenting the architectural masterpieces of medieval northern France, the author combines his description with reflections on the history of the period.

Initially written only for a small circle of friends, *Mont-Saint-Michel and Chartres* became so popular that Adams finally consented to have the American Institute of Architects publish a trade edition in 1913. The work's thought-provoking mixture of presentation of the religious monuments of medieval Normandy and the author's intelligent and often idiosyncratic reflections on the history and philosophy of a bygone era (and their potential applications to his own time, the early twentieth century) have lost nothing of their power to fascinate a reader.

Mont-Saint-Michel and Chartres opens with a powerful portrait of the Abbey of Saint Michael on the northern coast of France. As is the case throughout the text, the physical description of the abbey and its features is embedded in Adams' narration of the history of the place. In a move perhaps typical for the American view of Europe of the time, Adams tries to entice his readers into the narrative further by telling of the Norman migration across the English Channel into England after the battle of Hastings and then of the eventual immigration of the descendants of the builders of Mont Saint Michel to the New World, where they would become Adams' ancestors.

The oldest surviving parts of the abbey church serve as the starting point for Adams' reflections on the history, culture, and spiritual mindset of the eleventh century. In what is clearly his own reading, Adams sees the century united in its "masculine" Christian belief in power, heroic battle, and a philosophic materialism exemplified by the Romanesque style of architecture. Contemporary and later historians often have disagreed with this, and other of Adams' views, stressing disunity and civic strife where he saw harmony and community. Although later critics stressed individual ambition as central to the age, Adams' personalized account of one of the abbots is still in general accordance with the modern picture:

> One might linger over Abbot Robert of Torigny, who was a very great man in his day, and an especially great architect, but too ambitious. All his work, including the two towers [for Mont Saint Michel], crumbled and fell for want of proper support.

Thus, Adams' fascinating travel guide may still serve as one possible approach to the era; his own disclaimers that he writes for an intelligent and interested tourist, rather than crusty scholars, is the best antidote when his vision collides with treatments that stress abstract historic fact over feeling.

From the abbey church on the mount, the narrative moves to the great cathedral of Chartres near Paris. There, a fascinatingly detailed and extremely loving account of the outstanding features of the building captures the imagination of the reader, who is introduced to art still in existence in France. Again, the material objects are brought to life as Adams begins to render his interpretation of the meaning of this great architectural masterpiece:

> The Church at Chartres belonged not to the people, not to the priesthood, and not even to Rome; it belonged to the Virgin [Mary].

The cult of the Virgin Mary, whose "fetish power" has overcome the masculine obsession with God and his fiery Archangel Michael that is celebrated at Mount Saint Michel, is for Adams central for the period of the Transition Gothic of the twelfth century in France. A deep "feminine" mysticism has replaced rationalism, he says, and the veneration of the Virgin bestows a deep sense of unity on its culture—a unity, Adams is quick to point out, that his own early twentieth century has lost forever.

From the deeply sympathetic discussion of Chartres, Adams moves to show the depth of the cult of the Virgin in the medieval world. In the chapter "Les Miracles de Notre Dame" (the miracles of Our Lady), Adams guides the reader through a compilation of anecdotes and historical material enriched by his quotation and translation of medieval French texts related to his topic.

To conclude his spiritual and geographical tour of medieval northern France, Henry Adams adds three chapters dealing with the philosophy of the age. "Abelard" deals with the famous abbot and schoolmaster of that name, whose central debate with another scholar is playfully rendered by Adams much in the style of a senatorial debate in the Capitol. A chapter on the mystics of the twelfth century, among whom Francis of Assisi stands out, precedes his final discussion of Thomas Aquinas. For Adams, Aquinas presents the terminal point of scholastic philosophy; from his religious premises, nothing more than his attempted synthesis of faith and reason could be achieved. Adams directs his reader to then-current problems in theoretical physics, where people struggled again with the issues of unity versus multiplicity in the order of the cosmos.

What started out as a travel guide, then, has become a philosophical meditation on the state of the universe by the time Adams finishes *Mont-Saint-Michel and Chartres.* Even though his reading of French medieval history and culture has been criticized, Adams' vision of an age so different from an increasingly fragmented twentieth century remains a fascinating journey into a foreign country and a past mind-set. In Adams' celebration of a gentle, unifying Virgin, the reader can see a deep longing for a world different from that encountered at home in Washington, across the street from the White House.

THE EDUCATION OF HENRY ADAMS

First published: 1918 (privately printed, 1907)
Type of work: Autobiography

Obsessed with an apparent "failure" to be as successful as his ancestors, Henry Adams insists that his education did not prepare him for the rough reality of a new century.

The Education of Henry Adams, the most famous work of its author, was originally intended only for a small audience; after its posthumous publication in 1918, it promptly won the prestigious Pulitzer Prize in 1919, and it is still regarded as a masterpiece of American literature.

At the core of Adams' autobiography lies his concern that his education was rooted in the eighteenth century and thus was of little value in preparing the boy to become a success in what Adams calls the "twentieth" century (actually the second half of the nineteenth). Further emphasis is placed on the fact that in the newly emerging, rapidly changing world, all education will have to be continuous and can no longer guarantee success. Despite its author's focus on "failure," however, and its self-deprecating irony and gentle wit, *The Education of Henry Adams* chronicles a remarkably successful, productive, rich, and influential life.

The Education of Henry Adams opens with a skillfully drawn account of the author's youth in the family home of Boston and the summer residence of Quincy, where the historic legacy of his great New England family was always in strong evidence. Adams personifies the early factors of his development through a warm portrayal of his admired father; it was through him that the boy received an education which, the author half-mockingly insists, "condemned [him] to failure" because he was not educated to stoop to the low ways of a corrupt present.

Adams vigorously dismisses his formal schooling as dull memorizing and perceives personal experience as the true educator. Thus, a boyhood trip to Washington across the morally repulsive, slaveholding South is given more weight than the whole of his time at Harvard College. At Harvard, Adams insists, was bred "an inferior social type, quite as ill-fitted as the Oxford type for success in the next generation." Similarly, on his first trip to Europe, Adams' plan to study German law ends with his listening to the music of composer Richard Wagner; throughout his travels, his "accidental education" is worth more than carefully laid out schemes.

Following his young self back to Washington, Adams interprets the insights gained during practical work for his congressman father as an education in the corrupt and devious ways of contemporary politics; there, the narrative implies, morality and idealism are dangerously out of fashion. The author continues his account of his practical education—contrasting starkly to familial values—as the young man follows his father to England. There, his "education" acquaints him with the price of political scandal and compromise, alienating social customs, and the experience of the United States' sudden coming of age with the assassination of President Lincoln in 1865.

As a turning point in his career, Henry Adams depicts his decision in 1870 to accept a professorship at Harvard, after about two years back in the cauldron of Washington, where he was further educated in the corruption of the present day. His narrative—in a chapter significantly entitled "Failure"—reads like an apology for this act, which seemingly forever rejected any possibility that he would live up to his birthright of a shining political career. Accordingly, the narrator informs the reader that with this act, "Henry Adams' education, at his entry into life, stopped, and his life began." Characteristically, his self-assessment of the next seven years is carried by the familiarly self-mocking tone as he insists that "[a]s a professor, he regarded himself as a failure."

Against the dark vision of the failed eighteenth century man Adams, the narrative presents the fate of Clarence King, close friend of the author, who, as an enterprising geologist and self-made man, "had given himself education all of a piece, yet broad." Yet King's ensuing bankruptcy in 1893 and a confrontation with the gigantic dynamos of the Chicago Exhibition in that year seem to render hopeless all trust in education: What use can come of the cultivation of a mind in a world where the brute forces of capitalism and electricity threaten the very existence of a self hoping to live in harmony with a unified cosmos?

From this pessimistic vantage point, Adams develops the final third of his autobiography, which becomes increasingly theoretical and philosophical. The author connects the perceived failure of his life with a broader sense of chaos and vulnerability; he sees the "multiplicity" of the emerging twentieth century—symbolized by the dynamo—as opposed to the unity of medieval spiritualism and veneration of the Virgin Mary.

Adams' important observation of dramatically accelerating technological progress and its accompanying cultural change leaves his narrative struggling to produce a formula that could describe these processes with the same mathematical accuracy with which his contemporary scientists began to discover the rules governing the behavior of ideal gases. Mixing history and thermodynamics, Adams articulates a "dynamic theory of history" a "law of acceleration"; both theories convince in their analysis of the past but fall far short from being natural laws.

Henry Adams' autobiography ends on a note that is both resigned to the inevitability of the new and guardedly optimistic about the vistas the new powers serving humanity may open. Taking the death of a beloved friend as an occasion to conclude his autobiography, Adams ends with a vision of a future world which may be regarded "without a shudder."

Despite its obvious laments and occasionally massive self-deprecation, *The Education of Henry Adams* fascinates in its profound examination of a powerful mind growing up at a crucial period in American and human history. If his autobiography excludes important aspects of his life—his wife Miriam is not mentioned once—it is nevertheless a powerful meditation on how to prepare the mind to succeed in a rapidly changing, uncaring world. Taken as such, Adams' work is of a strikingly modern quality and has not lost its relevance for the reader of today.

Summary

The work of Henry Adams offers his readers a powerful view of a United States in transition and artistically examines the struggles of idealistic people who, aware of their cultural legacy, are trying to come to terms with the immense challenge of a new century and era. His fiction succeeds in combining entertaining stories with greater moral and philosophical concerns that are still relevant. His two late masterpieces blend discussion of architectural wonders and a presentation of the author's own life with fascinating reflections on the place of humanity in an ever-changing cosmos. Adams' gentle, ironic voice never lets a reader's interest lapse; it is full of wit and devoid of doctrine.

Bibliography

Conder, John. *A Formula of His Own: Adams's Literary Experiment*. Chicago: University of Chicago Press, 1970.

Contosta, David R. *Henry Adams and the American Experiment*. Boston: Little, Brown, 1980.

Decker, William Merrill. *The Literary Vocation of Henry Adams*. Chapel Hill: University of North Carolina Press, 1990.

Dusinberre, William. *Henry Adams: The Myth of Failure*. Charlottesville: University Press of Virginia, 1980.

Levenson, J. C. *The Mind and Art of Henry Adams*. Reprint. Stanford, Calif.: Stanford University Press, 1968.

Lyon, Melvin. *Symbol and Idea of Henry Adams*. Lincoln: University of Nebraska Press, 1970.

O'Toole, Patricia. *The Five of Hearts: An Intimate Portrait of Henry Adams and His Friends, 1880-1918*. New York: Clarkson N. Potter, 1990.

Samuels, Ernest. *Henry Adams*. Cambridge, Mass.: The Belknap Press of Harvard University Press. 1989.

Wagner, Vern. *The Suspension of Henry Adams: A Study of Manner and Matter*. Detroit: Wayne State University Press, 1969.

Wasserstrom, William. *The Ironies of Progress: Henry Adams and the American Dream*. Carbondale: Southern Illinois University Press, 1984.

Reinhart Lutz

JAMES AGEE

Born: Knoxville, Tennessee
November 27, 1909
Died: New York, New York
May 16, 1955

Principal Literary Achievement

Agee brought subtlety of thought and intensity of emotion to his portrayal of the people, issues, and sensibilities of the American South.

Biography

James Rufus Agee was born in Knoxville, Tennessee, on November 27, 1909. His father, Hugh James Agee, a warm and simple man, had worked for the U.S. Postal Service in Panama and later for the railroad in Tennessee. His mother, the former Laura Whitman Tyler, was from a wealthier family and kept a religious household. A turning point came early in Agee's life when, on May 18, 1916, his father died in an automobile accident.

Left alone to rear James and his sister Emma, Laura Agee's religiosity grew; it brought feelings of guilt and anger to James and led the family to a Catholic mountain retreat, where he found substitute parents in Father Harold and Grace Flye. A serious, lonely boy who loved reading, Agee experienced a spiritual crisis at the age of fourteen that further alienated him from his background and surroundings.

With his mother's remarriage in 1924 to a conservative churchman, Agee was ready to leave home. In 1925 he entered Phillips Exeter Academy in rural New Hampshire, where he wrote poetry and contributed stories to the school's monthly publication. Though his grades were poor, upon graduation in June of 1928 he was accepted to Harvard College. There he wrote for the newspaper and literary review and cultivated friendships with rising literary figures such as I. A. Richards, Bernard Schoenfeld, and Dwight Macdonald. Agee's college years, like much of his life to follow, were characterized by heavy drinking and severe depressions. Though he had felt occasional homosexual leanings, involvements with a series of women culminated in his courtship of Olivia Saunders, whose family had effectively adopted Agee, and the couple was married early in 1933.

A *Harvard Advocate* parody of *Time* magazine brought Agee to the attention of publisher Henry Luce, and upon graduation in 1932 Agee moved to New York to write for *Fortune*. Meanwhile, he worked sporadically on several autobiographical

novels. In 1934, some of his poetry was anthologized in *Modern American Poetry* and was selected for publication by Yale University under the title *Permit Me Voyage*. A *Fortune* assignment in 1936 to report on tenant farmers in Alabama led to a piece which was rejected by the magazine but developed into the book *Let Us Now Praise Famous Men* (1941).

In 1937, Agee met and fell in love with Alma Mailman; after years of discontent, he and Olivia divorced, and Alma became his second wife in 1938. This marriage lasted three years and resulted in the birth of a son, Joel. By 1940, Agee had met and fallen in love with Mia Fritsch, his third wife, to whom he remained married until his death, and by whom he fathered three children, Julia, Andrea, and John.

Having become a book reviewer at *Time* in 1938, Agee capitalized on his fascination with the cinema to become the magazine's film reviewer in 1941 and to accept the same post at *The Nation* in 1942. He also served as a steady consultant in the expansion of the Library of Congress Film Archives. He had always loved film, and his work as a reviewer and consultant led naturally to filmmaking itself. His first venture was "In the Street," made with photographer Helen Levitt in 1945. In 1948, Agee left his positions with *Time* and *The Nation* and turned his efforts to film and fiction. He established friendships with directors Charlie Chaplin and John Huston and was hired by Huston in 1950 to write a screenplay for C. S. Forester's novel *The African Queen*; the film was released in 1951. A coronary thrombosis in early 1951 interrupted Agee's work and precipitated his physical decline.

Agee's first novel, *The Morning Watch*, based on his years at St. Andrew's retreat, appeared in 1951. The following year, he penned a series on Abraham Lincoln for television, and in 1953 a film he wrote based on Stephen Crane's story "The Bride Comes to Yellow Sky" was released. With his constant smoking and drinking and frequent angina attacks, Agee took on numerous projects only to abandon them, and tried to complete others on which he had been working for years. On May 16, 1955, in New York City, a final heart attack took his life at the age of forty-five.

A Death in the Family, a novel published in 1957, received the Pulitzer Prize. Other posthumous publications include *Agee on Film: Reviews and Comments* (1958), *Agee on Film: Five Film Scripts* (1960), and *Letters of James Agee to Father Flye* (1962).

Analysis

During the course of his career, James Agee wrote in a wide variety of genres. It is difficult to place a single label on him, and even within a given genre his work often frustrates conventional expectations. Through the broad range of his poems, stories, essays, articles, novels, reviews, and screenplays, his voice expresses the clarity of thought and depth of passion that characterized his life.

Agee first considered himself a poet and as a young man admired the poetry of John Keats, William Blake, the seventeenth century "metaphysical poets"—John Donne, George Herbert, and Andrew Marvell—and, among his contemporaries, W. H. Auden. From these poets Agee took formal and stylistic influences—a devotion to metrical formulae, a meditative tone, complex thought and imagery, romantic lyricism—that give his poetry intellectual and spiritual elevation and sometimes an archaic or stilted quality. His volume of verse, *Permit Me Voyage*, includes portrayals of urban and rural scenes, a tragic narrative about an infertile farmwife, sonnets of marital discontent, versified prayers, and an impassioned "Dedication" to an exhaustive list of the poet's personal heroes, friends, and inspirations.

The ability to combine given forms with intense personal passion is seen beyond Agee's poetry. All of his works draw on his personal life or attitudes: His style is inherently subjective. This tendency to interpret his subjects in a personal and intimate manner is reflected even when he was on assignment to cover a luxury cruise, roadside America, the new Tennessee Valley Authority, or the Borough of Brooklyn, New York. By the same token, Agee's fiction is always partially or wholly autobiographical. He had little interest in making up or disguising stories; rather, he sought to observe and experience real life, and then to render and evoke it through the written word.

On the other hand, Agee's years as a staff and free-lance journalist inculcated in him the ability to tell a story simply and directly when necessary and to render detail with detached and even scientific precision. While his poetry betrays occasional emotional indulgence, his novels and essays exhibit steady control. Mere suggestions serve to add brief but vivid color, after which the narrative or thrust of the argument is duly resumed. In some cases, Agee's concern with maintaining the movement or structural integrity of a piece may seem to deny the emotional or evocative power inherent in the subject matter; however, the emotional power is enhanced through the subtle treatment, and realism is not sacrificed to artistic license. In this way, Agee's writing is often deceptive in its simplicity; character transformation and the depiction of mood are achieved not explicitly but gradually, almost imperceptibly.

Agee's family and educational background inform his unique style. Reared in a religious home, he spent his life defining his relationship to Christian institutions and beliefs. This background steeped him in the Bible, the catechism, the confession, and the sermon; his writing therefore often exhibits biblical simplicity and rhythm, an attention to detail, a relentless examination of moral condition, and a passionate rhetorical power. Similarly, Agee's wide knowledge of philosophy and music (above all, the music of nineteenth century composer Ludwig van Beethoven), along with the traditional canon of English and American literature, gave him a grounding in cultural history and a rich pool from which to draw intellectual or allusive power.

This cultured and literate background enhanced Agee's natural abilities with language, and his writing is masterfully crafted, with a subtlety of gesture and careful attention to detail. While capable of extremely economical usage in turning a striking phrase or image, Agee is not a particularly economical writer. His attention to detail and desire to replicate real people or situations with unflawed accuracy, in both external attributes and internal implications, result in long sentences, complex constructions, expansive catalogs, meticulously qualified arguments, and use of some of the finer technical devices of logic and rhetoric. While brevity was not a central concern of Agee, however, his writing is not verbose or diffuse, for the full and often dense prose reflects the precision and breadth of Agee's powers of observation and discernment.

Nowhere are these powers more evident than in his writings for and about film. On the one hand, his love of the quickly developing medium infused his journalistic and novelistic endeavors with the power to evoke images and entire scenes with cinematic fullness. On the other hand, it led him to devote his intellect and labor to elevating film as an art form, and Agee's reviews helped revolutionize attitudes toward film. He approached film with lucidity and treated it with as much respect and severe scrutiny as have been devoted to poetry and painting through the centuries. In writing about film, Agee found an eloquence that few others had—and that he himself often lacked elsewhere. Rather than simply report on a film's entertainment value or intellectual content, Agee brought to his reviews an inside, craftsmanlike approach. Even before he had begun making films himself, he saw and reviewed them with an eye to the specific cinematographic techniques involved in creating the series of images. Thus his reviews are often as informative and provocative as the works on which they focus.

LET US NOW PRAISE FAMOUS MEN

First published: 1941
Type of work: Essay

The lives of tenant farmers in Alabama, and their relationship to two journalists who come to report on them, are complex, difficult, and inspiring.

Let Us Now Praise Famous Men is a unique work of literature. It was first conceived as a feature article for *Fortune* magazine: In the summer of 1936, Agee was sent to Alabama along with photographer Walker Evans to document the lives of tenant farmers. The article they produced, however, was much too passionate and impressionistic for the editors of *Fortune*, so Agee worked on the project privately and eventually published the "article" as a four-hundred-page book. When it first appeared, only two years after John Steinbeck's novel *The Grapes of Wrath*, with which it shares certain similarities, the book received bad reviews and sold a mere six hundred copies. It was only after Agee's death, and especially in the political turbulence and social awareness of the 1960's, that the book achieved popularity and literary standing.

Let Us Now Praise Famous Men is as much about Agee's personal experiences among three poor sharecropping families as it is about their lives *per se*. For Agee, the two could not be considered separately, and the moral and emotional implications of his and Evans' presence among their subjects—seeing themselves as spies—are central to any meaningful contemplation of tenant farming during the Depression.

Thus, the piece moves back and forth, sometimes overtly in large sections, sometimes momentarily in parentheses, between precisely objective reportage and relentless self-examination.

The structure of the book reflects the care which Agee obviously invested in it. The composition is divided into various sections, and movements at times seem nearly spontaneous or improvised. Agee uses a series of prefatory pieces to create a sense of false beginnings that nullifies any expectations the reader may have and establishes the book's painstaking pace. Then, sections are introduced with titles, labels, and enumerations that reflect no overall pattern but rather mirror the complexity of the material they cover. They are not placed in chronological order, order of composition, or any order sequence of logical development. Each new section may be a new beginning, marked by an epigram, a poem, a list, or a dramatic shift in tone; transitions are often sudden and connections unclear. Such an unorthodox structure, far from being a gratuitous game devised to baffle, derives from the earnest effort to make sense of the experience of observing, interacting with, and living among sharecroppers.

In spite of this complexity, Agee is rigorously direct with the reader as to his purposes in the book and his awareness of the limitations its form places on him. He asks for no suspension of disbelief—the book is admittedly only paper—and makes no claims to extraordinary powers of insight or expression. He simply trusts in words. This trust and the earnest effort to be truthful, like so many attributes of the work, are relentless, and therein lies their emotional and philosophical power.

Within this context of moral and literary anxiety, Agee documents, with the help of Evans' photographs (which precede and are to be considered coequal with sections of the text), the poverty, aspirations, and pathos of the people he encounters. The Gudger, Ricketts, and Woods families live in poverty: Agee exhaustively details their surroundings, their clothing, their daily activities, their conversations, their work, their education, their diet, their health, and any other aspect of their lives he can attempt to portray. He also depicts his own interactions with them and the relationships that result. He contemplates the social and political implications of their lives for society as a whole and, through the intense and relentless examination of their existence, poses practical and philosophical questions of universal relevance.

A DEATH IN THE FAMILY

First published: 1957
Type of work: Novel

A man's sudden death in an automobile accident leaves his wife and small children to try to understand and continue without him.

A Death in the Family is a novel of delightful and deceptive simplicity. As the title implies, it is the story of a man's death and its effects on the family he leaves behind.

Jay Follet is happily married to his devout wife, Mary, and they have two children, Rufus and Catherine, ages six and four. Early one morning, Jay is summoned by his drunken brother Ralph to drive from Knoxville to their father's deathbed in rural LaFollette. As Jay suspects, the journey turns out to be unnecessary—Ralph exaggerated the severity of the old man's condition—so he sets out to return home, hoping to arrive before the children go to bed. Formerly an alcoholic, Jay may have had something to drink; apparently, high speeds and a loose pin in the steering mechanism cause his car to go off the road; Jay, with only two tiny bruises on his face, experiences a fatal concussion. His family is first alerted that he was in an accident, and then that he died. His body is returned to Knoxville, and the funeral is held. That, with several interpolated flashbacks (sections in italics which the editors, after Agee's death, placed where they thought best) is the entire action of the novel.

Within this bare plot, Agee uses careful and subtle detail to create character and emotional movement. The narrative voice is nearly absent; it either describes the external attributes of a particular moment or records the impressions and inner thoughts of any of a number of characters. From chapter to chapter, the point of view often shifts among Mary, Rufus, Catherine, Ralph, Mary's brother Andrew, and her Aunt Hannah. Each character brings to the narrative a particular sensibility through which events are viewed, and Agee often provides parallel, simultaneous perspectives on a given scene or moment. Contrasting with Mary's emotional spirituality are Hannah's evenheaded wisdom and Andrew's often bitter skepticism. Moreover, against the seeming clarity of the adults, Agee offers the perceptions of the children, who attempt to understand their elders, their own role in the world, and their father's disappearance with a balanced mixture of innocence, selfishness, and confusion.

Within the larger story of Jay's death and burial, most of which is recounted directly but from the distance of the Follet home, smaller events establish the novel's dramatic life and texture. Agee provides a wealth of otherwise ordinary incidents or encounters—Jay and Rufus seeing a Chaplin film, Jay's early morning departure, Hannah buying Rufus a hat, Rufus and Catherine bickering, Mary being comforted by the priest from Chattanooga—that take on special power or significance on this particular day in the life of the family. Agee portrays moments vividly but without pretension or fanfare; the moments both stand alone and accumulate to create a textured portrait of a group of people and a meaningful event in their lives.

A Death in the Family is a deeply autobiographical novel. Not only does Jay Follet's death mirror that of Agee's own father, but other details—the name Rufus and the taunting it occasions, the mother's extreme religiosity, and the priest's refusal to administer full rites—are drawn directly from the author's past as well. No effort is made to "fictionalize" the story; rather, Agee has given imaginative, artistic, and unsentimental expression to his vivid memories of a crucial period in his life.

Summary

As a man who lived somewhat too recklessly and died much too young, James Agee left behind a small body of work by no means commensurate with his extraordinary talents. His life was a tragedy of promise only partially fulfilled, and his writings offer, through careful examination of specific subjects, a universal vision of human suffering, longing, and hope.

Bibliography

Bergreen, Laurence. *James Agee: A Life*. New York: E. P. Dutton, 1984.

Coles, Robert. *Irony in the Mind's Life: Essays on Novels by James Agee, Elizabeth Bowen, and George Eliot*. New York: New Directions, 1978.

Doty, Mark A. *Tell Me Who I Am: James Agee's Search for Selfhood*. Baton Rouge: Louisiana State University Press, 1981.

Moreau, Genevieve. *The Restless Journey of James Agee*. New York: William Morrow, 1977.

Olin, Peter H. *Agee*. New York: Ivan Obolensky, 1966.

Ward, Joseph Anthony. *American Silences: The Realism of James Agee, Walker Evans, and Edward Hopper*. Baton Rouge: Louisiana State University Press, 1985.

Barry Mann

EDWARD ALBEE

Born: Virginia
March 12, 1928

Principal Literary Achievement

A prolific but controversial playwright, Albee's work in the modern theater has been acclaimed for its vigorous pursuit of the truth and the dramatic expression of the human condition.

Biography

Mystery surrounds the origins of Edward Albee. He was born somewhere in Virginia on March 12, 1928, and not in Washington, D.C., as is frequently listed. Two weeks after birth, Albee was given up for adoption to Reed A. and Frances Albee (twenty-three years younger than her husband). He was taken to Larchmont, New York, where he was reared in luxury. The name Edward was taken from Reed's father, wealthy theater magnate Edward Franklin Albee, who owned part of the Keith-Albee Theater Circuit until Joseph P. Kennedy forced him out in 1929. Despite several efforts, the playwright has never been able to trace his natural parents.

Albee grew up in a large, luxurious stucco Tudor house. He was surrounded by servants, horses, toys, tutors, and chauffeured limousines. His winters were spent in Palm Beach, Florida, or Arizona and summers sailing in Long Island Sound. Albee developed a love for horses and riding from his adoptive mother, whom he adored; she was a tall, beautiful woman who had once modeled for Bergdorf. He was also quite close to his grandmother. It was her trust fund that later enabled Albee to leave home and sustain his efforts as a writer.

Albee's love for the theater developed very early, fueled by his frequent trips to Broadway matinees (in a Rolls-Royce) and by the visits of famous theatrical guests to the Albees' sprawling estate. Excited by meeting such show business personalities as Ed Wynn, Jimmy Durante, and Walter Pidgeon, Albee began writing plays at an early age. He penned his first play at the precocious age of twelve—a full-length sex farce entitled *Aliqueen*, about passengers on an English ocean liner.

Albee suffered from a troubled childhood despite his apparent social, economic, and cultural advantages. Keenly aware that he was adopted, the future dramatist held a deep-seated resentment against his biological parents for abandoning him. That resentment would resonate throughout his plays. Albee's hostility, however, was not reflected toward his adoptive parents. Still, he gave them enough concern about his

disruptive behavior that Mrs. Albee enrolled the eleven-year-old boy in a strict boarding school in Lawrenceville. It would be the first stop of many schools, including Valley Forge Military Academy (termed by Albee the "Valley Forge Concentration Camp") and Choate School. An indifferent student at best, Albee received tremendous encouragement as a writer from his instructors at Choate. During his one-year stay there he wrote numerous pieces, including poems, short stories, a novel entitled *The Flesh of the Unbelievers*, and a play entitled *Schism*. Much of his work appeared in the *Choate Literary Magazine*, and one poem was published in *Kaleidoscope*, a Texas literary magazine.

Following graduation from Choate, Albee attended Trinity College beginning in 1946, but he did not apply himself to his studies. He became involved in dramatics, however, and played the role of Emperor Franz Joseph in Maxwell Anderson's *The Masque of Kings*. Midway into his second year, Albee left Trinity (actually, he was ordered to leave because he would not attend math lectures or chapel); he never completed his college education. His first job was at radio station WNYC, performing a variety of assignments. In 1950, he moved out of his adoptive parents' home, despite their entreaties to stay, and moved to Greenwich Village. He was determined to become a writer. For the next ten years he moved around frequently and took numerous positions, including office boy, bartender, book salesman, record clerk at Bloomingdale's, and Western Union messenger. All these jobs gave him ample opportunity to communicate with people. Albee also met and studied with playwright Thornton Wilder, who encouraged him to write for the stage. Saddled with job instability, Albee was able to survive because of the $100,000 trust fund established by his grandmother. Its provisions spelled out that Albee should receive fifty dollars a week until his thirtieth birthday, then the remaining sum.

Albee's coming of age as a playwright occurred in 1958, on his thirtieth birthday, when he quit his Western Union job, cashed in his grandmother's inheritance, and sat down and wrote *The Zoo Story* (1959) in three weeks. No Broadway producer was interested in it. Fortunately, William Flanagan (Albee dedicated the play to him), who had roomed with Albee for about nine years, sent the script to a friend in Italy, and it eventually ended up on the desk of German producer Boleslaw Barlog. Barlog presented it at the Schiller Theatre in Berlin on September 28, 1959. Albee attended the Berlin production, despite the fact that he could not understand German. Almost four months later, on January 14, 1960, the play received its successful New York premiere, in conjunction with Samuel Beckett's *Krapp's Last Tape* (1958). Albee's playwriting career was launched; he would soon be known as the "King of Off-Broadway."

In that same year, 1960, Albee would produce three more plays—*The Sandbox*, *The Death of Bessie Smith*, and *Fam and Yam*. Every year thereafter he wrote or adapted one or more plays for the New York stage, and each new Albee work would be eagerly awaited. His biggest success and first Broadway production occurred in 1962 with *Who's Afraid of Virginia Woolf?*, which won numerous awards. He won Pulitzer Prizes for *A Delicate Balance* (1966) and *Seascape* (1975). Albee continues to turn out new plays each year, conducts workshops for aspiring dramatists, lectures extensively in the United States and abroad, serves as artistic director for various theater companies, and often reads or directs revivals of his plays.

Analysis

Edward Albee is one of the most discussed and analyzed playwrights of contemporary American theater. Many books, countless reviews, and hundreds of articles have been published examining the artist and his plays. Most critics agree that Albee is an important writer whose recurring themes include the condemnation of cruelty, emasculation, social complacency, and vacuity. His characters appear to wallow in their own fantasies; the plays exhibit a pervading and overwhelming sense of loss, probably triggered by his own disturbed childhood. Albee is concerned with the illusions that keep people from seeing reality. He believes that he lives in a time when religious, moral, political, and social structures have collapsed. The dramatist is also preoccupied with the fear of death—a continuing motif since his first play. Albee's plays do not end happily, but he never strains to make them tragic.

Albee has a love-hate relationship with his critics, submitting to numerous interviews, in which he proceeds to give cryptic answers. He is alternately praised for his consummate craftsmanship, intelligence, and sensitivity and criticized for his clumsiness, dimwitted mentality, or crassness. Albee himself looks with scorn at attempts to analyze him or his work. He consistently reads all material written about him but derisively views it as well-meaning fiction. Probed about his own artistic credo, Albee is usually coy, but he has written that "the health of a nation, a society, can be determined by the art it demands." The statement may be a key to understanding Albee's own work, because he is openly critical at what passes for entertainment today on Broadway, in films, and on television. Albee praises the technological achievements in all three mediums and the high level of competence in acting and directing, but he decries the stereotyped, superficial, and sentimental literary material.

Albee's work is unusual for his attempts to fuse comedy and terror. He has said that he wants simultaneously to entertain and offend his audiences. In fact, audience indifference to his plays is one thing Albee abhors. He firmly believes that the theater must be "possessed" by the playwright rather than by the actor, director, producer, or audience. Throughout his career, he has steadfastly refused to condescend to changing theatrical fashions and resolutely follows his own inner visions.

Albee remains one of the great innovators of the theater, having experimented with various genres and techniques over the years, and he has been labeled at one time or another an absurdist, surrealist, existentialist, and satirist. He avoids easy labels or descriptions; about his own work, Albee has said that he does not concern himself with thinking about his style or direction:

> I'm interested in the fact that I write plays in such different styles from time to time. . . .
> I'm not doing it to avoid, or to revenge, or to confuse, or to be fresh in my own mind,
> even. I just do it because that is the way each one wants to be.

Whatever Albee's approach may be, he has not slowed his output of plays, creating at least one a year. Critics and audiences alike think that *Who's Afraid of Virginia Woolf?* remains his masterpiece, and *The Zoo Story* remains his most popular one-act work. Albee himself remains noncommittal about naming a favorite play, but he has expressed a fondness for *The Sandbox*, which he feels is his most perfectly written play (it is also his shortest).

Albee's weakest literary efforts have not been his own creations, but his championing of other writers through his role as stage adapter. He has adapted six works into plays—including *The Ballad of the Sad Café* (1963), *Malcolm* (1966), by novelist James Purdy, *Everything in the Garden* (1967), by playwright Giles Cooper, and *Lolita* (1981)—and only the first one, based on Carson McCullers' novella, received mixed reviews. The other three were rigorously criticized and have rarely been performed. Albee remained particularly incensed about the failure of the Broadway production of *Lolita*, based on Vladimir Nabokov's 1955 novel. In the introduction to his *Selected Plays of Edward Albee*, published in 1987, Albee assailed the production for its "combination of disrespect for Nabokov's and my text, directorial vulgarity . . . and a lax and insensitive turn by a leading performer." *Bartleby* (1961), an operatic adaptation of Herman Melville's short story "Bartleby the Scrivener," also failed. An Albee adaptation of Truman Capote's *Breakfast at Tiffany's* never opened.

Albee's work has rarely been adapted to the screen; it is viewed by filmmakers as too difficult, talky, uninteresting, and static. The one major exception was *Who's Afraid of Virginia Woolf?*, in 1966. It starred Elizabeth Taylor and Richard Burton and was well received by the public. The playwright had nothing to do with the film version, but he has stated that he enjoyed it overall despite certain liberties taken with the text. No one can say in which direction Albee's career will continue to develop. He refuses to be categorized, and each new work is different from the last. Albee says of his writing simply that "my mind fills with plays, and I write them down from time to time to unclutter my mind."

THE ZOO STORY

First produced: 1959 (first published, 1960)
Type of work: Play

A vagrant's death wish finds fulfillment after he meets a stranger in New York's Central Park.

The Zoo Story, Albee's first important play, was partially written on his thirtieth birthday, in 1958, as a present to himself. Albee composed the play in three weeks, but then could not find an American producer who would stage it. Albee had created a highly unusual and original work in his first venture that bears comparison with Samuel Beckett's first play, *Waiting for Godot*. Eventually, a German production of *The Zoo Story* was arranged on September 28, 1959, at the Schiller Theatre *Werkstatt* in Berlin. Four months later, the American premiere took place—on a double bill with Beckett's *Krapp's Last Tape*—on January 14, 1960, at the Provincetown Playhouse in New York City and ran for 582 performances. Albee won the Vernon Rice Memorial Award for *The Zoo Story.*

The Zoo Story is a stunning tour de force achievement by a new playwright. It is theatrically simple yet thematically complex. The long one-act play has only two characters, strangers to each other, who meet in Central Park on a summer Sunday afternoon. When the curtain rises, Peter is sitting on a park bench reading a book. Albee describes him as "a man in his early forties, neither fat nor gaunt, neither handsome nor homely." The other character, Jerry, walks in and sees Peter. Albee's brief description is as follows: "a man in his late thirties, not poorly dressed, but carelessly." He exhibits "a great weariness."

The Zoo Story is classically structured into three main segments that develop in a climactic order. The introductory section introduces Peter and Jerry and the many differences between them: their clothing, economic and social backgrounds, literary tastes, philosophies of life, and ways of communicating. In the middle section, Jerry narrates a long story about himself and an old, mangy dog that lives at his rooming house. The final section builds to a violent conclusion after Jerry tells Peter what happened to him at the zoo.

Peter and Jerry are oppositional characters in *The Zoo Story.* The only thing they have in common is their age. Albee's description of Peter is a man "moving into middle age," although "his dress and his manner would suggest a man younger." Peter is in no way remarkable or distinctive. He represents a kind of bourgeois Everyman who is comfortable with his sedentary life and avoids taking risks. Jerry, on the other hand, lives on the outer edge of society. He is a rootless person whose "fall from physical grace should not suggest debauchery." Jerry immediately goads Peter into conversation, a maneuver that the overly polite Peter finds disturbing, because he does not want anyone to penetrate his carefully polished façade. Peter tries to steer the conversation to duller topics, but Jerry will have none of it. Jerry eventually strips away all of Peter's protective layers and reveals the raging animal within him.

The separation of man from his true animal nature is an important theme in *The Zoo Story.* Peter remained blissfully ignorant of the animal within himself until Jerry, who always knew that he was an animal and that meaningful communication with others is difficult because of the individual's isolation, makes him face it. Hence the importance of the "Jerry and the dog" story, which reaffirms man's animal heritage and hatred of anything that invades personal security. Jerry finally goads the once-passive Peter into a fight in defense of his honor. The terrified Peter, responding like a savage beast, picks up Jerry's knife and is tricked into killing him.

Another important theme in *The Zoo Story* is the salvation of the individual through sacrifice. Jerry sacrifices himself, removing his isolation by reaching out to Peter, changing Peter for the better. The play ends with Jerry giving a Christlike exhortation to Peter, his disciple. *The Zoo Story* unfolds like a Greek tragedy that builds relentlessly to a horrifying and preordained conclusion. Peter's final howl, "OH MY GOD," amplifies Jerry's onstage whimper as the curtain falls.

THE AMERICAN DREAM

First produced: 1961 (first published, 1961)
Type of work: Play

A savage satire on the American family, which Albee portrays as substituting artificial values for real ones.

The American Dream was the fourth play written by Albee. It received its American premiere at the York Playhouse on January 24, 1961, and ran for 370 performances. Four of the five characters in the play—Mommy, Daddy, Grandma, and Young Man—also appeared in an earlier Albee work, *The Sandbox*. Unlike *The Zoo Story*, *The American Dream* is an absurd play.

The long one-act is structured into three major sections and eleven groupings of the five characters. The first part deals with the family unit itself—Mommy, Daddy, and Grandma—and the decision on whether Grandma should be put into a nursing home. The second section involves the introduction of Mrs. Barker, a social chum of Mommy, who once worked for the Bye-Bye Adoption Service. The final part begins with the arrival of the Young Man and Grandma's attempt to keep from being institutionalized. In *The American Dream*, Albee attempts to show that the much-vaunted American Way of Life is absurd. The playwright seeks to show how deprived of meaning Americans' normal human feelings and relationships have become. He points out that people go through the ritualistic motions of loving and caring for each other, sexual attractiveness, or neighborly concerns, but no feelings are engaged. All five characters may speak to each other, but they live in their own worlds, isolated from one another. Their repetitive language of endearments to each other is deflated and hollow.

The play opens with Mommy and Daddy waiting for someone to come and fix the toilet. Mommy tells a story about buying a beige-colored hat, but she exchanges it when her club chairwoman, Mrs. Barker, tells her that it is wheat-colored. Grandma enters carrying many neatly wrapped boxes; it appears that she spends her time wrapping these mysterious boxes. Soon, Mommy reveals her plan to send Grandma to a nursing home and convinces Daddy to agree. Grandma will not go quietly, however, and proves to be a stubborn match for her daughter. She tells Daddy that Mommy stated at age eight that she would marry a rich old man and even implies that their marriage is a disaster.

Albee pokes merciless fun at what he perceives to be a matriarchal society and at the impotence of the American family head. Sterility is an important theme: Mommy and Daddy cannot conceive a child. Daddy's character is vague, ineffectual, and without determination compared to the nightmarishly efficient Mommy. Mommy is the driving force in the family unit. Only Grandma can stand up to her daughter's wiles and match her. Into this feminine beehive of activity comes Mrs. Barker, the club chairwoman. She makes herself very comfortable and even removes her dress when asked. Through Mrs. Barker's arrival, it is revealed that Mommy and Daddy adopted a little child from her years ago. They systematically dismembered their "bumble of joy," however, because it behaved in a normal and natural manner instead of adapting to their artificial values.

Following that revelation, the Young Man enters and converses with Grandma. He is a handsome, vital, and completely empty-headed dolt whom Grandma calls "The American Dream." He wants to be a film actor and will do anything for money. He tells of an identical twin and of their separation at childhood; he feels as though he lost part of himself. In short order, Mommy and Daddy adopt him, with Mrs. Barker's blessing. The new adoptee will move into Grandma's old room, and Mommy will use him as a lover. Grandma closes the play with a short address: "So, let's leave things as they are right now . . . while everybody's happy . . . while everybody's got what he wants . . . or everybody's got what he thinks he wants. Good night, dears."

The American Dream is a less successfully realized and integrated work than *The Zoo Story*. Unlike the concise structure of *The Sandbox*, which it superficially resembles, the play is overly long and some of the speeches appear padded. Yet Albee has neatly skewered the American Way of Life, taking the false images promulgated by television, films, advertising, and political exploitation and revealing them to be totally empty and devoid of any meaning.

WHO'S AFRAID OF VIRGINIA WOOLF?

First produced: 1962 (first published, 1962)
Type of work: Play

Two married couples pass the night together hurling verbal abuse at each other until they come to a better understanding of themselves and their spouses.

Who's Afraid of Virginia Woolf? is regarded as Albee's most successfully realized play. It premiered on October 13, 1962, and ran for 664 performances. The original cast starred Uta Hagen, Arthur Hill, George Grizzard, and Melinda Dillon and was directed by Alan Schneider, who has been closely associated with staging Albee's work on the New York stage. The play was enthusiastically received by audiences and critics alike. The play won the New York Drama Critics Circle Award, the Antoinette Perry Award (Tony), and the Foreign Press Award. *Who's Afraid of Virginia Woolf?* caused a sensational controversy when it did not win the Pulitzer Prize as well. Two distinguished members of the Pulitzer committee resigned in protest. Albee subsequently won two Pulitzer Prizes, for *A Delicate Balance* and *Seascape*.

Who's Afraid of Virginia Woolf? was Albee's first full-length original play. It represents a departure for him not only in form but also in focus. In his earlier work, Albee stood outside society and vented his anger as an outraged social commentator whose passionate concern for justice and equality made him side with society's victims. He had been a champion for the lonely and oppressed. In *Who's Afraid of Virginia Woolf?*, Albee shifts his concern from the have-nots to the haves—college professors. They represent the core of civilized society (they educate their country's future leaders), and what he discovers there is perverse, cruel, hypocritical, immoral, and sterile.

Albee's play has little or no plot, but it moves forward rapidly. It has four characters: two married couples, with husbands teaching at the same small college. Martha is middle-aged, the daughter of the college president, and unhappily married to younger husband George. He has somehow disappointed her by not living up to her high expectations. Nick and Honey, the other (much younger) couple, are also locked into an unhappy marriage. Nick married her for money and what turned out to be a "hysterical pregnancy."

Throughout the long evening George and Martha (Albee names them after the childless George and Martha Washington) argue violently and trade insults with furious savagery. Albee has fashioned a highly fascinating battle of the sexes. The intense love-hate relationship of the couple is evident from the first moment, when they enter their house from a party slightly drunk and weary at 2:00 A.M. on a Sunday morning. Eager to go to bed, George is amazed that Martha has invited a new biology instructor and his wife over for drinks. It becomes clear that George and Martha enjoy verbally abusing each other, and the arrival of Nick and Honey only exacerbates the situation.

Albee has given subtitles to each of the three acts in *Who's Afraid of Virginia Woolf?* The first one is entitled "Fun and Games," the second, "Walpurgsnacht," and the third, "The Exorcism." Throughout the first act, George and Martha relentlessly bait and exasperate the other couple until Nick and Honey reluctantly enter into the spirit of it. Martha reveals to them that she and George have a grown, secretive son. In act 2, Albee draws a clear parallel between the two couples and shows that frustration is what fuels them—particularly sexual frustration, as exemplified by Nick's failure to satisfy Martha. During the first two acts, George has suffered the most abuse, but in act 3 he breaks free of his personal devils and attempts to exorcise the same from Martha; he tries to make her realize that there is not, and never was, a son. Martha's howling realization and acceptance of the truth brings the embattled pair closer together by the final curtain. Again, Albee reintroduces the recurring themes of the destruction of children by their parents and of men and women by each other.

Unlike other playwrights, who allow their characters to keep some of their lies and illusions—most notably Eugene O'Neill and Tennessee Williams—Albee strips all of them away from his characters. He makes it clear in *Who's Afraid of Virginia Woolf?* that he believes self-deception is evil and that no fraud should be entertained, no matter how comforting. Only the passionate search for the truth can nurture and fulfill human beings. Albee says that people must live without illusion and accept the inevitable consequences.

TINY ALICE

First produced: 1964 (first published, 1965)
Type of work: Play

A naïve lay brother of the Catholic church is seduced by the world's wealthiest woman.

Tiny Alice was first staged at the Billy Rose Theater on December 29, 1964, and it ran for 167 performances. It starred Sir John Gielgud, Irene Worth, William Hutt, Eric Berry, and John Heffernan; Alan Schneider directed. *Tiny Alice* provoked a fury of critical responses at its premiere, ranging from "brilliant" to "sophomoric." Most critics, as well as the performers involved, confessed to not understanding the play and called it a metaphysical muddle. One reviewer dismissed it as a Faustian drama written by a highly endowed college student. Subsequent revivals of the work have aroused the same acrimonious response. Albee, in introductory remarks to the published text in 1965, kept the controversy alive by writing:

> It has been the expressed hope of many that I would write a preface to the published text of *Tiny Alice*, clarifying obscure points in the play—explaining my intention, in other words. I have decided against creating such a guide because I find—after reading the play over—that I share the view of even more people: that the play is quite clear.

What is clear is that Albee did not include *Tiny Alice* as an important or representative work when he published *Selected Plays of Edward Albee* in 1987.

Despite its confusing allegorical structure, *Tiny Alice* has more of a plot coherence than most of Albee's other plays. Miss Alice is the world's richest woman; she will donate two billion dollars to the Catholic church if the Cardinal's secretary, lay Brother Julian, will be sent to her for further instructions. Brother Julian is a strange individual, dedicated to service in the church; however, he spent six years of his life in a mental institution. In time, Miss Alice seduces him into marriage, and that sacrament, blessed by the church, proves to be his undoing. He discovers that Miss Alice is a sham and is the personification of Tiny Alice, who lives inside a model house that is an exact replica of the real mansion. The play ends with Julian dying, alone and abandoned by everyone as he faces death.

The play is written in three acts; unlike *The Zoo Story*, which opens weakly and then builds in dramatic intensity, *Tiny Alice* has a strong first scene. It begins with the Cardinal and the Lawyer (church and state) crisply discussing the monetary gift to be bestowed on the church by Miss Alice. Unfortunately, the high level of tension introduced cannot be maintained in later scenes, as they are minor characters in the play. Later the audience is introduced to Brother Julian and Miss Alice, and it is their star-crossed union that forms the centerpiece of the action. Albee again brings in his familiar themes of aloneness, isolation, and the illusions to which people desperately cling. He also is concerned with the abandonment of one's faith and the relationship between sexual and religious ecstasies. Brother Julian, for example, spent six years in a mental institution because his faith left him. While there, he may or may not have had a hallucinatory sexual experience with a demented woman who believed she was the Virgin Mary. Miss Alice seduces Julian through her deeds rather than with words. Near the end of the play, having rejected him, she cradles the dying Julian in a Pietà embrace. Albee doubtless meant the model with Tiny Alice inside to represent a Platonic symbol of the bright world of ideals that people carry inside their minds. For Albee, Julian's confusion and penance at the end of the play give him absolution and a state of grace. Julian has examined his conscience, abandoned his delusions, and will make the necessary sacrifice to God and Tiny Alice. His acceptance of death finally releases Julian from a lifetime of doubt and gives him insight into himself. Albee makes it clear that Julian's illusory faith has finally been stripped away.

Summary

Edward Albee remains one of the United States' most important playwrights. A prolific dramatist, he produces work that is significant but controversial. What remains unique about Albee is his stunning integrity: He will not compromise his artistic ideals, and he resists efforts to become commercially successful. Albee continues following his own inner visions, and each new effort is different from its predecessor. Regardless of his popularity, however, Albee's place in theatrical history is secure.

Bibliography

Amacher, Richard E. *Edward Albee*. Rev. ed. Boston: Twayne, 1982.

Bigsby, C. W. E., ed. *Edward Albee: A Collection of Critical Essays*. Englewood Cliffs, N.J.: Prentice-Hall, 1975.

Hayman, Ronald. *Edward Albee*. New York: Frederick Ungar, 1973.

Kolin, Philip C., ed. *Critical Essays on Edward Albee*. Boston: G. K. Hall, 1986.

Paolucci, Anne. *From Tension to Tonic: The Plays of Edward Albee*. Carbondale: Southern Illinois University Press, 1972.

Roudane, Matthew C. *Understanding Edward Albee*. Columbia: University of South Carolina Press, 1987.

Stenz, Anita M. *Edward Albee: The Poet of Loss*. New York: Mouton, 1978.

Wasserman, Julian N., ed. *Edward Albee: An Interview and Essays*. Houston: University of St. Thomas, 1983.

Terry Theodore

LOUISA MAY ALCOTT

Born: Germantown, Pennsylvania
November 29, 1832
Died: Boston, Massachusetts
March 6, 1888

Principal Literary Achievement
Although she wrote for both adult and juvenile audiences, Alcott is most admired for her children's books, which were popular in her day and which continue as favorites with young adults.

Biography

While Louisa May Alcott is associated with the New England setting where she lived most of her life, she was born in Germantown, Pennsylvania, on November 29, 1832, the second of four daughters born to Amos Bronson and Abba May Alcott. Louisa's father, friend and admirer of Ralph Waldo Emerson and Henry David Thoreau, was a man of great vision and idealism but few practical skills. His inability to provide for his family of six became increasingly apparent as time went on. Soon after Louisa's birth, Bronson moved his family to Boston, where he organized the Temple School. While the school had much to recommend it, it was much more liberal than many Bostonians could accept, and six years later Alcott was forced to close its doors and personally shoulder many of the financial obligations incurred. This was the last time the Alcott family was to have a regular income. The financial instability under which Louisa lived provided material for many of her later writings.

After a trip to England, Bronson Alcott initiated a utopian communal experiment, Fruitlands, in Harvard, Massachusetts. This, too, ended in failure, only eight months after it was begun. Fruitlands was a pivotal experience for the whole Alcott family, for it taught them that Bronson simply would not be able to support them. Following her husband's nervous breakdown, Abba became the head of the household, and the women took on odd jobs. Louisa's abiding interest in women's work stems from this period.

Louisa's familiarity with poverty provided not only the content and substance of much of her later writing but also a serious incentive to write. Because her father was neither financially nor emotionally dependable, Louisa found herself increasingly at the center of the family. She assumed responsibility, living and working to support the family, a role she never relinquished throughout her life. After Fruit-

lands, the family lived in various Massachusetts towns—Still River, Concord, and Boston—and in Walpole, New Hampshire. When the family lived away from the business and intellectual center that was Boston, Louisa adopted the pattern of living for a few months in Boston, writing and picking up odd jobs to earn money, and then returning to be with her family. Family loyalty became tied to self-denial—a theme that was to run through some of her most successful writings.

Alcott had written since childhood, but publication came somewhat later. In 1851, her poem "Sunlight" was published in *Peterson's Magazine* under the pseudonym "Flora Fairfield." In the following year, her first story, "The Rival Painters: A Tale of Rome," appeared in *Olive Branch.* Other stories appeared in the *Saturday Evening Gazette* and in *The Atlantic Monthly.* As teacher for Emerson's daughter, Louisa had written several fairy stories, and in 1854 these were collected and published under the title *Flower Fables.* From an early age, Louisa had written and acted in family theatricals, and on May 4, 1860, her farce, *Nat Bachelor's Pleasure Trip,* was presented at the Howard Atheneum. During the decade of the 1850's, Alcott became the "spinster scribbler" about which she sometimes wrote in her later fiction. It was also during this period that she wrote the many sentimental stories that appealed to the audience at that time.

Thirty years old at the time of the Civil War, Louisa went to Washington in 1862 as a hospital nurse. Conditions were appalling. In six weeks she became ill with typhoid fever, and, when strong enough to make the trip, she was sent home to recuperate. This was a turning point in her life; she was never again in the exuberant good health of her youth. During her convalescence, she turned again to her writing, and she published the letters she had written home to her family from Washington (*Hospital Sketches* was published in 1863). During this period, too, she wrote the Gothic thrillers that Victorians clamored for; these sold well, but because she published them under a pseudonym, they did not acquire a reputation for their author. *Hospital Sketches,* however, did earn for Alcott the reputation of a serious writer, which encouraged her work on a serious novel, *Moods,* published in 1864.

After a European tour as companion to an invalid girl, Louisa once again turned to writing to support her family. She became editor of and contributor to *Merry's Museum,* a magazine for children. In 1867, Thomas Niles, a publisher with Roberts Brothers, urged her to write a novel for girls. Although Louisa balked, she turned out the first half of *Little Women,* drawn largely from family experiences. The novel became a great success when it was published in 1868. Encouraged, she moved to Boston and wrote a chapter a day until the second half of the book was finished early in 1869. *Little Women* established Louisa May Alcott's reputation as a writer of children's books.

Little Women was followed by *An Old-Fashioned Girl* (1870), *Little Men* (1871), *Work* (1873), *Eight Cousins* (1875), and *Rose in Bloom* (1876). By this time, Louisa had become interested in women's issues, including suffrage, and she expressed her opinions in *Woman's Journal,* founded by Lucy Stone and Henry Blackwell in 1870. In 1879, Louisa was the first woman to register to vote in Concord. After the death of her mother in 1879, Louisa and her father were thrown more upon each other. The family circle widened again, however, with the arrival of her sister's daughter from Europe, May Alcott Nieriker having died shortly after childbirth. With another person to care for, Louisa continued to write, but *Jo's Boys* (1886) was clearly intended to be her last novel. Both Louisa and her father suffered from ill health as they aged. On March 4, 1888, Bronson died during the night. Early on the morning of March 6, Louisa died in her sleep. Father and daughter had a joint funeral and were buried in Sleepy Hollow Cemetery in Concord.

Analysis

Because Louisa May Alcott is so well known for *Little Women*, much of her other work is generally overlooked. Yet she was a highly prolific writer who wrote throughout her life, virtually from childhood to the grave. The many stories and home theatricals that she wrote as a child constituted an apprentice period for her craft; much of her mature writing summons up this early period.

The mid-1850's found Alcott writing the sentimental stories popular in the Victorian era. Alcott was always especially attuned to her audience, writing what would sell to a publisher and be enjoyed by a real audience. While this shows a certain kind of sensitivity, it also restricted her writing. Victorian sentimentality was something she could always fall back upon, and in some of her later novels, when the modern reader hopes for a more mature engagement of ideas and testing of hypotheses, Alcott seems to take the easy way out into the old sentimentality that had worked so well in the past.

Although she was a hospital nurse for only six weeks during the Civil War, the experience was a turning point for Alcott. It had both good and bad outcomes. On the negative side, she never fully recovered her health from the typhoid fever she contracted or from the medication given to cure her. On the positive side, she had the time and the inclination to rewrite the letters she had written home, which were published in 1863 as *Hospital Sketches*. This work, published under her own name, established Alcott's reputation as a serious writer. Of particular note were her frankness and graphic detail, qualities that would continue to serve her well as her career developed.

At the same time, she was writing the Gothic stories that were published anonymously or under a pseudonym (frequently A. M. Barnard). In *Little Women*, when Jo March, generally considered to be Louisa's self-portrait, writes thrillers, she does so with a sense of shame and hides her identity from her publishers, her family, and friends. She soon abandons this form of writing, even though she is good at it and needs the money that can result from these stories, agreeing with Professor Bhaer that money earned in this way is not worth the moral degradation it necessitates. Jo no doubt betrays some of Alcott's own misgivings about the genre. The Gothic thriller and sensation stories were and are good reading material, however; they are fast-paced and full of suspense. Characterization is lively, although plots are sometimes unbelievable. With that willing suspension of disbelief demanded by all writers of the Gothic, Alcott created some memorable characters who play roles in dramatic and compelling plots. No doubt Louisa's own experiences as a hospital nurse, as traveling companion for an invalid woman in Europe, and as a woman attempting to earn money in and around Concord and Boston introduced her to a number of colorful personalities with rich stories, who provided inspiration for the heroes and heroines of her thrillers. The Gothic thrillers must have provided not only a rich outlet for her imagination but also a safe way of living vicariously experiences that conventions and responsibilities prohibited in real life.

Many of the Gothic thrillers feature strong, courageous, and independent heroines who are bent on carrying out some plot of revenge or ambition. Passionate and dramatic, these women manage to control and manipulate others to accomplish their dire ends. Generally, they succeed in their plans, although the outcome may entail more than originally intended. In *Behind a Mask*, for example, the bold heroine manages to entice several brothers to love her in order to humble them and teach them a lesson about their pride. Although her plot almost fails, she entices the uncle to marry her. She thus secures for herself a devoted husband as well as the security of becoming a legitimate member of a highly reputable, wealthy, and good family despite her own unsavory past. Although it is quite clear that the heroine is an evil woman, Alcott makes the reader appreciate her daring, her shrewdness, and her power to carry it all off. The reader ends up celebrating the villain's triumph. No doubt it is for this reason that Alcott chose to write these Gothic thrillers under a pseudonym and had moral qualms about them. Not all the Gothic thrillers flaunt quite so blatantly a different set of values from those conventionally upheld, but many deal with the bringing down of proud families by individuals with the boldness to use less than praiseworthy means to accomplish their ends. Sometimes these means are necessitated by personal desperation and social injustice, it is true, but the thrillers are intended to entertain rather than to invoke moral debate.

When she began writing for children, Alcott necessarily had to tone down the murders and ghosts, the passions and dramatic actions that marked the Gothic and sensation stories. Morality in Alcott's writings took a decided turn toward the conventional expectations of nineteenth century, middle-class America. The existence of the wealthy was no longer a call to arms, a challenge to use one's initiative to find the chink in the wall that would provide access for oneself; it became an opportunity to exercise virtues of patience, humility, and submission to one's own humble station in life. Poverty no longer was a condition to be overcome, but a reminder to appreciate other gifts—talent, family, loyalty and devotion, love, charity, and others.

Some critics have remarked that the stories written for children are saccharine, and undoubtedly this is so for the modern reader. It must be remembered, however, that Alcott was aware of her need to write what her publishers and audience desired. She did not have the luxury of a secure economic foundation, an independent income that would sustain her no matter whether she pleased an audience or not. Having tried her hand at other occupations (as teacher, governess, and companion), she turned to writing as one of a very few acceptable ways for a woman to earn a living. To write what would sell, she turned to novels that inculcated the "right" values and celebrated the virtues and delights of family life. The successes and accomplishments of individuals are measured against the backdrop of family and community responsibility and well-being. Another difference between the Gothic thrillers and the writings for children is the increased realism of plot and setting. One reason for the enormous success of *Little Women*, for example, is the fact that the personality types depicted and the situations in which they find themselves are detailed in such a way as to be credible. In writing such novels, Alcott relied upon incidents of her own childhood, and the authenticity of these experiences is verified by the tone and style of the novels.

Under different circumstances, Louisa May Alcott may have been a different kind of writer, one who would have ranked among the great artists of the nineteenth century. Nevertheless, most readers acknowledge the considerable talent evident in her work—her vivid characterization, her shrewdness in accommodating the fluctuating needs of various audiences, her expert management of plot events for interest, suspense, and dramatic effect, her lively description of setting, and the remarkable range of her subject matter and tone.

LITTLE WOMEN

First published: Part 1, 1868; part 2, 1869
Type of work: Novel

In the nineteenth century United States, a tightly knit family experiences the joys and disappointments of four young girls growing to adulthood.

Little Women was, and remains, Louisa May Alcott's best-known and most widely read work. It was her first novel for young girls and was so popular that her audience demanded sequels, a request that Alcott fulfilled, although most readers believe that *Little Women* is the most compelling of Alcott's novels about the March family.

As the novel opens, the four girls—the oldest, Meg (sixteen), tomboyish Jo (fifteen), sweet Beth (thirteen), and the youngest, Amy (twelve)—are sitting around the hearth contemplating a Christmas without presents, for their father is away serving as chaplain for a unit of men fighting in the Civil War and the family has very limited funds. From this opening dialogue, a reader gets insights into the basic personality types of the various characters. Meg feels most strongly the family's limited resources. It is she who struggles hardest with envy of the wealthier girls in town. Jo is the most spirited of the lot, physically the most active and psychologically the most independent; she nevertheless is most comfortable when she is safely ensconced within the family circle of Marmee (the girls' nickname for their mother) and her four girls. Beth is the sweetest and most generous of the girls, the one who complains least and tries hardest to ease the difficulties of the others. She is the character whom some readers think is really too good to be true. As might be expected, she dies an early death, as if she is too good for this world. The youngest, Amy, has rather grand visions of herself, but these are tempered as she tests her artistic skills abroad and eventually marries the boy next door.

Several themes emerge in the book as the girls develop into adults. One is the difficulty that women of the period had in finding suitable work. Marriage was the most obvious hope for economic stability, but for the woman who did not choose marriage, options were extremely limited and the pay not sufficient. The girls try a number of ways to earn money—as companion, governess, and writer, for example—but nothing that they can do succeeds very well. Another theme is the importance of maintaining the family circle. Even marriage is not greeted unhesitatingly, because it threatens to remove one sister from the family. Disruptions to the family circle are inevitable as children grow up, but in *Little Women* they are always greeted with only begrudging kindness. Materialism is decried, as are the frivolities of the dances and entertainments in which girls with only a little more money than the Marches indulge. The virtues of patience, submission, and devotion are lauded instead. Finally, no discussion of the novel is complete without mention of the spirited individualism of Jo. She is the most independent of the four girls, although she probably shocks everyone by turning down a very attractive marriage proposal from the wealthy young man next door. Her later acceptance of the older Professor Bhaer (in part 2) has been a source of some criticism for Alcott, because it seems a fictional denial of the feminism that grew ever stronger in Alcott's own life.

Perhaps the most important feature of *Little Women* is its depiction of domestic harmony in convincingly realistic detail. In the trivial daily activities and the modest goals and setbacks of family members, Alcott depicts a supportive family environment that anyone committed to the ideal of the family can approve. Further, although *Little Women* eschews the single-minded goals of revenge or passion that characterize the gripping Gothic tales, each of the four sisters' separate stories nevertheless determinedly marches along, with the various threads intertwining in a delightfully twisting, sometimes knotted, sometimes surprising, yarn of family life. For its adept juggling of subplots, the conversational dialogue of characters, the realism of setting and situation, and the idealism of personal morality and family harmony, *Little Women* will continue to be read for pleasure, for escape, and for education.

Summary

Louisa May Alcott was a productive and astute writer, assessing the needs of her audience and writing what would sell. Whether writing in the sentimental or Gothic vein, realistic novels for children or for adults, Alcott expressed her respect for individualistic women, her scorn for women's limited economic opportunities, and her esteem for the family unit. Her characters are memorable, her dialogues demonstrate an ear for conversation, her descriptions are strong and picturesque, and her narratives are unfailingly vivid and fast-paced.

Bibliography

Bedell, Madelon. *The Alcotts: Biography of a Family.* New York: Clarkson N. Potter, 1980.

Cheney, Ednah Dow. *Louisa May Alcott.* New York: Chelsea House, 1981.

Elbert, Sarah. *A Hunger for Home: Louisa May Alcott and "Little Women."* Philadelphia: Temple University Press, 1984.

_____. *So Sweet to Remember: Feminism and Fiction of Louisa May Alcott.* Philadelphia: Temple University Press, 1983.

MacDonald, Ruth K. *Louisa May Alcott.* Boston: Twayne, 1983.

Payne, Alma. *Louisa May Alcott: A Reference Guide.* Boston: G. K. Hall, 1980.

Stern, Madeleine B. *Louisa May Alcott.* Norman: University of Oklahoma Press, 1971.

Paula D. Kopacz

NELSON ALGREN

Born: Detroit, Michigan
March 28, 1909
Died: Sag Harbor, New York
May 9, 1981

Principal Literary Achievement
A lifelong critic of American society, Algren championed its victims in fiction renowned for an idiosyncratic style that is both realistic and lyrical.

Biography
Born Nelson Ahlgren Abraham, in Detroit, Michigan, on March 28, 1909, Nelson Algren is usually identified with Chicago, where his family moved in 1913. His mother, Goldie, was an ill-tempered, violent woman, and his uncouth mechanic father, Gerson, was an often remote presence. The emotionally insecure Algren preferred to identify with the wandering grandfather he never met, Nels Ahlgren, a Swedish convert to Judaism. A normal middle-class boy in most respects, Algren began frequenting pool halls, speakeasies, and gambling dens as a teenager.

His strongest family bond was with Bernice, the younger of two older sisters. It was she who encouraged his literary interests and insisted he attend college, and her death in 1940 left a space no one ever filled. Socially aloof, Algren discovered his love of books at the University of Illinois, Urbana, and led an ascetic and "spiritual" life of study, with the occasional lapse. In college, he wrote stories which demonstrate his identification with the oppressed—an identification that his experiences on the road would deepen. In 1931, with a degree in journalism, he went in search of a job that was not to be had during the Great Depression. Taking up the hobo's life, he traveled to New Orleans, the other major city of his fiction. There he sold door-to-door before accompanying two drifters to Texas, where he became involved in an ill-fated scheme to run a gas station and later worked at a carnival.

After further travels, gathering experiences that he would turn into fiction, Algren returned home, joined a writers' group, and started submitting stories using Nelson Algren as his pen name (only changing it legally during World War II). Politically radical, he frequented the John Reed Club, a Communist Party organization, and met writers such as Richard Wright, the future author of *Native Son* (1940). Over the years, he would have close ties with the Communist Party, but it is not certain that he was ever a member.

After several rejections, he was published by *Story* and *A Year* in 1933. When Vanguard Press paid him an advance for a novel, Algren, who always wrote best from immediate experience, went back on the road. In Alpine, Texas, he spent almost a month in jail for stealing a typewriter from the local community college. Though his stories and reporting enhanced his reputation, Algren was devastated when *Somebody in Boots* (1935) was not a success. Despite favorable reviews, the novel did not sell, and he attempted suicide during an extended period of depression. Tough but compassionate in his interviews, Algren was actually deeply insecure and very self-destructive; he did not spare those around him, either, about which he felt guilty even as he denied it. This is clearest in his three ambivalent, tortured marriages, two of them to Amanda Kontowicz, whom he met following the "failure" of his first novel.

In 1936, Algren took a job with the Works Progress Administration, or WPA, a federal program then providing writers and artists with jobs. In 1939, to write his second novel, he moved to the Polish "triangle," the setting of his Chicago novels, a world of taverns, pool halls, gambling dens, police line-ups, and brothels, where he recorded dialogue and anecdotes. With the success of *Never Come Morning* (1942), his confidence and spirits rose, though he made so little money that he was soon back on the public payroll with the Venereal Disease Control Project. During World War II, he served in the medical corps, seeing little action but enjoying wartime Marseilles, where he gambled away his black market profits. Returning to Chicago, he settled down to a more austere life to complete a collection of stories, *The Neon Wilderness* (1947).

His reputation growing in literary circles, he met Simone de Beauvoir, the French novelist and feminist author of *Le Deuxième Sexe* (1949; *The Second Sex*, 1953). This, the most fulfilling and passionate affair of his life, ended because of de Beauvoir's commitment to Jean-Paul Sartre, the French existentialist writer and philosopher.

The controversial *The Man with the Golden Arm* (1949) brought Algren to the height of his fame and success. Unfortunately, it did not solve his financial problems. He suffered gambling losses; in addition, he was so confident of his own shrewdness that he made several unfortunate financial deals, especially in Hollywood. Fame also isolated him from his subject, the dispossessed. Though he championed the downtrodden in his book-length essay *Chicago: City on the Make* (1951), he found it impossible to complete the novel with which he was struggling, *Entrapment*. Finally, he transformed *Somebody in Boots* into *A Walk on the Wild Side* (1956). Though its reputation continues to grow, it was not a success at the time, and Algren was almost as depressed by its failure the second time as the first, possibly going so far as a second suicide attempt.

Worse, he used popular rejection as an excuse to stop serious writing. Cashing in on his reputation, he lectured and taught. Aside from a few stories, he restricted his writing to journalism, magazine articles, and travel books, such as *Who Lost an American?* (1963) and *Notes from a Sea Diary: Hemingway All the Way* (1965). In

1968, he went to Vietnam, where, instead of covering the war, he had a disastrous experience with the black market.

As he became older, his writing turned bitter and satirical. Though he was often amusing and stimulating company, his physical condition deteriorated, which alarmed old friends, many of whom he snubbed without reason. Increasingly obsessed with money, he began a racetrack novel, but he seemed more interested in receiving advances than in actually finishing it; several segments came out in the collection *The Last Carousel* (1973). He was still politically committed enough to move to Paterson, New Jersey, in 1975 to write a nonfiction book on the black boxer Rubin "Hurricane" Carter, whom many considered unjustly convicted of murder. Failing to sell the manuscript, he turned it into the posthumous and poorly received *The Devil's Stocking* (1983).

With considerable help from friends, Algren moved to Sag Harbor, New York, in 1980. He relished this congenial town, but he had already suffered one heart attack that, characteristically, he refused to acknowledge. A second killed him the night before a party to celebrate his election to the American Academy of Arts and Letters.

Analysis

The work of Nelson Algren is best understood within the context of naturalism, a literary tradition deriving from realism's truthful representation of life darkened by "Darwinian" notions of survival of the fittest and determinism. Though naturalism began in nineteenth-century France with authors such as Émile Zola, a strong American tradition runs from Stephen Crane through Frank Norris, Theodore Dreiser, Upton Sinclair, and James T. Farrell to Algren. Their novels tend to foreground the marginal elements in industrial society, where factors of heredity, chance, and social conditions determine an individual's fate regardless of his or her will. Though characters are depicted as insignificant, their plight is often presented in a romanticized and melodramatic manner, as in some of Algren's writing.

During the Great Depression of the 1930's, with the apparent collapse of capitalism and the rise of Fascism, naturalism adapted easily to the left-wing dissent that blossomed at the time. Believing that "the role of the writer is always to stand against the culture he is in . . . with the accused," Algren, like many others, sympathized with the Communist Party. Despising capitalism's hypocritical rejection of addicts and criminals whose condition mirrored capitalism's materialist addiction and vicious competition, Algren put his pen at the service of the underdog, whom he saw as victim and scapegoat. This resulted in an often heavy-handed preachiness, though this element was less pervasive in his stories, usually, than the novels.

Algren claimed never to have been a Party member; his compassion for the underclass was more personal—as was that of Studs Terkel, his lifelong friend. At home with a segment of society that most people refuse to see—con men, drug addicts, prostitutes, and petty criminals—Algren regarded these people as victims of an economic system under which the rich are simply the successful hustlers. The only crime of the dispossessed is that they are losers, their guilt "the great, secret, and special American guilt of owning nothing, nothing at all, in the one land where ownership and virtue are one."

Doing what he called "emotionalized reportage," Algren wrote from life, speaking for those spiritually starved and trapped in the bleak struggle with their social surroundings. Always valuing the human over the theoretical, he lived in the urban settings he described—alley, bar, brothel, jail, tenements, and flophouses—just as he traveled the countryside of his novels, the poverty-stricken United States of the Depression.

In the world of Algren's fiction, there seems no way out except through the always imminent violence, and the only fatal weakness is the expression of doubt and compassion. For his main characters, never brutal enough, there is no hope for salvation except by trusting other people. Unfortunately, they are the product of a society in which trust, even self-trust, is impossible; the promise of love is counterfeit—or seems so until it is too late. Throughout Algren's work, characters destroy love; then, guilt-haunted, they are unable to escape their fates. Indeed, they seek their doom as expiation of their betrayal of love, while the policemen who hound them are burdened by their sense of shared guilt.

Though these themes remained constant, over time the tone of Algren's writing changed, irony giving way first to the comical before turning bitter and satirical, subsiding at times into slapstick and the bizarre. This reflected not only Algren's belief in the underlying absurdity of the human condition but also his growing despair that writing would ever change anything: Parody was ultimately his only response to society's callousness.

Though this cynicism suits naturalism, Algren was influenced stylistically by the poetry of Walt Whitman and Carl Sandburg, as well as the splenetic, free-form novels of the Frenchman Louis-Ferdinand Céline. Algren's prose catches what he called the poetry of human speech, its rhythms and repetitions, while repeated catch-phrases and song lyrics give it both a dreamlike quality and structural cohesiveness. A mix of specific details, low-life jargon, and well-observed idiosyncrasies of thought and behavior make this style both realistically exact and lyrically grim (though occasionally overwritten). Characteristic is the heavily symbolic and colorful imagery that conveys a nearly pervasive foreboding, as in *The Man with the Golden Arm*.

> Goggling upward at it, shivering a bit in the shabby coat, he felt for a moment as if he too were something impaled on city wires for only tenement winds to touch.

Leaving out the "spare parts," as he put it, Algren created an unorthodox grammar of fragments and short run-ons arranged to suggest the movement of thought and able to convey a wide range of moods, from the contemplative to the urgent. In these ways, he communicated mental states that his uneducated characters could not articulate for themselves.

From 1935 to 1981, Algren wrote only five novels. Though able to churn out stories and articles for money, he was never able to write his novels easily. Never planned, each developed by a process of aggregation as he expanded it from the inside. To complete this difficult process, Algren needed firsthand experience, but he became increasingly isolated. This partly explains why he completed so few long works; he was also hindered by increasing bitterness about his place in American letters. Identifying with the writers of the 1930's, who were poor but committed, Algren was critical of the literary scene after World War II. Not only was he ambivalent about the prosperity of other artists (which his gambling habit denied him anyway), but he also considered himself to be the victim of an anti-Communist backlash that he believed extended into literature through the auspices of the New Criticism. This movement removed writing from its social context, dismissing special pleading for a social cause in the belief that true art is self-contained. Attacking this as falsely limiting, Algren believed that "literature is made upon any occasion when a challenge is put to the legal apparatus by conscience in touch with humanity." Unfortunately, in the turbulent political climate of the 1950's, when to be liberal was to be suspect, many critics turned their backs on the social issues, dismissing Algren's work as sentimental and romantic. Yet the responsibility for his meager output was Algren's also, since he abdicated control of his own artistic life, choosing to see himself as a victim.

NEVER COME MORNING

First published: 1942
Type of work: Novel

A young boxer from Chicago's slums destroys himself in his struggle for identity and independence.

Never Come Morning, like all of Algren's novels, is a study of doom working itself out. Bruno "Lefty" Bicek is a young Polish-American imprisoned in the Polish slums of Chicago, so oppressively isolated that the outside filters through only in films and tabloids. These promise a glorified version of success, but the American Dream is closer to nightmare in this world of police lineups, gangs, petty crime, and brothels. Here everyone is either hunter or the hunted, who have nothing to lose but are too worried about being cheated of what they are owed to trust anyone else.

Like the rest, Bruno, hungering for boxing glory, scorns the Old World values of hard work and religious faith, but he is not strong enough to live by the New World's capitalistic code of violence and deception. Bruno thinks of himself as a wolf, but he is a dreamer instead of a schemer; though sensitive and humane, he is too crippled by conscience to protect himself and too insecure to protect others. Despite his boxing prowess, he cannot stand up to his more brutal inferiors, either the knife-wielding Fireball Kodadek or the blackmailing Bonifacy "the barber" Konstantine, who wants to control his boxing career.

In a world where everything is a cheat, love seems as false as every other promise, but to destroy love in Algren's novels is to destroy oneself. This is what happens when Bruno, asserting himself as a gang leader, seduces and betrays Steffi Rostenkowski. Steffi, born with the same limited choices, gives in to Bruno because he seems the best she can expect. Then Bruno, unsure of himself and afraid of Kodadek's knife, lets the rest of the gang have their way with Steffi. After this, Bicek's fate is sealed. Stubbornly proud, he channels his shame into rage, murdering a Greek outsider trying to join in the rape. Knowing that there can be no forgiveness for killing Steffi "in his heart," he is ready to accept any punishment and goes to jail for a crime he did not commit. Still in search of forgiveness, he returns and gets a job at Mama Tomek's brothel where Steffi, now Bonifacy's mistress, works. Hoping to free Steffi and himself, Bruno establishes his independence by arranging his own boxing match and proves his manhood by beating up Bonifacy's henchmen. All escape is illusory, however; Bruno wins in the boxing ring, but only for Bonifacy to denounce him to the police for the Greek's murder.

Never Come Morning is a stylistic improvement over *Somebody in Boots*, with complex shifts in tone and pacing, subtler characters, and well-developed scenes. The brothel scenes, in particular, are praised for their authenticity and compassionate understanding, conveying simultaneously the comic and the threatening. Critics differ about this and other digressions in the novel, however, which weaken the story's tension to dwell on capitalism's oppressive exploitation. To heighten the sense of futility and hopelessness, Algren uses images of imprisonment and rain. Equally bitter are the song lyrics whose cheerfulness is merely ironic in a dark world where people are compared to mutilated flies and decapitated dolls. In many parts, the story often pushed to the side, *Never Come Morning* reads like a mood poem on the imminence of violence and death.

THE MAN WITH THE GOLDEN ARM

First published: 1949
Type of work: Novel

Doomed from the beginning, card dealer Frankie Machine struggles hopelessly against drug addiction and guilt.

The Man with the Golden Arm, Algren's one great popular success, caught public attention because of the then-shocking drug addiction of its protagonist. For Algren, this aspect—a late addition to the novel—merely contributed to the story of the self-destructive relationship of Francis Majcinek, known as Frankie Machine because of his skill as a dealer, and his possessive, hypochondriacal wife, Sophie (or Zosh).

Like all Algren protagonists, Frankie is not as tough as he pretends; he talks big, but he is a coward who dreams of becoming a drummer. His fixer, Nifty Louis Fomorowsky, sees immediately that Frankie is among the world's sheep, not the shearers, and that like so many, he chooses his addiction and his doom. As always in Algren's work, when strength is used, it leads to violence and self-destruction; in an unthinking moment, Frankie kills Louie.

The wheelchair-bound Sophie is the most complicated female character in any of Algren's novels. Her pride stung by Frankie's indifference to her love, she had trapped him into marriage with a false pregnancy. Now, though there is nothing wrong with her legs, she insists that Frankie crippled her in a driving accident, binding him all the tighter to her through guilt. Throughout the book, she becomes more demanding and destructively compulsive, driving Frankie away while descending into insanity. Instead of abandoning her, Frankie makes halfhearted attempts to please her, because "a guy got to draw the line somewheres on how bad he can treat somebody who can't help herself no more just account of him." Unfortunately, Frankie does not know where to draw the line and so relies on morphine.

In another characteristic Algren touch, it does not matter that Frankie became addicted by chance in an army hospital. He is doomed anyway, because he cannot rid himself of this "monkey on his back" (a phrase introduced into general use with this novel). For Algren there are no fresh starts, even though trust and love always hold out hope. Molly Novotny offers love to Frankie, but he cannot accept it because his tortured guilt over Sophie alienates him more and more from himself.

In the novel's world, self-destruction is pursued in the hope of penance, and Frankie gets his one chance for redemption when he is caught shoplifting. In prison, he breaks his addiction, only to return to Division Street and find that Molly is gone, Sophie is crazy, and the one person he trusted, Sparrow "Solly" Saltskin, has betrayed his trust. When he loses his touch with cards, he goes back on drugs, while the tenacious police captain Record Head Bednar uses Sparrow, as well as Frankie's own addiction, to nail him for Louie's killing. On the run, wounded and exhausted, Frankie hangs himself in a flophouse.

In no other novel did Algren mix serious, lyrical, and comic elements to such effect. Writing it, he still thought that books could change society because "every man was secretly against the law in his heart . . . and it was the heart that mattered." Believing that there are no absolute moral values—only people—Algren rated compassion over justice, especially that based on property laws, and he tried in this novel to move the reader to believe that as well.

This is particularly clear in the example of the tortured police captain, Record Head Bednar, who has an answer for every pathetic excuse except when an arrested man says, "We are all members of one another." As the one responsible for arresting criminals, Bednar finally admits, but cannot embrace, his identification with the "guilty" who are closer to redemption than he is because he denies his connection with them. Instead, he continues his spiritual con game, apportioning society's justice when he is "more lost, more fallen and more alone than any man at all."

Though Algren was the grandson of a convert to Judaism and the son of a Jewish mother, it is Christian imagery that predominates in this book, though in an inverted manner. Everyone is guilty. Christ is the accuser, not the savior, since no one can be saved. All the characters feel crucified or impaled, but there is no afterlife, no point to the suffering, only death: " 'When you come to the end it's the end, that's all.' " There was some criticism of the book's loose two-part structure, and Algren regretted its chase ending, but the book excels in its focus on mood. The author cared more for changes of consciousness as the characters suffer the consequences of destroyed love than for plot. In depicting this, Algren's style is at its finest. Algren used jargon accurately and drew his lively images from the characters' lives: "He still looked like the business end of a fugitive warrant to Frankie."

At its best, the writing is both realistic in matter of detail and grim in tone, and it manages a lyrical quality with its freewheeling grammar.

> Caught between the dealer's slot and the cat-gray stroke of the years, Frankie saw a line of endless girders wet with the rain of those years to be. Where all night long, in that far time, the same all-night salamanders burned. Burned just as they had so long ago. Before the world went wrong. And any gray cat had purred at all.

At the same time, humor is used more and to more effect than in his earlier novels, in keeping with Algren's sense of the absurd in all human matters, even the tragic. Consequently, the comic elements provide more than laughs: They resonate with foreboding and the horror of life's meaninglessness. For example, the alcoholic dog Rumdum is redeemed, though Frankie is doomed, along with the whole colorful cast of grotesques at the Tug & Maul who drink their lives away. The near-slapstick affair between Sparrow and Vi, whose old husband, Stash Koskoska, is a slow-witted old man with a taste for day-old bread and cut-rate Polish sausage, affords more than comic relief. This travesty of marriage heightens, by contrast, the oppressiveness of Frankie and Zosh's mutual hell.

A WALK ON THE WILD SIDE

First published: 1956
Type of work: Novel

The wise fool Dove Linkhorn sets out to conquer women and the world, only to be thoroughly vanquished.

A Walk on the Wild Side started as a revision of *Somebody in Boots*, but as it progressed, Algren transformed his serious first novel into a parody of the American Dream. Algren justified this on the grounds that, times having changed, he had to entertain readers. Moreover, disgusted by the triumph of materialism, he no longer believed that writing could change attitudes, only mock them. This apparently defensive response betrays a lack of confidence in what some critics considered to be a great idiosyncratic masterpiece of the absurd that prepared the way for such writers as Thomas Pynchon, Ken Kesey, Joseph Heller, and Hunter S. Thompson.

Dove Linkhorn is the last of a line of poor Texas rebels against authority. Illiterate but canny, Dove is a loser who is too innocent to feel like a loser. Incapable of recognizing society's moral code, and so amoral, he does know when he has betrayed those who helped him. Deprived of any meaningful childhood, as Algren may have believed he himself was, Dove at sixteen wants two things, education and love, which he finds in Terasina Vidavarri. While trying to teach Dove the alphabet, she awakens his indefatigable virility, convincing him that he is a born world shaker. When she resists his later advances, he rapes her and flees, only to find he can escape neither his love nor his guilt for violating the reverence he feels for her.

In his subsequent adventures, he meets a cast of strange, but human, characters. He is as odd as the others, certainly, a wise fool, practically a cartoon figure. He learns the ways of the road from Kitty Twist; however, as so often happens in Algren, the man lets the woman down. She gets caught during a robbery while he manages to escape, selling door-to-door and working in a condom factory before having his great success as the Big Stingaree, "deflowerer" of "virgins" in a sex show. This rise to the top of the bottom is central to Algren's parody. In one scene, Dove watches a headless turtle crawl to the top of a pile of decapitated turtles before toppling to the bottom, where there is always room for one more. Dove himself slides to the bottom when he runs off with a teacher turned prostitute, whose lover, the legless Achilles Schmidt, will eventually blind Dove during a savage beating just after he learns to read.

Despite the many amusing and colorful scenes set in brothels and condom factories, the book's core is its examination of love and guilt. Love is resisted because it can kill, as it does the little girl who goes after her doll under the wheels of a train, or threaten one's self-sufficiency, as it does Schmidt's. Dove rebels against Terasina's power, only to learn that violence renders him permanently dependent through guilt. Initially, domination may seem the only basis for emotional relationships in a society that rewards deceit and force, but violence puts a man beyond salvation by destroying his contact with others.

Though less preachy than *Somebody in Boots, A Walk on the Wild Side* indicts a society where there is "self-reliance for the penniless and government help to the rich" and where the men who profit from vice are the very ones who inveigh against it and where the losers are jailed—having been given their "chance." During the Depression, the ladder of success was inverted; everyone was on the street hustling for a living and selling something. Dove is warned to watch out for trust and friends, but he comes to wonder if he wants success when it is always at the expenses of "them who have already been whipped."

At the end, as Schmidt beats Dove's face into a bloody pulp, others stand around and exult "as though each fresh blow redeemed that blow that his life had been to him." Algren believed that this is what capitalism reduces people to: the violence of despair. When the same crowd rushes Schmidt to his death, he goes as "a saint of the amputees," knowing that he has done their work for them. This Christ-like acceptance of guilt and connection with others is the only salvation the world offers; Dove returns home, ready for love at last and hoping Terasina will take him in.

THE NEON WILDERNESS

First published: 1947
Type of work: Short stories

In realistically grim and lyrically idiosyncratic portraits, Algren depicts America's down-and-out.

With *The Neon Wilderness*, Algren emerged as a mature and original spokesman for a whole class of people usually excluded from literature except as marginal and stereotyped caricatures. In place of the condescending tone of most writing about the poor, Algren demonstrates the compassion of a man determined to live up to the people he is writing about. The stories bristle with many of Algren's characteristic thematic and stylistic concerns. The more focused short-story form undermines his didactic, Communist streak, and though there are times when Algren sentimentalizes his characters, this does not diminish the overall power of these stories.

"So Help Me," his first published story, is a dramatic monologue using a favorite Algren device, the interrogation of a criminal. His use here of only the criminal's voice lessens the effect, but the solidity of detail and attention to human voice create a convincing account of man's isolation and the inevitability of violence, those constants of Algren's work. Another characteristic touch is the repeated use of the title phrase, prompting both sympathy and doubt. In "Design for Departure," one of his attempts to write an important story, Algren carefully creates the urban jungle motif and brings out the religious parallels in this story of Mary and Christiano, victims of psychological and economic deprivation. Born into a world of despair, Mary wants only to die, and her whole life is directed toward that departure as she succumbs to the pervasive sense of doom. Unable to connect with the world, she suffers through an unloving upbringing, drug addiction, and prostitution before finally committing suicide. Deaf Christy, who helps her die when he cannot save her, is one of a whole line of cripples in Algren's writing who are brutal yet not vicious so much as callous and spiritually starved.

The ending teeters between the moving and the sentimental, and some critics prefer Algren's more spontaneous stories. With "How the Devil Came Down Division Street," Algren dashed off one of his first comic masterpieces. Outrageous and bizarre, this supernatural story is told with a casual air that belies its grim moral, that the salvation of one character often necessitates the perdition of another. Irony is equally pronounced in "Depend on Aunt Elly," a bitter love story about a prizefighter and a prostitute. Despite their devotion to each other and their recognition that they are each other's only salvation, their lives are so determined that neither talent nor courage is proof against the simple bad luck of being who they are and being at the mercy of a greed more powerful than love.

Algren worked several of these stories into his novels. "A Bottle of Milk for

Mother," for example, tells of the accidental shooting for which Bruno "Lefty" Bicek takes the rap in the middle segment of *Never Come Morning*. Another interrogation story, this is an improvement over "So Help Me" because of the use of character interaction and an ironic narrator to depict Bruno's self-incrimination under Captain Kozak's masterful questioning. Kozak is one of Algren's weary, guilt-haunted, but clever cops, such as the captain in "The Captain Has Bad Dreams," used in *The Man with the Golden Arm*.

In "The Face on the Barroom Floor," later refashioned as the end of *A Walk on the Wild Side*, a thoughtless comment sparks a murderous brawl between Railroad Shorty, a powerful fighter cut in half by a train, and a callow young bartender. The story is a graphic tale of the inevitability of violence, given the desperate need for identity and self-respect in a world that denies them.

Throughout the book, characters are not seen as warped or degenerate, but as ordinary humans with their lives twisted by circumstances. Their aberrant behavior is for them the active expression of their individuality, their defense in a world where violence and deceit are necessary because the highest value is survival and morality is useless. In "A Lot You Got to Holler," for example, the protagonist says, "I was always in the clear so long as I was truly guilty. But the minute my motives were honest someone would finger me."

Summary

Termed "bard of the stumblebum" and "poet of the Chicago slums," Algren combined an idiosyncratic style and a keen eye for detail in his compelling depictions of the dispossessed. Convinced that "lost people sometimes develop into greater human beings than those who have never been lost in their whole lives," Algren created characters dignified even in defeat.

Bibliography

Bluestone, George. "Nelson Algren." *Western Review* 22 (Autumn, 1957): 27-44.

Carson, Tom. Introduction to *The Neon Wilderness*, by Nelson Algren. New York: Four Walls Eight Windows, 1986.

Cox, Martha Heasley, and Wayne Chatterton. *Nelson Algren*. Boston: Twayne, 1975.

Donohue, H. E. F. *Conversations with Nelson Algren*. New York: Hill & Wang, 1964.

Drew, Bettina. *Nelson Algren: A Life on the Wild Side*. New York: Putnam, 1989.

Edwards, Thomas R. "Underground Man." *The New York Review of Books*, June 28, 1990, 22-24.

Eisinger, Chester E. *Fiction of the Forties*. Chicago: University of Chicago Press, 1963.

Geismar, Maxwell. *American Moderns: From Rebellion to Conformity*. New York: Hill & Wang, 1958.

Philip McDermott

SHERWOOD ANDERSON

Born: Camden, Ohio
September 13, 1876
Died: Colón, Panama Canal Zone
March 8, 1941

Principal Literary Achievement

Though he wrote novels, autobiographies, and poems, Anderson is valued principally as a writer of short stories that penetrate the surface of undistinguished small-town characters unfulfilled in a materialistic society.

Biography

Sherwood Anderson was born in Camden, Ohio, a small town near Dayton, on September 13, 1876; he was the third of seven children of Emma and Irvin Anderson. His mother was of Italian descent. His father was a sign painter who was far from being an economic success but who had been a cavalryman in the Union army during the Civil War, where his training as a harness maker was particularly valuable. Gradually the local, independent saddlery was superseded by the harness factories, and craftsmen such as Irvin Anderson became redundant and impoverished; Mrs. Anderson took in laundry to supplement the family income. The social and economic circumstances of his parents clearly influenced the son's later thinking and his choice of themes for his stories. In 1884, the Anderson family moved from Camden to Clyde, Ohio, near Sandusky and the Lake Erie city of Cleveland, which is frequently mentioned in *Winesburg, Ohio* (1919).

For a time after 1896, Anderson worked in a Chicago warehouse before enlisting for service in the Spanish-American War, from which he was discharged with the rank of corporal. Thereafter, he enrolled in Wittenburg Academy at Springfield, Ohio, and was graduated in June, 1900, becoming an advertising salesman and copywriter in Chicago. In 1904, he married Cornelia Lane, the first of the four wives whom he tried "blunderingly to love." During those years he became a professional success writing what he called "rather senseless advertisements," but he was spiritually unsatisfied; accordingly, he moved to Elyria, a small town on the periphery of Cleveland, and founded the Anderson Manufacturing Company, which produced paint, in 1906. For a dozen years Anderson was rather successful economically, and he took satisfaction in his family; however, his success was not wholly fulfilling, and he engaged in extramarital affairs, overindulged in alcohol, and started writing a

novel. Soon he walked out of his office, was found walking the streets of Cleveland, and was hospitalized for a mental breakdown. Upon his release he returned to Chicago to join the band of writers (including Ben Hecht, Floyd Dell, Theodore Dreiser, and Carl Sandburg) who were the leading spirits behind the Chicago Renaissance.

The novel on which Anderson had been working before his breakdown he showed to his new acquaintances in Chicago. They recommended it for publication, and *Windy McPherson's Son* (1916), largely autobiographical, offered many indications of the nature of Anderson's subsequent writing, though it cannot be regarded as a major work of fiction. Windy McPherson is a thinly veiled portrait of Anderson's father; his son, Sam, gropes with the loneliness and oppressiveness of a small town (Caxton, Iowa) and tries to kill his father. He escapes, goes to Chicago, becomes successful, and marries advantageously—only to renounce the world of business and financial security in an endeavor to "find truth." In many ways the early episode imitates Huckleberry Finn's supposed killing of his father, Pap, which impels Huck's Mississippi River odyssey in *The Adventures of Huckleberry Finn* (1884), but the rest of the story, with its exploration of loneliness and aspiration, success and withdrawal, previews the very essence of *Winesburg, Ohio*.

In the same year, 1916, Anderson divorced Cornelia Lane and married Tennessee Mitchell. Then, in 1917, he published *Marching Men*, a novel set in the central Pennsylvania coal region that highlighted the failure of a movement to organize the miners against the oppressiveness of cheerless, stultifying routine. In *Mid-American Chants* (1918), Anderson attempted his hand at poetry, but with slight success. His models were *Spoon River Anthology* (1915), by Edgar Lee Masters, and the verse of Carl Sandburg, Vachel Lindsay, and Gertrude Stein. It was in the following year, 1919, that he first gained widespread recognition with the publication of *Winesburg, Ohio*, a series of frequently interconnected stories treating the unfulfilled potential, the unsatisfied craving for sexual satisfaction, and the tyranny of mediocrity and orthodoxy in small-town America.

During a trip to Europe in 1921, Anderson met writers Ernest Hemingway, Gertrude Stein, Ford Madox Ford, and James Joyce. During this year he became the first recipient of the *Dial* award; the next year it was awarded to T. S. Eliot for *The Waste Land* (1922). *Many Marriages* (1923) shocked some readers by its sexual frankness, which was considered an element of the new realism of literature that was most apparent in the work of D. H. Lawrence and that resulted, in large part, from the emphasis placed by Sigmund Freud on the role of sex in human personality and behavior. Anderson saw his characters suffering from thwarted emotions.

Anderson divorced Tennessee Mitchell in 1924 and married Elizabeth Prall. They went to live for a time in New Orleans (he had been there earlier, when he was writing *Many Marriages*); there he met William Faulkner, who was then working as a newspaperman, and he influenced Faulkner in both subject matter and style, encouraging him to become a novelist. Anderson's *Dark Laughter* (1925), a novel that contrasts the spiritual sterility of the white population with the irrepressible optimism and endurance of black people, is at once the most mature of his novels and the one closest in technique and philosophy to those of Faulkner, who was indubitably his superior in prose fiction technique and psychological exploration.

In 1927, Anderson settled in Marion, Virginia, and edited two local newspapers, one Democratic, the other Republican; in 1929, he divorced Elizabeth Prall. With the onset of the Depression, Anderson joined Theodore Dreiser, John Dos Passos, Edmund Wilson, Malcolm Cowley, and other distinguished "leftist" writers in advocating a new order based on workers' interests. His political interests were not new: In *Hello Towns!* (1929) and *Nearer the Grass Roots* (1929) he had sung the merits and shortcomings of the small towns of America, those sources of "every phase of life"; *Perhaps Women* (1931), a polemical study, proposed that a solution to the problem of the mechanical sterility of modern life might be found in the political leadership of women.

In 1933, Anderson was married for the fourth time—to Eleanor Copenhaver—and published a collection of short stories, *Death in the Woods and Other Stories.* Subsequently he wrote *Puzzled America* (1935), social essays; *Kit Brandon* (1936), a novel showing characters still trapped in constraining environments; *Home Town* (1940), essays; and memoirs. In 1937, he was elected to the National Institute of Arts and Letters. He died in Colón, Panama Canal Zone, on March 8, 1941, while on a tour sponsored by the Department of State.

Hart Crane, John Steinbeck, Thomas Wolfe, and many other modern American writers were directly or indirectly influenced by Sherwood Anderson; no less than William Faulkner declared that Anderson was "the father of my generation of American writers and the tradition of American writing which our successors will carry on."

Analysis

Winesburg, Ohio is dedicated to the memory of the author's mother, Emma Smith Anderson, who died when Sherwood was nineteen; she had exercised a crucial influence on her son's attitudes to life, for he wrote that her "keen observation on the life about her first woke in me the hunger to see beneath the surface of lives." This hunger persisted throughout Anderson's life and extended even to his attempts at autobiography. He continued to search for the wellsprings of the personality, the psyche, of all the characters in his grand drama of life, including himself.

In a prefatory sketch to *Winesburg, Ohio,* called "The Book of the Grotesque," Anderson offers an insight into his goal and method in the collection of stories that follows. An old writer offers an allegory about the early days of mankind, when there were many thoughts but no truths; people assembled thoughts and constructed their own tentative truths to live by, but in so doing each became a "grotesque" and "the truth he embraced became a falsehood." Anderson even enumerates some of the principal truths that made people into grotesques: "There was the truth of virginity and the truth of passion, the truth of wealth and of poverty, of thrift and of profligacy, of carelessness and abandon. Hundreds and hundreds were the truths and they were all beautiful." What is intended by this account is not unequivocal, but it seems to suggest that by taking a truth out of context and without regard to other truths, a person can follow a false philosophy and become eccentric and even pitiable. The two dozen stories about small-town folk who fail to conform to the norms of society and are accordingly alienated from their fellows never satirize those forlorn and unsatisfied people, those solitaries, those loners. They explore the roots of their disquietude, which are frequently found to have had their origins in some apparently insignificant experience, affront, or rejection that has been long denied or forgotten but is recalled for the edification of Anderson's persona, the youthful George Willard, newspaper reporter for the *Winesburg Eagle.*

None of Anderson's characters is a representative of power, authority, or success in the traditional sense—even the schoolteacher, Kate Smith, the clergyman, the Reverend Curtis Hartman, and the town doctors, Dr. Reefy and Dr. Parceval, are individuals of neither achievement nor authority. Their sullenness and reclusiveness, their very attitudes toward themselves, their neighbors, and life itself demand explication, and Anderson finds in the slightest indication of emotional stress (a sign, a movement, or a look) a means for opening his story. One critic has noted that Anderson was preoccupied by a desire "to describe the agonies and the failures of the unsuccessful, the deprived, and the inarticulate," and it became apparent early in the twentieth century that this could often be accomplished plausibly by the application of the insights of the great Viennese psychologist Sigmund Freud, who placed stress on both the role of dreams and the suppression of sexuality.

Anderson's immediate precursors in American fiction, such as Theodore Dreiser, Frank Norris, Ambrose Bierce, and Sinclair Lewis, had worked against the popular mode of sentimental fiction and had led a "revolt against the village" in favor of realistic portrayals of the expanding industrial society. Their realistic and naturalistic fiction was putting an end to the romanticism that had survived into the new century. They were less interested in the psychological than in the economic, political, and social influences on individuals, however; it was Sherwood Anderson who undertook the development of this approach to characterization. He sought, somewhat paradoxically, to do it within the modern equivalent of the village, the small town on the periphery of the great new industrial cities of the Midwest—the small towns that were the refuge of many of the former inhabitants of the cities.

The grotesques of Winesburg are not engaged in any grand enterprises or plots; rather, they are depicted in the smallest of human endeavors, and their traumatic experiences or socially disapproved actions in the past are—seen in proper perspective—either very minor aberrations or ones subject to multiple interpretations. Yet it seems that just such minor events, decisions, or traits are the ones that affect the lives of ordinary people. The focus of each story is not the solving of a complicated plot but rather the recognition of an epiphany, a special insight or revelation, that explains life's vicissitudes and failures. Action and plot are alluded to, but they are distant and merely set the stage for the discovery of the reasons for the inglorious lives of characters diminished by materialism and the mores of small-town provincialism and philistinism. Notwithstanding their epiphanies, none of Anderson's characters appears defeated and crushed; they all manage to continue, though much chastened and more philosophic.

The simplicity of Anderson's style has often been remarked upon, and many critics have supposed that it had a direct influence on the style of Ernest Hemingway and his many followers and imitators. At its best it has all the virtues of Midwestern speech: straightforwardness, honesty of statement, freedom from artificial flourishes and rococo constructions, demotic vocabulary, and the predominance of the simple declarative sentence. Yet his language is not without detail and vividness, as one can see in the opening of "An Awakening": "Belle Carpenter had a dark skin, grey eyes and thick lips. She was tall and strong. When black thoughts visited her she grew angry and wished she were a man and could fight someone with her fists." Anderson's simple vocabulary and syntax suit his subject to perfection: He captures the very essence of simple lives in simple language. It was Gertrude Stein, the famous mentor of American writers and experimenter with language, who commented that no one in America could equal Anderson for "a clear and passionate sentence."

WINESBURG, OHIO

First published: 1919
Type of work: Short stories

A newspaper reporter recounts significant episodes in the lives of the interesting and sensitive residents of his small town.

Although *Winesburg, Ohio* offers detailed analyses of more than twenty of the residents of a fictional town in the region of Dayton, Ohio, it introduces more than a hundred of the inhabitants of this community of some eighteen hundred people— the greatest number through incidental anecdotes and pointed, penetrating vignettes. The result is something akin to a novel, though there is no unifying story line and no central character or protagonist—George Willard, the young newspaperman, being merely the one through whose eyes the townsfolk are viewed.

The prefatory chapter, which concerns an old writer's dream of a procession of grotesques, sets the pattern for the sequence of twenty-two stories that follow; the writer's unpublished manuscript, "The Book of the Grotesque," set forth his theory that the moment one took a truth and tried to live by it, it became a falsehood: Anderson's book offers his implicit insight that any virtue that is overindulged or pursued uncompromisingly degenerates into its antithesis, a vice.

Winesburg, with its three doctors, three saloons, several churches, large residential hotel (the New Willard House, an ancient establishment), school, farms, newspaper office, and several specialty stores adjacent to the railroad station, is the quintessential small town of American legend. It is a quiet, gentle little town built upon the fundamental Protestant virtues and populated by industrious, frugal neighbors— or so it seems. Anderson, however, shows that Winesburg, representative of most small towns, harbors mainly people who are far from happy, successful, and contented. His stories explore the backgrounds and private aspirations or motivations of representative inhabitants—doctors, teachers, clergymen, retailers, telegraph operator, and shop assistants. All of them are, in one way or another, "alone and defeated" and living lives that are unfulfilled. They quietly nurse their hurts and failures, trying to hide them from others.

Most of the characters stand, lie, or sit by windows and doors: Symbolically they are separated, set apart from the town. Almost all are shown trying to reach out to touch others. Their hands are described in particular detail, as Dr. Reefy, with his "gnarled knuckles"; Elizabeth Willard, with her "long white hands," hands that are "white and bloodless"; and Tom Willy, the saloonkeeper, whose hands looked as though they had been "dipped in blood that had dried and faded." Kate Swift, the schoolteacher, desperately wants to touch her former student, George Willard, since she (now thirty) realizes that touching is a necessary preliminary to intimacy, and she realizes that sexual intimacy is an essential ingredient of a full and satisfying life.

Further, most of the characters at some point seek out George Willard as someone they believe will be interested in them as individuals and not only as sources of newspaper copy. Kate Swift sees him as "rapidly becoming a man," though he still has "the winsomeness of the boy"; that is, he has some of the qualities of the worldliness of age and some of the traits of the physically firm and attractive. It is this combination of characteristics—attractive mind and physique—that makes Willard appealing to many of the characters, even to the Reverend Curtis Hartman, the Presbyterian pastor whose wife is "afire with secret pride" in him. Hartman confesses, when he thinks about his wife, that he almost hates her because "she has always been ashamed of passion and has cheated me." Most of the other characters are aware of their lack of sexual fulfillment also; many obtain temporary satisfaction through illicit or occasional assignations in the woods beside Waterworks Pond.

Significantly, most are seen wandering the streets alone at night as they escape their confining homes and rooms: Almost all the houses in Winesburg seem to have back windows that look out on alleyways through which the lonely prowl, like scavenging animals, in their search for contact, companionship, and love.

One of the most interesting of the stories is "Hands," which offers a portrait of Wing Biddlebaum, a fat, bald little man with "nervous little hands" who had once been a teacher but had an innocent passion for caressing the hair or shoulders of his students. Biddlebaum has been a Winesburg resident for twenty years and is "the town mystery." As Adolph Myers, he had been run out of his Pennsylvania town when a half-witted boy misunderstood the motivation of his teacher's touching him, and he has since picked fruit and done farm labor to earn a livelihood. Yet he is something of an enigma, for when he talks to George Willard, his eyes glow and his hands rise: He sees beauty and he seeks to attach himself to it. Truly, as Anderson suggests in a phrase, this is "a story of hands"—as are many of the others.

Many of the characters in *Winesburg, Ohio* display outward signs of their inner conflicts and torments; they have nervous tics such as scratching an elbow until the coat sleeve is worn through, they chuckle incessantly, or they wear their clothes continuously for ten years. They have an irrepressible urge to talk to willing listeners; they run nude into the rain; they drink heavily; they use pillows as surrogate lovers. Even George Willard, after losing his virginity to Kate Swift, "courted" the young boy Seth Richmond. All the characters, as representatives of universal people, have their hidden, repressed desires, their stories of traumatic loss, their life-scarring memories of experiences that transformed their optimism, expectation, and potential satisfaction into failure, bitterness, and introversion.

Summary

Of her husband, George Willard's mother says, "Nothing he had ever done had turned out successfully." This appears to be true, also, of the characters into whose lives Sherwood Anderson's readers are allowed to peer. They all once had high hopes and expectations in life; through some quiddity, some misunderstanding, some quirk, their life plans were disrupted or destroyed. By means of the flashback and the introduction of minor players in the lives of the grotesque, the reader can appreciate the crucial weaknesses and decisions that have determined the present. Anderson's achievement is that he is not unrelievedly mechanical in his presentation: His simple prose style seems fully appropriate to the wide range of characters that he portrays, and Winesburg even today seems genuinely representative of America's small towns.

Bibliography

Anderson, David D. *Sherwood Anderson: An Introduction and Interpretation*. New York: Holt, Rinehart and Winston, 1967.

Appel, Paul P., ed. *Homage to Sherwood Anderson*. Mount Vernon, N.Y.: Appel, 1970.

Campbell, Hibert H., and Charles E. Modlin, eds. *Sherwood Anderson: Centennial Studies*. Troy, N.Y.: Whitston, 1976.

Howe, Irving. *Sherwood Anderson*. Palo Alto, Calif.: Stanford University Press, 1951.

Rideout, Walter B., ed. *Sherwood Anderson: A Collection of Critical Essays*. New York: Prentice-Hall, 1974.

Taylor, Welford D. *Sherwood Anderson*. New York: Frederick Ungar, 1977.

Townsend, Kim. *Sherwood Anderson: A Biography*. Boston: Houghton Mifflin, 1987.

Weber, Brom. *Sherwood Anderson*. Minneapolis: University of Minnesota Press, 1964.

White, Ray Lewis, ed. *The Achievement of Sherwood Anderson*. Durham: University of North Carolina Press, 1966.

Williams, Kenny J. *A Storyteller and a City: Sherwood Anderson's Chicago*. De Kalb: Northern Illinois University Press, 1988.

A. L. McLeod

JOHN ASHBERY

Born: Rochester, New York
July 28, 1927

Principal Literary Achievement

Recognized as one of the finest American poets of the last half of the twentieth century, Ashbery has been a major exponent and practitioner of the idea that poetry need not necessarily make sense or come to conclusions about philosophic problems.

Biography

John Ashbery was born in Rochester, New York, to Chester Frederick and Helen (Lawrence) Ashbery and spent much of his childhood on his grandparents' farm in northern New York, close to the shores of Lake Ontario. He attended Deerfield Academy and went on to Harvard University, from which he was graduated in 1949; his undergraduate thesis examined the poetry of the British writer W. H. Auden. During his early years he had wanted to be a painter, but he studied English literature at college, and in 1951 he was granted an M.A. by Columbia University for his study of English novelist Henry Green. He did further graduate work at New York University, and later in France, on the experimental writer Raymond Roussel. Between 1951 and 1954, he worked as a copywriter for the Oxford University Press in New York City; he was with McGraw-Hill in 1954 and 1955. During the 1950's he associated with a small group of young writers, including James Schuyler and Frank O'Hara, who attempted to bring the theories of abstract Impressionistic painting into literature and who came to be known as the "New York school" of poetry. Ashbery, however, has always rejected the suggestion that they were ever so cohesively organized as to be a "school."

In 1953, he published his first volume of verse, *Turandot and Other Poems*. From the beginning there was skepticism about the lack of clarity in his poems, although his enormous sophistication, his use of allusion, and his wittiness were quickly appreciated. In 1955, still pursuing his academic interests, he received a Fulbright scholarship to study in France at the university in Montpellier. In the following year he moved to Paris; he also published his second volume of poetry, *Some Trees* (1956). While in Paris, his interest in art, which had led him to his enthusiasm for abstract Impressionists such as Jackson Pollock and Willem de Kooning, drew him into writing art criticism for the Paris edition of the *New York Herald Tribune*, and he con-

tinued to do that work until 1965. He also formed a connection with *Art News.*

In 1962, his poems in *The Tennis Court Oath* brought the skepticism about his work to its sharpest response, and this book has retained a reputation for being the least sensible of all of his works. Despite formidable opposition, however, Ashbery began to win prizes. As early as 1960, he won the Poets' Foundation Award; in 1962, he won the Ingram-Merrill Foundation award; in 1963, the Harriet Monroe Memorial Prize and the Union League Civic and Arts Foundation Prize. This pattern of public recognition and critical praise, tempered by considerable critical disdain from certain quarters, was to continue. He reached his highest point of acceptance with *Self-Portrait in a Convex Mirror* (1975), which won the Pulitzer Prize, the National Book Award, and the National Book Critics Circle Award. The books of new poetry he has published since then have had his usual critical ups and downs over the matter of the poetry often not making sense. Ashbery seems unrepentant about this, and it is often a major theme in his work, since he wants his poems to reflect a world which he sees as lacking in coherence; he also wants his poems to have the formlessness, the nonrational element, which is common to abstract Impressionist painting.

In 1966, he returned from Paris to New York and took up the post of executive editor with *Art News.* In the 1970's, he broadened his activities to include teaching English at Brooklyn College and the poetry editorship of the *Partisan Review.* In 1978, he joined *New York* magazine as its art critic, and from 1980 to 1985, he reached an even wider audience as the art critic for *Newsweek.* He has continued to teach and to write both art criticism and poetry. In 1985, he received a MacArthur Prize fellowship and the Lenore Marshall/*Nation* Poetry Prize. In 1987, he published *April Galleons,* a collection of poetry; in 1989, a collection of his art criticism written between 1957 and 1987 was published as *Reported Sightings: Art Chronicles, 1957-1987.* He is a regular poetry contributor to *The New Yorker.*

Analysis

John Ashbery's poetry is a battleground for literary critics: Some consider him the finest poet of the late twentieth century; some consider him an occasionally good poet whose work is often of questionable literary quality; some critics dismiss him as entirely worthless. The main reason for this is quite simple: His poems often do not make sense. Ashbery knows this; indeed, his work is deliberately impossible to paraphrase much of the time, and he willingly admits that many of his poems are meaningless, given the way in which readers and critics ordinarily try to turn poems into prose as an element of their value as art. It is possible, for example, to identify certain Ashbery poems as clearly nonsensical. What confuses the issue is the fact that many of his poems are a teasing combination of what looks like sensible prose or poetry mixed with passages of seemingly arbitrary confusion. It is not a matter, however, of Ashbery's being unable to speak clearly; it is a deliberate element in his work, which he not only defends but also espouses as having literary and intellectual merit.

Perhaps the best way to approach the matter is through two ideas: that art in the twentieth century, particularly the plastic and aural arts, has been strongly inclined to move toward the nonrepresentational, and that Ashbery has spent a considerable amount of his time as an art critic, supporting the most experimental members of the American school of abstract expressionism in painting. Throughout his career as a commentator on contemporary painting, he has been a great admirer of Willem de Kooning, Franz Kline, and Jackson Pollock, and he has had an equal enthusiasm for the radical musical compositions of Arnold Schoenberg, John Cage, and Anton von Webern.

The history of art in general shows a close alliance between the artistic object and the world as it is generally perceived. In the mid-nineteenth century, particularly in painting and sculpture, the idea developed that the artist need not necessarily attempt to represent reality but could elaborate on it. That movement, which begins in Impressionism and moves on to cubism and ultimately to variations on the abstract had, by the time of Ashbery's coming of age, been fully manifested in many of the arts. The most difficult of the arts to so manipulate has been the literary art simply because the basic materials—the word, the sentence, and the paragraph—are by their very nature rational. Color or sound may be used arbitrarily; words are another matter, and the attempts to break the literary arts away from reality have been much more difficult—although not impossible, as the work of writers such as Franz Kafka and dramatist Samuel Beckett have shown.

Poetry, too, has had some success in repudiating sense. Poets such as T. S. Eliot, W. H. Auden, and Wallace Stevens, all of whom influenced Ashbery, are often very difficult to understand. The difference lies in the fact that there is some confidence in the fact that close study of these poets usually allows the reader to break the code—to get at what the poet is trying to say, however densely it may be expressed. With Ashbery it is not quite so simple; often he is clearly not expressing himself in a way that can be turned into sensible prose.

Ashbery is a poet of philosophic concern. He writes about the problems of life as human beings live it. That kind of poet is traditionally expected to express metaphysical questions, large or small, in elegant verse form and complicated imagery in which one metaphor leads reasonably to another and another; they ultimately lead to some sort of insight into the problem. The aesthetic pleasure lies in the poet's use of language, metaphor, and structure, all eventually making sense, if often on a very high plain of intelligence. Deciphering the secret, forcing the images to connect, leads to the secret in the center, and that has been the tradition of the poetry of ideas through the centuries (if somewhat more intensely formidable in the hands of twentieth century poets).

In Ashbery's case, however, the contemplation of the mysteries of life is complicated by the pose of diffidence, the not uncommon late twentieth century idea that one cannot know the truth. It is made even more difficult by Ashbery's constant determination to write poems about the diverse and devious experience of trying to discover truth in the making of a poem. Many of his best poems begin with the same kinds of questions about life which other poets address, but they quickly become studies of how difficult it is even to keep the subject straight. They usually conclude without the question being answered, and often with the clear suggestion that no answer is possible, at least through the medium of poetry.

An added difficulty lies in the way Ashbery uses figures of speech such as metaphors and similes. The trained reader expects that such poetic improvisations will illuminate the subject and will have some clearly logical connection to it. Ashbery often starts with figures that elaborate on the subject but quickly allows images into the poem which seem irrelevant. This practice is an aspect of his idea that his poems should be a record of how thoughts on the subject filter through his own mind, and that the seemingly irrelevant images are legitimate because they are part of how his mind jumps in and out of the subject—how one thing leads, not necessarily logically, to another. The poet bent on being clearly understood filters out the arbitrary thoughts, giving his readers an edited version of how the poetic flow operates. Ashbery leaves everything in, and as a result much of his material seems off the topic; indeed, much of it is, although there is often a crazy tonal logic about these maundering intrusions, just as there is in his sometimes maddening inclination to mix pronouns, shifting without any warning from "I" to "you" to "he" or "she." As a result, there is a feeling of constant flux, of spontaneity and witty vivacity, and a sense that the reader is implicated in the struggle to get things straight. Clarity, however, is only momentary and is often less important than the recording of the act of creation, however confused intellectually.

THE SKATERS

First published: 1966
Type of work: Poem

A poem about the difficulties and failures of the poetic process presented in the form of a confused journey through the alternatives open to the contemporary poet.

"The Skaters" has been sharply dismissed by many critics as being meaningless for the most part and being much less successful than the later poem "Self-Portrait in a Convex Mirror" (1975) as an attempt at dealing with the problem of the poem in the late twentieth century. Even its supporters are less enthusiastic about it than they are about "Self-Portrait in a Convex Mirror," in part because it is a much more difficult poem. On the other hand, it can be explicated, but only in part, and the reader must eventually accept Ashbery's refusal (stated more than once in the poem) to write what he considers the old-fashioned poem of sensible argument and appropriately obvious image.

If the best face is put upon the poem, as it has been by a few supporters of Ashbery, it can be read as his attempt to explain the difficulties of writing poetry of a new kind for an audience that expects philosophic poems to be clearly argued and intent on reaching sensible conclusions. The image of the skaters with which the poem begins can be seen as an example of the old style of art—graceful and skilled, but, significantly, going around in circles. This image will appear over and over in the poem as a reminder of how things used to be (at least for the poet), and against it is played out a search for a new way of dealing with reality.

The poem begins innocently enough, with a rather inflated description of the sight and sound of ice skaters. It may be a nod of compliment to the stylistic inclinations of Wallace Stevens, a poet much admired by Ashbery; it may, however, seem somewhat pompous in its fastidiousness, which would not be inconsistent with the main idea of the poem that art of that kind is no longer viable. Whatever the case (and with Ashbery much is left up to the reader), the skaters lead to a memory of childhood ribaldry and to the suggestion that little of the past is worth keeping and very much less is retained. Even music, however varied in form, has little long-lasting emotional purchase, and this statement leads to the virulent repudiation by the poet of any ability to express the emotional aesthetic that is so often expected of the poet: "'I am yesterday,' and my fault is eternal./ I do not expect constant attendance, knowing myself/ insufficient for your present demands/ And I have a dim intuition that I am that other 'I' with which/ we began." Time is seen as constantly fleeting, and nothing has much meaning in the long run: "Thus a great wind cleanses, as a new ruler/ Edits new laws, sweeping the very breath of the streets/ Into posterior trash." There are suggestions that these changes might make for a new optimism, but ultimately all fails. The section ends with the suggestion that the particular is irrelevant and that if there is to be poetry, it will be less perfect in its forms or conclusions:

> Hence, neither the importance of the individual flake,
> Nor the importance of the whole impression of the storm,
>   if it has any, is what it is,
> But the rhythm of the series of repeated jumps, from
>   abstract into positive and back to a slightly less
>   diluted abstract.
>
> Mild effects are the result.

The second section, however, continues the search into the romantic world of past poetry. For a time, it looks as if the imaginative dream might prevail, but difficulties occur, and the poet falls back into a kind of mild despair, recognizing that for him poetry is inadequate not only to discover meaning in life but also to deal with the serious social difficulties of the contemporary world. There are also problems with the poem of meaning simply because Ashbery allows his mind to wander through a maze of images which may seem quite incomprehensible.

The third section reveals a strong stylistic change. A kind of stolid, commonsense, step-by-step approach to the problem is tried in order to discover the secret of life and its relation to poetry. Some critics have seen touches of travel literature in the material, and it is a section in which adventures are essayed, if kept on a lower level than those of the second section by the insistence that only one thing, death, exists. The excursion into nature leads into a widening of experience, with Romantic implications, but it all ends with soaked clothing and the danger of the mundane head cold—the banality of real life. There is no room for the imagination; no one is interested in adventure, and the poet sees himself at the end "like a plank/ Like a small boat blown away from the wind."

The fourth section is the easiest to understand, since it is a kind of short story of depressed country life, a metaphor for the dreariness, the increasingly unimaginative particularities, of common experience in which, significantly, the trout (like the skaters) are circling aimlessly and the pump, which might be seen as a source of refreshment, is broken. The ending is particularly flat; the constellations, if rising in perfect order, have an arbitrariness about that order that suggests a meaningless universe, one in which the old kinds of poetry of metaphysical optimism have no place.

Ashbery is trying to create something like an abstract poem in which the accumulation of images support the occasional moments of clear statement, but with the kind of free-form looseness of association that has been so successful in abstract painting, in which objects do not necessarily mean anything specific. Instead, they add up to a sense of rightness that has very little to do with logic but much to do with an emotion which cannot be quite expressed in any other way. The poem is, in that sense, a metaphor for the failure of the old kinds of poetry to express the state of contemporary life, and the form it takes, a kind of surging, swaying movement in and out of sense and nonsense, is an example of poetic form imitating poetic meaning. It could be said that, in part, the form of this poem is its meaning.

SELF-PORTRAIT IN A CONVEX MIRROR

First published: 1975
Type of work: Poem

Ashbery contemplates the nature of the work of art and its relation to truth, memory, human souls, and the world in general.

"Self-Portrait in a Convex Mirror" is Ashbery's most popular and most critically honored poem, and it brings together some of the best and some of the most annoying elements in his work. From its beginning, it requires some basic knowledge of a specific painting that Ashbery (a well-known art critic) admires. Italian painter Parmigianino (1503-1540), whose real name was Francesco Mazzola, was one of the foremost mannerist painters. He produced a self-portrait, and in order to impress his Roman patrons with his technical prowess, he painted the likeness as it would appear in a convex mirror.

The poem begins with a charming, succinct description of the painting, rich with critical perception and including excerpts from comments which had been made about the work at the time of its presentation in the early sixteenth century. It is essential to remember that it is not a realistic portrait of the painter, since it is deliberately distorted as it would be in a convex reflection. This eccentric, tricky idea is consistent with the stylistic experimentations of mannerist painters, who often chose to present subjects in graceful distortion rather than attempt to record life with absolute accuracy.

The speaker in the poem is impressed in particular with the representation of the eyes, which are usually considered in art to give entrance to the soul. The eyes in this picture do not fully satisfy the speaker, however deftly they are painted, and it is this sense of failure to capture the soul which precipitates the main subject of the poem: How can one know reality, how does one record it in art or otherwise, given one's limitations as a human being?

It becomes clear that however much he enjoys the painting, he senses its inadequacy as a representation of reality. The flatness of the canvas, however cleverly manipulated, militates against the kind of three-dimensional experience of life: "But your eyes proclaim/ That everything is surface. The surface is what's there/ And nothing can exist except what's there." The problem of holding on to experience leads into a contemplation of past relationships and of how thin they are in the memory—how eventually everything sifts down into a kind of blurred mush without much significance. The poem juxtaposes the speaker's consideration of the painting (and that of other critics) with contemplation of day-to-day experience, attempting to come to some conclusion about the relation between art and life. The way in which the portrait, in its convexity, reaches out at the same time it recedes leads to the conviction that "art" may not necessarily be a satisfactory haven for truth about reality.

There is, as a result, an intellectual and tonal tussle in the poem as the speaker shuffles between the experience of the flux of life, in which constant accumulation never makes much sense, and his admiration for the world of art which is able to select and to idealize. That admiration is continually eroded by his uneasiness as to the truth of art, since the inexorable push of time and experience diminish any certainty that art has much to do with life as it is ordinarily lived:

> This always
> Happens, as in the game where
> A whispered phrase passed around the room
> Ends up as something completely different.
> It is the principle that makes works of art so unlike
> What the artist intended. Often he finds
> He has omitted the thing he started out to say
> In the first place.

Much of the poem is occupied with considering several different ways in which reality proves to be obdurate, not only in art but also in life. Ashbery tries to find some way in which the case for art can be made, and his comments upon the painting, and Parmigianino's work in general, are a kind of tour de force example of creating poetry and art criticism at the same time. More difficulty will be confronted in dealing with the examples of how life slips and slides about, because it is there, in the main, that the images are often incomprehensible. The reader must give up any attempt to understand fully what is being said and accept a vague, dreamy sense of emotional rightness. Clarity in those passages comes and goes as the poet allows his mind to roam about in and out of rational focus.

What does become cumulatively clear is that Ashbery is not simply concerned with the painting, but with all art, including poetry. This is a major theme in Ashbery's work: the inability of poetry to discover truth and to fix it once for all, since reality is always in flux and the work of art is static. Yet the poem goes even further in suggesting that Ashbery is also talking about the peculiar state of man—always searching for truth and always at the whim of constant change. Such a conclusion could be depressing, but in Ashbery's poem there is a kind of genial, sophisticated acceptance; there is a celebration of humankind's incapacity to "know," which makes humans, in a sense, captives like the figure in the Parmigianino painting, slightly distorted and unable to escape.

MIXED FEELINGS

First published: 1975
Type of work: Poem

The poet seems to be looking at an old photograph of some young women and imagines what they are like and how they would speak to him.

Ashbery's finest work may be in his long poems, where the space gives him time to develop a sense of what it is like to attempt to deal with a specific, recalcitrant subject. A shorter poem, such as "Mixed Feelings" (from the volume *Self-Portrait in a Convex Mirror*), while being a good poem, provides a kind of five-finger exercise in understanding Ashbery's peculiar charms as a poet. The idea is a simple one. The poet either thinks he is smelling frying sausages while looking at an old photograph, or he is, in fact, doing so. It hardly matters. What does matter is his attempt to date the picture, which is not too difficult, because he recognizes the aircraft in the photograph as one used in World War II. Some girls are leaning against it. He imagines their names, typically common names for girls at the time, and thereby provides a perceptive confirmation of the fact that times change, as does the style in choosing names for children. He wonders how he would explain to them how much the world has changed in more than thirty years. Would they want to listen, he wonders, standing as they do with that smart knowingness of young women? Perhaps they would tell him to get lost, using the slang of the day. Perhaps they would rather go to a café for a cup of coffee. Ashbery is, in fact, slyly evoking the social world of wartime, when servicemen tried to pick up young girls with a smart quip and were often rebuffed just as smartly.

He is not sure if his imagined setting is right. The picture reminds him of California, but his reference to the garment district suggests New York. The light looks Western, and the idea of the aircraft is strongly allied to the Pacific Coast for him. The Donald Duck cartoon on the airplane is a lovely touch, since it was common for combat aircraft to carry some kind of cartoon on the fuselage. He wonders about the girls in the photograph, but he is not going to spend much time at it. In the end, he imagines that sometime he will meet young women like them in an airport lounge and that they will then chat with him just as trivially as the women in the photograph might have done.

It is a very modest poem, and it shows that Ashbery can make sense if he wants to. It possesses the sort of tender stillness that often appears in short passages in his longer poems, and it has that peculiar eye for detail which is a mark of his work. It makes even his most obscure metaphors ring with associations that are hard to place but difficult to forget. The easy informality, the simple conversational style, and the cogent, economical way in which a complicated idea is presented with little sense of trickiness are elements that come and go in his longer poems, but they have a life of their own in many of his shorter works, in which a quiet moment is captured. It is a clever poem, but it is difficult to tell that from a quick reading. The poem is based on the association of ideas, but it is the way those ideas are dropped into place— with such seeming innocence, starting with the homely idea of the smell of sausages, a common kind of food for the troops—which leads to the photograph and beyond.

MORE PLEASANT ADVENTURES

First published: 1984
Type of work: Poem

The poem appears to be about the history of a personal relationship, perhaps a marriage, and its eventual failure; it may be a metaphor for life in general.

"More Pleasant Adventures," a poem from *A Wave* (1984), is one of those small performances by Ashbery which tempt critics into presuming that it stands for something other than itself, sometimes with preposterous consequences. On the surface it seems simple enough; the first two lines, for example, with the idea of the wedding cake looming behind them, are very smart, very succinctly sophisticated in their summing up of the way in which the romance settles down to living day by day. The following metaphors, tracing the gradual lack of mutual interest, round out the first verse with a poetic version of how couples stop communicating.

The second verse starts with a double example of how Ashbery makes use of nonpoetic language. "Heck" has a kind of down-home simplicity that is not expected in poetry. It is followed by an equally deflated idea, a line from the popular song from the 1940's, "Sentimental Journey." Serious poets are "supposed" to quote from opera, but Ashbery chooses the songs of the streets. There is a rightness about this; anyone who rationalizes a failed relationship with the word "heck" is hardly likely to possess a repertoire that transcends Tin Pan Alley. It surely places the failure as less than tragic, however, and the rest of the poem is a listing of minor failures, ending in a suggestion that whatever else the years have done, they have resulted in the accumulation of some property for the unhappy pair to fight over.

Ashbery is often distinguished from poets such as Robert Lowell and John Berryman because he is thought not to tell stories of human anguish and failure. Poems such as "More Pleasant Adventures," however, suggest the contrary. It may be possible to take this poem to a higher level of metaphorical gesture and claim that it makes a more portentous statement about human nature, but on its most obvious level it is a very wry, astringently cool, somewhat antiromantic look at the failure of love written from the point of view of one of the participants thereto. There is, however, a common theme in Ashbery which suggests that life tends to be less and less romantic as it passes by.

Summary

If art is to be, in part, a reflection of the time and place in which it is created, Ashbery's deliberate refusal to make meaning within a pleasingly complicated network of aesthetic and philosophic maunderings has a rightness about it. His digressions ask large questions but decline to answer them. The latter half of the twentieth century has lost that certainty, that assurance in social, political, religious, and familial structures, which was previously the source and basis of art. At the same time, Ashbery has managed to link the verbal arts with music and with the plastic arts in producing works which cannot be paraphrased and which stand for themselves as pure aesthetic gesture.

Bibliography

Donaghue, Denis. *Reading America: Essays on American Literature.* Berkeley: University of California Press, 1987.

Holden, Jonathan. *The Rhetoric of the Contemporary Lyric.* Bloomington: Indiana University Press, 1981.

Lehman, David, ed. *Beyond Amazement: New Essays on John Ashbery.* Ithaca, N.Y.: Cornell University Press, 1980.

Molesworth, Charles. *The Fierce Embrace: A Study of Contemporary American Poetry.* Columbia: University of Missouri Press, 1979.

Shapiro, David. *John Ashbery: An Introduction to the Poetry.* New York: Columbia University Press, 1979.

Charles H. Pullen

LOUIS AUCHINCLOSS

Born: Lawrence, Long Island, New York
September 27, 1917

Principal Literary Achievement

Extending the tradition developed by Henry James and Edith Wharton of examining twentieth century American society and its institutions, Auchincloss emerged as the preeminent "novelist of manners" of his time.

Biography

Notable for his dual career as practicing attorney and published novelist, Louis Auchincloss was born September 27, 1917, at Lawrence, Long Island (later a suburb of New York City), the third among four children and the second of three sons. The Auchincloss family, Scottish in origin, had grown both numerous and prosperous in and around New York City, initially engaging in the wool trade but later branching out into the professions. Louis' father, Howland, a 1908 graduate of Yale University, practiced law on Wall Street. Howland and his wife, the former Priscilla Stanton, saw to it that their children were reared "comfortably" but without ostentation, in relative ignorance of how well-off their family might possibly be.

Howland Auchincloss, although highly successful in a rather arcane field of legal practice, appears to have been what later generations would describe as a "workaholic" and suffered frequent nervous breakdowns in his fifties; well before that time, young Louis would seriously question the hold of Wall Street on his father's life and time. Priscilla Stanton Auchincloss was a strong, perceptive wife and mother despite numbing, often inexplicable inhibitions and "taboos," possibly deriving from guilt feelings over the death of a younger brother when Priscilla was no older than six. It is from his mother that Auchincloss claims to have derived his keen powers of observation and recall.

Beginning his education at the private Bovee School in Manhattan, Auchincloss enjoyed the companionship of such classmates as the future actors Mel Ferrer and Efrem Zimbalist, Jr., before Bovee closed its doors permanently just before the Wall Street crash of 1929, by which time Louis was old enough to follow in the footsteps of his father and elder brother by enrolling at the prestigious Groton School in Massachusetts, a training ground for diplomats and statesmen. Feeling ostracized by his classmates in the aftermath of a schoolboy prank early in his Groton career, young Louis worked hard to distinguish himself academically, earning the high grades he

sought but, as he later recalled, almost missing the real point of education. Auchincloss credits Malcolm Strachan, hired to teach at Groton toward the end of his own stay there, with reorienting his reading habits toward enjoyment and away from simple achievement.

Enrolling at Yale in 1935, again following the pattern established by his father, Auchincloss read widely for pleasure both inside and outside class, in time attempting a novel of his own based upon his social observations. When the manuscript was rejected by Scribner's, not without some words of encouragement for the aspiring author, Auchincloss saw fit to read the rejection as an omen of sorts and to follow his father into the practice of law without wasting any time. Skipping his senior year at Yale, he actively sought the best law school that would accept him without benefit of a bachelor's degree, enrolling at the University of Virginia as he turned twenty-one in the fall of 1938.

Avoiding the "temptations" of literature, either as reader or as writer, with all the resolve of a recovering addict, Auchincloss studied hard at Virginia, as he had done at Groton, soon discovering in legal prose and logic some of the same delights that he had found in literature. Determined to succeed both as student and as lawyer, he steered clear of the thriving "country-club" social scene but remained quite as observant of his surroundings as he had been during his "literary" days. In any case, his devotion to his studies soon paid off in high grades and honors; upon graduation in June, 1941, he was hired by the Wall Street law firm of Sullivan and Cromwell, where he had worked as a student clerk during the summer of 1940.

Auchincloss' seemingly impulsive decision to skip his senior year at Yale soon turned out to have been a wise one indeed: He was able to complete his studies and actually practice law for several months before the Japanese invasion of Pearl Harbor in December, 1941, with a secure job awaiting his return from military service during World War II.

Commissioned an officer in the Navy, Auchincloss was initially posted to an office job in the Canal Zone, a billet far removed from the war itself and, as he would demonstrate in both *The Indifferent Children* (1947) and some of his early short stories, an atmosphere conducive to petty politics and backbiting. Auchincloss in time saw action in both the European and Pacific war theaters, eventually assuming command of an amphibious vessel. While at sea, he made good use of his enforced leisure by reading widely from volumes purchased while on shore leave or from books left to gather dust in the ship's library.

Upon his return to civilian life, Auchincloss took a brief vacation to complete *The Indifferent Children* before returning to his job at Sullivan and Cromwell. Still unmarried, he remained close to his parents and felt the need to accommodate their wishes even as he opposed them; he agreed that his first novel, once accepted, be published under a pseudonym in order to spare the family name. In its first editions, therefore, *The Indifferent Children* appeared under the byline "Andrew Lee"—ironically named for an Auchincloss ancestor. The book's reviews, although mixed, were generally favorable—enough so, at any rate, that Auchincloss would continue to turn out fiction after office hours at Sullivan and Cromwell: *The Injustice Collectors*, an anthology of short stories initially published in magazines, appeared in 1950, followed by the novel *Sybil* in 1951. Still somewhat uncomfortable with his dual careers, Auchincloss felt obliged to choose between them and decided, toward the end of 1951, to devote full time to his writing, supported by an allowance from his father.

At the end of two years, however, having produced one novel (*A Law for the Lion*, 1953) and the short stories collected in *The Romantic Egoists* (1954), Auchincloss was ready to resume his career as an attorney, writing fiction during his spare time as before. Barred by company policy from returning to Sullivan and Cromwell once he had resigned, he eventually found a position with the firm of Hawkins, Delafield and Wood; elevated to partnership in 1958, he would remain with the firm for more than thirty-two years, from the spring of 1954 until his retirement in 1986.

In 1957, just before turning forty, Auchincloss married Adèle Lawrence, a Vanderbilt descendant then in her mid-twenties who in time would bear him three sons, John, Blake, and Andrew. Comfortable at last with the pursuit of two careers, Auchincloss proceeded to flourish in both, his elevation to partnership coinciding roughly with the publication of his generally well-received "Wall Street" novels, *The Great World and Timothy Colt* (1956; expanded from one of the longer short stories in *The Romantic Egoists*), *Venus in Sparta* (1958), and *Pursuit of the Prodigal* (1959). It was not until 1960, however, that Auchincloss would truly hit his stride with the remarkable efforts *The House of Five Talents* (1960), *Portrait in Brownstone* (1962), *The Rector of Justin* (1964), and *The Embezzler* (1966). Thereafter, Auchincloss continued to turn out novels, short fiction, and essays at the approximate rate of one volume per year, yet only rarely, in such novels as *I Come as a Thief* (1972), *The House of the Prophet* (1980), or *Watchfires* (1982), has his later work even come close to the standard that he set for himself in the four novels published between 1960 and 1966. Since his retirement from legal practice in 1986, Auchincloss has remained active as a writer, publishing nonfiction as well as such novels as *The Golden Calves* (1988) and the anthology *Skinny Island: More Tales of Manhattan* (1987).

Analysis

In 1960, the year that he broke new literary ground with *The House of Five Talents*, Auchincloss published an article in *The Nation* entitled "Marquand and O'Hara: The Novel of Manners," subsequently included in *Reflections of a Jacobite* (1961). Examining the work of both authors in considerable detail, Auchincloss concluded that the novel of manners, as developed by Henry James and Edith Wharton and refined by F. Scott Fitzgerald in *The Great Gatsby* (1925), had all but died at the hands of John P. Marquand and John O'Hara, whose works were then held in fairly high esteem. Both men, he argued, tended to invent social stratifications instead of merely observing them; more often than not, class distinctions exist only in the minds of individual characters, a tendency that caused Auchincloss to describe both authors as "psychological" as opposed to "social" novelists. Quite probably, he concluded, the social upheavals of the Depression and two world wars had rendered the convention more or less obsolete. Notwithstanding, Auchincloss was working even then to disprove his own suspicions, reaching back toward James and Wharton—and even French novelist Marcel Proust—for guidance as he sought to record and make sense of his own keen observations.

Although it was not until 1960 that Auchincloss reached full maturity as a novelist, he had spent most of the previous decade mapping out the fictional universe that his later characters would inhabit. Unlike O'Hara and Marquand, Auchincloss felt no need to invent social stratifications, finding them already in place. Of particular interest to Auchincloss, from his earliest novels onward, is the problematical question, or "myth," of an American "aristocracy"—an apparent contradiction in terms that has nevertheless been perpetuated in American society ever since the earliest settlers or their descendants began looking down their noses at other settlers more recently arrived in the New World. During the twentieth century, as Auchincloss observes in his fiction, the notion of an American aristocracy has tended to persist, yet not without challenge and change; increasingly, those born to what Thorstein Veblen described in 1899 as the "leisure class" have found themselves entering the work force, often in direct competition with those born to "humbler" origins.

A persistent Auchincloss "myth" is that of the Protestant minister's son, most commonly a native of New England, whose work ethic combines with ambition to drive him ever upward in the business or professional world. By the time he reaches the top, such a man is virtually indistinguishable, except perhaps for his continued commitment to the work ethic, from the hereditary "aristocrats" against whom he has successfully competed. His Harvard or Yale education, although acquired with scholarship aid supplemented by odd jobs, has been much the same as that of his richer peers. If anything, the minister's son has earned higher grades and learned more, the better to realize his own American Dream. Meanwhile, his white, Anglo-Saxon Protestant status and name have provided the clergyman's son with the perfect "cover," allowing him to blend in as he moves from the meritocracy into the perceived aristocracy, joining country clubs and sending his children to private schools as he wisely invests the residue of a steadily increasing salary.

From the 1930's onward, both Marquand and O'Hara had focused much of their attention on the business world, purporting to show how careers are made and broken. During the 1950's, Auchincloss covered much the same territory, inevitably inviting comparison with the two older, already established novelists. On close examination, however, Auchincloss' novels of the period seem rather more authentic and credible than those of O'Hara and Marquand, and with good reason. Unlike the two older authors, Auchincloss lived and worked in the world that formed the subject of his novels; what is more, he was well versed in the "novel of manners" tradition, which Marquand and O'Hara were not.

Beginning with *The House of Five Talents*, Auchincloss broadened and deepened his portrait of society, having laid the foundation of his fictional universe with the "Wall Street" novels of the late 1950's. The Wall Street setting is still very much in

evidence, often at the center of the action, but is complemented by historical and social background. Auchincloss began to experiment with viewpoint and narrative voice,
producing convincing "eyewitness" accounts: The main narrators of *The House of
Five Talents* and *Portrait in Brownstone* are elderly women, born during the nineteenth century; in *The Rector of Justin* and *The Embezzler*, the elusive nature of human "truth" is underscored by Auchincloss' skillful use of multiple narrators, both
male and female, no two of whom recall what they have witnessed in quite the same
way. Each narrator is fully delineated as a character in his or her own right, self-
revealing by choice of words and turns of phrase as well as by selective recollection.

A frequent reader of Proust, Auchincloss in his strongest novels approaches the
French author's remarkable blend of chronicle and art. In preparing *The Rector of
Justin* and *The Embezzler*, for example, Auchincloss began with lawyerly research,
reading thousands of pages of nonfiction dealing, respectively, with the history of
prep schools and with the notorious Richard Whitney fraud case of the 1930's; he
then proceeded to transform history into art, discarding or changing the "facts" as
he sought to tease out the archetypal meaning behind them. Of *The Embezzler*, he
recalls, "When I was sure I had my crime exactly right, I invented an entirely new
criminal and gave him an entirely new family, plus an entirely new motivation." A
similar approach would characterize most of Auchincloss' mature fiction; unlike the
historian, Auchincloss is concerned less with what happened than with why and how
it might have happened. A case in point is *The House of the Prophet* (1980), Auchincloss' first and only true *roman à clef*, loosely but frankly based on the life and
career of the columnist and pundit Walter Lippmann; upon learning that a Lippmann
biography was in progress, Auchincloss resolved to tell the story in his "own" way,
through art, altering certain facts and dates for dramatic effect, speculating upon the
thoughts and motivations of "Felix Leitner."

Among the more remarkable features of Auchincloss' fictional universe, from the
early 1950's onward, has been his thoughtful, credible portrayal of the changing role
of women in American society during the twentieth century. His second and third
novels, *Sybil* and *A Law for the Lion*, deal with the emergent female consciousness
as lawyers' wives begin to question the inequities of marriage and of the divorce
laws then on the books in the state of New York. In subsequent novels, Auchincloss
would go back in time, to his mother's generation and beyond, to trace the emer-
gence of the feminine consciousness and voice among the economically privileged,
showing also how certain women would deliberately reject the option of their own
"liberation." The author's sympathies, however, clearly remain with those who would
challenge stereotype in the interest of self-discovery.

Perhaps the most frequent criticism leveled against Auchincloss is that he writes
exclusively about New York, and about New Yorkers of a certain social class. On
reflection, however, such criticism tends to be short-sighted: For good or for ill, New
York, even more than Washington, D.C., is where major decisions are made, often
by people very like those of whom Auchincloss writes. Moreover, relatively few of
his main characters are "natives." Most commonly, the Auchincloss protagonist has

migrated to New York from New England or the Mideast in search of fame and fortune, much as a provincial European would settle in Paris or London. Auchincloss' New York is in fact a microcosm of American civilization, at once rebellious against, yet ever nostalgic for, its perceived European origins. Auchincloss' greatest achievement as a novelist would seem to be his credible, literate, and resonant portrayal of life behind the scenes of political and economic power.

THE HOUSE OF FIVE TALENTS

First published: 1960
Type of work: Novel

Writing in 1948, a rich, aging spinster recalls her life and times.

The House of Five Talents, announcing the full range of Auchincloss' skill as novelist and chronicler, is narrated in the first person by Miss Augusta Millinder, known familiarly as Gussie, a seventy-five-year-old heiress who, after the social upheavals of two world wars and a depression, sees fit to record her memoirs for posterity. Ostensibly penned during 1948, Gussie's testimony ranges from the "gaslight era" of her adolescence to the narrative present, providing an insider's view of society against the backdrop of history.

Unmarried by choice, having broken her engagement to a promising young architect for reasons best known to herself, Gussie Millinder emerges early in life as a keen observer and occasional meddler, using her spinsterhood as a vantage point from which to analyze and criticize the marital and parental misadventures of her relatives and friends. Gussie's meddling, however well-intentioned, fails more often than it succeeds, allowing the unseen Auchincloss to inject elements of plot into an otherwise linear narrative. In her twenties, for example, Gussie tries, unsuccessfully, to thwart her parents' divorce and her father's subsequent remarriage to an actress; later, in an incident presaging the plot of *The Embezzler,* she will offer to save a cousin's husband from bankruptcy and prison by covering his embezzlement with her own funds, on condition that the man retire permanently from business. Unhappy in retirement, the man pleads with Gussie to release him from his vow and soon reverts to his old ways, eventually disappearing abroad as a fugitive from justice. With the approach of old age, Gussie again intervenes to force a marriage between her scapegrace nephew Oswald, a Communist sympathizer, and the showgirl who is carrying his unborn child; the marriage predictably fails, leaving Gussie with little choice but to adopt the child herself.

Set mainly in New York City, with occasional excursions to such fashionable turn of the century "watering places" as Newport and Bar Harbor, *The House of Five Talents* credibly evokes both tradition and transition as Gussie meets the twentieth century, already "liberated" by her spinster status from constraints that still bind her married female relatives. As she approaches forty, for example, Gussie supplements her self-education with college courses and teaches in a girls' school, although she does not need the money; with the approach of World War I, she volunteers for auxiliary service in Europe, proceeding upon her return to develop a career of active if selective community service, giving as freely of her time as of her money.

Notable for Auchincloss' effective exploitation of first-person narration, *The House of Five Talents* also presents his first full-scale portrait of American society, showing how the would-be aristocracy defines itself, whether in its choice of sports and resorts or in the marriage of such rich Americans as Gussie's sister Cora to impoverished but titled Europeans. Gussie Millinder herself, meanwhile, remains among Auchincloss' most memorable and entertaining characters.

PORTRAIT IN BROWNSTONE

First published: 1962
Type of work: Novel

A broker's wife discovers her true strengths as she transforms herself from matron into matriarch.

Combining the narrative approach of *The House of Five Talents* with the general subject matter of his earlier Wall Street novels, Auchincloss in *Portrait in Brownstone* explores both office politics and the emergent female consciousness through the eyes of one Ida Trask Hartley who, around the age of sixty, begins at last to perceive the full extent of her experience and talents. Bookish and somewhat retiring, Ida has spent most of her life in the shadow of her hard-driving husband Derrick, a minister's son from New England, and her glamorous cousin Geraldine Denison, Derrick's sometime mistress. Indeed, it is Geraldine's suicide, following a long slide into alcoholism and depression, that begins the process of Ida's awakening and liberation, a process that forms the true plot of the novel.

Like Gussie Millinder in *The House of Five Talents*, Ida Hartley is a keen observer and gifted storyteller. In search of self-discovery, she revisits her past, recalling her mother's close-knit extended family, the Denisons, and her uncle Linnaeus Tremain, a brilliant, perceptive financier. Although all the male Denisons are gainfully employed and most have been to college, it is "Linn" Tremain's sustained generosity that enables them all to live in relative comfort and that allows Ida to attend college, the first woman in her family to do so.

Enrolled at Barnard College and interested in liberal politics, Ida soon finds herself debating political issues with Derrick Hartley, a Harvard graduate who, having made a small fortune with a Boston brokerage firm, has moved to New York with hopes of working for Linnaeus Tremain. Little deterred by Tremain's insistence that no vacancy exists in his firm, Derrick quite literally "dines out" on his accumulated savings while waiting for the older man to change his mind. It is at those dinners that Derrick makes the acquaintance both of Ida Trask, who will fall in love with him, and of Ida's mother, who will persuade her brother-in-law to give Derrick a job. As Tremain in time learns, much to his dismay, he has at last met his match.

Ida asks her cousin and perpetual rival Geraldine to entertain Derrick during a weekend in 1912 when she needs to be out of town. Derrick, studious and reserved, soon loses his heart and head to the flirtatious, fickle Geraldine, who does not return his love. In time, Ida wins Derrick back and marries him. A daughter and then a son are soon born to the Hartleys, whose marriage proceeds smoothly and without major incident until 1935, when Geraldine, recently widowed, entices Derrick into an affair with divorce and remarriage in mind. Derrick, meanwhile, has prospered in his work, somewhat at the expense of his chosen mentor Tremain; having in effect forced Tremain's retirement, he goes so far as to have the older man's name removed from the firm's corporate name after his death, a gesture which deeply offends Ida.

Following Geraldine's death early in 1950, Ida at last takes stock of her life, noticing that her daughter Dorcas and Dorcas' second husband are about to do to Derrick what Derrick once did to "Uncle Linn"; at the same time, she perceives that her son Hugo, still unmarried as he approaches forty, has embarked on a potentially dangerous affair with a divorce-bound married woman. Mustering all the accumulated resources of her intelligence, education, and experience, Ida moves quickly to intervene in both cases, assuming control of Derrick's firm after he suffers a sudden, provoked heart attack and buying for Hugo a sufficient share of stock in the company for which he works that he will be able to name himself president, thus assuring his eligibility for marriage to a much younger distant cousin and removing the married woman from his life. To be sure, Ida Hartley's sudden assertiveness stops somewhat short of "liberation" as perceived by later generations. Still, Auchincloss, through Ida, has successfully portrayed a moment of transition in American social history, when women of his mother's generation, at least the lucky ones, discovered at last the courage of their convictions.

Significantly, Ida Trask Hartley is the only character in *Portrait in Brownstone* allowed to speak for herself; the sections of the novel devoted to Derrick and their children are narrated in an affectless third-person style reminiscent of the author's Wall Street novels, providing counterpoint as Ida seeks within herself the resources needed to assume the control for which she has been well trained.

THE RECTOR OF JUSTIN

First published: 1964
Type of work: Novel

The New England prep school, a uniquely American institution formed on British models, is here caught and portrayed in all its ambiguity.

The Rector of Justin continues Auchincloss' analytical portrayal of American society and its institutions, here focusing upon the type of boys' boarding school that he himself attended and that has furnished the United States with much of its business and political leadership since the end of the nineteenth century. Told from a number of viewpoints, the tale of Justin Martyr Academy and its founder, the title character Francis Prescott, remains tantalizingly incomplete even at the end, showing the basic anomaly of an institution that seeks to foster "democratic" ideals while charging high fees and adhering to a selective admissions policy.

The unifying narrator of *The Rector of Justin* is one Brian Aspinwall; too frail of health to join his fellow Americans in preparing to fight the Nazis, he arrives to teach at Justin Martyr Academy during the eightieth year of the legendary founder's life. At first merely keeping a diary of his impressions and encounters, as of his own possible vocation to the Episcopal priesthood, Brian finds himself drawn to the old man by what he perceives as the latter's unwavering moral courage. In time he goes on to project a full-scale biography of Prescott, assembling spoken and written testimony from a variety of witnesses. Proceeding with his chosen task, Brian discovers that others before him have tried, and failed, to produce a Prescott biography; Brian too will fail, for want of life experience and objectivity. The book, as it stands, intersperses Brian's reflections with his steadily increasing, yet maddeningly inconclusive, documentation. Notably absent from the growing pile of written testimony is any word from Prescott himself; throughout his long life and career the old man has written little or nothing, preferring instead to be remembered by his actions. Yet it is precisely those actions, variously remembered and interpreted, that somehow fail to "add up," leaving even the elderly Prescott himself with the impression that he has somehow failed in his self-appointed mission.

Born during 1860 in New England, Prescott lost his father to the Civil War and his mother to disease while he was still a child, spending most of his youth in an early prototype of the type of school that would become his "dream." Completing his education at the University of Oxford, Prescott carefully studied the British "public schools" as potential models for his own academy, somehow missing the basic contradiction between British aristocratic ideals and the already ingrained democratic ideals of his New England boyhood. While at Oxford, moreover, Prescott momentarily lost interest in the religious studies that he deemed necessary for the founder/ headmaster of an Episcopal school, instead reading deeply in the Greek and Latin classics. Diverted from his dream, Prescott returned to the United States in 1881, embarking on a brilliant career with the New York Central railroad and planning marriage to a vivacious young woman from California, only to abandon both in great haste after a mysterious dream or vision during which his earlier ambition returned with a vengeance. Curiously, Prescott remains somewhat uninterested in theology, pursuing the prescribed course of study only to acquire what he sees as the teaching credential needed for his chosen task. While at Harvard, Prescott also met Harriet Winslow, an intellectually inclined "proper Bostonian" to whom he would remain married until her death nearly sixty years later. His wife and three daughters, however, would assume a distinctly secondary importance in his life, overshadowed by the creation—and preservation—of the "perfect" boys' preparatory school.

As Brian Aspinwall proceeds with his research, it becomes increasingly clear—to the reader, if not to Brian himself—that Prescott's single-minded perfectionism, ironically founded on imperfect principles, has left many human casualties in its wake, including family, friends, and former students. The school's alumni and trustees, represented in the novel mainly by the Wall Street lawyer David Griscam, continue to draw inspiration from Prescott's dream even as they perceive its limitations, going so far as to lie to Prescott about the school's business affairs in order to keep the shared dream intact. In his eighties, Prescott at last begins to perceive some of the flaws in his ideal, lamenting the fact that his students and alumni are in fact aristocrats of the sort that he instinctively distrusts and dislikes; still, he crucially fails to acknowledge, let alone examine, his own role in perpetuating those institutions that he professes to hold in contempt.

Thanks to the multiplicity of voices and viewpoints presented, *The Rector of Justin* emerges as both a readable, intriguing novel and a document of social history elevated to the dimension of myth. Although suspected of using his own alma mater, Groton, and its founder, Endicott Peabody, as his models, Auchincloss in fact cast his net considerably wider, studying the history of preparatory schools in general before concocting his own archetype, a school whose ingrained contradictions, embodied in the heart and soul of its founder, are all too plainly evident. For all of its implied criticism, however, *The Rector of Justin* is neither an exposé nor an indictment of the American prep school; throughout the narrative, the possible virtues of such an education are clearly delineated, showing that Prescott's vision, however flawed and unrealistic, is not without its merits.

THE EMBEZZLER

First published: 1966
Type of work: Novel

A notorious fraud case of the 1930's is recalled during the 1960's by its perpetrator, his former wife, and her current husband, once his best friend.

Building upon the strengths implicit in *The Rector of Justin*, Auchincloss in *The Embezzler* uses conflicting narrative voices and viewpoints to illuminate the mythical dimensions of recent American economic history. Departing from the recorded facts of the Wall Street fraud case that led directly to federal control of the American stock market, Auchincloss reinvents the case and its principal characters with credibility and skill, adding human dimension to an otherwise dry, if significant, historical event.

The Embezzler opens with the memoirs of Guy Prime, the title character, writing during 1960 to "set the record straight." Well into his seventies and living in self-imposed exile in Panama, Guy concedes the facts of his misdeeds but remains quite unrepentant, having paid his debt to society with a prison term; indeed, he reasons, the Franklin Delano Roosevelt administration could hardly wait for an excuse to enact laws already written, and Guy Prime just happened to provide that excuse.

Presumably discovered among Guy's effects after his death in 1962, his memoirs are subsequently read and commented upon by his former wife and her current husband in the two sections that complete the novel. As in *The Rector of Justin*, the confrontation of conflicting testimony concerning the same events and people casts considerable doubt upon the possibility of "truth" with regard to human nature; at the end it is doubtful indeed whether any of the characters involved could ever have understood the words or motivations of the others.

Recalling his youth in New York and later at Harvard University, Guy Prime evokes a setting and atmosphere similar to those of *Portrait in Brownstone*. At Harvard, Guy first meets Reginald "Rex" Geer, the industrious, ambitious son of an austere New Hampshire parson. Initially drawn to each other by the proverbial attraction of opposites, the sybaritic, gregarious New Yorker and the studious, reserved New England Yankee soon become close friends. When Rex is about to drop out of Harvard for financial reasons, Guy intervenes, unseen and unsuspected, to assure for Rex the scholarship aid that he needs. Indeed, it is Guy's persistent meddlesome streak (reminiscent of Gussie Millinder and Ida Hartley) that will in time cause most of his problems with Rex, as with other people as well. Easygoing and affable of manner, Guy often tries too hard to keep other people happy, little mindful that they might be happier, or better off, without his "help."

After Harvard, both Guy Prime and Rex Geer are hired by Marcellus de Grasse, a prosperous private banker and Prime family friend to whom Guy has introduced Rex. Rex rises quickly through the firm; Guy, although moderately successful, finds the work a bit too confining for his expansive temperament and draws on family connections to found his own brokerage house, inviting Rex to join him as full partner. When Rex, true to his own character, refuses, Guy simply cannot understand Rex's need to succeed on his own. Thereafter, the two men's differing needs and temperaments continue to strain their friendship, even as their professional relationship grows even closer. Guy's brokerage firm, soon prosperous, becomes a principal client of Rex's bank. During World War I, the two Harvard graduates again find themselves at odds: Guy, among the first to volunteer for combat, is instead assigned to a staff job, presumably because of his skill at meeting people; Rex, late to volunteer because of the pressures of his job, joins the war at the last minute but nevertheless emerges as a true hero. Thereafter, Guy envies Rex the latter's combat experience, even as Rex remains persuaded that Guy could have seen action had he so desired. During the decade to follow, the battle lines between Guy and Rex become even more sharply defined, as their respective approaches to finance come into conflict.

By Guy's own rueful reckoning, his own decade, the broker's decade, was that of the 1920's, an age of deals and speculation; Rex's decade follows, after the crash of 1929, when a banker's conservative instincts are needed to save whatever money might be left. A born salesman and trader, Guy is both ill-prepared and temperamentally ill-suited for the retrenchment of the Depression years. Still in good financial shape himself, he moves into the 1930's at full speed, investing in such then-risky ventures as tranquilizer pills and prefabricated housing. In order to keep his various ventures afloat, he borrows to the limit from a variety of institutions; once that limit is exceeded he becomes, in effect, the embezzler of the title, pledging securities that his firm holds in trust for various family members and for the Glenville Country Club, founded by Guy Prime himself. He intends to put the money back.

One fact upon which *The Embezzler*'s three narrators seem to agree is that Guy did not embark on the most reckless phase of his trading until after he discovered, or began to suspect, an affair between his wife, Angelica, and Rex Geer during 1934. Guy himself encourages Angelica to interest Rex in horseback riding as therapy for job-related stress. Whatever his suspicions may be, Guy soon begins borrowing heavily from Rex's firm, and then from Rex himself, to cover unanticipated losses in real estate and mining ventures. The ultimate confrontation between the two men begins during the spring of 1936, when Guy asks Rex to "cover" some embezzled bonds belonging to the Glenville Country Club; Rex, whose son is by then engaged to Guy's daughter Evadne, agrees to do so, on condition that Guy liquidate his firm and retire from business, the better to protect the market's trusting, unsuspecting clients. Left with little choice, Guy asks for a "reprieve" of several months to "set his affairs in order," proceeding instead with even riskier speculations in a desperate, reckless attempt to repair the damage himself and keep his firm in business. Predictably, he fails, and Rex, also predictably, refuses to bail him out; Guy's firm thus goes into bankruptcy, and Guy himself goes to prison, willingly and almost gleefully—he has not gone down without a fight.

A quarter of a century after the fact, Guy, Rex and Angelica—whom Rex has married after her divorce from Guy and the subsequent death of Rex's ailing first wife—have widely differing interpretations of what happened, why, and to whom. Both Guy and Rex feel betrayed by each other, Guy because Rex stole not only his wife but also his good name, Rex because Guy in effect "sold out" the stock market to the government, forcing the imposition of federal controls in place of the gentlemanly code of honor that had previously sufficed on Wall Street.

Angelica Hyde Prime Geer, whose memoir closes the novel, attempts to strike a balance between her husbands, seeing their conflict of wills not in absolute terms but as a clash of idiosyncrasies. She tends to favor Rex's interpretation of events, having long since concluded that Guy is something of a mythomaniac, an incurable romantic who tends to lose contact with reality. In the end, however, it matters little who may be "right" or "wrong"; Auchincloss, through his skillful use of shifting narrative viewpoints, has skillfully evoked and illuminated an otherwise puzzling incident in recent American history, showing how hard it is to know exactly where the truth lies.

Summary

Taken together, *The House of Five Talents, Portrait in Brownstone, The Rector of Justin*, and *The Embezzler* constitute the keystone of Auchincloss' fictional universe, providing a credible, authoritative portrait of American society and politics from the late nineteenth century until well past the mid-point of the twentieth, a period encompassing two world wars and the Depression. In such later novels as *The Country Cousin* (1978) and *The Book Class* (1984), Auchincloss has often returned to the temporal setting of *Portrait in Brownstone* and *The Embezzler*, evoking the transitional period of the 1930's with rare insight and skill. Nevertheless, it is upon the four major novels of the 1960's that his future reputation is likely to rest.

Bibliography

Bryer, Jackson R. *Louis Auchincloss and His Critics*. Boston: G. K. Hall, 1977.

Dahl, Christopher C. *Louis Auchincloss*. New York: Frederick Ungar, 1986.

Milne, Gordon. *The Sense of Society*. Rutherford, N.J.: Fairleigh Dickinson University Press, 1977.

Parsell, David B. *Louis Auchincloss*. Boston: Twayne, 1988.

Tuttleton, James W. *The Novel of Manners in America*. Chapel Hill: University of North Carolina Press, 1972.

David B. Parsell

JIMMY SANTIAGO BACA

Born: Santa Fe, New Mexico
1952

Principal Literary Achievement

Through his autobiographical poetry, Baca has gained wide recognition as a spokesperson for Chicano culture, particularly its poor and underprivileged.

Biography

Jimmy Santiago Baca, born in 1952 to Chicano parents in Santa Fe, New Mexico, had a deprived and unsettled childhood. He spent his early childhood first with grandparents, until he was five, and then in an Albuquerque, New Mexico, orphanage. He ran away from the orphanage when he was eleven and for the next nine years lived on the streets and in various detention centers.

In 1972, Baca was arrested and convicted for possession of heroin with intent to sell. He was sent to prison in Florence, Arizona, where he stayed for the next seven years. There, according to the Arizona Supreme Court, which ordered his release in 1979, he was subjected to "cruel and unusual punishment," including electric shock therapy.

Yet, despite its harshness, Baca's prison experience turned him around as a person and set his life on a new course. Poetry literally became his savior. In prison, he began reading and writing, first a journal and then poetry. He was encouraged by several people, including Will Inman, former publisher of *New Kauri* poetry magazine, who visited him in prison. He also submitted poems to *Mother Jones* magazine, where the distinguished poet Denise Levertov was poetry editor. Describing Baca as "an extraordinarily gifted poet," Levertov published three of his prison poems in *Mother Jones* and began a correspondence with him.

Louisiana State University Press, noted among academic presses for its support of poetry, published Baca's first collection, *Immigrants in Our Own Land* (1979). The peoms in *Immigrants in Our Own Land* center mostly on Baca's prison experience. After he left prison, Baca expanded his subject matter to include his whole autobiography and his identification with Chicano culture. His next major work, *Martín & Meditations on the South Valley* (1987), represented those expanded interests in a dramatic fashion. Introduced by Denise Levertov and published by a prominent New York publisher, New Directions, *Martín & Meditations on the South Valley* won the Before Columbus Foundation American Book Award.

Thereafter, Baca's literary reputation blossomed. Although some Chicano critics

described his poetry as prosy and self-engrossed, Baca's fame spread rapidly beyond Chicano circles. His poetry readings and workshops became popular across the country. He received a Ludwig Vogelstein Foundation Award, the 1989 International Hispanic Heritage Award, and a Wallace Stevens Yale Poetry Fellowship. He attracted media coverage, appearing on *The Today Show* and National Public Radio. He also began working on a number of film scripts, including scripts for actor Edward James Olmos and *La Bamba* (1987) producer Taylor Hackford.

Despite such national attention, Baca remains rooted in the Chicano culture of the Southwest. He has said, "Foremost and always until my last breath I'm going to be a Chicano." He has also closely identified with the region around Albuquerque, as some of his titles indicate; the collection *Poems Taken from My Yard* (1986) was incorporated into *Black Mesa Poems* (1989). Baca himself, with his wife and two sons, lives on a ranch in the Black Mesa area south of Albuquerque. Besides writing, he takes a strong interest in being a parent and in the Atrisco Land Rights Council, which represents claimants to the seventeenth century Spanish land grant.

Analysis

The charges that Baca's poetry is prosy and self-engrossed are, to some extent, justified; he has also been accused of misspelling the Chicano Spanish that his poems include. Some readers might also feel that Baca's empathy for convicts and members of youth gangs overlooks an important factor: What about their victims?

Yet these criticisms should not be allowed to obscure Baca's achievements. He is largely a self-taught poet who has shown tremendous development, and indicated the capacity for more, over his career. It has been said that Baca taught himself to read and write in prison. He got his schooling primarily from the streets and prison, so it is not surprising that his early work should reflect this background. Nor is it surprising that his early work should be prosy, documentary descriptions of his experiences.

The remarkable advances made by Baca are apparent in *Martín & Meditations on the South Valley*. There are still prosy passages, especially when Baca provides exposition and narrative transitions, but the description is sharper, more selective, and filled with striking, even surrealistic, metaphors:

> The lonely afternoon in the vast expanse of llano,
> was a blue knife
> sharpening its hot, silver edge on the distant
> horizon of mountains, the wind blew over
> chipping red grit, carving a pre-historic scar-scaled
> winged reptile of the mountain.

His subject matter, while still grounded in his own life, has also become more inclusive. It has even assumed, as Levertov notes in the introduction, a mythic quality.

Black Mesa Poems shows development in other directions. Here Baca takes on *machismo*, the cult of aggressive manliness, and redefines it. He depicts a man who grows out of his violent concept of *machismo*, exemplified by killing a bull, and accepts a nurturing, caring role, represented by fatherhood. In an interview in the *Albuquerque Journal*, Baca stated that "I see a sort of feminism permeating the Chicano male now."

In the same interview, Baca said that in rearing his children he was "learning how to reparent myself because I was so brutalized" by growing up on the streets. Baca's efforts to "reparent" himself and to redefine *machismo* are part and parcel of his overall poetic project—to reclaim himself, his heritage, and the Chicano culture.

In this context, Baca's autobiographical poetry is not simply self-engrossed; it takes on wider, even archetypal, meaning. The efforts of Baca and his hero Martín to reclaim themselves necessarily include identification with their culture, the Chicano culture, which must also be reclaimed. Therefore, the work of reclamation is interrelated, occurring along a spectrum that involves individuals, language, culture, history, and land.

IMMIGRANTS IN OUR OWN LAND

First published: 1979
Type of work: Poetry

Baca surveys his thoughts and experiences in prison.

Immigrants in Our Own Land provides samples of Baca's early work, which is indeed prosy. The collection includes a number of so-called prose poems, description divided into prose paragraphs. Other poems are in free-verse lines. In both kinds of poems, however, the description is somewhat flat, including too much direct statement and metaphors which are commonplace or trite.

Similarly, the point of view in the poems is limited. Centered on Baca's prison experience, the poems dwell on the plight of the inmates—on how Baca and the other inmates are ground down—but there is remarkably little concern with how they got there in the first place. It is as if readers are to assume that all these men are victims of mistakes and injustices. Baca may have even thought so at the time; he repeatedly expresses his solidarity with the other inmates and condemns the forces that oppress them.

The point of view, however limited, does have a positive side: "This is suffering, pain, anguish, and loneliness,/ but also strength, hope, faith, love, it gives a man/ those secret properties of the Spirit, that make a man a man." There is a determination in Baca to endure and remain "strong enough to love you,/ love myself and feel good." Despite harassment—in "It's Going to Be a Cold Winter," new guards ransack Baca's cell and subject him to a strip search—a healing process occurs, encouraged by the passing time, moments of quietness, the prison routine, and a new warden who brings reforms and new activities, including "a poetry workshop where the death house had been."

In "So Mexicans Are Taking Jobs from Americans," perhaps the best poem in the volume, Baca also extends his sympathies outside the prison. He reaches out to feel solidarity with poor Mexicans whose children are starving and to mock the economic fears of complacent, overfed "gringos":

> Mexicans are taking our jobs, they say instead.
> What they really say is, let them die,
> and the children too.

The volume's title poem, "Immigrants in Our Own Land," is also effective. It presents prison as a kind of reverse Ellis Island, where convicts are processed into a new land of "rehabilitation" that proves to be illusory. The title also seems to allude to Chicanos whose families have lived in the Southwest since the original Spanish land grant, but who are sometimes still treated like immigrants—legal or illegal. The poem thus connects prison to the Chicano situation, with the prison experience becoming a metaphor for the denial of Chicano land, language, culture, and identity.

MARTÍN & MEDITATIONS ON THE SOUTH VALLEY

First published: 1987
Type of work: Poetry

After life on the streets, Martín builds a home place for himself and his small family.

Martín & Meditations on the South Valley consists of two long narrative poems that form a sequence: They relate the story of Martín, a generic or mythic poor Chicano. In these poems, Baca came into his own as a poet. Although the poems are somewhat prosy, particularly at narrative junctures, he manages his language well: Chicano folk life is described in memorable, original metaphors and diction (including some Chicano Spanish) that form pictures like punched art in old tin. His style has developed considerably since *Immigrants in Our Own Land*, becoming what Denise Levertov called Gongoresque, with touches of native Hispanic surrealism: "The highway was a black seed split/ petals of darkness blossomed from."

The two poems are also peopled with a gallery of vivid characters, including Martín's grandmother, parents, and pals (mostly gang members). Inhabitants of barrios come forth with old stories about his parents—one-armed Pepín, blind Estela Gomez, Señora Martinez, Melinda Griego, Pancho Garza, and Antonia Sanchez, la bruja de Torreón. There are also stories of Martín's friends, who have suffered their separate fates—"Johnny who married,/ Lorenzo killed in Nam,/ Eddie en la Pinta,/ Ramon who OD'd in Califas." The main story, however, is Martín's, based on Baca's autobiography but freely changed and shaped to mythic purposes.

Like Baca, Martín is a deprived child from a broken family. Martín's parents abandon him; later, his mother is killed by her jealous second husband and his father dies of alcoholism. Martín himself lives first with his grandmother and then in an orphanage, but at the age of ten he runs away. He becomes an uprooted person, living a dissolute and sometimes violent life on the streets and wandering about the county. In the first section of *Martín*, he says, "I have been lost from you Mother Earth," but he promises to return.

Most of *Martín* recounts his wanderings and his efforts to return to his roots. He questions people about his parents, trying to reconstruct memories of them. He has a pleasant image of his mother "dancing in front of the mirror/ in pink panties, . . . / Her laughter rough as brocaded cloth/ and her teeth brilliant as church tiles." He also remembers some friendly visits with his father, but mostly the memories are bad. His mother, sexually abused by her own father, could never form close emotional ties: She left her husband and the newborn Martín and "ran away to California" with her lover. Martín also well remembers his last meeting with his father: His drunken father cuffed and cursed him, and "I kicked you down/ vomiting whiskey/ to the ground."

Martín's search for roots continues, and he finally finds them in Burque (Albuquerque), where he moves in with a good woman, Gabriela. They eventually buy "a small house/ along the river, in Southside barrio." Martín's rebuilding of the dilapidated home and clearing of trash from the "half-acre of land in the back" symbolize the reestablishment of his Chicano roots, and these are solidified by the birth of a baby, Pablito. In the poem's last lines, Martín cradles the baby and promises, "you and all living things,/ I would never abandon you."

In *Meditations on the South Valley*, the saga of Martín and his little family continues. Disaster strikes: Their home burns to the ground, and they are forced to move into a suburban apartment with middle-class tenants who have "ceramic faces" and walk manicured poodles. A test of how well Martín's roots are established, the experience only deepens his appreciation for the barrio: "I don't want/ to live here/ among the successful. To the South Valley/ the white dove of my mind flies,/ searching for news of life." With all its dirt and disorder, the barrio contains a vitality for which Martín longs:

> People live out real lives in the South Valley.
> Tin can lids patch adobe walls,
> the moon through a window
> smolders at St. Francis' statue feet
> on a dresser,
> and there is a quietness heavy as blood
> that spills over into each afternoon.
> and brims like flame over the fields.

Meditations on the South Valley reaffirms the richness of Chicano culture, even among the poor. It has substance and solidity, a rootedness in place and history and old things. In this spirit, Martín, with the help of his pals, sets about rebuilding his home, but even better this time around. In the poem's conclusion, Martín sums up his motivation: "I was stripped down to the essential/ force in my life—create a better world, a better me,/ out of love."

Summary

Jimmy Santiago Baca has developed into a powerful spokesperson for Chicano culture, enshrining life in the barrio and writing in a style with a distinctively Hispanic flavor. Embodying his vision in the character Martín, a down-to-earth man with mythic qualities, Baca urges Chicanos to reclaim and hold on to their culture.

Yet his vision is one that all readers can share and ponder. Like Wendell Berry, Gary Snyder, and the Appalachian poet Jim Wayne Miller, Baca provides a critique of mainstream but diluted American culture. Like those other writers, Baca speaks for an alternative way of life that is rooted in the land, a distinct culture, and loving relationships.

Bibliography

Bruce-Novoa, Juan. *Chicano Poetry: A Response to Chaos.* Austin: University of Texas Press, 1982.

Harris, Marie, and Kathleen Aguero, eds. *A Gift of Tongues: Critical Challenges in Contemporary American Poetry.* Athens: University of Georgia Press, 1987.

Levertov, Denise. Introduction to *Martín & Meditations on the South Valley.* New York: New Directions, 1987.

Martinez, Demetria. "Poet Started Expressing His Culture in Prison." *Albuquerque Journal,* November 19, 1989, p. G8.

Olivares, Julián. "Two Contemporary Chicano Verse Chronicles." *The Americas Review: A Review of Hispanic Literature and Art of the USA* 16, nos. 3/4 (Fall/ Winter, 1988): 214-231.

Shirley, Carl R., and Paula W. Shirley. *Understanding Chicano Literature.* Columbia: University of South Carolina Press, 1988.

Harold Branam

JAMES BALDWIN

Born: New York, New York
August 2, 1924
Died: St. Paul de Vence, France
December 1, 1987

Principal Literary Achievement
Through his novels, essays, plays, and poetry, Baldwin boldly and articulately documented the dilemma of race in the United States.

Biography
James Baldwin was born in New York City on August 2, 1924. His mother, Emma Berdis Jones, was unmarried at the time, and his illegitimacy would haunt him throughout his life. In 1927, Emma married David Baldwin, a former slave's son who had come north from New Orleans filled with bitterness toward whites. David worked in factories, preached on weekends, and reared his ten children with iron discipline and little warmth.

James grew to hate his father for constantly criticizing and teasing him. As a teenager, he rebelled in many ways, first by becoming a Young Minister at a rival congregation, then by rejecting the church to pursue writing. At the same time, he watched his father slowly descend into a mental illness borne of anger; days before Baldwin's nineteenth birthday, his father succumbed to tuberculosis.

From the first, Baldwin loved to read, and by the time he was graduated from the prestigious De Witt Clinton High School in the Bronx, he had written essays for his school and church papers and made friends, black and white, who later became important professional contacts. In 1942, to help support his family, he went to work laying railroad track for the Army in New Jersey. It was his first experience outside New York, and the bigotry he faced there infuriated him. He spent several years moving from job to job, exploring his sexual nature in brief affairs with other men, and writing his first novel.

In 1945, Baldwin received a Saxton Fellowship for the manuscript, but its rejection by publishers devastated him: He went into hiding and started a lifetime career of heavy drinking. He turned to writing smaller pieces—stories, articles, reviews—and by 1948 he was being taken seriously in periodicals such as *New Leader* and *Commentary*. The strain of being black among whites and homosexual among heterosexuals—he was at one point engaged to be married—were too oppressive, how-

101

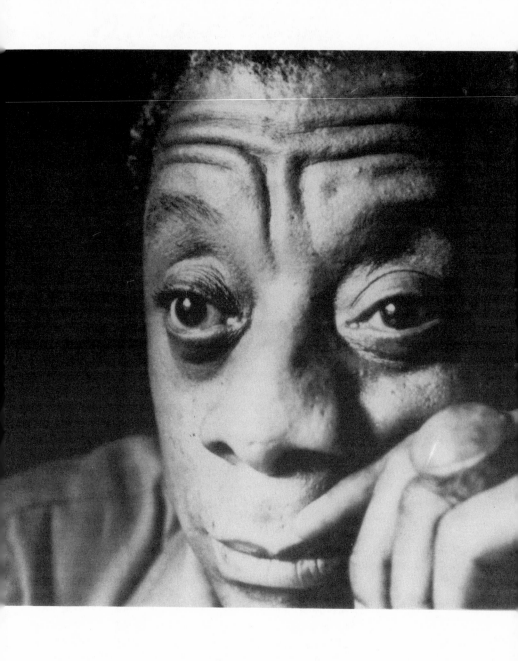

ever, so he left to join friends in exile in Paris. For the rest of his life he was constantly crossing the Atlantic.

In Paris he lived a penniless, bohemian life, and met such writers as Truman Capote, Saul Bellow, and Jean Genet. Black novelist Richard Wright, whom Baldwin had known in New York and both revered and resented, was also in Paris, and the rift between them, the old champion and the new, continued to grow. An article by Baldwin criticizing Wright's *Native Son* (1940) was published simultaneously in Paris and New York and attracted much attention.

Baldwin became great friends with a Swiss named Lucien Happersbarger, and it was in Lucien's Alpine village that he completed *Go Tell It on the Mountain* (1953), his first published novel. Returning to New York, he found readjustment difficult, again facing the racism he had crossed the ocean to escape. He wrote steadily, compiling topical essays into a collection called *Notes of a Native Son* (1955). His second novel, *Giovanni's Room*, published in England in 1955 and a year later in the United States, established his literary standing and identified him as an openly homosexual novelist.

With his mounting success, Baldwin remained deeply sensitive to the plight of blacks. In 1956 he covered a conference of black writers and artists in Paris and made his first trip into the Deep South, where he met the Rev. Martin Luther King, Jr., Rosa Parks, and other civil rights activists. These experiences confirmed his commitment to civil rights and led to a second volume of essays, *Nobody Knows My Name: More Notes of a Native Son* (1961). Two years later, he published *The Fire Next Time*, a piece about the extremist Black Muslims and Baldwin's own more moderate views. By virtue of his essays, he came to be considered a spokesman for his race. In 1963, Attorney General Robert Kennedy invited Baldwin and other prominent blacks to discuss the nation's racial situation. Despite good will on both sides, no common language could be found, and the meeting reminded Baldwin how far the nation still had to come.

Baldwin continued writing fiction. *Another Country*, his most candid and ambitious novel, appeared in 1962 to mixed reviews; his plays *Blues for Mister Charlie* (1964) and *The Amen Corner* (1954) were recognized for their vivid passion but faulted for poor structure; his sole volume of short stories, *Going to Meet the Man* (1965), and the novel *Tell Me How Long the Train's Been Gone* (1968) evoked the criticism that Baldwin was getting stale. He was accused by activist and writer Eldridge Cleaver of race hatred in *Soul on Ice* (1967) and he spared no mercy in an ongoing rivalry with novelist Norman Mailer. In many ways he was caught on the fence separating art and politics, and his articulateness and artistic vision were waning.

The final straw was the assassination of King on April 4, 1968. The loss, on both personal and political levels, profoundly affected Baldwin. Years of hope and struggle had only brought him back to the bitterness that had killed his father. In 1970, at the age of forty-six, he settled permanently in southern France. He still returned frequently to the United States, was still as devoted to friends and family as he had always been, and still wrote. None of his later works, however—*No Name in the*

Street (1971), further essays on race; a novel, *If Beale Street Could Talk* (1974); essays on film, *The Devil Finds Work* (1976); his last novel, *Just Above My Head* (1979); a book of poetry, *Jimmy's Blues: Selected Poems* (1983); and other articles, collections, and collaborations—garnered the praise of his earlier works. While he had myriad projects in mind, it became more and more difficult to write. He lectured and taught widely, but decades of liquor, cigarettes, constant travel, casual romance, publicity, and loneliness were taking their toll.

Baldwin developed cancer of the esophagus, and it claimed his life on December 1, 1987, in his home in France. His brother David, who had always been a close friend and support, was at his bedside when he died. A week later, more than five thousand people attended the funeral service held for him at New York's Cathedral of St. John the Divine, on the edge of his native Harlem.

Analysis

James Baldwin's turbulent and passionate life informs all of his writings. His life and art were inseparable; he wrote to understand the trials of the past and to articulate principles for the future. In his essays, he constantly depicted and expanded upon personal experiences, and in his fiction he drew on autobiographical events, issues, and characters, building dramatic situations that closely reflected his intimate experience of the world. He refused to lie, to shield, or to "prettify" reality. Though he limited his fictional settings to those he knew—a poor, religious Harlem home, the expatriate community in France, New York's jazz scene—he explored them deeply and critically. His experience with his friend Tony Maynard's legal battle against a false murder conviction inspired *If Beale Street Could Talk*, in which a young woman searches for the truth that will acquit her fiancé of rape, and his last novel, *Just Above My Head*, treats the anguished life of a homosexual gospel singer, a life not unlike his own.

Baldwin's early exposure to writers and writing helped him to become a skilled craftsman: His favorite childhood novels were Charles Dickens' *A Tale of Two Cities* (1859) and Harriet Beecher Stowe's *Uncle Tom's Cabin* (1852). His acquaintance with black writers Richard Wright, Countée Cullen, and Langston Hughes forced him to consider the particular problems of the black writer in the United States. Later, he was strongly influenced by the novels of Henry James—especially *The Ambassadors* (1903), *The Portrait of a Lady* (1881), and *The Princess Casamassima* (1886); though writing about wealthy white New Yorkers, James explored the same questions of individuality and nonconformity in a conformist society.

Baldwin was a precise writer: He chose words carefully and connected images with emotions in ways calculated to achieve maximum effect. His love of jazz music and appreciation of art infused his writing with evocative rhythms, colors, and textures, and his early training in the church is evident not only in the religious aspects of his stories but also in language replicating the simplicity, poetry, and ardor of the Bible and the traditional sermon. *The Fire Next Time*, perhaps his most renowned work, employs the biblical image of God's wrathful fire, as interpreted through a popular Negro spiritual song, to predict America's fate in the absence of meaningful progress toward a new racial order.

Race was always a crucial issue to Baldwin, but never a simple one. Though he often felt pure rage at the legacy of white supremacy, he strove in his life to speak to and treat black and white people in the same manner, and this determination to deal with people first as individuals helped him to create a language that is brutal but not unjust, objective but not detached. Baldwin never fully blames or exonerates anyone; as members of the human race, everyone is both guilty and innocent of shared history. For Baldwin, the color problem was not a problem for blacks alone, but for all members of society; the suppression of blacks and black culture has been a result of white fear and confusion, and it has inhibited the development not so much of black identity, but of a truly integrated and fulfilled American identity. Though keenly aware of both his African-American roots and his frequent voluntary exile, Baldwin considered himself American through and through, and he sought to express himself in American terms to an American audience.

In a similar fashion, though himself a homosexual, Baldwin tried to avoid all bias or prejudice in his treatment of sex, sexuality, and love. His curiosity and candor allowed sex and love to be used as meaningful modes for the expression of uniquely personal identity, and not simplistic ways of limiting or pigeonholing character.

Ultimately, the issues of race and sexuality become issues of identity and individuality. Baldwin, though a black homosexual, felt free to express himself through white, female, or heterosexual characters, and his voice, whether it be as the authoritative social observer of *Notes of a Native Son* and *Nobody Knows My Name*, the third-person narrators of *Go Tell It on the Mountain* and *Another Country*, or the intimately confessional protagonists of *Giovanni's Room* and *Tell Me How Long the Train's Been Gone*, is always searching for meaning, for a solution to the problem of expressing oneself forcefully and honestly in an imperfect world that bombards the individual with preordained roles and assumptions. While ostensibly writing about "exiles," "bisexuals," or "artists," all of which terms may have applied to Baldwin at points, he reserved for his characters the right to go beyond such labels and the freedom to feel and act according to the entire range of possible human behavior.

GO TELL IT ON THE MOUNTAIN

First published: 1953
Type of work: Novel

A young black man in Harlem begins to confront the legacy of anger and guilt that he is inheriting from his family.

Go Tell It on the Mountain, Baldwin's first published novel, tells a passionate story closely paralleling the author's own family background. It focuses on John Grimes, a black boy growing up in a religious home in Harlem under the stern hand of his preacher father Gabriel. The action of the novel takes place in 1936, on John's fourteenth birthday, with sections detailing previous events in the lives of John's aunt Florence, his father, and his mother Elizabeth.

Florence is a strident and bitter woman who left her ailing mother and irresponsible younger brother to come north. She married a man named Frank, who abused and abandoned her, and now she approaches old age feeling empty, living alone, and sharing in the life of her brother's family.

Gabriel, her brother, had been a wild young man, but he repented, became a preacher, and married a fallen woman named Deborah. Succumbing to temptation, however, he impregnated a young woman he worked with and then refused to acknowledge his paternity. He watched his son Royal grow before his eyes and heard of the boy's violent death in a knife fight. Gabriel drifted in despair, his wife passed on, and he came to New York to begin a new life. There he met Elizabeth.

Elizabeth was nine when her mother died, and, because her father ran a brothel, she went to live with her aunt in Maryland. There she fell in love with a young man named Richard; they moved to New York. Richard, wrongly accused of robbery, took his own life, leaving Elizabeth behind, alone and pregnant with John. Through Florence she met Gabriel, newly arrived from the South, they married, and Gabriel promised to treat John as his own. He preferred their other children, however, above all the fiery Roy, to his docile and pensive stepson John.

The character of Gabriel is a sharper version of Baldwin's own father, and, accordingly, his sternness and coldness elicit John's hatred. Everyone assumes that John will become a preacher like Gabriel, but, approaching manhood, John is having deep religious doubts. He is also feeling guilt over the sin of masturbation and is subtly becoming aware of his admiration for and attraction to Elisha, another young man in the church.

During the course of the day depicted in the novel, John's younger brother Roy is slashed in a fight, Gabriel strikes Elizabeth in anger, and Florence confronts Gabriel with his past in the form of a pained letter from his long-dead first wife. The novel's central action, however, is John's personal journey, culminating in the climactic third part entitled "On the Threshing Floor." Through a long night in the family's church, the Temple of the Fire Baptized, John experiences a frenzy of fear, inspiration, and awakening, a spiritual rite of passage before his family and congregation, in which he gives himself over to powers outside himself, infused as they are with familial and racial history, and begins to see the road he must travel.

The action of *Go Tell It on the Mountain* is not expansive; rather, it focuses on inner turmoils and private moments. Time moves slowly, and the interspersed flashbacks elucidate present moments or events. Through the accumulation of information, Baldwin slowly brings into focus how centuries of racial oppression—slavery, injustice, rape, violence—have shaped the lives of one Harlem family and how the complex family picture affects a sensitive young man at a crucial juncture in his life.

GIOVANNI'S ROOM

First published: 1956
Type of work: Novel

The inability of a young American in Paris to confront his bisexuality leads to his male lover's tragic downfall.

Giovanni's Room is an intimate, confessional narrative of an American named David who looks back on his turbulent experiences in France on the eve of his return to the United States. The novel works through two time frames simultaneously, for as past events are recounted the relevance of the present moment gradually emerges. By the end, night has become morning and only then does the story being told reach its conclusion.

Months earlier, David came to France with his girlfriend Hella, but uncertainty in their relationship and her wanderlust sent her traveling solo to Spain. David, with little money and none forthcoming from his father in the United States, befriends and exploits the generosity of a middle-aged homosexual, a Belgian-American businessman named Jacques. With Jacques he moves through the world of Paris gay bars, and at one of them he meets a handsome Italian bartender named Giovanni. David and Giovanni have an immediate rapport, and on the night of their meeting they stay out until dawn under the patronage of Jacques and Giovanni's boss Guillaume; they end up alone back at Giovanni's room, where they embark on a sexual relationship.

Having little money, David moves in with his new lover. Though David has had homosexual feelings and experiences before, the intensity of his fascination for Giovanni, and his own position in life—nearing thirty, and, ostensibly, marriage with Hella—make his relationship with Giovanni new and threatening. As so often has happened in the past, David ignores the possible consequences of his actions and continually reminds himself of his freedom, at any point, to abandon this new situation.

Giovanni's room, as the title suggests, has metaphorical significances for the story David is telling. It is cluttered with the debris of Giovanni's life—an unhappy past in Italy, an uncertain future in France, a superficial present of drinking and pandering among a subculture characterized by gossip, jealousy, and scandal. Just as Giovanni satisfies David's repressed desires, so does he find in David meaning and hope, and his room becomes, alternately, a haven or a prison, an Eden or a hell, a passageway to truth or a dead end, for both young men.

Throughout the telling of this history, the narrative returns to David's present in a rented house in southern France, alone, without either of his lovers. Time passes slowly; he measures the hours of the night drinking, preparing to leave, thinking mournfully of Giovanni, and waiting for morning to come. He recounts his panic and denial at Giovanni's growing dependence on him. Upon receiving news of Hella's imminent return from Spain, he cavalierly seduces a female acquaintance, for whom he feels no desire, to prove his independence and control. When Hella arrives, David abandons Giovanni; though they run into each other, he never admits to anything more than a casual friendship. Hella is puzzled but attributes David's behavior to the ambiguities of life in exile.

Meanwhile, Giovanni falls out of favor with Guillaume and loses his job. He has become "passe," a trifle no longer worth the attentions of the older men who frequent the bar. Without a job and without David, he becomes desperate; one night he comes to the bar drunk to demand his job back and in a moment of fury murders Guillaume. He takes to the streets and is covertly aided by David, but eventually is caught, tried, and condemned to the guillotine.

With Giovanni's crime, David becomes aware of how irresponsibly he has behaved and how much he has been evading the truth. He takes Hella to the south to escape the horrors of Paris, which for him has taken on the dimensions and associations of Giovanni's tiny room, but he cannot face Hella and runs away, only to be found by her days later among the homosexual subculture of Nice. His secret is revealed, and Hella departs for America, leaving David alone to face Giovanni's execution, which seems also to be his own, with the coming dawn.

In *Giovanni's Room*, Baldwin colorfully depicts the life of certain Paris milieus, but his focus is primarily on the three characters in the lovers' triangle. The dialogue is peppered with phrases of French that add atmosphere and reinforce the sense of anonymity and ambiguity so crucial to David's sensibility. Baldwin explores his chosen themes—bisexuality, exile, self-deceit, and guilt—with candor and boldness, remarkably so, given the age in which he wrote. The tone of the novel is one of rigorous self-examination and honest resignation; David has come to accept, although too late, responsibility for his actions. As such, his growth through the novel is a passage into maturity, a painful and tragic loss of innocence.

ANOTHER COUNTRY

First published: 1962
Type of work: Novel

A young black jazz drummer's suicide subtly affects the lives and loves of those he leaves behind.

Another Country is an intricate novel about a diverse group of idealistic but often troubled individuals in New York City. The novel is unified by the character of Rufus, a young black musician who commits suicide early in the novel but remains a vital presence in the awareness and memory of others.

Book 1, "Easy Rider," follows Rufus on the night of his suicide. Memories tell his history: growing up in Harlem and learning about racism, becoming a successful jazz drummer, meeting and falling in love with a simple, goodhearted Southern woman named Leona, feeling impotent against society's view of their interracial relationship, letting anger and alcohol inhibit his music, distrusting and abusing Leona, driving her to a mental hospital, losing his sense of worth, and, ultimately, jumping off the George Washington Bridge. The first book ends with Rufus' death.

The second book, "Any Day Now," follows the people closest to Rufus as they go on without him. His best friend Vivaldo, an aspiring writer of Irish-Italian descent, loved him and feels guilty for not saving him. At Rufus' funeral, Vivaldo is drawn to Rufus' younger sister Ida, and they soon become lovers. Ida is quiet, beautiful, proud, and bitter; whereas Vivaldo can accept individuals without regard to color or gender, Ida can never escape, even as she becomes a successful singer, awareness of her limited position as a black woman.

Losing Rufus brings Vivaldo and Ida closer to Vivaldo's friend and former teacher Richard and his wife Cass. Richard has just sold his first novel, a popular murder mystery, and Cass is realizing the limits of his artistic vision. It is Cass who sends news of Rufus' death to Eric, an American actor in Paris who was once his closest friend. After three years abroad, Eric is returning to New York to appear on Broadway, with Yves, his young French lover, soon to follow.

Another Country is unified not so much by a single action as by an interwoven pattern of events and themes. The story often jumps abruptly from scene to scene, and the narrative voice enters the minds of the characters—especially Vivaldo, Cass, and Eric. Seeking honest means to express themselves, they engage in parties and discussions, arguments and sex, with the mystery of Rufus always nearby. Vivaldo is plagued by jealousy when Ida spends time with her fast-talking producer, but she accuses him of making the racist assumption that all black women are whores. Eric, anxious about his future with Yves and somewhat dazed to be back in New York, becomes a haven for the disillusioned Cass; she comes to him and they begin an affair. As the weeks pass, Vivaldo's jealousy becomes more isolating, Cass's infidelity more frivolous, and Eric's future with Yves more certain.

In the culminating book 3, "Toward Bethlehem," Vivaldo comes to Eric for friendship and comfort and, both filled with the memory of Rufus, they spend a night of passion together. Meanwhile, Richard has confronted Cass and she must face her actions. Soon thereafter, Ida confesses to Vivaldo that she has indeed been unfaithful and realizes that in trying to vindicate her brother's death by exploiting the white system she has become a whore after all. Ida and Vivaldo come to a precarious understanding, and Cass predicts that she and Richard will do the same. The novel ends as Yves arrives from Paris to Eric's welcoming embrace.

Baldwin's careful structuring of his plot elements employs simultaneous action—different scenes occurring at the same time—and discrepant awareness—knowledge available to the reader but not to individual characters—to highlight the self-absorption, misunderstanding, and folly endemic to human interactions. Parallel situations, such as Vivaldo's courtship of Ida and Eric's courtship of Yves, Rufus' mistreatment of both Eric and Leona, Richard's and Ida's professional successes, and Ida's and Cass's infidelities, illuminate the complexity of Baldwin's world.

In *Another Country*, conventional racial and sexual assumptions are rejected, and the characters struggle on equal terms to make the connections they need. The novel's cryptic title functions on several levels, referring to exile (Eric's experience in France), to oppression (the black experience in America), to idealism (the yearning for a land free of social evils), and, most important, to the experience of love—entering, conquering, possessing, and inhabiting another person, tenderly or violently, emotionally or physically, with all that such otherness offers to the one who dares to love.

NOTES OF A NATIVE SON

First published: 1955
Type of work: Essays

Black people hold a precarious position in American political and artistic life, and their validation is essential to the fulfillment of the American identity.

Notes of a Native Son is a collection of essays published previously in various periodicals. Though not originally written to be published together, they share Baldwin's concerns over the resolution of the United States' racial dilemma and the question of American identity.

The first group of essays focuses on the black person as artist and on his image within the cultural canon. In "Everybody's Protest Novel," Baldwin, once an enthusiastic fan of Harriet Beecher Stowe, labels her an "impassioned pamphleteer" and criticizes *Uncle Tom's Cabin* and other "protest novels," including Richard Wright's *Native Son*, for falling short of their lofty aims, abusing language, and overtaxing credibility. Baldwin goes on in the second essay, "Many Thousands Gone," to recognize *Native Son* as a literary landmark but questions its actual power, given the depersonalization and mythification of blacks—Uncle Tom and Aunt Jemima. In essence, the "native son" is a monster created by American history, and it is American history that must confront and re-create him. The third essay in the group, "Carmen Jones: The Dark is Light Enough," criticizes an all-black production of a theatrical standard for perpetuating racial stereotypes.

The second group focuses on the socio-political scene. "The Harlem Ghetto," the earliest of the essays, documents the congestion and claustrophobia of 1948 Harlem. Baldwin considers token civic improvements—playgrounds and housing projects—to be at best superficial and at worst injurious. The position of black leaders is impossible, the black press merely models itself on downtown counterparts, and the popularity of churches only reflects the pervasive hopelessness.

This hopelessness is evidenced in "Journey to Atlanta," which recounts the experiences of a group of black singers, including Baldwin's brother David, as guests of the Progressive Party in Atlanta. The Melodeers, anticipating a week of open artistic exchange in the Deep South, encounter only disappointment and failed promises. They are coerced into canvassing for the party, have little opportunity to rehearse or perform, and are finally abandoned without support or return busfare.

In the title essay, "Notes of a Native Son," Baldwin juxtaposes his feelings upon his father's death—the end of a lifetime of racial bitterness—with images of Harlem in August, 1943, despoiled from widespread rioting after the controversial shooting of a black soldier. The private and public worlds merge to reflect the cycles of life in a tormented community. As Baldwin's father lay on his deathbed, Baldwin's mother lay waiting to give birth to her last child. Before the rioting, Harlem also lay in wait—tense, sweltering, and crowded with white policemen ready to strike and uniformed black soldiers heading off to war in Europe. With the passage of time, death, life, and rage came to fruition, and Baldwin surveys the results. He recalls first becoming aware of his violent feelings against whites, and he knows that with his father's death he must confront his filial hatred, just as Americans, black and white, must confront their shameful history.

The last group draws on Baldwin's experiences in exile. "Encounters on the Seine: Black Meets Brown" depicts the relations between American blacks and Africans— relations that are not automatically warm and fraternal—and the simplistic and pitiful attitude Baldwin met among the French. In "A Question of Identity," he analyzes what Americans such as himself seek in voluntary exile—an anonymity that expresses a longing for identity. Baldwin says that only by rejecting American values can one eventually affirm them, that the self-alienated discovers America by going to Europe.

The collection ends with two anecdotal essays. "Equal in Paris" relates Baldwin's false arrest for the theft of hotel bedsheets and his comic but demoralizing adventures in Parisian prisons and courts. Finally, "Stranger in the Village" tells of the summer Baldwin spent in his friend Lucien's Swiss village, a community that had never before seen a black person. The villagers approached him with curiosity and a bit of fear; he felt no malice, but he detected in their ignorance traces of the imperial and missionary traditions. Baldwin compares his experience there with the larger experience of blacks as supposed "strangers" in the "village" of the United States.

Notes of a Native Son demonstrates Baldwin's ability to connect disparate experiences and images—emotional and political, abstract and concrete, past and present— into persuasive arguments. His prose is full and textured, and ideas have the force of weight. At times, Baldwin speaks though the first-person singular of African-American history, an "I" that endured displacement, slavery, and all that followed. The tone becomes bitter, stubborn, and accusing. At other times, he adopts an empowered first-person plural, a "we" that assumes a white audience and refers to blacks from a distance. Yet Baldwin's characteristic objectivity, a more precise and color-free voice, is always available, and in these essays he acknowledges the complexity of these issues, the partial truth of cultural assumptions, and the shared responsibility for social transformation.

Summary

James Baldwin was very much a man of his era. By the time of his death, his message had been received and digested by the American populace; yet his vision, so passionate and articulate at its inception, will not lose relevance so long as prejudice and bigotry—oppression of those perceived as "other," "inferior," or "different"—persist. As a spokesman and activist, he helped to bring about the social transformation of his nation, to the benefit of all races, genders, and sexualities; as an artist, he found a unique and personal idiom for expressing the anguish and joy of his life.

Bibliography

Eckman, Fern Marja. *The Furious Passage of James Baldwin.* New York: Evans, 1966.

Kinnamon, Kenneth, ed. *James Baldwin: A Collection of Critical Essays.* Englewood Cliffs, N.J.: Prentice-Hall, 1974.

Macebuh, Stanley. *James Baldwin: A Critical Study.* New York: Third Press, 1973.

Porter, Horace A. *Stealing the Fire: The Art and Protest of James Baldwin.* Middletown, Conn.: Wesleyan University Press, 1973.

Pratt, Louis H. *James Baldwin.* Boston: Twayne, 1978.

Standley, Fred L., and Nancy V. Burt, eds. *Critical Essays on James Baldwin.* Boston: G. K. Hall, 1988.

_____. *James Baldwin: A Reference Guide.* Boston: G. K. Hall, 1980.

Sylvander, Carolyn Wedin. *James Baldwin.* New York: Frederick Ungar, 1980.

Weatherby, W. J. *James Baldwin: Artist on Fire.* New York: Donald I. Fine, 1989.

Barry Mann

Principal Literary Achievement

A founder of the Black Arts Movement, Baraka is acknowledged to be a major influence upon experimental twentieth century poetry and drama.

Biography

Born Everett LeRoi Jones in Newark, New Jersey, on October 7, 1934, Imamu Amiri Baraka was reared in the urban middle-class environment against which he has since rebelled. His father, Coyette (Coyt) LeRoi, was a postal employee, and his mother, Anna Lois Russ Jones, a social worker. Educated in the Newark public schools, Baraka began cartooning in junior high school and writing science fiction for the school publication in high school before graduating at the age of sixteen.

Although he had once considered the ministry for a career, Baraka accepted a science scholarship to Rutgers University. His experiences at Rutgers for one year, at Howard University for three years (where he earned a B.A. in English in 1954), and as an enlisted gunner in the air force (from 1954 to 1957) catalyzed his awareness of what he believed to be the illness of assimilation—that is, of black acquiescence and adaptation to white oppression. Consequently, after his discharge from the armed services, Baraka sought the supportive counter-cultural atmosphere of Greenwich Village in New York.

There, he founded Totem Press and cofounded the avant-garde magazine *Yugen* with Hettie Cohen, a Jewish woman who would be his wife for seven years, from 1958 to 1965. In those years, he achieved recognition as a jazz and blues critic, worked as a poetry and small-press magazine editor, and took graduate courses in philosophy and comparative literature at Columbia University. Under the influence of such bohemian experimental poets as Allen Ginsberg, Gregory Corso, and William Carlos Williams (as well as Ezra Pound), Baraka established his early poetic voice with his first volume of poetry, *Preface to a Twenty Volume Suicide Note* (1961). This collection reflected his resistance to the debilitating effects of white stereotyping and black assimilation, suggesting his eventual movement to a separatist philosophy.

Throughout his literary career, Baraka has served as a role model of his philosophy that art must lead to greater awareness and stimulate its audience to action. A

113

small sampling of his activities from 1959 to 1967 includes the following: 1959, compiling and publishing a pro-Castro anthology; 1960, touring Cuba with other artists at Castro's invitation; 1961, cofounding an experimental poetry group and magazine; 1963, seeing *The Toilet*, his first play, produced Off-Broadway and publishing *Blues People*, a book of music criticism; 1964, founding Black Arts Repertory Theatre and School; 1966, founding Spirit House, a black community theater with ongoing student workshops; and 1967, founding Jihad Publications for black nationalist writers.

Baraka's own nationalism was fostered by repeated arrests in which charges were dropped or, as in one case, a judge's decision was reversed by the United States Supreme Court on appeal. At the same time, recognition of Baraka's literary achievements was both national and international. The author was awarded a John Hay Whitney Foundation Fellowship for fiction and poetry in 1962, the Obie Award for best Off-Broadway play (*Dutchman*) in 1964, a Yoruba Academy Fellowship in 1965, a Guggenheim Fellowship for 1965-1966, and second prize at the Dakar International Arts Festival as well as a grant from the National Endowment for the Arts in 1966. Certainly, the dichotomy between the positive responses of the literary community and the negative responses of the legal professions served to fuel his anti-assimilationist beliefs.

In 1965, his interracial marriage was dissolved; in 1967, he married Sylvia Robinson, a black woman. The following year, LeRoi Jones became Imamu Amiri Baraka, thereby erasing his white heritage with Muslim and African words meaning "blessed poet/philosopher warrior"; his wife became Bibi Amina Baraka. For the next seven years, Baraka was to become increasingly active in nationalistic ventures and more fervid in his denunciations of white society. He called for non-pacifistic black attitudes and even for mass exterminations of whites, white organizations, and white culture so that blacks could create a totally independent country—in essence a black utopia. He endorsed black candidates in local elections, helped to found organizations for the protection and enhancement of black civil liberties and culture, and held high offices within both local and national activist groups.

Although he continues to be a fierce advocate of black rights, in 1974 Baraka dropped "Imamu" from his name in favor of the title "Chairman" when he adopted Marxism and socialistic beliefs. He also began to advocate a coalition of white and black proletariat against their middle- and upper-class oppressors. The need for a separate black state has been superseded by what Baraka perceives to be the capitalistic and imperialistic threat to the uninformed, disorganized masses. Consequently, Baraka's style in all of his writings shifted to a more didactic and less emotional function and content. What some critics have essentially termed rambling propaganda Baraka sees as rallying cries (predominantly to his black audience) for revolution.

Analysis

Amiri Baraka's writings divide into three distinctive patterns according to both form and content. His first literary period, although sometimes unconventional in dramatic subject matter, is his most conventional in form. Written under the name LeRoi Jones, the work of this early period is distinguished by a preoccupation with self-identity as well as a nascent concern for the lack of a collective black consciousness.

The work of his second literary period, during which he had begun to write as Imamu Amiri Baraka, is more experimental in form and is marked by strong advocacy of black separatism. A romantic with a profound belief in man's spiritual potential, the Baraka of this period sees whites as having distorted their spiritual capacities into materialistic oppression; therefore, he advocates the extinction of the white race (and its cultural artifacts) and the creation of a new black world. To that end, Baraka seeks to raise his readers' consciousness of history and racial identity so that, through dramatic involvement, they will be moved to active resistance.

The characteristics of this period (his most universally acclaimed) are based upon his belief that art is a dynamic, utilitarian process that must have an integral role in any "living" black community by virtue of the experiences it offers for growth. The white culture, according to Baraka, has already self-destructed from a pervasive, incurable emotional and spiritual paralysis.

Consequently, he rejects white American English through the re-creation of black speech patterns, whose words and sounds combine synergistically to produce a challenging syntax and a lyrical dramatic rhythm. Unlike his goal during his first literary period, Baraka's intent at this stage is predominantly ethnocentric. He employs inflammatory and obscene language to startle his readers, to force their emotional awareness. Perceiving violence as the only viable means to black rebirth, Baraka consciously chooses a multisensory, surrealistic style that can brutally assault his audience. His dramatization of historical injustices is uncompromising, as are his solutions. Furthermore, his consuming hatred of whites exacerbates the violence he advocates. Nevertheless, his concern for the black oppressed is balanced to some degree by his affirmation that blacks, as the superior race, can overcome their oppressors and can establish self-sufficiency.

Baraka's need to disavow the deceit and the deadliness he believes to be inherent in white English gradually leads to increased literary experimentation. Generally, his punctuation and his capitalization become extreme; for example, he uses open parenthesis and diagonals for pauses. He may capitalize every letter of a word for emphasis, spell phonetically, invent abbreviations, and pun. Another singular characteristic is his extensive use of present participles to connote the dynamic process of living.

In his nonfiction prose, he intermittently breaks the convolutions of his lengthy sentences with sentence fragments and asides addressed to the reader. His fiction is associational rather than chronological in content. In his poetry, he seeks the purest expression of his "beingness" by extending his verbal inventiveness, at times to the point of unintelligibility. His inversion of traditional symbols is particularly noteworthy. For example, the white god-figure and his dictums are false, created by the white race to victimize others; therefore, the sun, traditionally life-giving, becomes a symbol of black spiritual energy and a mortal threat to whites.

Slave Ship: A Historical Pageant (1967) is representative of his separatist ritual drama. As is typical of black nationalist theater, physical and emotional violence is portrayed in a series of evocative slave images meant to draw audience response on an emotional level. With little dialogue, the playscript depends heavily upon music, dance, sounds, and lighting to build—through horrifying black experiences—to the final affirmation of black beauty and power. When cast and audience unite, however, Baraka's script calls for a disembodied head to be thrown amidst the celebration, a graphic reminder that the struggle has not ended.

Baraka's third literary phase is characteristically Marxist; he no longer uses Imamu as a part of his name. He seeks an intellectual rather than an emotional response to his writing. His style is didactic and propagandizing, and he has enlarged the scope of his concern from a focus on black cultural victimization and racial identity to a socialistic focus on the world's oppressed. Instead of denouncing whites as the cause of America's ills, Baraka defends all who have been victimized, regardless of race, and blames the world's "dis-ease" on capitalists and imperialists. This does not, however, mean that he has abandoned his active participation in creating a unified black world of self-determination and nonoppression; in his third literary period he sees black nationalism being achieved as only one consequence of an inevitable socialist revolution.

DUTCHMAN

First produced: 1964 (first published, 1964)
Type of work: Play

On the New York subway, Lula, a thirty-year-old white female, seduces and murders Clay, a twenty-year-old black male.

Dutchman, winner of the 1964 Obie Award for best Off-Broadway production, is a riveting dramatization of psychosexual, interracial tensions. The title itself bears mythical implications supported by Baraka's own stage directions, which indicate a subway setting filled with contemporary myth. Despite Baraka's insistence that the two main characters are individuals, not allegorical creations, he confines them within this subterranean set. The Dutch sailed the first slave-bearing vessel to the American colonies. Moreover, the Flying Dutchman is the legend of a ship cursed to sail the seas eternally without ever finding safe harbor. Even if the first were a simple allusion, together these suggest that white America has doomed itself through its nonrecognition of blacks as human. If so, Lula as the white representative will inhabit the subway, preying upon her black victims until one galvanizes himself into action, freeing himself and both races through her murder.

Lula, the protagonist, controls scene 1. She enters from behind Clay, initiates their confrontive conversation, and sits beside him. Even though he is uncomfortable, she makes seductive overtures. Her accurate assessment of his middle-class background and assimilationist behavioral mask also fascinates him into continuing the conversation. Lula, the oppressor, condescendingly sees Clay as a stereotype and commands the topics with which they essentially talk at each other. By admitting that she is a liar—and later, that she is insane—Lula forces him into the untenable situation of having to process each of her statements as fact or fiction. Furthermore, it is she who offers Clay an apple that he accepts; critics have made much of the possible Adam and Eve analogy. Lula is also the initiator of physical aggression, first running her hand along Clay's leg and later harshly grabbing and shaking his wrist.

Clay, in suit and striped tie despite the summer heat, has assimilated into the white world. He does not wish to call attention to himself. Clay also sees Lula as a stereotype—of the liberal white female fascinated by fantasies of interracial sexual intercourse. Momentarily excited by her, he allows himself to become vulnerable by adapting to her mercuric emotional shifts.

In scene 2, as Lula describes her party plans in seductive detail, Clay begins to make physical advances. Their dialogue, strikingly fast-paced from the play's opening lines, intensifies into a dueling rhythm as they both become more openly confrontational. They even capture the attention of normally apathetic fellow subway riders, who watch their interaction with some interest. A major shift occurs when Lula unmasks Clay, accusing him of having escaped to her (the white) side. Clay assumes control, and Lula defends herself with hysterics, singing and dancing in the train aisle. Clay refuses every invitation to join her until she goads him to restrain her by warning him that he is dying because of his assimilation, that he must release himself from his self-imposed bonds. He wrestles her (as well as the drunk who attempts to defend her) into submission, slapping her with full strength.

Baraka sees dance as an ultimate expression of life. Lula's hysterical invitation, however, assumes a double meaning. Even though she may be offering Clay an apparent passageway out of his self-victimization, she is simultaneously inviting him into a new bondage: life on her terms. With no viable means of regaining his mask or escaping, Clay is finally free to expunge his rage. He erupts into a devastating diatribe that avows his contempt for those who surround themselves with illusions to avoid reality, his homicidal hatred of whites, and his need to assimilate so as not to commit mass murder. According to Clay, black art and music are escape valves that would be unnecessary if the artists would simply exterminate whites: "A whole people of neurotics, struggling to keep from being sane. And the only thing that would cure the neurosis would be your murders."

He defeats himself, however, by retreating tiredly from an insistence upon action to the safety of words. Clay concludes with a warning not to trust assimilated blacks because someday they will embark on a genocidal rampage, using as their justification the same white rationalizations they have been taught.

As Clay bends to gather his books, Lula stabs him twice; after he has destroyed her illusions of him, she must destroy him. Whether her actions are premeditated can be interpreted dramatically through her interactions with the other passengers. Her earlier admission that she knows them even more intimately than she knows Clay and their easy acquiescence in disposing of his body suggest either complicity or a compelling fear. That their presence as her "crew" is prearranged is in keeping with the Dutchman myths. Her preparation to start the cycle once more with another young black who enters the car further supports the mythical interpretation.

In *Dutchman*, Baraka dramatized two of his major themes. The first is that dehumanizing sexuality, in any form, leads to death. Clay and Lula's sexual interaction is simply another layer of masking. It is sterile, with no spiritual or emotional intimacy. Baraka's second theme is that psychic paralysis leads to annihilation. Clay has the opportunity to survive until he is caught in his own self-destructive trap. As a poet, he retreats into words and poetry when challenged because they are safe and comfortable, even when he recognizes the need for action. He does not see his art's potential as a motivating agent for change, and he reverts to passive resistance, giving up. Consequently, his art, too, is sterile. It is Lula who survives, by committing the extreme guerrilla action in murdering him.

AN AGONY. AS NOW.

First published: 1964
Type of work: Poem

From within a white metal shell, the poet views nature and remembers himself.

In "An Agony. As Now," from *The Dead Lecturer* (1964), Baraka describes in sensuous phrases his emotional and spiritual paralysis. The title of this poetry collection is a reference to the attempted suicide of the speaker. His sense of dissociation from the self who hates him is a normal part of the recovery process; however, Baraka adds another level of meaning. The inverted symbolism of white implies that assimilation, voluntary or involuntary, is a significant factor of the imprisonment.

Openings in the mask allow him to see, but the metal prevents any human contact. Introspectively addressing his ruminations to the soul he has sightlessly abandoned, he recalls a woman who ran from him to the forest of white "civilization" and a man decaying from psychic paralysis, "never beautiful." The speaker's mind races unencumbered to the sun in a series of associational images that offer a brief hope for resurrection with fragmented water imagery. Nevertheless, the torment escalates as he recognizes the corruption surrounding him. The sun is love, self-actualization, God, but the poet is trapped within himself and does not know how to reach the love, despite his need. Therefore, the sun reaches out to him, heating his white metal shell and burning awareness into him. His final scream is a scream of self-realization, a moment of truth, in which he relinquishes his detachment and accepts himself.

Baraka's characteristic devices include the use of open parentheses and commas to stop his reader and to increase the associational possibilities of his phrasing. Inverted symbolism and the repetition of key words and phrases reinforce his meaning as he guides his reader on a journey from mind, through sun, god, and soul, to beauty. The speaker's shell is the corrupting veneer of white civilization. To acknowledge his true identity, the black poet must reject the easy answers and accept his black consciousness as beautiful. Only after he destroys the façade will he again feel.

Summary

Amiri Baraka is a crucial figure in contemporary American literature. His indomitable insistence that the oppressed be freed and that art be an active factor in the process has led him to the creation of versatile forms of expression in poetry, drama, fiction, and nonfiction prose. A leading black aesthetician, he consistently extends his art into action. A critical concern, however, has been that he fails to reach his intended audience, the black masses. As his experimentation continues, his writing grows ever more esoteric and may become accessible to smaller and smaller audiences.

Bibliography

Benston, Kimberly W. *Baraka: The Renegade and the Mask*. New Haven, Conn.: Yale University Press, 1976.

——————, ed. *Imamu Amiri Baraka (LeRoi Jones): A Collection of Critical Essays*. Englewood Cliffs, N.J.: Prentice-Hall, 1978.

Brown, Lloyd W. *Amiri Baraka*. Boston: Twayne, 1980.

Fox, Robert Elliot. "LeRoi Jones/Amiri Baraka: A Scripture of Rhythms." In *Conscientious Sorcerors: The Black Postmodernist Fiction of LeRoi Jones/Amiri Baraka, Ishmael Reed, and Samuel R. Delany*. New York: Greenwood Press, 1987.

Hudson, Theodore R. *From LeRoi Jones to Amiri Baraka: The Literary Works*. Durham, N.C.: Duke University Press, 1973.

Lacey, Henry C. *To Raise, Destroy, and Create: The Poetry, Drama, and Fiction of Imamu Amiri Baraka (LeRoi Jones)*. Troy, N.Y.: Whitston, 1981.

Kathleen Mills

DJUNA BARNES

Born: Cornwall-on-Hudson, New York
June 12, 1892
Died: New York, New York
June 18, 1982

Principal Literary Achievement

Best known and most frequently celebrated for her dense, lyrical prose, Barnes was also an important contributor to expatriate culture of the 1920's and a significant modernist novelist.

Biography

Djuna Barnes was born into an eccentric, bohemian family at Cornwall-on-Hudson, New York, on June 12, 1892. Her mother, an amateur violinist who wrote poetry throughout her life, was perhaps the most conventional figure in the Barnes family. Barnes's father, Wald Barnes, rarely held any substantial employment, and he was a notorious philanderer. He adopted his mother's surname as a reaction against his own father, and his first name was merely one of many he employed throughout his early life. Wald's mother, Zadel, also lived with the family, and supported her son's interests in spiritualism. During her late childhood, Barnes's family moved to a farm on Long Island, but her parents soon separated, the eccentric and self-indulgent Wald having exceeded even his wife's amazing tolerance of his selfish behavior.

Partly as a consequence of her family's eccentric opinions, Barnes never attended public school, but she did move to Manhattan to attend art school. Her first book, a collection of poems and drawings entitled *The Book of Repulsive Women*, was published in 1915, and Barnes for a time considered the careers of artist and writer to be equally open to her. During much of World War I, Barnes lived in Greenwich Village and earned a living as a free-lance journalist for various small New York and Brooklyn papers. During this period, Barnes began to take women lovers, and her relationships with women were to remain the emotional center of her adult life.

With her expatriation to Europe in 1919, Barnes's life began a new chapter; no longer simply a member of an artistic community in the United States, she became a celebrated figure of international, although predominantly American, bohemian culture. It was in Europe that Barnes initiated longtime friendships with Natalie Barney, the famous lesbian advocate, and Peggy Guggenheim, the wealthy heiress, gallery owner, and patron of innumerable artists, including Barnes. She also interviewed

James Joyce, the great modernist novelist, and carried on distant acquaintanceships with luminaries such as Ernest Hemingway. In 1923, Barnes published *A Book*, a critically successful collection of poems, short stories, plays, and drawings. This text was subsequently republished with some alterations as *A Night Among the Horses* (1929), but it is best known by its earlier title. While living in Paris, Barnes began a love affair with the American artist Thelma Wood; this relationship, which lasted throughout the 1920's, was traumatic for Barnes emotionally, and it ultimately formed the basis for her novel *Nightwood* (1936).

Barnes's next book, *Ryder* (1928), was a best-selling novel in the United States, and it became the focus of post-office inquiries because of its sexual frankness. Like *Nightwood*, it is also biographical and draws upon Barnes's early familial experiences. In the following year, Barnes published a satire on the Paris lesbian community entitled *A Ladies' Almanack* (1928), which was privately printed and not widely available until a Harper & Row reprint in 1972. During the 1930's, Barnes lived in England, first in Peggy Guggenheim's household and later on her own in London. Her most important novel, *Nightwood*, was published during this period, and it gained for her the support of the profoundly influential T. S. Eliot. Having briefly returned to France in 1939, Barnes was almost trapped by the advancing German armies in their summer advance of 1940; however, she managed to escape with the financial aid and encouragement of Peggy Guggenheim, and she arrived in New York later that year. Returning to Greenwich Village, Barnes settled into a small studio apartment on Patchin Place, where she resided for the rest of her life. Initially, Barnes experienced extreme financial difficulties in New York and for a time returned to painting; however, she published a verse drama, *The Antiphon*, in 1958 and continued to work at various literary projects until her death. In her later years, Barnes became increasingly isolated, partly as a consequence of ill health and partly as the result of her alienation from a world which paid her small attention. She was, however, awarded a National Endowment for the Arts grant in 1981, and her *Creatures in an Alphabet* (1982), a collection of brief animal alphabet rhymes, was published shortly after her death on June 18, 1982, at the age of ninety.

Analysis

The American poet T. S. Eliot once described Djuna Barnes's *Nightwood* as a novel that in its stylistic prowess and its preoccupation with horror and fate very much resembles an Elizabethan tragedy. Although Barnes herself was widely read in the literature of the English Renaissance, the motivation for the preoccupation with decay and emotional trauma in her work stems from sources much nearer than the Elizabethans. Barnes herself insisted (in a 1919 interview with the American bohemian publisher Guido Bruno) that life was fundamentally morbid, particularly if one considers the life that goes on beneath the surface of everyday life. Although she was not a serious student of depth psychology, Barnes's work reveals a passing acquaintance with Freudian notions, and her concern with the morbid character of psychological experience is largely a consequence of her decision to explore the often possessive and aggressive aspects of the family dynamic and of romantic relationships. In this respect, the Freudian influence in her work only substantiates the impact of the other major influence in Barnes's fiction—*fin de siècle* literature.

In Barnes's early journalism, there are frequent references to Irish poet and playwright Oscar Wilde and to the drawings of English artist Aubrey Beardsley. Both figures are connected with the aura of exotic decadence that is commonly associated with European culture at the turn of the century, and Barnes's early poems and art definitely demonstrate the impact of the languid and often strangely animalistic figures that one characteristically finds in Beardsley's drawings. *The Book of Repulsive Women* is perhaps the best example of this influence in Barnes's own work, but it can also be found in the grotesque imagery that pervades her late verse drama, *The Antiphon*. Thematically, one might consider Barnes to be preoccupied with the process of decay and emotional estrangement, and this concern with impending doom and dissolution has led critics to consider her otherwise possibly eccentric fiction as very much in the mainstream of American fiction that runs from Herman Melville's tortured mariners to the apocalyptic vision of Hollywood that one finds in the fiction of Nathanael West.

While the thematic concerns in Barnes's work are very tightly focused, her stylistic and technical achievements are extravagant and wide-ranging. In this respect, Barnes is also very much in the mainstream of the spirit of literary experimentation that characterized the modernist movement of the 1920's. Her own interest in the work of Joyce is well known, and, as her novel *Ryder* demonstrates, Barnes is able to imitate effectively virtually every major writer in the history of English prose. In *Ryder*, this rhetorical exuberance is often entertaining and occasionally dazzling, but in *Nightwood* it is the motor that drives the novel. In *Nightwood*, Barnes largely eschews any interest in plot in favor of a detailed representation of the consciousnesses of the major figures. In her preoccupation with motivation and with the associative patterns that preoccupy her characters, Barnes's writing in *Nightwood* parallels what is often described as stream-of-consciousness prose, most frequently associated with the fiction of James Joyce and with the psychologically motivated passages in the work of William Faulkner.

Barnes's subsequent interest in verse drama reflects a further rhetorical development in her work, and it looks forward to her late return to poetry and short lyrics. In this respect, Barnes's career may be thought of as describing a circle that begins with short verse, passes through the prose experiments of the 1920's and 1930's, and returns to verse via the very demanding form of blank verse drama. It should not be forgotten, of course, that throughout her life Barnes continued to pursue visual art; her drawings form an essential part of novels such as *Ryder* and collections such as *A Night Among the Horses*, and they may well be studied for insights into the prose that they illustrate.

Finally, Barnes must also be read as an important example of lesbian writing and for her efforts to write a women's modernism and to use experimental techniques to explore the estranged and oppressed roles of women. Her world of gay women in

Nightwood is doubly distanced from the white heterosexual norms of modernist fiction, and as such this novel represents an important oppositional voice in the history of twentieth century literature.

RYDER

First published: 1928
Type of work: Novel

The eccentric and philandering Wendell Ryder attempts to assert patriarchal control over his family, but he ultimately fails.

Djuna Barnes's first novel, *Ryder*, is most significant for its display of technical virtuosity; it contains Elizabethan lyrics, audacious drawings, and enough ribald prose passages to have made it a minor scandal when it was first published. The plot describes the efforts of Wendell Ryder to found his own dynasty, but Wendell's successes are achieved largely at the expense of the women in the text; his wife, Amelia, and his mistress, Kate Careless, are ruthlessly exploited to fulfill Wendell's selfish ends. What impresses one most about Barnes's first popular success, however, is her early feminism and her ability to manipulate the novel form.

While many of her compatriots were celebrating the triumph of male sexuality, Barnes was concerned with exploring the ways in which women were exploited by men. Chapter 5 in this novel, "Rape and Repining," demonstrates her interest in early feminism in its mocking attack on women for their own misfortune. In addition, Barnes's novel reflects the influence of Joyce in its use of a narrative that abandons strict chronology in favor of digressive commentaries upon the various women and their roles in the novel. For example, Barnes devotes a considerable amount of space to Kate Careless, one of Wendell's mistresses and one of the most important figures in the text. At the same time, she recounts at great length the checkered career of Wendell Ryder, who is extravagantly indulged by his mother, Sophia.

Ryder is particularly significant for its narrative excesses, but it is also an important example of early feminist fiction. Perhaps most significant for the subsequent development of Barnes's career is the appearance in this novel of Dr. Matthew O'Connor, a figure that she would use to advantage in *Nightwood*. In contrast to the aggressively patriarchal and yet ineffectual Wendell, Dr. O'Connor embraces both the insight of a patriarch and the compassion traditionally associated with the feminine psyche, making his sexual ambivalence an important part of the novel's thematic concerns. The example of Dr. O'Connor does little to mitigate Wendell's excesses, however, and the novel concludes with Wendell alone and bewildered by the effects of his dominance. Barnes also suggests throughout the novel that the history of the Ryder family is indicative of a larger malaise, of which Wendell Ryder is only the latest manifestation. The first chapter, "Jesus Mundane," confirms this view by parodying the rhetoric of the Old Testament to insist upon humankind's fundamental ignorance and mediocrity. This first chapter is also indicative of the stylistic virtuosity and wit of the novel, which foregrounds language and style, frequently at the expense of plot development. In its bawdy imitations of Elizabethan lyrics and its allusive prose, the novel presents a series of different perspectives on the Ryder family, and these verbal portraits are accompanied by Barnes's own illustrations.

Ryder is primarily significant as an example of the influence of Joycean experimentation upon modernist American literature; although it has not received extensive critical attention, its concern with male dominance also makes it an important anticipation of the direction of much later feminist writing.

NIGHTWOOD

First published: 1936
Type of work: Novel

Robin Vote, a young, mysterious woman, is pursued by a series of lovers, particularly by an emotionally tortured American, Nora Flood.

Nightwood is Barnes's most important work and the one most frequently read and discussed. Although it has a reputation as a difficult novel, it has been widely and enthusiastically admired by important literary figures, most notably perhaps the modernist poet T. S. Eliot, who was instrumental in securing its publication, and the Welsh poet, Dylan Thomas. The primary focus in *Nightwood* is not plot but rather psychology, in that the narrative focuses upon the emotional reactions of its characters and their responses to Robin Vote. The novel's prose is dense and richly metaphorical, and two of its eight chapters consist solely of long conversations on the nature of lesbian love and sexuality.

The novel begins by considering the familial background of Felix Volkbein, the son of a Jewish Viennese merchant, who feels estranged and excluded from the snobbish world of European culture and society. Volkbein meets Robin Vote in the company of Dr. O'Connor, who is called to assist Robin after she has collapsed in a Paris hotel. Barnes's description of Robin consistently emphasizes her lack of volition; in this instance, for example, she is surrounded in her hotel room by exotic plants, and her skin is said to have a texture that is normally associated with plants. Mistakenly reading Robin's lack of volition as a sign of malleability, Volkbein later marries Robin in order to fulfill his aspiration of founding a familial dynasty. After the birth of their child, however, Robin withdraws into a solitary life of travel and immerses herself in Catholicism. Abandoning her child and husband, she reappears some months later in Paris with her lesbian lover, Nora Flood. Two features of these events are particularly significant for an overall understanding of the novel. The first is the notion of decline, as marked by Felix Volkbein's failed familial ambitions; the second is the use of religious imagery in connection with the unconscious, a connection that Barnes exploits throughout the novel.

The next section of *Nightwood* describes the tempestuous relationship of Robin and Nora Flood and the disintegration of that relationship as Robin is wooed away from Nora by the flighty and neurotic figure Jenny Petherbridge. Nora is distraught at this turn of events, and, in order to discuss her situation, she pays a visit to Dr. O'Connor. At this point, Matthew O'Connor emerges as a figure of great rhetorical prowess. An impoverished transvestite, Dr. O'Connor displays a profound understanding of Nora's dilemma, but his disquisitions on sexuality and love go far beyond Nora's emotional situation and become in themselves brilliant rhetorical exercises full of wit and self-mocking irony. Barnes based the character of O'Connor upon an actual figure from the expatriate milieu in Paris in the 1920's, but his conversation best recalls the rhetorical wit of *Ryder*, where he appears in a much more subdued form. Consistent with the thematic concerns of *Nightwood*, Dr. O'Connor's soliloquies revolve around the notions of decay and the psychodrama of sexuality, and his often grotesquely humorous but dark pronouncements foreshadow many of the subsequent events in the novel.

In the later sections of *Nightwood*, the narrator reveals that Felix Volkbein's child is physically and mentally weak, and the reader catches a final glimpse of Volkbein drunkenly nodding to aristocrats in a Viennese café. Dr. O'Connor is similarly last seen in a drunken collapse after a tirade in a Paris café, and Nora despairingly returns to America. There she encounters Robin Vote for the final time in a decaying chapel on her estate. As Nora looks on helpless, Robin bows before an altar to the Madonna and then sinks to her hands and knees to confront Nora's dog, which retreats, whimpering, at Robin's animal intensity. At the end of the novel, after a hysterical fit of laughing and weeping, Robin lies exhausted on the floor of the chapel.

Nightwood, through its often obscure associative patterns, demonstrates powerfully the dark and destructive side of emotional relationships; it is equally important for its consideration of love within a lesbian context. Barnes also reflects the intellectual climate of her contemporaries in her use of Freudian dream patterns to illustrate the preoccupations of her characters, and, as is her earlier work, the novel is filled with striking lyrical prose.

Summary

Djuna Barnes is perhaps the most important woman writer to emerge from the American expatriation in Paris in the 1920's. Her rhetorical mastery of a variety of prose forms and her concern with the unconscious enabled her to execute novels that are held together by their metaphoric associations rather than by the demands of plot or chronology. In this respect, her work is an important example of the modernist development of the novel form. In addition, her exploration of the roles of women, both through lesbian love and through the oppressive nature of patriarchal culture, make Barnes's work an important anticipation of the issues to emerge from later feminist writing.

Bibliography

Field, Andrew. *Djuna: The Formidable Miss Barnes.* Austin: University of Texas Press, 1985.

Frank, Joseph. *The Widening Gyre.* New Brunswick, N.J.: Rutgers University Press, 1963.

Friedman, Melvin. *Stream of Consciousness: A Study in Literary Method.* New Haven, Conn.: Yale University Press, 1955.

Kannenstine, Louis F. *Duality and Damnation: The Art of Djuna Barnes.* New York: New York University Press, 1977.

Messerli, Douglas. *Djuna Barnes: A Bibliography.* Rhinebeck, N.Y.: David Lewis, 1975.

Scott, James B. *Djuna Barnes.* Boston: Twayne, 1976.

Thomas Carmichael

JOHN BARTH

Born: Cambridge, Maryland
May 27, 1930

Principal Literary Achievement
Widely recognized for the formal ingenuity of his novels, Barth is a major contemporary novelist whose work perhaps best demonstrates the development of postmodern fiction in the United States.

Biography

John Barth was born in Cambridge, Maryland, in the second year of the Great Depression. After graduating from the local public schools, Barth spent the summer of 1947 studying theory and orchestration at New York's Juilliard School of Music. At the time, Barth's aspiration was to become a big band jazz arranger in the tradition of Billy Strayhorn, but he soon felt that in comparison with the sophistication of his peers his own talents were limited, so he abandoned music as a career. Returning to Maryland's Eastern Shore at the end of the summer of 1947, Barth found that he had been awarded a scholarship to The Johns Hopkins University, and he elected to attend Johns Hopkins in the fall of that year to pursue a major in journalism. Although Barth has suggested that his interest in working with past literature, particularly myth and historical narrative, is a by-product of his interest in musical arrangement, he first became seriously interested in writing fiction in the creative writing classes he took at Johns Hopkins. There he was also introduced to the world of literature and criticism, and by the time he had completed his A.B. degree, which was awarded to Barth in 1951, he had effectively decided to devote himself to the writing of fiction.

His first extended work of fiction, a novel entitled "The Shirt of Nessus" (unpublished), was Barth's master's project, for which he received an M.A. from Johns Hopkins in 1952. He then enrolled in the Ph.D. program in literary aesthetics at Johns Hopkins, but financial constraints forced him to abandon his studies and seek steady employment. In 1950, Barth had married Harriet Ann Strickland, and by 1953 they had two children, a daughter, Christine, born in 1951, and a son, John, born in 1952. A third child, David, was born in 1954. Barth joined the English faculty at Pennsylvania State University as an instructor in the fall of 1953, and he remained there until 1965. While teaching, Barth continued to hone his craft, and he began to produce quickly; his first two novels were both written in 1955. *The*

Floating Opera (1956), written during the first three months of that year, was nominated for the National Book Award, and his second novel, *The End of the Road* (1958) was made into a (very unsuccessful) film in the late 1960's. Although the sales of these novels were not large, Barth was encouraged by their critical success, and he followed them in 1960 with his third novel, *The Sot-Weed Factor*. This extravagant mock-historical fiction was praised effusively by Leslie Fiedler and others, and it marked Barth's arrival as a major contemporary writer, which was subsequently acknowledged by the "citation in fiction" Barth received from Brandeis University in 1965.

At the same time, Barth was becoming sought after professionally; after working his way up the ladder of academic promotion at Pennsylvania State, he accepted an appointment in 1965 to the English department at the rapidly expanding State University of New York, Buffalo, where he became Edward H. Butler Professor of English in 1971. In 1966, Barth published his perhaps best-known and most successful novel commercially, *Giles Goat-Boy: Or, The Revised New Syllabus* (1966). For a time, Barth was celebrated in popular weekly magazines such as *Time*, and his novel was highly placed on the national best-seller lists; however, Barth's fiction is often demanding and difficult, and *Giles Goat-Boy* was no exception. The novel has often been referred to as a largely unread best-seller, but *Giles Goat-Boy* nevertheless established Barth in the forefront of audacious American writing and placed him in the company of contemporary figures such as Thomas Pynchon. His next volume of fiction, *Lost in the Funhouse* (1968), is a collection of often experimental short narratives, and these marked a further step for Barth into the field of metafiction, or the literature of extreme narrative self-consciousness.

Barth was divorced from Harriet Ann Strickland in 1970, and in 1971 he married Shelly Rosenberg. He published *Chimera* (1972) in the following year, for which he was chosen as cowinner of the National Book Award, and in 1973 Barth returned to Baltimore and Johns Hopkins, this time as a faculty member in The Johns Hopkins University Writing Seminars. His next novel, *Letters: A Novel* (1979), was followed by *Sabbatical: A Romance* (1982), then *The Tidewater Tales: A Novel* (1987). Barth has also been an important spokesman for contemporary experimental fiction, and his most significant essays have been published together in *The Friday Book* (1984).

Analysis

In his 1987 introduction to the Anchor Literary Library editions of his early novels, Barth remarks that his first novel, *The Floating Opera*, reflects the influence of French existentialist thought in post-World War II American culture. Most conspicuous in Barth's assimilation of existentialist influence is the notion of the world's absurdity, or what Barth describes elsewhere as the ultimately arbitrary nature of existence and the accompanying human recognition that this absurd existence is the ground of our experience. This view is repeated throughout Barth's fiction; in his first novel, *The Floating Opera*, it finds its expression in Todd Andrews' despairing reflection over his inability to exclude any fact from the vast research he has amassed in preparation for the writing of his own narrative. For Andrews, every fact has significance, but none has any ultimate importance because the world itself is finally without any absolute principle of order. Similarly, Ebenezer Cooke, the protagonist of Barth's third novel, is plunged into spiritual paralysis by his awareness that every choice is equally valid but that no choice is necessary or compelling. These same dilemmas haunt George, the central figure in *Giles Goat-Boy*, and Ambrose, the protagonist of one series of stories in *Lost in the Funhouse*. Thematically, these ideas are most significant in Barth's fiction for their impact upon his consideration of questions of value and the motive for action in the world.

In Barth's first novel, his protagonist is able to avoid suicide in part by his own incompetence; however, his subsequent principled rejection of suicide is more significant. Reasoning that nothing has intrinsic value, Todd Andrews concludes that all decisions based upon value judgments about the world are ultimately matters of opinion, including the decision to take his own life. Each of Barth's subsequent protagonists confronts this dilemma in some form, and, while his novels are often ribald and extravagantly humorous, Barth finally endorses what he describes as a "Tragic View" in his work. This view can be said to be tragic in the sense that it posits death and fragmentation as the horizon against which existence is plotted; it also entails an acknowledgment of the absence of any final answers to the questions that Barth poses, together with a refusal to give in to resignation in the face of uncertainty.

Barth's fiction is consistently organized so that these ideas are also suggested by the formal strategies of narration, structure, and representation in each novel. For example, Barth frequently employs a self-conscious narrator in his later work who calls attention to the facts that the text is a work of fiction, not a simple transcription of the real world, and that fictional narration is itself governed by conventions which have nothing to do with reality. In this way, the self-conscious in Barth's fiction suggests that language reveals the way that reality or representations of it are inventions and have little to do with what is actually the case. Self-conscious narration is thus always for Barth a representational strategy, designed to signal all forms of order as impositions upon a fundamentally arbitrary world.

Barth's landmark 1967 essay, "The Literature of Exhaustion," presents his most cogent description of the relationship of fictional technique to these thematic concerns, and the same view is restated in his later essay, "The Literature of Replenishment" (1980). In both essays, Barth insists that the novel must affirm the artificial elements in art, but he also asserts that fiction does represent the world in approximate ways. For many, the questioning of the authority for values and the interrogation of language in Barth's fiction has made his work exemplary of the postmodern aesthetic, and Barth's use of parody and elaborate structural devices has reinforced this view. Barth himself is acutely aware of the relationship between literary history and the history of civilization and ideas. He has suggested, for example, that the Chartres cathedral or Beethoven's Sixth Symphony would be embarrassing if they were created today. For Barth, literary techniques live in history and are subject to historical change, but change, for Barth, simply reflects the ways in which culture is a direct consequence of the ideas that motivate it.

In addition to exploring the relationship between fiction and reality and the question of value in individual action, Barth's work has exhibited recurring patterns and motifs. The role of the love triangle, for example, is central to Barth's first three novels, as well as the notion of twinship as the metaphorical representation of opposites that yearn to be united. Barth's work from *The Sot-Weed Factor* on also demonstrates a singular preoccupation with the pattern of ritual heroic adventure; again, this pattern is employed as a metaphor for the path of individual life experience, often ironically so. This ironic use of ritual or legendary material is also conspicuous in Barth's retelling of classical myths in *Lost in the Funhouse* and *Chimera*. In these stories, the principal concern is very much one of self-doubt and the stability of individual identity. This is consistent with Barth's insistence upon the absurd nature of the world outside the self, but it is also part of Barth's consideration of the nature of love and the ground for human relationships.

What finally impresses one most in Barth's fiction are his technical virtuosity and his willingness to pursue the implications of his dramatized ideas relentlessly.

THE FLOATING OPERA

First published: 1956
Type of work: Novel

An Eastern Shore lawyer confronts the absurdity of existence and is driven to attempt suicide.

Barth's first published novel, *The Floating Opera*, anticipates much of his subsequent development in its playful devices and tone and in its thematic preoccupation with absurdity. The first-person narrator and protagonist, Todd Andrews, recounts the experiences of his life leading up to his decision not to commit suicide in 1937; although Todd is currently fifty-four and the present time of the narration is 1954, the novel is principally concerned with the events leading up to his fateful decision on June 21 or 22, 1937. Todd has been living with the possibility that he may die at any moment as a consequence of his chronic heart condition, a subacute bacteriological endocarditis with a tendency to myocardial infarction, first diagnosed when he was released from the army at the end of World War I. This fact—the unpredictable nature of his own continued existence—prompts Todd's recognition of his inability to order and control his own experience, but this alone does not lead to suicide.

Todd also becomes convinced that there is no rational basis for human values and actions as a consequence of his conviction that sexuality is simply hilarious and his experience of killing a German soldier who had befriended him during the battle for the Argonne Forest. In Todd's view, humankind is literally a species of animal; at the same time, he insists that there is no justification for any action. Any line of questioning, he argues, maintained long enough eventually ends in an unanswerable question which reveals that there is no ultimate reason for the opinions and values people hold.

Consistent with this view, Todd's narration signals repeatedly that his ordered story is simply a fabrication, put together from any number of possible interpretations and orderings of the facts of his life. In the chapter entitled "Calliope Music," for example, he begins with two columns of print placed side by side on the page. The left column comments upon the absurd law case that Todd is currently considering, while the right column comments upon the rational basis for suicide. Though Todd excuses this device as a symptom of authorial ineptitude, this typographical arrangement demonstrates that no single account is definitive or conclusive in arranging all the facts relevant to his experiences. At the same time, it emphasizes Todd's awareness of his role as the narrator of his own story. In addition, Todd repeatedly refers to the indeterminate nature of his experiences; frequently, he is unable to remember an exact date or precise time.

Despite these assertions of indeterminacy, Todd persists throughout *The Floating Opera* in attempting to impose a rational order on his own existence and to find a rational basis for a single human action. This latter endeavor is represented in his *"Inquiry"* into the causes of his father's own suicide, the result of his financial ruin in the stock market crash of 1929. In the same spirit, he adheres to a principle of limited inconsistency in his daily habits. He breaks daily habits as a matter of principle and maintains others for their sheer absurdity. In a similar vein, he adopts a series of masks to govern his life, but when his final mask, that of cynicism, collapses, his awareness of the absence of any ultimate rational justification for moral actions and values presses in on him, and he decides to commit suicide.

Ironically, it is only through a rigorous application of his philosophical insight that Todd is able subsequently to reject suicide. His original plan is to blow up a visiting showboat, Captain Adam's *Original and Unparalleled Floating Opera*, with its entire cast and audience aboard. As his name aptly suggests, Captain Jacob Adam fulfills a patriarchal role in presiding over a metaphorical image of life and the world. It is certainly significant that Hamlet's "To be, or not to be" soliloquy and Jacques' enumeration of the seven ages of man ("All the world's a stage," from *As You Like It*) are part of the performance. The importance of these speeches is belittled by the audience's hostile reaction to the second-rate actor who performs them; however, Todd appropriates the latter speech as a felicitous metaphor to substantiate his assertion that Hamlet's question is meaningless. In strict point of fact, Todd does not reject suicide; his attempt is thwarted for reasons he never discovers, but he does mark this failed attempt as a provisional turning point. After this event, Todd suggests that in the absence of absolutes of any kind, relative values might be lived by; it is with this tentative assertion that the novel closes.

The formal ingenuity in *The Floating Opera* and its mixture of bawdiness, low comedy, and intellectual seriousness identify it as a typical Barth novel. Although less extravagant than his subsequent large fictions and less involved technically than *Lost in the Funhouse*, *The Floating Opera* is essential to any understanding of Barth's development, and it is perhaps the most concise presentation of the ideas that form the dramatic and formal motivation for much of his later work.

THE SOT-WEED FACTOR

First published: 1960
Type of work: Novel

In the early eighteenth century, a young immigrant tobacco planter loses and then regains his Maryland estate.

Barth's third novel, perhaps his most widely acclaimed critical success, is written as a flamboyant imitation of an eighteenth century novel. His narrator adopts the tone and the locutions of eighteenth century narrators, and his descriptions of early colonial life in Maryland and of life in the London of the period are designed to recall the descriptions known of those places from contemporary literature of the period. The importance of this narrative strategy is twofold and distinctly contemporary: on the one hand, the parodic imitation of an earlier novelistic style draws the reader's attention to the ways in which this narrative is purely a product of fictional conventions; on the other hand, the density of authentic historical detail in the text also consistently suggests to the reader that Barth is re-creating a plausible, although wildly humorous, colonial milieu. By exploiting the tension between these competing claims, Barth is able to suggest the absence of any but a fictional order and at the same time present a compelling necessity for choice and action, as suggested by the realistic aspects of the novel.

One of the most conspicuous features of *The Sot-Weed Factor* is its immensely complicated plot, itself a feature of the assertion of artifice in Barth's fiction; like Barth's earlier fiction, *The Sot-Weed Factor* demonstrates his preoccupation with value and action. Ebenezer Cooke, the novel's protagonist and the son of a Maryland "sot-weed factor," or tobacco planter, is reared as an orphan in England together with his twin sister, Anna. After an education at home supervised by the family's tutor, Henry Burlingame, himself educated at the University of Cambridge but without familial connections, Ebenezer goes off to Cambridge, where his wild imagination and inability to take the world seriously make him an indifferent student at best. Ebenezer's disposition here recalls the problems of Todd Andrews in Barth's first novel and will be the source of many of his future difficulties. After returning from Cambridge, Ebenezer embarks on a career as a poet in London. Hopelessly naïve, he takes his own innocence and literal virginity as a sign of his calling, and he obtains a commission as the poet laureate of Maryland before he is sent to that colony to oversee his father's estate. Again, Cooke's career as a poet is significant: There was a historical Ebenezer Cooke, who wrote well-known satires on life in colonial Maryland, including one that shares the title of Barth's own novel. Parts of these poems are included in this narrative.

Cooke and his scheming servant are intercepted by pirates while crossing the Atlantic, and, after being taken prisoner, they are forced to walk the plank. They manage to swim to shore and make their way to Malden, the site of Cooke's father's estate. Ebenezer then manages to lose his estate in a bizarre afternoon of impromptu colonial justice, and he only regains it with great difficulty, with the considerable help of Burlingame, his former tutor, who is embroiled in dark political intrigues in the American colonies involving Lord Baltimore, William Penn, the French, and the Indians. These political schemes are an important part of Barth's thematic concern with the absence of any sure knowledge in the world and with the often obscure effects of any single human action. These political machinations are complemented in the novel by the presence of Barth's rewriting of the journal of Captain John Smith, the early Virginia explorer and adventurer, which calls into question the Pocahontas legend—and by implication much early American history.

Ebenezer's sister Anna follows him to America, largely to pursue her passion for Burlingame, and these three are reunited at Malden after the estate has been wrestled away from those who had turned it into a brothel and an opium den. In large part, Ebenezer's successful reclaiming of his plantation is dependent upon the good graces and legal authority of Joan Toast, a former London prostitute (and Ebenezer's first near-mistress). Although syphilitic and dying, she is married to Ebenezer, and it is his consummation of this marriage that allows him to regain legal title to his inheritance. At the end of the narrative, Burlingame disappears into the machinations of political life, and Joan Toast dies along with her infant son, but Ebenezer's sister's son, Andrew, lives and is reared by Ebenezer and his sister at Malden. With the publication of his satire upon Maryland, Ebenezer's laureateship is withdrawn, but it is offered again later in Ebenezer's life by one of Lord Baltimore's heirs. Ebenezer declines this offer, however, and dies with little recognition. Barth's narrator uses this ending to assert the distance between fiction and fact by drawing attention to the regaining of Ebenezer's estate, which should be the natural conclusion to the story, and the ambiguous and inconclusive events which he describes at the end of the narrative. In this way, the structure of Barth's narrative and the narrator's commentary upon that structure are employed to reinforce the thematic preoccupations so consistently found in his fiction.

The Sot-Weed Factor marks an important advance in Barth's fiction. The use of parody, the elaborate structural devices in the novel, and the self-conscious narrator all point to strategies that Barth subsequently found increasingly congenial to his aesthetic program.

GILES GOAT-BOY

First published: 1966
Type of work: Novel

A young boy, reared among goats, attempts to transform the allegorical world/ university in which he lives.

One of the attractions that *Giles Goat-Boy* held for its initial readers and that certainly contributed to its early commercial success was its sustained allegory. Barth employs the metaphor of the university as the ground of his setting so that the Cold War world is divided into Eastern and Western campuses, and the various quads are identified with the major powers of post-World War II politics. For example, the United States corresponds to New Tammany, Germany to Siegfrieder College, Asia to the monastic world of T'ang, and the Soviet Union to Nikolay College. In Barth's novel, New Tammany is lead by Lucius Rexford, also known as "Lucky," a thinly disguised portrait of President John F. Kennedy. In addition, various political ideologies are presented in allegorical fashion: For example, Communism is described as Student-Unionism. Events of twentieth century history are also represented in Barth's allegory so that, for example, World War II becomes Campus Riot II. The Eastern and Western campuses of Barth's world-as-university are each controlled by a separate computer, which is known by the acronym of WESCAC in the west, and Barth's own novel is presented as a transcription of tapes from WESCAC's files. Like the manipulation of eighteenth century novelistic conventions in *The Sot-Weed Factor*, the use of allegory in *Giles Goat-Boy* is designed to assert the fictional nature of Barth's narrative and to suggest at the same time a correspondence between this elaborate fiction and the historical world of the early 1960's.

Into this world Barth injects George, a young man who is initially reared by Max Spielman in the New Tammany goat barns. Max was essential to the New Tammany effort in Campus Riot II, but he has since been blacklisted and expelled from any place of power. George himself spends his early life as a goat, and his narrative gains much of its humor from its caprine perspective. After realizing his true calling, however, George sets off to pursue a human career in the world of New Tammany. He becomes convinced that his mission in life is to become Grand Tutor of the Western Campus and to achieve his own education, or commencement, with the ultimate aim of discovering his true identity and of setting New Tammany straight. In his quest, George follows loosely the pattern of heroic adventure outlined by Joseph Campbell, the comparative mythographer, in his study *The Hero with a Thousand Faces* (1949); according to Campbell's pattern, or monomyth, the typical hero traces a course that leads him from initiation to illumination to disillusionment, and while Barth's George conforms to this course, he often does so ironically. This elaborate structural pattern is mocked in part to demonstrate the very limits of all imposed order. Despite the efforts of the False Tutor, Harold Bray, to thwart his education, and although often misled by his own misunderstandings, George does achieve a moment of mystical transcendence in the belly of WESCAC, the computer. Yet, like all mystical moments, this one is short-lived, and although George enjoys some brief notoriety, little changes in New Tammany. By the end of the novel's epilogue (or "Posttape"), George is saddened by his experiences, despairs of the future, and has withdrawn from active life in New Tammany.

Among the more interesting narrative devices in Barth's novel is the self-conscious commentary provided by the text's various framing devices. *Giles Goat-Boy* begins not with the story of George, but with letters from various readers in a publishing house commenting upon the quality of this novel and upon the character of its author. This "Publisher's Disclaimer" is followed by a "Cover-Letter to the Editors and Publisher" written by a "J.B.," who then describes how he received his manuscript, entitled *The Revised New Syllabus*, from one Stoker Giles. This series of frames suggests the confusion surrounding the question of authorship of the transcriptions, and it thereby echoes the preoccupation with truth and the impossibility of arriving at absolute certainty that haunts George's quest. These frames also provide a self-conscious commentary on the narrative that they introduce; much the same effect is achieved when, at the height of George's quest, he asks a librarian for directions to Tower Clock. The librarian complies, but her response is read from a book, which appears to be *Giles Goat-Boy*—thus Barth's novel itself appears as an object in his narrative. This narrative moment dramatizes the thematic preoccupation with patterns and the struggle for the knowledge of order in the world.

While *Giles Goat-Boy* has not maintained the large reputation it enjoyed when it was published, it was an important book for Barth's career because it first signaled his growing interest in the ironic possibilities of myth and it demonstrated a further step in his manipulation of structure and narrative techniques as formal correlatives for his thematic concerns.

LOST IN THE FUNHOUSE

First published: 1968
Type of work: Short stories

Through a series of stories that range from Homeric Greece to the contemporary United States, successive artist figures question their lives and their vocation.

The most experimental of Barth's works, *Lost in the Funhouse* employs an extreme narrative self-consciousness and the manipulation of narrative voices to dramatize Barth's continuing concern about values, action, and the absence of sustaining order in the world. At one point, Barth considered including a tape of his readings of these short narratives along with the book itself; this idea was abandoned, but it does suggest the extent to which Barth was exploring the limits of written narrative in the late 1960's. *Lost in the Funhouse* is a series of short narratives designed to be read together, like a novel, in the order that they are arranged. This notion is graphically represented by the first narrative, a Möbius strip entitled "Frame-Tale," which, when cut and pasted according to the instructions, is emblematic of the cycle. As the protagonists grow older in this series, the actual settings recede into the past, from twentieth century Maryland to classical Greece to the Homeric Greece of the Trojan War. Yet the quest to understand the self and achieve a basis for value and action remains a central concern.

An early series in *Lost in the Funhouse* describes the childhood experiences of Ambrose Mensch in Maryland immediately prior to and during World War II. Ambrose is a sensitive child whose keen awareness and nagging doubts recall the disposition of Ebenezer Cooke in *The Sot-Weed Factor*, and three stories describe the ironic circumstances of his naming, his call to become an artist, and his great moment of existential doubt as he is lost in the funhouse of the collection's title during a family vacation. As Ambrose's awareness and doubts grow, Barth's narrative techniques also become increasingly self-conscious, mirroring on the formal level the concerns he presents thematically. This pattern is repeated in the other narratives in the collection, and perhaps reaches its climax in the convoluted frame structures of his "Menelaiad," a story about the self-doubts that plague the Greek hero Menelaus and his love for Helen of Troy.

Some of the narratives in this collection are quite gimmicky, while others are either extremely short or wildly complicated, but there is an overall unity in *Lost in the Funhouse* that revolves around the questions of individual identity, the possibility of value, and the limits of human knowledge. It is also significant in that it suggests the audacious climate of experimentation that characterized advanced American literature of the late 1960's.

Summary

As perhaps the most sophisticated practitioner of postmodern fiction in America, John Barth is a central figure in the literary history of the contemporary period. Each of Barth's books is consistent with the others in its pursuit of ideas and problems that Barth first considered, in their nascent form, very early in his career. Yet each Barth novel or short story is also distinctive in demonstrating a distinctive aspect of his technical prowess as a writer. While experimentation in and for itself has never been Barth's aim, it is nevertheless true that Barth's success as a novelist in large part has depended upon his willingness to take risks and to experiment—and to do so with a keen sense of the literary tradition in which he writes.

Bibliography

Harris, Charles B. *Passionate Virtuosity: The Fiction of John Barth*. Urbana: University of Illinois Press, 1983.

Joseph, Gerhard. *John Barth*. University of Minnesota Pamphlets on American Writers, no. 91. Minneapolis: University of Minnesota Press, 1970.

Morrell, David. *John Barth: An Introduction*. University Park: Pennsylvania State University Press.

Tharpe, Jack. *John Barth: The Comic Sublimity of Paradox*. Carbondale: Southern Illinois University Press, 1974.

Waldmeir, Joseph J., ed. *Critical Essays on John Barth*. Boston: G. K. Hall, 1980.

Weixlmann, Joseph. *John Barth: A Descriptive Primary and Annotated Secondary Bibliography*. New York: Garland, 1976.

Ziegler, Heide. *John Barth*. London: Methuen, 1987.

Thomas Carmichael

DONALD BARTHELME

Born: Philadelphia, Pennsylvania
April 7, 1931
Died: Houston, Texas
July 23, 1989

Principal Literary Achievement

One of the most influential of the American avant-garde fiction writers of the post-World War II era, Barthelme produced four novels and a children's book but became most widely known for his highly distinctive short stories.

Biography

Donald Barthelme was born in Philadelphia, where his parents were students at the University of Pennsylvania. His father was an architect; his mother had been a student of English. A few years later, the family moved to Houston, where his father became a professor of architecture at the University of Houston.

Texas may seem an unlikely place for one of the most-discussed writers of non-linear, "experimental" fiction to have developed, but Barthelme credits his father's interest in what for the time were advanced architectural styles with fostering his interest in the avant-garde. The house they lived in was designed by his father, and it was remarkable enough for Houston that, Barthelme has said, people used to stop their cars and stare at it. It was this interest of his father that Barthelme credited with being the most influential element of his early years on his later development. In high school, Barthelme wrote both for the newspaper and for the literary magazine. In 1949 he entered the University of Houston, majoring in journalism. During his sophomore year (1950-1951) he was the editor of the college newspaper, the *Cougar*. During this year he also worked as a reporter for the *Houston Post*.

In 1953, he was drafted into the U.S. Army, arriving in Korea the day the truce was signed—at which point he became the editor of an army newspaper. Upon his return to the United States, he once again became a reporter for the *Houston Post* and returned to the University of Houston, where he worked as a speechwriter for the university president and attended classes in philosophy. Although he attended classes as late as 1957, he ultimately left without taking a degree. Barthelme has said that he read extensively during this period in a number of fields which he later integrated into his fiction: literature and philosophy, as well as the social sciences. In 1956, he founded a literary magazine called *Forum*, where he developed an interest

in the layout and design of the magazine as well as its literary content. This interest became evident in later years, when he began to incorporate graphics, usually nineteenth century lithographs, into his short stories. At the age of thirty, he became the director of Houston's Contemporary Arts Museum.

In 1962, he moved to New York to be the managing editor of the arts and literature magazine *Location*. His first published story, "The Darling Duckling at School" (later revised and printed as "Me and Miss Mandible"), appeared in 1961. His first story for *The New Yorker*, entitled "L'Lapse," appeared in 1963. Since then, most of his works have appeared first in this magazine, to the point where Barthelme's name became almost a synonym for an ironic, fragmentary style that characterized its pages in the late 1960's and early 1970's. Erudite, brief, fragmentary, disjointed: His stories seemed to many to epitomize a certain New York (or *New Yorker*) attitude toward life in general. Barthelme also wrote film criticism for the same magazine.

Barthelme's first collection of short stories, entitled *Come Back, Dr. Caligari*, appeared in 1964. His first novel, *Snow White*, a modern take-off on the fairy tale, appeared in 1967. Further short stories were collected in *Unspeakable Practices, Unnatural Acts* (1968), *City Life* (1970), *Sadness* (1972), *Amateurs* (1976), *Great Days* (1979), and *Overnight to Many Different Cities* (1983). Many critics see the height of his short story production in the volume *City Life*, noting a tendency of his later stories either to repeat the techniques of the earlier ones or to become more like traditional short stories. Barthelme published two other novels before his death, *The Dead Father* (1975), which some commentators regard as his masterpiece, and *Paradise* (1986). A fourth novel, *The King*, appeared posthumously (1990). The first of two anthologies of previously published stories, entitled *Sixty Stories*, appeared in 1981; a companion volume, *Forty Stories*, appeared in 1987.

Barthelme married twice. His only child was a daughter, Anne Katharine, born in 1965 to his first wife, Birgit. It was for Anne that he wrote his children's book, *The Slightly Irregular Fire Engine: Or, The Hithering Thithering Djinn*, which won a National Book Award in 1972. At his death from cancer on July 23, 1989, he was survived by his second wife, Marion.

Barthelme was a member of the American Academy and Institute of Arts and Letters, the Authors League of America, the Authors Guild, and PEN (International Association of Poets, Playwrights, Editors, Essayists, and Novelists). In addition to the National Book Award for his children's book, he was the recipient of a Guggenheim Fellowship in 1966 and the PEN/Faulkner Award for Fiction for *Sixty Stories*. Barthelme taught for brief periods at Boston University, the State University of New York at Buffalo, and the College of the City of New York, at the last of which he was Distinguished Visiting Professor of English from 1974 to 1975.

Analysis

For the reader new to Barthelme, the most productive way to approach his works is in terms of what they are not: what they avoid doing, what they refuse to do, and what they suggest is not worth doing. Nineteenth century literature, and indeed most popular ("best-seller") literature of the twentieth century, is structured according to the two elements of plot and character. These two Barthelme studiously avoids, offering instead a collage of frequently amusing fragments whose coherence is usually only cumulative, rather than progressive.

The typical Barthelme story is brief and is based on an intellectual idea rather than an emotional one. Its plot is inevitably interrupted by seemingly unrelated subplots (or fragments of them) and contains elements whose presence is not immediately explicable—and indeed, whose only justification is precisely that they are without explanation. Its characters are usually little more than names attached to strings of talk, and the talk usually changes character many times during the course of the piece so that these hollow personages express themselves in a bewildering array of contents and tones of voice. Many times they are quoting, implicitly or explicitly, well-known philosophers who were much discussed in the 1960's and 1970's or mouthing the empty phrases of the advertising media. (Several commentators have pointed to Barthelme's training in journalism and speechwriting to explain his fascination with the verbal detritus of modern society.)

Barthelme's works are not for those whose formal education is deficient, nor are they for those who have lived in ignorance of the philosophical currents of Western thought in the second half of the twentieth century. For example, the title of "Kierkegaard Unfair to Schlegel" plays on the names of two nineteenth century European thinkers; "A Shower of Gold" refers to the way in which, according to the classical poet Ovid, Zeus appeared to a woman named Danae. "The Abduction from the Seraglio" quotes the title of an opera by Wolfgang Amadeus Mozart, and "The Death of Edward Lear" introduces as a character the author of nonsense verse. Barthelme's works, moreover, may not be for those from areas of the country untouched by New York's peculiar brand of edgy energy. Commentators have pointed out that Barthelme's works presuppose and celebrate a position of ironic distance from the demands of a competitive society. They will probably speak most directly to readers who have noted the debased status of words in Western industrial nations and noticed that the most widely disseminated utterances of our time seem to be the most trivial.

Barthelme is frequently classified as a "postmodernist" author, one of a generation of writers who came to international prominence in the late 1960's and the 1970's. Among other things, this label means that his most immediate predecessors are the modernist authors of the early years of the century such as T. S. Eliot, James Joyce, and Franz Kafka. Yet critics have split regarding whether Barthelme is doing fundamentally the same things as the earlier modernist authors or whether his works represent a significant development of their method. A number of the modernist authors, Gertrude Stein and Virginia Woolf among them, also rejected the nineteenth century's linear plot, with its development of characters and a definable beginning, middle, and end. Stein, for example, joined fragments into seemingly random strings or structured them by the sounds of the words themselves or by the associations they created in her own mind. Woolf emphasized the individual fragmentary moment of perception and the associations of the minds of her characters instead of the development through societally determined factors. T. S. Eliot wrote a poetry of fragments (especially in *The Waste Land*, 1922) structured, according to some commentators, by contrast with a mythical world that had been lost. Joyce's *Ulysses* (1922) is certainly structured on this principle.

In addition, it is usually asserted with respect to Barthelme that his works evoke the fragmentary nature of modern urban life or the alienation of consciousness that such nineteenth century thinkers as Karl Marx and Friedrich Engels thought inevitable in industrial societies. This, too, was suggested by the modernists as a reason for the nature of their own works, most notably by T. S. Eliot. Yet, at the same time, Barthelme diverges from the modernists in that he seems to lack their belief in the power of art to change the world: His stance is ironic, self-deprecating, and anarchistic. The only reaction to the "disassociation of sensibility" of which Eliot spoke that is now possible, Barthelme seems to say, is the cackle of laughter. If there is a "message" in Barthelme's fiction, it would surely have to be that the problems of the late twentieth century lie (in William Wordsworth's phrase) too deep for tears and are, at any rate, beyond the capacities of the artist to affect them.

A SHOWER OF GOLD

First published: 1963
Type of work: Short story

A young artist appears on a television quiz show and suffers a series of strange intrusions into his life.

"A Shower of Gold," one of the stories from Barthelme's first collection of short stories, is a meditation on themes developed most fully by the existential philosopher Jean-Paul Sartre, whose influence on American thought was especially strong in the 1950's and 1960's. The story has more of a plot than do many of Barthelme's works, and it has a somewhat recognizeable situation; its departures from reality are in the twists of situation and in the episodic interruptions by seemingly unconnected characters and plot developments.

The protagonist, a struggling New York artist named Peterson, is trying to get on a television program called *Who Am I?* The only qualification necessary is that he have strong opinions about some subject—a criticism on Barthelme's part of the premium that contemporary society places on novelty over depth, and on the emphasis on the individual that is implied by making the fact of belief so important. Peterson gets on the show by citing surprising factual data as his opinion, and he is praised by the woman running the program, a Miss Arbor, to the extent that he mouthes the platitudes of Sartrean philosophy.

Miss Arbor eagerly asks Peterson if he is alienated, absurd, and extraneous: all the depressing things that Sartre held to define man's position in the universe. Nothing is so negative or weighty, Barthelme is saying, that it cannot be turned into glossy ad hype. Peterson resists her attempt to pigeonhole him but agrees to go on the show. While waiting to do so, he has run-ins with a number of people: his exploitative manager, who wants him to compromise his artistic integrity by sawing his artworks in half so that they will sell better; his barber, who continues the flow of prepackaged Sartre; the president (whose secret-service men invade Peterson's loft and attack him); the player of a "cat-piano" (made by pulling the tails of cats held fast in a frame); and three girls from California who preach a philosophy of "no problem" but exploit his kindness as do all the others.

Despite these flickering, clearly absurd and dreamlike happenings, Peterson continues to look for meaning in life; however, he sees the error of his ways when finally he does appear on the show and listens to the monologues of the other contestants. He then begins to free-associate, trailing off in the middle of a fairy-tale version of the tale of Zeus and Danae from which the story's title is derived, and which constitutes Barthelme's simultaneous evocation of and brushing away of the myth of wholeness that will forever evade Peterson.

THE INDIAN UPRISING

First published: 1965
Type of work: Short story

Comanche Indians are attacking a city that seems to be Paris; the situation has echoes of an insurrection in a Third World country.

"The Indian Uprising" is Barthelme's vision of a world under siege, of civilization defined as perennially under attack from the forces of disorder that have entered into its very streets and define its mode of existence. The characters alternate an artistic café life with moments in which they torture and interrogate the Indians. The unnamed protagonist, referred to only in the first person, asks a woman identified as Sylvia whether she thinks they are leading a good life. Her answer is in the negative, yet neither the protagonist nor the story suggests a means by which that life could be altered.

While the siege continues, the protagonist, whose descriptions of cafés and night life echo those of Ernest Hemingway writing of Paris, discusses the situation with a number of people, mixing battle reports with references to the nineteenth century French composer Gabriel Fauré, echoes of the so-called hyacinth girl in T. S. Eliot's *The Waste Land*, and quotations from Shakespeare. He stops to analyze the composition of one of the barricades (which results in a lengthy list of detritus); his conclusion is that he knows nothing. His main occupation, however, seems to be making a table.

One of his companions, a Miss R., echoes the Austrian philosopher Ludwig Wittgenstein and discourses on the nature of words. A cavalry regiment plays music from a series of Italian composers in streets named for American military men (in the fashion of streets and squares in Normandy). At the end the Indians may have completely penetrated the city, but it seems as if the protagonist is readying himself to enter prison (he is asked for his belt and shoelaces), and in any case it may not matter.

This mixture of places and times seems intended to focus attention on the only thing that ties them all together: the fact that for the inhabitants of this city, torture and battle have become normal and are integrated into daily existence. Life has become defined as the response to a threat and would have no meaning without it. On a general level, this can be read as a repetition of Sigmund Freud's insistence that civilization is founded on repression; on a more specific level, it may be a portrait of a society that could not exist without its mobilization in war.

AT THE END OF THE MECHANICAL AGE

First published: 1973
Type of work: Short story

An unnamed narrator weds a woman he meets at the grocery store; God comes to their wedding, but the couple divorces before their child is born anyway.

"At the End of the Mechanical Age" is Barthelme's teasing meditation on the necessity and impossibility of conceptualizing human existence in the inhuman terms of "age" or "era." His point of departure is certainly the suggestion, first developed in the 1960's and 1970's, that industrial society was evolving into a state that would be fundamentally different from that which had defined it for the last two centuries—what some commentators have called "post-industrial" society. Barthelme pokes fun at this notion without fundamentally overturning it by having the two main characters, the unnamed "I" and his eventual wife, "Mrs. Davis," speak of "the end of the mechanical age" as if it were the same thing as talking about the end of the day, a precise thing with a particular nature and schedule.

They speculate on what will come after the mechanical age, as if an "age" were like a day or a season, but Barthelme's feelings come through in their agreement that whatever it will be, the age to follow will not be pleasant. In response to the question of whether there is anything to be done about all this, Mrs. Davis replies that the only solution is to "huddle and cling." Clearly, whatever will happen to mankind, it is not something that can be controlled, at least not by the average citizens that make up middle-class society.

The protagonist has met Mrs. Davis at the grocery store in front of the soap display; they hold hands before they speak, and when they do talk it is for Mrs. Davis to express an opinion, as if on a television commercial, regarding one of the brands of soap. Later, they converse by singing songs of male and female savior figures named Ralph and Maude, who will redeem the world after the mechanical age has come to an end. Before it does so there is a flood, which echoes the end of the world that Noah survived; the two pass the time by drinking drinks of "Scotch-and-floodwater" in their boat.

Even marriage as an institution is part of the mechanical age, which is why theirs must end. God, as much a character in all these developments as either of the human beings, comes to their wedding. The protagonist tries to get a clear view of the situation by asking Him about the state of things, but He does little but smile and disappear. Predictably, neither their marriage nor their child has had an effect on the alteration of ages, and at the end each leaves in search of his or her savior.

THE EDUCATIONAL EXPERIENCE

First published: 1973
Type of work: Short story

Students wander about a great fair where the products of Western civilization are being offered in slipshod profusion.

"The Educational Experience" offers Barthelme's view not only of what current education consists—random facts with no coherence—but perhaps also of the worth of the entire sum of mankind's history: nothing. Barthelme's theory of history is contained in a fractured quotation from Wittgenstein that is offered by the "group leader" toward the end of the story: "The world is everything that was formerly the case." People are nothing but the bodies of their predecessors, which do not form into a coherent whole, as the chunks of citation and reference remain undigested. This past ranges from the Fisher King of the Holy Grail quest legends (whom T. S. Eliot claimed to have included in *The Waste Land*) to Sergeant Preston of the Yukon.

Yet time has itself changed all those things from the past of which education consists. Another of the grail motifs that Eliot appropriated, the Chapel Perilous, has been turned into a bomb farm, and Antonio Vivaldi's concerto *The Four Seasons* has become *The Semesters*. Education is clearly no fun. The students are not allowed to smoke, but the narrator reflects that this is undoubtedly "necessary to the preservation of our fundamental ideas." Both the pretensions of the educators and the disinterest of the students are criticized: The students are told that they will be both more beautiful and more employable, but they are only in a hurry to get back on the bus that has brought them to this exposition. Those doing the educating are similarly in the dark: Several of the students are "off in a corner, playing with the animals," and the professors are unsure whether to "tell them to stop, or urge them to continue." As the narrator concedes, "[p]erplexities of this kind are not infrequent, in our business."

Neither the students nor the teachers believe what is being said, but both groups bravely play along as if they do. Both, it is clear, have lost touch with the real history of Western civilization, given that it has to be visited on a whirlwind tour. At the same time, however, this history has become both more trivial and more threatening, so that recovering it may not be as simple a thing as merely a change of method.

SNOW WHITE

First published: 1967
Type of work: Novel

A modern-day retelling of the German fairy tale of Snow White that ends badly.

Snow White is the first of Barthelme's four novels and is one of his most lucid works of any length, largely by virtue of the clarity with which he indicates to the reader at all points what it is that he is doing—or rather, what he is avoiding. The work includes references to what is being avoided so that the reader is aware of the avoidance.

Every reader knows the characters of the standard version of the fairy tale: Snow White, the handsome prince of whom she dreams, the wicked stepmother, and the seven dwarfs who live in the forest and with whom Snow White finds refuge. Indeed, all of these have their equivalents in the characters of Barthelme's version, along with several others not in the fairy tale. In this version of the story, Snow White is twenty-two, lives with seven men with whom she regularly has unsatisfying sex in the shower, and seems to have confused herself with Rapunzel from another fairy story, as she continually sits at her window with her hair hanging out. Her dwarfs have modern names such as Bill (the leader), Clem, Edward, and Dan, and they suffer from a series of ailments, of which the most important seems to be that Bill no longer wishes to be touched. During the day, the seven men work in a Chinese baby-food factory.

The closest thing this retelling of the tale has to a prince is a man named Paul, who does not seem to want to fulfill his role of prince. Avoiding Snow White, he puts in time in a monastery in Nevada, goes to Spain, and joins the Thelemite order of monks. Ultimately he does end up near Snow White, but only as a peeping Tom in a bunker before her house, armed with binoculars. The story's version of the wicked queen is named Jane; she writes poison-pen letters and ultimately makes Snow White a poisoned drink, which Paul drinks instead. He dies. There is another character named Hogo (for which there is not a prototype in the fairy tale), who makes a play for Snow White; she rejects him, but he ends up taking on the role of chief dwarf, which Bill has vacated.

The underlying point of the contrast generated by these modernized versions of the fairy-tale characters is clearly that which was the point of Joyce's version of *Ulysses*—namely, that there are no heroes today. This in fact forms the center of the personality problem both of Paul, who does not want to act like a prince though he is one, and of Snow White, who is unsure about the nature of her role as Snow

White: She continues to long for a prince, but at the same time she feels it necessary to undertake the writing of a lengthy (pornographic) poem that constitutes her attempt to "find herself."

Snow White is a somewhat more accessible work than many of the short stories, partly because its greater length dilutes the quotations and echoes of philosophers, and partly because the use of the well-known story as a prototype gives the reader a sense of a larger structure. This fact also clears some space for Barthelme to fill with his verbal jokes, most of which are directed at pointing out to the reader how language constructs that which people take to be reality. The book also abounds in the same kind of mindless repetition of stock phrases by characters that characterizes "A Shower of Gold" and which was partly explained by "The Educational Experience."

Summary

Donald Barthelme was one of the most innovative and original writers of the second half of the twentieth century, drawing on and developing the themes and techniques of the modernists who preceded him. Avoiding plot and developed characters, his works are collages of the high and low, the sublime and ridiculous, of which modern society is constituted. In his short stories and novels, the fragmentary nature of modern society is both exemplified and exploited for comic effect, becoming both subject matter and technique of his writing.

Bibliography

Bellamy, Joe David, ed. *The New Fiction: Interviews with Innovative American Writers.* Urbana: University of Illinois Press, 1974.

Couturier, Maurice, and Regis Durand. *Donald Barthelme.* London: Methuen, 1982.

Gordon, Lois. *Donald Barthelme.* Boston: Twayne, 1981.

Klinkowitz, Jerome. *Literary Disruptions: The Making of a Post-Contemporary American Fiction.* Urbana: University of Illinois Press, 1980.

_____. *The Self-Apparent World: Fiction as Language/Language as Fiction.* Carbondale: Southern Illinois University Press, 1984.

McCaffery, Larry. *The Metafictional Muse: The Works of Robert Coover, Donald Barthelme, and William H. Gass.* Pittsburgh: University of Pittsburgh Press, 1982.

Stengel, Wayne B. *The Shape of Art in the Short Stories of Donald Barthelme.* Baton Rouge: Louisiana State University Press, 1985.

Bruce E. Fleming

ANN BEATTIE

Born: Washington, D.C.
September 8, 1947

Principal Literary Achievement

Sometimes called a voice of the "Woodstock generation," Beattie writes indirect short stories and novels that depict "numbed" characters struggling to find happiness.

Biography

Ann Beattie was born in Washington, D.C., on September 8, 1947, the only child of Charlotte Crosby Beattie and James A. Beattie. She attended the Lafayette Elementary School and was graduated from high school in Washington, D.C., in 1965. Her father was a grants management specialist for the Department of Health, Education, and Welfare. If Beattie did not find her early schooling very stimulating, she seems to have been preparing in some fashion for writing even during her childhood. In an interview with Patrick H. Samway, Beattie explained:

> I was an only child. . . . It is often true of only children that they become watchers because they belong to small families and are tightly bonded to those units. . . . I am continually squirreling away situations that I don't consciously realize are registering.

It was in college that she began to take literature seriously. She took a course with Frank Turaj, who, she says, "taught me how to read." She received a bachelor of arts degree from the American University in 1969 and matriculated as a graduate student in English at the University of Connecticut. It was there that she started submitting stories for publication; she received her master's degree in 1970. "A Rose for Judy Garland's Casket" was her first story published, and in the same year, 1972, she withdrew from the doctoral program. Beattie later explained that she was "miserable" and that she simply decided to write instead of "reading criticism about writing all day."

In 1973 she married David Gates, a fellow University of Connecticut graduate student and a musician and writer as well. A "major" story, "Victor Blue," was published in *The Atlantic Monthly* that same year, and a first story in *The New Yorker*, "A Platonic Relationship," appeared a year later.

Ann Beattie has been a visiting writer as well as a lecturer at the University of Virginia. At Harvard University she held a Guggenheim Fellowship and was a Briggs-

Copeland lecturer. Doubleday brought out the short story collection *Distortions* and Beattie's first novel, *Chilly Scenes of Winter*, almost simultaneously in 1976. United Artists released *Chilly Scenes of Winter* as a film in 1979, calling it *Head Over Heels*. *Falling in Place*, a second novel, received an award from the American Academy and Institute of Arts and Letters when it appeared in 1980, and Beattie was again invited to be a visiting writer at the University of Virginia. Not surprisingly, her alma mater, the American University, recognized her as one of its distinguished alumni.

A third short story collection, *Secrets and Surprises* (1978), was followed four years later by a collection entitled *The Burning House* (1982). In May of 1982, Beattie and Gates were divorced. *Love Always*, a third novel, was published in 1985, and a fourth short story collection, *Where You'll Find Me and Other Stories*, was published in 1986. With her fourth novel, *Picturing Will* (1989), Beattie extended her literary domain dramatically; the novel was well received, gaining a front-page review in the book review section of *The New York Times*. Beattie lives in Charlottesville, Virginia, with her husband, painter Lincoln Perry.

Analysis

Critic Christina Murphy has called Ann Beattie a neorealist who uses an equivocal voice. Unlike the univocal narrator, the equivocal narrator does not offer the reader a particular perspective or interpretation; the equivocal narrator simply offers accumulated detail. Therefore, readers must approach Beattie's works actively—they must be acutely aware of Beattie's fine distinctions of character and circumstance.

Critics do not challenge Beattie's characters' credibility; an occasional critic, however, challenges her interest in her milieu. If many of Beattie's characters closely resemble a select segment of her generation's college graduates, some certainly do not. "Dwarf House," one of the short stories in *Distortions*, provides one example. Unlike his self-pitying mother, his confused brother, and several other miserable characters outside the Dwarf House, James accepts his physical limitations and his options realistically—though he must stand on a chair to meet people of normal height eye to eye, he has found work, friendship, and love. James can be happy.

Even before she gave readers a small clue to her complex irony and seeming detachment by using as her copyright "Irony and Pity, Inc.," Beattie revealed an extraordinary understanding of human personality and the dynamics of human relationships. Engaging readers by forcing them to verify behavior and events with their own experiences before they can understand her fiction seems to be Beattie's technique. The reader need not be as nonjudgmental as Beattie seems to be.

Most of Beattie's characters are engaged in some kind of struggle for happiness. Often they are self-alienated. A great number of characters in *Distortions* seem to think and function inappropriately; they are doomed to struggle and fail. None of the lovers in "Four Stories About Lovers" seems happy; few are faithful. "The Lifeguard" is the story of the drowning of four children whose boat is set afire by one who has brought along gasoline.

It is only those characters like the dwarfed James and his bride in "Dwarf House" who may love and marry in anything near ecstasy. There is some gift in a capacity for love. Sam, in "Snakes' Shoes" in the same collection, can help the child of estranged parents by using the magic of imagination and love to transform antagonists into friends. Like Sam and James, Noel in "Vermont" empathically consoles the narrator when her husband leaves her. "You're better off," he reassures her, and she is certainly better off when Noel is ready to love her. A young Georgetown student, Sam, in "A Platonic Relationship," can give Ellen, a music teacher, a more fulfilling, if not a permanent or conventional, relationship.

In the collection entitled *Secrets and Surprises*, the struggles continue. For the main character in "Shifting," for example, happiness is synonymous with independent movement and eventual sexual freedom. In *The Burning House*, several key characters learn to recognize their own pain, a certain requisite to alleviation of suffering. In those instances they are far more aware of the reality of their own experience than are all the characters in *Falling in Place*, who probably terrify more than one reader (and critic) by their disengagement.

In more recent writing, such as *Where You'll Find Me*, a short story collection, and *Picturing Will*, a novel, Beattie retains her equivocal narrative stance, but her important characters show courage in finding and losing love; they act as foils, distinguishing responsible nurturing from wanton irresponsibility in their behavior.

DWARF HOUSE

First published: 1975
Type of work: Short story

A dwarf and his new bride seem to have found the happiness that eludes the "normal" members of his family.

"Dwarf House," which first appeared in *The New Yorker* magazine, was included in the first collection of Beattie's short stories, *Distortions*, the following year. Since in this story James and his bride, both dwarfs, alone have found happiness, Beattie seems to pose a question about the essentials for contentment. In contrast to James and his bride-to-be, MacDonald, the "normal" brother, returns from a visit to the "dwarf house" (inhabited by his brother, several other dwarfs, and a giant) to report to his self-pitying mother not only that James refuses to return to the home of his previous misery, but also that James is working, he is in love, and he plans to be married. When MacDonald telephones his own wife from his office with the usual "late-night meeting" excuse, after which he takes his secretary for a drink, he discovers that more things are askew. His secretary manages to smile only with the help of drugs, and she has recently had an abortion.

When the family assembles for James's wedding, the minister releases a bird from its cage to symbolize "the new freedom of marriage and the ascension of the spirit." This is marvelously apt, for the bride's true radiance challenges all the "normal" characters—MacDonald, his wife, MacDonald and James's mother—to a painful awareness, but only if they can perceive it.

VERMONT

First published: 1975
Type of work: Short story

A woman whose husband has just left her ponders whether she loves a male friend enough to move in with him.

In "Vermont," characters in a typical Beattie milieu are revealed in intimate relationships. Noel, whose wife Susan has finally had to tell him that she has been having an affair, comforts the narrator when her own husband David announces his imminent departure. Although Beattie seldom describes her characters physically, Noel, the more generous and understanding lover, appears to be physically awkward and unattractive compared with David, who, early in the story, pities Noel for his "poor miserable pajamas."

Noel tells the narrator that she "will be better off" without David, and he does his best to take David's place as a father and friend. When he eventually suggests that she and her young daughter move in with him, she considers and finally protests that she cannot say that she loves him. He answers, "Nobody has ever loved me and nobody ever will. What have I got to lose?" If the narrator really does not love him, however, she has much to lose. When she later reveals that she has been considering his comment carefully, possibly because she does not find him unlovable (and cannot accept the bleak outlook he has for himself), he comments, "Well, I've told you about every woman I ever slept with. Which one do you suspect might love me?" They are speaking by telephone, and the narrator whispers to herself, "Me!"

David appears again at the story's end to visit his former wife and his daughter and to reveal the extent of his confusion in his current relationship; he is not happy with his new girlfriend.

SHIFTING

First published: 1978
Type of work: Short story

A teenage boy teaches a woman married to a controlling husband how to shift.

"Shifting," in the collection *Secrets and Surprises*, is about the focal character's need for emotional change as well as her means of finding it: being taught to drive a standard transmission Volvo by a teenager who likes and perhaps understands her.

Natalie is in a bind: She has a rigid, controlling husband who does not even laugh at her jokes. Although both she and her husband have agreed to sell the old Volvo left to them by Natalie's uncle, she puts prospective buyers off and secretly learns to drive the car. Sharing her husband's car has been too restrictive.

Michael is a local teenager who delivers the evening newspaper to the old lady next door and is puzzled that Natalie's husband has not taken the trouble to teach his wife to "shift." Telling her, "You can decide what it's worth when you've learned," he charges her four dollars after her fourth and final lesson. She has allowed him, not herself, to assess a value for her lessons. Natalie finds the money she gave him neatly folded on the floor mat when she returns to the car two hours after entering Michael's house for a drink: Shifting need not apply exclusively to driving.

LEARNING TO FALL

First published: 1979
Type of work: Short story

Ruth, a single parent, and a friend of hers contemplating a new relationship are both learning that grace is an aspect of courage.

Characters in two of the short stories in *The Burning House* represent definitive types that appear in Beattie's novels. Ruth in "Learning to Fall," the collection's first story, is a loving, nurturing, single parent and friend. She is "learning to fall"— literally, in a dance class, but figuratively as well—to accept the inevitable. Her husband left her while she was still pregnant, and her lover admires her but does not want any of the responsibility of Ruth, whose son Andrew was damaged in the process of being born.

The narrator of the story, a friend of Ruth, has a sometime lover, Ray, who visits with Andrew and the narrator, showing great gentleness to the two; they regularly take the excursion to New York so that Ruth can entertain her lover in Westport. In a restaurant with Andrew and the narrator, Ray patiently tries to help Andrew locate his gloves. When all three leave the restaurant to return to the street, the narrator sees herself with Ray and Andrew and imagines the possibility of the inevitable relationship. Perhaps she is falling. She decides that at least she can be like her friend Ruth and "aim for grace."

In "The Burning House," the title story of the collection in which "Learning to Fall" appears, there is a character who may be called a second definitive type. Frank behaves in a way that suggests to the narrator, his wife, that her frustrating marriage is deteriorating. Frank has called the important shots: He has even "chosen the house," and the house is burning. In the final scene, with the couple in bed, Frank delivers to his wife what some critics have recognized as the ultimate insult—his conception of the difference between the sexes:

Men think they're Spider-man and Buck Rogers and Superman. You know what we all feel inside that you don't feel? That we're going to the stars. . . . I'm looking down on all this from space. . . . I'm already gone.

FALLING IN PLACE

First published: 1980
Type of work: Novel

A frustrated teacher of summer school gets to know an unhappy family in which the father and mother are separated and the young son wounds the daughter with a gun.

In Greek myth, Icarus' exuberantly beating wings hurl him toward the sun, where they melt, and he plunges to his death in the sea. The Icarian figure adorning the cover of *Falling in Place* suggests the downside of youthful aspiration; the major characters in *Falling in Place* do not take control of their lives. Instead, they seem to fall numbly into place through indirection.

Of all the major characters in the novel, Cynthia Forrest alone seems fully aware of how disappointing she finds her own life: From her standpoint, she is wasting a very good mind trying to teach summer school students about literature. Perhaps ironically, her students dub her "Lost-in-the-Forrest"; from their standpoint, the name is apt. Cynthia does not usually concern herself with students as individuals, and she is using an anthology of excerpts, so the literature may seem unreal and the students' personal experience irrelevant. The students' welfare does not seem to be an issue. Cynthia only becomes involved with a student, Mary, when Mary's father, John Knapp, expresses concern about Mary's summer school work and makes a date to talk to her teacher.

The conference between parent and teacher is not without some sexual overtones, and it takes place in a restaurant. If Mary's welfare is really at issue here, it is lost in the dynamics of multiple protocols: the protocol of the business lunch; the protocol of the relationship between parent and teacher; and the unstated protocol between a young, attractive woman and an ostensibly successful man.

The summer school class has disturbed Cynthia. One of her common nightmares, dreamed often after teaching, is that she is falling. Cynthia (realistically) believes that she is not reaching her students. She does not seem to realize that she has failed to help them link literature to their lives. The best Cynthia Forrest can do is to keep herself minimally functional. Her own love life is disappointing until the very end of the novel, when her whimsical, immature lover, Spangle, returns from Madrid, where he had rescued his wayward brother, and New York, where he failed to rekindle an old flame.

Most of the characters in *Falling in Place* are dying in their tracks. At the instigation of a friend who has proved himself monstrous in many respects, John Knapp's ten-year-old son John Joel shoots his sister Mary. He had not known the gun was loaded.

John Knapp has been living with his mother in Rye, New York, where he is close to work and to his mistress, Nina. The family remains in Connecticut to be visited on weekends. The youngest of the Knapp children has been brought to his paternal grandmother's house to cheer her when it is first thought that she may have cancer. Louise, who is John's wife and the children's mother, does not attempt to keep her child. She even relinquishes John Joel after the shooting, and she accepts her divorce from John with philosophical stoicism.

The one time the readers see Louise in close contact with one of her children is when she takes John Joel berry picking and picnicking. On that occasion, Louise and John Joel speak of intimate things. Included in the heavy baggage that John Joel needs to unload is the revelation that his friend Parker has found his mother's diaphragm and put a pin hole in it. Parker is hardly a good friend for John Joel, but there are no others available; Mary does not have a choice of friends either. Except for one unsatisfactory friend each, the Knapp children are alienated. The shooting, although it is technically an accident, is a climax of a great deal of mutual hostility.

John Knapp is having an affair with a woman named Nina, not very much older than his daughter; she is stronger than he is in many ways, but she is dissatisfied with her job, as well as her home—a small womblike apartment where John feels safe and she feels cramped. Nina cannot understand how John can be materially rich and yet so dissatisfied. Nina believes that money will make her happy.

By the novel's end, John Knapp has left his family to be with Nina; John Joel has joined his baby brother at their grandmother's house; Louise is helping Mary recover; and Cynthia is greeted by the returned Spangle. No problems have been resolved, and it is not likely that anybody will be very happy. On the very last page of the novel, however, there is an upbeat answer to what seems to be a trivial question. Greeted by her old boyfriend, Spangle, and hearing about his brother's lost keys and money, Cynthia asks what was wished for when everything was thrown into the fountain. Spangle's answer is, "The usual, I guess."

PICTURING WILL

First published: 1989
Type of work: Novel

A woman photographer whose husband has left her rears her son Will, although the reader learns that her second husband, Mel, is the most nurturing "parent" in the novel.

Will's mother, Jody, is a professional photographer; the novel's title is eventually seen to be both apt and ironic. Human growth certainly requires love and devotion more than it does the commercial virtues of glitz and promotion. In the opening chapter of the section entitled "Mother," the reader is told, "Only a baby—someone who truly needed her care—could have made [Jody] rise to the occasion" when Wayne leaves her. Jody does become a famous and gifted photographer who shows extraordinary insight, a sense of drama, and an unusual capacity for composition. She is a successful wedding photographer as well. It is significant, however, that the picture of Will that she carries with her is actually rubbed out and almost indecipherable; the real picture is an internal one. It is with intuitive accuracy that Jody chooses the right community for her early success, the suitable parent (not the biological one) for her son, and the agent who (though a child molester) successfully promotes her artistic career. In this novel, one good apple, Mel, the adoptive father, decontaminates the bunch.

If petty, vain, irresponsible men are unfit fathers, then Wayne has done both his wife and son the greatest service by abandoning them. Originally having met Jody by accident, Wayne is incapable of growth: "Wayne read books—not to expand his horizons . . . but to reinforce the limits of what he believed." Wayne finds purpose in neither work nor close, trusting relationships.

The final portion of the novel describes Wayne's life: his relationship with his third wife, his attitude toward his male coworkers and bar chums, and his affairs with other women. He is "lucky" with other women, but he otherwise feels sorry for himself. His resentment of Jody's refusal to have an abortion and his consequent resentment of Will is made clear in his relationship with Will when he visits with him in Florida. Corky, Wayne's third wife, and Zeke, his working associate, are far more supportive and nurturing to Will than Wayne is.

Wayne's affairs are given sexually explicit treatment—unusual in Beattie's works. The details emphasize Wayne's vanity and selfishness, no less his immaturity. When one of his lovers allows Wayne to use her estate for a pool party, he entertains Will and all of his own friends. His ultimate act of bravado is to urinate in the pool.

When Wayne's luck with women turns, he is erroneously charged with drug dealing, a charge appropriate only to his former girlfriend. As Will is being prepared for an early return flight to New York to pose with his mother for a picture for *Vogue*, he looks out a bathroom window to see his father being taken into custody by two policemen. This, a strange experience involving Haveabud, the man who becomes his mother's agent, and his disappointment in not being able to see his dear friend, Wag, are heavy childhood agonies.

Mel is an intellectually as well as an emotionally sustaining force in the novel. What Christina Murphy calls "inner narratives" in *Picturing Will*—italicized whole chapters—are found finally to be journal entries of Mel's; he beautifully describes the parent's plight. One often-quoted passage is worth repeating:

> Do everything right, all the time, and the child will prosper. It's as simple as that, except for fate, luck, heredity, chance, the astrological sign under which the child was born, his order of birth, his first encounter with evil, the girl who jilts him in spite of his excellent qualities, the war that is being fought when he is a young man, the drugs he may try once or too many times, the friends he makes . . . and animals with rabies.

Mel is a true lover and a devoted father. It is he who drives Will to Florida to visit his natural father Wayne and who willingly works for Haveabud because he will promote Jody's artwork in New York. In the last section of the novel, "Child," the reader sees that Mel's faith that he and Will can "stand firm" and make it is justified. The now happily married Will is coaxing his own son to continue the cycle as he urges, "Come on, baby. Throw me the ball."

Summary

Ann Beattie's stories and novels demonstrate that she is, as she herself said she hoped to be seen as, "astute about human behavior." Her stories about people struggling to make their peace with the world and find contentedness have struck a strong chord with a generation of readers that came of age in the 1960's and 1970's. In her novel *Picturing Will*, she moved beyond her indirect portrayals of alienation to a depiction of a nurturing parent, a universal father.

Bibliography

Beattie, Ann. Interview by Patrick H. Samway. *America* 162 (May 12, 1990): 469.

Boyle, T. Coraghessan. "Who Is the Truest Parent?" *The New York Times*, January 7, 1990, sec. 7, p. 1.

Friedrich, Otto. "Beattieland." *Time* 135 (January 22, 1990): 68.

McCaffery, Larry, and Sinda Gregory. "A Conversation with Ann Beattie." *Literary Review* 27 (Winter, 1984): 165-177.

Murphy, Christina. *Ann Beattie.* Boston: Twayne, 1986.

Parini, Jay. "A Writer Comes of Age." *Horizon* 25 (December, 1982): 22.

Shapiro, Laura. "Through a Zoom Lens Darkly." *Newsweek* 115 (January 22, 1990): 62.

Judith Schnee

SAUL BELLOW

Born: Montreal, Canada
July 10, 1915

Principal Literary Achievement

Critically recognized as one of the most significant American novelists of the twentieth century, Bellow has depicted the hero as a sensitive sufferer pitted against the values of a materialistic age.

Biography

Saul Bellow's parents were Russian Jews who had emigrated to Canada. A precocious, intelligent child, he had learned not only English but also Yiddish, Hebrew, and French by the time the family moved to Chicago in 1924. Bellow has always considered Chicago his spiritual birthplace. In 1933, he was graduated from Tuley High School and enrolled in the University of Chicago, where, by his own account, he was peripatetic in his studies, drifting from one course to another, registering for one but finding another more interesting. Among novelists, Theodore Dreiser and Joseph Conrad were particular favorites, though Bellow seems to have read widely, especially in sociology. He received his bachelor's degree with honors in sociology and anthropology in 1937.

During those years before World War II, Bellow was living in Chicago and learning his art, writing on a bridge table in a back bedroom of his apartment during the day. His first wife, Anita Goshkin, was a social worker, and she helped support him while he wrote. By 1938 he had gotten a job with the Works Progress Administration (WPA) as a biographer of local novelists and poets, a position that not only paid some of the bills but also satisfied his intellectual appetite for wide reading, which included novelists such as Sherwood Anderson and "homespun" poets such as Edgar Lee Masters and Vachel Lindsay. Bellow's interest in Anderson is significant, since the grotesque, alienated characters of Anderson's works can be seen as being transmuted into the suffering human beings seeking meaning that appear in Bellow's own novels.

Bellow's first story, "Two Morning Monologues," appeared in 1941; it is a short, slight tale in which Bellow clearly showed that he was still an apprentice. Meanwhile, he served a brief term in the U.S. Merchant Marine, and, like Joseph, the main character in his first novel, *Dangling Man* (1944), Bellow waited out World War II. His intellectual breadth secured for him a job on the editorial staff of the

"Great Books" project of the *Encyclopædia Britannica*; he also taught English briefly at the University of Minnesota in 1946. *Dangling Man* is a self-consciously austere work, tracing its hero's growing disaffection from society, his wife, and himself as he waits to be drafted. The diary format, reflective of Joseph's thoughts and tensions, is skillfully handled and allows Bellow to portray Joseph's conflicts in psychological rather than chronological time.

Set in New York City, *The Victim*, Bellow's second novel, was published in 1947. It focuses on Asa Leventhal, a Jew, who tries to come to terms with the guilt imputed to him by his Gentile friend Allbee, who accuses Asa of complicity in Allbee's failure in life. The themes of guilt and responsibility intertwine and deepen the character of Asa as "sufferer with dignity," one of the characteristics of the so-called Bellovian hero. The book brought its author a more solid reputation and helped earn for him a Guggenheim Fellowship in 1948. Bellow went to live in Paris. For the next few years, he traveled about Europe and began work on his third novel.

The Adventures of Augie March (1953) won the National Book Award and established Bellow as one of America's most important novelists. Augie became a new kind of literary cult hero—the intellectual vagabond whose travels across the United States revealed him to be a sensitive soul driven to find a higher reality amid the soul-killing materialism of modern society.

Throughout the 1950's, Bellow lived in New York City, teaching at several universities and publishing a number of short stories, articles, and book reviews. Another marriage came and, in 1955, another Guggenheim award. In 1956 Bellow brought out his fourth novel. *Seize the Day* is recognized as one of its author's most important works. Powerful in its economy, the book is a forceful account of a day in the life of Tommy Wilhelm, a loser with a soul. Like Gimpel the Fool, the hero in Isaac Bashevis Singer's classic short story (which Bellow had translated from the Yiddish in 1953), Tommy engages the reader's sympathy in spite of his foolishness and his failures because of a capacity for turning his suffering into a meaningful form of endurance. Tommy prevails, saddened and chastened, the representative of mid-twentieth century man.

By the time of his fifth novel, *Henderson the Rain King* (1959), Saul Bellow had achieved that rare distinction of being both popularly acclaimed and critically recognized. In that novel, the theme of success, already treated in *Seize the Day*, is reworked. Eugene Henderson is a success—a millionaire who sets out for Africa in an attempt to find spiritual coin as a replacement for the tedium of his personal affluence.

In the early 1960's, Bellow served as coeditor of a short-lived periodical, *The Noble Savage*, an intellectual journal of human culture. He also continued to teach, now at the University of Chicago, an institution with which he became regularly associated throughout the 1960's and 1970's. *Herzog* (1964), his sixth novel, is often regarded as his best. It won the National Book Award, and with it Bellow came to be regarded as America's foremost contemporary novelist. Moses Herzog, whose letters to the world-at-large are both a plea for understanding and a commitment to life, spoke to the world of the 1960's as Augie and Tommy had to the world of the 1950's.

The mid-1960's saw also the production of several plays, notably *The Last Analysis* (1964), which had a short run on Broadway. Three one-act plays in 1965 also met with failure. Dramatically confusing, the plays drift from heavy-handed portentiousness to farce. This brief experience as dramatist was Bellow's last attempt at writing for the stage.

By contrast, his next novel, *Mr. Sammler's Planet* (1970), became a best-seller and won for Bellow a third National Book Award. In spite of critical acclaim, however, the novel was puzzling to many readers because of its "metaphysical" cast—it contains long passages of philosophical speculation by its protagonist, Mr. Sammler, an old man whose main interest is the study of a thirteenth century mystic, Meister Eckhardt. With the publication of *Humboldt's Gift* (1975), Saul Bellow reached the pinnacle of his literary career. This comic novel of great zest and insight garnered the Pulitzer Prize for 1975, in the following year, Bellow, then sixty-one, received the highest accolade in literature, the Nobel Prize.

His first nonfiction work also appeared in 1976. *To Jerusalem and Back: A Personal Account* describes the novelist's visit to Israel, and it deals with the special problems of survival faced by that nation. *The Dean's December* (1982) is viewed as a disappointing novel. Void of the comic gusto that marks Bellow's best work, the book is a novel of ideas in the spirit of *Mr. Sammler's Planet*, recording the philosophical meditations of its protagonist as he contends with the destructive political and social forces represented in the Communist city of Bucharest, to which he travels, and the American city of Chicago, to which he returns.

Him with His Foot in His Mouth and Other Stories appeared in 1984, and the decade concluded with three more novellas. *More Die of Heartbreak* (1987) features, once again, one of Bellow's intellectual heroes, this time a college professor of Russian literature who comes to America from Paris in search of his visionary uncle. Written when Bellow was in his early seventies, the book typifies the author's continuing affirmation of human values amid the crushing dysfunction of contemporary life. *A Theft* and *The Bellarosa Connection* appeared in 1989. Though lacking the scope of his earlier work, these novellas, especially the latter, probe the connection between guilt and responsibility and insist, finally, on the primacy of the human spirit.

Analysis

What sets Saul Bellow's novels apart from those of his major contemporaries, such as Thomas Pynchon, John Barth, and Norman Mailer, is primarily the treatment of the hero. The critical consensus is overwhelming in its assessment of the Bellow protagonist as a sensitive, thinking being who contends with the soul-destructive forces of modern society. Though often a victim and a spiritual alien in a materialistic world, Bellow's protagonist is nevertheless capable of dignity, sympathy, and compassion.

In his critical essays as well, Bellow calls for a more positive vision of man as a sort of glorious sufferer wounded by his own aspirations and ideals in a world that has lost its belief in both. Bellow's vision of man's conflict with the world is not presented as a journey into chaos, as such a conflict is often portrayed in contemporary works. Unlike his contemporaries, Bellow does not locate his hero in a world where meaning and purpose are nonexistent or, at best, random. In Pynchon's *Gravity's Rainbow* (1973) or Barth's *Giles Goat-Boy* (1966), for example—or even in the works of the South American "magical realists" such as Julio Cortázar and Jorge Luis Borges—reality is a virtual fictoid, a fabulous construction, an existential hall of mirrors against which the hero or antihero bumps his psyche.

By contrast, Bellow's world has substance. The settings of his novels—New York, Chicago, or even the countryside—are fully realized, authentically felt places. These environments, in fact, thrust the hero into a kind of moral laboratory in which to test his own values and gradually come to terms with life. For Bellow, it is not the world that is illusory, but the hero's ability to achieve certainty of comfort and intellectual ease. The hero, in fact, must always strive to understand his place in the order of things. "The fault, dear Brutus," as William Shakespeare wrote, "is not in our stars, but in ourselves, that we are underlings."

The hero as underling, what Bellow himself called the greatness of man's "imbecility," is explored in the novels not with naturalistic gloom but rather from a point of view that is, above all, genuinely comic. Bellow is one of America's supreme comic novelists. His vision of man's plight entails an awareness of the contradiction between desire and limitation, between aspiration and ability. Such a contradiction has been, throughout Western literature, a vital source for the comic temper. It is interesting to note that among the novelist's other pursuits is his translation from the Yiddish of Isaac Bashevis Singer's "Gimpel Tam" (1945; "Gimpel the Fool," 1953), a work spiritually akin to Bellow's own point of view. Gimpel is the schlemiel, the loser with the soul whose place in heaven is assured by the genuine humility of his earthly naïveté, a humility amounting to a holiness through submission. The Bellovian hero is the intellectual schlemiel, aggrieved by the madness of contemporary life but unable to submit with Job-like serenity as Gimpel does.

Bellow is thus at odds with the naturalistic writers who preceded him and from whose tradition he emerged. Those writers, such as Theodore Dreiser, saw man as basically a victim, a creature irredeemable by any imaginative aspiration because the weight of social forces—dramatized as economic imperatives or as ethical and emotional bankruptcy—keeps him down.

The problem for Bellow's heroes is not the lack of imagination or the inability to feel, but the reverse. Protagonists such as Tommy Wilhelm in *Seize the Day*, for example, suffer—like Gimpel—not only because the world is a pitiless place, but also because they refuse to submit to the pitilessness, striving instead for some humanistic ideal. Tommy Wilhelm wants sympathy; he demands it as a human being. Yet his expectations lie fallow in the stony ground of his father's heart and in the heartlessness of Tamkin and the commodities exchange.

Another intellectual schlemiel, Moses Herzog, whose name in German suggests "heart," is a scholar of Romanticism who writes letters to the world to keep from going mad. His alienation from the world can only partly be explained as neurosis. Much of it stems, as does Tommy Wilhelm's, from his own moral insight, which places him above the world while keeping him enthralled by the demands of the world.

Ultimately, what places Bellow in the mainstream of classic novelists—if one can label a contemporary as "classic"—is his concern with a theme common in the work of the great novelists: the inherent contradiction between the hero's potential as a human being and the moral value of his actual experience. Such a theme, sometimes expressed as the conflict between illusion and reality, has been characteristic of great literary works from Miguel de Cervantes' *Don Quixote de la Mancha* (1605; *Don Quixote of the Mancha*, 1612), whose hero jousts with windmills in the belief that they are giants, to Gustave Flaubert's *Madame Bovary* (1857; English translation, 1886), whose heroine finds the illusion of romance stronger than the reality of daily life. All Bellow's protagonists joust, metaphorically, with windmills. A seeker such as Charlie Citrine in *Humboldt's Gift* has a romantic, imaginative point of view which is counterpoised by the hardened realism of his mistress and of his mentor, Humboldt; the huge, corporeal reality of Sorella Fonstein in *The Bellarosa Connection* contrasts ironically with her own spiritual delicacy; even the freneticism of Augie March betrays at ground level Augie's sense of human decency.

Finally, Saul Bellow is one of the great wordsmiths of the American novel. His prose style varies with the nature of the protagonist and the dilemma. The euphoric, Whitmanesque breathlessness of *The Adventures of Augie March* simmers into the quiet restraint of *Seize the Day*, expands into Moses Herzog's tempered frustrations, and dilates into the metaphorical considerations of *Mr. Sammler's Planet*. In each work the prose is often a startling mix of erudition and slang, of the analytically precise and the casually colloquial; yet it is also effective and always right. His work is irresistibly entertaining, containing accurate portrayals of contemporary life dramatized by dialogue of unerring naturalness.

THE ADVENTURES OF AUGIE MARCH

First published: 1953
Type of work: Novel

Through a skein of events, from Chicago of the Depression to postwar Paris, Augie March experiences life as an affirmation of the human spirit.

Bellow's third work is not only a picaresque novel of great zest but also a kind of *Bildungsroman*, an autobiographical record of physical experience as it relates to intellectual and emotional growth. Augie's own exuberant narration of his life, beginning in Chicago during the Great Depression, reveals a personality who is in some ways a reckless and amoral character reminiscent of the rogue-heroes of the Spanish picaresque novel of the sixteenth and seventeenth centuries. Yet he is also a man who must define himself by his relationship to others and who views the world at large as basically sound. Many critics have likened the book, and Augie in particular, to *The Adventures of Huckleberry Finn* (1884), and certainly Augie's status as folk hero, his take-the-world-as-it-is attitude, and his earthy narrative "talk" are very much influenced by Mark Twain's classic American novel.

Yet Augie is deeper than Huck because he is less naïve and, because of his origins, more cynical. He is not easily drawn into others' sphere of influence, as, by contrast, Huck was credulously drawn to the Duke and the King. Augie's adventures—his various jobs as stock boy, coal salesman, petty thief, prize-fight manager, union organizer, and even eagle trainer—are attempts to taste all of life. Augie is the embodiment of nineteenth century American poet Walt Whitman's belief in the value of all men and professions. All labor is valuable in a democracy; all occupations play a part in the positive force that is life itself. The various jobs are also, for Augie, a means to an end—the end being, as he says, "a better fate."

A better fate was also what the heroes of a previous literary generation sought for themselves. Clyde, in Theodore Dreiser's *An American Tragedy* (1925), however, climbed the social ladder only to end a literal prisoner to his own ambition: That there was no way out but death was the naturalistically logical conclusion to Clyde's ambition. Unlike Clyde, Augie is not merely a product of his environment, not only the sum total of his experiences (equalling zero). The "better fate," as Augie implies, is, indeed, worldly success, but success tempered by insight. Though he ends his story in Paris, involved in some international business ventures of questionable legitimacy, Augie comes to understand the value of commitment to humanity, the need for involvement with life.

This sense of commitment is ultimately missing in Augie's life. He is a hero the reader can admire for his individuality and sense of independence, but he does not learn by the novel's end to cease his wandering ways—emotional, intellectual, or physical. His major love affairs, first with Thea, then with Stella, whom he marries, are largely failures. Even his ability to accept people as they are—Einhorn, for example, whose crippled body Augie carries about—does not encourage him to commit himself to a creed or code.

Augie can see people objectively; he is capable of giving them the benefit of the doubt. The world is thus not a valley of despair. Beyond this passive acceptance of people for what they are in a world clearly teeming with life, however, Augie has no goal, no plan. Lacking commitment, he drifts from one adventure to another, hoping for the right "feel." He is akin to a latter-day knight-errant, seeking adventures in the vague hope of discovering the Holy Grail.

SEIZE THE DAY

First published: 1956
Type of work: Novella

Like a Greek tragedy, this novella is an intensely compact work examining one day in the agonized life of loser Tommy Wilhelm.

Set in the Gloriana Hotel on Broadway during one morning and in the commodities exchange on Wall Street later in the day, *Seize the Day* begins with its suffering hero, Tommy Wilhelm, seeking the company of his father, Dr. Adler. Dr. Adler does not love his son and views him as a failure and a dreamer. Adler disdains his son's misery: Tommy's marriage has failed and his career at Rojax Corporation has floundered. In seeking out his father, Tommy does not so much want financial help, though he needs it and even expects it. What he really seeks is his father's approval and love. At the very least, he seeks understanding from the old man, a compassion that Tommy has not found from anyone—especially his wife, who is stonily demanding further alimony. Adler is pitiless, disdainful, and sententious. One of Bellow's most consummately realized villains, he is a soulless creature who is himself ironically effete, living in tight-fisted retirement in a second-rate hotel.

Broke and desperate, Tommy turns to another father figure, a wily, fast-talking con man, Dr. Tamkin. Tamkin wearies Tommy with his incessant talk, an overwhelming mixture of Emersonian bromides on self-reliance and psychoanalytic jargon about money as a type of aggression. He convinces Tommy to invest the last of his money on the commodities market—ironically, in futures.

Tommy's inevitable failure is depicted in a brilliant scene in which he anxiously watches the exchange board for signs of profit while Tamkin, ever talking, preaches on the evils of greed. When Tommy is wiped out, Tamkin disappears and Tommy is left a pathetic victim. He is, in his father's words, a slob. In the final scene, the broken Tommy wanders into a funeral chapel. There, unknown to the mourners, he weeps aloud for the dead, a gesture symbolizing his own dead end and suggesting his deeper, personal loss of love, compassion, and human sympathy.

Seize the Day is rich in character portrayal. Reminiscent of Einhorn in *The Adventures of Augie March*, Tamkin is a characteristic mix of the comic and the villainous. Fast-talking, full of trite sayings, and even shrewdly understanding of his victim's needs, Tamkin is the con man *par excellence* because he has almost convinced himself of his own sincerity in preaching against the evils of materialism. He cheats Tommy not only out of his money but also out of his beliefs, his ideals. Dr. Adler, whose name means "eagle" in German, is indeed a predator of sorts. Like Tamkin, he preys on his son's weakness as a way of preening himself. Lofty, aristocratic, and fiercely aloof, Adler has become ignoble by divorcing himself from human feelings.

The novella's title provides a final ironic commentary on the story's central idea.

The *carpe diem* theme—literally, to "seize the day"—was a classical pronouncement that urged man to make the most of his time, to extract from each moment the joy of life that time was ever stealing away. Tommy's dilemma is that he cannot subscribe to that pronouncement. His failed investment in futures is an ironic assertion of Tommy's need to live beyond the day, beyond the commercial grind—to seek for a deeper meaning of life and its sufferings.

HENDERSON THE RAIN KING

First published: 1959
Type of work: Novel

A millionaire goes to Africa in search of meaning, eventually finding it in sympathy for humankind.

Henderson the Rain King is a mad, antic fantasy, perhaps the most comic of Bellow's novels. Rich, world-weary Eugene Henderson, like the heroes of myth, seeks escape from the burden of the world and embarks on a journey to unknown lands in search of meaning and peace. The unknown land is Africa, and Henderson arrives there in poverty of spirit, having, like Ishmael in Herman Melville's *Moby-Dick* (1851), the need to find purpose in his life. Henderson is a kind of Tommy Wilhelm in reverse, except that Henderson, a graduate of an Ivy League university, has a broader perspective, a core of reference that is beyond Tommy's imagining. Whereas Tommy seeks meaning in the financial markets and then in the urbanized coldness of his father's disapproval, Henderson, already financially secure, seeks meaning in the pastoral and the primitive. Where Tommy seeks relief in futures, Henderson seeks salvation in a kind of past, a land primeval and innocent.

His first adventure is in the land of the Arnewi, in a village in the midst of mountains and clean air. The landscape suggests a primordial world of Edenic innocence, and Henderson at first is a kind of Adam, ready to start fresh. The novel, in fact, is rich in suggestive allusions to biblical and secular literary characters. As a new Adam, however, Henderson is a failure. As Moses, armed with his faith, had parted the waters of the Red Sea to save his people, so Henderson, armed with the weapons of technology, attempts to rid the life-giving well of an infestation of frogs. His role as savior backfires: He blows up the well, bringing destruction rather than life. Like Mark Twain's "Sir Boss" in *A Connecticut Yankee in King Arthur's Court* (1889), Henderson has tried to improve mankind by the beneficence of civilization; he has tried to impose a modern system of values on a primitive but honest culture.

In this first adventure, however, the destruction that Henderson wreaks teaches him little about his own place in the world. Continuing his quest for meaning, he comes next to the Wariri, among whom his most telling lessons in self-wisdom occur. Though he has become a "rain king" by the notable feat of moving a stone rain goddess, his exalted position comes only at the price of his physical humiliation—

he is flayed and thrown into the mud of a cattle pond.

Additionally, Henderson comes under the influence of the tribe's philosopher-king, Dahfu, who ponders metaphysics and is convinced that his destiny is to return, in the afterlife, as a lion. King Dahfu is a puzzling character. He seems genuinely humble in the face of universal mysteries revealed to him in his philosophy, yet his incessant talking reminds the reader of the stream of con men who appear in Bellow's novels, from Einhorn and Tamkin to the gangster, Rinaldo Cantabile, of *Humboldt's Gift*. Dahfu's effect on Henderson is both serious and wildly comic. Convinced that Henderson must free himself from his fears of inadequacy, Dahfu prescribes a therapy entailing Henderson's confrontation with a lioness. The scene in which the rain king finally learns to imitate the courage of the lioness, even to the point of getting down on all fours and roaring, is both comic and pathetic. Again, Henderson is humiliated, this time spiritually, but he has learned the meaning of man's noble fragility in a crazy world.

The novel ends with one of those physical epiphanies typical of Bellow's work. Henderson is at an airport in Newfoundland—note the significance of the place name, suggestive of Henderson's own newfound self. He has escaped from the Wariri and from the "past" of Africa, and he has taken under his wing an American child who is flying back to America, alone and frightened. He cares for the child, gives it comfort, and embraces it. He has found his meaning: sympathy for the family of man.

HERZOG

First published: 1964
Type of work: Novel

A student of Romanticism, Moses Herzog, tries to come to terms with the material, unromantic world.

Considered by many to be Bellow's masterwork, *Herzog* may well be Bellow's prototypical novel, and Herzog himself the prototypical Bellovian hero. Like Emily Dickinson, who wrote poems as a means of opening a communion with the world, Moses Herzog, sensitive student of Romanticism, writes letters to the world-at-large in an attempt to keep his sanity and to measure his need for compassion and empathy in a world devoid of both. Like Gimpel the Fool, Herzog is a true schlemiel, a loser by the standards of the world but a noble spirit.

Though capable of anger and self-pity at the break-up of his marriage, and of lust in his relationship with his mistress, Ramona, Herzog can still yearn for a deeper, richer life. Like the great thinkers to whom he writes his imaginary letters, Herzog seeks meaning and peace. Even amid the bustle of the urban life of New York and Chicago, Herzog is withdrawn into the private bustle of his mind, remembering events from his broken marriage and formulating rebuttals to the negative, spirit-killing philosophies of men such as Sandor Himmelstein, whose surname means "stony heaven," and even seventeenth century philosopher Baruch Spinoza. His letters come to him like bursts of inspiration and serve as antidotes to his own fears that he is out of his mind.

The novel thus represents a form of psychoanalysis: Herzog's remembrances are transferred into the actual world of his letters. The direction of the plot is thus not chronological but psychological: Events have meaning not in relation to time but in their association with other events or ideas. The main action of *Herzog* is not physical but mental, and despite brilliant evocations of city life, the real power of the book is the revelation of Moses Herzog's mind.

The incisive treatment of the effects of the urban experience on a sensitive, troubled spirit, however, is finely contrasted in *Herzog* with scenes of almost idyllic calm. Scenes of Herzog enjoying the pleasures of his country retreat in the Berkshires serve both to reinforce the traditional aspects of Bellow as a novelist—his use of nature as a corrective to Herzog's troubled mind, for example—and to strengthen the psychological truthfulness of his hero. Herzog is, after all, a student of Romanticism, and nature for the Romantic was curative, an agency or force by which man, by attuning himself to its power, could find inspiration, illumination, and genuine spiritual sustenance.

Nowhere is the redeeming force of nature more explicit than in the scene in which Herzog, from his country retreat, recalls the time Valentine Gershbach (his former wife's lover) is bathing Herzog's child. The scene is presented with the feeling of a pastoral. The purity, the gentleness implicit in Gershbach's action, gives pause to Herzog's anger. Herzog sees his rival as a human being, a fellow-creature, as much to be pitied as contemned. He releases his anger and comes to terms with Gershbach; Herzog thus survives not by hating but by forgiving.

HUMBOLDT'S GIFT

First published: 1975
Type of work: Novel

Two writers try to reconcile their poetic ideals with the demands of the world of popular taste and the lure of success.

Humboldt's Gift is a kind of Gothic novel in the sense that its protagonist is haunted by a ghost. The ghost is both a living man and the spirit or ideals that the man, an older writer named Von Humboldt Fleisher, represents.

Humboldt is a writer whose talent—or genius—has been corrupted by the American vision of success. Modeled closely on Bellow's recollections of a friend, poet Delmore Schwartz, who in the late 1930's had produced a first book of poetry that was hailed as a work of promising genius but who died with the promise unfulfilled, Humboldt has also produced a first volume of poems, *Harlequin Ballads*, but has since lived off his early reputation. Humboldt had "made it big," as the narrator Charlie Citrine remarks, but had produced nothing since. Instead, he had lived the good life, which included fast cars, women, and other trappings of materialistic success.

Yet Humboldt was aware of his entrapment by the overpowering world of things. Sensing his own surrender to materialism, he had taken to playing the role of the great Romantic nonconformist. The paradox of Humboldt's condition was that as a poet he was an example of unfulfillment and failure, but as a man and public figure he represented the idea of poetry as a spiritual, revivifying force capable of saving a sick society.

It is this paradox that haunts Citrine. He too is a writer, but unlike Humboldt, his idol, he has not produced any significant work—he has written histories, biographies, and political essays, the residue of other men's ideas. Citrine dreams of producing his own great work, a philosophical treatise on the human mind; like Humboldt, however, he gives in to the demands of public taste. He writes a Broadway play which becomes a smash hit and secures a lucrative motion-picture contract. Now wealthy, Citrine has become another Humboldt of sorts. When Humboldt himself dies and becomes, in Citrine's words, one of his "significant dead," Citrine renews his aspiration, believing that he has been singled out to produce a great work.

Ironically, Citrine's aspiration remains largely unfulfilled. He falls to the lure of the flesh. His mistress, Renata, is flesh personified, and his passionate enjoyment of her is his only genuinely poetic experience. In fact, the poetry of Charlie Citrine is in his natural zest for the physical quality of living, a total, rhapsodic immersion in *things*.

This expression of the intensity of life is one of the hallmarks of the novel. The villains, for example, are depicted with a Dickensian verve and sprightliness. Rinaldo Cantabile, the gangster who ensnares Citrine into subjection by a gambling debt, is portrayed with such fearsome energy that he is wonderfully comic in his wickedness. Charlie Citrine's "adventures" amid the likes of Cantabile and Renata and her gorgonic mother can be viewed as latter-day depictions of the hero in the underworld, a hell of soulless materialism.

Humboldt's Gift is thus the most Gothic of Bellow's novels. Just when Charlie has met defeat—broke, dejected, and deprived even of the luscious Renata, who has married an undertaker (perhaps from the underworld)—he is visited by a final ghost: Humboldt's gift, a legacy of a film script from the dead poet. Citrine submits the script to a producer, makes a fortune from the sale of the rights, and once again is on his feet, independent, ready to continue the pursuit of the good life. The old Romantic dream, however, is gone. Citrine realizes that he will never produce art, that he is too addicted to the popular taste and the world of the flesh. In the final scene, Citrine is at Humboldt's graveside. He has buried his idol and with him the dream of producing poetry in the materialistic land of America.

THE BELLAROSA CONNECTION

First published: 1989
Type of work: Novella

Sorella Fonstein hounds showman Billy Rose into an interview during which she hopes Billy will admit his responsibility—and thus admit his common humanity—in saving Sorella's husband from the Nazis.

As Saul Bellow had used the traditional, even old-fashioned narrative structure of the picaresque for his first major work, *The Adventures of Augie March*, so thirty years later Bellow shows his interest in and adaptation of more contemporary narrative forms. *The Bellarosa Connection* is an example of the so-called new journalism, in which real events and people are treated in broadly fictional ways. E. L. Doctorow, for example, had used such historical personalities as Harry Houdini, Henry Ford, and J. P. Morgan in the fictional tapestry of his *Ragtime* (1975).

In *The Bellarosa Connection*, Bellow creates a series of events based on the historical atrocity of the Holocaust during World War II. The action centers on Sorella Fonstein's persistence in gaining an interview with impresario Billy Rose, who was responsible—through his anonymous underground railroad—for bringing a number of Jews to America as they escaped from the Nazis. Among those who were saved was Sorella's husband, Harry. Fonstein is snubbed by Billy Rose (the European Jews had called their savior "Bellarosa") but Sorella herself, with tigerlike tenacity, ultimately succeeds in confronting Billy and blackmailing him, through her knowledge of a scandal, into meeting with Harry.

Billy's ignorance and crudity as a human being are portrayed with insight, for if human character is fraught with contradiction, then Billy's character is contradiction personified. His motive for underwriting his sole example of generosity and unselfishness in a life of hustling selfishness is never fully explained; Billy himself is not really sure of his motive. As a Jew, Billy may have truly acted in sympathy with his fellow Jews, as if (as the narrator points out) "the God of his fathers still mattered." For one time in his life, this obsessively vulgar person begrudgingly freed the font of human goodness within him.

In spite of his complexity, however, Billy Rose is not the main character. He is seen by the reader only in the climactic interview with Sorella. It is, in fact, Sorella who commands the reader's—and the narrator's—attention. Like many of Bellow's women, she is fierce, tenacious, and in absolute command over her husband. With an animal obesity to match, she is bright and yet oddly gentle, even humble. What Sorella achieves by the interview is not only Billy's consent to meet with her husband so that Harry can thank him. At bottom lies Sorella's extorting from Billy a sense of responsibility for the life he had saved, a responsibility that extends to all humanity. Billy thus shares kinship with Harry, with Jews, and with all humankind.

Sorella seems to have understood this connection—the real Bellarosa connection— the chain of mutual responsibility, of recognition of human suffering, of compassion for the human condition.

This connection is ultimately clarified by the novella's point of view. The narrator is a distant relation of Fonstein, who tells the story in an effort to purge his memory. He is the founder of Mnemosyne Institute, a company engaged in training business- men and government leaders in memory techniques. Like Billy Rose, the narrator is a self-made millionaire. His working motto being "memory is life," he is now on the eve of retirement, about to pass on the business to his son. His recollections of the Fonstein and Billy Rose story thus close the circle of relationship. The narrator's memory forms the link connecting the participants of the drama with the rest of humankind. Like the narrator, the reader is vicariously involved. Humanity, through memory, is being tested and vindicated.

Summary

Saul Bellow summarized his own literary goals as well as his achievement in his 1976 Nobel Prize acceptance speech. In it he declared that the novelist's duty is essentially to affirm the value of the human soul, to record the ultimate triumph of the spirit in the midst of materialism. Indeed, Bellow's novels insist on the primacy of the hero—suffering, questioning, doubting, and yearning— always central to the plot, not a peripheral element subject to its randomness.

Bellow's distinction as a contemporary novelist is precisely his concern for character in conflict with society. His insistence on human values puts him at odds with many latter-day novelists and places him, instead, in the tradition of the great nineteenth century novelists who saw character as the central focus of the novel.

Bibliography

Bradbury, Malcolm. *Saul Bellow*. New York: Methuen, 1982.

Braham, Jeanne. *A Sort of Columbus: The American Voyages of Saul Bellow's Fic- tion*. Athens: University of Georgia Press, 1984.

Clayton, John Jacob. *Saul Bellow: In Defense of Man*. 2d ed. Bloomington: Indiana University Press, 1979.

Cronin, Gloria, and Leila H. Goldman, eds. *Saul Bellow in the 1980's: A Collection of Critical Essays*. East Lansing: Michigan State University Press, 1989.

Newman, Judie. *Saul Bellow and History*. London: Macmillan, 1984.

Porter, M. Gilbert. *Whence the Power? The Artistry and Humanity of Saul Bellow*. Columbia: University of Missouri Press, 1974.

Trachtenberg, Stanley, comp. *Critical Essays on Saul Bellow*. Boston: G. K. Hall, 1979.

Edward Fiorelli

WENDELL BERRY

Born: Henry County, Kentucky
August 5, 1934

Principal Literary Achievement

As a poet, essayist, and novelist, Berry has become widely recognized as an advocate of responsible farming and environmental practices.

Biography

Wendell Berry was born in rural Henry County, outside Port Royal, Kentucky, on August 5, 1934. His father, John Berry, was a respected lawyer and attorney for the Burley Tobacco Growers Association. The Berrys—Wendell's mother, two sisters, and brother—were all readers, and they were a lively and well-informed family. His father was a keen judge of farmland and often spoke with his sons about the merits of various local farms.

Wendell attended local public schools and entered the University of Kentucky in Lexington, where he earned his B.A. in 1956 and his master's degree in English in 1957. He married Tanya Amyx in May, 1957, and taught for a year at Georgetown College, a small liberal arts school in Georgetown, Kentucky. Deciding to pursue a career as a writer, he applied for a Wallace Stegner Writing Fellowship at Stanford University, studying under Stegner in 1958-1959, and then serving as E. H. Jones Lecturer (in creative writing) in 1959-1960. Berry's first novel, *Nathan Coulter*, was published by Houghton Mifflin in 1960. A Guggenheim Foundation Fellowship allowed him to travel with his wife and family in France and Italy for a year in 1962.

Berry returned to accept an appointment as assistant professor at New York University, where he directed the freshman English program from 1962 to 1964. By this time he was actively publishing poetry, earning the Vachel Lindsay Prize from *Poetry* magazine in 1962. His elegy on John F. Kennedy's death, "November Twenty Six Nineteen Hundred Sixty Three," first published in *The Nation* and reprinted with illustrations by Ben Shahn, won special recognition.

In 1964, Berry made a momentous decision to leave the New York literary scene and return to Kentucky, where he purchased a run-down farm near his boyhood home of Port Royal and joined the English department at the University of Kentucky. Berry describes the complex reasons behind this decision in his autobiographical essay, "The Long-Legged House." He rebuilt a small summer house on the banks of

the Kentucky River as a study and began to restore Lane's Landing Farm as a working farm. By that time he was well into his second novel, *A Place on Earth* (1967), which he completed with the assistance of a Rockefeller Foundation Fellowship. He also published his first poetry volume, *The Broken Ground* (1964), that same year. Berry's return to Kentucky marked a reaffirmation of local family ties that stretched back five generations to when his great-grandfather had emigrated from Ireland and settled in Port Royal in 1803.

Though his New York friends warned him against returning home, Berry has never regretted his decision. In returning to his native community to reclaim his heritage, Berry made a decision to write about what he knew best: the land and people of his native Kentucky hill country. His fictional Port William was his "undiscovered country," but he had to discover how to write about his native region, how to free himself from the Southern romantic clichés and to see things clearly. In *The Hidden Wound* (1970), Berry writes about the crippling legacy of slavery and the destructive attitudes toward the land that it fostered. The book is also a meditation on race relations and a tribute to Old Nick and Aunt Georgie, black tenants on his father's farm who had influenced Berry as a boy. In a broader sense, the book is about how Americans have exploited both men and land.

Writing and organic farming became twin vocations for Berry. He consciously decided to restore his hillside farm by farming it organically. He claims that his training as a poet helped him to become an organic farmer, to view farming as a way of life and not merely as an exploitation of the land for profit. He views both a farm and a poem as a complex of living structures that "mutually clarify and sustain each other."

Berry was clearly inspired by his return home, publishing four poetry volumes in the next decade—*Openings* (1968), *Farming: A Hand Book* (1970), *The Country of Marriage* (1973), and *Clearing* (1977), as well as a third novel, *The Memory of Old Jack* (1974), and a third essay collection, *A Continuous Harmony: Essays Cultural and Agricultural* (1972).

Along with his teaching at the University of Kentucky, Berry periodically accepted visiting appointments, returning to Stanford University in 1968-1969 as a visiting professor of creative writing and subsequently serving as writer in residence at the University of Cincinnati in the winter of 1974, at Centre College in the winter of 1977, and at Bucknell University in 1987.

In 1977, Berry published his fourth essay collection, *The Unsettling of America: Culture & Agriculture.* He resigned his professorship at the University of Kentucky in order to accept a position as contributing editor for two of the magazines at Rodale Press, *Organic Gardening* and *New Farm.* He has continued to be a leading spokesman for small-scale family farming and sound conservation practices, opposing the wastefulness of large-scale corporate farming. His essays have appeared in publications as diverse as *The Hudson Review, Harper's Magazine,* and *The Nation* on one hand, and *Blair and Ketchum's Country Journal* and *Organic Gardening* on the other.

In 1980, Berry changed publishers and went to North Point Press, a small, well-respected West Coast publisher in Berkeley that published his work, including the revisions of his early novels, until 1991. The 1980's were an active decade for Berry, with two poetry volumes appearing, *A Part* (1980) and *The Wheel* (1982), as well as an essay collection, *The Gift of Good Land* (1981), and a book of literary essays, *Standing by Words* (1983). North Point Press also published another essay collection, *Recollected Essays: 1965-1980* (1981), and his *Collected Poems: 1957-1982* (1985). A collection of Port William stories, *The Wild Birds* (1986), appeared the next year, followed by *Sabbaths* (1987), a poetry volume; *Home Economics* (1987), another essay collection; *Remembering* (1988), a novella; and *What Are People For?* (1990), an essay collection. Berry returned to teach part time at the University of Kentucky, but he guards his privacy as a writer and is reluctant to accept engagements that will take him away from his writing or farming.

Analysis

Wallace Stegner has written of Wendell Berry's work, "It is hard to say whether I like this writer better as a poet, an essayist, or a novelist. He is all three, at a high level." What connects all Berry's work is a tough-minded regional vision whose constituents are not the traditional Southern pieties but the integrity of language, farming, marriage, labor, and place. His regionalism is more akin to that of William Carlos Williams than that of William Faulkner. It has less to do with mythologizing a region than with the complex cultural memory of a particular place that comes from many generations of continuous settlement in that place. He is not interested in evoking a mythic past or recounting the decline and fall of a planter aristocracy, but rather in describing an ethic and a way of life based upon devotion to land and place.

Berry's decison to return to his native region was based on his desire to avoid the rootless, urban nomadism of modern American life. In *A Continuous Harmony*, he criticizes the restless mobility of modern motorized culture. Deserts may produce nomadic cultures, but for the rich, fertile, well-watered land of Kentucky to do so is preposterous. Berry's regionalism might almost be described as ecological:

> The regionalism that I adhere to could almost be described simply as *local life aware of itself.* It would tend to substitute for the myths and stereotypes of a region a particular knowledge of the life of the *place* one lives in and intends to *continue* to live in. It pertains to living as much as writing, and it pertains to living *before* it pertains to writing. The motive of such regionalism is the awareness that local life is intricately dependent, for its quality but also for its continuance, upon local knowledge.

All Berry's writing has derived from this vision of stubborn loyalty to a particular place. It has its roots in Thomas Jefferson's ideal of the intelligent yeoman farmer and in the Southern Agrarian ideals articulated by Allen Tate and others in *I'll Take My Stand* (1926). To these political and literary antecedents, Berry brings a keen ecological awareness along with a profound respect for the culture of farming—in the root sense of "agri-culture." His interest is in developing long-term sustainable methods of agriculture that will not exhaust the land or harm the environment and will allow a rural village culture to reestablish itself in the United States. He is opposed, therefore, to the powerful economic and social forces that have combined to disrupt rural American life since the end of World War II.

In his novels, Berry celebrates three families of his fictional Port William community—the Coulters, the Feltners, and the Beechums—who farm the rolling hillsides and rich bottomlands of the Kentucky River Valley region, west of the Appalachians. In a carefully controlled, meticulously detailed style, he recounts the small triumphs and disappointments of their lives. They are all small tobacco farmers with mixed livestock and grain crops who struggle from year to year, sustained by the pride and discipline of their work. Berry evokes the strengths and continuities of the community that sustained this way of life until recently. Economic issues often pit the greed and indifference of outsiders against local farmers who struggle to produce a livelihood and preserve their farms.

In his first novel, *Nathan Coulter*, Berry recounts the growth of a young Kentucky farm boy whose loveless home is dominated, after his mother's death, by a harsh father driven to over-work his farm and himself. In this brutal, male environment, young Nathan Coulter finds nurturance in his carefree Uncle Burley, who is not driven by the obsession to own and dominate the land.

In Berry's next novel, *A Place on Earth*, Mat Feltner tries to come to terms with the loss of his only son, Virgil, during World War II. In the seasonal idylls of work and family, Mat struggles to continue working his land in memory of his son. *The Memory of Old Jack*, Berry's third and perhaps most accomplished novel, traces the life of Jack Beecham, a retired farmer of ninety-two, who relives his life as farm boy, husband, father, lover, farmer, and community figure on a radiant day in September, 1952. A short story collection, *The Wild Birds*, recounts six more stories of the families of the Port William fellowship, and a novella, *Remembering*, tells the story of a crisis of faith experienced by farmer Andy Catlett after he loses his right hand in a corn picker. In all these works, Berry's fictional style is spare and deliberately understated, in the formalist tradition, with carefully chosen narrative and symbolic incidents.

Berry's poetry celebrates the lyrical dimensions of his agrarian vision of the farmer as husband to farm and land as well as to wife and family. Stewardship is the major unifying theme—between the farmer and his family, community, land, and region. As a pastoral poet, Berry writes about the land, the seasons, the cycle of the agricultural year. His root metaphor is husbandry—caring, rearing, nurturing, growing, and harvesting what the land yields. In the vision of his poems, the mythos of male generativeness finds its response in female receptivity. The voice in his poems is in turn pensive, meditative, celebratory, and affirming. One of his chief personae, "the Mad Farmer," sometimes voices radical or whimsical agrarian social or political positions that reflect the more polemical arguments in Berry's essays, but there is a quiet, elegiac mood in his poetry as well, one that celebrates the richness of the moment in the poetic perception and gives thanks for his marriage, his land, and his community.

Berry's essays are his most assertive genre; in them he voices most directly his concerns about the ravages of strip mining, corporate farming, agribusiness, racism, and consumerism, balancing these against the virtues of small, self-contained farms and rural communities. His *The Unsettling of America: Culture & Agriculture* has become a basic text of the environmental movement.

For Berry, environmental responsibility begins with personal frugality, careful land use, and intact farming communities. The environmental crisis, he argues, is at heart a human problem, rather than an economic or technological one. It is a problem of optimal scale, of knowing how to farm in a sustainable manner, rather than exploiting and ruining the land. The healthiest farms and rural economies are the most diverse; they are not the huge, one-crop monocultures encouraged by corporate farming. Such diversity depends upon the kind of family farms that survived in the United States until the end of World War II. In his essay collections, Berry traces the social and economic decline of the family farm and its environmental consequences. Water pollution, pesticide contamination, and topsoil runoff are but a few of the adverse consequences of poor farming practices. With the demise of small, carefully run farms and the subsequent loss of farm labor, corporate farmers were forced to adopt wasteful practices. Berry's Kentucky countryside was once a good farming region, with many small farms lovingly tended. Now there are abandoned farms and rural poverty. In *What Are People For?*, Berry concludes that "we have nearly destroyed American farming, and in the process have nearly destroyed ourselves."

NATHAN COULTER

First published: 1960 (revised, 1985)
Type of work: Novel

Nathan Coulter, a young Kentucky farm boy, faces the loss of his mother and a harsh, demanding father as he grows to maturity.

Berry's first novel, *Nathan Coulter,* is a spare, lean *Bildungsroman* that traces the development of the young protagonist, Nathan, as he grows from childhood to adulthood in a Kentucky farming family. Narrated by Nathan in the first person, the novel recounts the working lives of the Coulters, who raise tobacco on a hill farm outside Port William. The action is set in the earlier part of the twentieth century, when the farm work was done by hand and with mules. Each person's value was known by his labor. Nathan and his older brother Tom are slowly initiated into this work of farming. The novel re-creates the mythos of a pre-World War II farming community.

Nathan Coulter is the story of a male-dominated family, of a father who drives himself and his sons too hard in a continual struggle to force his farm to yield. Jarrat Coulter is competitive and driven, as his father was before him, and he tries to instill in his sons the same stern discipline of work. Unfortunately for him (and for them), there is no joy in his labor or his land, nor any real nurturing for his sons or his farm.

After his wife's death, Jarrat unconsciously blames his sons for their mother's death. He leaves his sons in the care of their grandparents and withdraws into sullen resentment. His resentment of his children culminates in a terrible fight with his older son, Tom, during the tobacco harvest, after he has driven his help beyond endurance. Beaten and humiliated, Tom leaves home, and Nathan is left in the care of his Uncle Burley, who has refused the burden of landownership. Burley is virtually the only kind and humane figure in this bleak novel.

In his portrait of Jarrat Coulter, Berry reveals the limitations of this harsh work ethic. Jarrat has attempted to dominate both his land and his family, to the detriment of both, without any compassionate attachment to either. In his "severe and isolated manhood," he has closed himself off from healing relationships with his sons or his land. When the break comes with his children, it is complete. Jarrat's brother Burley, on the other hand, lacks the ambition to farm, preferring instead to hunt and fish when he is not working for others. Burley has a kinder and gentler nature, however; each brother has something that the other lacks, and each is by himself incomplete.

There is much cruelty in this novel—much agrarian violence—toward men, animals, and the land. The two boys blow up a friend's pet crow with a dynamite cap and fuse, Uncle Burley shoots the heads off live ducks at a carnival, fish are blown out of the river with a stick of dynamite, and Burley's hunting dogs tear apart a live raccoon. This cruelty seems to emerge from a masculine agrarian culture that is bent on dominating the land rather than living within its limits. Women are scarcely mentioned in the novel except as background figures, and there are few community customs or celebrations to soften this harsh frontier ethic.

Berry writes about the succession of generations on the land, but the Coulters are too competitive to work the same land, so Jarrat buys the farm adjoining his father's land. In the original 1960 version of the novel, Berry traced Nathan's maturation until he starts to farm himself, but in the condensed version of the novel, published in 1985, he cut the novel considerably, ending it with the death of Nathan's grandfather after the fall tobacco harvest. Unable to live with his father, Nathan's older brother Tom has already left to farm elsewhere and the novel ends with the hope that Nathan and his father will eventually be reconciled.

THE COUNTRY OF MARRIAGE

First published: 1973
Type of work: Poetry

Berry's fourth volume of poetry contains thirty-five lyric poems that celebrate farming, marriage, and nature.

The lyric poems in *The Country of Marriage* celebrate Berry's rich and complex sense of place through the interlocking relationships of birth, marriage, livelihood, and heritage. The quiet, contemplative poems collected in this volume celebrate the land in its different moods and seasons. Through the dominant metaphors of marriage and husbandry, Berry invokes the deep and enduring relationship of his poetic persona, the "Mad Farmer," to family, land, and place. Berry's poems recall another poetic commitment to a particular place: the growth of William Carlos Williams' poetry from his lifelong service as a pediatrician in Paterson, New Jersey.

In the opening poem, "The Old Elm Tree by the River," Berry proclaims: "In us the land enacts its history." These sentiments are later echoed in his lyric tribute to Agrarian writer Allen Tate, "The Clear Days," in which Berry intimates that the poet and lover will remain distracted "Until the heart has found/ Its native piece of the ground." In the final selection, "The Anniversary," he concludes, "What we have been becomes/ The country where we are." These poems are about Berry's multiple marriages of commitment: to a region, a human relationship, a vocation, and a vision. The firmness and certainty of his commitment are reflected in the quiet, contemplative serenity of his lines. Berry's commitment to place is reinforced in his adulatory "To William Butler Yeats," which celebrates the Irish poet's loyalty to his native region: "Poet, you were but keeping faith/ With your native truth and place." In "The Wild Geese," the poet affirms that "What we need is here." Another lyric, "A Homecoming," concludes, "Show me/ my country. Take me home."

The title poem, "The Country of Marriage," is a long, intimate courtship poem, written in the first person and presumably addressed to the poet's spouse. His promise to her provides him, like a wanderer, with "the solace of his native land/ under his feet again and moving in his blood." The common life shared by the poet and his wife renews him like the hospitable welcome of a house, orchard, and garden. She is the one to whom he always returns, like one who is lost and wanders into a forest. The bond of their relationship is much more than a pragmatic exchange of love and work; it is a partnership of loving mutuality. They drink the renewing waters of their relationship, planting their lives together in the place they have consecrated by their marriage. Its abundance survives their thirst, for "like the water/ of a deep stream, love is always too much." The discerning reader may hear in this lovely contemporary marriage poem faint echoes of Edmund Spenser's great Elizabethan nuptial poem, "Epithalamion" (1594), particularly in the theme of marriage standing as a firm bulwark against the mutability of time. A companion piece, "A Marriage, an Elegy," contains echoes of the classical myth of Baucis and Philemon, the faithful old couple whose hospitality was rewarded by the gods, who granted their wish that they never be separated even after their death.

The nurturing care of farming husbandry is celebrated in such poems as "Planting Trees," "The Gathering," "Planting Crocuses," and "The Asparagus Bed." Farming is seen as an honorable livelihood, worthy of being passed on from father to son. Other poems reflect a Frostian response to the various moods of nature, as in listening to a song sparrow singing in the fall, admiring the wild geese flying overhead, or marveling at the mist rising from a river in the bitter cold of winter.

The mood of Berry's poems is not always lyrical or meditative, however; some poems take on a more strident or polemical tone, particularly those spoken by his

"Mad Farmer" persona. "The Mad Farmer Manifesto: The First Amendment" celebrates responsible land ownership as an antidote to the abstract greed of consumerism. "Testament," a poem calling for a simple death and burial, echoes William Carlos Williams' "Tract," a poem on the same topic. The triptych "Inland Passages" recalls the frontier transition from hunting to homesteading, farming, and finally a settled rural culture, contrasting restless wandering with contented settlement in one place. The closing poem in the volume, "An Anniversary," recalls in the cycle of the seasons the Edenic myth of innocence, fall, loss, and redemption.

THE GIFT OF GOOD LAND

First published: 1981
Type of work: Essays

A collection of twenty-four essays that explore the cross-cultural relationships between culture and agriculture.

Berry's fourth essay collection, *The Gift of Good Land*, continued to address many of the same issues that he had touched upon in earlier volumes. Many of these essays first appeared in *The New Farm* or *Organic Gardening* during Berry's period of association with Rodale Press in Emmaus, Pennsylvania. These essays nicely balance theory and practice, both reflecting Berry's criticism of prevailing assumptions of modern American agriculture and offering cultural alternatives to large-scale, mechanized single-crop farming. A more sensible economy of scale, according to Berry, would favor small, diversified farms such as those of the Amish and of others who practice alternative farming methods.

One must defend the small farm, Berry argues in his foreword, on more than economic terms. One must judge economic health according to the overall health and vitality of human and natural households:

> Like a household, [the small farm] is a human organism, and it has its origin in both nature and culture. Its justification is not only agricultural, but is a part of an ancient pattern of values, ideas, aspirations, attitudes, faiths, knowledges, and skills that propose and support the sound establishment of a people on the land. To defend the small farm is to defend a large part, and the best part, of our cultural inheritance.

Throughout the volume, Berry stresses the indivisibility of culture and agriculture: A culture's farming methods will invariably reflect the values and assumptions of that culture. The United States has tended to stress bigness, impersonality, mechanization, and exploitation of the land. For Berry, however, small is better. Emphasizing the interconnectedness of humans, land, climate, animals, and local culture, Berry values small-scale, labor-intensive agricultural techniques that allow the land to be used continuously while still maintaining its fertility and yield.

Berry cites a number of diverse examples of local, native farming cultures that are admirably suited to their local soil and climate conditions—those of the Indians of the Peruvian Andes, the Hopi of the southeastern Arizona desert, and the Amish farmers of Pennsylvania. In each of these diverse examples, the scale, balance, diversity and quality of the agriculture are appropriate for the local environment. Good farming, he emphasizes, involves communal techniques, craftsmanship, and artistry evolved over long periods of time, not merely drudgery. Each of these is a small-scale solution, markedly in contrast with the factory system of modern American agriculture.

In his essays, Berry stresses small-scale solutions for agricultural problems. He asks how much technology is enough and what is too much. He advocates a wise restraint in the use of large-scale farm machinery, preferring instead to work with hand tools or with horses at a slower, more deliberate pace. Berry praises the homestead, the garden, the small, intensively worked farm as best achieving the ideal of long-term sustainable yield. The best farms imitate nature in their variety. The organic farm, according to Sir Leslie Howard, is one whose structure is formed in imitation of a natural system. Soil fertility can best be studied by understanding the nutrient cycle of a woodland. In "Solving the Pattern," Berry lists fourteen critical standards for solving agricultural problems that are equally valid as general ecological principles.

In his title essay, "The Gift of Good Land," Berry attacks the traditional notion of land ownership, suggesting that the land is lent to humanity and brings with it the responsibility for good stewardship. He compares the Judeo-Christian heritage with the Buddhist doctrine of "right livelihood" or "right occupation," his purpose being to establish a biblical argument for ecological and agricultural responsibility.

To practice good stewardship, Berry argues, is to imitate God's love for his creation and to respect that creation as something which exists beyond human understanding and exclusively human purposes. To attempt to dominate and exploit the land is to commit exactly the same kind of sin of hubris or pride that was exemplified in Satan's rebellion against God's order. To calculate the success of modern agribusiness solely in economic terms, apart from the long-term health of the land and the human community, is to commit the equally serious sin of abstraction. By this, Berry means the reduction of a greater good, the continued vitality of the land, to a lesser good, short-term economic profit. The economics of agribusiness, Berry charges, ignores the complex disciplines necessary to traditional farming practices and ultimately destroys the land, the farming communities, and the culture on which they are based. He defends the small farm because its smallness is a prerequisite of diversity, which is in turn a prerequisite to the care and nurture of the world as God's creation.

Summary

"My work has been motivated," Wendell Berry has written, "by a desire to make myself responsibly at home in this world and in my native and chosen place." This theme of a responsible and self-sufficient regionalism, rooted in the skills and knowledge of Berry's native Kentucky farming communities, is at the heart of his vision. As a poet, novelist, and essayist, Berry has celebrated the virtues of farming as a vocation, of the dignity of marriage, and of the rich diversity of local communities. His moral vision is based on the enduring Jeffersonian ideal of a nation of independent yeoman farmers, and Berry is a wise and perceptive cultural critic. His works range beyond agriculture and regionalism to offer a commonsense prescription for restoring the wholeness and vitality of rural American communities.

Bibliography

Cornell, Robert. "*The Country of Marriage*: Wendell Berry's Personal Political Vision." *Southern Literary Review* 16 (Fall, 1983): 59-70.

Ditsky, John. "Wendell Berry: Homage to the Apple Tree." *Modern Poetry Studies* 2, no. 1 (1971): 7-15.

Hass, Robert. "Wendell Berry: Finding the Land." *Modern Poetry Studies* 2, no. 1 (1971): 16-38.

Hicks, Jack. "Wendell Berry's Husband to the World: *A Place on Earth*." *American Literature* 51 (May, 1979): 238-254.

Morgan, Speer. "Wendell Berry: A Fatal Singing." *Southern Review* 10 (October, 1974): 865-877.

Nibbelink, Herman. "Thoreau and Wendell Berry: Bachelor and Husband of Nature." *The South Atlantic Quarterly* 84 (Spring, 1985): 127-140.

Andrew J. Angyal

JOHN BERRYMAN

Born: McAlester, Oklahoma
October 25, 1914
Died: Minneapolis, Minnesota
January 7, 1972

Principal Literary Achievement

Berryman's *The Dream Songs* (1969) reconciles features of the long poem and the short lyric in an idiom which is tragicomic, classically formal, yet idiomatic.

Biography

John Berryman was born John Allyn Smith, Jr., on October 25, 1914, in McAlester, Oklahoma, the elder son of John Allyn Smith, Sr., and Martha Shaver Little Smith. The Smiths would have one other child, Robert Jefferson Smith, born September 1, 1919. Between 1914 and 1926, the Smith family moved about every two years to various Oklahoma farming communities, the elder Smith holding a series of banking positions. In 1924, a scandal involving the senior Smith's brother's theft of funds forced Berryman's father to resign from the First State Bank in Anadarko, Oklahoma. By 1925, Berryman's parents and grandmother had moved to Tampa, Florida; the boys remained in Oklahoma at a Roman Catholic boarding school, St. Joseph's Academy. Tempted by cheap land and quick profit, Berryman's father began to speculate in Florida real estate. By mid-1926, however, the land boom collapsed, Smith went bankrupt, and the entire family, including the boys (by this time recalled from Oklahoma), moved to Clearwater, Florida. It was there that they rented an apartment in a building owned by John Angus McAlpin Berryman.

The Smiths' marriage was by then all but ended. Smith, increasingly despondent over his business failures and his wife's obvious romantic involvement with their landlord, threatened suicide. On June 26, 1926, Smith was found shot dead outside their apartment, apparently a suicide. By September 8, 1926, his wife had married Berryman and had changed her own first and middle names to Jill Angel. She also changed her elder son's name to John Allyn McAlpin Berryman, though this was not done legally until 1936, when Berryman filed for a passport to study in England. Thus it was that at the age of twelve, the future poet had to abandon the name of his father and assume that of his mother's lover. His stepfather, whom he called "Uncle Angus," was a distant but never cruel man; even so, his father's apparent suicide

186

continued to affect Berryman throughout his life. It certainly contributed to his pre-occupation with death by suicide and foreshadowed his own manner of death.

After a generally unhappy stay at South Kent School, South Kent, Connecticut, Berryman had the good fortune to attend Columbia College, Columbia University, starting in 1932. It was there that he studied under Mark Van Doren. Van Doren, himself a poet as well as a scholar, encouraged Berryman to write verse, took him as a protégé, and was instrumental in helping him obtain the Euretta J. Kellett Scholarship for two years of study in England at Clare College, University of Cambridge. Berryman spent 1936 through 1938 at Clare College, pursuing his studies in the alternately brilliant, erratic, and lackadaisical way that typified his entire school career. The two most important events of this period of his life were his engagement (despite a previous commitment to American Jean Bennett) to Beryl Eaman, a young English actress (for whom he would write a verse play, *Cleopatra*, in 1937) and his winning of the Oldham Shakespeare Prize. Eaman would stay with the Berrymans in 1938 and early 1939, but her doubts, coupled with the onset of World War II, led to her breaking the engagement.

The war years were difficult for Berryman. His mother had separated from his stepfather. Though he had managed to place several poems with *The Southern Review* in 1938, he was without any work until the fall of 1939, when he managed (through Van Doren) to obtain an instructorship in English at Wayne University, Ann Arbor, Michigan. By December, however, he was having fainting spells, misdiagnosed as petit mal, a form of epilepsy. Things seemed better in the fall of 1940, but only for a short time. He obtained an instructorship at Harvard University and published some of his poems in *Five Young American Poets* (1940), but he was not generally liked by his Harvard colleagues because of his irascible temperament and his firm refusal to pursue doctoral studies. He did not endear himself to James Laughlin, publisher of the poetry anthology, when he objected to his work being published with other poets, despite the fact that the others were Elizabeth Bishop, Randall Jarrell, W. R. Moses, and George Marion O'Donnell.

Berryman's poor eyesight and medical history meant exemption from military service, but with the United States' involvement in the war, college classes were small. He married his first wife, Eileen Patricia Mulligan, in 1942, but Harvard did not renew his contract, so at the end of spring term in 1943 he was without a teaching post and had little hope of finding one. He accepted a temporary position teaching English and Latin at Iona Preparatory School in New Rochelle, New York, in the fall of 1943 but resigned three weeks after the term had begun to accept an instructorship in English at Princeton University.

Largely on the strength of his promise, for he had as yet published relatively little and nothing of a scholarly nature, Berryman obtained a two-year Rockefeller Foundation Research Fellowship in 1944 to prepare an edition of William Shakespeare's *King Lear* (1608). It was at this time that he first met the American poet Robert Lowell and Lowell's wife, author Jean Stafford. He never would complete his Shakespeare text, but the postwar years would bring a series of works which would dramatically illustrate Berryman's evolving style: *The Dispossessed* (1948), an anthology of verse that resembles the poetry of William Butler Yeats and Robert Frost; *Homage to Mistress Bradstreet* (1953), a long poem in which the poet attempts to seduce an unhappy and frustrated Anne Bradstreet (an American Puritan poet); and *77 Dream Songs* (1964), later supplemented, rearranged, and published as *The Dream Songs* (1969). This last is his masterwork, and it introduced "Henry," a Berryman persona, as its antihero.

Despite the steadily increasing fame he won through these works and the tenured position he held as Regents Professor of Humanities at the University of Minnesota, Minneapolis, Berryman's personal life grew ever more chaotic. His second marriage, to Elizabeth Ann Levine, the mother of his only son, Paul, lasted less than three years (from 1956 to 1959). His third marriage, in 1961, to Kathleen Donahue, was more stable than his second; his two daughters, Martha and Sarah Rebecca, were born in 1962 and 1971, but Berryman's drinking and despondency threatened even this relationship in the months before his death. Lukewarm critical reaction to *Love & Fame* (1970), which is a sober view of Berryman's pursuit of both as avenues to happiness, raised fears concerning his power to create verse. Though the critics had been kinder to *Berryman's Sonnets* (1967), those were twenty-year-old poems about a 1947 love affair.

Amid fears that his creative life was over, that his third marriage was failing, and that he was no longer effective as a teacher, Berryman closed the covenant that much of his poetry indicates he believed he had with his father. On a bitterly cold morning in Minneapolis, January 7, 1972, he leaped from the Washington Avenue Bridge, which connects the University of Minnesota's east and west campuses. His life thus ended as violently as had those of several poet colleagues he most admired: Hart Crane, Randall Jarrell, and Sylvia Plath.

Analysis

Berryman sought a distinctive poetic voice throughout his career. As a young man, he particularly admired Yeats's ability to make poetry intensely personal yet mythic. He also admired Frost as a distinctly American and non-academic poet who believed that what a poem implied was as important as what it literally expressed. Consequently, in the beginning of his career, Berryman was wary of T. S. Eliot's objective universal themes and characterizations. He also considered Eliot's use of learned allusions artificial. Neither was Berryman fond of Eliot's mentor Ezra Pound or "new poets" such as William Carlos Williams. He loved the gaudy imagery and eclecticism of Wallace Stevens.

Berryman would modify his negative positions considerably in the latter half of his career. Even late in his life, Berryman obliquely criticized Williams' understanding of the function of narrative and history in a typically outspoken interview published in the *Harvard Advocate*, but he also wrote a never-published, scholarly introduction to the poems of Pound, came to love Pound's *Hugh Selwyn Mauberley* (1920) and *Cantos* (1917-1970) as forerunners of his own *The Dream Songs*, and was himself admired by Pound as a new voice in American poetry. Berryman's contacts with Eliot became more amicable over the years as well. His intense dislike for Eliot's poetry when Berryman was a student at Cambridge was still apparent in 1953 when Berryman wrote that he considered *Homage to Mistress Bradstreet* a reaction to long poems as they were then written—a veiled thrust at Eliot's *The Waste Land* (1922) and Williams' *Paterson* (1946-1958). Berryman courted Eliot's approval in the late 1940's when both were residents at Princeton University, but it is noteworthy that Eliot disliked Berryman's introduction to the Berryman anthology as originally submitted to Faber & Faber, where Eliot held a directorship, and that Eliot rejected *77 Dream Songs* outright.

Clearly, Berryman identified most consistently with poets who were social outcasts, whose verse, like his own, was intensely personal and guardedly self-revelatory. He often began his literature courses with Walt Whitman's "Song of Myself" (1855, 1881). He had lifelong empathy with fellow suicide Hart Crane and the flamboyant style and way of life of drinking companion Dylan Thomas. He pitied but also admired Delmore Schwartz and Randall Jarrell, and he wished that he had met Sylvia Plath, whose life so closely resembled his own.

Berryman's early verse, written before and during World War II, is personal but derivative. An attentive reader will note echoes of Whitman, Frost, Pound, Eliot, and even Williams in *The Dispossessed*. The sonnets to Lise, written to a woman named Chris with whom Berryman had a love affair during the late 1940's while at Princeton University, are in the Petrarchan mode. They were published in the late 1960's, and in reprintings the name Chris appears instead of the Petrarchan echo (Lise for Laura). These poems are important in Berryman's oeuvre primarily because they show his turning toward specific personalities as well as actual locations and events. They also reveal something of the poet's chaotic life, his frantic and tawdry attempts to keep the affair secret, yet his decided attempt to couch every rendezvous in terms of high art. The Berryman persona also appears as seducer in *Homage to Mistress Bradstreet*. Berryman received guarded critical approval for this long poem. He took the American Puritan poet Anne Bradstreet as its subject, primarily because he considered her personal frustrations overwhelming and her poetry mediocre. In this sense, she represents the way Berryman saw his own life and art at the time. That he was having an affair with his own "Ann," the woman who would become his second wife, allows the poet's attempt at the seduction which frames the poem a personal level of meaning.

The Dream Songs, begun in 1955 and continued through 1968, represents the full realization of Berryman's style. Its 385 lyrics, which Berryman insisted should stand as a single poem, tell in disjointed narrative the life story of "Huffy Henry," a Berryman persona. Henry is an antihero, invariably thwarted by the circumstances of his life but inevitably rising to meet a new challenge, only to be struck down again. Berryman injects various details from both small and major incidents of his life, though a reader unacquainted with the poet's private life will miss many of the details. That Berryman successfully mixes various styles and achieves a distinctive tone which is simultaneously tragic and comic is a measure of the degree to which the poet had refined his style and altered his methods of composition.

The Dream Songs came to be a curse as well as a blessing for Berryman. It catapulted his verse to international attention, and fellow writers such as Saul Bellow, Adrienne Rich, and Ralph Ellison helped circulate the individual poems as they appeared. Berryman's old friend, publisher Robert Giroux, encouraged the poet at every turn, publishing *77 Dream Songs* as an interim text and promising publication of the larger collection once Berryman had determined the number and final arrangement of poems he wanted to include. The literary world realized that Berryman's most important work was imminent, and by 1966 even *The New Yorker*, which had repeatedly rejected most of Berryman's submissions, was accepting new dream songs as soon as they came from his pen. The Guggenheim Foundation provided two year-long grants, in 1966 and 1967, specifically to free Berryman from teaching and to hasten completion of *The Dream Songs*.

The problem was that Berryman had fallen so completely into the distinctive style of this verse that he literally became unable to write in any other manner. What is more, he became unable to stop writing. In the desperately manic way that characterized so much of his literary life, Berryman would telephone fellow writers in the early morning hours to read the poem he had just written. Ellison bore the brunt of many of these telephone calls, almost always for advice on the poems employing black dialect, but Bellow and Rich also had to render immediate critical opinions on matters of arrangement and choices for inclusion in the final edition. Berryman came to fear that he would never finish, so he arbitrarily closed the collection at 385 songs. His fear that he would never be able to write in other styles led him to rush his next two collections into print; the consensus of critical opinion holds that this was a mistake.

His Toy, His Dream, His Rest (1968) and *Love & Fame*, published two years later, represent Berryman's attempt to deal with larger, more serious subjects inappropriate to the format of *The Dream Songs*. Berryman's struggle with alcoholism was greatest at this time; despite his involvement with Alcoholics Anonymous, he never permanently conquered his addiction. Similarly, his return to Roman Catholicism, nominally the religion of his boyhood, was short-lived. General despondency over indifferent reaction to his last works, widespread student dissatisfaction with his teaching, and a third marriage nearing collapse because of his alcoholism likely hastened the suicide that he had feared would inevitably conclude his life.

THE DISPOSSESSED

First published: 1948
Type of work: Poetry

The best example of Berryman's early style, this volume's poems are solidly written and of good quality but derivative.

Many of the poems in *The Dispossessed* date from Berryman's student days. Their method of composition is conservative, betraying adaptations from Yeats, Frost, and Eliot. This is not to imply, however, that they stand outside Berryman's thematic canon. The title of the collection, followed by the dedication to his mother, imply the themes of estrangement and alienation which would become familiar elements in Berryman's later verse. The dedication ironically reveals Berryman's bitterness at never having known his father and, legally as well through a changed name, having effaced his father's memory. The poetry, as a collection, implies that, all attempts notwithstanding, no genuine rebirth is possible in the world of the 1930's and 1940's.

The opening poem, for example, "Winter Landscape," establishes the scene of a weary, frozen world in which "three men . . . in brown" return from the hunt and are at once frozen in time. Like the figures of John Keats's Grecian urn, they are unaware of "the evil waste of history/ outstretched." Some readers will recognize in Berryman's setting the details of Pieter Brueghel's painting *Hunters in the Snow* (1565), but the poet also allows the reader to see the men as Adolf Hitler's brownshirts. Human beings participate in the march of history, continuing the cycle from epoch to epoch, but history is forever on a demoralized and degraded course. Even worse, the actors in Berryman's human comedy have neither the consolations of art and civilization, which one finds in the gyre poems of Yeats, nor the power to act as interpreters of the cause of their malaise; no hidden spiritual life, Eliot's solution for the same problem, ever appears as an avenue of escape.

More telling is the resemblance of "Winter Landscape" to "The Return," a poem from Ezra Pound's early collection *Ripostes* (1912); Pound's poem was itself inspired by a poem of Henri de Régnier. It was written on the eve of World War I and is a prophecy of the ennui and exhaustion felt by hunters returned from the hunt. Berryman's poem was written immediately before the beginning of World War II. Like Pound, Berryman was experimenting with symbolism at the early stage of his career, and this variation, twice removed from Régnier's original, underscores Berryman's conviction, derived via Yeats, that Western civilization is doomed to repeat its mistakes in ever more degraded variation.

Both poems utilize the same setting, that of weary hunters returning in the snow. Pound's imagery is more overtly classical—the invincible hunters were "Gods of the wingèd shoe," recalling Hermes, the swift messenger. Berryman's image is that of the invincible Fascist brownshirts. A stanza drawn from each poem reveals quite clearly the degree of Pound's influence. Pound's second stanza reads:

> See, they return, one, and by one,
> With fear, as half-awakened;
> As if the snow should hesitate
> And murmur in the wind,
>   and half turn back;
> These were the "Wing'd-with-Awe,"
>   Inviolable.

Pound's stanza may be compared with the first stanza of Berryman:

> The three men coming down the winter hill
> In brown, with tall poles and a pack of hounds
> At heel, through the arrangement of the trees,
> Past the five figures at the burning straw,
> Returning cold and silent to their town.

Consequently, disfigurement and distortion are recurring images, particularly in the poems of the first part of the collection. "The Statue" of the volume's second poem is "tolerant through years of weather," and it cynically looks at passersby though it is never considered by those who glance at it. The person it commemorates is long dead, and no one knows or cares that it immortalizes someone named Humbolt. "A Point of Age" marks the start of a life's journey in a world where all the travelers are uncertain of their destination. "The Ball Poem," literally about a boy's lost ball, sets forth Berryman's epistemology of loss: that one can replace missing elements in life, but these replacements never duplicate what is gone. Berryman saw life as a series of losses, the first and most significant for him being the death of his father.

"Fare Well," written in December, 1946, represents Berryman's attempt to lay the ghost of his father to rest. The poem juxtaposes the mysterious rebirth imagery of Yeats (the phoenix, the tree of life, and fire) with the warm snow of Eliot's *The Waste Land*.

> O easy the phoenix in the tree of the heart,
> Each in its time, his twigs and spices fixes
> To make a last nest, and marvelously relaxes, —
> Out of the fire, weak peep . . .
> Father I fought for Mother, sleep where you sleep!
> I slip into the snowbed with no hurt
> Where warm will warm be warm enough to part
> Us. As I sink, I weep.

The poems of parts 2 through 4 continue these themes. "Canto Amor," a love song written when Berryman was thirty, expresses the poet's hope that his marriage will survive the uncertainties of the world. "The Lightning," which concludes part 4, reproduces the terza rima of "Canto Amor," the three-line rhymed-verse form of Dante's *La divina commedia* (c. 1320). The poet's sister-in-law, Marie Mabry, fears a violent lightning storm, but the poet sees the lightning as simply one manifestation of the violent chance of nature. The title poem of *The Dispossessed* ends part 5. Part of the poem dates from August 6, 1945, the day of the bombing of Hiroshima, Japan. The new dawn of the nuclear age is as lifeless as the winter landscape of the collection's opening poem. The child of the nuclear age is deformed and grotesque, a "faceless fellow."

HOMAGE TO MISTRESS BRADSTREET

First published: 1953
Type of work: Poem

A long poem that uses the figure of Anne Bradstreet to portray human temptation, guilt, grief, suffering, and pain.

It was irrelevant to Berryman whether or not the historical figure represented in his *Homage to Mistress Bradstreet* ever actually experienced the discontent described in the poem. The Bradstreet it describes is a montage of frustrations, temptations, and feelings of guilt, very much like those of the poet who created her. Though Berryman had written the poem's first stanza and several lines of the second in March, 1948, he set them aside for nearly five years until the tone of Saul Bellow's *The Adventures of Augie March* (1953) gave him inspiration for the idiom he sought. Using notes he had made on the historical Bradstreet during this hiatus, Berryman wrote fifty new stanzas during the first two months of 1953, completing the entire poem on March 22 of that year. He was fond of saying that he finished the poem five years to the day after he had started it.

Berryman had been fascinated with Bradstreet as early as 1937. He read her poems and letters to her husband, and examined as much historical detail as he could find about daily life in Puritan Massachusetts. Bradstreet's mediocrity as a poet, coupled with the severe moral code of the society in which she lived, predisposed him to see an affinity with his own circumstances. To a degree, then, she is a mask for Berryman, whose guilt for his marital infidelity was strong following the affair he described in the sonnets; however, she is also "Lise" herself and at least one other lover. By 1953, these distinctions had become relatively unimportant: Bradstreet had become every person who doubts or feels guilt, frustration, and estrangement.

Berryman considered both himself and Bradstreet to be poets in societies hostile to their art. He portrays her as rejecting both her husband and father and the Puritan deity which sanctions their view of life. Even so, Berryman knew that this was taking great liberties with the historical evidence available. The historical Bradstreet's letters portray her as a model of devotion to her husband; members of her family encouraged her writing of poetry and (without her knowledge) saw to the first publication of her poems. This is likely the reason Berryman chose to have his heroine's dilemma resemble that of the woman in the Scottish ballad "The Demon Lover." His Bradstreet also faces a demonic tempter, the male poet persona, another mask for Berryman himself. Such temptation, never acted upon but remaining wholly within the mind of the woman tempted, allows the poem to remain within the realm of historical possibility.

The structure of the poem is distinctive, though its stanza form resembles the eight-line configuration Yeats favored. The poet tempter's voice blends with Bradstreet's thoughts, and the tension is unremitting. Bradstreet mentally renounces family, faith, and life in Puritan Massachusetts; she desires to yield to her poet tempter, and realizes that in the very thought she has sinned. Even so, she does nothing overtly; to those who know her, she remains among the elect and is destined for salvation. That she lives for many years after the temptation, though she has privately succumbed, adds the burden of hypocrisy to guilt.

Homage to Mistress Bradstreet represents the poet's final departure from the Poundian symbolism of his earlier verse. He sought in its movements from formal rhetoric to low idiom a means of personalization that would yet allow him to mask the individual he personified. The result allows his Bradstreet to function simultaneously as unfulfilled wife, unfulfilled poet, and vicarious lover who sins in thought though not in deed. She is, therefore, a more particularized creation than Eliot's J. Alfred Prufrock; she is associated with the strictures of her Puritanism yet is also a reflection of the same moral scruples in which Berryman was reared. Berryman's Bradstreet is, like her creator, the domesticated but sorely tempted poet. She is heroic because, unlike her creator, she never succumbs to her temptation; yet, because she never actually experiences forbidden love, she never rises above mediocrity. Her tragedy is that she bears all the burdens but reaps none of the artistic rewards of her sin. She remains, like Berryman himself, tied to her unhappy domestic conventions in an environment hostile to creativity.

Berryman's marriages and love affairs became, to his own mind at least, a means of pursuing fame through love. At the latter stage of his career he admitted this openly, but in the early 1950's he still required a mask. The Bradstreet poem allowed him to explore his personal situation from a nominally feminine point of view. His discussions with William Carlos Williams, a personal friend with whom he largely disagreed on matters poetic, clearly show his amusement at Williams' belief that historical references needed to be scrupulously faithful to documented facts. Though Berryman knew Bradstreet's background and the history of American Puritanism in astonishing detail, he believed that his verse portrait need only be consonant with what might have been.

Berryman intended *Homage to Mistress Bradstreet* as his response to the theological underpinnings of Eliot's long poems, particularly *The Waste Land*. He also objected to the anonymity of Eliot's characterizations, what Eliot would have considered correlative objectivity. Aiming for a tone never before produced in long poetry, Berryman sought possible historicity, while avoiding Williams' strict understanding of the historical, such as one finds in *Paterson*. Though she is sorely tempted and guilty in her own eyes, Berryman clearly considers his Bradstreet a heroine, if only because she has endured life.

BERRYMAN'S SONNETS

First Published: 1967
Type of work: Poetry

These poems constitute an important shift in Berryman's style, away from a rhetorical mode and toward a sustained nervous idiom.

Berryman's Sonnets, a cycle that traces a five-month love affair that began in April, 1947, contains poems that were written in 1947 while Berryman was teaching at Princeton University. The cycle was not published until 1966, primarily because of its explicit references to persons, places, and events of that time. The woman who is its subject was called "Lise" in the first printing of the work, perhaps a Berryman equivalent for the "Laura" of Petrarch's sonnets. In reprintings which followed upon the success of *The Dream Songs*, however, Berryman restored his subject's actual name and changed the title of the collection to *Sonnets to Chris*.

In isolation from Berryman's other works the cycle is not impressive; it follows the predictable pattern of meeting, anticipation, love, and loss that one finds in Petrarch. What makes it important is Berryman's discovery of the "nervous idiom" he would develop in *Homage to Mistress Bradstreet* and, still more successfully, in *The Dream Songs*. Berryman uses this technique to describe the poet's increasingly agitated state of mind as his mistress first yields, then rejects her lover's advances, and ultimately abandons him. Berryman's sonnets mark the poet's movement toward the greater use of idiom and what he had called as early as 1934 "a more passionate syntax." They betray a young poet still searching for his voice and indicate a veering away from Poundian symbolism. Berryman clearly used the discipline that the sonnet form imposed as a means of tempering his tendency to expand relentlessly and to control the jarring effects of the idiom he was coming to prefer. He candidly admits as much in sonnet 66 when he "prods our English" to "cough me up a word" that will "justify/ My darling fondle."

Readers of *The Dream Songs* will recognize in the sonnets several characteristics of Berryman's fully realized style. First, there appears a fascination with the method of composition. Language becomes a lexicon or thesaurus from which the poet, in vestigial homage to Pound, must select *le mot juste* ("the precise word"). The French phrase, which Pound repeatedly used to describe his own process of composition, becomes anglicized in Berryman's sonnet as "justify." Then too, the process by which the proper word arrives is fundamentally unattractive, fitful, and spasmodic; in this case, the language expectorates it. Clever as it is, the imagery is fundamentally ugly, with the lover's word becoming so much phlegm. On the other hand, the poet is aware that the adulterous meetings the sonnets commemorate are also ugly. Thus, in this roundabout way, the poet justifies his "darling fondle."

Berryman's real fascination with Lise/Chris was perhaps the new direction in which it took his poetry. Even as the relationship destroyed his marriage, it gave rise to new opportunities to explore the tormented mind of the lover. Lise/Chris was no Dantean Beatrice, nor was she a Petrarchan Laura. The Berryman anima inspires lust and infidelity. In the final analysis, Lise/Chris provides a poet whose greatest fear is creative infertility with the opportunity to write. If there were any doubts that the process of composition underpins the entire cycle, they are dispelled by sonnet 117, the last in the collection. As fall turns to winter and the attraction, too, begins to chill, the poet waits in the grove—with more than a hundred sonnets in his pocket—for his mistress to appear. When "my lady came not/ . . . I sat down & wrote."

As in a classical sonnet sequence, development of the love relationship is keyed to the changing seasons: the beginnings in spring, with reference to "all the mild days of middle March"; an awareness of death, even at the affair's zenith in July (sonnet 65); bitterness in the aftermath of dying love (sonnet 71), written in September. The concluding poems, written in 1966 specifically for publication, note the acute, unhappy aftermath of the experience but settle upon another beginning, "free . . . of the fire of this sin" (sonnet 111).

THE DREAM SONGS

First published: 1969
Type of work: Poetry

The life, misfortunes, and utter optimism of Henry, Berryman's most original creation, are presented.

The Dream Songs, a work that Berryman always maintained is one poem in 385 parts, is the poet's tragicomic view of his chaotic existence. Its distinguishing features are its humor and its idiom, both portrayed by Henry, the Berryman "I and not I" of all the songs (Berryman identified Henry this way in the *Harvard Advocate* interview). Berryman chose the name Henry precisely because he did not like it, which allows Henry's occasional identification as "Henry Pussycat," the compliant one on whom the world unloads all its woes, as well as "Huffy Henry," who sulks, is arrogant, but ultimately accepts every calamity. The only other character in *The Dream Songs* is "Mr. Bones," who appears as minstrel interlocutor in the black dialect poems. All the particulars of the individual songs refer to specific events in Berryman's life. Often these are obscure or seem relatively unimportant in themselves—a film he sees, the weather, a trip to Ireland—but even these neutral or happy events reveal Henry's predisposition to sadness and depression. Significant events, such as the birth of a child or the death of a friend, elicit the same serious doubts and questions.

Berryman sought to represent in modern form many of the elements one finds in classical heroic epic. For this reason, *The Dream Songs* presents skewed time sequences and a heroic prospectus that is the tragicomic counterpart of the typical mythic hero. For example, Henry dies in section 4, approximately a quarter of the way into the songs; the entire section, written as fourteen posthumous poems (numbers 78 through 91), tells of his struggle toward heroic resurrection. Henry being what he is, he naturally never achieves a classical heroic apotheosis; if anything, his despair appears more pronounced in the episodes that follow. The best he manages, though he does so with relative consistency, is a small spark of hope, most often in the poems which concern his daughter's birth and growth.

The poems written in black minstrel dialect, which employ jazzlike rhythms and sometimes a minstrel show format with Mr. Bones as interlocutor, are especially effective in maintaining the tragicomic tone. Bones is not only the classic minstrel show figure, he is also a tragicomic persona of death and reveals the bitterly comic features of life, as in the final lines of song 50:

> —Mr. Bones, your troubles give me vertigo,
> & backache. Somehow, when I make your scene,
> I cave to feel as if
>
> de roses of dawns & pearls of dusks, made up
> by some ol' writer-man, got right forgot
> & the greennesses of ours.
> Springwater grow so thick it gonna clot
> and the pleasing ladies cease. I figure, yup,
> you is bad powers.

Though Berryman's break with symbolism was complete by the time he began composition of *The Dream Songs*, he retained to the end of his career the conviction (shared by Robert Browning, another poet he admired) that life is action and that the best verse portrays not character but character in action. For this reason, Berryman tells his readers relatively little about Henry as a person. It is enough that his subject bears a name the poet dislikes intensely. It is equally revealing that Henry lives his life on a much more mundane level than Pound's own mask, Hugh Selwyn Mauberley. Mauberley, like Pound, is Ulysses, a heroic figure who relentlessly combats Philistinism in all its forms. Henry, on the other hand, is a lovable nonentity who is usually defeated before he begins. The fact that neither character is an accurate self-portrait of its creator is unimportant.

Berryman saw the writing of poetry as a practical matter—as a process whose primary purpose was to dispel fear. For him, as for Stephen Crane, the subject of a Berryman biographical study, verse was an "anti-spell," a kind of word magic. Berryman's fears, like those of Crane, were essentially three in number: abandonment, uncertainty, and death. This view of poetry as ritual is a consistent element in Berryman's development. It explains his fascination from boyhood with the Roman Catholic liturgy, his admiration for Yeats's verse plays, and his relentless pursuit of his created persona, Henry.

As happened with almost everything Berryman did, *The Dream Songs* became an obsession, so much so that he feared he would never again be able to return to writing more conventional forms of poetry. His fears are understandable, since there are clearly poetic subjects which do not yield to a tragicomic mode. Also, Berryman came to realize the limitations of Henry as a recurring presence in his work. It was largely for this reason that Berryman wrote *Love & Fame*, which details his personal search for what he considered the only rewards of life, and *Delusions, Etc. of John Berryman* (1972), whose first section is structured according to the hours of the Roman Catholic liturgical office. This last work is his most overtly spiritual, and it coincides with his return to Roman Catholicism in the year before his death.

Summary

Berryman sought to achieve a distinctly American idiomatic style which, nevertheless, maintained the structures of classical verse forms. He moved toward this goal steadily in the years following World War II, and by the early 1950's he believed that American rather than British poets constituted the last great hope for poetry written in English. The disorder of his personal life inspired the themes of his poems, but it never affected their craftsmanship. Berryman came from a different tradition from that of academic poets such as Eliot or W. H. Auden; he was an irascible maverick from birth to death, a genius who was at once pitiable and admirable.

Bibliography

Arpin, Gary Q., ed. *John Berryman: A Reference Guide*. Boston: G. K. Hall, 1976.
Haffenden, John. *John Berryman: A Critical Commentary*. New York: New York University Press, 1980.
—————. *The Life of John Berryman*. Boston: Routledge & Kegan Paul, 1982.
Halliday, E. M. *John Berryman and the Thirties*. Amherst: University of Massachusetts Press, 1987.
Kelly, Richard J., ed. *John Berryman: A Checklist*. Metuchen, N.J.: Scarecrow Press, 1972.
Linebarger, J. M. *John Berryman*. New York: Twayne, 1974.
Mariani, Paul. *Dream Song: The Life of John Berryman*. New York: William Morrow, 1990.
Stefanik, Ernest C., Jr., ed. *John Berryman: A Descriptive Bibliography*. Pittsburgh: University of Pittsburgh Press, 1974.
Thomas, Harry, ed. *Berryman's Understanding: Reflections on the Poetry of John Berryman*. Boston: Northeastern University Press, 1988.
Thornbury, Charles, ed. *John Berryman: Collected Poems, 1937-1971*. New York: Farrar, Straus & Giroux, 1989.

Robert J. Forman

AMBROSE BIERCE

Born: Horse Cave Creek, Meigs County, Ohio
June 24, 1842
Died: Mexico
1914 (?)

Principal Literary Achievement

One of American literature's most overlooked writers, Bierce has earned limited recognition for a small number of bizarre and much anthologized short stories, many of which are set against the backdrop of the Civil War.

Biography

Ambrose Bierce was born in Horse Cave Creek, in Meigs County, Ohio, on June 24, 1842, to Laura and Marcus Aurelius Bierce. When Bierce was four years old, the family moved to northern Indiana, and it was there that the writer grew up. He inherited an interest in books from his father and was instructed in religion by his mother.

A career in journalism and an involvement and interest in things military began early for Bierce. He left home at fifteen and worked as a printer's devil for two years for a local newspaper. At seventeen he entered the Kentucky Military Institute. Shortly after he left the institute, the Civil War broke out, and Bierce was one of the first to enlist in the Ninth Regiment of the Indiana Volunteers, which he served off and on for three years, during which time he received numerous citations for bravery, was wounded in the head, and rose to the rank of first lieutenant.

After being discharged, Bierce tracked down confiscated Confederate cotton for the federal government and then accompanied his former commander, General W. B. Hazen, a hot-headed leader whom he admired, on a mapping expedition to the West. It was on this trip that Bierce settled in San Francisco, where he was able to begin his writing career in earnest. In 1868 he took a job with a newspaper called the *News-Letter*, for which he wrote a column entitled "Town Crier," in which he employed satire and wit to expose and attack both public figures and institutions he deemed guilty of hypocrisy. The column was a rousing local success.

Bierce married Molly Day in 1871, and a honeymoon trip to Europe (courtesy of Molly's father) took the writer to London, where he went to work for Tom Hood's *Fun* and for *Figaro*, writing under the pen name Dod Grile. He also published three collections of columns, sketches, and fiction under this name while in London: *The Fiend's Delight* (1872), *Nuggets and Dust Panned Out in California* (1872), and

Cobwebs from an Empty Skull (1874). The cynicism displayed in the pieces which make up these books and the articles he wrote for the London papers earned the writer the nickname "Bitter Bierce."

Bierce returned reluctantly to San Francisco in 1877 and wrote for and edited various newspapers over the next nine years, all the while producing articles that enhanced his reputation as a witty, even cruel social satirist. During this period he became the mentor of several aspiring writers and put together a collection of pessimistic and satirical definitions which he entitled "The Devil's Dictionary." In 1886, he went to work for the San Francisco *Examiner*. His marriage dissolved in 1888.

The high point of Bierce's career in terms of his fiction writing came in 1891 with the publication of *Tales of Soldiers and Civilians* (subsequently altered and published under the title *In the Midst of Life* in 1898). It is the bizarre, even supernatural, violent, and cruelly ironic stories of this collection which have earned for Bierce his place, limited as it is, in American literature; the stories, much to the author's chagrin, inspired comparisons with those of Edgar Allan Poe. Though captivating reading, they did not fit into the mold of the realist, local-color literature of the time.

Other creative collections followed (*Black Beetles in Amber*, a book of satirical poems, in 1892, and *Can Such Things Be?*, a varied collection of stories, in 1893), but Bierce continued his journalistic writing, in part because he enjoyed it and in part because his creative work did not win the national attention he believed he deserved. Bierce moved to Washington, D.C., in 1896. Between 1896 and 1913, he wrote for the *Examiner* and later for the magazine *Cosmopolitan* while assembling the various volumes of his collected works. During this period as well, his "The Devil's Dictionary" was published under the title *The Cynic's Word Book* (1906).

In 1913, Bierce left Washington, D.C., and headed to Mexico, where he planned to observe the Mexican Revolution before moving on to Europe. He attached himself to Pancho Villa's revolutionary army and, in December of 1913, sent a letter from Chihuahua, Mexico, concerning his experiences with Villa's company. By most accounts, this letter was the last that anyone ever heard of the American writer. A number of obituaries appeared over the years, all providing different details concerning the author's demise. It is not certain, however, when, where, or how Bierce died.

Analysis

Ambrose Bierce wrote almost all of his fiction during the height of the realist movement of American literature. Bierce, however, was emphatically nonrealist, rejecting virtually all tenets of the movement, particularly that concerning the use of "local color." Bierce believed that fiction, in the tradition of great literature, should make use of and engage the imagination rather than merely attempt to paint a detailed picture of contemporary reality. It is precisely this belief and the exercise of it in his works that placed Bierce outside the mainstream of American literature during his lifetime. It is also precisely this belief which makes his stories seem ahead of their time and which makes them so much more appealing to the twentieth century, post-Sigmund Freud, reader than they were to late nineteenth century readers.

The majority of Bierce's stories are intense, detailed, and objectively told; they are sharply focused narratives which present protagonists faced with a psychologically challenging situation. Bierce penetrates the inner world of his characters and often places them in a macabre, even supernatural, and often cruelly ironic world (frequently set against the backdrop of the Civil War) both reminiscent of Edgar Allan Poe and anticipating a whole host of twentieth century writers, from Franz Kakfa to Jorge Luis Borges. At their best, the stories both captivate and surprise the entranced reader. At their worst, they are marred by coincidences so improbable that even the reader capable of the most profound suspension of disbelief finds them impossible to accept, even within the context of their fictional world.

No collection of Bierce's stories so vividly displays both the strengths and the weaknesses of the author's fiction (often within the same story) as does *Tales of Soldiers and Civilians* (or *In the Midst of Life*, as it is more commonly known). "An Occurrence at Owl Creek Bridge" and "Chickamauga" are included in this collection, as are "The Affair at Coulter's Notch," in which a Civil War artillery captain fires, unknowingly, on his own plantation, "The Man and the Snake," in which a man dies of fright of what turns out to be a stuffed snake with shoe buttons for eyes, and "The Suitable Surroundings," in which a man dies after reading a ghost story in a haunted house.

Beyond fiction, Bierce's literary writings, from essays to poetry, are characterized by the pessimism, cynicism, and wit for which Bierce the journalist was more known than was Bierce the short story writer. It is his stories, however, particularly the much-anthologized "An Occurrence at Owl Creek Bridge" and, to a lesser degree, "Chickamauga," which have earned for Bierce his place in the history of American literature.

AN OCCURRENCE AT OWL CREEK BRIDGE

First published: 1891
Type of work: Short story

During the Civil War, a Confederate spy is about to be hanged; he seems to escape, but his escape is only a dream.

"An Occurrence at Owl Creek Bridge" is by far Bierce's most widely read story, and it may also be his best. It focuses on Peyton Farquhar, a Southern planter and part-time Confederate conspirator, who, as the story opens, is about to be hanged on the Owl Creek bridge for having attempted to burn it. As Farquhar is being hanged, the reader is told, the rope breaks and he plunges alive into the water below. The rest of the story recounts his escape down the creek and then through the forest toward his home. Just as he reaches his house, where his wife awaits him, he feels a sharp blow to the back of his neck. In reality, he is not home at all: He hangs dead, of a broken neck, beneath the Owl Creek bridge. The rope has not, in fact, broken. Farquhar's escape has been only a momentary illusion.

What makes this plot so successful, as it lures the reader into the story, and what makes the whole story so captivating, is the technical brilliance of the narration. Bierce begins the story, for example, with a very objective, unadorned, strikingly dispassionate, and minutely detailed description of both the soldiers and Farquhar on the bridge as the former prepare for the latter's execution. The objectivity of the prose lends an official air to the narrative, almost as though it were not a piece of fiction at all but a military report. This objectivity combines with the detail with which the scene is set, including everything from an explanation of the various postures of the soldiers to the exaggerated ticking of the prisoner's watch, to lend a profound degree of realism to the story. The reader is thus led to believe from the beginning of the story that what is being told is minutely accurate.

Once Farquhar is in the water, the tone is far less dispassionate, however, as the narrator enters the head of the fleeing prisoner, focusing on Farquhar's reactions both to the soldiers who pursue him and to the task of escape. Details abound here as well, though, ironically, it is through these details that the reader is provided with hints (extremely subtle ones, almost certainly imperceptible to the first-time reader) that Farquhar's escape is but a dream and not real at all. Farquhar's senses as he escapes, for example, are heightened beyond those of a normal human being, as he can even see the insects on each leaf of the trees on the creek bank from his position in the water. Later, Bierce's description of the forest as Farquhar heads homeward becomes dreamlike. The reader is told that the road Farquhar takes "was as wide and straight as a city street, yet it seemed untraveled." Elsewhere, the narrator reports that the forest "on either side was full of singular noises, among which— once, twice, and again—he distinctly heard whispers in an unknown tongue." As Farquhar gets closer to home, he feels pain and swelling in his neck. While much of this description may be attributed to a prisoner actually fleeing from his near execution by hanging, some of it is plainly nonrealistic in nature. The reader thus has the information necessary to decipher the story but is in all likelihood unable to do so, lured into Farquhar's compelling tale of flight.

Another element of the story's presentation that merits mention is its structure. Bierce divides the story into three numbered sections, the content and division of which serve to intrigue the reader. The first section describes the setting of the execution right up to the point when the plank below Farquhar's feet is removed. The second section abruptly shifts to background information on Farquhar and how he came to commit the act for which he is being executed. The narrator reveals that a Confederate soldier had told Farquhar of the vulnerability of the bridge, thus planting the seed for Farquhar's action. The last line of the section reveals that the Confederate soldier was in fact a Federal scout. The third and final section picks up where the first section left off, with Farquhar apparently plunging into the water, and it concludes with the abrupt and surprising ending.

"An Occurrence at Owl Creek Bridge" is, in both content and presentation, a tour de force, a story that lures, captivates, and surprises its reader. It is a perfect Biercean story in that it is an intense and detailed narrative that mixes both real and unreal and ends in violent death and cruel irony. Whether Bierce is a master of the short story genre is debatable. This story, however, is undoubtedly a master work.

CHICKAMAUGA

First published: 1891
Type of work: Short story

During the Civil War, a small boy plays at war, gets lost in the woods, falls asleep, and awakens to a macabre and horrifying reality.

Like "An Occurrence at Owl Creek Bridge," "Chickamauga" possesses classic Biercean features, including the violence of war and a bizarre version of reality. The chief difference in this story, however, is that the bizarre reality, for all its appearance as such, is no dream; it is all too real.

The story tells of a small boy, who, with toy wooden sword in hand, wanders off into the woods to fight invisible foes, just as his ancestors have battled real ones. The boy strays too far and becomes lost. Finally, he lies down to rest and sleeps for several hours. Soon after he awakes, he is joined by hundreds of wounded and dying soldiers making their way in macabre fashion through the twilight near where the boy lies. Rather than being frightened by them, he is entertained. He even tries to play with them and eventually, sword in hand, takes a position in front of the group and "leads" them. Soon he and the soldiers come upon a fire. He then recognizes the buildings of his own plantation and runs in search of his mother, whom he finds, her

white face turned upward, the hands thrown out and clutched full of grass, the clothing deranged, the long dark hair in tangles and full of clotted blood. The greater part of the forehead was torn away, and from the jagged hole the brain protruded, overflowing the temple, a frothy mass of gray, crowned with clusters of crimson bubbles—the work of a shell.

The child attempts to scream, but it is revealed that he is a deaf mute, a fact which explains how the soldiers have managed to lay waste to his family's plantation, fight throughout the area where he lay, and begin their retreat, all while he slept.

The most intriguing aspects of "Chickamauga" concern the bizarre world it creates and the fact that this bizarre world is not illusion but reality. Ironically, the story begins almost as a story for children, as the narrator tells of the boy's innocent foray against make-believe enemies. When the boy does encounter a real "foe"—a rabbit—he begins to cry and flees. The innocence which pervades this section, however, is accompanied by a dark, or at least more serious, underside, as both the boy's motivation in his play and his actions are described in military terms, if only in mock fashion. Once the boy awakens, however, the story becomes dreamlike—or, more accurately put, nightmarelike—as the hundreds of wounded soldiers stumble their way through the "ghostly mist." Even more bizarre is the playful manner with which the boy regards the soldiers. The reader is even told that the boy

> laughed as he watched them. But on and ever on they crept, these maimed and bleeding men, as heedless as he of the dramatic contrast between his laughter and their own ghastly gravity.

The chief irony in all of this is that as bizarre as the reality painted by the narrator is, it is indeed reality. This is particularly surprising to the reader familiar with "An Occurence at Owl Creek Bridge." Certainly the reader of that story would expect the child to awaken or in some other way reveal that he has only dreamt the horrifying scenes described by the narrator, but the dreamlike scenes are worse than any nightmare because they are real. It is an interesting irony, and almost certainly one that Bierce, the staunch opponent of realism, appreciated, that one of his most bizarre stories, in spite of its apparent nonrealist qualities, turns out to be one of his most coldly realistic tales.

Summary

Ambrose Bierce's fiction never earned the fame that he believed he deserved. A nonrealist writing during the realist movement, he wrote in the shadows of more famous and more mainstream writers, such as Mark Twain and William Dean Howells. The lack of fame accorded Bierce, however, in no way detracts from the quality of his stories, some of which have appeared in numerous anthologies. While it is quite easy to find writers in American literature more celebrated than Bierce, it is difficult to find stories that can captivate and surprise the reader more than those of Bierce, whose works will be more appreciated, particularly for their portent of the nonrealist, psychological fiction of the twentieth century, as more readers discover this overlooked writer.

Bibliography

Davidson, Cathy N., ed. *Critial Essays on Ambrose Bierce.* Boston: G. K. Hall, 1982.

Grattan, C. Hartley. *Bitter Bierce: A Mystery of American Letters.* Garden City, N.Y.: Doubleday, 1929.

Grenander, M. E. *Ambrose Bierce.* New York: Twayne, 1971.

Wiggins, Robert A. *Ambrose Bierce.* University of Minnesota Pamphlets on American Writers, 37. Minneapolis: University of Minnesota Press, 1964.

Woodruff, Stuart C. *The Short Stories of Ambrose Bierce: A Study in Polarity.* Pittsburgh: University of Pittsburgh Press, 1964.

Keith H. Brower

ELIZABETH BISHOP

Born: Worcester, Massachusetts
February 8, 1911
Died: Boston, Massachusetts
October 6, 1979

Principal Literary Achievement

Highly praised for a small output of carefully crafted poems, Bishop is known as an accessible modern poet with an eye for detail.

Biography

Elizabeth Bishop was born in Worcester, Massachusetts, the daughter of Thomas and Gertrude Bulmer Bishop. Both of her parents were of Canadian heritage, but her paternal grandfather had left Prince Edward Island to establish a well-known building firm in Worcester that was responsible for such landmark buildings as the Boston Public Library and Museum of Fine Arts.

Her father died a few months after her birth, and as a result of this her mother suffered a breakdown and was treated in a sanatorium in Boston. In 1916, her mother returned to Canada for further treatment in proximity to her family, but the result was another breakdown that required her incarceration in a mental hospital in Nova Scotia, where she remained until her death in 1934. Effectively an orphan, therefore, Elizabeth passed her early childhood with her mother's family in Great Village, Nova Scotia; some of her poems reflect memories of this time.

At the age of six, she was taken to live with her paternal grandparents in Worcester. Some critics have suggested that Elizabeth sensed the move as something like an expulsion from paradise and that images of simplicity and family affection such as she had known in Great Village continued all of her life to represent life's highest good. In Worcester she began to be frequently ill, suffering again from the bronchitis she had contracted in Great Village, to which were added asthma and a number of other diseases. In order to give her happier surroundings, her grandfather arranged for her to live with her mother's sister in Boston. From the age of eight, she began to read poetry and fairy tales; she has mentioned Walt Whitman and Gerard Manley Hopkins as early poetic favorites.

She entered boarding school at the age of sixteen, at the Walnut Hill School in Nantick. There she read the works of William Shakespeare and the English Romantic poets. She entered Vassar College with the intention of studying music, but later

she told an interviewer that she was so terrified by the thought of recitals that she gave up the idea. In college she founded a literary review, called *Con Spirito*, with other literary-minded students, among them Mary McCarthy and Eleanor Clark, both of them subsequently well-known novelists. Her first poems appeared there and later in the *Vassar Review*; many of these appear in the standard volume of Bishop's life work, *The Complete Poems, 1927-1979* (1983).

The greatest poetic mentor of Bishop's early years was Marianne Moore, who helped to get some of her poems published in an anthology called *Trial Balances* (1935). Bishop's first volume was *North & South* (1946) which was chosen for the Houghton Mifflin Poetry Award and which includes her most anthologized single poem, "The Fish." In 1949 Bishop moved to Washington, D.C., in order to accept the post of poetry consultant to the Library of Congress. It was then that she visited the poet Ezra Pound, incarcerated in St. Elizabeths Hospital; the result of this was the poem "Visits to St. Elizabeths." Further awards came soon after, including the American Academy of Arts and Letters Award in 1950 and the Lucy Martin Donnelly Fellowship from Bryn Mawr College in 1951.

With the money from her prizes, Bishop set out for a trip to Brazil, where allergic attacks forced her to stay for a number of months. Once cured, she decided to stay on and, in fact, lived in Brazil for most of the rest of her life, returning to the United States only some years before her death. In 1955 she published her next book, which included *North & South*, by then out of print, as well as her newer poems; the volume was entitled *North & South—A Cold Spring*. Among the new poems was the widely acclaimed "In the Fishhouses." Much of her subsequent work, until the mid-1970's, touched upon her life in Brazil, including the volume *Questions of Travel* (1965). This was followed, in 1976, by *Geography III*. The prematurely titled *The Complete Poems* of 1969 won the National Book Award, and *Geography III* won a National Book Critics Circle Award. Bishop was the recipient of honorary degrees from Rutgers University and Brown University. She died of a cerebral aneurism in Boston in 1979.

Analysis

Elizabeth Bishop held a unique place in American poetry during her lifetime, and after her death she has come to seem one of the few truly durable and original voices of twentieth century poetry. An accessible voice in a period of frequently puzzling poets, Bishop's style was marked by precision and clarity, so that many critics have spoken of her work as a logical development of Imagism, the short-lived school of precise observation and clipped phrases of Ezra Pound and F. S. Flint in the early years of the century. The single most frequently evoked model, however, is Marianne Moore, with whom Bishop was friends, and whom she addressed directly in one of her poems ("Invitation to Miss Marianne Moore," in *A Cold Spring*). Certainly the link between the two comes readily to mind, not only because of the biographical connection between the two poets, but also because of Moore's equally effective choice of precise words to evoke unitary states of things. Recently, however, some critics have challenged this linking.

The particular qualities of her poetry aside, it certainly added to Bishop's mystique that during the period of her greatest fame she lived in Brazil and was rarely seen in the United States. Another factor contributing to her reputation, perhaps paradoxically, was the fact that she wrote relatively little: Her complete poems are contained in a single volume, like those of T. S. Eliot, and can conceivably be read through in a single sitting. In the glut of print in the modern world, the very parsimony of her production came to seem a virtue, as did her insistence on continual revision of the poems.

The impression that an initial reading of her poetry makes is certainly that of the polished surface. Her words are carefully chosen, her evocations of the physical world precise, ranging from the description of scales on the floor of the fish house ("At the Fish Houses") to the sensations of a child reading *National Geographic* in a dentist's waiting room ("In the Waiting Room," from *Geography III*). Her poems lack an easy moral; critics tend to agree that they avoid coming to overall, or perhaps overly pat, answers about the great themes of human existence. The reader must tease out the meaning, if indeed there is such, from under the shining surface.

As a result, some critics have found that her poetry lacks substance, an accusation more frequent with respect to her earlier, pre-Brazil poetry (which nevertheless contains many of her most celebrated single works). It is a refusal to disclose secrets, if secrets there be, that the reader senses in these early poems, or an unwillingness on the part of the author to get involved with the world. This changed to some degree when Bishop began to write about Brazil, from whose culture she evidently felt sufficient distance to allow herself to characterize it from the outside, as she was not able to do with North American culture. From the poems about Brazil, as a result, a number of more elemental, slightly less intellectualized human themes emerge, longing for other climes and satisfaction with daily living among them.

A number of critics have therefore seen the theme of her poetry taken as a whole to be that of involvement or noninvolvement with the world. By and large, the earlier poems are perceived as remaining within the bounds of the self, and the later poetry as being willing to step outside of these bounds. Such easy dichotomies are not satisfactory, however, as there are early poems which clearly do take stands on human issues and later ones which do not seem to do so at all.

Critical stances such as these underline the curiously negative quality of most attempts to place Bishop in a larger context, whereby what she does not do becomes more important than what she does. Many social critics understand the twentieth century to be a time when previously hard and fast moral and social values were questioned, and they see relativity as the rule not only in physics but also in the world at large. Such critics praise Bishop precisely for having had the taste and sensitivity to avoid giving easy answers. In short, they praise Bishop for not committing certain faults or (as a variation) see the slight air of authorial absence in her poems as itself an indication of the built-in alienation or fragmentation of modern thought. One critic has suggested that she successfully subverts the now outmoded heroic/masculine vision of the hero, substituting for it a more rational female version. Other critics, more accustomed to poems that contain what has been called "the reek of the human," fault her poems for seeming to have been written by a "lady" (as well as a woman)—they seem too gentrified, too rarefied. What is certain is that her works avoid vulgarity of surface and vulgarity of message as well, itself an accomplishment of no mean measure.

THE FISH

First published: 1946
Type of work: Poem

The narrator catches an old fish that he or she subsequently lets go.

"The Fish" is Bishop's most anthologized poem, perhaps in part because it echoes a work widely familiar to concertgoers, the nineteenth century German poem called "The Trout" that Franz Schubert set to music in his celebrated song, which in turn provided the theme for his equally well-known "Trout" quintet. These echoes aside, however, the work is popular because it avoids the surrealism that makes puzzling some of the other poems published in Bishop's first collection. It is devoted in large part to a description of a fish that the narrator catches and, in the last line, lets go. The moral suggested is somewhat closer to the surface than is usual for Bishop; in addition, the slight but undeniable sententiousness of the narrator may make it easier for the reader to identify with him or her than with the less characterized and virtually invisible narrators of many of her other poems.

The work opens with a simple statement: The narrator has "caught a tremendous fish." The fish immediately comes to seem somewhat noble, or perhaps resigned: "He didn't fight./ He hadn't fought at all." The reader sees the fish immediately as humanized, both through the male pronoun as well as through the author's ascription to it of the adjective "venerable." The narrator clearly reacts to this creature as an equal to an equal, on one hand totally within his or her power, on the other hand a creature into whose eyes he or she looks; the reader is told that the fish's eyes are "far larger" than those of the narrator, "but shallower, and yellowed." The most intimate communication with another person frequently takes place through the eyes—so too this contact of fisherman and fish.

This fish, however, is the veteran of many previous combats; from his lip hang the remains of five fish hooks. As a result, it seems that the narrator has been victorious where others have failed; the reader is told that "victory filled up/ the little rented boat." Yet this victory may perhaps be that of the fish, whose hooks have been referred to as "medals"—the fruits of military victory. The last line reads: "And I let the fish go." Why "and," the reader may wonder. This suggests that the narrator's letting the fish go is the anticlimactic natural result of the fish's victory, an acknowledgment of the greater nobility of the natural world with respect to the human one. This reaction seems a bit extreme for the situation described; indeed, the slight discomfort the reader may feel with this poem lies in precisely this self-effacement of the narrator before the minutely described denizen of the deep. One may wonder whether human beings are nothing more than creatures to plague a fish.

AT THE FISHHOUSES

First published: 1965
Type of work: Poem

An unnamed narrator describes a visit to fish houses and talks with an old man.

Although "At the Fishhouses" consists largely of description, it also seems to offer a formulation of the relation between man and nature, or man and truth, which approaches that achieved by some of the poems of Robert Frost, in which daily occurrences are also made to yield deeper meanings through a juxtaposition with larger themes. In this poem, furthermore, the precise descriptions that in many of Bishop's works are simply a fact of style come to take on the quality of content, being put in context by the sudden shift to abstraction of the work's final six lines.

The self-effacing narrator begins by description, sketching the old man who sits mending his nets, until nearly halfway through, where he or she appears for the first time in a possessive pronoun: The reader is told that this man "was a friend of my grandfather" (the word "I" is not used until even further down). The reader is given the silver surface of the sea, the benches, the lobster pots; even the tubs are lined with iridescent scales on which walk iridescent flies. Suddenly the man becomes real: He accepts a cigarette, a Lucky Strike. A line break introduces the reader to the theme of the water, that element from which come all these silvery riches and that forms the source of this man's life and livelihood. This separate section of six lines is tied to the first through the theme of color: In the water lie silver tree trunks.

The next section starts again with the water, an "element bearable to no mortal." The narrator waxes whimsical with memories of singing hymns to a seal, then returns again to the water. This is the same sea that the narrator has seen all over the world, yet here it is so cold that no one would even want to put in a hand, for it would make one's bones ache; if one tasted it, the water would burn the tongue. This, the narrator reflects finally, "is like what we imagine knowledge to be." The narrator then enumerates the qualities ascribed to knowledge that in fact are possessed by this water:

> dark, salt, clear, moving, utterly free,
> drawn from the cold hard mouth
> of the world, derived from the rocky breasts
> forever, flowing and drawn, and since
> our knowledge is historical, flowing, and flown.

Knowledge, one imagines, is all around, but at the same time it is an element in which one cannot live or even dip one's limbs. Knowledge, furthermore, is inherently historical: a great stream of time that surrounds humankind, relative to an individual's own precise situation.

The suggestion seems to be that knowledge, paralleled to this translucent and inviting—but, in fact, inhospitable—element, is ultimately unreachable. The best one can do is live on the land, scraping the scales from fish that have been taken from this medium. One may imagine knowledge to flow all around, and in fact it is the font of those things necessary for human sustenance. Yet at the same time one can never attain it; indeed, it is a medium too fine for such corporeal creatures as humans to experience directly.

QUESTIONS OF TRAVEL

First published: 1965
Type of work: Poem

A meditation, taking a tropical scene as its point of departure, on the merits and disadvantages of travel.

"Questions of Travel" provided the title for Bishop's third volume of poetry, and it comes from a group of works that were written in, and take as their theme, Brazil. The poem is at once a series of very precise observations and, obliquely, a meditation on movement in place that suggests movement in the imagination. The dichotomy that is thereby set up between mind and body comes perhaps from the French philosopher René Descartes and echoes earlier literary treatments of the question of travel in Emily Dickinson, Ralph Waldo Emerson, and Marcel Proust.

In this poem the narrator remains submerged, emerging only briefly in the pronoun "we" in the poem's second group of lines and then again before the final, italicized section as "the traveller," who (like Romantic poet John Keats's Grecian urn) writes his or her own motto on which neither the narrator nor the author comments further. The result is that the reader is left with the ambiguity of knowing merely that this is what the traveler thinks, without knowing whether this is what the reader is to think. Yet since the final section consists largely of questions, it may be precisely these questions that are the final "answer."

The poem's first line situates the reader immediately in an alien place, identified only as "here." All things are relative: From the narrator's point of view, the streams seem to be waterfalls, but from the point of view of the streams (if one can imagine this) the mountains become far away and tiny. In the second section begin the questions. Is it better to think of there from here? Would it have been better to think of here from there? Why do people travel? What, after all, are they looking for? The ultimate decision of the poem seems to be for travel, enumerating as it does the strange, tiny details that can be perceived only outside the frames of one's normal life. The last of these is the rain, which produces a silence during which "the traveller" writes the question which closes the poem: "*Is it lack of imagination that makes us come/ to imagined places, not just stay at home?*" Is there a point, that is, to physical displacement? Should one travel only in the mind? Is the imagination not better than reality? Though the poem ends on this question, Bishop's skill at evoking the details which precede it somehow suggests that travel in reality is better, or at least more interesting, than travel in imagination. Nevertheless, her vote remains somewhat hesitant, with the final image one of the person thinking of the inherent limitations of the human body: "*Continent, city, country, society:/ the choice is never wide and never free.*"

VISITS TO ST. ELIZABETHS

First published: 1965
Type of work: Poem

A visit to a hospital for the insane and to a poet (known to be Ezra Pound) who is incarcerated there.

"Visits to St. Elizabeths" is the result of Bishop's visits, while in Washington, D.C., as the poetry consultant to the Library of Congress, to see the great modernist poet Ezra Pound, who had been incarcerated in this mental hospital as an alternative to conviction for treason; he had made purportedly pro-Fascist radio broadcasts on Italian radio during World War II. Bishop's reaction, characteristically enough, has nothing to do with politics and focuses only on the man in the hospital, who is never named. Yet the poem seems to lose a great deal if the reader is unaware of the poetic stature of Ezra Pound (for some literary historians, the single most original figure of Anglo-American modernism, and at any rate a figure without whom the shape of twentieth century literature would have been vastly different). It helps to have a sense both of Pound's literary grandeur and stature and of the circumstances to which he had been reduced. The narrator's meditation involves a realization of both these extremes, of both the splendors and miseries of the poem's central figure.

The poem is stylistically somewhat peculiar in that it takes a particular metrical prototype as the model which it adopts and then varies, namely the childhood add-on song, "The House That Jack Built." The echo is made clear by Bishop's repetition of its basic structure of one line, separated by a blank line from the next group of two, separated in turn from the next group of three, and so on to the final stanza of twelve lines. For example, the first reads, "This is the house of Bedlam," the second, "This is the man/ that lies in the house of Bedlam."

Already the reader can recognize the reference to the British mad hospital at Bethlehem, called Bedlam, whose chaos before the reforms of the nineteenth century has been preserved in the lower-case use of the noun "bedlam." The evocation is of lack of order; the man "lies" in this house, rather than, say, living there, as if slumped or quiescent, clearly not a fully functioning human.

As the poem progresses, details are added, but the adjectives applied to the man alter. At first he is "honored," then he is "old," "brave," then "cranky," "tedious," and "busy," and he ends up simply "wretched." The crazy round of the madhouse is evoked in this alteration of adjectives, as it is in the repetitive, sing-song rhythm of the increasing numbers of lines and details.

In reacting to one specific person's situation, the narrator in this poem (essentially Bishop herself) seems to express a sense of human empathy that is sometimes lacking in Bishop's more cerebral poems, a realization both of the heights to which individual humans can rise and of the depths to which they can sink. The reader may be left thinking that the wretchedness of this person is not totally unmerited, a situation that may or may not correspond to one's understanding of the historical Pound but which at any rate makes the contemplation of the situation described in the poem possible rather than merely unbearable.

Summary

Elizabeth Bishop carved a secure niche for herself in twentieth century poetry through the careful craftsmanship of her few, meticulously polished works. If some of her poems seem to evade involvement with the world in favor of a highly polished surface that will be most attractive to those who find refuge from action in words, others pose more centrally the very questions and problems that the more distant ones seem to avoid. Critics are united in their praise for her technique, and admiration for her understatement in an age of loudness continues to grow.

Bibliography

Bloom, Harold, ed. *Elizabeth Bishop: Modern Critical Views*. New York: Chelsea House, 1985.

Kalstone, David. *Five Temperaments: Elizabeth Bishop, Robert Lowell, James Merrill, Adrienne Rich, John Ashbery*. New York: Oxford University Press, 1977.

MacMahon, Candace, ed. *Elizabeth Bishop: A Bibliography, 1927-1979*. Charlottesville: University Press of Virginia, 1980.

Motion, Andrew. *Elizabeth Bishop*. Wolfeboro, N.H.: Longwood, 1986.

Schwartz, Lloyd. *That Sense of Constant Readjustment: Elizabeth Bishop's "North & South."* New York: Garland, 1987.

Schwartz, Lloyd, and Sybil P. Estess, eds. *Elizabeth Bishop and Her Art*. Ann Arbor: University of Michigan Press, 1983.

Travisano, Thomas J. *Elizabeth Bishop: Her Artistic Development*. Charlottesville: University Press of Virginia, 1988.

Wylie, Diana E. *Elizabeth Bishop and Howard Nemerov: A Reference Guide*. Boston: G. K. Hall, 1983.

Bruce E. Fleming

ROBERT BLY

Born: Madison, Minnesota
December 23, 1926

Principal Literary Achievement

Bly is respected as one of the principal architects of postmodern American poetry, rejecting New Criticism and seeking a more politically active role for the generation of poets that emerged after 1945.

Biography

Robert Elwood Bly was born in Madison, Minnesota, on December 23, 1926, to Jacob Thomas Bly and Alice Aws Bly, second-generation Norwegian immigrants. He grew up on the family farm and, after completing high school in Madison, enlisted in the navy, serving in a special radar program until the end of the war. According to Bly, one of the few positive memories he had of his experience in the navy was the purchase of his first books of poetry, especially Carl Sandburg's *Chicago Poems: Poems of the Midwest* (1946) and Walt Whitman's *Leaves of Grass* (1855-1892).

After the war, using the G.I. Bill, Bly attended St. Olaf's College in Northfield, Minnesota, and studied writing under Arthur Paulson. Wanting to pursue his studies in a more concerted way, Bly transferred from St. Olaf's after only one year and entered Harvard University in 1947, where he majored in English. His education consisted of traditional English literature, augmented by courses in Latin, Greek, and German; however, he also read respected contemporary poets, such as Robert Lowell (especially *Lord Weary's Castle*, published in 1946) and Richard Wilbur. His interest in modern poetry led to an appointment during his junior year as literary editor of *The Harvard Advocate*, where he met other young writers and poets, among them Donald Hall, John Ashbery, Kenneth Koch, Frank O'Hara, Adrienne Rich, and John Hawkes. Bly was graduated from Harvard magna cum laude in 1950, and he delivered the class poem.

After spending seven months in a cabin in northern Minnesota, Bly decided to begin his career as a poet by moving to New York City, where he supported himself with a series of part-time jobs. At night, alone in his rented room, he read the Austrian poet Rainer Maria Rilke and classical poets Horace, Vergil, and Pindar; he also began work on his first book, *Silence in the Snowy Fields* (1962).

Tired of New York and eager to continue his academic studies, Bly enrolled in the

University of Iowa's M.A. program in creative writing in 1954, under the direction of the midwestern poet Paul Engle. While there, he met several young, emerging poets, such as W. D. Snodgrass, Kim Yong Ik, and Marguerite Young. Also while at Iowa, Bly married Carolyn McLean, a young woman whom he had met while editing *The Harvard Advocate* in Cambridge. The couple moved to a farm in Minnesota in June of 1955, while Bly continued working on his master's thesis. Completed in 1956, his collection of poems entitled *Steps Toward Poverty and Death* earned for him the M.A. in English from Iowa.

The following year, Bly received a Fulbright Grant to translate Norwegian poetry and traveled to Oslo, where he read, for the first time, poets such as Pablo Neruda, Georg Trakl, Juan Ramón Jiménez, and Gunnar Ekelof, all of whom he would later translate into English and publish in the United States. Not only did the translations serve Bly as a means of income upon his return to Minnesota in the late 1950's, but also the poetry itself influenced his own work, invigorating it with new ideas on form and a new understanding of the poet's role in society. Bly's poetics began to take shape as early as 1958, when he and a friend, William Duffy, founded the literary journal (and subsequent publishing house) *The Fifties*. Bly's journal began by publishing poets such as James Wright, Donald Hall, and Louis Simpson, placing it among the most avant-garde of academic journals at that time. Changing its name to the Sixties Press in 1961, Bly began to publish translations of Georg Trakl, Selma Lagerlöf, and others, collections of poems by emerging American poets, and his own *Silence in the Snowy Fields.*

In the early 1960's, after an extensive stay in Europe financed by an Amy Lowell Traveling Fellowship, Bly returned and became politically active against the Vietnam War. He organized antiwar poetry readings at many colleges and universities and organized American Writers Against the Vietnam War, which sponsored an anthology, *A Poetry Reading Against the Vietnam War* (1966). The Sixties Press continued to publish antiwar anthologies, such as *Forty Poems Touching on Recent American History* (1967), most of which were edited and introduced by Bly. His own activities became increasingly public, as he read at demonstrations and draft-card burnings. Academically, he continued to gain notice, however, receiving a Rockefeller Grant in 1967 and winning a National Book Award for his 1967 collection, *The Light Around the Body.* Even these academic honors, however, Bly turned into political statements, donating all prize money to the draft resistance movement and using his acceptance speeches as opportunities to denounce the publishing world for not taking a more active role in the antiwar movement.

During the 1970's, the Seventies Press continued to publish translations, and Bly continued to publish volumes of his own poems. His poetry readings took on a softer quality, with Bly reciting poems from memory and accompanying them on the dulcimer. When he was not reading or writing, Bly was founding and directing symposia on various topics, such as the Annual Conference on the Great Mother, later called the Conference of the Great Mother and the New Father. In the late 1970's, he began to travel to poetry festivals and gatherings all over the world.

By the late 1970's, his family had grown to include two daughters, Mary and Bridget, and two sons, Noah and Micah. Despite his love of family and the close ties he had with his children, Bly and his wife, Carolyn, were divorced in 1979, after twenty-four years of marriage. In 1980, Bly married Ruth Ray and moved to Moose Lake, Minnesota. Bly's activity during the 1980's centered on his conferences for men, which he has sponsored at various universities around the United States. His purpose has been to counterbalance the tendency of modern society to do away with appropriate role models for men. His readings and symposia, as always, have been well attended and well received across the country.

Analysis

Rejecting the rather bleak view of T. S. Eliot's *The Waste Land* (1922), which set the tone for a generation of modernists, and further rejecting the obsessive, confessional writing of others in his own generation, Bly has chosen to write poetry that is inclusive, expansive, and, he believes, conducive to psychic healing. His career seems dedicated to offering opposition to the New Critics and their tendency to separate the artist's life from the art itself. Bly believes that such separation allows the art to be amoral and destructive—choking its ability to speak in the present tense about the great issues that society faces and will continue to face. For him, the modern desire to take an objective stance, to view the world from a comfortable distance, is dangerous; he has argued, therefore, for an approach to experience that has been called subjectivism—that is, an attempt to do away with the barrier between the subject and the object, to merge the two so that people can once again participate in the world in a more responsible, more spiritual, way.

In his collection *News of the Universe: Poems of Twofold Consciousness* (1980), Bly elucidated his position that one could divide Western literature using the philosopher René Descartes as a marker. Prior to Descartes, according to Bly, Western literature reflected a people whose sensibility was not divided, a people who did not separate themselves from nature or from those elements in their own individual natures they could not explain rationally, such as intuition, superstition, and spirituality. He cited the epic Anglo-Saxon poem *Beowulf* as an example, showing that when the poet describes the monster Grendel, he does so without having to explain its existence and without doubting that his audience will believe in such a creature; the *Beowulf* poet had complete "faith in nighttime events." This proximity to the darker side of the human psyche, this lack of separation from nature, was destroyed, said Bly, when Descartes declared in 1619, "I think, therefore I am." After Descartes, Western literature would forever divide the autonomous self from nature. As Bly described it in his preface to *News of the Universe*:

> What I've called the Old Position puts human reason, and so human beings, in the superior position. . . . Consciousness is human, and involves reason. A serious gap exists between us and the rest of nature. Nature is to be watched, pitied, and taken care of if it behaves. . . . In such language the body is exiled, the soul evaporated, the mind given executive power.

The danger of this philosophical stance in the West is that humans have become alienated from nature, alienated from that part of the psyche which participates in nature at the unconscious level, and alienated from an understanding of spirituality, which Bly maintained was also, for the most part, unconscious. This alienation leads to an amoral position regarding the natural world; people become observers merely, not participants.

Bly saw this tendency in the Western tradition culminating in the philosophy of the New Critics, a group of literary critics who sought to view art as artifact—that is, to view it aesthetically, without considering its historical or cultural context. What mattered to the New Critics was a work's position in the ongoing dialogue of literary achievement—its place in the established canon—and its allusions to the earlier traditions. Another important consideration for the New Critics was form—the existence of an identifiable, aesthetically satisfying form. Bly believes that New Criticism drew the lifeblood from poetry, causing it to be uninspired, even dead. He opposes the view that one can separate the artist, or the artist's world, from the art itself: The artist's overriding goal, after all, is to integrate the two. He objects to what he considers the New Critics' obsession with form. Bly himself is conscious of form—changing form often, after lengthy deliberation and study—but views a concern with form as a natural function of the process of writing, rather than as the imposition of some preselected frame upon which one hangs one's work to please the makers of canons.

Mostly, however, he has objected to the absolutely amoral position of New Criticism when it comes to evaluating literature in its historical context. Bly believes that literature (and literary criticism) has a responsibility to face its political implications, to argue politically charged issues, and ultimately to take a stand on those issues. His propensity to do just that has been perhaps his single greatest achievement for those poets who have come after him; they have almost uniformly confronted political issues, refusing to shy away from the dialogue of the present, and this is true largely because of Bly's championing of the writer's political obligations during the 1960's and 1970's.

Unwilling to take as his literary models the traditional form and language of English literature as it descended to him via the established canon, Bly has chosen to find his models from pre-Cartesian sources, such as fairy tales, Anglo-Saxon and Norse poetry, and poetry from other cultures, especially more primitive (that is, non-Western) cultures. What he has searched for in these works has been referred to as the "deep image"—archetypal images that speak on a level beyond the cultural, beyond the superficial. Bly's understanding of the deep image and its significance came from his reading of the philosopher Carl Jung, with his theory of a collective unconscious to which all humans have access via these mythic, archetypal images. Using such images as darkness, water, and death to represent experiences common to everyone, Bly attempts to write poetry that will ultimately heal, on the level of the psyche, Western society's tendencies toward alienation and destruction that he finds so unnecessary. In his poem "Sleepers Joining Hands," he wrote of the healing power of poetry, using an archetypal image of optical illusion: "For we are like the branch bent in the water . . . / Taken out, it is whole, it was always whole. . . ."

THE TEETH MOTHER NAKED AT LAST

First published: 1970
Type of work: Poem

Using surrealistic images of destruction and bits of political speeches, Bly angrily denounces the Vietnam War as a manifestation of the United States' own psychic disintegration.

Published separately in 1970, then later incorporated into *Sleepers Joining Hands* (1973), *The Teeth Mother Naked at Last* has been described as one of the best antiwar poems written in the twentieth century. Bly's strategy in the composition of the poem was to undermine somehow the sterility of the language the United States used—both in its nightly news broadcasts and on its political lecturns—when discussing the Vietnam War and the issues surrounding it. He did this by revealing these familiar phrases and familiar political statements to be false.

After a series of descriptive images from the war in Indochina, descriptions which move from the striking—almost beautiful—to the increasingly bloody and grotesque, Bly tells his reader, "Don't cry at that." Would one cry at other natural phenomena, he asks, such as storms from Canada or the changing of the seasons? The language used publicly to discuss the war was similar to the language reserved for inevitable, natural things. Bly forces the reader to admit that fact by exposing the harsher reality of war.

The language he uses was drawn from many sources: the phrases of the military ("I don't want to see anything moving. . . . [T]ake out as many structures as possible"); the standard phrases of columnists and television commentators; and the rhetoric of politicians, especially President Lyndon Johnson, whose Texas drawl Bly mimics by using hyphens. Then Bly, almost in a rage, warns that all such language conceals the truth. He catalogs those who lie, from the ministers to the reporters to the professors to the president, equating their willingness to lie with a kind of societal death wish. Bly sees in Americans' capacity to kill, and to kill in such a sterile, casual way, a profound psychic rift, a demonstration of their own spiritual inadequacy.

The myth embodied in the title of the poem is also the myth by which Bly understood that spiritual poverty. The myth of the Great Mother, first discussed at length by Carl Jung, and later by several prominent anthropologists including Claude Levi-Strauss, reveals the Western attempt to disavow the more feminine aspect of the psyche and embrace the masculine, that is, logical, instead. In an essay entitled "I Came Out of the Mother Naked," which appeared as a section of *Sleepers Joining Hands*— the section immediately after *The Teeth Mother Naked at Last*—Bly argued that the

Great Mother, the embodiment of feminine consciousness in mythology, actually has four manifestations, which he listed as the Good Mother, the Death Mother, the Ecstatic Mother, and the Teeth Mother. He validated these aspects by taking examples from archaeology, mythology, and primitive poetry. The Good Mother is the image of the hearth, the one most familiar to the West; the Death Mother Bly described as the mother figure responsible for evil and for evil witch and hag images; The Ecstatic Mother Bly equated with the muse of Greek literature, the feminine part of the consciousness which grants creativity; and the Teeth Mother, her opposite, is the aspect that destroys the spirit and forces people into a catatonic state, depriving them of the joy of life.

This aspect of the feminine had perhaps the most importance for Bly, because he saw in her image the spiritual bankruptcy of the American psyche—to him, the war in Vietnam revealed that as a people Americans had chosen the Teeth Mother over the Ecstatic Mother; they had chosen to destroy rather than create. Bly's poem *The Teeth Mother Naked at Last* is perhaps the most remarkable antiwar poem of the Vietnam War era, precisely because it argues against the war on this most psychological, most fundamental level.

SLEEPERS JOINING HANDS

First published: 1973
Type of work: Poem

Using autobiographical images, Bly embarks on a psychic journey into the darkness of his own consciousness to reveal the development of his inner personality.

"Sleepers Joining Hands," the title poem of Bly's 1973 collection, marks a departure from the type of poetry for which Bly had been known previously. His antiwar poetry, remarkable for his energetic, manipulative handling of the language of politics and political thought, had served as a training ground for the more mature, more personal poetry that distinguished this volume. Here language was used to uncover the truth of the psyche on a personal level. The use of Jungian psychology became more than a mere feature of the poetry; it becomes a central impetus—a tool for digging into the unconscious to discover the self.

The imagery of the poem is essentially autobiographical—recounting Bly's days in New York reading the Austrian poet Rainer Maria Rilke in solitude, recalling his relationship to his mother and his father, describing his life at home with his wife and children. To say that this poem is autobiographical is misleading, however, since the poem was not written in normative language, but written instead in a crazy-quilt juxtaposition of images in a tone Bly calls "psychic." The language in the poem is like the language of dreams—bits and pieces of memory alongside half-thoughts and inner, often unvoiced, fears.

The poem has been described by the critic Richard Sugg as an epic quest seeking selfhood, but to understand this quest, one must first turn to the ideas of Carl Jung. Jung believed each personality was made of three features: the individual consciousness (experiences and memory, of which one is aware), the individual unconscious (experiences and memory one has suppressed or forgotten), and the collective unconscious (inherited, universal experiences and memories of ancestors which are passed down to each individual). Archetypes, or images which reveal or reflect the collective unconscious, function as indicators of that part of the personality that is most strong, but usually inaccessible. Jung believed (as does Bly) that an individual who could integrate the three aspects of personality would obtain an enlightened state (Jung's examples were Christ and Buddha) whereby his personality would be whole and intact.

It was this sort of integration Bly sought in the lines of his poem, which uses images from his memory (consciousness); images from his dreams, fears, and unspoken feelings (unconscious); and archetypal images from mythology and religion (collective unconscious) to fuse the three into an overall understanding of the self. He often uses images of digging, of plunging down beneath the surface, of seeking the roots of the self. The journey takes place at night, and images of night prevail— owls, nocturnal animals, and moonlight. It is a journey taken when one is in a dreamlike, unconscious state. What one finds at the end of the journey, at the core of the self, is communion with all other selves—full participation in the collective unconscious: One becomes the night creature, one becomes the archetypal image, one becomes a "sleeper," joining hands with "all the sleepers in the world."

Bly's poem "Sleepers Joining Hands" attempts this participation in the collective unconscious. The poem, and the other poems in the volume, marked a new plateau for Bly's achievement, not so much in form, but in terms of poetic subject. Rather than seeking a more mature political voice, Bly turned his attention inward, writing what some critics have called psycho-spiritual poetry. Of this kind of poetry, which seeks to heal psychic wounds and regain the unconscious that has been lost, Bly has been recognized as an undisputed master.

THE ANT MANSION

First published: 1975
Type of work: Poem

Coming upon a piece of wood inhabited by ants, the poet speculates on the mystical and metaphoric significance of the objects of human labor.

"The Ant Mansion," one of the longer prose poems included in Bly's volume *The Morning Glory: Another Thing That Will Never Be My Friend: Twelve Prose Poems* (1975), contains a short narrative in which the poet, after waking in his sleeping bag, takes a walk through the forest. He comes upon a "wood chunk" that has started to decay, providing a home to a colony of ants. He takes the object home and, after studying it, begins to speculate on its significance as a metaphor for human existence.

This poem, as well as the entire collection *The Morning Glory*, was the culmination of a series of poems Bly began in the early 1970's. After his psychological journeys in *Sleepers Joining Hands*, Bly began to experiment with the form he called the "prose poem," a form the French poet Charles-Pierre Baudelaire claimed would be the major poetic form of the twentieth century. The prose poem offered Bly several new options, introducing new elements into his poetry. First, it introduced the element of plot—the poems became more narrative in nature. Second, the emphasis was not on the form at all, but on the content—not on the language, but on the thought. Third, it allowed Bly the best medium in which to write what had been called, for lack of a better phrase, the "thing poem," or the object poem.

In his essay "The Prose Poem as an Evolving Form" (1986), Bly pointed out that the main difference between usual poetic forms and the prose form is that the basic unit of the usual poem is the line. In the case of the prose poem, the basic unit is the sentence. According to Bly, the sentence allows the poem to proceed at a calmer, more relaxed pace; the prose poem establishes a more intimate, more natural, state for contemplation. According to Bly, the form's closest antecedent—although it resembles the fable, the short story, and the essay—is the haiku. Like the haiku, the prose poem (or object poem) "is evidence that the poet has overcome, at least for the moment, the category-making mentality that sees everything in polarities: human and animal, inner and outer, spiritual and material, large and small." The prose poem allows a kind of participation in nature that more structured poetry does not allow.

Bly begins "The Ant Mansion" by describing a dream in which the rubbing of his sleeping bag causes him to dream of being bitten by a rattlesnake. This wakes him, and he heads to the pasture, veering into some nearby woods. There he discovers the chunk of wood; he takes it back to his house, placing it on his desk. He begins to study the object, noting its many cavities, the color of each various shade of brown or black. He speaks of the wood as an apartment house for ants, speaking of the cavities as "floors" and the bark strips as "roofs."

In the second half of the poem, Bly remarks that the "balconies" created by the half-decayed wood would make excellent "places for souls to sit" and begins to consider inviting all those souls he has known that are now dead to come and live in the ant mansion. He includes villagers he has known, his brother, his grandmother, and eventually such large masses as those who died in the Civil War. By the end of the poem, it becomes clear that the ant mansion has become a symbol for the objects of human labor, the fruit of human life on earth, which no one (or very few) is ever likely to see or use. Bly ends the poem thinking of his father's labor and wishing that it, too, could be found by a pasture and somehow validated.

FIFTY MALES SITTING TOGETHER

First published: 1981
Type of work: Poem

Employing dark, shadowy images, the poet descends into the psyche to unlock the mechanism that invigorates personality on the level of gender.

Bly's poem "Fifty Males Sitting Together," first published in *The Man in the Black Coat Turns* (1981), embodies a theme that occupied him throughout most of the 1980's and beyond: the significance and inadequacies of being male in Western culture. In a preface to *The Man in the Black Coat Turns*, Bly claimed that in its poems he had "fished in male waters, which [he] experienced as deep and cold but containing and nourishing some secret and moving life down below." Bly's concern with maleness stems from his anthropological study of the Great Mother. It is Bly's contention that for the first forty thousand years or so of human existence, humans lived primarily in matriarchal cultures in which the female retained the bulk of social, political, and religious power. These primitive cultures worshiped the Great Mother, symbol of the forces in nature and of life itself.

According to Bly, recorded history began when the masculine began to fight against the Great Mother, asserting its superiority instead, the superiority of masculine thinking (logic and reason) over more natural (even more divine) patterns. This movement away from the Great Mother has left humans detached from nature, unsure of their strength, and intensely alone.

How this historical process manifests itself in modern life has preoccupied Bly since early in his career. He writes often of the male's relationship to the father, writing of it in terms of frustration, incongruity, and disunity. His own relationship with his father had been nonexistent, remarked Bly during an interview with Bill Moyers for a 1988 Public Broadcasting Service documentary entitled "A Gathering of Men," until he realized—later on in life—that he had been involved in a sort of conspiracy with his mother to exclude his father. Once he realized this, he began a dialogue with his father that continued until his father's death. The problem, according to Bly, was that older males have very few ways in which to initiate younger males into society. Initiation—the integrating of the younger generation into the mainstream of cultural life—has become so haphazard and arbitrary in modern society as to be nonfunctioning. Part of the purpose of the seminars and symposia Bly organized across the country was to enlist older males to be initiators of their younger brethren; he also sought to encourage younger males to understand their shared dilemma.

In the poem "Fifty Males Sitting Together," Bly describes a young male witnessing a ritual of descent—shadowy in nature—which takes place by a dark lake at night. Fifty males participate in the ritual, while the wives wait at home. Because he is of the woman's world, and because the darkness of the masculine ritual frightens him, the young male cannot participate in the older males' descent into the darker regions of the psyche; he "loses courage" and turns to nature instead. Using poetic irony, Bly refers to this turn as an ascent, but in the world of Bly's imagery, ascent is a defeat—true self-awareness and knowledge can come only from the psychic descent. When the young man turns away, he moves far away from the world of men and feels cut off from them, alone. Yet in a last line, characteristic of Bly, the young man looks back and sees the night descending on the other shore, as if to say that even though he can not participate, he is at least aware of what he needs to heal his wounded psyche.

Summary

More than practically any other poet of his generation, Robert Bly has sought to enact what he believes is the proper role for the poet in society: a consciousness-raising, outspoken advocate for change and a moral conscience for a society often too willing to be morally and spiritually complacent. As a culture, the Western world, particularly the United States, tends to shirk its responsibilities to humanity and to its own future generations, Bly believes. New Criticism and the poetry it championed encouraged this lack of responsibility. Bly's criticism offers an effective counterstatement, to borrow a term from Edmund Burke, and his poetry offers a highly convincing, alternative voice.

Bibliography

Altieri, Charles F. "Varieties of Immanentist Experience: Robert Bly, Charles Olson, and Frank O'Hara." In *Enlarging the Temple: New Directions in American Poetry During the 1960's.* Lewisburg, Pa.: Bucknell University Press, 1979.

Friberg, Ingegard. *Moving Inward: A Study of Robert Bly's Poetry.* Goteborg, Sweden: Acta University Gothoburgensis, 1977.

Howard, Richard. "Robert Bly." In *Alone with America.* New York: Macmillan, 1969.

Lensing, George S., and Ronald Moran, eds. *Four Poets and the Emotive Imagination: Robert Bly, James Wright, Louis Simpson, and William Stafford.* Baton Rouge: Louisiana State University Press, 1976.

Malkoff, Karl. *Escape from the Self: A Study in Contemporary American Poetry and Poetics.* New York: Columbia University Press, 1977.

Mersmann, James F. "Robert Bly: Watering the Rocks." In *Out of the Vietnam Vortex: A Study of Poets and Poetry Against the War.* Lawrence: University of Kansas Press, 1974.

Sugg, Richard P. *Robert Bly.* Boston: Twayne, 1986.

Edward W. Huffstetler

PAUL BOWLES

Born: Jamaica, Queens, New York
December 30, 1910

Principal Literary Achievement

With powerfully surreal, sensual images taken from his expatriate experiences, Bowles portrays the landscapes and people of North Africa and Central and South America as well as the drifters who encounter them.

Biography

Paul Bowles was born to Rena Winnewisser Bowles, a homemaker, and Claude Dietz Bowles, a dentist, on December 30, 1910, in the Borough of Queens, New York City. His father was, as he later recalled, a bad-tempered man, easily given to child beatings to enforce his will. Perhaps it was fortunate, then, that Paul's father was so addicted to his golf game that he was away from home on weekends whenever the weather permitted. Rena Bowles excused her husband's child abuse, but she showered attention on her son, devoting considerable time to reading poetry and playing music for him. She realized he had artistic proclivities and wanted to encourage them.

Like many creative young people who are abused, however, Paul retreated into himself, refusing to socialize with other children and, out of spite, beating weaker classmates symbolically to get revenge on those who beat him at school. Life was hellish, but it did encourage him to develop his creative powers.

After finishing secondary school in New York in 1928, he attended New York's School of Design and Liberal Arts for a matter of months, then went on to the University of Virginia; he stayed there only six months, however, before leaving the United States for Paris in 1929. He went to Paris at the behest of famous composer Aaron Copland, and it worked well for him: In Paris he discovered not only what pursuits he would follow but also where he would spend most of the remainder of his life (in Morocco). It would take another trip home to New York, then another semester of studies at the University of Virginia before he would become a true expatriate. The restless young man traveled to Berlin, Germany (in 1931 and 1932), where he studied music under another great composer, Virgil Thomson.

Nevertheless, it was his return to Paris in 1933 (he would stay there for a year) that gave him his twin missions in life: He would compose serious music and he would write. While there, either Gertude Stein, American expatriate novelist, or her

227

lover, Alice B. Toklas (the story varies), advised him to find the perpetual summer weather he craved as well as the splendid isolation from Western ways he also sought by moving to Morocco. In 1937, he turned to writing music in Tangier, Morocco, a small but highly international city across from Spain on the Mediterranean Sea. Yet, though he turned his attention to composing scores for Tennesse Williams' *Summer and Smoke* (pr. 1947, pb. 1948) and *The Glass Menagerie* (pr. 1944, pb. 1945), among other plays, he never forgot what he was advised to do with his life when he lived in Paris: to write.

Though he had written reviews for the *New York Herald Tribune* as well as experimented with poetry, Bowles did not do any sustained writing until 1938, when he married another talented writer, Jane Auer, who as a girl had spent several years abroad. It was her encouragement and example that enabled Bowles to focus upon writing rather than musical composition. Their relationship lasted until her death in 1973. It was apparently a combination of opposites—she, the emotional one, and he, the cool, distant one.

In 1949, Bowles created the work for which he is best known, *The Sheltering Sky*, a magnificent depiction of the lack of real communication between people that brought Bowles significant recognition from critics such as Gore Vidal, who became a staunch advocate of his prose. *Let It Come Down* (1952), another novel, furthered Bowles's preoccupation with the horrors of life lived inauthentically and the drugged ennui of Western urbanites faced with life as it is lived in Morocco. Upon its publication, comparisons were made between his work and that of French existentialists Albert Camus and Jean-Paul Sartre.

A third novel, *The Spider's House* (1955), is a lament for a vanishing way of life and a celebration of the Morocco that was passing away under Western influence, influence that Bowles despises. The novella *Up Above the World* (1966), which deals with the brutal murder of North Americans by a South American psychotic bent on getting rid of any witnesses to a murder he perpetrated, also included what was by now becoming Bowles's literary signature: a depiction of the violent meeting between the oversophisticated, soft Westerner and the life-hardened, primitive native of a Third World nation.

An autobiography, *Without Stopping* (1972), followed; its title gave succinct testimony to the pattern of Bowles's life, a life in motion and a life in flight. This work explained his preoccupations, but it did not clarify much about his private life. Along with his acclaimed novels, Bowles has been writing short stories and novellas since he moved to Morocco in the 1930's, and some of them have received as much attention as his longer works. In 1950 came his short story collection *The Delicate Prey and Other Stories*, followed by a novella, *The Time of Friendship* (1967), and two more collections of stories, *Pages from Cold Point and Other Stories* (1968) and *Midnight Mass* (1981). In these strange tales of life in lands far distant from the United States, he deepens his development of the thesis that there is no real order in the natural world—that people are usually prey to one another and to natural forces beyond their control.

Bowles's *Collected Stories, 1939-1976* (1979) offers readers many of his best tales, all of which demonstrate the cruel ferocity of nature and those living closest to her. His naïve Westerners pay heavily for their ignorance about or condescension toward them. In addition, Bowles published a collection of poems entitled *Next to Nothing: Collected Poems, 1926-1977* (1981).

Throughout his life's work, Bowles has explored the terrain of the countries about which he writes, carefully interweaving sights, smells, and sounds in ways one might expect from a person with so much musical talent. Certainly, Bowles has shown no remorse in having abandoned American life, which he considers no life at all. It has primarily been Morocco which has given him the raw material of his art.

Analysis

Though widespread acclaim has eluded Paul Bowles, his impact upon contemporary fiction has been a lasting one and a significant one—more than any other American writer, he introduced existentialist concepts to American fiction. His main themes are those of existentialist fiction: the isolated self, the impossibility of meaningful communication between people, and the terrifying void beyond this world which can drive people insane.

Bowles's writing concerns, for the most part, people of frail identity searching for something to relieve the intense monotony that comes from being caught up in the self. These ennui-ridden searchers come to Third World countries to have something to do, somewhere to go, even if they do not find meaning in this flight from familiarity.

The professor of "A Distant Episode," for example, a linguist with all the cultural sophistication and pride of the educated Westerner, wants to do a language survey in Morocco. What he finds is not what he seeks. Captured by wild, cruel Reguibat tribesmen, his tongue is cut out, and he is further mutilated so he can be sold as a comic curiosity piece. In order to survive, he soon learns to do what they say. Finally, however, a French soldier, thinking him a mad religious character, tries to shoot him. The story closes with him running toward the desert sun and certain death; the professor's personality disintegrates in the Sahara.

So, too, the personality of Kit Moresby of *The Sheltering Sky* falls apart under the harshness of imprisonment, and she adopts a new identity: helpless Arab concubine. Like Kit's, her husband's identity is destroyed by the filth, misery, and horrifying isolation he finds in the town of El Ga'a. Dying of typhus, he is completely alone: The natives of El Ga'a do not care whether he lives or dies because he is an outsider and a "Nazarine" (Christian). In his final moments he forgets who he was and turns into something without past or future.

Certainly, Bowles's characters talk to one another, but real communication is lacking. Their talk is fragmented, superficial, transitory. People in Bowles's stories do not say what they mean because they do not know anything important about themselves or the wider world around them. It is not that they do not wish to communicate, but that words fail them, leaving them locked in anguish.

Cruelly projected behind the merciless white sky of Bowles's stories is the void. This meaninglessness he envisions hides just behind the "sheltering sky" and terrifies those who are aware enough to sense its presence. It is the same void that haunts the fiction of existentialist writers Albert Camus, Jean-Paul Sartre, and Samuel Beckett. The void is mirrored on earth by Bowles's terrible jungles and deserts, the places most hostile to human beings, with their cliffs, bad weather, and deadly creatures— scorpions, vipers, and poisonous lizards. Yet the meaningless quality of the void is also found in the labyrinthine streets of the villages and towns of North Africa and Central and South America, where boredom and terror breed.

The flight of Bowles's characters from this void brings them no rewards, no respite; it brings them only frustration and a sense of futility, fragility, and absurdity. The only exception seems to be Fraulein Windling of *The Time of Friendship*, whose strong Christian beliefs give her an inner sense of purpose and integrity missing in Bowles's secular drifters. Bowles's people are never satisfied, and this dissatisfaction leads them to dissipation, crime, and death. The sterility within them grows until it overtakes them. They try to amuse themselves as they drift downward toward death, never connecting with others, never understanding how special life really is.

THE SHELTERING SKY

First published: 1949
Type of work: Novel

An American couple's travels in North Africa lead to the husband's death from typhus and the wife's sexual enslavement by a wealthy African.

The Sheltering Sky, arguably Bowles's best work, has as its setting his terrible yet hauntingly lovely depiction of the Sahara Desert. The chief protagonist could be said to be the desert itself: an aloof, indomitable, compelling, disorienting, killer landscape—a killer waiting for new victims. All is mystery, despite the clarifying sunlight. A kind of anarchy reigns in the chaotic towns on the desert's periphery, and the farther one travels from coastal cities, the more anarchic and mysterious things become for Bowles's dissolute, bored Americans and Europeans.

Into this strange part of the world Bowles introduces his Americans, Port and Katherine (Kit) Moresby, a young husband and wife from New York, wandering aimlessly, supported by considerable funds. Port, whom Kit likes to insist is a writer, actually is no such thing: He really does nothing with his life. Cynical and jaundiced by fruitless years spent in the United States, Port begins his African sojourn at the Café d'Eckmühl-Noiseux in a town somewhere close to the coast of Morocco.

Kit, his intelligent, attractive wife, is not quite as dissatisfied with life as is he, for she has lingering expectations of some kind of life illumination to come from this exile of theirs. She is alert to the people she encounters; her lively interest in her surroundings counters her husband's boredom, yet she also struggles to find meaning in her life and sometimes falls into a bored silence.

A fellow American simply called Tunner meets the Moresbys, then attempts to befriend them; however, he turns traitor to his new "friend," Port, when he seduces Kit on a train ride to the interior. Like Port and Kit, Tunner is a drifter drawn to North Africa by restless yearnings not quite identifiable but nevertheless persistent. Also entering the picture are the Lyles, a bizarre couple supposedly composed of a mother and her spineless son who, it is found out, sleep together (whether they are incestuous is not stated). The boy, Eric, is a liar, a cheat, and a thief, and his mother is a loud-mouthed, obscene, overly aggressive woman, proud of herself to the point of narcissism.

The Lyles, however, serve only as distractions. The main focus of the novel is upon the contest of wills between Port and Kit, a contest which results first in Kit's committing adultery with Tunner, then later in her leaving his deathbed in order to rediscover personal freedom as well as escape Port's dying from typhus in an ugly, dirty hotel room. Port, though one to proclaim his insularity and self-sufficiency, relies to a marked degree on Kit for companionship. Any strength in their relationship comes from them finding themselves stranded in a strange land, one that is both intriguing and hateful. Death, more often than not veiled in the United States, here stalks the streets openly and conspicuously. Among stinking hotel patios and filthy, disease-bearing alleyways disguised as city streets, Port and Kit come to a temporary understanding.

Yet, when temptation comes (in the banal form of Tunner), their self-serving relationship begins to fall apart; when Port is felled by the typhus, it is in ruins. Kit, having cuckolded her husband, deserts him completely, heading for the high desert outside of El Ga'a. Here, with the great blank sky surrounding her, she wanders lost and alone in the desert, realizing that death will surely come if no one rescues her.

Rescuers do appear: an old man and a young man, riding across the wastes on camels on the caravan route. The young, virile man, Belqassim, who has twenty-two wives and many servants, gives her a ride in exchange for sexual favors, their lovemaking taking place first in the evening after a long ride, then by day. Slowly but surely, Kit loses her mental bearings, bewitched by sand and distance; she comes to depend upon her "benefactors" despite the fact that they see her as no more than an exotic white slave. She realizes that her part of their unspoken bargain is to be an unprotesting concubine, paid in gold bracelets and big rings for her services.

Taken, disguised as a boy, into Belqassim's house, Kit is installed as a mistress (unbeknown to his wives, who accept this "young man" as a pathetic case shown kindness by their husband). Kit, depressed over her servitude and her sexual humiliation, plans a daring escape, which is foiled by Belqassim; he beats her to the point where she begins to lose her mind. Crazed and desperate, she tries again, and she succeeds in escaping. She makes her way to a French outpost, where she is placed in touch with the American legation.

Delivered against her will out of North Africa, she flies to an unnamed Western country—possibly France—and once again is surrounded by the wave of violent noise that is the hallmark of the West. Her mind distraught and her personality severely altered by the trials she endured abroad, she irritates the legation official sent to pick her up at the airport. It is painfully obvious that the desert and its inhabitants have stolen away her mind and soul and that she will live out her half-life in a place she hates.

LET IT COME DOWN

First published: 1952
Type of work: Novel

A dark tale of an anti-heroic expatriate's descent into corrption, theft, and murder.

Let It Come Down greatly reinforced Paul Bowles's growing reputation as a consummate "writer's writer," a craftsman who could capture the ambiguity, terror, and dangerous fascination of developing foreign countries. This novel, his second, has as its setting Tangier, Morocco, prior to its loss of International Zone status in the early 1950's. Like many locales featured in Bowles's novels and stories, Tangier appears dirty, divided (into a slovenly native sector and a prosperous Western one), and sinister—a haven for drug addicts and smugglers. The physical division mirrors a political, economic, cultural, and spiritual division, for the city represents not only Moorish Morocco but also the whole Muslim culture of Africa. Its streets wind sinuously, like intricate designs in the mosaics of the Sultan's Palace, and the city echoes to the sounds of distant calls to prayer from minarets.

To Bowles, Muslim Tangier has a mysterious presence lacking in the Christian part of town; in a sense, it defies Western understanding. The isolation of people seems, to outsiders, more intense than it is in the cities of the West, and death hovers closer. The smells of Tangier are a violent assault: a mixture of garbage, urine, open-air meat and vegetable stands, and the perfume from exotic plants. Bowles's old Tangier, a city behind walls, retains the imprint of past conquerors, both Phoenician and Arab. Yet Europeans have also made their impression upon the city, bringing with them what the author sees as a dangerous materialism represented by seedy, neon-lit night spots, big cars, and drunken, raucous public conduct. To Bowles, this new Tangier has a soullessness about it, its bourgeois comforts partially protecting Westerners from thoughts of death and destruction.

Let It Come Down tells the story of Nelson Dyar, a former New York City bank clerk. A self-acknowledged loser, misfit, and victim, Dyar spends the first half of the novel trying to lay claim to a beautiful, illiterate peasant girl, the prostitute Hadija. Hadija, however, is also pursued by another American expatriate living in Tangier, Eunice Goode, a lesbian who (like Dyar) has enough money to get by without doing much work. Goode (her surname as much an intended pun as Dyar's) is furious over Dyar's "interference" in her life; she intends to possess Hadija totally and make her a kind of white slave. She plans to involve Dyar with a known Soviet agent, Madame Jouvenon—and the plan works. Goode suggests to Jouvenon that she enlist Dyar's services, since he, as an American living in Tangier, is bound to have contacts valuable to Soviet spymasters. Jouvenon, convinced, easily manages to convince the bankrupt Dyar to betray his country by offering him regular paychecks in exchange for information.

Goode calls the American Legation of Tangier and informs them of Dyar's perfidy. No immediate steps are taken to apprehend him, and events keep him from being apprehended by the legation. Then, in an interesting twist of plot, Dyar's sometime employer, Wilcox, wants Dyar to exchange some currency for him at a black market dealer's. Sensing an opportunity to elude the Soviet spies who now employ him as well as a chance to be (temporarily, at least) rich, Dyar joins with a young native of Tangier, Thami, a thoroughly dissipated ne'er-do-well whose hashish habit frequently takes him away from his neglected wife and abused children. Thami spirits Dyar away in a leaky boat, and Thami's partner leaves them on a narrow strip of deserted beach below high cliffs, a locale not far from Thami's home village and his ancestral cottage, perched on a cliff above the sea.

When the ravenous Thami goes after food in his old village, the equally ravenous Dyar, out of boredom, takes up Thami's hashish pipe. Drugged and in a dream, he then wanders away from the house on the cliff; at the nearest town, Dyar accidentally meets Thami. Thami appears not to blame Dyar for stealing his pipe and its contents, so together they go back to the abandoned house on the cliff. After both take up heavy hashish smoking, Dyar, driven by unknown demons, accidentally (or possibly intentionally, Bowles not making it clear which) kills Thami by sticking a nail in his ear as he sleeps and pounding the nail into his skull with a hammer stolen in the village.

Morning arrives and Dyar, dazed and somewhat disconcerted rather than overwhelmed by guilt, attempts to move the corpse so that curious villagers will not find it, only to be interrupted by the unexpected arrival of a nymphomaniacal former lover from Tangier—Daisy, the Marquesa de Valverde. She, horrified after discovering the corpse of Thami, leaves Dyar to fend for himself and returns to Tangier. The novel ends as rain comes down. Dyar, standing in the ruined patio of the deserted house, confronts his imminent death from starvation or angry villagers.

In his characteristically meticulous way, Bowles has created yet another of his visions of a Western exile bereft of purpose or morality who is destroyed in the cruel desert of North Africa. Yet Bowles does not want his characters—in this case, Dyar—to elicit reader sympathy, for there is nothing with which to sympathize. Instead, Bowles wants his readers to see their own baseness and spiritual vacuity mirrored in the plight of the characters.

Dyar loses himself in the surreal chaos of Tangier; it is his choice to do so. A pathetically inert figure, he acknowledges the fathomless emptiness of his existence, finding solace in alcohol, hashish, and fly-by-night affairs. Dyar is at once victim (of drugs, of his own stupidity and lack of insight, of circumstances) and victimizer. He victimizes young Hadija as if he were a predator and she were prey, yet finds himself the prey of another of Tangier's predators, the man-hungry Daisy. Dyar is victimized by Wilcox, whose promises of an easy life in Tangier turn out to be as meaningless as anything else he tells his "friend." Yet Dyar entices Thami to help him escape Tangier with Wilcox' money by pandering to his greed and then, accidentally or intentionally, kills him. Though Dyar has a chance to show internal fortitude by turning down the offer to spy for the Soviets, he forfeits it. He lives solely for himself, with no regard for the needs or feelings of others, and in this he is a true Bowles character.

Nothing is resolved in *Let It Come Down*; Bowles permits no satisfying, neat conclusion. The reader is left with ambiguity and questions as well as a sense of dread. Readers are left with a character living in a universe that neither wants him nor needs him. The earth is, in Bowles's radical estimation, much like the claustrophobic place depicted by French poet Charles Baudelaire, who envisioned earth as having a gigantic, smothering pan cover above it, sealing humankind in. To speak of plot, then, is difficult, because, as Bowles might say, "Everything happens, yet nothing happens." His people do not have meaningful experiences which somehow lead to a catharsis; instead, they lurch from accident to accident. Things happen to people, in a dislocated way, but nothing connected to purpose can occur in this limbo of defeat.

THE DELICATE PREY

First published: 1950
Type of work: Short story

Hideous deaths come to a young desert traveler and the tribesman who kills him.

Bowles's most celebrated short story is a brutal, ironic tale of fatal misjudgment, of deceit, of appalling cruelty, and of the destruction of a destroyer. Nature, in the form of the Sahara Desert, is as much a protagonist as is young Driss, the tale's victim. Its silence is that of the tomb: static and eloquent.

"The Delicate Prey" revolves around three members of the Filala tribe, two brothers and Driss, the son of their sister, who make a fateful journey to the desert town of Tessalit. Driss is a young, virile man who enjoys the bordellos of the town in which he resides. His uncles decide to take a short route to Tessalit through country that comes perilously close to the dreaded Reguibat warriors, a bloody-minded group of land pirates known for their horrible murders of those traveling through their domain.

On the journey, the three meet a lone camel rider whom no one seems to suspect except Driss; Driss questions his motives in serving as their guide, but he remains quiet about these fears. The man identifies himself as a Moungari, a man from a supposedly peaceful, well-respected place. On a pretext of going hunting for gazelle, the Moungari lures one brother, then the next, to their deaths, shooting each in turn. Imagining the distant shots to be harbingers of a feast to come, Driss meanwhile drifts off to sleep; he awakens in horror when he finally realizes what the earlier shots signified. He sets off toward distant Tessalit, only to stumble across the camp of the Moungari and his friends.

As he hails them, they shoot him in the arm; as he tries to rise and shoot his enemies, he is suddenly pushed to the ground. The Moungari ties his hands, binds his feet, then, to Driss's horror—and the reader's—castrates him and makes a deep incision in his stomach, in which he places the organ. Driss is then raped and, after a time, his throat is cut.

Yet the rapacious Moungari makes the mistake of taking the wares he has stolen to Tessalit, where he is apprehended by French authorities, then handed over to the Filali merchants for punishment. They bind him, drink all of his water, giving him none, then take him to the desert, where they place him, bound, into a pit from which only his head emerges. One day later, the head, maddened by the heat, is portrayed as singing.

In this dark story, Bowles captures both the bleak hostility of the Sahara and the even more bleak nature of man, a creature given to heinous deeds done in the spirit of celebration. The Sahara may be a killer, but it kills without malice. The Moungari and the Filali, on the other hand, are deliberate in their cold, astonishing acts of cruelty—true monsters from a desolate land.

THE TIME OF FRIENDSHIP

First published: 1967
Type of work: Novella

A platonic friendship between a North African boy and a middle-aged European woman ends as war approaches.

"The Time of Friendship" is a marked departure for Bowles, for instead of his usual bleak assessment of human nature, readers are given a glowing tale of mutual respect and love between two very different people. The story ends without betrayal, cruelty, or death. Yet death does hover just beyond the story's horizon as the two main characters, Fraulein Windling and her platonic love, the young desert-dweller, Slimane (Arabic for Solomon), enjoy their time together.

One winter, this middle-aged Swiss woman and this Muslim youth form a mutual attachment. She enjoys his rapt attention to her stories, and he enjoys hearing her tell them. When she, a devout Christian, indirectly challenges his Muslim assumptions about Jesus, he reacts without anger; instead, he tells her an apocryphal story about Jesus, a man he regards as a Muslim prophet. Sensing her young protégé's religious nature and wanting to set him straight about Jesus Christ's true identity, she lovingly creates a crèche scene, carving Mary and baby Jesus, wise men, and shepherds from native clay, creating a floor from chicken feathers, and decorating the scene with candies from Switzerland.

While Fraulein Windling's back is turned, however, her friend inadvertently beheads the camels and other figures while trying to get at the candy. Deftly, subtly, Bowles uses the devastated manger scene as an omen of what will come. War is coming: The French occupiers of the area are engaged in battle against local patriots, a lopsided conflict in which the heavily-armed French are almost certain to prevail. When Fraulein Windling leaves her North African friend behind as a result of her forced repatriation home to Europe, she leaves him with real grief in her heart, for she realizes that when she returns—if she ever will—he may be dead, a victim of the conflict. Thus, the last meeting is a sad affair. Unspoken feelings speak the loudest as the two try to make conversation. As the train moves, she impulsively kisses Slimane's forehead and, by so doing, offers him evidence of her love.

In this story, Bowles's ability to convey stifled emotion and lost hopes with an astonishing economy of words is on full display; character and situation are carefully delineated. "The Time of Friendship" reverberates with lostness, but also with a kind of wild joy as two people share moments of intimacy and understanding.

Summary

Paul Bowles is an innovator of the first order whose masterful works deserve far more critical attention than has been given them. This slighting of Bowles, as some critics suggest, may be attributable to his strong anti-American bias, to his choice of locales ("too foreign," some say), or to his pessimistic view of human nature and man's destiny. His works, while difficult and painful to read at times, offer readers a window on a strange, bizarre world that no other writer has offered; his is writing that will endure.

Bibliography

Bertens, Johannes Willem. *The Fiction of Paul Bowles: The Soul Is the Weariest Part of the Body.* Amsterdam, The Netherlands: Humanities Press, 1979.

Pounds, Wayne. *Paul Bowles: The Inner Geography.* Berne, Switzerland: Lang, 1985.

Review of Contemporary Fiction 2 (1982). Special Bowles issue.

Sawyer-Laucanno, Christopher. "An Invisible Spectator." *Twentieth Century Literature* 32 (Fall/Winter, 1986): 259-299.

Stewart, Lawrence D. *Paul Bowles: The Illumination of North Africa.* Carbondale: Southern Illinois University Press, 1974.

John D. Raymer

T. CORAGHESSAN BOYLE

Born: Peekskill, New York
1948

Principal Literary Achievement

Boyle is widely recognized for his comic picaresque novels and his satiric absurdist short stories.

Biography

T. Coraghessan Boyle was born in 1948, in Peekskill, New York, a small town on the banks of the Hudson River in the area made famous by Washington Irving in such stories as "Rip Van Winkle" and "The Legend of Sleepy Hollow." His father was a schoolbus driver, and his mother was a secretary. Boyle's grade school and high school education gave no indication of his future as a writer; in fact, he has said, in a typical facetious exaggeration, that he never read a book until he was eighteen, that he mostly read comic books and watched television. Music was his primary interest.

Boyle went to the State University of New York at Potsdam as a music major, studying the clarinet and saxophone. He has said that he really was not good enough to be a professional musician and did not have the discipline to practice. He drifted rather aimlessly into a creative writing class, where he discovered writers such as John Barth, Thomas Pynchon, Donald Barthelme, and Gabriel García Márquez, all of whom have influenced his work.

When he was graduated from college, the Vietnam War and the pressure of the draft made him decide to become a teacher to qualify for a military deferment. Although he has characterized himself as a "wild, radical hippie" at the time, he got a job teaching English at a junior high school in Peekskill in what Boyle has described as a tough slum school, where he often had to get violent to maintain discipline. It was during this time that he says he began taking drugs.

Feeling himself at a dead end and having gained some encouragement by publishing a story in *The New American Review*, he applied to the creative writing graduate program at the University of Iowa and was accepted on the basis of his work. At Iowa he studied under such writers as John Cheever, Vance Bourjaily, and John Irving, receiving his Ph.D. in 1977. Boyle also won a Creative Writing Fellowship from the National Endowment for the Arts in 1977, and his dissertation creative project, *Descent of Man*, was published in 1979. The book was well enough received

to give Boyle a significant underground reputation and to earn for him a job as a creative writing professor at the University of Southern California in Los Angeles. The stories also won the Coordinating Council of Literary Magazines Award for Fiction and the St. Lawrence Award for Fiction.

Boyle's first novel, *Water Music* (1981), a picaresque work based on the adventures of Mungo Park, an eighteenth century Scottish explorer, was received by critics as a virtuoso performance. Boyle's delight in playing with the language was infectious, and the book was admired more for its exuberant style than for its thematic depth. Turning to a more realistic approach and a more contemporary setting in his second novel, Boyle published *Budding Prospects: A Pastoral* (1984), a satiric treatment of the American Dream in which hippies growing marijuana in the Northern California backwoods are presented as modern models of Benjamin Franklin and Henry David Thoreau.

Boyle continued to write short stories during this period, publishing his collection *Greasy Lake and Other Stories* in 1985, which was widely praised for its satire and humor. A particularly ambitious work is *World's End* (1987), a sprawling picaresque novel covering several generations of Hudson Valley families; the book won the PEN/Faulkner Award for American Fiction and was called Boyle's "peak achievement" in *The New York Times Book Review*. Boyle's third collection of short stories, *If the River Was Whiskey* (1989), was not so well-received, with critics complaining that it did not contain any stories equal to some of the masterpieces in his first two collections. *East Is East* (1990), about a young Japanese half-breed who jumps ship and lands on a small island near Georgia, similarly received only lukewarm response.

Boyle has said more than once that he yearns to be famous. Every book he writes he expects will end up on the best-seller list and make people forget the name of millionaire horror writer Stephen King forever. It is not the money that interests him, he claims. "I want to be read," insists Boyle. "I would like to have about four or five times the audience Michael Jackson has for his records—and out-dance him publicly." T. C. Boyle (The middle name, pronounced kuh-RAGG-is-son, is an admitted affectation; his real name is Thomas John Boyle) now lives in Los Angeles with his wife and his three children. Although he still presents himself for publicity purposes as a latter-day hippie, complete with shaggy hair and beard, a metal clip in his ear, and voodoo bracelets on his wrist, Boyle lives a hard-working middle-class life in the suburbs; he continues to teach at USC and to write books which he hopes will become best-sellers.

Analysis

T. C. Boyle's most pervasive fictional theme is the importance of history; his most predominant fictional method is satire. His two most ambitious novels to date, *Water Music* and *World's End*, are both sprawling picaresque novels deeply rooted in history. *Water Music* is based on the actual adventures of Mungo Park, a Scottish explorer who became the first white man to explore the Niger River in Africa and who published a best-selling account of his adventures entitled *Travels in the Interior*

Districts of Africa in 1797. *World's End* begins with seventeenth century native Indians and Dutch and American settlers of the Hudson River Valley of New York and traces the descendants of three families into the twentieth century.

Whereas *Water Music* is modeled after both the eighteenth century picaresque novel of Laurence Sterne and the twentieth century send-ups of the picaresque novel by such writers as John Barth, *World's End* builds on the American myth-making tradition originated by Washington Irving as well as such modern American myth makers as Thomas Berger. Even Boyle's least mythic novel, *Budding Prospects*, a satiric send-up of the American Dream and the male escape fantasy, is deeply rooted in both the history of the founding fathers and the history of the hippie movement of the 1960's.

Boyle's stories, as is typical of the short story in general, are less dependent on history than are his novels, standing alone as independent satires, mostly on modern society and popular culture. Boyle's first collection, *Descent of Man*, features such absurd situations as the film star dog Lassie leaving her master Timmy for a love affair with a coyote, a woman falling in love with a brilliant chimpanzee who is translating Darwin and Nietzsche into Yerkish, and a group of teenagers who are so stoned on drugs that they do not notice that it is literally raining blood.

Boyle continued this kind of absurdist satire and parody in his second collection, *Greasy Lake and Other Stories*, but some of the stories in this collection have such control and achieve such a powerful significance that they go beyond simple satire. Although the collection contains parodies of Sherlock Holmes and Gogol's famous story "The Overcoat," as well as such absurd stories as one about a secret love affair between Dwight Eisenhower and the wife of Nikita Krushchev and a story about the mating of whales, it also contains such surrealistically sublime pieces as "The Hector Quesadilla Story," about a baseball game that goes on forever, and such classic tragicomic nightmares as the title story. Critical response to Boyle's 1989 collection of stories, *If the River Was Whiskey*, and his novel *East is East* (1990) indicated that Boyle had not moved much beyond his earlier works. According to several critics, these stories often seem self-parodies and do not have the scope of his earlier picaresque efforts.

WATER MUSIC

First published: 1981
Type of work: Novel

The lives of Mungo Park, a Scottish explorer, and Ned Rise, a thief, intertwine in eighteenth century England.

Water Music is based on the real-life adventures of eighteenth century Scottish explorer Mungo Park as told in his book *Travels in the Interior Districts of Africa*. It also focuses on the imagined adventures of Ned Rise, a member of Park's final exploration party, who uses his wits to survive on the streets of London. Both men are classic picaros, one in the mode of the adventuring nobleman and the other in the mode of the unscrupulous rogue. The first part of the novel centers on Boyle's moving back and forth between Park's harrowing adventures in Africa as he escapes mutilation and death at the hands of savages and Ned Rise's exploits as he evades the clutches of fellow criminals and the gallows on the no-less-dangerous streets of London. Each chapter ends in a traditional cliff-hanger as the reader is whisked from the Niger to the Thames and then back again until the twin picaresque streams of the story merge when Park returns to England a hero and Rise narrowly escapes death. Both feel the need to escape England and civilization, such as it is, which they do when Park makes his final (for him, fatal), disastrous expedition to the Niger River.

The novel has much purely visceral appeal; it is filled with sufficient sex and violence to hold the interest of even the most superficial and adolescent reader. Boyle is only following in a tradition, however; such violence and degradation were the stock and trade of the picaresque novel, which constituted the pulp literature of the eighteenth and nineteenth century. Boyle uses the picaresque mode only as the means by which he can play with fictional conventions in an exuberant way. It is the language of the book that most catches the discriminating reader, combining as it does high-flown eighteenth century rhetoric with the flat and slangy language of the twentieth century. Other writers, such as John Barth and Donald Barthelme, have tried this technique with more success, but Boyle seems to take a great delight in his play with language, a delight the reader often shares.

Water Music is black humor at its blackest and most humorous. Called "High Comic Book Fiction" by one reviewer and a virtuoso performance on a grand scale by another, the book was both hailed for its inventive use of the picaresque/experimental mode and blasted for its comic-strip bathos and superficiality. Regardless of this mixed response, it is the book that made T. C. Boyle a name to reckon with in modern American literature.

GREASY LAKE

First published: 1985
Type of work: Short story

Three young men looking for adventure on a Saturday night find more than they bargained for.

"Greasy Lake," the title story of Boyle's best-received collection of stories, takes its title and its epigraph— "It's about a mile down on the dark side of Route 88"— from Bruce Springsteen's song "Spirit in the Night." It focuses on three nineteen-year-old men living in a time (probably the 1960's) when, the narrator says, it was good to be bad, when young people cultivated decadence like a taste. Driving the family station wagon, they search for some escape from their suburban shopping-center lives at Greasy Lake where, on the banks of festering murk, they can drink beer, smoke marijuana, listen to rock and roll, and howl at the moon. On the particular night of this story, however, at 2:00 A.M., these extremely "bad" characters meet someone more "dangerous" than they are. When they try to embarrass a friend in a parked car, they find out too late that it is instead a "bad, greasy" stranger, who begins beating them up. Things go from bad to worse when the narrator loses the key to his mother's station wagon and cracks the greasy stranger on the head with a tire iron. When the three, caught up in the violence, begin tearing the clothes off the girl in the car, they are interrupted by the arrival of another man—who threatens to kill them.

All this intense physical action is described in a combination of fear-filled seriousness and silly slapstick—that is, until the narrator, trying to escape, is driven into the primeval swamp of Greasy Lake itself, only to find himself stumbling over a floating dead body. As he crouches there in the shallow water, he listens to the "greasy stranger" taking the tire iron to his mother's Bel Air station wagon like an avenging demon. The story ends when the three boys start to leave and are stopped by the arrival of two young women in a silver Mustang who ask them if they want to party. By this time, however, they have had enough of "being bad" and drive away in the wrecked car, leaving one of girls standing there in the dirt road with drug-filled hand outstretched.

"Greasy Lake" is a realistic, yet surrealistic, story about the posturing efforts of young men wanting to be tough. Boyle has said that it is about strutting around thinking you are bad and then finding someone who is tougher than you are. The proposition the story raises, says Boyle, is where is the bottom and do you really want to get there? The metaphor for the "bottom" is the Greasy Lake itself, the ultimate end of the basic ironic dichotomy in the story between the suburban clean-cut and greasy primitivism. Although there is a distinction between the pretense of danger and real danger, the story suggests that the pretense can itself be dangerous. The progression from comic posturing and slapstick comedy to Gothic horror and final bathos is handled so deftly that the reader is irresistibly carried along by it.

THE HECTOR QUESADILLA STORY

First published: 1985
Type of work: Short story

An aged, overweight Mexican baseball player yearns for a final heroic gesture but gets caught in a game that lasts forever.

The hero of the slightly surreal "The Hector Quesadilla Story" is a typical Boyle antihero. Although the story is in the tradition of mythic tales of Babe Ruth and Joe DiMaggio, Hector Quesadilla, in his fifties, is no Sultan of Swat; he has shin splints, corns, and hemorrhoids. He is not only old, he is also fat, a man who eats as though there were some creature inside him made of nothing but jaws and guts. He has not played regularly in ten years, but he wants one more season; he refuses to admit that he is old. In baseball, Hector believes, the grass is always green and the lights are always shining, for it is a game that never ends.

The story focuses on one particular day late in the season; it is Hector's birthday, and there is a home game at Dodger Stadium in Los Angeles. His entire family attends—his wife, his grandchildren, even his son, Hector Jr., who studies English at USC and is writing a thesis on a mystical British poet Hector has never heard of. Hector's own mystic adventure begins when the game is tied up at 5 to 5 at the bottom of the ninth and seems headed for extra innings. As the game goes into its twenty-second inning, Hector begins to feel, with a sense of wonder, that he is destined to be the hero of the longest game in history.

The story moves toward its transcendent climax at the top of the thirty-first inning when finally Hector is sent out to bat and thus, it is hoped, to bring the game to an end. It is not to be. Although he connects with the ball, sending it over the center fielder's head to slam off the wall, his legs give out, and he is cut down at third. Stunned and humiliated, he staggers to the dugout to the jeers of the remaining crowd. Still it is not over, however, and Hector goes in again. The story (but not the game) ends with him stepping up to the plate, the bat flashing in his hands like an archangel's sword; the game goes on forever.

Although this story begins in Boyle's typical comic play, this time as a parody of the baseball hero biography, the magic of the game itself takes over. Instead of a comic parody, what results is a truly transcendent hymn to the national pastime and an objectification of the yearning in the heart of everyone to have that one moment in the sun. What makes the story work is its metaphoric objectification of the mythic ideal of "the game that goes on forever." The language moves from satiric flippancy to a poetic evocation of those countless Sunday afternoons on baseball fields all across America when little boys look for heroes and old men try to hold on to youth.

Summary

T. C. Boyle is probably one of the most ambitious and enthusiastic American authors writing today. Both in the scope of his picaresque novels and in the perception of his satiric short stories, he has carved out a place for himself in the comic experimental tradition of John Barth and Donald Barthelme. He is not a slavish imitator of those writers, however; he has a unique voice that manages to hover delicately between the serious and the satiric, and he has his own vision of the importance of history in the American psyche.

Bibliography

Abrams, Garry. "T. C. Boyle Would Be Famous." *Los Angeles Times*, October 7, 1987, pp. B13-14.

Adams, Michael. "T. Coraghessan Boyle." In *Dictionary of Literary Biography Year-*

book: 1986, edited by J. M. Brook. Detroit: Gale Research, 1987.

DeCurtis, Anthony. "A Punk's Past Recaptured." *Rolling Stone*, January 14, 1988, 54-57.

"T. Coraghessan Boyle." In *Contemporary Authors*. Vol. 120, edited by Hal May. Detroit: Gale Research, 1987.

"T. Coraghessan Boyle." In *Contemporary Literary Criticism*. Vol. 36, edited by Dan Marowski. Detroit: Gale Research, 1986.

Charles E. May

RAY BRADBURY

Born: Waukegan, Illinois
August 22, 1920

Principal Literary Achievement

Bradbury is credited with playing a leading role in winning a large readership for science fiction in the 1950's by producing works with well-developed characters, provocative themes, and an attractive literary style.

Biography

Ray Bradbury was born in Waukegan, Illinois, on August 22, 1920, the son of Leonard Bradbury and Esther Moberg Bradbury. One of his older twin brothers died before his birth, and a younger sister, Elizabeth, died in infancy when he was seven.

Despite economic problems that took his family twice to Arizona in search of work, and despite the deaths of two siblings, Bradbury's memory of his early years is positive. In *Dandelion Wine* (1957) and other works, his boyhood home in Waukegan becomes Green Town, an idyllic if somewhat fragile Midwestern town, where children enjoy the pleasures of playmates their age balanced with the opportunity for solitary explorations of a surrounding countryside.

In 1934, the family moved permanently to Los Angeles, California, where Bradbury soon adapted to his second beloved home. Los Angeles attracted him in part because it was a center of the entertainment industry that Bradbury had loved since at least the age of three, when he remembered seeing actor Lon Chaney in *The Hunchback of Notre Dame* (1923). Throughout his life, Bradbury devoured the fiction of wonder and adventure: radio, motion pictures, comic books, pulp and slick magazines, and the novels of such authors as Edgar Rice Burroughs and Jules Verne. At the age of twelve, he and a friend found themselves unable to await the next sequel in Burroughs' Mars series and, therefore, wrote their own.

Bradbury began writing stories and poems as soon as he learned how to write. He made his first sale as a teenager, contributing a sketch to the George Burns and Gracie Allen radio comedy show. In high school, he also developed an interest in theater that continued throughout his writing career.

After finishing high school, Bradbury plunged into writing, trying to make himself quickly into a professional. He joined a science fiction organization, studied with science fiction writer Robert Heinlein, and worked with several other successful pulp fiction and screenwriters. He set himself the task of writing a story a week,

while living at home and earning money selling newspapers. His first published story was "Hollerbochen's Dilemma," which appeared in *Imagination!* in 1938. He wrote his first paid science fiction story, "Pendulum," in collaboration with Henry Hasse, and it appeared in *Super Science Stories* in 1941. Soon he was publishing regularly in pulp magazines such as *Weird Tales.*

When he married Marguerite McClure in 1947, he was a well-established writer, publishing more than a dozen stories each year. "The Big Black and White Game" appeared in *Best American Short Stories* in 1945, and "Homecoming" was selected for the O. Henry Awards *Prize Stories of 1947.* In the year of his marriage, Arkham House published his first story collection, *Dark Carnival* (1947); many of these stories were reprinted in the highly regarded collection *The October Country* (1955). From then on, his fiction was regularly recognized with awards and selected for anthologies. In 1949, the year the first of his four daughters was born, the National Fantasy Fan Federation selected him best author of the year.

His career continued to advance and then to diversify after 1949. *The Martian Chronicles* (1950) became one of the first science fiction novels to receive serious attention from the mainstream literary establishment when reviewer Christopher Isherwood praised it highly. Then followed a pattern of publishing collections of stories interspersed with new novels and other activities that included screenplays, musical theater, drama, and poetry. His best-known fiction appeared before 1963: *The Martian Chronicles, Fahrenheit 451* (1953), *Dandelion Wine, Something Wicked This Way Comes* (1962), and five collections of short stories. Each of the novels either grew from earlier published stories or was constructed of earlier stories worked together into a longer work. During this period, he also traveled to Ireland, where he worked on the screenplay for director John Huston's 1956 film version of Herman Melville's classic novel, *Moby-Dick* (1851).

After 1963, he continued to publish short story collections, but he devoted more of his energy to other areas, especially drama. His first collection of short plays, *The Anthem Sprinters* (1963), grew out of his six months in Ireland. He produced two shows based on his own works: *The World of Ray Bradbury* (1964) and *The Wonderful Ice Cream Suit* (1965). His other works in the 1960's included a cantata and a film history of America for the 1964 New York World's Fair. Though his interests in fiction and drama continued into the 1970's, he also turned his attention more decisively toward poetry, publishing three volumes and then collecting them into a single volume, *The Complete Poems of Ray Bradbury* (1982). During this period, he wrote much nonfiction prose for magazines ranging from *Life* to *Playboy.*

Film productions of his works began to appear in the 1960's and continued into the 1980's: *Fahrenheit 451* (1966), *The Illustrated Man* (1969), *The Martian Chronicles* (1980), and *Something Wicked This Way Comes* (1984). Of these adaptations, only French filmmaker François Truffaut's *Fahrenheit 451* was widely praised by film critics. Many of his short stories have been adapted for television, some with great success. His own animated short film, *Icarus Montgolfier Wright*, was nominated for an Academy Award in 1962.

After 1980, Bradbury collected some of his early detective stories in *A Memory of Murder* (1984) and then published a detective novel, *Death Is a Lonely Business* (1985), and a Gothic thriller set in Hollywood, *A Graveyard for Lunatics* (1990). In 1985, he began a series of adaptations of his own stories for a cable television series *The Ray Bradbury Television Theater*. In this period, he also received some coveted writing awards: a life achievement award from the World Fantasy Convention (1977); a Gandolf "Grand Master" award at the Hugo Award Ceremonies of 1980; the Jules Verne Award (1984); and the Valentine Davies Award for film (1984).

Bradbury's achievements are mainly in fantasy and science fiction. His drama and film scripts have been well-received, but his poetry has not. Continuing attention from literary scholars and cultural historians suggests that he will surely be remembered for the powerful and thoughtful storytelling that brought him to prominence in the 1950's. Bradbury's achievement opened a generation's hearts and minds to the worlds of imagination and wonder in fantasy and science fiction, beginning an era of wide popularity for and of scholarly interest in genres that had been on the fringe of modern culture.

Analysis

Literary critic David Mogen has characterized well the central motif of Ray Bradbury's fiction: joyous absorption in the experience of living. In each of his major works, this joy in living plays a crucial role. Mogen sees this attitude toward life in Bradbury's own life—in his prolific career with its many directions and in his non-fiction accounts of his life and career. One could guess this about Bradbury merely by looking at his book titles—not only those that recommend enthusiastic exploration or offer medicines for melancholy, but also those that are drawn from visionary poets such as Walt Whitman and William Butler Yeats.

The dominant thematic note in Bradbury's fiction is a kind of hopefulness for humanity. Mogen and another critic, Gary K. Wolfe, have noted that Bradbury's optimism has roots in two major Western myths that have been important to many American writers: the frontier and the Garden of Eden. For Bradbury, the stars are the new frontier, humanity's next field of exploration and expansion. The stars also become a new Eden, an extension of the hope for new beginnings that idealistic explorers saw in America and that F. Scott Fitzgerald so eloquently captured in his description of the "fresh, green breast of the new world" at the end of a novel Bradbury admired, *The Great Gatsby* (1925).

Mogen sums up Bradbury's hopefulness by describing him as a visionary "who believes the human race will conquer death through spiritual rebirth in unearthly new frontiers." Bradbury's readers are aware of the dark elements in his fiction, however: the tales of terror collected in *The October Country*, the threatening ravine that cuts through Green Town, and the technological dystopias (of which *Fahrenheit 451* is the main example). Bradbury is acutely aware that human beings are capable of evil and contain darkness. He seems to see humanity as destined ultimately for transcendence of the kind described by nineteenth century American Romantic authors such as Walt Whitman and Ralph Waldo Emerson, in which humanity approaches becoming God-like. Yet he also sees humanity in the present as blind to its best interests, selfish, turning technology to destructive rather than creative and imaginative ends, in continuous danger of self-destruction.

In a discussion of *The Halloween Tree* (1972), a lesser-known fable for young readers, Mogen illustrates what Bradbury sees as one of the greatest dangers facing modern humanity, the paralysis of imagination before the fear of death. This is also one of the main themes of *Fahrenheit 451*, and it appears in many of Bradbury's works. The purpose of the tale of terror, for Bradbury, is to help the individual human imagination symbolically confront its mortality. If people fail to face and deal with their deaths, they become the victims of terror, and the results of this victimization often include a drive for meaningless power and the impulse to impose a single order upon human experience. In several of his works, this imposition of order appears as attempts to turn off the imagination, which is a source of multiple ideas of order. *Fahrenheit 451* offers a vivid picture of a society so afraid of death that it attempts to be a happiness machine, filling people's lives with empty, supposedly painless electronic stimuli and censoring all the great ideas and great books in the history of civilization. While such a society believes that it is escaping death somehow, it is in fact running directly toward death in the form of a military holocaust. The two major Green Town novels, *Dandelion Wine* and *Something Wicked This Way Comes*, show individuals facing death and the temptation to grasp evil power to evade death.

Bradbury's works show his optimistic faith in a fulfilling human destiny in some future time and place, but they also show his understanding of the barriers that humanity must overcome on its journey to this destiny and of the human limitations people are likely to carry with them into any future.

THE MARTIAN CHRONICLES

First published: 1950
Type of work: Novel

Americans explore and colonize Mars, then abandon the colony when atomic war breaks out on Earth; a few refugees return to Mars after Earth civilization is destroyed.

In the 1940's, Bradbury had established himself as a highly popular story writer. When a Doubleday editor encouraged him to try connecting some of his stories into a unified, novelistic collection, Bradbury quickly responded with *The Martian Chronicles*, a group of stories about people from Earth colonizing Mars.

The idea of the colonization of Mars fascinated Bradbury throughout his career. When he produced *The Martian Chronicles*, he had published more than ten Martian stories, and he continued to produce more after the book was published. This book became the first of several Bradbury works that are called novels not because they have the traditional plot characteristics of the novel but because they are somewhat unified collections of related stories, rather like Sherwood Anderson's *Winesburg, Ohio* (1919). Bradbury repeated this form with varying success in *The Illustrated Man* (1951) and *Dandelion Wine*.

The Martian Chronicles is an apt title. Bradbury structured the book as a loose chronicle, beginning in 1999 with the first expedition to Mars and ending in 2026, with what is probably the last. The chronological ordering establishes a strong forward movement in the first one-third of the book, which deals with four exploratory expeditions from 1999 to 2001. Roughly the middle one-third contains stories and episodes which, though placed from 2001 to 2005, are not very sequential. They seem more like a gathering of incidents illustrating aspects of a colonial period. The final third of the book, though it spans 2005 to 2026, really concentrates on the beginning and the end of this period. In 2005, atomic war begins to destroy Earth civilization, draws most of the Martian colonists back to their home planet, and effectively brings an end to space travel. In 2026, Earth is devastated, but a remnant of idealists from Earth escapes to Mars, hoping to start over.

While the overarching structure of a chronicle binds the book together at the beginning and end, there are other important unifying elements. One major element is the metaphor of the frontier. Bradbury repeatedly returns to the idea of Mars as a new frontier. The planet is a new world (like America), populated at first by predominantly peaceful, intelligent beings much like humans, though they have telepathic powers and a slightly different technology. The Martians find themselves playing the role of Native Americans in the frontier metaphor, resisting invasion somewhat haphazardly until almost completely wiped out by a plague of chicken pox accidentally brought from Earth. There are no "Indian wars," but the abandoned cities and artifacts of Martian civilization become objects of interest, wonder, exploitation, and wanton destruction by the later colonists. The Martians, after their demise, produce converts, people who believe that the Martian civilization was better than their own and set out in various ways to imitate what they believe it was. This motif of conversion into Martians remains important throughout the book and becomes its final note.

The colonial phase begins with a Johnny Appleseed character who dreams of the desert world becoming a green world and sets out on foot to plant trees over large areas. Bradbury's episodes and sketches present positive and negative aspects of America's colonial history. On the negative side are exploiters and materialist dreamers who ignore the spiritual significance of this new beginning and seize upon the dross—the chances for wealth and power available on a comparatively free frontier. On the positive side are those who come to Mars in search of spiritual freedoms denied on Earth. Among them is a large group of Southern blacks who see in Mars the chance to gain what the United States has denied them. Their story, told in "Way in the Middle of the Air," may seem rather naïvely conceived when read by late twentieth century readers, but sketches such as this one gave Bradbury a reputation for radicalism in 1950. Among the spiritual questers is William Stendahl, who in "Usher II" prefigures themes in *Fahrenheit 451,* using Mars to escape from anti-imagination book censors on Earth and to take a poetically just revenge upon some of them.

In the last third of the book, Bradbury complicates the frontier metaphor by fore-grounding the Eden myth that stands behind it and mixing in the new terror that existed during the period following World War II when he produced this book—the threat of atomic holocaust. In long years of war, Earth finally reduces itself to rub-ble, and at the last a small group of people flees to Mars, determined to start over and do things right this time. The image of a remnant of the spiritually pure leaving behind a hopelessly corrupt civilization to start anew is, of course, at the center of the American myth of the frontier. "Pioneers" bringing their purity to an innocent and empty place evokes the idea of Eden regained, where a truly new start is possi-ble. Added to these elements, however, is a feature that points to the profundity of the optimism behind this book that so vividly portrays humanity's failures and weak-nesses. Remaining on Mars are the remnants of an ancient and wise Martian civili-zation and perhaps even some actual Martians. For humans to be converted into Martians, to become products of the place and its native spiritual presences, may lead to a true advance for humanity beyond the blind and selfish passions that have once again produced holocaust.

The idea of a saving remnant of the spiritually chosen pervades the Bible and the Judeo-Christian tradition. It also is important to Bradbury and appears regularly in his stories. This mythic pattern is one of the more important indications of optimism in Bradbury's fiction. He often tells stories such as this one, in which civilization dies because of its failures of wisdom, compassion, and imagination. Nearly always, however, the pattern includes a small new beginning by those whose vision is cleansed by suffering and who vow to preserve the best of the past and leave the worst behind, and this pattern converts Armageddon into a step toward salvation.

As the first work of American science fiction to gain a truly broad reading public, this book is of considerable historical importance in modern American literature. Although literary critics disagree about the book's artistic merits, *The Martian Chron-icles* promises to remain in print as a popular favorite.

FAHRENHEIT 451

First published: 1953
Type of work: Novel

> In a future America, a man dedicated to burning all of humanity's great writing discovers he has been mistaken.

Fahrenheit 451—named for the temperature at which paper ignites and burns—is Bradbury's best-known novel and is probably also his best. Based on an earlier story, "The Fireman" (1950), and developing the censorship theme that appears in several other Bradbury works, this novel presents the dystopia that Bradbury may fear most.

In a future America, the lowest common denominator of culture has imposed its ideas of happiness upon the whole culture. The universal idea of happiness has become an extrapolation of sitting in front of a television with a six-pack of beer, free of hard work, of complex human relationships, and of the disturbing stimulation of the ideas and images of the great artists and thinkers. In the future, television screens can be all four walls of a room. There, the viewer participates in the families and adventures that appear on "the walls" by subscribing to and then acting out a viewer script. When the walls fail to interest, one places receivers in the ears and blankets the mind with pleasant sound that blocks out awareness of self and world.

Montag, the protagonist, is a fireman. His team's job is to burn books and arrest their possessors. Not all books are outlawed—only those that stimulate the imagination with their complex ideas or vivid images of human possibility, those books that encourage people to aspire toward thought and experience beyond the ordinary.

Though this story is often compared with George Orwell's dystopia, *1984* (1949), the two books differ significantly. An especially important difference is the role of government. The tyranny of an oligarchy in *1984* is matched by the tyranny of the anti-intellectual majority in *Fahrenheit 451*. Bradbury's novel partakes of the atmosphere of anti-Communism following World War II. The government seems distant, unconcerned with life in Montag's city, involved instead in the threat of atomic war that hangs over the nation. Beatty, Montag's boss, in a series of lectures on the history and theory of the firemen's work, makes clear that the firemen act on behalf of ordinary people who know what happiness is, who want to be sure that everyone is happy, and who want to extirpate any who fail to conform to this idea of happiness. Book collectors are discovered and exposed by their neighbors, acting from a sense of civic duty; no secret police are required.

Montag's story develops rapidly and inexorably in three stages.

Part 1, "The Hearth and the Salamander," presents a series of discoveries that lead Montag to steal and read from the books he is supposed to burn. He meets an imaginative young girl, Clarisse, who opens him to ways of seeing that he finds attractive. He discovers that his wife, Mildred, is not happy, despite her self-deluding assertions to the contrary, and that he is not happy either. Their lives are empty and teeter on the edge of self-destruction, held back only by the constant vacuous stimulation of electronic media and drugs. Montag is the salamander, the dragon of dangerous fire, but he discovers that his hearth is cold, that his home lacks spirit and love; it has no central animating principle. When he sees a woman who prefers to be burned with her books rather than to give them up, he realizes that they must contain something of great importance. He begins to read the books that he has almost unconsciously been hiding away in his home.

In part 2, "The Sieve and the Sand," Montag tries to understand the wisdom he believes is in his books, which include the Bible and poems such as Matthew Arnold's "Dover Beach" (1867). He finds that, in several ways, his mind is like a sieve; he does not know how to make sense of what he reads without any intellectual training or context. Frustrated at the futility of his efforts, he takes dangerous risks. He contacts Faber, an unemployed professor in whom he once confided, and becomes aware of the possibility of rebellion. He finds himself bursting to talk about what he has read and tries communicating with his wife. These activities bring him increasingly to the attention of Beatty, who has long suspected that Montag does not fit the fireman mold. Part 2 ends when Montag's team answers an alarm that brings them to his own house.

Part 3, "Burning Bright," tells of Montag's escape from his job and the imprisoning city. He becomes a fugitive when he kills Beatty rather than betray Faber. Montag concludes that Beatty wanted to be killed, that he manipulated the crisis before Montag's burning home in order to bring about his own death. This observation highlights one of the more puzzling aspects of the novel, which is how to read Beatty's character. Beatty is the spokesperson for the majority point of view, yet the arguments he offers for keeping literature out of people's hands and destroying those who insist upon reading are filled with references to and quotations from the very works he opposes. Montag's final realization seems to suggest that Beatty, like Mildred, deludes himself into believing he is happy. Beatty, however, unlike Mildred, may come to understand his duplicity, leading him actively to seek death.

Montag's harrowing flight brings him finally to a hearth, where vagrants gathered around a fire warm themselves and form a community. He soon learns that they have met there to receive him into their fragile underground—a group of rebels who survive relatively unmolested in the countryside and whose rebellion consists essentially of memorizing great books in preparation for the day when they can be written again. These people can help him understand the books they remember, and he himself can become a "book" by sharing what he has managed to remember from Ecclesiastes and the Book of Revelation. As he joins this community, atomic war comes to the nation, and the city he has left behind is consumed in flames. They believe that all the other cities are also being destroyed and therefore that their rebel group represents the phoenix, the new civilization to arise from the ruins of the old.

Bleak as this novel may appear, emphasizing as it does some of the worst things people can do, it nevertheless ends with an expression of hope that goes beyond the idea of the biblical saving remnant suggested by the phoenix image. One of the rebels speaks for them all, and probably for Bradbury, when he says, "We know all the damn silly things we've done for a thousand years and as long as we know that and always have it around where we can see it, some day we'll stop making the goddam funeral pyres and jumping in the middle of them." In order to know what those silly things are and where they lead, one must have the books that tell about them. One of the reasons the society of *Fahrenheit 451* fails is that it made a happiness machine that erased the past and prevented people from imagining the future. With their minds locked in the present, they could do nothing to stop the fiery holocaust from falling upon them.

DANDELION WINE

First published: 1957
Type of work: Novel

Twelve-year-old Douglas Spaudling and his friends in Green Town, Illinois, in the summer of 1928 have adventures that teach them about the joys and the pains of living.

Dandelion Wine, like *The Martian Chronicles*, was constructed from previously published stories. Bradbury made a significantly greater effort to turn these stories into a unified book, however, by revising the stories with care and by writing connecting material. Bradbury also provided a greater impression of unity than in *The Martian Chronicles* by dropping the stories' original titles and using no table of contents. *Dandelion Wine* is perhaps the most autobiographical of his novels. Elements of Bradbury can be seen in both Douglas Spaulding and his younger brother Tom. Green Town, on Lake Michigan, is similar to Bradbury's childhood home, Waukegan, Illinois, and the Spaulding family is like the Bradbury family.

Readers have noticed the similarities between *Dandelion Wine* and Sherwood Anderson's *Winesburg, Ohio*. Bradbury's book differs in that the predominant point of view is pre-adolescent, so that the spiritual anguish and the problems of sexuality that are important in Anderson's book are virtually absent in Bradbury's. The childish exuberance in the feeling of being alive that is a central theme both exceeds the energy and falls short of the profundity one sees in George Willard, Anderson's youthful protagonist. Bradbury presents a vivid picture of a boy's life in a small Midwestern town early in the twentieth century. In the summer of 1928, Doug awakens to the momentous sense that being physically and spiritually alive is a great gift, and he begins to keep a written record of his life. This consists of two lists: One contains events that happen every summer like rituals—"Ceremonies"; the other contains new and unprecedented events—"Revelations."

Once Bradbury has established Doug as a boy awakening to a sense of the wonder of life and wanting to understand it in his imagination, the structure of the book falls into a collection of sketches and stories, roughly chronological. Each story is well-connected to the over-arching structure, often in several ways. The story may contain a ceremony, a revelation, or a combination of the two, and it may contribute as well to one of several thematic patterns that structure Doug's awakening.

One of the main patterns is that of loss. Doug, his brother, and their friends interact with a number of very old people during this summer. One ancient man becomes their time machine, transporting them to the wonderful places he has been by telling stories. A Civil War veteran who cannot remember which side he was on, Colonel Freeleigh can nevertheless still picture and describe vividly the day he saw a giant herd of bison on the prairie or a battle in the war. Before the summer is over, he dies. So does Doug's great-grandmother, who loved to repair the shingle roof each summer. His best friend moves away. A pair of elderly ladies permanently park their electric car after hitting a pedestrian. The trolley makes its last run and is replaced by a bus. Doug is almost present at two killings. The arcade's ancient mechanical prophetess, the Tarot Witch, finally breaks down. Great and small, parts of Doug's world slip away, and with the realization that he is richly alive comes the realization that he must die.

At the end of the summer, Doug becomes mysteriously ill. Brother Tom realizes that Doug wants to die because he has lost so much during the summer. This will-to-death also arises from a deeper source, Doug's fear of facing and accepting his own mortality, an experience that Bradbury says he had when he was thirteen: "I discovered I could die, and that scared the hell out of me. And I thought, 'How do you escape *that* knowledge? Well, I'll *kill* myself.'"

Doug is cured by a kind of magic, when his friend the local junk man gives him two bottles of fragrant air to breathe in. Like the bottles of dandelion wine that the boys and their grandfather produce throughout the summer, these bottles contain reminders of the richness of life to be enjoyed in those moments when it might be forgotten. Doug realizes this; he also comes to feel an obligation to live in order to pass on to others the wonderful if temporary gift of life that he has received. His first success at passing on this gift comes when he restores his grandmother's magical power to produce delicious meals out of a chaotic kitchen after the too-orderly Aunt Rose ruins her cooking by organizing her. *Dandelion Wine* is a particularly rewarding novel for younger readers, but its fanciful humor and vivid portrait of small-town life can be enjoyed by older readers as well.

SOMETHING WICKED THIS WAY COMES

First published: 1962
Type of work: Novel

Jim Nightshade, Will Holloway, and his father, Charles Holloway, must face their deepest fears and desires when a dark carnival tempts them to surrender their souls in exchange for meaningless power.

"By the pricking of my thumbs,/ something wicked this way comes." In Shakespeare's *Macbeth* (c. 1605), the witches speak these lines as Macbeth approaches for his second meeting with them. He has come because he has found his ill-gotten power empty and insecure. The witches speak out of sympathy for the evil they have cultivated in him. When Charles Holloway quotes these lines in *Something Wicked This Way Comes*, he is also speaking of the sympathy of the evil that lurks always in the hearts of the good for the greater evil in the hearts of those who have given in— who have agreed to trade something for nothing, thus converting themselves into grotesques who feed on the pain and fear of others.

Quasi-allegorical in form, this novel, like *Dandelion Wine*, is set in Green Town and seems aimed at young readers. Two boys deal with the temptations of evil presented by Cooger and Dark's Pandemonium Shadow Show. Will Holloway and Jim Nightshade are best friends and neighbors. Will, son of Charles, was born just before midnight, Jim, just after midnight on Halloween Day. Will seems the natural child of reason and goodness, but fatherless Jim finds in himself an attraction to danger, to power, and to evil. Their friendship binds them together in mutual dependence and defense.

The novel is divided into three parts. In the first, "Arrivals," the Cooger and Dark carnival comes to Green Town at 3 A.M. on a Friday, the week before Halloween. No sooner does it arive than impossible things begin to occur. Miss Foley, a teacher, is terrified upon seeing her treasured little-girl identity eaten away by age in the maze of mirrors. The boys meet a boy who is revealed to be Cooger, having somehow returned to the age of twelve, and through their accidental interference with the magical carousel that changes people's ages, they age him to 120.

The mirror maze and the carousel are the main instruments that the carnival uses to capture those lonely people who dream of gaining power by transforming themselves. The mirror maze shows them what they want to be and makes them fear old age and death. The carousel, by carrying them backward or forward, makes them the age they believe they wish to be; however, Dark, the show's proprietor, a version of the illustrated man from Bradbury's second story collection, always cheats, never giving people exactly what they believe they want, but rather some extreme version of it. As a result, they tend to become his slaves, wanting another ride on his machine, and so they become part of his traveling freak show.

In Jim, Dark sees a potential partner, one who might help him carry on the show. Jim's desire is to become instantly older and more powerful. Bradbury does not explore this desire; rather, Jim seems to be a projection of the otherwise invisible dark side of Will. By the end of the first part, Will and Jim have gained enough knowledge of Dark's work to realize that he will catch and destroy them to use them if he can. In the second part, "Pursuits," the boys hide from him and try to discover a way to deal with him. By themselves, they find they cannot, though they are resourceful in their opposition. They enlist the help of Charles, Will's father.

Charles Holloway combines elements of both Jim and Will in his own past. He married late, after trying to make himself into his own ideal for thirty-nine years. He found eventually that life is not simple and fine, that one never becomes the ideal one dreams. Instead, as he tells Will, a person makes choices from one moment to the next, living into the future in a constant struggle against the temptations of nonbeing. There is no final arrival, only pursuit. Will's struggle to stay with Jim and protect him is parallel to Charles's struggle to come to terms with himself. Charles's main regret is that he took so long to begin his life so he is susceptible to the carousel's temptation to roll back the years.

Charles is janitor at the Green Town library. There the most intense phase of the struggle begins. The second part ends when Dark makes his way into the library early Sunday evening, disables Charles, and captures Will and Jim. Charles almost gives in to death in this scene, to the power of the Dust Witch, one of Dark's accomplices, to stop one's heart. In the face of death, Charles realizes that human life is a bleak and meaningless joke. This nihilism leads him not to despair, however, but to laughter, for in the face of mortality, desire and temptation appear ridiculous. His laughter repels the witch and becomes the weapon by which he defeats Dark in the last part, "Departures."

Charles rescues Will and, together, they finally recover Jim from Dark's power, using the forces of laughter, kindness, and joy. With Dark's death, the freaks become free of their magic prison, represented by the tattoos that cover Dark's body. The carnival dissipates. Charles points out, however, that humanity is not free of temptation, for the desire for empty impossibilities is in them all, and there will be many other attempts to exploit this desire in their long lives.

Critical reaction to Bradbury's second traditonal novel was mixed. Those who disliked it found it overwritten. There are many passages in the novel that remind one of Walt Whitman's *Song of Myself* (1855), with sentences of many clauses celebrating and elaborating a scene or realization. As a result, the novel is not efficient in its development and, to some readers, seems inflated with unnecessary poetic prose. Others, however, respond positively to the fast pace of the action and to the marshalling of fantasy elements that produce an entertaining adventure/allegory.

Summary

Throughtout his career, Ray Bradbury has exhibited both an enthusiasm for experience and an awareness of the weaknesses that repeatedly bring humanity to the brink of self-extinction; those elements are the hallmarks of his fiction. In his science fiction and in the fantasies based on his childhood, Bradbury has produced a memorable and influential body of writing, notably in *The Martian Chronicles* and *Fahrenheit 451*. With moving and imaginative stories told in a lively, poetic style, he brought American science fiction and fantasy to the attention of a mass audience, helping to make possible a renaissance in these genres.

Bibliography

Johnson, Wayne L. *Ray Bradbury.* New York: Frederick Ungar, 1980.

Mogen, David. *Ray Bradbury.* Boston: Twayne, 1986.

Nolan, William F. *The Ray Bradbury Companion.* Detroit: Gale Research, 1975.

Olander, Joseph, and Martin H. Greenberg, eds. *Ray Bradbury.* New York: Taplinger, 1980.

Slusser, George E. *The Bradbury Chronicles.* San Bernardino, Calif.: Borgo Press, 1977.

Toupence, William F. *Ray Bradbury and the Poetics of Reverie.* Ann Arbor: University of Michigan Research Press, 1984.

Terry Heller

ANNE BRADSTREET

Born: Northampton, England
c. 1612

Died: Andover, Massachusetts Bay Colony
September 16, 1672

Principal Literary Achievement

Blending Puritan religiosity, an awareness of the English literary tradition, and a talent for depicting domestic themes, Anne Bradstreet, one of the earliest Massachusetts Bay settlers, became America's first authentic poet.

Biography

Despite the prominence of both her father and her husband in the Massachusetts Bay Colony, facts about Anne Bradstreet are scarce, and her poems are the major source of biographical information. She was born Anne Dudley, probably in Northampton, England, in 1612. From the age of seven, she lived in the household of the earl of Lincoln, whom her father served as a steward for more than a decade. As the child of a Puritan family, she became conscious of sinfulness early in life. Her physical health also suffered. She regarded smallpox, which afflicted her at age sixteen, as a punishment for her "carnal" desires. In 1628, she was married to Simon Bradstreet. Two years later, the Bradstreet and Dudley families sailed to the New World on the *Arbella* along with John Winthrop and the original Massachusetts Bay colonists.

In the New World, the Bradstreets lived in several places before settling permanently in Merrimac (now Andover). Both her father and husband assumed leadership roles in the colony from the start. The former remained politically active into his seventies, serving four one-year terms as governor between 1634 and 1650 as well as thirteen terms as deputy governor. Her even more durable husband began as secretary of the colony, served thirty-three years as a commissioner of the New England Confederation, and in his seventies and eighties served as governor. He was also interested in frontier trading, and his frequent absences from home became the subject of two of his wife's best poems.

For some years after her marriage, Anne Bradstreet continued to suffer from poor health and the added humiliation of not being able to bear Simon any children. It is not clear when she began writing poetry, but by the late 1640's she had written enough to justify, at least in the opinion of her admirers, a book. A family member

THE
TENTH MUSE

Lately sprung up in AMERICA.

OR

Severall Poems, compiled with great variety of VVit and Learning, full of delight.

Wherein especially is contained a compleat discourse and description of

The Four
{
Elements,
Constitutions,
Ages of Man,
Seasons of the Year.
}

Together with an Exact Epitomie of the Four Monarchies, viz.

The
{
Assyrian,
Persian,
Grecian,
Roman.
}

Also a Dialogue between Old England and New, concerning the late troubles.

With divers other pleasant and serious Poems.

or friend, probably her brother-in-law, John Woodbridge, carried a manuscript of her poems to England. In 1650, the first book of poems by an American author, Bradstreet's *The Tenth Muse Lately Sprung Up in America*, appeared in England.

In the meantime, one of her concerns had been resolved, for she gave birth to eight children. From the evidence of her poems, she was a conscientious wife and mother. As Simon Bradstreet's wife, she was probably spared the worst household drudgery, but colonial life imposed severe hardships on a woman in any station. Nevertheless, she found time to compose long poems with such titles as "The Four Elements," "The Ages of Man," "The Humours," "The Four Seasons of the Year," and "The Four Monarchies." Today these poems seem derivative and amateurish, but "The Prologue," which is a defense of her resolution to pursue the male-dominated literary profession, remains an intriguing work.

Once it was in print, Bradstreet, conscious of the defects of her earlier work, revised it for a possible second edition. In "The Author to Her Book," she expresses chagrin over poems she characterizes as "ill-formed offspring"; she also composed additional poems of a quite different sort, including love poems to her husband and poems to and about her children. Her inclination to memorialize family events such as illnesses, deaths, and "deliverances" from these troubles sheds light on her life. Because she wrote a poem on the incident, for example, it is known that her house burned down on July 10, 1666. She also wrote religious meditations in both prose and verse. These more personal poems are much more concrete and vital than her earlier ones.

Bradstreet did not live to see the second edition of her book in print. She died on September 16, 1672, six years before the publication of the expanded edition. Another set of poems and prose meditations remained in manuscript until 1867. Bradstreet's legacy also includes her numerous descendants, among them such distinguished Americans as Wendell Phillips, the great abolitionist; Richard Henry Dana, Jr., author of *Two Years Before the Mast* (1840); the poet Oliver Wendell Holmes and his son, who served as a United States Supreme Court justice; and one of America's most important twentieth century poets, Edwin Arlington Robinson.

Though delicate in health, Bradstreet proved to be a woman of great interior strength and endurance. She not only ranks as America's first woman poet but also was America's first poet of indisputable literary quality.

Analysis

Anne Bradstreet benefited from an education unusually thorough for a woman of her time. Knowledgeable about history, theology, and science, she also demonstrates a familiarity with numerous earlier poets. She wrote an elegy on the famed soldier, diplomat, and poet Sir Philip Sidney that displays a keen interest in his sonnet sequence *Astrophel and Stella* (1591). She also appears to have been influenced by the English meditative poets of her own century. The poet she honors most highly, however, is the French religious poet Guillaume de Salluste (Seigneur du Bartas), whose epic *La Semaine* (1578; *The Divine Weeks*, 1608) was a favorite among Puritans.

In her early writing, Bradstreet favored quaternions, poems with subject groups of four. For centuries, the material world was believed to be composed of four elements: fire, air, earth, and water. Thus, human temperaments and physiological types were explained as various mixtures of these elements and were called "humours." Two of Bradstreet's quaternions consist of successive speeches by the respective elements and humours in which they boast of their own importance. "The Ages of Man" follows a similar pattern, with Childhood, Youth, Middle Age, and Old Age speaking in turn. While rather stiff and uninspired, these poems show that Bradstreet had accumulated considerable astronomical, geographical, historical, theological, medical, and psychological information. "The Four Seasons of the Year," though occasionally betraying a love of nature, is similarly conventional and bookish. Her longest poem, "The Four Monarchies," versifies in 3,432 lines a portion of ancient history for which her chief source was Sir Walter Raleigh's *History of the World* (1614). The last and shortest history is of the Roman monarchy, and it culminates in "An Apology" for being unable to carry it out to its projected length. The loss is not great, for "The Four Monarchies," which labors to show the vanity and futility of ancient pre-Christian ambition, is a tedious poem.

Those and a dozen other shorter poems make up her *The Tenth Muse;* except for the introductory poem, "The Prologue," however, which provocatively asserts her commitment to poetry even as it seeks to disarm masculine criticism of her pioneering work, this collection was not responsible for establishing her reputation as one of the two most significant poets of the colonial era in America (Edward Taylor being the other). Readers must turn to the posthumously published poems to appreciate Bradstreet's poetry.

Motherhood became a paramount fact of her life and also one of her favorite metaphors. In "The Author to Her Book," her book is an ill-favored child whom she has labored to improve. She wittily bids her child not to fall into a "critic's hands" but to explain that her mother has had to turn her "rambling brat" out of the house because of poverty. This metaphor is useful in establishing the mock-modest tone that she employs when referring to her own work. Bradstreet is not being hypocritical; rather, she enjoys assuming the role of the hard-working amateur—a role made somewhat more difficult to sustain by the publication of her book. She reminds her critically inclined readers that few parents would care to be held completely responsible for their offspring.

Her own children are often her true subject as well. Her family poems avoid sentimentality and brim with the honest sentiment of a woman who trusts in heaven but loves her husband and children beyond any other earthly thing. If her book becomes her child, her children in one poem become the birds of her nest. Inevitably the theme of death arises. "Before the Birth of One of Her Children," which is addressed to her husband, expresses the fear of the colonial housewife—for whom each pregnancy is the prelude to a possible death. Several other poems memorialize grandchildren who died in infancy or early childhood. The feeling in these poems is artistically restrained, and the attitude is one of resignation to God's mysterious will, yet there can be no doubt of the genuineness of her grief on each occasion.

Two poems occasioned by her husband's absence on business focus on her intense love for him. In one, she argues that her love exceeds that of the female deer, dove, and fish for their absent mates; when he returns, they will "browse," "roost," and "glide" together. In the other, "A Letter to Her Husband, Absent upon Public Employment," she uses the sun to describe her husband and her love for him.

Like most of the 1650 poems, "Contemplations" is conventional and rather general in its thought, but the voice is unmistakably Bradstreet's. It is a compact spiritual autobiography affirming that the hope of heaven is the only security worth striving for. Her fine prose work, "Meditations Divine and Moral," addressed to her son Simon and unpublished until 1867, demonstrates her good sense, poet's ear, and talent for grounding her religious outlook in close observations of the world around her.

Anne Bradstreet was a poet of considerable talent who, lacking fruitful contact with other poets, nevertheless learned to write by studying the works of past poets. Discovering her true subject matter in religious and domestic themes, she also fulfilled the demanding role of a colonial housewife with a large family. American critics were somewhat tardy in recognizing her accomplishments, but it is safe to say that her best poems will be long remembered.

THE PROLOGUE

First published: 1650
Type of work: Poem

A colonial woman begins her book of poems by defending it against captious criticism.

"The Prologue" is Anne Bradstreet's apology for her book of poems. At first, it seems like an apology in the common sense of the word, for she refers to her "foolish, broken, blemished Muse" and begs elaborate pardon that her poems are not so fine as those of other poets, although she insists that she is doing the best she can. Upon closer inspection, "The Prologue" turns out to be an apology in the literary sense of a defense of her art. One of her favorite poets, Sir Philip Sidney, also referred to his own work condescendingly. This attitude has a special meaning when expressed by a woman writing in a New World Puritan outpost before 1650.

"The Prologue" is written in eight six-line iambic pentameter stanzas, using the rhyme scheme ababcc. She begins by advising her reader that she has no ambition to write an elaborate, important poem such as an epic. She lauds the sixteenth century French poet du Bartas but notes that her work will be much simpler. She hopes it will not be judged too harshly, for her ability is severely limited.

In the second half of the poem, she modifies her defense. She acknowledges that men expect women to practice feminine arts such as needlework and refuse to recy value in a woman's poem. She intimates that the Greeks, in making the Muses feminine, had more regard for feminine creativity, but concedes that this argument will not convince the men. She then concludes with two stanzas confessing the superiority of male poets but asking "some small acknowledgement" of women's efforts. After all, Bradstreet's "lowly lines" will simply make men's poetry look better by comparison.

Even read literally, as it often has been read, this poem displays clever strategy. How could any fairminded person expect competent poetry from uneducated people who had no opportunities to travel or associate familiarly with other poets and who spent most of their lives bearing children and serving their needs and those of their husbands? Even when blessed with talent and sufficient leisure to compose, such writers offered no threat to the male poets, many of whom could take education, frequent association with their peers, and leisure for granted. By displaying humility at the beginning of her book, Bradstreet hoped to forestall or at least minimize the inevitable criticism of a woman poet.

It is difficult, however, to escape the conviction that irony lurks everywhere in this poem. In the first place, it is scarcely possible that Bradstreet considered her brain "weak or wounded" as she styles it in the poem; talented people are usually aware of their talent. If she cannot write "of wars, of captains, and of kings," she has the resources to write about her husband, children and grandchildren, domestic life (including the cruel experience of watching her home burn), and the spiritual struggle common to all Puritans.

The last four stanzas of the poem betray signs of an ironic counterattack upon her critics. Her fifth stanza almost undermines the effect toward which she is working by nearly boiling over with indignation at men's refusal to accept the woman poet. Such criticism is "carping"; it maintains that any feminine poetic success must be the result of either plagiarism or "chance." Why did men call poetry "Calliope's own child"? The answer that she attributes to the men—that the Greeks did nothing but "play the fools and lie"—mimics a weak-kneed response.

In her final stanza, she catches the true satiric tone. Addressing "ye highflown quills that soar the skies," she asks not for the "bays," or traditional laurel wreath honoring poetic achievement, but for a "thyme or parsley wreath" befitting the woman who is expected to reign chiefly in the kitchen. She might as well have asked for a bay leaf, the common kitchen spice, but such a request might have reminded her audience that the laurel leaf and the bay leaf are closely affiliated. In effect, Bradstreet has asked for a recognition less humble than it seems. Her final point— that her "unrefinéd ore" will make the male poets' "gold" appear to shine more brightly—taunts the egotism of the males, who are probably flying too high to notice.

A LETTER TO HER HUSBAND, ABSENT UPON PUBLIC EMPLOYMENT

First published: 1678
Type of work: Poem

In a verse letter to her absent husband, a woman affirms her love.

"A Letter to Her Husband, Absent upon Public Employment" is one of two Bradstreet poems on this subject. She must have been familiar with the classical epistle, or verse letter, which English poets had begun imitating in the sixteenth century. She addresses her husband by a series of metaphors, the main one being the sun. She likens herself to the earth in winter, lamenting "in black" the receding light and feeling "chilled" without him to warm her. She is home with only "those fruits which through thy heat I bore"—her children—as reminders. With her husband "southward gone," she finds the short winter days ironically long and tedious.

She continues to project her sun metaphor into the future. When he returns, the season will be summer figuratively and perhaps literally: "I wish my Sun may never set, but burn/ Within the Cancer of my glowing breast," a zodiacal allusion to early summer. She closes by reaffirming their married oneness: "Flesh of thy flesh, bone of thy bone,/ I here, thou there, yet both but one."

Though neither so intricate in form nor elaborate in imagery as John Donne's famous "A Valediction: Forbidding Mourning," published in 1633, this poem on the same theme shows Bradstreet's resourcefulness with imagery and able handling of her favorite pentameter couplets. While exhibiting great devotion to Simon, this poem succeeds because it also reflects devotion to the art of lyric verse.

IN REFERENCE TO HER CHILDREN, 23 JUNE 1659

First published: 1678
Type of work: Poem

A mother bids a loving farewell in turn to each of her eight children.

One of Bradstreet's most charming poems, "In Reference to Her Children, 23 June 1659" distinguishes and describes each of the "eight birds" from her "nest." Several times she indicates precise dates for her poems or the events they describe; this one suggests a time of relative leisure after five of the eight have left home.

She maintains the bird metaphor throughout the poem's ninety-six lines, describing the various "flights" of five of her children and her concerns about those re-n the nest. Four are "cocks," four "hens." The oldest having flown "to regions far," she longs for his return. The next two, both girls, have been married, while the second son is at "the academy," where he will learn to sing better than nightingales. Number five is "mongst the shrubs and bushes," which may mean that he has taken up farming. She hopes that the youngest three will not fall victim to birdcatchers, stone-throwers, or hawks.

Recalling the pains and cares of their early childhood, she notes that their growing up has not ended her constant concern for their welfare. Going on to remind the children that her own days are numbered, she tells them that she expects to be singing among the angels soon. The closing lines beg her brood to emulate in their own families the loving attention and moral instruction she has bestowed on them, thus keeping her alive in a way. She ends by bidding her offspring farewell and assuring them that she will be happy if all goes well with them.

Forty-eight tetrameter couplets might seem rather a long time to keep the bird metaphor going, but Bradstreet's light touch sustains the reader's interest. Because she evokes her children as individuals and conveys her tender feeling for each of them, this poem written on a particular day for a particular family expresses the universality of mother love.

Summary

Beginning with ambitious but uninspired poems on remote subjects, Anne Bradstreet proceeded to discover her vocation as a poet of more personal matters. Of the poems in the first edition of her book, only "The Prologue" anticipates the more intimate kind of poem for which she is now best known. Her typical subjects became birth, illness, recovery, death, leavetakings, and her love for her husband, her children, and God. Her witty elaborations of basic metaphors—her book as her child, her children as birds, her husband as the sun—show Bradstreet's poetic imagination at its best.

Bibliography

Cowell, Pattie, and Ann Stanford, eds. *Critical Essays on Anne Bradstreet*. Boston: G. K. Hall, 1983.

Jantz, H. S. *The First Century of American Verse*. Worcester, Mass.: American Antiquarian Society, 1944.

Morison, Samuel Eliot. *Builders of the Bay Colony*. Boston: Houghton Mifflin, 1958.

Piercy, Josephine. *Anne Bradstreet*. New York: Twayne, 1965.

Stanford, Ann. *Anne Bradstreet: The Worldly Puritan*. New York: Burt Franklin, 1974.

_____. "Three Puritan Women: Anne Bradstreet, Mary Rowlandson, and Sarah Kemble Knight." In *American Women Writers: Bibliographical Essays*, edited by Maurice Duke et al. Westport, Conn.: Greenwood Press, 1983.

Robert P. Ellis

RICHARD BRAUTIGAN

Born: Tacoma, Washington
January 30, 1935
Died: Bolinas, California
September, 1984

Principal Literary Achievement

Known for his gentle narrators and the unusual central characters of his novels, Brautigan is the principal transitional figure between the Beat writers and the youth culture of the 1960's.

Biography

Richard Brautigan was born in Tacoma, Washington, on January 30, 1935, the son of Bernard Brautigan and Lula Mary Keho Brautigan. A series of stepfathers made Brautigan's early life rather chaotic and unstable. He began to write while attending high school, and the Beat movement drew him to the San Francisco Bay area in the mid-1950's. There he met Philip Whalen, with whom he shared an apartment for a period, Allen Ginsberg, Lawrence Ferlinghetti, and most of the other poets and fiction writers who congregated in the book stores and coffee houses. While Brautigan is primarily remembered as an offbeat novelist, he was first published as a poet; *The Return of the Rivers* appeared in 1957, the same year he married Virginia Dionne Adler. *The Galilee Hitch-Hiker* was published in 1958, *Lay the Marble Tea: Twenty-four Poems* in 1959, and *The Octopus Frontier* in 1960, the year his daughter Ianthe was born. During this period he worked at a succession of odd jobs while writing a considerable body of poetry.

During the four years Brautigan was married to Virginia Adler, he completed two of the three books of fiction upon which his literary reputation rests and began the third. Donald Allen was instrumental in bringing two of Brautigan's novels to the attention of an editor at Grove Press in New York, which published *A Confederate General From Big Sur* in 1964. When this work sold poorly, Grove had second thoughts about handling a second book. Allen acted on Brautigan's behalf again by publishing *Trout Fishing in America* himself in 1967, and Richard Brautigan's literary career quickly started to take shape. The "love generation" soon began to think it heard its own voice in the thoughtful, eccentric characters that peopled Brautigan's novels; Brautigan became a cult writer to a social and political movement with whom he shared only a few preoccupations.

Though he had never attended college, Brautigan became poet-in-residence at the California Institute of Technology in 1967. In 1969, the novelist Kurt Vonnegut helped Delacorte Press secure rights to *Trout Fishing in America* as well as Brautigan's new book, *In Watermelon Sugar*, which had been published by a smaller press a year before. With *The Abortion: An Historical Romance* (1971), Brautigan began to base more and more of his fictional works either on particular subgenres of the novel, such as the romance, or on specific earlier literary works, such as F. Scott Fitzgerald's short story "The Diamond as Big as the Ritz" (in *Tales of the Jazz Age*, 1922).

His popularity grew, his book sales soared, and Brautigan began to wander more widely and more frequently than he had been able to before. In addition to his house in Bolinas, California, Brautigan acquired a strip of Montana ranch land near Livingston. The writer's fascination with this section of the country influenced both *The Hawkline Monster: A Gothic Western* (1974) and *The Tokyo-Montana Express* (1980).

Brautigan married again, in Japan, and brought his bride Akiko back to live with him in Montana. Like his first, this marriage was short-lived; the couple separated in 1981. Brautigan had begun to drink heavily even earlier, and he grew despondent when the sales of his books declined steadily and critical reaction to his writing grew cool.

Experiments in fictional form and subgenre mark almost all the later and less important novels. *Willard and His Bowling Trophies* (1975) Brautigan subtitled *A Perverse Mystery*. *Sombrero Fallout* (1976) is subtitled *A Japanese Novel*, and *Dreaming of Babylon: A Private Eye Novel 1942* (1977) is an odd reworking of the 1940's private eye story. *So the Wind Won't Blow It All Away* (1982) seems to be based, at least in some ways, on Henry David Thoreau's *Walden* (1854). During this period, Brautigan grew more and more moody and reclusive, granting no interviews and delivering no public lectures on his works. Only with *The Tokyo-Montana Express*, his next to last book, did Brautigan again achieve anything resembling the brilliance, effervescence, and wit of his early works.

Self-absorbed, deeply depressed, troubled by debts, and abrasive even to those who cared for him, Brautigan went from bad to miserable. After the commercial failure of *So the Wind Won't Blow It All Away* (it sold fewer than fifteen thousand copies), no publisher was interested in a work that he offered them in 1983. In his house in Bolinas, sometime late in September of the following year, when even his closest friends did not know where he was, Brautigan put a borrowed Smith & Wesson .44 Magnum to his head and pulled the trigger. His body was not found until October 25, 1984.

Analysis

The principal themes of Brautigan's fiction are concerned with different aspects of the same classical philosophical question: What constitutes the good life? For example, in *A Confederate General from Big Sur*, Brautigan explores the role of friendship in life—its obligations as well as its joys and tribulations. Lee Mellon, the book's central character, is an entertaining ne'er-do-well whose complex, disorganized life brings the first-person narrator, Jesse, as much trouble as it does pleasure—perhaps more. Lee is inventive and funny, but his behavior and morals are an increasing strain on Jesse's patience and sense of right and wrong. Lee Mellon's spontaneity and his direct contact with life cement the friendship, but it is in almost constant danger of coming apart toward the close of the story. Though the narrator feels "a sudden wave of vacancy go over me" when Lee treats another character harshly, Jesse remains loyal. One needs friends in this world, and sticks with them (the book implies) whether they are good or bad, right or wrong. Such a youthful answer to one of life's tougher questions did not go unnoticed by those readers wearing bell-bottomed trousers or miniskirts.

Brautigan was concerned as well with the individual's need for a sense of community. In *A Confederate General from Big Sur*, community comes in the form of the little group that gathers around the bogus general Lee Mellon at his Big Sur encampment. Community nurtures the individual and helps both to create possibilities for each person and to establish the boundaries of his or her reality. *Trout Fishing in America* is concerned with this same question, though here the individual's "community" is national rather than local. *In Watermelon Sugar*, set as it is in a fantasy-embroidered commune, is especially concerned with how life is best lived in relation to other lives. The community of iDEATH represents for Brautigan one answer to the problem of how men and women may relate meaningfully to one another within a social unit. Freedom, respect, and gentleness are all-important qualities of the sort of social construct that fosters growth and trust, that makes life worth living. Just as important as community, however, in bringing meaning and purpose to life is a sound, deeply shared love between a man and a woman.

The narrator of *The Abortion* had drifted through a purposeless existence until he met and fell in love with Vida, a beautiful woman who brings him back in contact with life. Love gone sour and the consequences of this on the soul are the principal concerns of both *Willard and His Bowling Trophies* and *Sombrero Fallout*. Without love, Brautigan's books imply, life is a gray, pointless affair. Both his poetry and his prose point to healthy love and sexuality as a very important part of the good life.

Despite the strength and the consistency of themes in Brautigan's novels, this element is seldom if ever the emphasis in his fiction, and his readers probably did not buy his books for their ruminations on particular ideas. Instead, Brautigan was a scintillating prose stylist whose humor ran toward a zaniness that was seldom lame or strained. Lee Mellon, despite his flaws as a human being, is entertaining and fascinating because he is at the same time likable and humorously fantastic. In *Trout Fishing in America*, the narrator goes to a strange sort of retail business establishment that sells trout streams by the foot (trees and birds are optional and at extra charge). Like Lee Mellon, the Cleveland Wrecking Yard is funny and sad at the same time; the reader is encouraged to laugh and ponder the odd ways of America—how it treats everything as commodity even as Americans (both the reader and the author) try to imbue everything with meaning. Even in Brautigan's later books such as *The Hawkline Monster*, the humor of situation and character is frequently entertaining. A wry view of life animates Brautigan's early novels, and when that disappeared, so too did the joy that readers found in his books.

Besides being humorous, the writing is richly metaphoric. When he began writing fiction, Brautigan retained both the insights and the methods of poetry. The Cleveland Wrecking Yard shows Brautigan's use of figurative language as well as it shows his humor. This establishment represents the way America "does business," packaging myth with environment and selling both at a profit. As in all good metaphors, the point is both clear and striking.

Often, however, Brautigan's figurative language is harder to interpret. Every reader of *In Watermelon Sugar* has the impression that something besides a post-nuclear-war hippie commune is the topic under discussion, but even the critics have not been able to agree on what this extended figure of speech is intended to illuminate. Another type of figurative complexity is found in Brautigan's frequent analogies. The "Ice Age Cab Company" chapter of *The Tokyo-Montana Express* finds the narrator struggling to describe how a sunset on the mountains constantly changes as it is being watched. To help readers understand his problem, he tells the story of a woman cab driver who seems preoccupied with an entirely different kind of change in the appearance of the mountains—that brought about by successive ice ages. At the end of her monologue, the narrator says, "When she started talking about the mountains, they looked one way and when she finished talking about them, they looked another way. I guess that's what I'm trying to say about this sunset." On the superficial level, one learns how long it takes her to tell her tale—in terms of the sunset. On another level, one is informed about the kinds of changes that take place in the mind as one views things from different perspectives. On the poetic level, one experiences an abrasion, one kind of change (a relatively rapid one, the sunset) grinding against a very different kind (the very slow change that glaciers bring about over aeons). The result of such carefully wrought poetic language, though it often seems simple on the surface, is a discourse that is lean and spare and drenched in nuance.

A CONFEDERATE GENERAL FROM BIG SUR

First published: 1964
Type of work: Novel

A small band of bizarre nonconformists searches for Lee Mellon's connection with the past and, not finding it, survives with whatever comes to hand.

A Confederate General from Big Sur, Brautigan's first published novel, focuses the reader's attention on its characters. The narrator is Jesse, a young man whose gentle, strange personality has the capacity to delight the reader with metaphoric insights and uncommon attitudes toward love, friendship, and life in general. The central character of the novel, however, is Lee Mellon, a true eccentric. In the first part of the book, he tries to gather information about an ancestor, Augustus Mellon, who (at least as family history would have it) was a general in the Civil War. Jesse tries to help Lee in his quest and thus becomes enmeshed in Mellon's chaotic, rough-hewn life. At one point, Jesse calls his friend a "Confederate General in ruins," echoing Ralph Waldo Emerson's description of man as a god in ruins. Lee Mellon is something of a narcissist and a bounder, but his character is compelling because he confronts life directly and leads the kind of wild, wide-open existence that invites the reader to fantasize that he too could be more this way if he chose. Lee comes short of being truly offensive, because he brings no lasting harm to anyone else.

Despite Jesse's and Lee's intensive search, they find no evidence that anyone by the name of Augustus Mellon was ever a Confederate general. Throughout the work Brautigan uses analogies from the Civil War, and particularly writings about that mythic struggle, as an underlying conceit. As in Brautigan's later novels, an underlying literary work, a repeated allusion, acts as a source and inspiration, giving both information to the account and tone to the writing style. In fact, Brautigan identifies the principal source as Ezra J. Warner's *Generals in Gray* (1959).

After their failure to uncover any information about the hypothetical general, Lee and Jesse retreat to Mellon's ramshackle place on the coast at Big Sur and ponder the possibilities of life while they have affairs with local women, help control a psychotic millionaire driven from home by his greedy family, and generally share whatever adventures and misadventures come their way. Jesse, however, is troubled by the chaos and uncertainty of life at Big Sur with Lee Mellon in charge. He is further unsettled by Lee's increasing aggression toward others, especially the erratic millionaire Johnston Wade, who is also referred to as Roy Earle, the character portrayed by Humphrey Bogart in the film *High Sierra*. Despite all Lee Mellon's flaws, his rebelliousness, zaniness, and originality make him compelling and appealing.

This frankly experimental work is further complicated by Brautigan's providing not one but several endings for the book. In the first ending, the two friends and their girlfriends are high on marijuana and Jesse is unable to complete the sexual act initiated by the woman he is with. The second ending resembles a still photograph of the foursome on the beach. By the time readers reach the sixth ending, they learn that the book has more and more endings unraveling faster and faster—"186,000 endings per second," the speed of light.

While Brautigan's decision to provide multiple endings may adequately describe marijuana intoxication (through confusion and disorientation), it nevertheless forces readers to select their own version of how the tale ends and thus casts some of the burden of the meaning of the story on them. No matter which ending (or endings) readers select, the conclusion of the book is desolate. One is alone, though one may find oneself among friends, and the isolation is painful and lacking in hope. Intoxication, sex, or activity may numb the pain for a while, but eventually each individual must face whatever hollowness exists within his or her soul. The contrast between the pervasive humor and the desolation of the ending (that desolation is also found elsewhere in the book) gives the novel a tense, haunting quality. The contrast oddly blends the angst that is often found in the Beats and the joyous, carefree attitude that characterized the American youth movement of the 1960's.

TROUT FISHING IN AMERICA

First published: 1967
Type of work: Novel

Trout fishing becomes an extended metaphor for much that is either good or strange in the American experience: friendship, nature, commercialism, growing up, and love.

Trout Fishing in America is Richard Brautigan's best-known and probably most important novel, but it is organized in a manner different from his other novels and from more conventional examples of the genre. For one thing, it has no easily recognizable plot structure. Rather, it weaves together (with apparent randomness) about forty episodes in the unnamed narrator's life and juxtaposes these with a few miscellaneous sections that illuminate the chapters in their vicinity. One thread of the story deals with the experiences of the narrator's boyhood. From these the reader gains a sense of his unusual personality—especially his separateness, vivid imagination, and highly individual way of viewing life. Another thread consists of the narrator's trout fishing experiences, though these sometimes overlap with the boyhood episodes. Chapters set during the narrator's adolescence show him seeking comfort and meaning from nature, well outside organized American society. Yet another thread in this complexly textured novel deals with the narrator's life in beatnik San Francisco. By this point he has married and fathered a child. The reader will quickly notice that the chapters are not presented chronologically; instead, they occasionally form small thematic packets or sometimes appear to be arranged for the humorous relationships to one another.

The themes of *Trout Fishing in America* are at least as complex and various as the book's structure. Many values that can be observed in Brautigan's other books are upheld here. Certainly, friendship is important in life, the book implies, but so too are love, a direct contact with nature, freedom, individuality and a good sense of humor.

Central to grasping the meaning of the novel is an understanding of Brautigan's many uses of the term "trout fishing in America." At its most fundamental level, the term refers to the actual act of fishing for trout—specifically, how this very act can rehabilitate a troubled mind. The term also represents nature itself in some sections and a state of mind that rises above the ordinary in others. Furthermore, the phrase is used as both a mythical character's name and a spirit of adventurousness in which freedom and rebellion combine to produce an idealized view of the possibilities of life. While this last use of the term tends to give the work a zestful quality in some places, the book is not fundamentally optimistic.

At the heart of *Trout Fishing in America* is a critique of contemporary American life and culture. Rampant commercialism, the packaging and selling of both the body and the myth of America, is shown in all its ugliness in the important "Cleveland Wrecking Yard" chapter as well as in several other parts of the novel. Nature and the environment have become secondary concerns in a country where an abundance of wildlife (including trout) and the purity of air and water have been taken for granted for centuries. Restrictions to personal liberty and the pressures on the individual to conform to American society's accepted roles are also criticized.

Such themes are not unique to this work; Brautigan's ideas are closely related to those of other artists of the Beat movement. Brautigan's extravagant humor masks the criticism implied by the work, however; the narrator never preaches, and if he does moralize, it is by means of a joke—often aimed at someone very much like himself. What is unique in the work is Brautigan's method of making both story and meaning.

Trout Fishing in America is probably best understood if it is viewed as a novel that owes much to poetry. While it was published after *A Confederate General from Big Sur*, it had been written previously, when all that Brautigan had published to that point were volumes of verse. The key phrase of the work, "trout fishing in America," acts much like an incantation or refrain in poetry—providing an echo of the main topic from beginning to end while changing its meaning as the tale progresses and the reader sees more deeply into the theme. This refrain acts also as a unifying element in the work, as does the image of grass in Walt Whitman's *Leaves of Grass* (1855), itself a sprawling, seemingly disorganized work of poetry. Finally, the book is highly metaphorical, from its often repeated key phrase to the details of its description. *Trout Fishing in America* is a novel that only a modern poet could have written.

IN WATERMELON SUGAR

First published: 1968
Type of work: Novel

In a fantasy commune, the gentle, shy narrator tries to find peace and a sense of community while writing a book.

In Watermelon Sugar takes place in a world where life is lived simply and everything is made from watermelon sugar, a substance refined from both the watermelons grown on the commune and Richard Brautigan's considerable imagination. The central character, another of Brautigan's gentle narrators, is the only writer in what seems to be the only settlement left on the planet. In fact, intellectual and artistic pursuits are allowed but not encouraged in the commune called iDEATH.

Most of the residents live their lives on a more literal, physical plane: making stew for the gang, turning watermelons into building materials, and constructing transparent underwater tombs. Life at iDEATH moves at a leisurely, idyllic pace.

The novel consists of three books. In book 1, the reader is introduced to the gentle lives of most of the main characters. Pauline, whom the narrator describes as "his favorite," spends the night with him. When he was a child, a band of speaking, ironic tigers ate his mother and father—after sending him outside to play. Book 1 ends with the narrator wishing his former girlfriend Margaret would leave him alone.

Book 2 is both a dream and a flashback. In the narrator's dream, a band of misfits led by inBOIL, who seethes internally, rummages through the debris in the Forgotten Works, a place that seems to represent the remains of a demolished culture that placed its primary value in things instead of people. In its profusion of objects and its physical complexity, the Forgotten Works resembles a demolished twentieth century America. The residents of iDEATH seem to represent a postmodern settlement that has survived some great catastrophe by placing values where they rightfully belong—on simple living, friendship, and love. *In Watermelon Sugar*, more strongly than any other of Brautigan's books, espouses the ideals of the youth movement of the 1960's.

The drunken gang that follows inBOIL believes that they represent the real iDEATH. In an effort to prove this, they cut off their fingers and noses and consequently bleed to death. The residents of the commune watch this bloodletting with more relief than horror, finally collecting the dead and burning them in their cabins close to the Forgotten Works. At the end of book 2, after the carnage, the narrator realizes that all of his feelings for Margaret have turned sour.

The opening of book 3 shows the narrator awakening from his flashback dream. He joins his friends from the commune and appears to be little affected by it. Later, while gazing at the Statue of Mirrors, he has a vision of Margaret hanging herself. Margaret's body is found (she actually has hanged herself) and brought back to the commune for burial.

Margaret is buried on a Thursday; in the bizarre world of *In Watermelon Sugar* the sun shines black on Thursdays and no sounds can be heard. At the conclusion, all the members of the commune are waiting for the setting of the black sun so that the social dancing, which customarily concludes a funeral, can begin. The narrator has finished his book, and the poetic wording of the ending reminds the reader of a similar incantation in the opening. One finds oneself reading the very book the narrator has been working on all along.

Upon publication of *In Watermelon Sugar*, many readers were tempted to see the work as a drug-induced fantasy. While the story may indeed by viewed as a many-colored distortion of the everyday world, it is doubtless a mistake to interpret it as a hymn to hallucinogens. Nothing in the content of the work suggests that drugs are either an issue here or a means to an end.

One of the main problems of interpreting this work accurately involves determining the meaning of the term "iDEATH." The death of "I" seems to represent the suppression of the ego, a feature of the Zen philosophy that was held in very high esteem by the Beats. In this system of thought, the ego is identified with selfishness and aggression. Surely inBOIL and his gang have misunderstood iDEATH. The ego is not to be done away with by self-torture or by punishing oneself. Those who value material objects above human values—kindness, love, and community—are on the wrong path. Instead, Brautigan's book recommends the simple life, as does Henry David Thoreau's *Walden* (1854). Where Brautigan differs from Thoreau is in his view of society. Whereas *Walden* depicts a utopia for one, Brautigan suggests that life can be lived—indeed, is more meaningfully lived—in the company of others.

A key to attaining the death of the ego seems to consist of living in the present moment. Intellectual pursuits and even art apparently hinder this process. It is probably for this reason that the narrator's writing is considered something of an unnatural act in the commune. Since his scribbling harms no one, though, his foible is tolerated (if not encouraged). Important to this interpretation is the personality of the narrator; he is certainly more troubled than are the mainline iDEATH people with whom he associates. After the black sun sets and the writer concludes his work, he will be able to put aside whatever it was in his ego that made him want to write his book in the first place. In this way he moves toward greater and greater acceptance by those in the commune, and in the ending, with the completion of the book, the reader is in fact witnessing his final immersion into the community.

THE ABORTION

First published: 1971
Type of work: Novel

A reclusive male librarian meets a beautiful woman who moves him farther and farther into the world by means of her having an abortion.

The Abortion: An Historical Romance was Brautigan's first book to which he gave a subtitle; by doing so he clearly indicated that the work was based on an already established subgenre. A writer of such originality, however, does not produce the sort of romance that most readers might expect. Instead, he infuses the form with his own themes and zany humor.

The unnamed narrator of *The Abortion*, though distinguished by eccentric attitudes and gentleness, is not as fully developed a character as the narrators of several other of Brautigan's books, most notably Jesse of *A Confederate General at Big Sur* and the unnamed narrator of *In Watermelon Sugar*. While he is admirable for his view of humanity, a self-imposed isolation and his chosen role in life reduce him in stature. Distant from most of society and remote in his feelings, he lives a life apart, both in the depths of his distinctly odd library (where he also lives) and in the labyrinth-like rooms of the Mexican abortion doctor later in the story.

Early in the story, the narrator describes his strange library: The books are all donated by the people who write them, society's sad losers and misfits, and Brautigan goes into considerable detail with titles (*Growing Flowers by Candlelight in Hotel Rooms*, *The Stereo and God*) and descriptions of the often unhappy or disturbed people who get to shelve their books themselves. Included in the catalog is a book called *Moose*, written by one Richard Brautigan, "who looked as if he would be more at home in another era."

In a flashback, the narrator relates how he met Vida, the extremely beautiful woman with whom he is living when the story opens. She too had brought her story, a tale of how her body does not really suit her, to be dutifully accepted and cataloged. Wherever she goes, even on the abortion trip to Mexico, her beauty brings chaos by the attention men pay to it. The stereotype of the mayhem-producing beautiful female can be traced in American literature from Katrina Van Tassel in Washington Irving's "The Legend of Sleepy Hollow" (1819) to Eula Varner in William Faulkner's *The Hamlet* (1940). Vida, as a character name, is derived from the Latin *vita*, meaning life.

This allegorical naming of a character is matched by the allegorical nature of the library itself. The narrator is the thirty-fifth or thirty-sixth librarian, which corresponds to the numbering of American presidents at the time the work was written— a split term for one president accounting for the confusion. In addition, the library is run by America Forever, Etc.

After they discover Vida's pregnancy, she and the narrator travel by plane to Mexico for the abortion, and this trip ironically represents the quest found in traditional romances. From beginning to end, Brautigan adheres closely enough to the traditional romance form so that readers familiar with it can recognize the various necessary items and feel its subjective intensity. At the same time, Brautigan's treatment of these essential forms is humorous, which casts an ironic light upon the entire novel.

Upon returning to San Francisco after the abortion, the narrator learns that he has lost his position at the library. While this forces him into the harsh realities of life outside his pleasantly numbing cocoon, where he had essentially retreated, Vida and his friend Foster welcome the change. He will become a hero in Berkeley, they assure him, and the final scene finds him outside among the students, contentedly collecting money for America Forever, Etc. Like the better-known *Trout Fishing in America*, this work deals with the problem of creating a meaningful life in the United States during the middle of the twentieth century.

The Abortion is the story of a man who has been strongly influenced by the literature he has read and obviously absorbed. The difficulties he encounters in the broader world are caused in part by his belief that life is—or ought to be—like literature. Literary forms, Brautigan suggests, provide a framework for thoughts and expectations. *The Abortion* shows how skewed a life based on these kinds of expectations can become.

Summary

In his early novels, Richard Brautigan searched for the meaning of America. What he found was a country debased by commercialism, shaken in its values, and haunted by loneliness. For the individual, love, humor, and the imagination can bring meaning to life.

Brautigan explored the American soul in the middle of the twentieth century; he believed gentleness and peace to be both means and end in this quest. His highly original, richly metaphoric books show him to be much more than a transitional literary figure. His finely crafted prose bears witness to his unique way of viewing the world.

Bibliography

Boyer, Jay. *Richard Brautigan*. Boise, Idaho: Boise State University Press, 1987.

Chenetier, Marc. *Richard Brautigan*. New York: Methuen, 1983.

Foster, Edward H. *Richard Brautigan*. Boston: Twayne, 1983.

Malley, Terence. *Richard Brautigan*. New York: Warner, 1972.

Pütz, Manfred. *The Story of Identity: American Fiction of the Sixties*. Stuttgart, Germany: J. B. Metzlersche Verlagsbuchhandlung, 1979.

Tanner, Tony. *City of Words: American Fiction 1950-1970*. New York: Harper & Row, 1971.

Charles Hackenberry

HAROLD BRODKEY

Born: Staunton, near Alton, Illinois
1930

Principal Literary Achievement
Concerned with examining his own life in close detail, Brodkey writes short stories largely about growing up as an adopted child near St. Louis and about his later life at Harvard University and in New York State.

Biography
Harold Roy Brodkey was born Aaron Roy Weintraub across the Mississippi River from and slightly to the northeast of St. Louis, Missouri, in Staunton, Illinois, in 1930. His father, a junk man, was illiterate. Aaron's mother died when he was an infant, and his father, unable to care for the child, allowed Joseph and Doris Brodkey to adopt him. They changed his name to Harold and gave him their surname, a corruption of the family's original Russian name, Bezborodko.

In Brodkey's fiction, Joseph and Doris Brodkey become Leila and S. L. (perhaps to suggest St. Louis) Cohn. They figure prominently in early stories in which Leila is portrayed as having adopted Aaron/Harold largely as a means of reclaiming her husband, from whom she was separated. Leila (variously Leah and Lila in Brodkey's stories) is shown as a woman too self-absorbed to offer much love to anyone else. There apparently was a daughter, somewhat older than Harold, who becomes Nonie in his stories.

One can speak only tentatively about the life of Harold Brodkey; he has kept the details of his personal life completely private except as they are revealed in his stories. The date of his birth, for example, remains a secret, although the year, 1930, has been established. In an interview, *Esquire* journalist D. Keith Mano asked Brodkey if he had ever worked. Brodkey replied that he had but would provide no other details because he had not yet written about that experience. So intensely personal are Brodkey's stories that he guards assiduously the autobiographical details of which they are composed. His stories are generally thought to record with diarylike authenticity the actual events in his coming of age.

If one is to believe the information given in "Largely an Oral History of My Mother," Brodkey, in the persona of Alan Cohn, was discovered to have a remarkably high IQ—so high, in fact, that special training was recommended for him. The adoptive parents, by now having had their fill of Alan/Harold, used this opportunity

279

to try unsuccessfully to return the boy to his birth father.

Brodkey apparently lived a childhood that was in many ways typically Midwestern. He went to school, earned money as a babysitter, and belonged to the Boy Scouts. His family situation, however, was not typical. Having lost his real mother so early as to be unable to remember her, he tried to construct her in his imagination, using the small pieces of information that he was able to glean from people who knew her. Although she was not well-educated, his birth mother was bright, bookish, and fluent in five or six languages. Brodkey invented her and thus stirred his ability to create characters and situations by paying special attention to small details. This talent would later become the hallmark of his stories.

Having sustained the early loss of his real mother and, because of his adoption, also of his father, Brodkey would sustain similar losses in adolescence through the deaths of his adoptive parents. Joseph Brodkey had a stroke when Harold was nine and was an invalid thereafter. He lived on for five years and required considerable attention. One year before her husband died, Doris Brodkey developed cancer. She lived a painful and increasingly isolated existence until her death, which occurred during Harold's undergraduate days at Harvard University. Never an easy or outgoing person, she became increasingly embittered as her health deteriorated.

A scholarship to Harvard and a small inheritance enabled Brodkey to live outside the Midwest for the first time, persumably beginning in 1948. Shortly after that, he spent part of a summer in Europe, which was his first trip outside the United States. The events of his life upon leaving college remain a mystery.

In 1957, Dial Press published his first collection of stories, *First Love and Other Sorrows*, which became an alternate selection of the Book-of-the-Month Club. This collection was received with considerable enthusiasm and word was out that Brodkey was at work on a Proustian kind of novel, "Party of Animals," under contract to Farrar, Straus & Giroux. On June 4, 1976, *The New York Times* announced that Brodkey had delivered the more than two thousand-page manuscript of this sprawling work to the publisher—sixteen years after the original contract was signed. Major sections of "Party of Animals" have been published in *The New Yorker, Esquire*, and *New American Review*. The three segments that make up *Women and Angels*, published in 1985, are from "Party of Animals," as are many of the stories in *Stories in an Almost Classical Mode*, published by Alfred A. Knopf in 1988. The latter, like his first collection, was a Book-of-the-Month Club alternate selection.

Brodkey regularly publishes short stories and poems, particularly in *The New Yorker*. His output is small but well-wrought. Typically, he takes his stories through at least twenty revisions before he considers them finished. His attention to detail and the easy unfolding of his prose have attracted a loyal following despite there being only three collections in print over three decades of publication.

Brodkey was awarded both the Prix de Rome Magazine Award and the Brandeis Creative Arts Award in 1974. He received first prize in the O. Henry short fiction awards in 1975 and again in 1976. Brodkey has been a fellow of the American Academy in Rome, the John Simon Guggenheim Memorial Foundation, and the National Endowment for the Arts. He has taught writing and literature at Cornell University and at the City University of New York. Brodkey married Ellen Schwamm, a novelist, in 1980 and lives with her and her daughter, Emily, in New York City. He has a desk at *The New Yorker* and is an occasional lecturer on the college and university circuit.

Analysis

Harold Brodkey writes about the commonplace. His slow, sometimes agonizingly detailed unfolding of the commonplace has distinguished him as a credible analyst of growing up Jewish and adopted in the Midwest. In the early stories, the cast of characters is identical: The story is told from the point of view of a boy, with an adoptive mother and father and an older sister given to tormenting him. Added to this ordinary American family configuration in some of the stories is a maid.

The first three stories of the nine that make up *First Love and Other Sorrows* are really the beginning of what might be called a *Bildungsroman*. They detail the childhood of the first-person narrator, who longs for love but is unable to attract it. The narrator was adopted by his foster parents in part because he was very attractive. In "The State of Grace," however, he is thirteen years old, six feet tall, weighs 125 pounds, and his ears stick out. He is displeased with the way he looks and extremely self-conscious of being the gangly teenager new to adolescence. As baby-sitter of the seven-year-old Edward Leinberg, he realizes that Edward needs love as much as he does. Despite this realization, he is unable to give it.

These first three stories reveal the themes that Brodkey will pursue in his later work and presage the focus of "Party of Animals." Five of the stories in the volume focus on Laura (sometimes Laurie) Andrews as protagonist.

A recurrent theme in Brodkey's work is that true selflessness does not exist. In his stories, as presumably in his early life, all Brodkey's characters have motives for what they do, and these motives are inextricably tied to self-interest. This attitude may seem cynical, but in Brodkey's work it appears more realistic than cynical. Sometimes he confuses reciprocity with selfishness. For example, in "Innocence," one of the later stories in *Stories in an Almost Classical Mode*, the protagonist is determined to give Orra Perkins her first orgasm, not so much to provide her with pleasure but rather to get a stronger hold on her and to increase the intensity of his own sexual pleasure with her. It is difficult in this story to know where the line is drawn between selfishness and selflessness.

Brodkey does not develop strong plots. His stories are essentially concerned with descriptive details about places and emotions. His prose style has been shaped considerably by the style of *The New Yorker*. His style is unadorned, lean, and direct, and is carefully calculated and assiduously polished to the point that it reads easily and is generally convincing. He succeeds best when he writes about his Midwestern childhood, perhaps because his uncomplicated style reflects the commonness of the situations in his life.

Verbal and typographical invention are an integral part of Brodkey's technique.

He is always conscious of how sentences look on a page. He uses punctuation in a unique and extremely calculated way. A typical example of his technique is found in a description of his adoptive mother in "A Story in an Almost Classical Mode":

> What she did was get your attention; she would ask you questions in a slightly high-pitched pushy voice that almost made you laugh, but if you were drawn to listen to her, once you were attentive and showed you were, her voice would lose every attribute of sociability, it would become strained and naked of any attempt to please or be accept-able; it would be utterly appalling; and what she said would lodge in the center of your attention and be the truth you have to live with until you could persuade yourself she was crazy: that is, irresponsible and perhaps criminal in her way.

This complex sentence reveals Brodkey's fascination with semicolons and his typical use of the colon to emphasize that what follows is the most important part of the sentence. The colon simultaneously connects and separates. Brodkey sometimes combines his affection for semicolons with a fondness of parentheses, lodging a semicolon in the exact center of a parenthetical section of a sentence; he then places the parenthetical section in the exact center of the sentence.

In *Women and Angels*, Brodkey explores his real mother in the story "Ceil" and his adoptive mother in "Lila." The philosophy that emerges from those stories, particularly the latter, is what one critic has dubbed the "tyranny of need." Brodkey views dependence as an essential ingredient of love. Close human relationships seem to be based on reciprocal weaknesses between two people rather than on the strengths of one or both of them.

Although Brodkey's parents, both real and adoptive, were Jews, it is difficult to classify his stories as notably Jewish. He was a Jewish boy growing up beside the Mississippi near the Missouri-Illinois border, but his life was shaped more by the convoluted emotions of the people who surrounded him for his first fifteen years or so than by the fact that he was Jewish. Formal religion did not play a significant role in his life. He had to handle larger, more personal discriminations as he grew up than anti-Semitism. His most developed statement of a religious philosophy occurs in "Angel," the last story in *Women and Angels*.

FIRST LOVE AND OTHER SORROWS

First published: 1957
Type of work: Short story

The adolescent first-person narrator sees love around him and seeks it himself.

The title story of *First Love and Other Sorrows* takes place in the springtime when its narrator is sixteen years old and is dealing with a budding sexuality. He lives with his adoptive mother and his twenty-two-year-old sister, who seems as unhappy with her looks as the narrator is with his. She complains that her face is too round and that she does not look good in suits. The brother has peach fuzz and admits to shaving every three days; his mother and sister think he needs to shave more often. The adoptive father is dead.

The boy's mother warns him against playing too hard and about getting over-heated in the springtime. This admonition seems to be a veiled warning that the heat of youthful sexuality can be as dangerous as the heat of April, which is the usual met-aphor for youth. The boy certainly seems to feel that such is the case. The sister is dating Sonny Bruster, who, as the son of one of the town's leading bankers, is a good catch, in the eyes of the mother. The romance between the two of them is not with-out problems; at one point, they stop seeing each other for several weeks. They get back together, however, and are engaged before the story ends.

The boy feels like an intruder in his mother's house. She makes it clear that she cooks only because he is there; were it only the two women, they would eat sand-wiches. The family situation is not a hostile one, but little love is apparent. The mother, a controlling woman, is vitally concerned with having her daughter marry someone prosperous. She had known genteel living in a large house overlooking the Mississippi River, but the house was lost during a financial crisis and she was re-duced to living in humbler surroundings.

The boy's best friend is a schoolmate named Preston, who is shy, and—although the same age—more heavily bearded than the narrator. He is unimaginative and suspicious of imagination in others. The narrator is the aesthete, and Preston is the scientist who aspires to a career in physics.

Preston is the narrator's safe, dependable friend, with whom he enjoys athletics and double dating. Another boy in the school, however, is much more enticing. Joel Bush is so handsome that the other students can scarcely bear to look at him. He is described in ecstatic terms, but he is so perfect that people avoid him and admire him from a safe distance. Brodkey's effusive description of Joel may be read within a homosexual context, particularly when compared with his description of Orra Per-kins in "Innocence."

One day, Joel reveals to the narrator that he had sex with an older woman the night before. He describes the event as masturbation with bells. Juxtaposed to this sexual revelation is a strenuous physical workout on the school's playing field, which serves as a sex substitute for many budding adolescents. The narrator spends an eve-ning with Eleanor Cullen, who previously had had an uneventful date with Joel. Elea-nor reveals that she does not regard herself as a basically happy person, which echoes the narrator's earlier statement that he is not popular because he is too gloomy.

The story ends with the narrator's sister engaged to Sonny Bruster and wearing an heirloom engagement ring that she does not like. Her mother is in the kitchen writ-ing letters to send to all of her relatives telling them of the engagement. The boy and his sister come into the kitchen and the mother offers to heat up some soup for them. Her eyes fill with tears of emotion, and the three embrace and kiss.

This story is typical of Brodkey's early work and gives a strong indication of the course his future work has followed. Nothing much happens in the story except that an adolescent boy makes tentative moves toward growing into manhood. He is uncertain and fearful of rejection and therefore cannot approach Joel. The closest he can get to him is to be friends with Eleanor. The story deals with situations and emotions but has little plot. The descriptions are accurate and evocative, filled with the carefully observed and presented sights, sounds, and textures that characterize most of Brodkey's writing.

SENTIMENTAL EDUCATION

First published: 1957
Type of work: Short story

This third-person narrative is a delicate story of how two inexperienced college students discover love.

"Sentimental Education," one of the stories in *First Love and Other Sorrows*, was first published in *The New Yorker*. It is a tentative step in the direction of "Innocence," which was published sixteen years later. Set in Cambridge, Massachusetts, the story features the nineteen-year-old Elgin Smith, who is an undergraduate at Harvard University. The only other character to appear directly in the story is Caroline Hedges, a freshman at Radcliffe College.

The action takes place within a college year, during which time both Elgin and Caroline are forced to reassess their values. Their relationship grows, but the direction of their growth is not always toward each other. When the school year ends, they go their separate ways, although they do not break from each other decisively. They agree to meet again in the fall, but as friends rather than as lovers.

Elgin first sees Caroline on the steps of Widener Library and is instantly smitten. She does not know of his existence until two weeks later. Elgin drops his course in the Victorian novel and enrolls in a class on metaphysical poets because he knows that Caroline is also taking that course. He borrows a pencil from her during several class meetings and finally impresses her by his classroom contributions, though she is disturbed by his nasal, Midwestern twang. When he invites her to have coffee with him, she declines, but decides to say yes to his next invitation.

The relationship develops slowly, which gives Brodkey room to incorporate all the subtle detail that characterizes his stories. The detail in this story involves a careful analysis of the human emotions that are evoked by young love, particularly when both parties are unsure of themselves.

The relationship is platonic for some weeks, although both Elgin and Caroline want more. Both are too reserved, however, to move toward expressing their feelings physically. Finally, however, after weeks of daily study sessions in Widener Library and of going out onto the Fenway, where Caroline tries to give Elgin elocution lessons, Elgin confesses his love to Caroline. Although Caroline does not immediately confess a reciprocal love, she does feel love for him, and they soon find their way into his bed.

The relationship initially surprises both of them. They have the feeling that such a drastic expression of love should offer something more than it has given them. Although they continue their affair, Caroline feels increasingly cheapened by it. She hates to admit to and surrender to her animal appetite, but she cannot deny that it exists. As time passes, the relationship changes; Elgin talks of marriage, but Caroline realizes how impractical that would be. She also thinks that she has lost her dignity by giving herself to Elgin and that he will not continue to love her because of that lost dignity.

During their last five weeks before the summer holiday, the two are chaste, although they see each other daily. They kiss, and touch, but they restrain their desires. On their last day together, they drink champagne. Caroline has to catch the night train to Baltimore and later go to Europe for the summer. Elgin is leaving too, presumably to return to the Midwest. They agree to see each other in the fall but only as friends. The story ends as Caroline walks back to her dormitory alone, at her own request. Walking away from Elgin, she feels a certain release, for she has shed the pressures of love and close daily association.

This story is different from any of the others in the collection. Unlike the first three, it is a third-person, author omniscient narrative. It is perhaps the most delicately presented of all the stories in *First Love and Other Sorrows*.

INNOCENCE

First published: 1973
Type of work: Short story

The first-person narrator struggles doggedly to give Orra Perkins her first orgasm.

Unlike many of Brodkey's short stories collected in *Stories in an Almost Classical Mode*, "Innocence" was not first published in *The New Yorker*. Instead, it appeared in *New American Review*, presumably because of *The New Yorker*'s reluctance to publish the common four-letter word that is used for copulation. "Innocence" is a story of young lust—as opposed to young love—in which the protagonist, a Harvard undergraduate, achieves what he feared was the unachievable: a sexual encounter with a very popular and beautiful Radcliffe undergraduate, Orra Perkins.

Orra is not inexperienced; she has been intimate with seven or eight men before she meets the narrator. She has never achieved an orgasm with them, because, according to her, she is too sexual to have orgasms. She is not overly distressed by this omission and strenuously discourages the narrator from trying to give her the orgasm that he so much wants her to experience. His motive is twofold: He thinks that he will own Orra if he achieves his end, and he also thinks that his own sexual pleasure with her will be enhanced if she can respond more fully to his penetrations.

This story, generally considered to be among Brodkey's best, is some thirty pages long, of which two-thirds is devoted to presenting a highly detailed account of how Orra is brought to the pinnacle of passion. Before the story ends, Orra not only has her orgasm but, thinking back on it, has another, multiple orgasm. Despite all the explicit physical detail the story contains, the result is neither prurient nor clinical. Rather it is realistic, direct, and detailed—so detailed, in fact, that the reader begins to long for Orra to achieve the orgasm.

This longing is part of Brodkey's technique. He does not seek to titillate his readers; rather, his aim is to walk them through the experience. As the two participants in the event strain through the seemingly endless encounter to achieve a climax, the reader is dragged along. Eventually, the reader is so worn down by the detailed narration of the event that he or she feels as physically spent as the perspiring participants when the moment of ecstasy finally arrives.

Brodkey's interest in beautiful people such as Orra reminds one of the fiction of F. Scott Fitzgerald. Brodkey's characters usually are well-to-do or quest after those who are. The original description of Orra is remarkably similar to that of Joel Bush in "First Love and Other Sorrows," leading one to speculate on whether Joel in that story was a first, unfulfilled homosexual love.

The title, "Innocence," may seem ironic, but it really is not. Despite having had some sexual experience, Orra is a neophyte in the bedroom. The narrator is little more experienced, although he knows his way around sufficiently to manipulate Orra's body to achieve the ultimate aim of giving her an orgasm.

True to the concerns in many of his other stories, Brodkey's theme involves dependency and achieving union through weakness—in this case, Orra's past inability to reach sexual fulfillment. The narrator's ability to bring her to the point of climax makes her dependent upon him in ways that she has never before been dependent upon anyone.

This story, virtually without plot, is an intricate depiction of both the physical and emotional details of a crucial event in the lives of two twenty-year-olds. The description engages all the senses, moving slowly through every second of the prolonged encounter and showing Brodkey as the recognized master of protraction.

CEIL

First published: 1983
Type of work: Short story

Through the recollections of others, Wiley Silenowicz attempts to know the mother he lost when he was two.

It is difficult to say definitively whether "Ceil," one of the three stories in *Women and Angels*, is a success. Some would question whether it is a story or merely a collection of fragments. "Lila" and "Largely an Oral History of My Mother," both depictions of Brodkey's adoptive mother, are more complete works.

Despite this caveat, "Ceil" is among Brodkey's most important works, for it reveals more than any other story the inner Brodkey, who yearns to establish a link with his past. Although the writing in "Ceil" is uneven, some of Brodkey's best images appear in the story, particularly when he writes about the great plains of the Midwest near Staunton, where his mother lived.

Ceil was the youngest of twenty or twenty-five children. Her father was a charismatic, highly intelligent rabbi and her mother was remembered as long-suffering and remarkably fertile. Born in Russia near Odessa, Ceil was her father's favorite. He arranged a marriage for her, but she refused to go through with it. She was a bright, independent girl who, after her father had simultaneously forgiven her and put a curse upon her, set sail from Odessa for New Orleans.

Upon her arrival in New Orleans, Ceil goes directly to the beauty shop. Unhappy with the result, she is in another beauty salon within an hour having it redone. Although appearances are important to her, success means more to her than anything else. She moves quickly from being a waitress to a housemaid to a successful businesswoman.

She is married to Max, a man much beneath her, who is originally from the Odessa area. Her success becomes legendary. Her self-satisfaction culminates with the birth of her son. Soon afterward, she falls ill and dies after a painful and lingering hospital confinement.

Brodkey strives in this story to capture a background of which he has only glimmerings. He sketches scenes of Russia by quoting passages from Anton Chekhov. He searches his own subconscious and ressurects a faint memory of having lived with his mother in a wooden house beside a single railway track; he recalls how its rooms shook as trains passed.

Part of "Ceil" is little more than fragmentary snatches, short single paragraphs set off from the rest of the story. Another part consists of italicized conversations with Lila or Ruthie, Wiley's adoptive mother and grandmother. What emerges is an incomplete portrait of a long-dead woman who necessarily remains sketchy in the eyes of her grown son. Part of Brodkey's creative genius is his ability to capture this quality so well.

Summary

Critics have compared Harold Brodkey with such noteworthy American authors as Nathaniel Hawthorne, Ralph Waldo Emerson, Walt Whitman, F. Scott Fitzgerald, and Thomas Wolfe. In contrast to them, however, Brodkey is neither an eclectic nor a derivative writer. He brings to his writing a singular gift for detailed description of the commonplace and a frequently eerie penetration of the human psyche. A plodding perfectionist, Brodkey is clearly the son of the highly competent, intelligent, energetic, hardworking woman he describes in "Ceil." Though not as prolific as his counterparts, Brodkey has and will probably continue to produce highly polished prose.

Bibliography

Bawer, Bruce. "A Genius for Publicity." *The New Criterion* 7 (December, 1988): 58-69.

Kakutani, Michiko. "First-Person Stories, Tidy and Not." *The New York Times*, September 14, 1988, C25.

Kermode, Frank. "I Am Only Equivocally Harold Brodkey." *The New York Times Book Review*, September 18, 1988, p. 3.

Mano, D. Keith. "Harold Brodkey: The First Rave." *Esquire* 87 (January, 1977): 14-15.

Shiras, Mary. "Accessible Dreams." *Commonweal* 77 (February 7, 1958): 493-494.

Weiseltier, Leon. "A Revelation." *The New Republic* 192 (May 20, 1985): 30-33.

R. Baird Shuman

CHARLES BUKOWSKI

Born: Andernach, Germany
August 16, 1920

Principal Literary Achievement
Recognized as one of the twentieth century's most influential and imitated writers, Bukowski, cult figure and "underground" poet, vividly documents the pain of the poor and dispossessed of urban Los Angeles.

Biography
Charles Bukowski was born in Andernach, Germany, on August 16, 1920, the only child of a German mother and an American soldier. Because of social and economic difficulties, his parents brought him to the United States when he was three years old. They settled in Los Angeles, where he was reared and educated and where he presently resides. His father spent most of his working life as a milkman till he lost that job during the Depression, a tragedy that turned an already difficult family life into an unbearable one. Bukowski's father was obsessed with pushing his son into attaining the American Dream to such an extent that young Charles left home after he was graduated from high school in 1939. Their relationship was an extremely difficult one, since his father regularly beat him.

Though *Ham on Rye* (1982) purports to be a novel, it unquestionably documents the early life of Charles Bukowski—his childhood, adolescence, and early manhood. The main character-narrator, Henry Chinaski, is certainly Bukowski himself as he records in vivid detail the poverty and oppression of the Depression years and the damage done to the poor and dispossessed during that bleak period.

Both of Bukowski's uncles died young because of their excessive drinking, though his grandfather lived into old age in spite of an irresponsible life of drinking and womanizing. One of young Charles's earliest memories is the contrast between his family's disgust with his alcoholic grandfather and his own memory of him as a warm and generous presence. Young Charles Bukowski identified with the outcasts early, the isolated and the alienated and, indeed, became the writer whose major subject matter documented those empty, wasted lives.

His early family life is a litany of violent beatings from his father, who was unfaithful to his wife and beat her as well when she uncovered the marital infidelities. His grammar school days in the poorest sections of Los Angeles also consisted of endless battles with bigger and stronger boys who mercilessly taunted him because

he was awkward, unattractive, and German. He spent much of his time alone, hiding out from the brutality of the daily routine of school.

While his teen years brought more self-assurance on the athletic field, they also brought violent bodily reactions in the form of acne and boils that became so inflamed that he had to be hospitalized. His face was permanently scarred, pitted and ravaged by the skin disease; in the shower room, his fellow athletes cruelly mocked his naked body covered with suppurating boils. During a time following surgery on his face and back, he first felt driven to create an alternate, imaginative world in which he could live outside the agony of reality. He realized that he could become a hero only in his imagination and that within that world nothing could hurt him. In short, he had found a refuge and power within himself that answered only to him. This realization propelled him eventually into the life of a writer.

Several other key incidents reinforced his decision to become a writer. One took place in the fourth grade, when the teacher was asking all the students what their fathers did for a living; young Charles was struck by the fact that virtually everybody in the class lied, since most of their fathers had lost their jobs during the Depression; the teacher seemed to be accepting the lies at face value. The other incident occurred several years later when a sensitive teacher realized that young Charles's "eyewitness" account of Herbert Hoover's visit to Los Angeles was an elaborately constructed hoax and, instead of punishing him for lying, rewarded him for how accurately he presented his fiction.

Bukowski became a frequent visitor to the local library and would read a book a night. His early literary heroes were writers such as Sherwood Anderson, Theodore Dreiser, John Dos Passos, Aldous Huxley, and especially D. H. Lawrence and Ernest Hemingway. There is certainly little question which of these writers have influenced Bukowski's literary style. His work is frequently compared to that of Hemingway not only because of the journalistic prose and distinctly lean sentence style but also because of such shared obsessions as violence, alcohol, and sex.

The young Bukowski did attend some classes at Los Angeles City College but learned little from his teachers there, preferring the company of the novels of Fyodor Dostoevski, Ivan Turgenev, Louis-Ferdinand Céline, and John Fante. He did, however, excel in college drinking contests and gained a reputation, which he retained for many years, for drinking everybody under the table. He left school without a degree and worked at many different menial jobs—as a stock boy, dishwasher, elevator operator, postman, slaughterhouse worker, and baker. His novel *Factotum* (1975) documents the variety of banal occupations he practiced during his post-high school years. Except for some prolonged working periods in the postal service, he never stayed at one job for very long. He seems to have chosen a life of insecurity so that he could write without the distractions of duty and career. In fact, his work generally records the life of a rootless writer, a drifter whose only duty is to the poem or the story. In between the writing comes an endless round of drinking, barroom brawls, visits to the track, and short-lived liaisons with alcoholic women. These affairs take place in cheap hotels or boardinghouses that cater to such lost souls.

In 1955, however, Bukowski's excessive drinking landed him in the charity ward of one of the city hospitals, where he nearly died of a bleeding ulcer. After numerous blood transfusions, he left the hospital a shaken realist; he began compulsively writing and publishing poems in the many "little magazines" that were flourishing during the late 1950's and early 1960's. During the 1960's, in the literary ferment created by the Beat writers, such as Allen Ginsberg, Jack Kerouac, Lawrence Ferlinghetti, and William Burroughs, Charles Bukowski, who aligned himself with no literary or political group, became a prime example of the artist as maverick. Since he was completely isolated and owed allegiance to no one, he could write about anything he wished. He became the quintessential "underground" writer and, as a result, a major cult figure, having won the "outsider of the year" award in 1962 from the prestigious "little magazine," *The Outsider*. He produced fourteen books during the 1960's, mostly poetry of uneven quality. Several volumes of poetry, however, such as *It Catches My Heart in Its Hands* (1963) and *The Days Run Away Like Wild Horses over the Hills* (1969), contained a number of highly moving poems that convinced the most anti-Bukowski critics that he could create poetry of deep feeling and substantial literary merit.

In 1970, John Martin of Black Sparrow Press convinced him to quit working at the post office after fourteen years to devote himself to writing full-time. Bukowski continued to produce prolifically during the 1970's, writing three highly acclaimed novels, *Post Office* (1971), *Factotum* (1975), and *Women* (1978), and many volumes of poetry and short stories. The 1980's brought forth two major novels which have met with generally high critical praise: *Ham on Rye* (1982) and *Hollywood* (1989). Bukowski gained further renown because of his screenplay for the motion picture *Barfly* (1987), starring Mickey Rourke and Fay Dunaway. Known for wasting nothing, Bukowski wrote a comic novel, *Hollywood*, which was essentially about the making of the film.

Bukowski has continued to publish volumes of poetry, his first love, and many short stories in spite of becoming wealthy as a result of his royalties. He is still considered a major cult figure, especially in France and Germany, where his books are consistent best-sellers. Though he suffered poor health in the late 1980's, he continued, as he put it, "playing with the poem."

Analysis

Charles Bukowski seldom comments on his own work, since most of his readers know that virtually all the novels, short stories, and poems are thinly veiled approximations of his actual life. Indeed, his highly acclaimed novel *Ham on Rye* (1982) is not only his autobiography but also an American portrait of the artist as a young man. Literary critics find his work difficult to interpret because it so closely resembles the actual day-to-day routine of an unapologetic, hard-drinking, womanizing gambler who loves playing the horses and brawling in barrooms. His work records the despairing life-styles of the poor and infamous in Los Angeles in unrelenting detail. In *Hollywood*, his alter ego, Henry Chinaski, announces himself as "a historian of drink" who has no peer and wryly adds that he has outlived his drinking companions principally because he "never gets out of bed before noon."

The great French playwright and novelist, Jean Genet, called Charles Bukowski "the best poet in America," words of high praise from an artist who rarely commented on another poet's work and is considered the archetypal "underground" writer of the twentieth century. Bukowski's themes are the same in most all of his poetry, novels, and short stories: violence, despair, poverty, hopelessness, alcoholism, suicide, madness, and how alcohol, sex, gambling, and, most important, writing can intermittently relieve the agony of these lives of dramatic desperation. He is the United States' best-known existential writer and, many would claim, its most influential and imitated poet. Bukowski owes allegiance to no one for the success of his work except the persistent integrity of the small presses that first published him and to Black Sparrow Press, which has continued to publish his work. The only literary assistance he ever received was from the books he read in his local public library.

Bukowski's work must continue in spite of the psychological or physical traumas he is experiencing at any given moment; his fictive alter ego, Henry Chinaski, always finds time to jot down a few lines of a poem on the back of an envelope or a paper bag. What motivates Bukowski's commitment to the life of the imagination is his unflinching realization that without it, his life would be as meaningless and absurd as the rest of the trapped creatures he writes about. Wallace Stevens, one of the most important poets of the twentieth century, defined the imagination as the "violence within that protects us from the violence without." There is little doubt that Bukowski views its function in exactly the same terms, yet in an even more profoundly personal way. He survived on the mean streets of Los Angeles, after all, not (as did Stevens) in the comfortable safety of the office of vice-president of one of American's largest insurance companies.

One of the more compelling poems from what is perhaps his best-known collection of poetry, *The Days Run Away Like Wild Horses over the Hills,* concerns the plight of a poor man who discovers his beloved wife's infidelities and proceeds to castrate himself in her horrified presence, flushing his testicles down the toilet yet continuing to drink his wine while holding a bloody towel between his legs with a look of utter indifference on his face. The poem is called, ironically, "Freedom." The ruling passions of the poor, the ugly, and the hopeless are, in Bukowski's view, much more significant to them than those of the wealthy are to themselves simply because they are all they have. In one of his finest collections of poems, *It Catches My Heart in Its Hands,* he presents a world in which the young are "fenced in/ stabbed and shaven/ taught words/ propped up/ to die"—an existence in which "you and I ain't living well/ or enough."

Critics often compare Bukowski to several of the so-called Beat writers (such as Jack Kerouac, William Burroughs, and Allen Ginsberg) but fail to mention that Bukowski comes out of a working-class background. He never had the opportunity to attend such prestigious universities as Columbia or Harvard as did those three writers. A number of his public school friends' fathers committed suicide during the Depression, while many others drank themselves into an early grave. Though Kerouac emerged from a working-class New England background, he did attend Columbia University on a football scholarship, while Allen Ginsberg and William Burroughs came out of college-educated families with a tradition of reading and culture. Though he is frequently compared to Henry Miller in his graphic depiction of drinking and sexual freedom, one never feels that Bukowski is in any way romanticizing that life-style. Miller's characters could, if they chose, move on to an economically more rewarding life and, because of their intelligence, charm, or sexual prowess, find any number of amorous partners in countless cafés of the Latin Quarter of Paris during the 1930's.

What brings couples together in most of Bukowski's works is that nobody else wants them; they are social outcasts who are desperate for sexual contact, but also for any kind of momentary intimacy that will temporarily assuage their pervading sense of empty despair. In the novel *Post Office*, the transient sexual liaisons with Betty, Mary-Lou, Joyce, and Fay do not last long, but they are vital in creating a meaningful life for Henry Chinaski (though he never thinks of his life in anything but temporary terms, because people are going mad or dying around him constantly). There is no aunt back east to whom Sal Paradise, the fictive alter ego of Jack Kerouac in *On the Road* (1957), continually returns for solace, comfort, and forgiveness. Bukowski's heroes are denied the luxury of despair because there is literally no physical place to indulge in that kind of self-pity.

The desperate and unvarying pattern of lives that Bukowski presents in most of his novels, short stories, and poems can be summarized quite bluntly in an excerpt from his volume of poems entitled *Dangling in the Tournefortia* (1981): "it was 11 a.m. and I was puking/ trying to get a can of ale down/ the whore in the bed next to me/ in her torn slip/ mumbling about her children in/ Atlanta." It is these stark imagistic scenes, repeated in book after book, that call to mind the literary advice from another stark poet, William Carlos Williams, and his rule for writers: "No ideas but in things." Bukowski's action immediately moves into image with no intervening philosophical speculations; his language records with unflinching accuracy scenes that tell all. The critic John William Corrington captures the effect of Bukowski's direct language when he calls it "the spoken voice nailed to the paper." Not all of Bukowski's language, though, is so brutally naturalistic. He regularly offers a bittersweet comic side to the dreary life of cheap boardinghouses and the eternal quest for the rent check. In a poem entitled "The Tragedy of the Leaves," he talks about the necessity for laughter in spite of depressing circumstances:

> what was needed now
> was a good comedian, ancient style, a jester
> with jokes upon absurd pain; pain is absurd
> because it exists, nothing more;
>
> . . . .
>
> and I walk into the dark hall

> where the landlady stood
> execrating and final,
> sending me to hell
> waving her fat sweaty arms
> and screaming
> screaming for rent
> because the world has failed us
> both.

There is also in these lines an empathetic quality of the poet as spokesman for all members of his tribe of down-and-outers, the losers in this world. The cadences are reminiscent of a bardic voice. One could certainly view Bukowski as the bard for his people in the poorer sections of Los Angeles where he originated. Bards have traditionally been viewed as the voice of their people, but always of people in a very specific physical locale. Allen Ginsberg and William Blake project bardic voices and attempt to reconnect their readers to the truth of their own experience. Bukowski's bardic voice, like that of William Carlos Williams, functions in a much more specific geographical place using the energies of the local, depleted though they may be, to generate utterance.

Though his message is consistently pessimistic, it is not the hopelessly bitter pessimism of his poetic idol, American poet Robinson Jeffers. Even in the midst of violence and death, Bukowski continues to offer hope. In lines reverberating with E. E. Cummings and William Carlos Williams, he declaims: "I want trumpets and crowing, . . . I want the whirl and tang of a simple living orange/ in a simple living tree." The great poet Robert Duncan once defined the word "responsibility" by breaking it down into its etymological units as "response-ability: that is, keeping the ability to respond." If one defines the word in those terms, Charles Bukowski is arguably the most "responsible" poet that America has produced since Walt Whitman. He has unquestionably kept and even celebrated his ability to respond vividly to his own life and the lives lived in his bardic realm with an affection, dedication, and faithfulness rarely encountered in contemporary American literature.

POST OFFICE

First published: 1971
Type of work: Novel

The normally jobless, transient Henry Chinaski attempts to live a normal life with a permanent position in the postal service.

Post Office is Charles Bukowski's first novel; it became one of his best-selling works. He had published approximately twenty books of poems and short stories during the 1960's, with his hero, Henry Chinaski, as the major character in most of the stories. *Post Office* breaks no new literary ground but offers amplified versions of his typical narratives, now covering a fourteen-year period of employment in the postal service. The plot moves through various episodes of crises with his supervisors, coworkers, and lovers; *Post Office* presents a domesticated version of the picaresque hero. Chinaski certainly fits the major requirements of the typical picaresque hero, since he is a rogue who satirizes his authoritative supervisors in a series of loosely connected episodes. While his tone is consistently cynical, he usually projects a morally superior attitude.

The plot moves along on the intensity and energy of the particular crisis that involves Chinaski at any given moment. He initially seeks employment with the postal service because the monotonous work appears easy, and he seems exhausted with his transient living conditions; his betting at the race track has also drained his financial resources. The opening line, "It began as a mistake," sets the tone for the entire novel, which is divided into six major sections.

The first two sections present his beleaguered contacts with overly demanding customers and inflexible supervisors such as the thirty-year postal veteran, Mr. Jonstone, known throughout the remainder of the novel as "The Stone." A bureaucratic bully of monstrous proportions, he spends most of his day doggedly carping at Chinaski and "writing him up" for the smallest infractions of postal rules. Chinaski, while suffering from "The Stone's" consistent pettiness, is clever enough to know exactly how far to go and when to utilize similar bureaucratic tactics to intimidate his supervisor into temporarily modifying his mean-spirited behavior. Chinaski's only solace during his apprenticeship is the warmth and sexual security that Betty offers him as they drink their way through most evenings.

As Chinaski's financial condition improves, he concentrates on playing the horses and begins to miss work. Betty, who has become jealous of his attentions to an attractive neighbor, gets a job and leaves Henry. His next amorous partner is a sexually indefatigable Texan, Joyce, who insists on marriage in Las Vegas and moving them to her small Texas hometown directly next door to her millionaire father. There, Chinaski works as a shipping clerk and eventually at the local post office. Joyce becomes bored with Chinaski's inability to keep her sexually satisfied and divorces him. He then returns to Los Angeles, moves back in with Betty, and goes back to the postal service. Betty quickly succumbs to the effects of her alcoholic binges and dies in the city hospital.

Chinaski meets a number of interesting but irksome fellow workers in the sorting room, including David Janko, a novice writer who bludgeons him night after night with the infinite details of both his sexual life and his novel in progress. He relates all these details in a strident vocal narrative that nearly pushes the regularly hungover Chinaski over the edge. The remaining three sections detail Chinaski's relationship with Fay, an aging hippie who bears his child and eventually moves into a commune in New Mexico. His highly successful performance at the track, letters of warning from his supervisors written in impeccable bureaucratic jargon, and his eventual resignation from the post office conclude the novel.

Adding a level of self-consciousness to this work, the concluding paragraph proposes that the seemingly pointless episodic nature of the narrative will be organized into a literary structure: "Maybe I'll write a novel, I thought. And then I did." The concluding paragraph of *Post Office*, though only three short sentences, qualifies this first novel as an embryonic version of a *Künstlerroman*, or a novel about the education and growth of the artist. A number of Bukowski short stories from the 1970's and 1980's such as "Scum Grief," "How to Get Published," and "Scream When You Burn," concern the specific day-to-day problems of the writer; he compares himself to his literary heroes and colleagues of the past and present, such as Dylan Thomas, Ginsberg, and Hemingway. In many stories and novels after *Post Office*, he frequently includes references to his creative work along with the typical drinking, gambling, and sexual scenarios that remain standard subject matter for virtually all his work.

HAM ON RYE

First published: 1982
Type of work: Novel

Bukowski's literary alter ego, Henry Chinaski, chronologically records his brutally poor childhood and adolescence in Los Angeles during the Depression.

Ham on Rye (1982) is not only a loosely constructed autobiographical novel of Charles Bukowski's distressingly poor childhood during the Depression, but it also qualifies as the novelist's version of both a *Bildungsroman* and *Künstlerroman*. A *Bildungsroman* is a literary genre that usually deals with a young protagonist's growth, development, and education into the sometimes harsh realities of life—a fall from innocence into experience, from a condition of blissful ignorance into the potential agony of self-consciousness. D. H. Lawrence's *Sons and Lovers* (1913) is a classic example of this type of novel.

Ham on Rye can also be viewed as a *Künstlerroman*, or a novel that presents the growth and development of the young hero as an artist. James Joyce's *Portrait of the Artist as a Young Man* (1916) and Thomas Mann's *Tonio Kröger* (1903) are two of the better known examples of this kind of apprenticeship novel. Even though Bukowski's second novel, *Factotum*, recorded Henry Chinaski's failure to keep even the most menial of jobs, and *Women* documented a similar inability to maintain consistent relationships with his numerous female lovers, *Ham on Rye* goes back to his earliest childhood memories, predating the chronic personal failures of Chinaski's middle years.

The structure of *Ham on Rye* resembles the episodic, loosely organized plot of his three earlier novels. It is divided into fifty-eight chapters, some as short as a page and a half. The title is a fairly obvious pun on Bukowski's legendary reputation as a "ham"—that is, a dramatic self-promoter—and his equally infamous reputation as a drinker of heroic proportions. His drink of choice is whiskey or rye. It is also quite obvious that the "wry" or comic attitude that Bukowski/Chinaski projects toward a life steeped in unrelenting pain and misunderstanding saves him from the madness and suicide that have swallowed up less resilient characters. His sense of humor and his ability to view himself ironically help him objectify his sufferings and enable him to accept his condition and work within it rather than hopelessly resigning himself to its despair. His comic imagination, then, transforms the merely grotesque into a vividly compelling work of literature.

While the time frame of the novel covers the young Chinaski from his birth in 1920 to the Japanese attack on Pearl Harbor in 1941, the major focus is on his relationship with his father and other authority figures during his elementary and secondary school years. It is unquestionably his father's sadistic cruelty toward him that becomes the novel's emotional and psychological core. Henry Chinaski somehow creates an interior life that generates an alternate kind of benign violence that enables him to regulate and utilize the destructive energies of his father for his own artistic growth rather than his self-destruction. Though he finds temporary solace in heavy bouts of drinking and mindless barroom brawling, he also discovers, in his local public library, fellow sufferers such as D. H. Lawrence, Ernest Hemingway, and for humor, James Thurber. A sympathetic teacher encourages his precocious ability to create "beautiful lies"—that is, fictions that fulfill his imagination's yearning for some kind of satisfaction even though he seems buried in a life of poverty, violence, and hopelessness.

Again and again, Chinaski's wry or sardonic sense of humor saves him from the uncertainty and chaos of the Depression years:

> The problem was you had to keep choosing between one evil and another, and no matter what you chose, they sliced a little bit more off you until there was nothing left. At the age of 25 most people were finished. A whole god-damned nation of assholes driving automobiles, eating, having babies, doing everything in the worst way possible, like voting for the presidential candidate who reminded them most of themselves.

It is precisely Henry's resolution not to be "finished" by the time he is twenty-five that drives him to read and write himself out of the despair. It is in a scene in which he attends his high school prom as an onlooker because he has neither money for formal attire nor a female with whom to go, that Henry comes into his deepest realization of his isolation and alienation. He sees himself infinitely separated from the rich "laughing boys" and confesses his hatred of their beauty, their untroubled lives, and their unconscious participation in the joys of youth. He resolves at that moment that "someday I will be as happy as any of you, you will see."

Ironically, *Ham on Rye* dramatically documents that Charles Bukowski has not only survived but has prevailed by transforming his brutally isolated childhood and adolescence into a critically acclaimed novel for the more privileged members of the class of 1939 to read and envy.

HOLLYWOOD

First published: 1989
Type of work: Novel

A novel about writing a screenplay and the chaos of trying to deal with Hollywood producers who are only interested in huge financial profits.

Hollywood is Charles Bukowski's version of a subgenre of the novel called a *roman à clef*, or a "novel with a key or secret meaning." The key will be immediately apparent to anyone who has seen the film *Barfly*, since the content of the novel *Hollywood* concerns the difficulties in writing and producing that film (Bukowski wrote the screenplay).

Though Bukowski has altered the proper names in the novel, many of them are easily recognizable if the reader uses some imagination. The film *Barfly* is called *The Dance of Jim Beam*, and certain well-known foreign directors appear from time to time with names such as Jon-Luc Modard and Wenner Zergog. The major difference between Bukowski's four previous novels and *Hollywood* is that most of the action takes place in Beverly Hills and Hollywood rather than the usual sordid neighborhoods of urban Los Angeles. Some of the sleazier film scenes, however, are actually shot in several of Bukowski's favorite gin mills, which have now become "sets" for the film. The French director, Jon Pinchot, in his quest for authenticity, also decided to use the real inhabitants of these places, the barflies themselves, instead of Hollywood actors. Chinaski himself is regularly called in to demonstrate to the actor portraying him exactly how he conducted himself during his habitual barroom brawls.

The plot consists of the endless ups and downs of acquiring funds for producing the film. Bukowski also reveals that greed, and greed alone, constitutes the primary motivation for filmmaking and that producers and backers will do anything to increase profits. Hollywood has nothing to do with art, truth, or beauty in any form.

The comic aspects of *Hollywood* work on a number of complex levels because the content of the novel is also its form: It is a novel about writing a screenplay, but it is also a novel written by a barfly trying to write a screenplay about the life of a barfly. Not only is the barfly, Henry Chinaski, drinking to excess and trying to recover long enough to produce some acceptable scenes, but also one of Chinaski's major complaints is that everyone else involved in the direction, production, and promotion of the film is also debilitated by their alcoholic drinking. Indeed, when Chinaski is first asked what the screenplay is about, he states unequivocally: "A drunk. Lots of drunks." Later, he adds: "But the whole movie is *about* drinking." He then summarizes quite clearly his attitude toward drinking during an interview just before the preview of the finished film:

"Isn't drinking a disease?"
"Breathing is a disease."
"Don't you find drunks obnoxious?"
"Yes, most of them are. So are most teetotalers."

Finally, Henry honestly admits to himself as he watches his film, *The Dance of Jim Beam*, in his local theater: "I only wanted to show what strange and desperate lives some drunks live and I was the one drunk I knew best."

Although Henry Chinaski's financial situation has improved by the conclusion of the novel, he and his companion, Sarah, still enjoy going to the films together, coming home to the five cats, and watching Johnny Carson on television. Sarah asks him what he intends to do now that the film is completed, and he responds that he will now write a novel about "writing the screenplay and making the movie." When asked what he might call the novel, he answers that it will be entitled *Hollywood*.

Summary

The literary quality of the novels of Charles Bukowski has progressively improved principally because each became more refined and sophisticated in terms of its form. The structure of *Post Office* consisted of a raw chronology of his years in the postal service, while *Ham on Rye* adhered to the pattern of a *Künstlerroman*. *Hollywood* has the advantage of being a full-fledged modernistic work because its form and content are virtually identical: it is a novel about writing a screenplay as it simultaneously records the difficulties that people encounter who drink too much. What saves Bukowski's work from becoming a dreary record of the hopeless lives of a group of helpless alcoholics is his refreshing sense of humor, his ability to see the irony of his own behavior, and his complete lack of self-pity. His work moves more clearly toward satire with each new novel and demonstrates his ability to see himself and his world in increasingly objective and compassionate terms.

Bibliography

Dorbin, Sanford. *A Bibliography of Charles Bukowski*. Los Angeles: Black Sparrow Press, 1969.

Easterly, Glenn. "The Pock-Marked Poetry of Charles Bukowski." *Rolling Stone* 215 (June 17, 1976): 28-36.

Fox, Hugh. *Charles Bukowski: A Critical and Bibliographical Study*. Somerville, Mass.: Abyss, 1969.

The Outsider 1, no. 3 (1963). Special Bukowski issue.

The Review of Contemporary Fiction 3, no. 3 (Fall, 1983). Special Bukowski/Butor issue.

Patrick Meanor

JAMES M. CAIN

Born: Annapolis, Maryland
July 1, 1892
Died: Hyattsville, Maryland
October 27, 1977

Principal Literary Achievement

Cain's best work exemplifies the definitive American mastery of the so-called hard-boiled style of writing, which gained prominence during the 1930's and won international favor for economy of expression.

Biography

James Mallahan Cain, son of James William and Rose Mallahan Cain, was born in Annapolis, Maryland, on July 1, 1892. He was the eldest of five children, including his three sisters—Rosalie, Virginia, and Genevieve—and his brother, Edward. His youthful aspirations, neither of which he completely surrendered during his entire life, were music and playwriting. He abandoned his plans to sing professionally but retained a critical appreciation of music that is evident in works such as *Serenade* (1937), *Career in C Major* (originally "Two Can Sing," 1938), and *Mildred Pierce* (1941). His exceptionally good ear for dialogue failed to ensure his success as a playwright. Between 1926 and 1955, his five attempts to write for the stage all resulted in failure of one kind or another; yet the effective dialogue and swiftly paced plots that did not function for him in drama became the core of his best-selling and most critically praised fiction.

In 1910, Cain was graduated from Washington College (in Chesterton, Maryland), of which his father was president and to which, after unsuccessful forays into the world of professional singing, he returned as a teacher of English and mathematics from 1914 through 1917.

During the next decade, Cain worked as a newspaperman for the *Baltimore Sun*. After military service in France, where he worked on the newspaper of his World War I infantry company, he returned to the *Baltimore Sun* as a columnist and feature writer. He published articles in *Atlantic Monthly*, *The Nation*, and, as a protégé of H. L. Mencken, *American Mercury*. Mencken recommended him to Walter Lippmann, who subsequently installed him as an editorialist for the *New York World*.

Cain's marriage to Mary Rebekah Clough in 1920 came to an end in 1927, at which time he married Elina Sjostad Tyszecka, who was to be his wife during the

302

golden years of his career, 1927-1942. His first short story, "Pastorale," appeared in 1928. He published his first book in 1930, a collection of satirical dialogues entitled *Our Government*. In 1931 he served briefly as managing editor of *The New Yorker* magazine and then moved to Hollywood. It was while he was earning his living as a scriptwriter that he produced the novels which, along with his first short story, guaranteed his inclusion in the canon of American literature. He achieved national fame in 1934 with his first novel, *The Postman Always Rings Twice*. This was followed by *Double Indemnity* (1936), *Serenade* (1937), *Mildred Pierce* (1941), and *Love's Lovely Counterfeit* (1942). His second marriage ended in divorce in 1942.

Cain remained in Hollywood for five more years, during the last three of which he was married to Aileen Pringle, a former actress. The marriage, troubled in large part by Cain's drinking problem, ended in divorce in 1947. This was the year in which the last of his best novels, *The Butterfly*, was published. It was also the year of his marriage to Florence Macbeth, the last of his four wives—by none of whom he had any children of his own.

As a writer, Cain had begun to aim at higher creativity, to which end he intensified not so much the profundities of style and thought as the niceties of research. *Past All Dishonor* (1946) was a heavily researched novel set in California and the silver boom of the 1860's. Following his determination to devote himself to serious literary enterprise, he moved with Florence to Hyattsville, Maryland, in 1948. The best of his post-Hollywood fiction, *Galatea* (1953) and *Rainbow's End* (1975), merely echo his achievements of the 1930's and 1940's. The major effort of his later period was *Mignon* (1962), his first published novel in the ten years that followed *Galatea*; like *Past All Dishonor*, it is set in the 1860's, and it entailed painstaking research. The setting is the Red River Expedition to western Louisiana in the last year of the Civil War. Unlike *Past All Dishonor*, which, at the peak of Cain's fame, enjoyed mixed but generally enthusiastic reviews and a successful market, *Mignon* was a disappointment in both areas. Florence Macbeth Cain died in 1966; Cain himself, writing constantly to the last, died in Hyattsville on October 27, 1977, at the age of eighty-five. *Cloud Nine*, a novel published posthumously in 1984, adds nothing to his reputation.

Analysis

The substance of James M. Cain's fiction coincides with the undercurrents of Greek tragedy—violently satisfied ambitions, incest, hubris, adultery, murder, betrayal, and nemesis. Greek tragedy is also drama and music, the two modes of artistic expression to which Cain vainly aspired. Cain's work is best approached in this context of tragedy and auctorial frustration, even if one agrees with W. M. Frohock that the tragedy is "bogus" or "tabloid." (Frohock judges all Cain's work to be "trash" yet recognizes in it a readability to which many first-rate writers are drawn.) Like the major figures in his stories, Cain never got what he truly wanted; yet, in creating those figures, he wrote what he truly wanted to write and, although he did not become a dramatist and creator of high literature, he fathomed the currents of truth that may be the consciously or unconsciously sought goal of all art.

Cain's antiheroes mainly achieve, not their true desires, which may or may not remain unknown to them, but the surfaces of their dreams; the coalescence of the dreamer with the surface of the dream is the guarantee of disaster. Cain appears to have detected the fallacy of the American Dream, which rises brightly but upon unseen and unadmitted props of crime, violence, promiscuity, and sexual waywardness. The first sentence of *The Postman Always Rings Twice* encapsulates the quality and direction of Cain's fiction: "They threw me off the hay truck about noon." In addition to immediately arresting the reader's interest with perfect verbal economy, the sentence connotes the alienation of the unsettled individual ("me") from the Establishment ("They"), those who have harvested the fields of the American Dream at the temporarily shadowless (it is "about noon") surface of a society that has been wounded by the dream-destroying reality of the Depression of the early 1930's. The story that follows is, at the literal level, the working-out of Cain's fictional formula: A man and a woman seek sexual gratification and monetary profit from the murder of the woman's husband. At the emblematic level, it presents the American Dream as a sublimation of the quest for sex and cash.

The hard, lean, unembellished, and fast-paced narratives of Cain's characteristic works earned for his fiction the epithets "tough-guy" and "hard-boiled." He objected to these terms both because they placed him in a specific category, which placement as a critical device he abhorred, and because they were also associated with Ernest Hemingway, whose works Cain admired but whose influence upon himself he sternly denied in his preface to *The Butterfly*. In that preface, Cain, differentiating himself from Hemingway, says, "I . . . write of the wish that comes true, . . . a terrifying concept." The terror derives from the fact that it is chiefly the materialistic surface of the wish that comes true, not the true wish. There are precedents in Greek tragedy. The wish of Sophocles' Oedipus for material success, for example, comes true, but only by way of patricide and incest, the factors which ultimately defeat him; his true wish, unknown to himself until he is brought down by his wish come true, is for spiritual peace, which he learns at last is found in love. Cain's antiheroes fulfill their wishes for sex and money but, in doing so, must contend with the destructive forces loosed by the woman—the equivalent of "the first woman," as Cain says in the preface to *The Butterfly*, naming the Greek mythical Pandora.

The woman in *Serenade* murders a man's homosexual lover and restores to the man, through his heterosexual relationship with her, the fine singing voice which readers are given to understand his homosexuality had flattened. Then the basis of the man's successful new career asserts itself as the very destruction of that career. The man learns, after his singing voice reveals his identity and the law then finds and kills his fugitive woman, that his love for the woman was the real meaning of his life. Love for a woman whom a man mistakenly assumes to be his daughter is the nexus of the tragedy in *The Butterfly*. Here the true love is incestuous, although to himself the man does not acknowledge it as such. His love increases in direct proportion to the strengthening of the unadmitted assumption that she is his daughter.

A virtual companionpiece to *The Butterfly* is *The Moth* (1948), in which a man's love for a twelve-year-old girl is as true as it is conventionally exceptionable. *The Moth* antedates Vladimir Nabokov's *Lolita* by seven years. Oddly, Nabokov's comic novel about a middle-aged man in love with a twelve-year-old girl ends unhappily, while Cain's novel is one of the few to which he gave a happy ending.

The happy ending is not Cain's specialty. His murder mysteries, *Sinful Woman* (1947) and *Jealous Woman* (1950), end happily and are both among Cain's least effective accomplishments. *Sinful Woman* is representative of another of Cain's infrequent devices, third-person narration. *Mildred Pierce* and *Love's Lovely Counterfeit* carry the device creditably, but the same cannot be said of either *Sinful Woman* or *The Magician's Wife* (1965). Departures from the techniques of *The Postman Always Rings Twice* were, except in the composition of *Mildred Pierce*, not felicitous for Cain. He is essentially a master of the short, brisk, unsentimental, first-person narrative tragedy of persons pulled to destruction by the inevitable consequences of their fulfilled material wishes, which at first obscure and then either delay or preclude the experience of their true subjective wishes.

THE POSTMAN ALWAYS RINGS TWICE

First published: 1934
Type of work: Novel

Adulterous lovers who get away with murder cannot escape their fate.

The Postman Always Rings Twice was Cain's first novel and came to stand as his finest work of fiction. It is both classical Cain, with its hard-boiled first-person narrative of a wrenching love triangle, wish fulfillment, and retribution, and classical in its tragic theme and episodic structure. A very attractive young woman, Cora, is unhappily married to Nick Papadakis, the proprietor of a restaurant. A drifter, Frank Chambers, falls in love with Cora, hires on as Nick's employee, and enjoys Cora's requital of his love. The adulterers successfully conspire to murder Nick, thereby gaining his restaurant business and their own life together. Much of their planning materializes through fortuitous as well as engineered accidents. It is also an accident that finally destroys both of them, Cora as accident victim and Frank as the victim of circumstances: Having been acquitted of contriving the accident that was supposed to have taken the life of Nick Papadakis, a charge of which he was actually guilty, he is now ironically convicted of contriving the accident that killed Cora, despite his innocence. The structure, like that of Greek Tragedy and classical literature in general, is symmetrical: Cora and Frank are denied free union by societal and economic restrictions, Cora and Frank achieve free union through their crime, Cora and Frank are destroyed precisely in the context of their achievement of free union. The symmetry is that of separation-union-separation.

Cain's special skill is in presenting a story with the immediacy and relevance of a news item. Stories, historical or otherwise, which did not speak to his own time defeated his interest. He insisted in a Hearst newspaper column for November 11, 1933, that he could not sustain his interest in certain regarded contemporary novels — among them Ernest Hemingway's *A Farewell to Arms* (1929), William Faulkner's *Sanctuary* (1931), and Nathanael West's *Miss Lonelyhearts* (1933) — because "they bear no relation . . . to the times in which I live." He believed that "the destiny, the national purpose of the deal" had to be there before a writer could have anything to say; the destiny of the American Dream antecedes *The Postman Always Rings Twice.* The "they" who throw Frank Chambers off the hay truck also give him a cigarette. He is then given a job by Nick, a businessman whose financial security Frank would like to have, but without the attendant responsibilities; he would also like to possess Cora. Frank does not understand that Nick and Cora are extensions of the "they," reversing the process of gift-giving — Nick tendering a job, Nora her body — and causing him to be thrown. The classical symmetry appears as thrown-gift-gifts-thrown.

Behind or beneath Frank's wish for money and sex is his true wish, unrecognized until too late, for love. The Establishment, moreover, as the repository of superficial wishes, always defeats the individual whom it ostensibly accommodates. The last paragraph of the novel begins with "Here they come." (These are also the very last words of *Past All Dishonor.*) The "they" of the novel's beginning have at the novel's ending become Frank's executioners. Cain makes use of appropriate names in *The Postman Always Rings Twice*: "Nick" and "Cora" are both Greek names, and their characters embody the money and sex that Frank Chambers, whose name is not Greek, wishes to have. Frank's error is much the same as that of the Trojans who refused to share Laocoön's apprehension about Greeks bearing gifts.

DOUBLE INDEMNITY

First published: 1936
Type of work: Novel

A woman and her lover murder the woman's husband for insurance money, after which their mutual desire culminates in a death wish.

Double Indemnity was written by Cain in approximately two months; it appeared initially in *Liberty* magazine as an eight-part serial. It was, as Cain himself admitted, practically a rewriting of *The Postman Always Rings Twice.* In both novels, a man, obsessed with desire for a married woman and tempted by the prospect of easy money, contrives under the woman's encouragement a scheme to murder the husband and profit from the murder. In each novel the effect of the successful criminal enterprise is the self-destruction of the principals in tandem with their ultimate realization of their true love for each other.

Although neither title was Cain's inceptive selection — the original title of *The Postman Always Rings Twice* was *Bar-B-Que*, and *Double Indemnity* was suggested to Cain by James Geller—both include an ironic play on types of dualism. Fatal accidents happen twice, one staged and one actual, in the first novel; in the later novel, there are two double compensations for an accidental death that is actually a murder: The first is the double-indemnity insurance award, and the second is the self-execution decided upon by the two murderers who collected the insurance.

Despite the similarities, the novels remain distinct; each has its special characteristics, and each is a masterwork. The murderers in *Double Indemnity* are Phyllis Nirdlinger, a very attractive, unhappily married woman, and Walter Huff, an insurance agent who falls in love with Phyllis and whom she uses as the instrument of gaining her ends. Phyllis is more cunning and venomous than Cora Papadakis, and Walter is superior to Frank Chambers in both industry and intelligence. The intricacies of the legal profession inform the plot of the earlier novel, and the complexities of the insurance business inform the plot of *Double Indemnity*. The love story in *The Postman Always Rings Twice* is fashioned against images of purgative swimming (off the seashore) and fertility (Cora is pregnant when the accident takes her life). In *Double Indemnity*, the love story is cast against images of sterility (hearth fire, the moon, Phyllis's thinking of herself "as Death") and culminates in the suicide pact of leaping from a ship into shark-filled waters.

Double Indemnity has other elements that are absent from Cain's first novel. There is a deep friendship between Huff and a father-figure named Keyes, who is head of the insurance company's claims department. There is a subplot involving Phyllis' stepdaughter Lola and Beniamino Sachetti, Lola's suitor. Huff's affection for the stepdaughter results in a double love triangle: Phyllis-Huff-Lola and Lola-Sachetti-Huff. These elements add depth to the story without even slightly curtailing its pace. Raymond Chandler, who wrote the screenplay for *Double Indemnity*, considered the novel, and Cain's work in general, to be "the offal of literature." The judgment, although seconded by not a few critics of Cain's fiction, is rash. In *Double Indemnity*, Cain manages not only to tell a gripping story in very few words but also to introduce a credible love story and a moving friendship into the lives of its concisely sketched characters. Furthermore, Cain's theme, materialistic and selfish dreams as leading eventually to an awakening into the reality of human affections, is far from negligible.

MILDRED PIERCE

First published: 1941
Type of work: Novel

A businesswoman sublimates an erotic need for her unconscionably selfish daughter.

Mildred Pierce is a domestic tragedy in which wife-husband and mother-daughter relationships are perversely confused. Mildred Pierce's husband, Herbert (or Bert), is not a good provider, and his need in a wife is for maternal solicitude. Mildred is a capable and intelligent woman who suffers an obsession with her daughter, Veda, which she thinks is mother love. Veda is a talented coloratura soprano whose obsession is herself. Bert deserts his family for a woman who is a mother figure. Mildred, thrown upon her own resources, becomes a successful entrepreneur in the restaurant business and finances her daughter's musical education, which leads to a bright career. When Veda, constantly betraying her mother, finally deserts her, Mildred is crushed, having lost her unconsciously desired love mate. Cain handles the incest motif more subtly, or perhaps more covertly, and decidedly more effectively here than he does in *The Butterfly*, published six years later. The novel concludes with Mildred and Bert reunited.

The transformation of Mildred from a mother who would be wife to her daughter to a wife who resigns herself to mothering her husband is signalled in two keynote episodes. The first is the one in which Mildred learns that Veda is pregnant. Her immediate reaction is neither maternal protectiveness nor the murderous anger that Bert will feel toward the man responsible, but a fierce "jealousy . . . so overwhelming that Mildred actually was afraid she would vomit." This response is a betrayed lover's reaction, not a mother's. The distraught Mildred asks Veda "if she'd like to sleep with her, 'just for tonight.'" Veda declines, and Mildred spends a wakeful night "with the jealousy gnawing at her." The second episode is the conclusion of the novel. Bert says to Mildred "to hell with" Veda, and Mildred, sensing his meaning, manages to swallow her sobs "and draw the knife across an umbilical cord." The indefinite article is functionally ambiguous, referring both to Veda, whose frustrated lover Mildred ceases to be, and to Bert, whose resigned mother she now becomes.

Mildred Pierce, as a long novel in third-person narration which is not a crime story or thriller, is not standard Cain; its pessimism, however, is standard Cain. Its emphasis upon vacuous materialism in the worlds of business and professional entertainment and its disclosure of affections transmuted by sublimation make it Cain's most pessimistic work. That it is, at the same time, not bitter or misanthropic in its effect is attributable to the author's sympathetic understanding of the forces and the emotions that move its characters; in this novel, Cain created his finest characterizations.

Summary

James M. Cain was an observer of the American character and a commentator on its dark vagaries. The height of his career coincided with the arrival of *film noir*, of which the film versions of *The Postman Always Rings Twice* (1946), *Double Indemnity* (1944), and *Mildred Pierce* (1945) are examples. What Ruth Prigozy, in her article on the film version of *Double Indemnity*, says about *film noir* is equally descriptive of the direction of Cain's fiction:

> The murder-detective story crime film was popular in the war years, for it enabled filmmakers to depict . . . the violent, nightmarish quality of the era, without explicitly criticizing America. In *film noir*, the optimism of the previous decade was rejected, perhaps unconsciously, in favor of an overtly skeptical view of human nature and society.

With his antiheroic characters and his theme of successfully but self-destructively pursuing the material side of personal gratification, Cain exposes the treacherous shoals of American aspirations.

Bibliography

Bradbury, Richard. "Sexuality, Guilt, and Detection: Tension Between History and Suspense." In *American Crime Fiction: Studies in the Genre*, edited by Brian Docherty. New York: St. Martin's Press, 1988.

Frohock, W. M. "James M. Cain: Tabloid Tragedy." In *The Novel of Violence in America: 1920-1950*. Dallas: Southern Methodist University Press, 1950.

Hoopes, Roy. *Cain: The Biography of James M. Cain*. New York: Holt, Rinehart and Winston, 1982.

_____, ed. *Sixty Years of Journalism by James M. Cain*. Bowling Green, Ohio: Bowling Green State University Popular Press, 1985.

Madden, David. *Cain's Craft*. Metuchen, N.J.: Scarecrow Press, 1985.

_____. *James M. Cain*. Boston: Twayne, 1970.

Prigozy, Ruth. "Double Indemnity: Billy Wilder's Crime and Punishment." *Literature/Film Quarterly* 12, no. 3 (1984): 163.

Roy Arthur Swanson

ERSKINE CALDWELL

Born: White Oak, near Moreland, Georgia
December 17, 1903
Died: Paradise Valley, Arizona
April 11, 1987

Principal Literary Achievement

Enormously popular in the 1930's and 1940's, Caldwell brought to millions of Americans his bawdy, forcefully written, grimly comic stories of injustice and human irrationality, set chiefly in the South.

Biography

Erskine Caldwell was born in the community of White Oak, near Moreland, Georgia, on December 7, 1903, the only child of Ira Sylvester and his wife, Caroline Bell Caldwell, of Staunton, Virginia. In following years, the little family moved often about the South, wherever Caldwell's father's duties as a minister and troubleshooter for his denomination took him, until they settled in Wrens, Georgia, in 1918, less than thirty miles southwest of Augusta. Caldwell's mother, like Ernest Hemingway's and Thomas Wolfe's, kept her son in shoulder-length curls; odder still, however, was her refusal to allow the boy to attend school until the seventh grade.

In Wrens, the nearest thing to a hometown Caldwell had, the family lived an uneventful life. His father assumed a permanent pastorate, and both parents took jobs at the institute (or high school). Ira Sylvester, a man of great good will and unflagging philanthropy, though modest athletic ability, organized the school's first sports program and served for many years as its football, basketball, and baseball coach. Mrs. Caldwell was a teacher of English. Known as "Skinny," as much for his elongated frame as his first name, Erskine attended school under the watchful eyes of his parents and found his first job writing one summer on the *Jefferson Reporter*. In time he advanced to "stringer" status, serving as a correspondent for some city newspapers, covering mainly baseball games.

As son of a minister and teachers, Caldwell enjoyed a respectability in tiny Wrens very different from the reputation he was later to achieve after the shocking success of *Tobacco Road*'s stage version (1933). Misled by whoppers that Caldwell himself told the gullible—as did so many of his literary contemporaries—and by the subject matter of *Tobacco Road* (1932) and *God's Little Acre* (1933), books often read "behind the barn," Americans came to believe that he had himself emerged from

311

the people he depicted. The tall, redheaded, freckle-faced youth who ran in the Wrens One-Mile Relay on New Year's Day, 1920, became in following decades the nemesis of the Watch and Ward Society, "America's No. 1 cracker-barrel pornographer" (*Time* magazine, 1957), and a suspected agent of the Kremlin. In Wrens, Caldwell wrote newspaper copy and an occasional story and chauffeured a doctor on rural house calls, where he saw how blacks lived and discovered the living conditions of tenant farmers on the sandy roads that crisscrossed the countryside outside the town. In Wrens he developed the searing social conscience that boils below the apparent indifference of his fiction.

Finishing high school, Caldwell left for his father's alma mater, Erskine College, in South Carolina. He stayed there only a year and a half, however, before transferring to the more challenging University of Virginia on an obscure scholarship for the descendant of a Confederate veteran. At Charlottesville, Caldwell discovered the "little magazine," the trying ground for young writers, that he was soon to deluge with short stories from his own typewriter. There, too, he read Theodore Dreiser's powerful *Sister Carrie* (1900), some of the stories of the young Ernest Hemingway (just coming into prominence), and a book that affected his whole generation, Sherwood Anderson's *Winesburg, Ohio* (1919). He also studied writing formally.

At the end of his second year, he pushed north as far as Philadelphia, where he spent a summer term at the Wharton School of Finance before moving to Scranton to unpack crates in the cellar of Kresge's—a discount store, the predecessor of K Mart. On the basis of limited football experience at Erskine College, he played right end for three games on a semi-professional team, where he found himself completely outclassed. Experiences such as these, greatly exaggerated, eventually adorned his book jackets to serve as evidence of a life colorful enough to rival Jack London's.

The next spring he eloped with the first of his four wives and took a twenty-dollar-a-week job on the *Atlanta Journal*. In addition to reporting, Caldwell wrote book reviews that he sent to other papers and worked on short stories at night, determined now to be a writer himself. After a single year, he quit Atlanta for rural Maine to write only stories, and he sent them out until in 1929, he got the first one published and then anthologized. Soon F. Scott Fitzgerald, author of *The Great Gatsby* (1925), recommended that his own editor, Max Perkins of Scribner's, accept Caldwell's work. Not only did Perkins then print several of Caldwell's stories in *Scribner's Magazine*, but he also arranged for Caldwell to publish a collection, *American Earth* (1931). Further, he accepted Caldwell's new novel, *Tobacco Road*, which became a smash Broadway hit in Jack Kirkland's version the next year. The notoriety the sexy play received guaranteed a huge audience for Caldwell's next novel; suddenly Caldwell's name was on everyone's lips and the term "tobacco road," meaning a run-down white neighborhood, entered the American language.

As his marriage began to founder, Caldwell accepted offers from Hollywood and produced more short story collections, another novel, and a book of reportage. These were less enthusiastically received. World War II gave brief impetus to his career as servicemen devoured his earlier risque novels and Caldwell broadcast from Moscow while the Nazis poured into Russia. By then he had married Margaret Bourke-White, the photographer known for her combat photos in the pages of *Life* magazine. The end of the war marked the end of his critical acclaim, however, and soon after, his popularity as well. Caldwell himself refused to acknowledge any decline, deliberately ignoring the judgment of those whom he felt were late to recognize him in the first place and whose opinions were not worth much anyway.

Although he wrote many more books he had been so completely forgotten by the time of his death on April 11, 1987, that the obituaries of major American newspapers were obliged to explain in great detail who he was.

Analysis

Erskine Caldwell is one of few American writers to achieve both enormous popular and critical success. Known to millions of his countrymen, many of whom actually read *Tobacco Road* or *God's Little Acre*, Caldwell's name mentioned on a radio program in the 1930's or 1940's would instantly evoke howls of snickering laughter, since his books suggested raw humor and sex. Ensign Pulver in Thomas Heggen's hit novel and play *Mister Roberts* (1946) was probably one of countless World War II sailors who had memorized the most scandalous passage in *God's Little Acre*, which he could recite "flawlessly."

Yet if Caldwell meant "dirty books" to large numbers of Americans, he was something quite different to students of literature. Many considered him chiefly a protest or proletarian writer, one of those socially committed novelists of the Depression era who exposed injustices in American life, the plight of tenant farmers, or the outrageous conditions under which cotton mill workers or Southern blacks lived. Left-leaning critics championed his work as properly Marxist, but they were often disappointed by what they considered irrelevant elements in his writing. What, they wondered, did all the slapstick and sex have to do with the class struggle? They wished he would simply concentrate on exposing the evils of capitalism. Even before World War II, the Soviet Union had put its stamp of approval on his work, and after the war the countries of Eastern Europe joined in so clamorously that Caldwell became a figure of some suspicion during the Cold War years.

On the other hand, many compared him to William Faulkner, whose critical reputation was growing in the early 1930's, but who could not command the sales that Caldwell could, saying that Caldwell's Southern Gothic tales were as profoundly metaphorical as Faulkner's. Faulkner himself joined the chorus of praise, calling him the best writer in America. Other critics insisted on comparing him to James Farrell, whose naturalistic novel *Young Lonigan* (1932), the first in his trilogy about Studs Lonigan, appeared the year of *Tobacco Road*. Like Farrell, Caldwell wrote about heredity and poor families whose unhappy destinies were largely determined by the environment around them, a world where a man was strictly on his own.

Still others stressed Caldwell's humor. Not since Mark Twain, they said, had a Southern writer made readers laugh so in showing man's hopeless irrationality. They pointed to stories such as "Mid-Summer Passion," in which Ben Hacket, fortified with fermented cider, pulls a pair of pink panties on Mrs. Fred Williams in a sort of panty raid in reverse or to the shenanigans of "A Country Full of Swedes," which won for him a Yale Award for Fiction in the mid-1930's. Certainly readers found Jeeter Lester's attempt "to get on the good side of the Lord" with the help of the zany evangelist Sister Bessie Rice or Ty Ty Walden's gold mining schemes—to mention only two of the obsessions of Caldwell's simple-minded characters—hilariously funny.

Like Mark Twain's, too, was Caldwell's interest in American places in a period when regional distinctions were much stronger than they have become since two generations of television and a mobile society have worked their homogenizing effects. Caldwell wrote about the South, where he was born, and northern New England, where he spent the most productive decade of his life. In his later years he continued to travel about the United States and the world, showing interest in regional writers and expressing great pride in his editing in the 1940's *American Folkways*, a collection of studies of regional America by a host of writers. Although he left the South while still in his twenties, never to return except for temporary visits or Florida residencies, readers inevitably think of him still as a "Georgia boy."

Caldwell's writing, both his short stories and his novels, is uneven. It is not fair, however, to say that his muse abandoned him early in his career or that he sold out for big money after *God's Little Acre*, charges that were often leveled against him. Neither accusation is true. He wrote weaker stories, such as "Dorothy" (1931) and "Strawberry Season" (1930), as well as strong ones from the start. Two little-known novelettes that he published on small presses before *Tobacco Road*, *The Bastard* (1929) and *Poor Fool* (1930), most readers will find unrewarding. Indeed, Scribner's lost Caldwell as an author when the company decided not to accept his decidedly minor "Maine novel," the book he wrote after *Tobacco Road*, published years later as *A Lamp for Nightfall* (1952). Although he could command generous advances and profitable contracts in his heyday, he continued to write just as dutifully when there was little demand for his work.

Caldwell wrote a plain style of American English that F. Scott Fitzgerald perceptively recognized as resembling Hemingway's and told his stories, often about country folk, from an objective point of view—so objective, in fact, that many mistakenly thought he sympathized little with his characters. While the bulk of his writing is "realistic," providing recognizable details of everyday life, his use of grotesquerie, like that of such moderns as the Czech novelist Franz Kafka, is meant to show that the reaches of human experience cannot be captured by the photographic realism of the past, that something more is needed to depict, for example, the iniquity of the perverse preacher Semon Dye in *Journeyman* (1935) than merely faithful reproduction of externals.

Although he believed in the primacy of feeling and often seemed to view sex, as did the slightly older English novelist D. H. Lawrence, as bringing out the god in man, Caldwell's view of life is often as pessimistic as that of any naturalist: Jeeter

Lester and his wife are killed in a fire in *Tobacco Road*; Will Thompson, the charismatic labor leader, is shot to death in *God's Little Acre*, as is Clem, the saintly black Christ figure in "Kneel to the Rising Sun" (1935); and Semon Dye successfully bilks the town of Rocky Comfort in a revival meeting before moving on.

Thus an unresolved contradiction underlies much of his work. Caldwell trusts that social justice will eventually bring better times to poor whites and blacks; he believes that the spirit of man is indomitable, that there is a mystic force in the blood and soil, and that in listening to one's deepest instincts one listens to the voice of God Himself. At the same time, he acknowledges that man is irrational and the world is a cruel place where the wicked often triumph over the good. Yet Caldwell himself saw no such contradiction; rather, he called his work only a realistic balance between "the depiction of the violent and ugly, of poverty and class conflict" and "spasms of laughter, the horseplay of humor, and the enjoyment of living."

TOBACCO ROAD

First published: 1932
Type of work: Novel

Jeeter Lester and his wife, Ada, dirt-poor Georgia tenant farmers, lose their family and their lives at planting season.

Tobacco Road, Caldwell's fourth novel (counting *The Bogus Ones*, discovered in 1978), remains the book for which he is best remembered. Narrated in an episodic fashion, it quickly reveals more of theme and meaning than would a more organically developed effort. In *Tobacco Road*, Jeeter Lester and his wife, Ada, live in a decaying cabin with his silent mother and two of their fifteen children, the harelipped Ellie May and her younger brother Dude. Like the tobacco road on which they live, once a means of delivering hogsheads of tobacco to the Savannah River, and like the fields around them, they are obsolete and worn out.

When Lov Bensey arrives to seek Jeeter's help in getting his child-wife to speak to him and sleep with him, his father-in-law regards the visit as an opportunity to steal turnips he suspects are in the sack Lov carries. Times in Georgia are so hard that "Captain" John has moved to Augusta, cutting off the credit that his tenant farmers like Jeeter need to eat and to acquire seed cotton and fertilizer for the tired soil. In no more than three brief chapters of *Tobacco Road*, Caldwell reveals the silent, loveless existence of his exploited country people and exposes the obsolete sharecropping system that controls their empty lives.

Lov is soon robbed of his turnips and seduced by Ellie May in a scene that is mostly suggested in the novel but was graphic enough to have titillated a decade of theatergoers. Seen from another perspective, Ellie May's seduction appears only the desperate act of a neglected teenager, starved of affection. Indeed, Caldwell later suggests that Ellie May is the proper mate for Lov, who married her sister mostly because she lacked Ellie May's disfigurement. In *Tobacco Road*, Caldwell comments obliquely and with great economy on a number of problems: human sexuality and love, agriculture in the South, hunger in America, the plight of the old, the place of labor in human life, and man's relation to God.

With the appearance of Sister Bessie Rice he investigates this latter theme, though not to the extent that he does in *God's Little Acre*. Bessie, almost forty, decides that God has directed her to marry Dude and conduct a revival crusade. Like so many Protestants of fundamentalist background, Caldwell distrusts clergy, believing that a person's relation to God must be direct, not attained through the office of fallible intermediaries—let alone via half-baked ignoramuses such as Bessie.

Although he is lazy, dishonest, mean-spirited, and lecherous, Jeeter Lester often provides the reader with the author's viewpoint. Caldwell approves of Jeeter who, despite his myriad faults, obeys his deepest instincts and trusts in God and the land. Strangely enough the reader comes to feel the same way. Although there is little reason to believe that Jeeter will ever change his ways, in death he seems a sacrificial victim. Ultimately one is ready—or almost ready—to believe Dude, who, in eulogizing his father, suddenly speaks about growing "a bale to an acre like Pa was always talking about doing."

GOD'S LITTLE ACRE

First published: 1933
Type of work: Novel

Shifting again the acre consecrated to God, Ty Ty Walden makes a last effort to find the gold he believes lies beneath his Georgia farm.

God's Little Acre, published on the heels of *Tobacco Road*, appeared in 1933 to favorable reviews and a highly publicized fracas with the New York Society for the Suppression of Vice that focused enormous public attention on the new novel. To it Caldwell brought in more concentrated form many of the ideas that had interested him in the earlier book. Again he sought to explain that "feeling," trust in oneself and in God—a state very similar to Ralph Waldo Emerson's self-reliance—is the natural goal of man. In *God's Little Acre*, as in *Tobacco Road*, he treads an uneasy line between preaching that a divinity waits inside human beings to be freed and showing humans at their most irrational. In other words, he is never quite sure if he is a romantic who believes that man is limitless or a naturalist who sees him as a helpless victim of economic forces, his emotions, and his biology.

In depicting Will Thompson, the visionary leader of men, Caldwell resorts to an even more poetic style than he used in describing Jeeter's love for the soil, one that recalls his early ambitions as a poet and his impressionistic prose poem *The Sacrilege of Alan Kent*, privately printed in 1936, though written in stages much earlier. When Will Thompson reluctantly appears at Ty Ty Walden's farm to help his father-in-law in his foolish search for gold, Caldwell's episodic story takes an aberrant turn. What at first seems to be only a rollicking story of rural eccentrics becomes an account of labor unrest, infidelity, and murder.

In *God's Little Acre*, as in *Tobacco Road*, a patriarchal figure embodying a host of contradictions becomes a sort of spokesman for Caldwell in the solemn stillness of the book's conclusion. Ty Ty Walden endorses the strength, *joie de vivre*, and sexual vitality of his daughter's husband and recognizes (unlike his jealous sons) Will's qualities of leadership. Though Will represents a threat to familial unity and to the virtues of his sister-in-law Griselda (his other sister-in-law, Darling Jill, has no virtue to worry about), Ty Ty must acknowledge the divinity he discerns within him. And Will's raging libido becomes, in the course of the novel, a positive force, since it is from the love and admiration of three women that he acquires the strength to lead the mill workers in opening the mill, shut by selfish monied interests.

After Will, who has gradually been identified with Christ, has distributed his garments (by throwing his torn-up shirt out the window of the seized mill), he is killed by soldiers (out-of-state guards hired by the mill owners). In the aftermath of his death comes more tragedy, but readers are left with the belief, haltingly explained by Ty Ty, that Will's life has been a model for all and that conventional morality plays little role in the lives of heroes whose lives are at the service of the masses.

Summary

Caldwell's two-fisted stories of baffled rural Americans struggling to survive in the merciless world around them won him the devotion of millions of readers who found his voice strong, his depictions honest, his prose style readable, and his courage admirable. He wrote forcefully about subjects other writers were afraid to confront, and he did so with a wild comic touch. If he emphasized sex, he did not neglect to expose the injustices everywhere in American life in the Depression years. Called a sensationalist by his detractors, he conveyed what Thoreau called "the stark twilight and unsatisfied thoughts which all men have."

Bibliography

Caldwell, Erskine. *Call It Experience*. New York: Duell, Sloan and Pearce, 1951.

_____. *With All My Might*. Atlanta: Peachtree, 1987.

Cowley, Malcolm. *—And I Worked at the Writer's Trade*. New York: Viking Press, 1978.

Devlin, James E. *Erskine Caldwell*. Boston: Twayne, 1984.

Jacobs, Robert D. "The Humor of Tobacco Road." In *The Comic Imagination in American Literature*, edited by Louis D. Rubin. New Brunswick, N.J.: Rutgers University Press, 1973.

Korges, James. *Erskine Caldwell*. Minneapolis: University of Minnesota Press, 1969.

James E. Devlin

TRUMAN CAPOTE

Born: New Orleans, Louisiana
September 30, 1924
Died: Los Angeles, California
August 25, 1984

Principal Literary Achievement

Capote's greatest accomplishment was his merging of the dramatic narrative techniques of fiction with the objective reportage of journalism in what he termed "the nonfiction novel."

Biography

Truman Capote was born Truman Streckfus Persons, the only child of J. Archulus Persons and Lillie Mae Faulk Persons. During the first six years of his childhood, the boy frequently was handed off to the care of relatives by his carefree and irresponsible parents. Following his parents' permanent separation when the child was six, he was left fully in the care of relatives in Monroeville, Alabama.

Being reared by a series of relatives, Capote had a lonely childhood existence; the experience forced him, as he said in many interviews as an adult, to create his own world, personality, and sense of identity. The search for that sense of selfhood was to be a frequent theme in his literary work, both fiction and nonfiction. One imaginative influence on the young Capote was his eccentric cousin Sook Faulk, who encouraged the boy's propensity for fantasy invention, and he was later to recall Sook as the doting parent surrogate in his short story, "A Christmas Memory." Capote's childhood days can be seen in the novel *To Kill a Mockingbird* (1960), written by his childhood friend, Harper Lee, where the youthful Capote appears as the character Dill. Following his parents' divorce in 1931, Capote spent most of his time in Monroeville until his mother remarried in 1932 to Joseph Capote. Following their marriage, the boy was to change his name legally to "Capote" and eventually move to New York to live with his mother and stepfather.

Capote attended private schools in Manhattan and ultimately was graduated from the Franklin School, although his attendance had been, at best, irregular. The boy's time in an exciting metropolitan New York environment came at an impressionable age, and Capote, like one of his later heroines, Holly Golightly in *Breakfast at Tiffany's* (1958), loved the pace, sophistication, and glamour of New York.

Capote's childhood fascination with the style of words continued in his teenage

319

years as he served as a copyboy and file clerk at *The New Yorker* magazine. Although none of Capote's early work in fiction was published by *The New Yorker*, in 1945, the twenty-one-year-old writer published several short stories which gained for him almost instant literary attention: "Miriam," which appeared in *Mademoiselle* magazine; "A Tree of Night," in *Harper's Bazaar*; and "My Side of the Matter," in *Story* magazine. The appearance of these stories, and the subsequent publication in 1948 at age twenty-three of his first novel, *Other Voices, Other Rooms*, achieved for the young writer overnight international acclaim. Capote often described the novel as a poetic version of his own lonely childhood—sensitive, abandoned, and isolated. The book was, he said, an emotional, or spiritual, autobiography, if not an actual literal one. The novel's romanticized treatment of a homosexual theme made it a sensation in the late 1940's, when only one other contemporary novel, Gore Vidal's *The City and the Pillar* (1948), had dealt with homosexuality. The controversy over Capote's book was further intensified by the now-famous picture of the youthful author on its back cover sprawled seductively on a *chaise longue* with his blond bangs hanging over his elfin face. Capote quickly added to his reputation as a master of prose style with his 1949 short story collection, *A Tree of Night and Other Stories*, and the 1951 novella, *The Grass Harp*.

In the 1950's, Capote began to explore a variety of journalistic approaches to writing, including the travel recollection of *Local Color* (1950), an extended account of an American opera company's tour of the Soviet Union in *The Muses Are Heard* (1956), and his 1959 volume of commentary accompanying the photographs of Richard Avedon, *Observations*. In 1958, he produced his successful novella *Breakfast at Tiffany's*, which further enhanced his reputation as a fiction writer. An equally popular film version of the novella followed in 1961. In the 1950's and 1960's, Capote applied his talents to other literary forms, adapting two of his works for the theater—his novella, *The Grass Harp*, and later his short work, *House of Flowers*, which was made into a musical. He also wrote two screenplays for films, *Beat the Devil* and a film version of Henry James's Gothic novella, *The Turn of the Screw*, released under the title *The Innocents*. During the 1960's, Capote also published the first two parts of what was to be a trilogy of emotionally etched stories of his childhood in the South: *A Christmas Memory* appeared in 1966 (it had originally been printed in *Mademoiselle* in 1956), followed by *The Thanksgiving Visitor* in 1967. A year before his death, a third volume, *One Christmas* (1983), was published, dealing with the visit of a boy to see his father, separated from him by divorce.

Capote's major achievement in the 1960's, however, was to be the 1966 nonfiction book *In Cold Blood: A True Account of a Multiple Murder and Its Consequences*, a work that required six years of research by the author. Many critics view *In Cold Blood* as Capote's finest work; the author maintained that he had created a new art form, the "nonfiction novel." This new form combined the detached observation of journalistic reportage with the dramatic story-telling techniques of fiction. Capote spent years in Kansas after the crime was committed and, upon the capture of the two men charged with the killings of the Clutter farm family, more time investigating the lives and motives of the killers right up to the time of their execution. The publication of *In Cold Blood*, first in installments in *The New Yorker* and later as a book, made Capote wealthy and gave him unparalleled celebrity as an author.

Following the success of *In Cold Blood*, Capote announced that the next literary project he would undertake was to be a *roman à clef* about New York and the international jet set with which he personally had become so familiar. Its title was to be *Answered Prayers*, and when completed, Capote predicted, the work would rival the achievement of French novelist Marcel Proust's monumental *À la recherche du temps perdu* (1913-1927; *Remembrance of Things Past*, 1922-1931), a claim he made repeatedly in television talk show appearances. His personal life and physical well being, however, became increasingly chaotic during the 1970's. He wrote in a personal reminiscence, an interview with himself in his 1980 volume, *Music for Chameleons*: "I'm an alcoholic. I'm a drug addict. I'm homosexual. I'm a genius." The complications from all those conditions simultaneously caused erratic behavior by the writer in his last decade and greatly diminished his writing volume, which was never great because of his insistence on perfection of style.

In 1973, he had published a collection of short pieces, *The Dogs Bark: Public People and Private Places. Music for Chameleons* included not only more personal profiles but also a new short account of another true crime, "Handcarved Coffins," a kind of *In Cold Blood* in miniature. In 1983, the third of his childhood recollections appeared, a slender story in book form, *One Christmas.*

Only four portions of *Answered Prayers* ever appeared. These four parts ran in 1975 and 1976 in *Esquire* magazine, and their appearance created a personal disaster for the writer, since many of the thinly disguised portraits of persons he thought to be his friends grievously offended their original models. Many of the writer's wealthy friends simply cut all contact with Capote.

In his last years, Capote was subject to frequent bouts and recuperations from his many substance dependencies; he had a chaotic personal life. He died in 1984, shortly before his sixtieth birthday, while on a visit to Los Angeles, California. Following Capote's death, an extensive search was made for the missing portions of *Answered Prayers*, those segments the author so often said that he had completed. No portions of the work—other than those already published in magazine installments— were ever found. Some believe that Capote did write the complete book and destroyed the remaining sections. Others think the missing portions may exist somewhere, but the majority opinion holds that Capote never really wrote the rest of what he had promised would be his most revealing, most stylistically controlled work. The existing segments were published after his death under the title *Answered Prayers: The Unfinished Novel* in 1986.

Analysis

In the preface to the last collection of his work published in his lifetime, the 1980 volume *Music for Chameleons*, Truman Capote discussed in detail his views about the ordeal of writing as a creative activity and his own lifetime commitment to that pursuit. Writing was an occupation with a great risk to it: One had to take chances or fail. Indeed, Capote compared writing to professional pool playing and to a professional card dealer's abilities. He also explained that he began writing as a child of eight and was, by his view, an accomplished writer at seventeen; thus, when *Other Voices, Other Rooms* appeared in 1948, he viewed it as the end result of fourteen years of writing experience.

The substance of writing—and its accompanying pain of creation—Capote explained with a phrase he borrowed from Henry James; it was the "madness of art." All imaginative writing was, he explained, the artist employing his creative powers of observation, of description, of telling detail; it was that act that led Capote in his later writing to see the possibilities of journalism (which is factual, detailed observation of truth) as an art form that could be as powerful as fictional writing. So it was that he shifted from fiction to nonfiction in mid-career with works such as *The Muses Are Heard* and his most famous work, *In Cold Blood*.

For Capote, the writer is, by nature, an outsider, the observer seeing and hearing that which is about him but comprehending the witnessed events with an artistic sensitivity unknown to others. The outsider's perspective is—simply because it is detached from the observed society—more comprehensive. As he was an artist "outside," it was natural that Capote's works often dealt with the conflict between vulnerable persons similarly outside their more conventional environment. This theme can be seen in a number of his works, such as *Other Voices, Other Rooms*, and even in the real-life killer of his masterwork, *In Cold Blood*. Often this theme is played out in his work through a confrontation of an unconventional outsider with the conforming, ordered world.

In *Other Voices, Other Rooms*, Cousin Randolph, the homosexual older relative, states the outsider's lament as he attempts to explain the search for love to the youthful Joel, explaining that all men are isolated from one another, that everyone, in the end, is alone:

> Any love is natural and beautiful that lies within a person's nature; only hypocrites would hold a man responsible for what he loves, emotional illiterates and those of righteous envy, who, in their agitated concern, mistake so frequently the arrow pointing to heaven for the one that leads to hell.

A similar idea occurs in *The Grass Harp* when Judge Cool, having joined a rebellious group hiding in a tree house, speaks of those who are pagans or spirits and defines them as accepters of life, because they are those who grant life's differences.

Some of the more flamboyant examples of the free, nonconforming spirit are seen in Capote's female characters, specifically Idabel, the tomboy twin of *Other Voices, Other Rooms*, who outwrestles young Joel in one scene and whose lack of femininity is an obvious counterpoint to Joel's boyhood homosexual longings. Another such unconventional personality is Holly Golightly of *Breakfast at Tiffany's*, who has run away not only from her background of poverty to seek glamour, but also from a childhood marriage to indulge her New York encounters with a series of wealthy men. Holly's defiance of convention is as meaningful as Joel's and Idabel's or, for that matter, the runaways in *The Grass Harp*, whose tree house retreat is Capote's symbol for all places of security for those who may be yearning for a place for their differences, their individual spirits, their ideal fantasies to be at home.

Capote frequently said in interviews in his lifetime that he saw in the real-life killers—particularly Perry Smith—of *In Cold Blood* the man he might have become had his own life taken a different turn. His realization was that the killers were the evil side of the same yearning for love, acceptance, even artistic achievement (especially with Smith) that he had known. That desire is seen in a key scene in Miami after the murders, as Perry realizes that all his hopes and ambitions are a dead end:

> Anyway, he couldn't see that he had "a lot to live for." Hot islands and buried gold, diving deep in fire-blue seas toward sunken treasure—such dreams were gone. Gone, too, was "Perry O'Parsons," the name invented for the singing sensation of stage and screen that he'd half-seriously hoped some day to be.

In Capote's musical, *House of Flowers*, one of the characters sings a song of yearning for escape from the everyday entitled "I Never Has Seen Snow," and snow is a recurring image in many Capote works for the elusive dreams of life. One of the young boyfriends of the Clutter girl recalls becoming lost in a snowstorm in *In Cold Blood*, while the cook Missouri ("Zoo") hopes to run away north to see snow in *Other Voices, Other Rooms*; Judge Cool's distant wife had died in the snows of Switzerland in *The Grass Harp*. Ultimately, in a world that fails to understand or make room for the sensitive, artistic spirits, the "different," Capote returns frequently to the idea, stated by Judge Cool, that whatever passions compose them, private worlds are good—that is, unless turned to evil ends by the greater uncomprehending world.

OTHER VOICES, OTHER ROOMS

First published: 1948
Type of work: Novel

A young boy, seeking his lost father, moves into a strange household in Mississippi where he encounters bizarre relatives while trying to find love.

Other Voices, Other Rooms, Truman Capote's first published long work, is a moody and atmospheric tale characterized both by its strange setting—a decaying mansion in rural Mississippi—and by the host of peculiar characters it presents to the reader.

The book details the encounters of thirteen-year-old Joel Knox Sansom, who travels to an old mansion, Skully's Landing, in rural Mississippi, where he hopes to meet his long-lost father, Edward Sansom. In its emphasis on romantic and ghostly settings and its use of strange, eccentric characters, *Other Voices, Other Rooms* is typical of what has been termed the "Southern Gothic" school of fiction, a style of fiction marked by its use of the grotesque both in locale and in characterization. This category can be seen in the works of other Southern-born fiction writers such as William Faulkner (his short story "A Rose for Emily" and his 1931 novel *Sanctuary* both offer elements of Southern Gothic), Tennessee Williams (his 1958 play *Suddenly Last Summer* deals with incest, homosexuality, insanity, lobotomy, and cannibalism), Carson McCullers (her 1941 novel *Reflections in a Golden Eye* and her story "Ballad of the Sad Café" both have grotesque situations and characters), and Flannery O'Connor (her 1952 novel *Wise Blood* deals with religious obsession and madness). In *Other Voices, Other Rooms*, Capote uses this sense of the strange and the mysterious to convey the loneliness, isolation, and naïveté of Joel.

When Joel arrives at Skully's Landing, he meets a variety of unusual characters: an ancient black man, Jesus Fever; Jesus Fever's granddaughter, a twenty-one-year-old cook named Missouri (nicknamed "Zoo"); Joel's father, the bed-ridden invalid Edward Sansom (who communicates with the rest of the household by rolling red tennis balls down the stairs); his father's new wife, Miss Amy; and a much-talked-about cousin, Randolph. En route to the Landing, Joel also has met two young girls, the twins Florabel Thompkins and her tomboy twin sister, Idabel. (Many interpreters of Capote's work see Idabel as Capote's fictional version of his own childhood friend, Harper Lee, later destined herself to be the author of *To Kill a Mockingbird*.)

While the main plot of the book appears to be dealing with Joel's attempt to find and, later, to talk with his father, Capote really is presenting the plight of Joel as a lonely, sensitive youth who is, in fact, trying to come to terms with his own identity in an environment where he has no moorings. In one key scene, he tries to pray; he finds it almost impossible to ask God for someone to love him, yet that is really what the boy is seeking.

It is the search for love that defines the lives of many of the characters in *Other Voices, Other Rooms*: Cousin Randolph, Joel's homosexual older relative, still laments the loss of his great love, a boxer named Pepe Alvarez, and Miss Amy has married Joel's father—even though the man is an invalid—to have someone to love and care for. These aspirations to love are reflected in the desperation of other characters: At a carnival, the boy Joel is pursued by the midget woman, Miss Wisteria, who, throughout her tragic life, has never found anyone her own size to love. Similarly, the cook, Zoo, has suffered from her first experience with love; at age fourteen, she had married a man named Keg Brown who tried to kill her. Zoo seeks a place of beauty and purity, which, in her fantasy, she believes she will find in the North, where she hopes to go to see snow for the first time.

At the end of the novel, Joel, after recuperating from a severe illness during which he was cared for by Cousin Randolph, makes a decision about his life. He realizes that Randolph is, in many ways, a child like himself who has simply sought love in his life. Joel decides that he must abandon his childhood and accept his own sexual nature; at the end of the novel, the mature Joel ascends from the haunted garden at Skully's Landing to Randolph's room to embrace Randolph, leaving behind both his youth and his own sexual longing.

THE GRASS HARP

First published: 1951
Type of work: Novella

In a rigid small-town Southern setting, an odd assortment of local people attempt to assert control over their lives by their defiance of convention.

The Grass Harp, Truman Capote's sadly humorous tale about a curious collection of small-town Southern eccentrics, continued the romantic and occasionally bizarre mood of his earlier *Other Voices, Other Rooms*, but his emphasis in this work more often is on the possibilities for humor in such strange behavior rather than on shock value. Indeed, Capote captured the same tone of Southern small-town hilarity that one also finds in many of the short stories of Eudora Welty.

Eleven-year-old Collin Fenwick, from whose point of view the work is told, is sent as a young boy by his grieving father to live with two unmarried cousins, Verena and Dolly Talbo. The father was distraught over the death of Collin's mother, so much so that he took off his clothes and ran naked into the yard the day of her death.

Collin is similar to Joel Knox Sansom of *Other Voices, Other Rooms* (and to the real-life youthful Capote) in that he is a lonely boy handed over to be reared by odd relatives. The Talbo household consists of Verena, the domineering force, who also has a head for business activities in the town; Dolly, the somewhat addled but good-hearted sister; a black woman, Catherine Creek, a companion to Dolly, who insists that she really is an Indian; and Collin, the boy who frequently spies on the household residents in different rooms through peepholes in the attic floor.

As a study of human loneliness, *The Grass Harp* echoes the themes of *Other Voices, Other Rooms*: the isolated, unloved, and unwanted child as well as the quiet desperation of many adults in small communities who suffer their own private terrors and despair. Dolly, Catherine, and Collin spend time regularly on picnics held in the hidden tree house of two lofty China trees outside the town. The tree becomes a vehicle for their transport away from their real lives in the constricting town and into worlds of their imaginings. Verena too—though not in their group—has suffered rejection; her intense friendship for another woman, Maudie Laurie Murphy, was lost when Maudie married a liquor salesman from St. Louis, left on a wedding trip (paid for by Verena), and never returned.

While *The Grass Harp* covers Collin's life from age eleven to age sixteen, the primary conflict of the work develops when sisters Dolly and Verena quarrel over a dropsy medicine formula known only by Dolly but which Verena hopes to develop commercially with a new man friend, Dr. Morris Ritz, a confidence man she met in Chicago. Dolly, viewing her formula as her own, decides to leave the house, taking both Collin and Catherine Creek with her. With no real destination or other home, the group moves into the tree shelter while Verena arouses the town in a search for the runaways. There are several comical encounters as a posse, including the local sheriff and a stuffy minister, attempts to get the group out of the tree. The group's rebellious independence is attractive to others, however, including a teenaged loner, Riley Henderson, and the elderly Judge Charlie Cool, and both soon join the tree dwellers in their defiance of the town's authority figures. At one point, the Judge summarizes the shared plight of the tree's inhabitants, telling them that there may not be a place in society for characters such as they are; he thinks there may be a place for them somewhere, however, and that the tree just might be the spot.

The search for that true, spiritual, home—for a place of real belonging—haunts each of the sympathetic characters in *The Grass Harp.* The Judge further defines for the group their role in life, as "spirits," or persons willing to grant differences in human behavior. He recalls, too, how he once almost had to imprison a man because that man defied custom and wanted to marry a black girl he loved. He reveals that his family views him as scandalous because he once maintained a long, friendly correspondence with a lonely thirteen-year-old girl in Alaska.

Capote sketches a variety of townspeople—some curious types, others mean and petty. There are the owners of the Katydid Bakery, Mr. and Mrs. C. C. County, and there is the traveling evangelist Sister Ida, the mother of fifteen children, one of whom is a star in her religious show and regularly lassoes souls for Christ. Ultimately, Sister Ida's troupe joins forces with the tree-house group in a battle with the town's conformist faction. A reconciliation becomes possible when Dolly realizes that she truly is needed by her sister, Verena. Verena, by this time, has been robbed of her cash and bonds by the smooth-talking Dr. Ritz, whom she had hoped to marry.

The last sections of the work deal with the maturing of Riley Henderson, his falling in love, and his eventual marriage to Maude Riordan. As Collin also matures, he plans to go away to law school and thus leave the town. Dolly, Verena, and Catherine Creek live together until a stroke kills Dolly, after which Catherine retires to live in seclusion in her own cabin. As Collin prepares to leave the town, he notes that the town remains—like the stories of the people in it—in memory. *The Grass Harp* reverberates with themes of alienation, loneliness, and the search for a secure and meaningful place in life, ideas Capote used in *Other Voices, Other Rooms* and was later to employ in *Breakfast at Tiffany's.*

BREAKFAST AT TIFFANY'S

First published: 1958
Type of work: Novella

A romantic, nonconformist runaway seeks glamour, self-identity, and freedom in Manhattan during World War II.

Breakfast at Tiffany's is a first-person narrative with a young male writer as its single point of view. The narrator relates what he observes of the life and experiences of

Holly Golightly, a young Texas woman who has come to New York in the early 1940's seeking new life, excitement, and glamour, which she feels is more in keeping with her freewheeling, sometimes irresponsible, approach to life.

Like *Other Voices, Other Rooms*, which preceded it, *Breakfast at Tiffany's* presents a free-spirited person trying to escape from the tawdry aspects of a past life by finding a life-style more compatible with her dreams and fantasies. Capote's story of Holly develops as a remembrance triggered in the writer-narrator's memory by an encounter with a Lexington Avenue bar proprietor who had known Holly as a frequent and colorful patron of his bar. Bell reports to the narrator that Holly in 1956 may have been seen in East Anglia, in Africa, where a Japanese photographer (who also had known Holly in New York) has encountered a wooden replica of Holly's face in a remote native village. The writer then recalls his first encounter with Holly when he had rented an apartment in the same building with her (and the photographer) during the early years of World War II.

The writer (whom Holly calls "Fred," after her brother, who is in the military service) grows more familiar with the irrepressible Holly after their first meeting. He finds that she views life essentially as a continuing party; some of the noisier parties occur in Holly's apartment. Holly first met the writer as she slid into his apartment from the fire escape one evening. He soon learns that Holly plays host to a wide assortment of mostly male friends, ranging from soldiers to Hollywood agents to an occasional gangster. Holly also is a regular visitor to Sing Sing Prison, where she is a paid messenger for a gangster named Sally Tomato. Sally is a vivacious blonde who speaks in a kind of butchered French-English which is her attempt at city sophistication.

Holly fascinates everyone who meets her: the young writer, her former agent, the bar owner, a rich playboy named Rusty Trawler, and a handsome Brazilian, Jose Ybarra-Jaegar, whom she hopes to marry. Holly is, in effect, a kind of free-spirited female earth goddess, the kind of myth men tend to worship, a myth suggested by the wooden carving of the story's opening. The freedom to love as one desires is one of Holly's obsessions. She tells the narrator that she believes people should be allowed to marrry as they like, either male or female. In another conversation, she expresses her open-minded attitude toward lesbians and even considers taking in a lesbian roommate. She further reveals that she is attracted to older men (such as Wendell Willkie) but that she could as easily be interested in, ideally, Greta Garbo.

The novella is a slowly unfolding character study of Holly through a series of episodic events: her parties; her free life-style; her taking in a model, Mag Wildwood, as a roommate; the visit of her older Texas husband, Doc; her aspirations to marry the rich Brazilian Ybarra-Jaegar; and her arrest and scandal because of her associations with Sally Tomato. Most important of all these casually related events is the sudden death of Holly's brother, Fred, killed in overseas combat. Faced with scandal and the end of her planned marriage, Holly, at the end of the story, leaves New York, abandoning her only commitment—the pet cat with no name—and heads to South America to seek further that glamorous place of safety for which she yearns.

The book's title is a symbol of that search; Holly likes the environment of Tiffany's jewelry store in New York, since nothing bad (she thinks) could happen to anyone there. A quiet, assured place of the security, wealth, and glamour—a place of calm belonging—that Holly so desperately seeks, she sees as an alternative to the despair that grips her, the depression she calls the "mean reds." Although frivolous and exasperating to those who know her, Holly Golightly (her name obviously suggests her attitude toward life) captivates all who meet her so that, in their minds, she takes on the substance of an elusive mythic dream, her appeal carved in their memories just as it was in the African wooden figure.

IN COLD BLOOD

First published: 1966
Type of work: Nonfiction

A Kansas farm family is mysteriously murdered by two ex-convicts who flee the scene but are eventually captured, tried, and executed.

In Cold Blood was created as a work of deliberate literary experiment. Having written extensive journalistic reportage in his account of an opera company's tour of the Soviet Union (*The Muses Are Heard*) and in various travel writing, Capote desired to combine the reportorial techniques of journalism—the gathering of extensively detailed factual material by observation and interviewing—with the narrative and dramatic scene devices of fiction. The grisly, senseless murders of a Kansas farm family (Herbert W. Clutter, his wife, and two children) on November 15, 1959, in Holcomb, Kansas, provided the opportunity for the writer to test his theory.

In Cold Blood is a documented record of those murders, but it is also a documentation of the backgrounds, motives, attitudes, and perspectives of hundreds of local townspeople as well as those of the two killers, ex-convicts, Richard Eugene Hickock and Perry Smith who are arrested eventually for the crime, tried, and executed. Shortly after the crime was committed, Capote arrrived in Kansas to begin the massive accumulation of material that forms the substance of the book. At the outset, the murders were baffling because of the lack of any apparent motive for the slayings. There also were few clues.

Initially Capote envisioned his work as a short one in which he would explore the background of the murders and the reaction of the town to them. With the discovery, capture, and confession of the two killers, however, his concept changed focus and became not only a study of the crime and its impact on the community but also an investigation into the lives and motives of the two killers. While describing present action—the arrest, incarceration, trial, and conviction, then the appeals process, and finally the execution by hanging in Lansing, Kansas, in 1965—Capote also delves back into the murderers' past—their families, aspirations, and personal defeats. The completion of his book took more than six years.

The organization of the material has been ingeniously handled. Capote once said he had taken more than six thousand pages of notes. The book has four sections, all of which offer the reader shifts in time and place, rather like the cinematic technique of parallel editing, thus allowing the reader to experience simultaneous events with different persons in different locales. The four sections are entitled "The Last to See Them Alive," "Persons Unknown," "Answer," and "The Corner." In the first section, Capote traces each member of the Clutter family through their activities on the last day of their lives, going through their routine in remarkable detail (even clothing is noted, as is music heard on the radio.)

While following the family, Capote also allows the readers to follow the ongoing progress of the two killers, Dick and Perry, as they move inexorably toward their victims in Kansas. The shifts between the killers' activities and those of their intended victims come to seem as fatalistic as Greek tragedy, and they add to the sense of tension and suspense (even though the reader is aware of the outcome of the impending meeting). Capote further heightens the reader's sense of dramatic anticipation by having section one end with the finding of the bodies by local people. He carefully withholds the actual murder scenes until much later in the work; once the killers have been captured, they are revealed in their confessions.

Part 2 catalogs the investigation of the crimes and the town's reaction to them. Against the ongoing investigation, the reader also follows the travels of Dick and Perry as they flee from Kansas—first to Mexico, later to Florida, and eventually back to Texas. As the authorities try to find leads to what seems a motiveless act, the reader sees the murderers as they fish, drink, and go to beaches. Capote also begins to introduce background information about the killers; a letter by Perry's father is included, as are a letter from Perry's sister written to him in prison and another convict's lengthy commentary on her letter. These revelations are juxtaposed against the frustration of investigator Alvin Dewey as he tries to find leads in the case.

Part 3, "Answer," brings the break in the case: A convict in prison reveals that Dick Hickock once told him of a plan to rob the Clutter household and leave no witnesses. As the net draws slowly about the killers after that revelation, the reader is given a sadly humorous episode in which a young boy and his ailing grandfather are given a ride by the murderers. The meeting of the open, honest, good-natured child with the killers is an example of how Capote has skillfully manipulated his material for maximum ironic effect. The killers join with the boy in a game to find empty soft-drink bottles in the barren Texas countryside.

Part 4 deals with events after Dick and Perry's arrest: their trial and conviction, the innumerable appeals in the courts as they seek to avoid execution, and, finally, their deaths by hanging in the Kansas State Penitentiary. Of particular interest in this section of the book is Capote's study of Dick and Perry's time on death row and his look at the lives of others who were death-row prisoners at the same time.

Capote's book does not end with the hanging of Dick and Perry; instead, there is a tranquil scene back in Holcomb, at the cemetery where the Clutter family was buried. Detective Alvin Dewey visits the graves and, while there, meets a young girlfriend of the Clutter girl. Their talk is routine—about school, college plans, marriages, hopes, aspirations, ambitions, the stuff of everyday life. These are exactly the details of routine life that have been denied the Clutter family and, indeed, even their killers, by the tragic turns that fate works in people's lives. With the contrast between retribution and innocent hope, the book's final irony is eloquently achieved.

Summary

Truman Capote frequently depicted isolated, alienated personalities engaged in a desperate pursuit of love and seeking a place of security and belonging. That search is seen in the plight of characters as varied as Joel Sansom, Holly Golightly, and Judge Cool and the tree dwellers of *The Grass Harp*; it is found even in the real-life personalities of the killers in *In Cold Blood*.

The sense of personal desolation and anxiety is depicted with varying styles; Capote's early work has a romantically dense and suggestive metaphorical style, whereas later in his career, he developed the stylized but factually based approach that he called the "nonfiction novel." All writing, Capote often said, like all art, has at its center a perfectly wrought core and shape, and it was this distilled essence in his writing coupled with his theme of the individually bruised soul seeking safety that gives his works their almost unbearable tension.

Bibliography

Brinnin, John Malcolm. *Truman Capote: Dear Heart, Old Buddy.* New York: Delacorte Press/Seymour Lawrence, 1986.

Clarke, Gerald. *Capote: A Biography.* New York: Simon & Schuster, 1988.

Fox, Joseph, ed. Editor's note to *Answered Prayers: The Unfinished Novel*, by Truman Capote. New York: Random House, 1987.

Grobel, Lawrence. *Conversations With Capote.* New York: New American Library, 1985.

Hallowell, John. *Between Fact and Fiction: New Journalism and the Non-Fiction Novel.* Chapel Hill: University of North Carolina Press, 1972.

Moates, Marianne M. *A Bridge of Childhood: Truman Capote's Southern Years.* New York: Henry Holt, 1989.

Nance, William L. *The Worlds of Truman Capote.* New York: Stein & Day, 1970.

Rudisill, Marie, with James C. Simmons. *Truman Capote.* New York: William Morrow, 1983.

Jere Real

RAYMOND CARVER

Born: Clatskanie, Oregon
May 25, 1938
Died: Port Angeles, Washington
August 2, 1988

Principal Literary Achievement
In his relatively short career as a professional author, Carver established a critical reputation as one of the most powerful and innovative short story writers of his generation.

Biography
Raymond Carver was born on May 25, 1938, in the small town of Clatskanie in northwestern Oregon; however, before he started school, his family moved to Yakima, Washington, where his father worked as a logger. Carver went to elementary school and high school there and spent his leisure time fishing and hunting. Carver once said that growing up in the rugged and rural Pacific Northwest made him want to be a "writer from the West." He also once declared that the most important, although in many ways the most negative, influence on his early hopes to become a writer was the fact that he married and became a father before he was twenty. The pressures of supporting his young family made it almost impossible to find time to write.

Carver once said that he could not remember when he did not want to be a writer; he even took a correspondence course in writing when he was a teenager. He was never really interested in writing a novel, but rather liked short stories—a form which he said best suited the circumstances of his life, for they could be finished in a few sittings. As a young man, his reading tastes were relatively unformed and undisciplined. He read Zane Grey westerns, the science fiction works of Edgar Rice Burroughs, and such men's magazines as *True*, *Argosy*, *Sports Afield*, and *Outdoor Life*—a masculine reading list which may partially account for the laconic, no-frills style of his short stories.

Carver moved his wife and two children to California in 1958, where he registered as a student at Chico State College, a small school in the California State University system. An important positive influence on his career while at Chico was his enrollment in a creative writing class taught by John Gardner, who was soon to make a name for himself as a writer. Carver was lavish in his praise for the help

Gardner gave him, comparing him to the great maestros of the past who nurtured their apprentices. Because of Gardner, Carver began to think of writing as a high calling, something to be taken very seriously.

Carver transferred to California's northern coastal college, Humboldt State, where he studied under short story writer Richard Day and received his B.A. degree in 1963. Soon after, he left for the University of Iowa Writers Workshop with a small graduate grant of five hundred dollars. Unable to support his family and write, however, he returned to California before the end of the academic year. After returning to California, Carver held a number of minor jobs in Sacramento as a mill hand and a delivery boy, but perhaps his most fortunate job was a two-year stint as a night watchman at a hospital, where he was able to squeeze in some time writing. In 1967, Carver got a better job, as a textbook editor for Science Research Associates in Palo Alto, California. In 1968, the English Club at Sacramento State College, where he had taken a poetry-writing course, published twenty-six of his poems in a collection entitled *Near Klamath*.

Although Carver was busy writing during the 1960's and was publishing his poetry and fiction in various small magazines, his big break did not come until 1970, when he was fired from his Science Research Associates job and when he received a National Endowment for the Arts Discovery Award for Poetry. With the money from the grant (plus his unemployment benefits and severance pay), he found the time to revise many of the stories which appeared in his first important book, *Will You Please Be Quiet, Please?* (1976). Carver was soon publishing in reputable journals and better-paying slick magazines such as *Esquire* and *Harper's Bazaar* and gaining recognition by having his stories chosen to appear in the O. Henry Award collections.

In 1971 and 1972, Carver had a lectureship at the University of California, Santa Cruz, and in the fall of 1972 he held a Wallace Stegner Creative Writing Fellowship at Stanford University. During the fall semester, 1973, he also had a visiting writer's appointment at the Iowa Writers Workshop. By this time, however, he was plagued with the disease of alcoholism. He has said that he and his colleague, well-known writer John Cheever, were drinking so heavily during their tenures at Iowa that they never took the covers off their typewriters.

In 1977, when *Will You Please Be Quiet, Please?* was nominated for the National Book Award, Carver had to be hospitalized several times. He has said that June 2, 1977, was the date he stopped drinking for good. Carver's professional career began to blossom in the late 1970's and 1980's: He received a Guggenheim Fellowship in 1979, published a highly praised collection of stories entitled *What We Talk About When We Talk About Love* in 1981, and another significant collection entitled *Cathedral* in 1983. Moreover, his personal life improved significantly. Following his divorce from his first wife in the late 1970's, Carver met and began living with the writer Tess Gallagher. Also in 1983, he was awarded the Mildred and Harold Strauss Living Award, a five-year grant of $35,000 a year. His works have been translated into more than twenty languages. In 1987, after he had put together still another collection of both old and new stories, Carver, a heavy smoker, was diagnosed as having lung cancer. He underwent surgery in the fall, then radiation treatments. His condition had already gone too far, however; he died in Port Angeles, Washington, on August 2, 1988. His final collection, *Where I'm Calling From*, was published that same year.

Analysis

Raymond Carver's first two collections of short stories shocked readers with their violence and puzzled them with their laconic Chekhovian style. *Will You Please Be Quiet, Please?* contains twenty-two stories that provide stark images of lives lived in quiet desperation. In many of the stories in this collection, the characters are thrown out of their everyday routine and caught in situations in which they feel helpless and estranged.

Whereas the stories in Carver's first important collection are relatively drained of imagery and recall the style of Ernest Hemingway, the stories in his second major collection, *What We Talk About When We Talk About Love*, are even more radically sparing in their language; indeed, they are so minimal that they seem mere dehumanized patterns with no life in them at all. Whatever theme they may have is embodied in the bare outlines of sometimes shocking, sometimes trivial, events, and in the spare and reticent dialogue of the characters, who seem utterly unable to articulate the nature of their isolation. Characters often have no names or only first names and are so briefly described that they seem to have no physical presence at all.

The lyricism of Carver's style lies in a "will to style" in which reality is stripped of its physicality and exists only in the hard, bare outlines of the event. Carver's stories have more of the ambience of dream than of everyday reality. They are unconcerned with social issues, yet the stories are not parables in the usual sense. His characters give a feeling of emotional reality that reaches the level of myth, even as they refuse to give a feeling of physical or simple psychological reality. The most basic theme of Carver's stories is the tenuous union between men and women and the mysterious separations that always seem imminent.

The stories that appear in Carver's last two collections, however, *Cathedral* (1983) and *Where I'm Calling From*, perhaps because they were mainly written after Carver had been cured of alcoholism and had met Tess Gallagher, are more optimistic and hopeful than the earlier stories; they also are more voluble and detailed, exhibiting an increasing willingness by Carver and his narrators to discuss, explain, and explore the emotions and situations that give rise to the stories. Instead of separation, Carver's later stories move toward union or reunion. They are characterized by a mood of reconciliation and calm self-knowledge and acceptance. Although this shift in moral perspective moves Carver's fiction toward a more conventional short story form, all of his stories are told in such a way that the universal human mystery of union and separation is exposed, even if it is not always explained. The simple, yet complex, humanity revealed by Carver can neither be understood nor cured by the pop psychology of modern life; as in the great short stories of his predecessors, it can only be captured in the pure and painful events of human beings who mysteriously come together and come apart.

Raymond Carver was the most important figure in the renaissance of short fiction sparked in American literature in the 1980's. He belongs to a line of short story writers that begins with Anton Chekhov and progresses through such masters of the form as Sherwood Anderson, Katherine Anne Porter, Ernest Hemingway, and Bernard Malamud. On the basis of a small output of stories, Carver will remain a significant figure in the history of modern American literature.

NEIGHBORS

First published: 1976
Type of work: Short story

A young couple fantasize about taking the place of their vacationing neighbors.

"Neighbors" is one of the most puzzling and shocking stories in Carver's first collection, *Will You Please Be Quiet, Please?* It focuses on Bill and Arlene Miller, a young couple who feel that the lives of their neighbors Harriet and Jim Stone are somehow brighter and fuller than their own. The story begins when the Stones go on a trip and ask the Millers to look after their apartment and water the plants. When Bill begins routinely to perform this task, however, his visits to the apartment make him sexually aroused. Moreover, he begins to stay longer and longer in the apartment, taking trivial things such as cigarettes and a container of pills, and nibbling food from the refrigerator.

Bill's fascination with the apartment becomes more bizarre when he secretly takes time off from work and slips in to spend the day alone there. He first tries on a shirt and Bermuda shorts belonging to Jim Stone, then a brassiere and pair of panties belonging to Harriet. The story comes to a climax that evening when his wife goes over to the apartment and the reader discovers that she is similarly fascinated, telling her husband that she found some pictures in a drawer. Although the reader is not told what kind of pictures they are, one may assume they depict the secret life of the Stones. When the couple go back across the hall to their own apartment, they consider that maybe the Stones will not come back. When they discover that they have locked the key to the Stones' apartment inside, they feel desperate:

> "Don't worry," he said into her ear. "For God's sake, don't worry."
> They stayed there. They held each other. They leaned into the door as if against a wind, and braced themselves.

Typical of Carver's early work, the story offers no explanation for the fascination the apartment holds for the young couple; the closest Carver will come to an explanation is Arlene saying, "It's funny . . . to go in someone's place like that," to which her husband replies, "It *is* funny." This is not a story about a sexually perverted couple; rather, it is a story about the fascination of visiting the secret inner reality of someone else and the excitement of temporarily taking on their identity. To enter into the dark and secret world of the "neighbors" is to experience a voyeuristic thrill.

The dissatisfaction that everyone feels at times with being merely themselves and no one else and the universal inner desire to change places with someone else is delicately handled in the story. For example, Bill's fantasy of changing places with his neighbor is suggested by the simple act of his looking into the bathroom mirror, closing his eyes and then looking again—as if by that blink, a transformation could take place. Moreover, the fact that Bill wants to make love to his wife after visiting the apartment reflects the erotic thrill of peeking into the life of someone else and then, almost in an act of autoeroticism, fulfilling that fantasy with whomever is at hand. The desperation the couple feel at the end as they find themselves locked out of the apartment, bracing themselves "as if against a wind," points to the impossibility of truly entering into the lives of others, except to visit and inevitably to violate.

WHY DON'T YOU DANCE?

First published: 1981
Type of work: Short story

A young couple inspect the furniture a man has set up on his front lawn, but more is at stake than a yard sale.

This first story in Carver's controversial collection *What We Talk About When We Talk About Love* is characteristic of the qualities of his short fiction at the high point of his career. The story begins with an unidentified man who has, for some unexplained reason, put all of his furniture out on his front lawn. What makes this event more than merely a mundane yard sale is the fact that the man has arranged the furniture exactly as it was when it was in the house and has even plugged in the television and other appliances so that they work as they did inside. The only mention of the man's wife is the fact that the bed has a nightstand and reading lamp on his side of the bed and a nightstand and reading lamp on "her" side of the bed; this is Carver's typical unstated way of suggesting that the man's marriage has collapsed and that his wife is no longer around.

The story begins its muted dramatic turn when a young couple who are furnishing their first apartment stop by and begin to inspect the furniture. As the girl tries out the bed and the boy turns on the television, their dialogue is clipped and cryptic, reminiscent of the dialogue of characters in a story by Ernest Hemingway. When the man returns from a trip to the store, the dialogue continues in its understated and laconic way as the couple make offers for some of the furnishings and the man indifferently accepts whatever they offer. The man plays a record on the phonograph; the boy and the girl, then the man and the girl, dance. The story ends with a brief epilogue as, weeks later, the girl is telling a friend about the incident. The story ends: "She kept talking. She told everyone. There was more to it, and she was trying to get it talked out. After a time, she quit trying."

The story is an embodiment of the way that modern short fiction since Anton Chekhov has attempted to embody inner reality by means of the simple description of outer reality. By placing all his furniture on his front lawn, the man has externalized what had previously been hidden inside the house. When the young couple arrive, they embody the ritual process of replacement of the older man's lost relationship with the beginnings of their own, creating their own relationship on the remains of the man's.

The story is not a hopeful one, however, for the seemingly minor conflicts that the dialogue reveals between the two young people—his watching television and her wanting him to try the bed, her wanting to dance and his drinking—presage another doomed relationship exactly like the one that has ended. Indeed, there is more to it, as the girl senses, but she cannot quite articulate the meaning of the event; she can only, as storytellers must, retell it over and over again, trying to get it "talked out" and intuitively understood.

THE BATH

First published: 1981 (revised as "A Small, Good Thing," 1983)
Type of work: Short story

A couple lose their son in an automobile accident and are plagued by a mysterious telephone caller.

"The Bath," which originally appeared in *What We Talk About When We Talk About Love*, reappeared in the *Cathedral* collection, revised and renamed "A Small, Good Thing." The second version is also reprinted in Carver's final collection, *Where I'm Calling From*. Both versions of the story focus on a couple whose son is hit by a car on his eighth birthday and who is hospitalized in a coma. This horrifying event is made more intolerable by the fact that the couple receive annoying anonymous telephone calls from a baker from whom the wife had earlier ordered a custom-made birthday cake for the child. "The Bath" is a brief story, told in Carver's early, neutralized style, focusing less on the feelings of the couple than on the mysterious and perverse interruption of the persistent anonymous calls.

The revision, "A Small, Good Thing," is five times longer than "The Bath." It develops the emotional life of the couple in more sympathetic detail, suggesting that their prayers for their son bind them together in a genuine human communion that they have never felt before. The parents are given more of a sense of everyday human reality in the revision, and their situation is made more conventionally realistic. The father feels that his life has gone smoothly until this point, and the story thus suggests that neither he nor his wife has ever had their comfortable middle-class life threatened by such a terrifying disruption before. Much of the detail of the revision follows the parents as they anxiously wait for their son to come out of his comatose state. Whereas the mysterious voice on the phone throughout "The Bath" suggests some perverse interference in their lives, in "A Small, Good Thing" the voice suggests a more concerned presence who always asks them if they have forgotten about their son Scotty.

The most radical difference in the revision, however, can be seen in the conclusion. Whereas in the first version the child's death abruptly ends the story, in the second, the couple discover that it is the baker who has been calling and go visit him after the boy's death. He shares their sorrow; they share his loneliness. The story ends in reconciliation in the warm and comfortable bakery as the couple, in an almost Christian ritual of breaking bread together, eat the baker's bread and talk into the early morning, not wanting to leave—as if a retreat into the communal reality of the bakery marks the true nature of a healing unification.

Although the earlier version of the story seems to have been repudiated by Carver, the revisions that created the new story, "A Small, Good Thing," provide a striking example of how Carver's writing style and thematic concerns changed since his first two collections. Whereas "The Bath" is a story about a mysterious eruption into any life, "A Small, Good Thing" is a story that moves toward a more conventionally moral ending of acceptance. The image of the parents in the warm, sweet-smelling bakery, momentarily reconciled by their sense of communion with the baker, is a clear indication of Carver's moral shift from the skeptical to the affirmative, from the sense of the unspeakable mystery of human life to the sense of how simple and moral life is after all.

CATHEDRAL

First published: 1983
Type of work: Short story

A cynical man has his prejudices challenged by an encounter with a blind man.

This title story of Carver's third collection is typical of how his technique and thematic concerns changed after his own personal life became more stabilized. The story contains much more exposition and discussion, more background and efforts at clarification, than the stories in Carver's first two cryptic collections. "Cathedral" is told by a first-person narrator, a young man who resents the visit of an old friend of his wife—a blind man for whom the wife once read.

Unlike Carver's earlier stories, which focus primarily on the immediate situation detached from its background, the first quarter of "Cathedral" recounts the narrator's knowledge of his wife's previous married life, her friendship with the blind man (especially the fact that they have sent audio tapes back and forth to each other), and even of the blind man's wife Beulah, who has recently died. Although the relevance of all this information to the final epiphanic revelation of the story is not made clear, it does reveal the cynicism of the narrator, who obviously resents his wife's relationship with the blind man. It also reveals him as an insensitive character who has prejudiced notions about a variety of subjects; for example, his only notion of blind people comes from films, and he asks if the blind man's wife was "a Negro" only because her name was Beulah.

The conversation among the narrator, his wife, and the blind man that makes up the center of the story is inconclusive, mainly devoted to the blind man's dispelling many of the prejudiced expectations the narrator has about the blind. The climax toward which the story inevitably moves—a confrontation between the narrator and the blind man—begins when the wife goes to sleep and the two men drink and smoke marijuana together. The encounter is created by a program on television about the Church in the Middle Ages—which the narrator watches because there is nothing else on. When the program features a cathedral, the narrator asks the blind man if he knows what a cathedral is. The blind man says he has no real idea and asks the narrator to describe a cathedral to him. When the narrator fails, the blind man asks him if he is religious, to which the narrator says he does not believe in anything.

The blind man then asks the narrator to find some paper and a pen so that they can draw a cathedral together. The blind man puts his hand over the hand of the narrator and tells him to draw, with the blind man's hand following along with him. The blind man even asks the narrator to close his eyes as they continue drawing. When they finish, the blind man asks him to look at the drawing and tell him what he thinks; the narrator keeps his eyes closed. He knows that he is in his house, but he says that he does not feel like he is inside anything. His final statement is typical Carver inconclusiveness: "It's really something."

"Cathedral" is a much-admired Carver story, often finding its way into literature anthologies for college classes; however, it is less experimental and innovative, more explicit, and more conventionally optimistic and moral than his earlier stories. The narrator has obviously reached some sort of traditional epiphany at the end; ironically, whereas he had been morally blind before, now he is able to see. The story is about his ultimate ability to identify with the blind man, about the two men blending together into one entity. The narrator's experience is a religious experience in the broadest sense; the fact that a cathedral brings the two men together makes that clear enough. The story is much more "talky" than Carver's earlier stories, partially because it is a first-person narrative in which the personality of the narrator is the very thematic heart of the story itself, but also because Carver seems to believe he has an explanation for things that he did not try to account for previously. The tendency toward explanation moved his later work closer to the kind of moral fiction of which his first mentor, John Gardner, would have approved.

ERRAND

First published: 1988
Type of work: Short story

The death of Russian writer Anton Chekhov is imagined by Carver with a poignant Chekhovian touch.

"Errand" has special significance in the Carver canon, for it is the last story in his last collection, *Where I'm Calling From.*" Because it was published not long before Carver's death, when he knew he had cancer, and because it deals with the death of one of Carver's most treasured progenitors, Anton Chekhov, it takes on a particular poignancy as a kind of farewell tribute to the short-story writer's craft and art.

Much of the story seems less a unified narrative than a straightforward report of Chekhov's death in a hotel in the resort city of Badenweiler, Switzerland. The story recounts without comment Chekhov's last hours, as a doctor visits him in his room and as his wife, Olga Knipper, stands by helplessly. Knowing that it is hopeless and that it is only a matter of minutes, the doctor orders champagne and three glasses from the kitchen. A few minutes after taking a drink, Chekhov dies.

Up to this point, "Errand" is not really a story at all, for it does not have the implied "point" that is always typical of the short story—especially since the innovations were introduced by Chekhov himself. What makes it a story is the appearance of the young waiter who brings the champagne. When the young man returns to the room the next morning to bring a vase of roses and to pick up the champagne bottle and glasses, Olga Knipper, who has spent the remainder of the night sitting alone with Chekhov's body, urges him to go into the town and find a mortician, someone who takes great pains in his work and whose manner is appropriately reserved.

The young man listens as Olga tells him in great detail what to do. He should behave as if he is engaged on a great errand, moving down the sidewalk as if he were carrying in his arms a porcelain vase of roses that he has to deliver to an important man. He should raise the brass knocker on the mortician's door and let it fall three times; the mortician will be a modest, unassuming man with a faint smell of formaldehyde on his clothes. As the young man speaks to him, the mortician will take the vase of roses.

As Olga tells this "story" of the errand the young waiter must fulfill, it becomes so real that it seems to be actually happening—it becomes, in itself, an example of the storyteller's art. Meanwhile, the boy is thinking of something else: On the previous night, just after Chekhov died, the cork which the doctor had pushed back into the champagne bottle had popped out again; it now lies at the toe of the boy's shoe. He wants to bend over and pick it up, but he does not want to intrude by calling attention to himself. When Olga finishes the storylike description of the errand she wishes the boy to perform, he leans over—still holding the vase of roses—and without looking, reaches down and closes his hand around the cork.

It is this single, simple detail that makes "Errand" a story rather than a mere report and thus a fitting tribute to the short-story writing art of both Chekhov and Carver. The cork is not a symbol of anything; it is a concrete object in the world that one can almost tangibly feel as the boy closes his hand around it. It is the unique and concrete act of picking up the cork that humanizes the otherwise abstract report of Chekhov's death. It not only fulfills Chekhov's dictum that if a gun is described hanging on a wall early in a story, then it must be fired before the end, it also embodies the most important lesson that Carver learned from Chekhov—that human meaning is communicated by the simplest of gestures and the most trivial of objects.

Summary

After years of neglect, the short story enjoyed a true renaissance in the 1980's; Raymond Carver was arguably the most important figure in that revival. His understanding of the merits of the short story form and his sensitivity to the situation of modern men and women caught in tenuous relationships and inexplicable separations has made him a spokesperson for those who cannot articulate their own dilemmas. Although critics are divided over the relative merits of Carver's early, bleak, experimental stories and his later, more conventional and morally optimistic stories, there is little disagreement that he is a modern master of the "much-in-little" nature of the short story form.

Bibliography

Boxer, David, and Cassandra Phillips. "*Will You Please be Quiet, Please?*: Voyeurism, Dissociation, and the Art of Raymond Carver." *The Iowa Review* 10 (Summer, 1979): 75-90.

Carver, Raymond. "The Art of Fiction." Interview by Mona Simpson. *The Paris Review* 88 (Summer, 1983): 192-221.

_____. "Raymond Carver." Interview by Nicholas O'Connell. In *At the Field's End: Interviews with Twenty Pacific Northwest Writers*. Seattle: Madrona, 1987.

Meyer, Ann. "Now You See Him, Now You Don't, Now You Do Again: The Evolution of Raymond Carver's Minimalism." *Critique* 30 (Summer, 1989): 239-251.

Stull, William L. "Beyond Hopelessville: Another Side of Raymond Carver." *Philological Quarterly* 64 (Winter, 1985): 1-15.

Charles E. May

WILLA CATHER

Born: Back Creek Valley, Virginia
December 7, 1873
Died: New York, New York
April 24, 1947

Principal Literary Achievement

Known primarily for her literary portraits of frontier life, Cather has achieved critical recognition as one of the leading American novelists of the twentieth century.

Biography

Willa Cather was born in Back Creek Valley, near Gore, Virginia, on December 7, 1873. Christened Wilella and called by the nickname "Willie" throughout her childhood, Cather later adopted the name Willa. The daughter of Charles Cather, a farmer, and his wife, Mary Virginia Boak Cather, she was the eldest of the couple's four children, who also included brothers Roscoe and Douglass and a second daughter, Jessica.

Although the Cather family had long been established in the small Virginia community where Willa was born, a general westward migration of family members, sparked by the railroad's opening of the Great Plains states to increasing numbers of settlers, was already under way at the time of Cather's birth. Cather's aunt, uncle, and grandparents had already left Back Creek for the Nebraska farming community of Red Cloud when Charles Cather decided to follow suit in 1883. Auctioning off the family farm, the Cathers left Virginia and traveled by train to Red Cloud; at the age of nine, Willa Cather arrived in the region that would provide the setting for most of her best-known works.

The tiny area where the Cathers and their relatives established homesteads had already come to be known as Catherton, but that did not increase Charles Cather's luck as a prairie farmer. After an unsuccessful first year, he sold his homestead and moved his family into Red Cloud, where he began a farm loan and insurance business. It was in Red Cloud that young Willa passed the next six years of her life, becoming an avid reader and diligent student whose sharp intellect and forceful personality left a lasting impression on friends and teachers alike.

In 1890, at the age of sixteen, Cather left Red Cloud for Lincoln and the University of Nebraska. After a year's preparatory study, she entered the school and quickly

established herself as one of its brightest—and most individualistic—students. Severe and mannish in her dress, she was self-confident and sometimes aloof in her manner, and she was already beginning to establish herself as a writer. An editor and contributor to the campus' two literary magazines, she also had two articles published in the *Nebraska State Journal*, to which she began contributing a regular column during her junior year. That assignment soon changed to one as the paper's theater reviewer, a post she held until after her graduation, earning a reputation as a tough and eloquent critic impatient with the third-rate fare often served up by touring companies from larger cities.

A year after her graduation, Cather moved to Pittsburgh, where she would remain for the next ten years. For much of that time she lived with the family of her close friend, Isabelle McClung, with whom she made her first trip abroad in 1902. During this period, Cather worked as an editor of *Home Monthly* magazine and taught high school. She continued the writing she had begun in Nebraska and published a book of poetry, *April Twilights*, in 1903, and a collection of short stories, *The Troll Garden*, in 1905. The following year, Cather moved to New York to work for *McClure's* magazine and six years later published her first novel, *Alexander's Bridge* (1912).

That same year, Cather made the first of many trips to the American Southwest, where her brother Douglass worked for the Sante Fe railroad. There, she visited cliff-dwelling Indian ruins and discovered the striking vistas and ancient culture that would play an important role in several of her later novels. Cather's next work, however, was *O Pioneers!* (1913), a story set among the landscapes and people of her Nebraska childhood. The book earned critical acclaim, as did her 1915 novel, *The Song of the Lark*, which examines the career of a singer.

Cather's next novel, *My Ántonia*, published in 1918, is still recognized as one of her major works, and its story of an immigrant girl's life on the Nebraska plains draws its inspiration from many actual people and events remembered from her own youth. After publishing a collection of short stories entitled *Youth and the Bright Medusa* (1920), Cather wrote *One of Ours* (1922), a novel set against the action of World War I, for which she was awarded the Pulitzer Prize in Fiction.

Throughout the 1920's, Cather's popularity grew with critics and readers alike. She had achieved international recognition as one of America's finest writers, and her work continued to reflect the important influences on her life. *A Lost Lady* (1923) takes as its theme the end of the frontier days in the Midwest, while *The Professor's House* (1925) includes a long segment on the discovery of Southwestern Indian ruins. Now in a period of great productivity, Cather published *My Mortal Enemy* in 1926 and, in 1927, *Death Comes for the Archbishop*, which many critics regard as one of her finest works. Set in the Southwest, its story chronicles the life of a priest ministering to the Indian tribes.

In 1930, Cather was awarded the Howells medal for fiction by the Academy of the National Institute of Arts and Letters. During the decade that followed, she published three novels, *Shadows on the Rock* (1931), *Lucy Gayheart* (1935), and *Sapphira and the Slave Girl* (1940), a book of short stories entitled *Obscure Destinies*

(1932), and a collection of essays, *Not Under Forty* (1936). In 1944, she received the National Institute of Arts and Letters' gold medal. Despite the increasingly fragile state of her health, Cather continued to write until the time of her death from a cerebral hemorrhage on April 24, 1947, and two volumes of her later work—essays and short stories—received posthumous publication.

Analysis

Willa Cather is a rarity among writers: a woman who has managed to escape classification as a "woman writer" and a novelist closely identified with a particular region who has nevertheless avoided the label "regional writer." It is the depth and universality of the themes that run through her work that have allowed Cather to transcend such limiting definitions of her voice as a writer, permitting its individuality to achieve full critical recognition.

Central to much of her work is Cather's fascination with the men and women who struggled to build a life for themselves and their families in the sometimes hostile environment of the American frontier. As the daughter of a farmer and, briefly, a homesteader, Cather was intimately acquainted with the conditions faced by the pioneers, many of them immigrants adjusting to a new life far from their native lands, and the level of courage, endurance, patience, and strength that was demanded of them in their efforts to tame the frontier. In books such as *O Pioneers!* and *My Ántonia*, Cather creates vivid fictional portraits of the individuals who peopled the world of her Nebraska childhood. Her sensitivity to the problems faced by the immigrant homesteaders is especially acute, and her admiration for their ability to outlast the difficulties awaiting them in their new land is boundless.

In Cather's world, the pioneer experience draws on the depths of an individual's character. Cather's particular talent lies in her ability to translate this experience into universal terms, turning a pioneer woman's simple life into a glowing tribute to the human spirit. Cather sees in her characters—as she did in the figures surrounding her in her youth—people whose individual stories of courage and endurance form a heroic pattern that changed the face of a nation.

Yet Cather also recognizes, certainly to some extent from personal experience, that a life tilling the soil can be restrictive and unfulfilling for anyone whose aspirations lie beyond the horizons of the Midwest's farms and small towns. Claude Wheeler, the central character in *One of Ours*, is ill-suited to the life of a farmer and finds his escape in the battlefields of France, while Jim Burden, the narrator of *My Ántonia*, is impatient to leave his small community for the larger world.

Cather also deals in her work with the passing of the frontier spirit as larger communities drew an influx of people to the region. There is a strong nostalgia for times past in many of her novels and an increasing dislike of modern society and modern ways that sometimes drew critical fire later in her career. In *A Lost Lady*, the charming Marian Forrester—a gracious, aristocratic presence in the small town of Sweet Water—gradually enters a decline that leads her to an affair with her husband's friend and an association with the town's unscrupulous lawyer. The book is sympathetic in its portrait of Marian, who represents the fading past, and harsh in its portrayal of Ivy Peters, the attorney whose ways represent a break with traditions such as honor and respect.

Hand in hand with Cather's reverence for the pioneer spirit is her admiration for individuality. One of the recurring themes in her work is the individual whose dreams and ambitions place him or her at odds with society. The choices a person makes, and the repercussions those choices have, is the theme of both *The Song of the Lark* and *The Professor's House*. In the former, a singer sacrifices everything for her career, leaving behind her Midwestern home and family and relegating her personal life to secondary status in order to pursue her dream. When she has achieved her goals, she is able to look back clear-eyed on the decisions she has made along the way and accept that they were necessary in obtaining her goal. For Cather, this was a highly personal subject, and the novel's storyline has many similarities with her own life.

The Professor's House examines the life of a man who has not made such a decision and who reaches the beginning of old age only to come face to face with the unique individual spirit he suppressed years ago. Although outwardly successful, he feels less and less at home in the life he has gradually allowed to become his own until he at last releases his connection to his earlier self and resigns himself to living out what his life has become. His own choices are contrasted with his reminiscences concerning a former student, Tom Outland, whose ability to live in harmony with his own spirit reminds the professor of what he has lost.

Cather also had a strong feeling for the land itself, both the Midwestern prairies and the more dramatic landscapes of the Southwestern region she later came to love. The land is an intrinsic part of several of her best works and it was frequently the inspiration for the poetry she wrote earlier in her career. It is in her descriptive passages that Cather's prose style is at its most eloquent, capturing with vivid imagery the colors, physical features and shifting moods and impressions that a particular landscape evokes in its human inhabitants. In *O Pioneers!* and *My Ántonia*, the unique and subtle beauty of the prairie landscape is strongly felt throughout the stories, while *Death Comes for the Archbishop* and *The Professor's House* both offer striking portraits of the Southwest.

The latter two books also draw on Cather's fascination with Indian culture and the history of the land prior to the arrival of white settlers. Tom Outland's discovery of the cliff-dwelling Indian ruins in *The Professor's House* and his complete absorption in them over the next year of his life provide the book with its most compelling segments. *Death Comes for the Archbishop* is a historical novel that brings to life the missionary work of two priests whose lives span the dramatic changes in the Southwestern frontier that took place in the latter half of the nineteenth century. The love they come to have for the land and its people reflects Cather's own feelings even as the book gives voice to a unique period in American history.

MY ÁNTONIA

First published: 1918
Type of work: Novel

An immigant pioneer woman's life is recalled by a childhood friend.

One of Cather's best-loved novels, *My Ántonia* is a moving tribute to the spirit of the pioneers whose strength and endurance made possible the settlement of the American frontier. In its portrait of its title character, the book gives an individual face to the myriad experiences facing the immigrants who composed a large portion of the Midwest's early homesteaders.

The story is told from the point of view of Jim Burden, a young boy from Virginia who has lost his parents and arrives in Nebraska to live with his grandparents. On the same train is an immigrant family, the Shimerdas, whose oldest daughter, Ántonia (pronounced in the Eastern European manner, with accents on the first and third syllables), will become the companion of Jim's childhood days. Through Jim's eyes, the reader sees the family's early struggles as they suffer cold and deprivation in a dugout house, lose the sensitive Mr. Shimerda to suicidal despair, and gradually begin to pull free of hardship through diligence and hard work.

Ántonia Shimerda is an intelligent girl who must forgo any thought of serious study in order to work for her family. First in the fields and later as a "hired girl" in Red Cloud, she is cheerful and uncomplaining, shouldering her share of the backbreaking work required to support a family farm. Ántonia's patient, gentle spirit stays with Jim long after he has left his small community, coming to represent for him the very best of what the pioneer experience can draw from the individual.

Yet Ántonia is not a simplistic character or a lifeless symbolic figure. Cather brings her fully to life, flawed and warmly human, and her story is both specific in its details and universal in its larger themes. A practical, sensible girl, she is nevertheless passionate in her love of the dances that provide all the hired girls with one of their few pleasures, and her trusting nature leads her into trouble — in the form of an illegitimate child — when she is unable to recognize dishonesty, so foreign to her own nature, in the man she loves.

My Ántonia draws its inspiration from Cather's own childhood memories, and Ántonia herself is modeled after a woman named Annie Sadilek, who worked as a maid for the Cathers' neighbors in Red Cloud. Like Ántonia, Annie's father had tragically committed suicide when faced with the hardships and cultural deprivations of his new home, and Annie's own strength and perseverance left a deep impression on Cather over the years. The book's narrator, Jim Burden, who leaves his small community first for college and then to become an attorney for the railroad, is essentially Cather herself, and Jim's growing understanding in the book's later passages of the importance of those early years parallels Cather's own.

My Ántonia is also filled with a wealth of memorable supporting characters: Jim's strong, loving grandparents, the family's colorful farm hands, Ántonia's friends, Lena Lingard, who becomes a successful dressmaker, and Tiny Soderball, who makes her fortune in the Alaska gold rush, and Cuzak, the good-hearted immigrant who marries Ántonia and makes his life as a farmer although he longs for the city life he knew as a boy. The novel is peopled with a rich cast of characters culled from Cather's memory and transformed by her writer's imagination.

There is perhaps no other book that captures quite as well as this one does the look and feel of the prairie. An eye accustomed to more spectacular landscapes may miss the subtleties of the land's beauty, but Cather's deep feeling for the Midwest, with its rolling plains, wildflowers, and open sky, creates an almost palpable picture of her story's setting—one that is crucial to the reader's understanding of the characters and their lives. In the beauty of its language and the humanity of its characterizations, *My Ántonia* remains a major achievement among Cather's work.

A LOST LADY

First published: 1923
Type of work: Novel

An aristocratic woman's gradual decline mirrors the changes in the life of a small Midwestern town.

A Lost Lady is Willa Cather's elegiac portrait of the spirit of an earlier age. In her depiction of Marian Forrester, the much-admired figurehead of culture and society in the town of Sweet Water, Cather evokes a quality of life that began, for her, to vanish sometime around the beginning of the twentieth century. To Cather, much of what was wrong with twentieth century life was the absence of those qualities that Mrs. Forrester embodies: charm, warmth, and a certain graciousness of manner that has no place in the harsher climate of an industrialized society.

The novel traces the fortunes of the Forresters from their position in the book's opening chapters as wealthy and prominent citizens who divide their time between Sweet Water and the more sophisticated society of Denver, to their financial ruin and the decay of spirit that it precipitates. As in *My Ántonia*, Mrs. Forrester is seen through the eyes of a young man, Niel Herbert, although the voice here takes the form of a third-person narrator. From the time he is twelve and is nursed by Mrs. Forrester after a fall from a tree, Niel regards Marian as the standard against which all other women are measured. His devotion to her continues throughout his teenage years until the morning when he becomes aware that she is involved in an affair with a friend of her husband. For Niel, the shock is overwhelming. As Cather phrases it, "It was not a moral scruple she had outraged, but an aesthetic ideal."

The revelation of Mrs. Forrester's secret life is accompanied by the Forresters' financial ruin, brought on in large part by Captain Forrester's sense of honor. The captain had made his money in railroads and is serving on the board of directors of a bank when the bank's failure threatens to wipe out the savings of many investors for whom the captain's name has been an important draw. Determined not to let his investors down, Forrester liquidates his own fortune and pays it out to the investors. The strain brings on a stroke from which he never fully recovers.

The change in their fortunes quickly takes its toll on Marian Forrester. Ill-equipped to cope with a life uncushioned by her former wealth, she quickly declines to the point where Niel returns from school to Sweet Water to stay with the couple and see them through their difficulties. No longer able to travel, Marian soon feels the narrow constraints of small-town life and begins to drink. As time passes, she comes to rely more and more on Ivy Peters, an unscrupulous lawyer with a longstanding grudge against the Forresters, who takes advantage of Marian's helplessness.

It is clear that, for Cather, Marian Forrester represents a way of life that has been lost in the face of changes in modern society. Ivy Peters personifies those changes, emerging as an unsavory representative of an age in which money has replaced loyalty and honor as the standards by which a man is judged. The contrast between Captain Forrester and Peters is stark and not at all favorable to the latter, making the reversal in their fortunes—one beginning the novel in a position of wealth and authority and the other having seized the reins by its close—all the more painful. In an episode that saddens Niel greatly, Marian invites several of Ivy Peters' group of friends to dinner for an evening which seems to Niel a coarse mockery of the earlier days when an invitation to the Forresters was a much-sought-after prize.

Yet Marian Forrester rallies, surprisingly, at the book's close, leaving Sweet Water and marrying again, to a husband who treasures her as Forrester had. Ultimately, however, she remains for Niel—and for Cather—a figure from a lost era and a reminder of the ways in which the world has changed.

THE PROFESSOR'S HOUSE

First published: 1925
Type of work: Novel

An older man reassesses the choices he has made in his life, comparing himself to a former, much-loved student.

In *The Professor's House*, Willa Cather explores the thoughts and emotions of a man making the difficult transition from middle to old age and finding, as he looks back over his life, that he has lost sight of the person he once was. The first symptom of Professor Godfrey St. Peter's growing internal crisis is his reluctance to leave his attic study when he and his wife move to a new house. For St. Peter, the study— uncomfortable and inconvenient as it has always been—represents the constancy of his working life and the years devoted to his massive history of the Spanish explorers in North America. Unwilling to relinquish this tie to the past, the professor continues to rent his old house and visit it when he works.

As time passes, however, a growing sense of alienation from his family and even his work seems to overtake him. His two daughters have grown and have developed qualities with which he is impatient, and his relationship with his wife has become a matter of habit rather than interest. Questioning whether he has followed the right path in his life, he finds himself thinking that he has lost the boy he once was, opting instead for a set of social conventions. The spiritual malaise that has seized hold of him very nearly brings the professor to tragedy when he realizes that his life is in danger from a gas stove and he chooses to do nothing. Saved by the family's long-time sewing woman, St. Peter finds that he has somehow let go of those remnants of his boyhood self and is now able to resign himself to the years ahead of him.

Many critics feel that *The Professor's House* is Cather's most revealing book in terms of her state of mind and her own conflicts regarding the artist's uneasy relationship with society. For Cather, it was essential that her work remain the top priority in her life, and she was prepared to make whatever sacrifices that decision might require. For the professor, social obligations in the form of a family have deflected him from the path he originally set out to follow.

Yet although they make up the greater portion of the book, Godfrey St. Peter's self-doubts and psychological quagmire are not the most memorable segments of *The Professor's House*. The remarkable section of the novel entitled "Tom Outland's Story" comes alive in a way that the longer sections dealing with St. Peter never do. Indeed, Outland's presence—or memory—is the spark that enlivens even those sections of the book in which he does not play a prominent role.

An outstanding student and self-made scholar, Outland has already invented a lucrative engine when he is killed in World War I. The money from the invention leaves his fiancée, St. Peter's daughter Rosamond, a wealthy woman, yet it is a source of great strife within the family. A close friend as well as a student, Outland has come to represent for the professor a man who followed his natural inclinations wholeheartedly. At the time of his own turmoil, St. Peter is editing Outland's journal account of a year spent exploring and excavating Indian ruins. Outland is from Cather's beloved Southwest, and his discovery of a long-vacant village of cliff-dwelling Indians has a transforming effect on his life, one which illuminates his segment of the book and gives it a tone of energy entirely different from those devoted to the professor.

It is a difference that captures the contrast between the way in which the professor has lived and the total absorption that marks Outland's own approach. Recalling his young friend, St. Peter cannot help but find his own life pale and unfocused by comparison, and Cather illustrates this contrast with the marked shift in tone that characterizes Outland's segment—and, indeed, his every appearance—in the book. Whereas the novel as a whole needs the segment to balance and inform its storyline, "Tom Outland's Story" could stand alone as a novella.

The Professor's House is interesting both for its insights into Cather herself and for its reflective quality, which marks its author's own approaching later years. Yet it is Tom Outland that one remembers—a fact that eloquently bears out Cather's premise regarding the merits of each man's chosen path.

DEATH COMES FOR THE ARCHBISHOP

First published: 1927
Type of work: Novel

Two missionary priests, sent by Rome to bring order to the American Southwest, experience a growing love for the land and its people.

Death Comes for the Archbishop is the book that Willa Cather herself believed to be her finest work. Like *The Professor's House*, it is a novel that explores the life of a man and draws on the American Southwest for its setting. Here the similarity ends, however, since the tone of the two books is quite different. Unlike the earlier books, *Death Comes for the Archbishop* celebrates the life choices of its central characters, finding in the lives of Father Joseph Vaillant and Father Jean Marie Latour a simple dignity and extraordinary fulfillment.

Cather based her story on William Howlett's account of the life of Father Macheboeuf, vicar to Archbishop Lamy of New Mexico. Set in the mid-nineteenth century, the book follows the fortunes of Father Latour and his assistant and friend, Father Vaillant, as they organize the disjointed religious structure of the Southwestern missions. The two face a formidable task, made more difficult by powerful priests long in power in the area who are loathe to abandon the corruption into which they have fallen. Working together diligently and with an unshakable faith, Father Latour and Father Vaillant eventually reclaim the region and bring its far-flung communities under the guidance of a single diocese.

The actual course its story takes, however, is less important than the novel's moving exploration of the human spirit as it is revealed in the two priests. Father Latour and Father Vaillant, both men of deep faith and dedication, willingly sacrifice much in the way of personal desires for the sake of the mission they have undertaken, and the book shines with the integrity and nobility of their efforts.

Cather was often asked how much of the story of the two priests was based on historical fact. Perhaps the most accurate answer would be that the skeletal outline of the book is drawn from reality, but everything else is what Cather referred to as a "work of the imagination." The book could be described as historical fiction, or perhaps fictionalized history, but whatever term one chooses to apply, it is clear that those elements that make *Death Comes for the Archbishop* remarkable are Cather's. Her extraordinary prose style is much in evidence, painting vivid literary portraits of the Southwestern landscapes and bringing to life a chapter in frontier history.

Cather's love for the Southwest is evident throughout the book and it reverberates in the love the two priests come to feel for the land and its people. Father Vaillant, in particular, is a man of the people—a dedicated priest who is happiest when he is able to minister to those cut off from the Church by distance or circumstance. Father Latour is a reflective man who sees his greatest dream accomplished in the building of a stone cathedral in Santa Fe, a building that combines the Romanesque architectural style of the Old World with the raw building resources of the New. In the novel's moving final image, it is at the altar of this cathedral that Father Latour is laid after his death.

Death Comes to the Archbishop is rich in unforgettable set pieces and unique secondary characters. Among the book's most memorable segments is the priests' encounter with a dangerous man who offers them shelter for the night, fully intending to murder them and steal their mules. They are warned by his Mexican wife, whom they later assist after she, too, has fled. This event leads to an encounter with frontiersman Kit Carson, in an effective blending of fiction and history that typifies the skill with which Cather brings the past to life.

Ultimately, *Death Comes for the Archbishop* is, like much of Cather's work, a tribute to the courage and perseverance of those who settled the American frontier. What Cather evokes so well in her depiction of Father Latour and Father Vaillant is the depth of purpose that led these men, and so many others like them, to leave behind the world they knew and undertake a mission that would transform their lives into an act of faith.

Summary

In novels as varied as *My Ántonia* and *Death Comes for the Archbishop*, Willa Cather created eloquently written portraits of individuals whose lives achieve a universality of experience and feeling within the confines of very specific, and often unremarkable, settings.

In Cather's best works, the courage and strength of the human spirit are brought vividly to life in stories that capture crucial moments in the history of the American frontier. In the midst of situations that test the limits of their endurance, Cather's characters are helping to shape the face of a changing nation as the threads of their quiet, individual stories are woven together in the fabric of history.

Bibliography

Bennett, Mildred R. *The World of Willa Cather.* New York: Dodd, Mead, 1951.

Brown, E. K., and Leon Edel. *Willa Cather: A Critical Biography.* New York: Alfred A. Knopf, 1953.

Gerber, Philip L. *Willa Cather.* Boston: Twayne, 1975.

Murphy, John Joseph. *Five Essays on Willa Cather.* North Andover, Mass.: Merrimack College Press, 1974.

Woodress, James. *Willa Cather: Her Life and Art.* New York: Pegasus, 1970.

Janet Lorenz

RAYMOND CHANDLER

Born: Chicago, Illinois
July 23, 1888
Died: La Jolla, California
March 26, 1959

Principal Literary Achievement
Chandler helped to shape the American school of detective fiction in the 1930's, attempting to write detective novels that could be considered serious literature.

Biography

Raymond Thornton Chandler was born in Chicago, Illinois, on July 23, 1888. He was the only child of Maurice Benjamin Chandler, a railroad worker, and Florence Dart Chandler (née Thornton), an Irishwoman who immigrated to Plattsmouth, Nebraska. Maurice was an alcoholic, and he and Florence were divorced when their son was seven years old. Raymond and his mother moved to London to live with his severe grandmother and his unmarried Aunt Ethel. His uncle, Ernest Thornton, an Irish solicitor, reluctantly supported this entire household. Chandler felt abandoned by his father, and so developed a strong loyalty to his mother and a sense of justice that manifested itself later in his novels.

Chandler attended Dulwich College, a typical English public school. There he studied the Bible and the Greek and Roman classics, a course of study designed to teach a strict Victorian moral code emphasizing honor, public service, and self-denial. This code profoundly affected Chandler's personality, and it formed the basis for the character of Philip Marlowe, the hero of Chandler's best-known works.

In 1905, when he was seventeen, Chandler was graduated from Dulwich near the head of his class. He wanted to go to a university to study law, but his uncle refused to pay his tuition, deciding instead that Chandler should seek a career in the government. Chandler spent a year studying in France and Germany and became a British citizen to qualify for the civil service examination, which he passed easily. Yet, after six months in his job as an accountant for the Navy, he quit to become a writer, much to the chagrin of his Uncle Ernest.

He spent the next few years writing for newspapers and submitting articles and reviews to literary magazines but made very little money from his writing. In 1912, when he was twenty-three years old, he borrowed five hundred pounds from his

uncle and sailed to the United States. Chandler went to St. Louis, then to Nebraska. He soon moved on to Los Angeles, however, to stay with a family he had met on his passage to America. Warren Lloyd, the father, was a Ph.D. in philosophy who became moderately wealthy from his dealings in the oil business. He found Chandler a job, and Chandler joined his social circle. There Chandler met Cissy Pascal, who was then married to one of Lloyd's friends.

Chandler's mother joined him in Los Angeles in 1916. In 1917, he went to Canada to join the Army to fight in World War I. He was the only member of his unit to survive a German artillery barrage in France in June, 1918. By 1919, he was back in the United States. He felt rootless, and he wandered up to the Pacific Northwest, then to San Francisco, where he worked in a bank. He soon returned to Los Angeles, however, and began his affair with Cissy Pascal. She was divorced from her husband in 1920, but she and Chandler did not marry until 1924, after his mother died. At this time, Chandler was thirty-five years old—Cissy was fifty-three, although she looked younger. Their marriage was often troubled, but they remained together for thirty years, until she died.

By this time, Chandler had taken a job with the Dabney Oil Syndicate, where he eventually became vice president. During his years in the oil business, he developed a problem with alcoholism that eventually led to his dismissal. He was now forty-five years old. He gave up drinking and began to write for the pulp magazines, contributing his first story to *Black Mask* magazine in 1933. He supported his family this way for six years. Finally, in 1939, when he was fifty years old, his first novel, *The Big Sleep*, was published.

Although the book sold well, Chandler made only two thousand dollars on it. His second book, *Farewell, My Lovely*, published in 1940, received good critical reviews, but sold sluggishly, as did his third novel, *The High Window* (1942). He achieved his best sales with his fourth book, *The Lady in the Lake*, published in 1943. Now he had established himself as a novelist, and he had attracted the attention of Hollywood.

In 1943, Chandler went to Paramount Studios to work with Billy Wilder on the screenplay for the novel *Double Indemnity* (1936) by James M. Cain. Both this script and the script he wrote for *The Blue Dahlia* in 1946 were nominated for Academy Awards. The years in Hollywood were profitable for Chandler, but they were also destructive. In the sociable studio atmosphere, he began to drink again, and he had several affairs. His screenwriting career ended in a series of bitter, petty quarrels.

Chandler escaped Hollywood in 1946, when he and Cissy moved to La Jolla, California. He gave up alcohol again and wrote two more novels: *The Little Sister*, published in 1949, and *The Long Goodbye*, published in 1953. Although he finally had fame and enough money to be comfortable, he could not be happy. He became ill with shingles and developed a skin allergy that caused the tips of his fingers to split open. It was so painful that he had to wear gloves to read and bandage his fingers to type. When this allergic rash spread over his chest, he required morphine to withstand the pain. Cissy's health also deteriorated, and she died of fibrosis of the lung in 1954.

Cissy's death drove Chandler to despair, and he began drinking again in earnest. He attempted suicide early in 1955. During the last four years of his life, he divided his time between London and La Jolla. Under the influence of his literary agent, Helga Greene, he remained sober long enough to publish one last novel, *Playback*, in 1958.

In February, 1959, the Mystery Writers of America elected him president, and he flew to New York to accept his office. He caught a cold there and returned to La Jolla alone. He secluded himself and began drinking heavily. His cold developed into pneumonia, and he died at the Scripps Clinic in La Jolla on March 26, 1959.

Analysis

In May, 1948, in an article in *Harper's* magazine entitled "The Guilty Vicarage," W. H. Auden wrote, "Chandler is interested in writing, not detective stories, but serious studies of a criminal milieu, the Great Wrong Place, and his powerful but extremely depressing books should be read and judged, not as escape literature, but as works of art." This assessment pleased Chandler, for it confirmed that he had moved detective fiction toward the realm of literature.

Chandler's education in an English public school taught him high standards for writing. It also left him with a distinctly British writing style. In the five years he worked for *Black Mask* magazine, Chandler taught himself to write in the voice of the American vernacular. He both transmitted and invented colloquialisms. Chandler's hero, Philip Marlowe, the narrator of all seven of Chandler's novels, speaks in colorful slang that captures and holds the reader's interest. He is famous for his startling similes, such as the one at the beginning of *Farewell, My Lovely* in which he describes the thug Moose Malloy: "[H]e looked about as inconspicuous as a tarantula on a slice of angel food."

Mystery stories often rely on dramatic irony—that is, the reader knows something that the detective does not know. Chandler sets himself a difficult problem when he makes Marlowe the narrator, because the reader cannot have any knowledge of events that occur outside the detective's perceptions. On the other hand, the reader becomes privy to Marlowe's thoughts and emotions, which lends Chandler's novels a greater depth than most other mystery stories.

The name "Marlowe" may be a play on the name of Sir Thomas Malory, who wrote the Arthurian romance *Le Morte d'Arthur* in 1485. Indeed, Philip Marlowe behaves like a valiant knight fighting evil in the tradition of chivalry, and there are references to the world of knights in shining armor throughout Chandler's novels. In *The Big Sleep*, Marlowe approaches his client's house and notices a stained-glass window above the entrance that shows "a knight in dark armor rescuing a lady who was tied to a tree and didn't have any clothes on but some very long and convenient hair." Marlowe speculates that he might eventually have to go up and help him. Later in the novel, he looks down at his chessboard and comments, "The move with the knight was wrong. . . . Knights had no meaning in this game. It wasn't a game for knights." The title of the novel *Lady in the Lake*, in fact, refers to the woman who gave King Arthur the sword Excalibur. In *The High Window*, when Marlowe rescues a secretary held captive by her domineering boss, her attending physician calls him a "shop-soiled Galahad."

Philip Marlowe remains true to his knightly code of honor in a sinful world by avoiding its temptations: money and sex. He will never accept more than his standard fee, though he works overtime and often gets beaten up. He always refuses a bribe. He is working, not out of a desire for money, but out of a sense of compassion for the weak victims of the world. He expresses contempt for the idle rich and for policemen who allow themselves to become corrupt.

He remains chaste through most of the novels as well. Beautiful blonde women often tempt him, but they usually turn out to be evil or crazy. When Carmen Sternwood shows up naked in his bed in *The Big Sleep*, he kicks her out of his apartment. Then, in a fit of revulsion, he savagely tears the sheets off his bed. When Marlowe meets a nice girl, such as Anne Roirdan in *Farewell, My Lovely*, he describes her by saying, "Her nose was small and inquisitive, her upper lip a shade too long and her mouth more than a shade too wide." Her hair is brown, not blonde, however, so Marlowe is not really attracted to her. "She looked as if she had slept well. . . . Nice teeth, rather large." He is trapped in that traditional male quandary: He respects the nice woman, the madonna, but he is sexually attracted to the whore.

Eventually Marlowe does sleep with a woman: Linda Loring in *The Long Goodbye*. Their encounter is a perfunctory one-night stand during which she begs him to marry her and he refuses. In *Playback*, Chandler's last and least respected novel, Marlowe actually marries. Yet his sexual escapades seem gratuitous and sadistic. His "romantic" interlude with the character Berry Mayfield sounds almost like a rape:

> She started for the door, but I caught her by the wrist and spun her around. . . . I must have been leering a little because she suddenly curled her fingers and tried to claw me. . . . I got the other wrist and started to pull her closer. She tried to knee me in the groin, but she was already too close. Then she went limp and pulled her head back and closed her eyes.

Some critics have suggested that Marlowe remains chaste, not because he is following a code of honor, but because he really prefers men to women. In *Farewell, My Lovely*, Marlowe meets a sailor, Red Norgaard, and describes him in a way that leaves no doubt that Marlowe finds him attractive:

> He had the eyes you never see, that you only read about. Violet eyes. Almost purple. Eyes like a girl, a lovely girl. His skin was as soft as silk. Lightly reddened, but it would never tan. . . . His hair was that shade of red that glints with gold.

Yet Chandler defended his creation, Philip Marlowe, against accusations of homosexual tendencies. In fact, Marlowe's chastity can be understood as a manifestation of the moral code of an English public schoolboy.

THE BIG SLEEP

First published: 1939
Type of work: Novel

In a corrupt 1930's Hollywood, Philip Marlowe, a hard-boiled detective, solves the mystery of the disappearance of his client's son-in-law.

The Big Sleep was Chandler's first novel, and some critics argue that it is his best. In it, Chandler's knightly hero, Philip Marlowe, fights vice, particularly materialism and sex, and champions the virtues of loyalty and friendship.

Everything in this unseasonably wet October in Southern California is damp and unnaturally green, a color that Chandler associates with corrupt female sexuality. Marlowe meets his client, General Sternwood, an elderly invalid, in a steamy greenhouse filled with plants "with nasty meaty leaves and stalks like the newly washed fingers of dead men." Sternwood wants Marlowe to find out why he is being blackmailed for his daughter Carmen's gambling debts. Marlowe soon discovers that the blackmailer, Arthur Gwynn Geiger, is a pornographer who uses Carmen as a model. Carmen's boyfriend, Owen Taylor, kills Geiger, and then gets killed himself.

Joe Brody, a small-time racketeer, steals some nude photos of Carmen and tries to blackmail the Sternwoods. Carol Lundgren, Geiger's male lover, murders Brody in mistaken revenge for Geiger's death. The blackmail case is resolved. Yet, out of a sense of loyalty for General Sternwood, Marlowe continues work on the case, now to solve the disappearance of Sternwood's son-in-law, Rusty Regan, whom the old man loved.

Carmen has killed Rusty Regan, and her sister Vivian, Regan's wife, knows this. Vivian's loyalty to her father causes her to call on Eddie Mars, the most powerful mobster in Hollywood, to help her cover up her sister's crime. In return, Mars expects to be able to blackmail Vivian out of much of her father's fortune. Marlowe despises Mars because he values only money and power and will do anything to get it. Mars disguises the disappearance of Rusty Regan by holding his own wife prisoner, then spreading the rumor that she ran off with Regan. In contrast, Mona Mars is loyal to her husband and readily goes along with his plans because she loves him. Marlowe falls in love with her, as much for her moral beauty as her physical appearance.

Marlowe deduces that Carmen killed Regan; she is insane and will do anything to get sex. Carmen had propositioned Regan, her sister's husband. When he refused her, she killed him. Out of the loyalty Marlowe feels for General Sternwood, he agrees to protect the general from the knowledge that his daughter killed his only friend. In return, Marlowe extracts a promise from Vivian to put Carmen in a mental hospital.

Marlowe has solved the crimes he was hired to investigate. Yet the two major criminals, Carmen and Eddie Mars, remain unpunished, so Marlowe is discouraged. All his effort and sacrifice did not make much progress against the evil and chaos in the world. General Sternwood, whom Marlowe worked so hard to protect, is old and nearly dead. Marlowe fell in love with Mona Mars, but in vain. Marlowe concludes by saying, "On the way downtown I stopped at a bar and had a couple of double Scotches. They didn't do me any good."

FAREWELL, MY LOVELY

First published: 1940
Type of work: Novel

Philip Marlowe helps a good-hearted thug find his old girlfriend among the demi-monde of Los Angeles and Bay City (Santa Monica).

Farewell, My Lovely, Chandler's second novel, is filled with murder and corruption, yet it is essentially a love story. It begins on a warm day near the end of March in south central Los Angeles. Moose Malloy, a huge, dim-witted ex-convict, enters a bar called Florian's searching for Velma Valento, the girlfriend he left behind eight years before when he entered prison. Marlowe happens to be there to see Malloy kill the manager of the bar and maim the bouncer. Malloy escapes, and Marlowe makes a report to the police.

Curiosity drives Marlowe to look for Velma. He follows the leads to the home of Jessie Florian, the alcoholic widow of the former bar owner. She acknowledges that Velma used to sing at the bar, and she gives Marlowe a photograph of the missing woman. Marlowe receives a call from Mr. Lindsay Marriott. Marriott hires the detective to accompany him to a remote canyon in Malibu, where he will deliver the ransom for a stolen jade necklace. When they arrive, Marriott is killed and Marlowe is knocked unconscious.

When he comes to, he is met by Anne Roirdan, a spunky, intelligent woman who happens by to check out the unusual lights in the canyon. She is the daughter of the former police chief of Bay City, and she decides to help Marlowe solve the case, although he balks at the idea. She discovers that the jade necklace belongs to Mrs. Lewin Lockridge Grayle (Helen), the wife of a very rich man.

Marlowe discovers that Lindsay Marriott holds a mortgage on Jessie Florian's house; this is the indirect connection between Helen Grayle and Moose Malloy. Mrs. Grayle invites Marlowe to her house. She is a beautiful blonde, and Marlowe finds her very attractive. She is married, however, and so, according to Marlowe's chivalrous code of honor, she must remain as unattainable as the Holy Grail. It is probably no accident that her name is homophonous with the elusive goal of the medieval knights. She throws herself into Marlowe's lap, and he succumbs to the temptation and kisses her. Just then, her husband walks in. Marlowe exits, embarrassed.

When he returns to his office, he is met by a Native American named Second Planting. Planting drives Marlowe to the home of Jules Amthor, a phony psychic. There, Marlowe is beaten unconscious. He comes to, only to be beaten again by two Bay City police officers. When he reawakens, he realizes that he has been drugged by Dr. Sonderborg, a Bay City drug dealer. Marlowe escapes Sonderborg's clutches and flees to the home of Anne Roirdan. She feeds him, dresses his wounds, and offers him her bed. His principles make him refuse and return to his apartment alone.

Lieutenant Randall of the Los Angeles Police Department warns Marlowe off the case. Marlowe continues anyway, by going to interview the corrupt chief of the Bay City Police, John Wax. Marlowe discovers that the town is being run by the racketeer Laird Brunette, who owns the Bay City Belvedere Club and two gambling ships anchored in international waters three miles offshore. Brunette is a friend of Helen Grayle.

That night, Marlowe hires attractive sailor Red Norgaard to take him out to one of the gambling ships so that he can talk to Laird Brunette. He gives the racketeer a message on his card for the missing Moose Malloy. Marlowe returns to his apartment at about ten at night. He telephones Helen Grayle and invites her over for a drink. He falls asleep waiting for her, and, when he wakes, Moose Malloy is in his apartment.

When Grayle arrives, Malloy hides in Marlowe's dressing room. Marlowe accuses Grayle of killing Marriott, and Grayle pulls a gun on Marlowe. Malloy comes out of the closet because he recognizes Helen Grayle's voice as that of Velma Valento, his lost love. He suddenly realizes that she was the one who betrayed him to the police eight years previously. Grayle shoots Malloy five times in the stomach, then escapes and disappears. Malloy dies.

Anne Roirdan congratulates Marlowe, but he still refuses to kiss her. Three months later, a detective finds Velma/Helen Grayle in Baltimore; she shoots him, and then herself, rather than be taken prisoner. Marlowe relates this story to Lt. Randall at the end of the novel. He ends on a note of regret:

> I rode down to the street floor and went out on the steps of the City Hall. It was a cool day and very clear. You could see a long way—but not as far as Velma had gone.

Velma is the "lovely" of the title to whom Marlowe is bidding farewell. He could never love the homey Anne Roirdan as long as the dangerous, blonde Velma obsessed him, as she did both Moose Malloy and Lindsay Marriott. Those two men loved her, and, in return, she murdered them.

THE HIGH WINDOW

First published: 1942
Type of work: Novel

A rich Pasadena widow hires Philip Marlowe to find an old rare coin.

Chandler's third book, *The High Window*, tells a story of personal tyranny and the misuse of money and power. The novel begins in front of an old, redbrick home in Pasadena. It is summer and much warmer there, in the San Gabriel Valley, than it is over the hill in Hollywood, where Philip Marlowe lives.

Marlowe is in Pasadena at the request of the wealthy widow Elizabeth Bright Murdock, a drunken, domineering matron. She wants Marlowe to find a valuable coin, the Brasher Doubloon, that has disappeared from her safe. She asserts that her flamboyant daughter-in-law, the former Linda Conquest, a nightclub singer, stole the coin. Linda's marriage to Elizabeth's son, Leslie Murdock, has been faltering, and she has moved out of the Pasadena house and gone into hiding.

Elizabeth Murdock has a secretary, Merle Davis, who intrigues Marlowe. She is blonde and could be beautiful, but she wears no makeup. Merle is afraid of men, because she suffered sexual harassment at the hands of Horace Bright, her former employer and Elizabeth's first husband. Marlowe feels attracted to Merle and protective of her. She gives him the names of Lois Magic, who was Linda Conquest's former roommate, and Louis Vannier, Lois's escort.

Leslie Murdock follows Marlowe to his office to find out why his mother hired a detective. His father was Horace Bright, who supposedly committed suicide when he lost all of his money in the stock market crash of 1929. Leslie is tied to his mother's purse strings, and he has rebelled by marrying a nightclub singer and running up twelve thousand dollars worth of gambling debts at Alex Morny's Idle Valley Club, a gambling house in the San Fernando Valley.

Marlowe discovers that Lois Magic, Linda's former roommate, has married Alex Morny. He confronts a man who has been tailing him, who turns out to be another detective, George Anson Phillips, who claims he has been hired to tail Leslie. Phillips asks for Marlowe's help on the case, but when Marlowe shows up at his apartment, he finds Phillips shot dead.

Marlowe goes downtown to interview a coin dealer, Elisha Morningstar, who, curiously, offers to sell him the Brasher Doubloon for a thousand dollars. When Marlowe returns to his office, however, he finds that the Brasher Doubloon has been delivered to him through the mail. He puts it in hock at a pawn shop for safekeeping. He telephones Elizabeth Murdock, who tells him that the doubloon has been returned to her. Returning to Morningstar's office, Marlowe finds him murdered.

The police are now suspicious of Marlowe, because he has discovered two dead men in as many days. After they interrogate him in his apartment, he receives a call inviting him out to the Idle Valley Club to talk to Alex Morny. He meets with Morny and with Linda Conquest-Murdock, who explains that she hates her husband's mother because she mistreats Merle, her secretary.

Marlowe is summoned to his apartment, where he finds Merle, who is hysterical. She believes that she murdered Horace Bright in 1929 by giving him a fatal push out a window. Elizabeth has encouraged that idea in Merle and has let her believe that Elizabeth was protecting her by making the blackmail payments to Louis Vannier to keep that truth hidden. Now Merle has discovered Vannier dead in his house, and she believes that she killed him, too.

Marlowe calms Merle and goes to Vannier's place. There he discovers some photographs proving that Elizabeth pushed her husband out the window and that Leslie killed Vannier, who had previously killed Phillips and Morningstar. Leslie stole the doubloon from his mother to copy it with Vannier. They hired Phillips to sell the coin to Morningstar. Phillips got nervous and sent it to Marlowe. The other Brasher Doubloons were fakes. Marlowe returns the coin to Elizabeth, but he refuses to return her secretary. He personally drives Merle back to her family in Kansas, where she recovers from her big-city neuroses within a week. The "shop-soiled Galahad" had done his duty again.

THE LONG GOODBYE

First published: 1953
Type of work: Novel

A beautiful woman hires Philip Marlowe to protect her alcoholic husband, a successful author, from his self-destructive actions.

The theme of *The Long Goodbye*, the sixth of Chandler's seven novels, is, again, the corruption of American society, especially its rich. It is also about alienation and the need for love and friendship.

Marlowe befriends a charming drunk, Terry Lennox, in the parking lot of a swank Beverly Hills Restaurant. Terry comes to him a few months later and Marlowe takes him down across the border into Tijuana. It seems that Terry's wealthy wife, Sylvia, the daughter of Harlan Potter, a newspaper magnate, has been murdered, and the police suspect Terry. The police arrest Marlowe as an accessory when he pulls into the driveway of his Hollywood Hills home after the long trip back from the Mexican border.

The police release Marlowe after they receive a written murder confession from Terry, as well as the news that he has died in Mexico. The police warn Marlowe off the case, as do several others, including Linda Loring. Linda, the disenchanted wife of a physician, is the sister of the murdered Sylvia. Later, she becomes Marlowe's lover for a single night.

Meanwhile, Eileen Wade, the beautiful wife of a successful writer, Roger Wade, hires Marlowe to rescue her husband from a disreputable clinic for wealthy alcoholics. After Marlowe does so, Eileen begs him to stay with her husband to keep him sober long enough to finish another novel. Marlowe remains for a while but then leaves, disgusted with Roger's drunken confessions of adultery with Sylvia Lennox and with Eileen's seductive behavior. Marlowe returns to the Wade house a week later to have lunch with Roger. Roger gets drunk and passes out, and Marlowe stays near the house to watch over him. When Eileen returns from shopping that afternoon, however, Roger is dead in the study, with a bullet through his head.

Lieutenant Bernie Ohls, Marlowe's old friend, investigates the death. He disagrees with the official finding, which ruled that Roger's death was a suicide. Instead, Ohls points out evidence to Marlowe that Eileen Wade sneaked into the house and shot her husband while Marlowe was outside and a noisy motorboat was passing by, covering the sound of the gun.

Marlowe and Howard Spencer, Roger's publisher, go to Eileen's house and confront Eileen with this evidence. Marlowe also reveals the fact that, in England during World War II, Eileen had been married to Terry Lennox, who used the name Paul Marston then. She thought that he had been killed by the Nazis. She learned that he was alive only after she met him accidentally in Idle Valley (Chandler's name for the San Fernando Valley), after he had married Sylvia.

That night, Eileen commits suicide by swallowing an overdose of sleeping pills. She leaves a note confessing that she killed Sylvia Lennox because she felt that Sylvia had stolen both of her husbands. Eileen killed Roger because she was angry about his affair with Sylvia and she wanted to make it look like he was guilty of her murder.

Marlowe publishes her confession to clear Terry Lennox's name of guilt for Sylvia's death. He makes love to Linda Loring, who is divorcing her husband, yet he refuses to marry her and live on her father's money. Lennox, who supposedly died in Mexico, comes to Marlowe with a darkened complexion and a new name, Señor Maioranos ("Mr. Better Years"). He faked his suicide with the help of some gangsters to make his murder confession seem more plausible.

Marlowe despises Lennox for his lack of integrity. He returns the five-thousand dollar bill that Lennox had sent him earlier in payment for helping him escape the country. When Lennox asks him why he refuses the payment, Marlowe tells him,

> You had standards and you lived up to them, but they were personal. They had no relation to any kind of ethics or scruples. . . . you were just as happy with mugs or hoodlums as with honest men. . . . You're a moral defeatist.

When Lennox leaves Marlowe's office, Marlowe realizes that he has lost a friend. He feels as empty as he had when Linda Loring left him after their one night of passion, when he said, "To say goodbye is to die a little."

Summary

Raymond Chandler's hero, Philip Marlowe, is a perfectionist who hates the shallow values of American society. By the time of *The Long Goodbye*, set in 1951, the pockets of corruption that Chandler had depicted infecting Hollywood and Bay City in the 1930's had spread over all Los Angeles, like the smog that now blanketed the city. Marlowe has grown tired and cynical. Still, he battles on, even while questioning his own motives and integrity.

Throughout Chandler's seven novels, the character of Marlowe becomes increasingly complex. *The Long Goodbye*, Chandler's penultimate book, is concerned more with theme, characterization, and description than it is with the mechanics of a mystery novel. It represents the fulfillment of Chandler's desire to lift detective fiction to the realm of serious literature.

Bibliography

Durham, Philip. *Down These Mean Streets a Man Must Go: Raymond Chandler's Knight*. Chapel Hill: University of North Carolina Press, 1963.

Gross, Miriam, ed. *The World of Raymond Chandler*. New York: A & W Publishers, 1977.

MacShane, Frank. *The Life of Raymond Chandler*. Boston: G. K. Hall, 1986.

Marling, William. *Raymond Chandler*. Boston: Twayne, 1986.

Wolfe, Peter. *Something More Than Night: The Case of Raymond Chandler*. Bowling Green, Ohio: Bowling Green State University Popular Press, 1985.

Pamela Canal

JOHN CHEEVER

Born: Quincy, Massachusetts
May 27, 1912
Died: Ossining, New York
June 18, 1982

Principal Literary Achievement

Cheever is one of the very few postwar American writers to have achieved major status both as a novelist and as a writer of short stories.

Biography

John Cheever was born in Quincy, Massachusetts, on May 27, 1912. He was descended not, as he liked to claim, from Ezekiel Cheever, master of the Boston Latin school eulogized by Cotton Mather, but instead and more prosaically from Daniel Cheever, one of Ezekiel's cousins and the keeper of the prison at Cambridge. Cheever grew up during what he called the twilight years of Athenian Boston culture. The accelerating pace of the decline that another Quincy man, Henry Adams, had noted a few years earlier in his *The Education of Henry Adams* (1907) manifested itself not only in the Boston area but in Cheever's personal life as well. As a result of the stock market crash of 1929, Cheever's father, Frederick, lost first his position as a shoe salesman (not a shoe manufacturer, as his son liked to claim), then his investments, and finally his self-esteem when his independent-minded wife Mary opened a gift shop in order to support the family. As their parents grew gradually apart, Cheever and his brother Fred, seven years senior, grew closer—unnaturally so, Cheever came to believe. Dismissed from Thayer Academy for smoking and poor grades, Cheever wrote a semi-autobiographical, quasi-Cubist story, "Expelled," which Malcolm Cowley selected from a pile of unsolicited manuscripts for publication in the October 1, 1930, issue of *The New Republic*. After a walking tour of Germany, the brothers settled in Boston, where Fred supported them both while Cheever devoted himself to his writing. By 1934, "Jon" (or "Joey") as he then styled himself, decided to make a break.

He spent part of the summer at Yaddo, the writers' retreat in Saratoga Springs, New York, thus beginning what was to be one of the several long and immensely useful literary relationships. It was Cowley who helped him secure a foothold there and it was again Cowley to whom Cheever turned upon his arrival in New York in July. Living in a squalid room on Hudson Street, Cheever, helped by Fred, sup-

ported himself by writing book reviews and synopses of novels for Metro-Goldwyn-Mayer. The money was meager, but friendships with E. E. Cummings, John Dos Passos, Sherwood Anderson, Walker Evans, James Agee, Gaston Lachaise, and Cowley (his mentor and surrogate father) were rich. His story "Brooklyn Rooming House" appeared in the May 25, 1935, issue of *The New Yorker*, the magazine that would over the next three decades publish more that one hundred Cheever stories (only John O'Hara would publish more). His efforts to publish a novel at this time were hampered as much by conservative literary tastes as by Cheever's need for the quick money that the writing and the sale of stories could provide. He could still not support himself by fiction writing alone and so spent part of 1938 in Washington, D.C., on the staff of the Federal Writers' Project. Back in New York the following year he met Mary Winternitz, daughter of the dean of Yale Medical School. The couple were married on March 22, 1941. Cheever enlisted in the Army the following year and was serving in the South when his first book appeared on March 8, 1943. Although this collection of thirty short stories (including one of his best, "The Brothers") netted its author only four hundred dollars, *The Way Some People Live* received a number of encouraging reviews and soon resulted in his transfer to a Signal Corps staff that included William Saroyan and Irwin Shaw and was stationed in Astoria, Queens. (Since nearly half of Cheever's infantry regiment died in the war, the book and transfer may very well have saved his life.)

After the war, Cheever continued living in New York, writing stories and working on a novel. The Boston opening of *The Town House*, a play adapted from several Cheever stories and produced by George S. Kaufman, seemed promising, but the New York production soon folded and whatever financial relief Cheever had hoped to realize came to nothing. In 1951, the Cheevers moved to suburban Scarborough. Getting a grant from the Guggenheim Foundation to support his writing proved easier than getting his next book, *The Enormous Radio and Other Stories* (1953), accepted; rejected by Random House in 1952, it was published by Funk & Wagnalls the following year to less than enthusiastic notices. Although Cheever would later claim that "something went terribly wrong" in the mid-1950's, in all outward respects his prospects seemed to be brightening: a $2400 advance from Harper & Brothers for a novel, the Benjamin Franklin Award for "The Five-Forty-Eight," an O. Henry Award for the "The Country Husband," election to the National Institute of Arts and Letters (Cheever was elevated to the American Academy of Arts and Letters in 1973), sale of the film rights to "The Housebreaker of Shady Hill," a year in Italy (at Cowley's suggestion), the birth of his second child, Ben (Susan, his first, was born in 1943; Frederick, his third, in 1957). His first novel (something of a psychological as well as financial necessity), *The Wapshot Chronicle* (1957) was a Book-of-the-Month Club selection and winner of the National Book Award. *The Housebreaker of Shady Hill and Other Stories* appeared in 1958; two years later he received a second Guggenheim and, with Phillip Roth and James Baldwin, spoke at *Esquire* magazine's "Writing in America" symposium. Despite misgivings and after a for-money-only stint in Hollywood writing a screenplay of D. H. Lawrence's *The*

Lost Girl (1920), Cheever purchased a restored late-eighteenth century house in Ossining, New York, some forty miles north of New York City. The house was expensive enough to fuel his anxieties over money but also provided exactly the right setting for the myth of the refined, well-to-do country squire which Cheever, with the unwitting help of interviewers and writers of feature articles, would perpetuate over the next twenty years.

Soon after the publication of his strangely titled fourth collection, *Some People, Places, and Things That Will Not Appear in My Next Novel* (1961), Cheever suffered two emotional setbacks: the discovery of his brother Fred's alcoholism and his wife Mary's decision to work, teaching part-time at nearby Briarcliff College. Cheever, mindful of his mother's act of financial independence, was prepared to take the latter as something of a sexual attack and a further blow to an already shaky marriage; his marriage, however, would somehow manage to survive rebuffs, talk of divorce, and Cheever's infidelities for forty years. Although his second novel, *The Wapshot Scandal* (1964), earned for its author a *Time* magazine cover story and a Howells Medal for the best novel of 1960-1964, financial worries led Cheever to break with *The New Yorker* and to sell the film rights to the two *Wapshot* books and to "The Swimmer." (The latter was made into a feature-length film starring Burt Lancaster in 1968. Cheever much preferred to sell the rights but have no film made; the two forms are, he maintained, entirely different.) He traveled with John Updike to Russia in 1964 as part of a cultural exchange, thus beginning his love affair with Eastern Europe. By the end of the decade he found a love more sexual than cross-cultural (though at times hardly less distant), beginning a long-term affair with the actress Hope Lange.

The writing of *The Wapshot Scandal* had depressed Cheever; writing *Bullet Park* (1969) exhilarated him, but when Benjamin DeMott's remarkably wrongheaded review appeared in *The New York Times Book Review*, the author became severely depressed. The early 1970's became for Cheever a time of continued financial worries and sexual anxieties, much drinking, and little writing. The serenity which the poet Asa Bascomb achieves in the title story of *The World of Apples* (1973) collection eluded Cheever as he taught writing at Sing Sing Prison from 1971 until his first heart attack (brought on by his drinking) in 1972. He taught (when sober) in 1973 at the University of Iowa Writers' Workshop, where John Irving and Raymond Carver were also on the faculty; T. Coraghessan Boyle and Allan Gurganus were in his classes. His teaching stint at Boston University the next year ended prematurely with Cheever's complete physical collapse. He entered a detoxification unit and afterward spent a month at Smithers Rehabilitation Clinic in New York. Free of his addictions to tranquilizers and alcohol, Cheever, now a regular at Alcoholics Anonymous, completed *Falconer* (1977), hailed as "Cheever's Triumph." *Falconer*'s success freed Cheever from the financial worries that had plagued him since his father's ruin and, like the novel's protagonist, from a number of other fears as well. As the awards and honors poured in—an honorary doctorate from Harvard; a Pulitzer Prize; the National Book Critics Circle Award and American Book Award for *The Stories of John*

Cheever (1978); the National Medal for Literature—Cheever became less reticent and more willing to be interviewed and to discuss his personal life, except his bisexuality. The triumph was, unfortunately, short-lived. Cheever suffered two epileptic seizures in 1980 and was found to have cancer the following year. The illnesses were especially devastating to a man who had enjoyed physical activity his entire life. Despite the illnesses, he wrote an original screenplay, *The Shady Hill Kidnapping*, broadcast on the Public Broadcasting Service in January, 1982, and a novel, *Oh What a Paradise It Seems*, published in May of that year. Cheever died in his home on June 18, 1982. With the appearance of his daughter Susan's memoir, *Home Before Dark* (1984), his son Ben's selected *Letters of John Cheever* (1988), and Scott Donaldson's excellent *John Cheever: A Biography* (1988), the facts of Cheever's life have become nearly as accessible as his fiction. Excerpts from his journals appeared in *The New Yorker* in 1990.

Analysis

"Fiction is not cryptoautobiography," Cheever warned with the insistence of a man either with a mission or with something to hide. Posthumously published biographical materials make it abundantly clear that Cheever's fiction follows Cheever's life rather closely but never reductively. "Fiction," he claimed, "is our most intimate and acute means of communication, at a profound level, about our deepest apprehensions and intuitions on the meaning of life and death"; it is "our only coherent and consistent, continuous, history of man's struggle to be illustrious." For Cheever, then, fiction was much more a spiritual than a biographical or psychoanalytical exercise, closer to hymn and prayer than to either confession or disclosure. His essentially affirmative vision and lyrical style are not merely and superficially willed; rather, they are earned. His description of fiction as "the bringing together of disparate elements" places as great an emphasis on the apparent randomness of contemporary experience as it does on the elusive wholeness of being for which his characters yearn. "The most useful image I have today," Cheever noted in 1959, "is of a man in a quagmire, looking into a tear in the sky." One year later, Cheever would flatly assert that life in the United States in 1960 "is hell." This apprehensiveness is every bit as much cultural as personal and could, Cheever felt, be attributed to a "loss of serenity in our lives," to a "loss of tradition," that has forced Cheever as well as his characters and readers into a ceaseless act of moral (and, for Cheever, aesthetic) improvisation. The decorous surface of his prose stands in marked contrast to the non-linear development of his plots and his characters' lives. At its worst, this decorum (evident as well in the veneer of respectability of Cheever's suburban stories, the mask of a veneral itch that is itself a mask for or symbol of something deeper still) seems little more than a form of what in *Bullet Park* Cheever, perhaps not-so-tongue-in-cheek, calls "spiritual cheerleading." This spiritual cheerleading may seem especially odd to find in the fiction of a writer whose early work was strongly influenced by that of Ernest Hemingway; Hemingway distrusted the very words—honor, love, courage, valor, and so forth—on which Cheever's lyrical vision came more and more to rely. Cheever's fiction convinces the reader on the basis not of what it denies but instead of what it affirms by virtue of its emotional effect and cumulative power. It evokes a nearly liturgical dimension that leads the reader to believe, as Cheever did, that the purpose of both writing and living is to enlarge man rather than to diminish him.

Because his vision is earned rather than willed, the fiction operates not at the extreme of faith but between the poles which Cheever variously described: expansion and constriction (or confinement), "grossness and aspiration," a world which "lies spread out around us like a bewildering and stupendous dream" versus a world grown suddenly incoherent, inhospitable, even "preposterous." In Cheever's stories and novels, opposites meet but do not necessarily merge as the narrative teeters precariously between the prosaic and the poetic, the practical and the visionary. Even Cheever's distinctive narrative voice proves hard to pin down, managing to be at once compassionate yet detached, celebratory yet satirical. Cheever's characters often find themselves similarly (ambivalently, even ambiguously) situated—not so much placed as displaced, or what Cheever's friend, novelist Ralph Ellison, would call dispossessed. They suffer, often serio-comically, from loneliness and from a loss of self-esteem; often (but by no means always) they live well (if precariously) financially, but they are generally bereft emotionally and spiritually impoverished. The discontinuity of their lives often drives them to an earlier time, to tradition, and to memory, but their nostalgic desire to recover what they have lost—a sense of purpose and security—is often one-sided and therefore mistaken in that they fail to realize that nostalgia is as much "a force of expectation" as it is a longing to recover the past. At their most successful, the search for spiritual wholeness leads them "to build a bridge" in an effort to connect the discontinuous facts of their lives, including the unruliness of their sexual desires. Asked by John Hersey to explain the "blurted quality" of his prose, Cheever responded by attributing it to "some ungainliness in my spiritual person that I cannot master," least of all by psychoanalysis, which Cheever, like many of his characters, had tried and which, he believed, places too much emphasis on motivation and not enough on aspiration.

The critical response to Cheever's work has been uneven and unsure, less because of any difficulty (as opposed to ambiguity or ambivalence) in the fiction than from attempts on the part of reviewers and critics to apply the right kind of rigid formulas which Cheever's work both invites and resists. For example, closely associated with *The New Yorker* magazine, he was soon classified and accordingly dismissed as a "*New Yorker* writer." Reading him as a realist, critics paid scant attention to the strong element of fabulism in his fiction. Judged a writer of short stories, he had his novels discussed as proof of his failure to make the leap to the "more demanding" form of the novel. Seen as a comic writer, he was judged a literary lightweight, a naïve optimist, an apologist for the suburbs, or alternately a satirist of those same suburbs. In fact, Cheever's settings kept changing—city, country, St. Botolphs, suburbs, Italy, prison—but his characters' predicament remained essentially the same. At a time of considerable literary experimentation, Cheever found himself either praised or damned as a conservative in terms of both values and style—this despite the fact that his achievement derives in large measure from his having so successfully managed either to transcend or to undermine the very formulas used to pigeonhole his work. Cheever not only gave new life to the short story and, thanks to the immense success of his retrospective *The Stories of John Cheever* (1978), opened up the market for other short fiction writers, he also broke down the line separating story from novel, realism from fabulism, convention from innovation (or what he liked to call "improvisation") so unobtrusively that his efforts largely went unnoticed as he went about his chosen task of communicating modern man's deepest apprehensions and aspirations.

THE WAPSHOT CHRONICLE

First published: 1957
Type of work: Novel

In this family chronicle, the youngest generation of Wapshots encounters the waywardness of love and of contemporary life.

The Wapshot Chronicle, Cheever's first novel, begins with a Fourth of July celebration in St. Botolphs, "an old river town," a world of the imagination modeled loosely on Cheever's birthplace, Quincy, Massachusetts. Mishap—a firecracker exploding underneath the horse pulling a wagonload of the town's most upright women—is turned to narrative advantage; it is the excuse the novel needs to take the reader on a tour of the area. The pace will soon change and the continuity dissolve as the novel moves through three progressively shorter parts of seventeen, then ten, and finally five, chapters to end back in St. Botolphs on yet another Fourth of July a few years later. Against the discontinuity of the intervening narrative, the novel's frame takes on a special but nevertheless ambiguous significance. It adds an element of ceremony, but also of arbitrariness, that corresponds to the relation between St. Botolphs and the world outside its borders where much of the novel takes place. The relation between these worlds and between tradition and independence (itself an American tradition), between a past which both sustains and confines and a present which frees but also dismays and displaces forms the thematic center of a novel that is very much about the need "to build a bridge" between the two worlds and all they represent.

Descended (in a double sense) from a long line of New England sea captains, the mythically named Leander Wapshot stands at the novel's moral center. Lusty, sometimes drunk, but always ceremonious, he is Cheever's diminished hero, captain of the *Topaze*, a barely seaworthy tourist ferry owned by his eccentric, sexless sister, Honora. When Leander loses his boat, he loses his usefulness and therefore his self-esteem and thus becomes the tragi-comic epitome of "man's inestimable loneliness." His civic-minded wife, Sarah, like his sister Honora, plays her part in Leander's temporary fall from grace when she turns the *Topaze* into a floating gift shop. His sons, Moses and the younger, "ministerial" Coverly, fare no better in their relations with women in the world beyond St. Botolphs.

Once the brothers leave St. Botolphs (Honora, who controls the family inheritance, demands that Moses leave; Coverly departs because he cannot live at home without his brother), their lives become nomadic, and the novel's plot ever more wayward, serving up several divergent yet oddly parallel and at times intersecting stories rife with chance meetings—a sign on the one hand of life's versatility and romantic possibilities and on the other of its inexplicable randomness. Moses goes to Washington, gets a government job that is so secret that the narrator cannot discuss it, has an affair with a married woman named Beatrice, gets fired, leaves Washington, goes fishing, comes to the aid of a wealthy man whose gratitude includes hiring Moses, and falls in love with and marries Melissa, the ward of a distant cousin, Justina Wapshot Molesworth Scaddon. Justina is the widow of a five-and-ten-cent store king, caricature of the American nouveau riche, and the novel's comic version of Charles Dickens' Miss Havisham. Meanwhile, Coverly has gone to New York, where he does not get a job in the carpet business owned by the husband of yet another wealthy cousin (Coverly fails the days-long psychological testing), works in a department store, goes to night school to become a computer "taper," and falls in love with and marries his Georgia-born "sandwich shop Venus," Betsey Macaffery, like Melissa an orphan. (Absent parents, especially fathers, figure prominently in Cheever's fiction.) Moses' and Coverly's marriages are as full of interruptions as Cheever's narrative. Melissa soon turns aggressively asexual as the couple continues to live under the vast but confining roof of Justina's Clear Haven mansion. Coverly's marriage begins to deteriorate when Betsey's efforts to make friends at the planned community of Remsen Park (where Coverly's work has taken them) all fail. Stylistically and narratively, *The Wapshot Chronicle* is as "fractious" as the brothers' marriages: Straightforward narrative sections alternate with Wapshot journals, lists, letters, phony biographies, catch-22 logic, and frequent addresses to the reader, including such announcements as "now we come to the unsavory or homosexual part of our tale and any disinterested reader is encouraged to skip."

The ending of *The Wapshot Chronicle* proves no less curious than the chapters which precede it. Both couples reunite, and both Moses and Coverly father sons and so fulfill the terms Honora set for establishing trusts in their names, part of which the brothers will use to buy Leander a new boat. Before the boat can be bought, however, or the boys (now men) even return, Leander drowns, but his death becomes the occasion of Cheever's (and the town's) celebration of all that Leander represents. At the very end of this novel in which tragedy is undercut by humor and the absurd heightened by pathos, Leander finally gets what neither Sarah nor Honora ever let him have in life—the last word—when quite by accident Coverly finds Leander's handwritten "Advice to my sons," which mixes practical advice with liturgical intensity, ending with the words, "Trust in the Lord."

THE WAPSHOT SCANDAL

First published: 1964
Type of work: Novel

The comic waywardness of *The Wapshot Chronicle* gives way to the confusions and discontinuities of the contemporary world.

Similarities between *The Wapshot Scandal* and the work to which it serves as sequel, *The Wapshot Chronicle*, are readily apparent: the similar cast of characters (though Leander and Sarah are both dead), the use of a framing device (two Christmases at St. Botolphs), and the interweaving of multiple narratives. Honora, still eccentric but now more sympathetic, tries to escape persecution for nonpayment of taxes by traveling to Italy, where she finds herself homesick rather than free and, in the company of an equally lonely IRS agent, returns to St. Botolphs, where she must forfeit the family fortune and soon drinks herself to death (a death which Cheever somehow seems to make funny). Cheever depicts the lives of Coverly and Betsey in a missile-site housing complex named Talifer and of Moses and Melissa in affluent Proxmire Manor. The differences between the two books, however, are of greater importance than the similarities. In *The Wapshot Scandal*, the narrative is more discontinuous (so much so that Cheever once described it as "an extraordinarily complex book built upon non sequiturs"). The temporal vagaries of *The Wapshot Chronicle* here seem more pronounced, resulting in a more mythified realism, a fictive world that is simultaneously now and never. (In this sense it resembles the strangely familiar setting of Shirley Jackson's "The Lottery," which significantly first appeared in *The New Yorker* in the 1940's.) The narrator's relation to his story has also grown more problematic: It is at once more intimate and more detached. He claims to have personal knowledge of the Wapshots, who, he says, always made him feel like an outsider. Most important, *The Wapshot Scandal* is a darker and at times blackly humorous novel haunted by death, as the now vacant Wapshot house is said to be haunted by the ghost of Leander, described here as a man who always looked like a boy but who in his last years "looked like a boy who had seen the Gorgon." Coverly cannot understand why his father would want to come back, least of all to a decidedly fallen world which seems to promise nothing ahead and offer nothing to which to return. The modern world has almost entirely displaced the "old river town" of the earlier novel, but the potency of this new world is almost entirely destructive, as figured most clearly in Dr. Lemuel Cameron, né Bracciani, director of the Talifer missile site and believer in the inevitability of nuclear war, who is more than willing to dispose of all who do not measure up to his intellectual and physiological standards, including his own son.

With Leander's death, the moral center of the Wapshot books shifts to Coverly, whose efforts to build a bridge between past and present and to adapt to the rootlessly and ruthlessly modern world without succumbing to it are fraught with difficulties. As his world grows increasingly resistant to his sense of what that world should be and as Betsey, still frustrated in her efforts to make friends with her neighbors, grows ever more distant, Coverly searches for some way to prove himself useful, even illustrious. A "computer taper" misassigned to a public relations department as the result of a computer error, Coverly does succeed in building a bridge of sorts when he runs a computer analysis of Keats's poetry and discovers that in their order of frequency the most commonly used words yield their own poetry— proof, Coverly believes, "that some numerical harmony underlay the composition of the universe."

Moses is neither so fortunate nor so optimistic. Having given up his study of banking for a job in "a shady brokerage house," he finds himself morally as well as financially in debt, soon to become both a cynic and a drunk. Moses, however, appears very little, Melissa very much, in this novel; the reader detects a corresponding shift from Betsey's loneliness to Melissa's boredom and disappointment. The bland assurances and apparent security of middle-class life in well-to-do Proxmire Manor come up against Melissa's all-consuming fear of death which in turn releases her "unruly lusts" and "ruthless greed for pleasure." Her problem is not so much sexual as it is spiritual, but when her minister advises her to see a psychiatrist, Melissa takes matters into her own hands and begins an affair with a nineteen-year-old grocery boy, Emile Cranmer. Each sees the other as divine, which is to say as representing the life neither has but for which both yearn. The yearning of Melissa, Emile, and indeed of the novel's characters is real enough even if it generally manifests itself in bizarre, ultimately unfulfilling ways: in supermarket purchases or the golden egg which, thanks to Emile, Melissa finds and so wins a trip to Rome. Rome, however, will not satisfy Melissa, any more than it does Honora. Nor will Emile, who, thanks to one of Cheever's numerous and entirely self-conscious plot contrivances, ends up in Italy on the block at a sex auction, where Melissa buys him. Last seen at the Supramarketto Americano in Rome, Melissa appears still dissatisfied, still yearning, still buying, still absurd.

At novel's end Coverly, evicted from his house, returns to St. Botolphs, where, after Honora's death and in the company of a nagging Betsey and a randy, drunken Moses, he honors Honora's request to preside over a Christmas dinner for guests from the Hutchins Institute for the Blind. The sense of ceremony is played against the novel's second ending, however, in which the narrator claims that he will "never come back" to St. Botolphs and that even if he did there would be "nothing" to return to, "nothing at all." His words recall Prospero's speech at the end of William Shakespeare's *The Tempest* (1611) as spoken by Coverly over Leander's grave in accord with his father's request at the end of *The Wapshot Chronicle*. Here, however, those words do not so much comfort as disconcert, and in this sense seem strangely linked to the "large, ugly, loaf-shaped and colorless escarpment of granite" around which a housing development has been built that Emile sees earlier in the novel and which Cheever ambivalently describes as "triumphantly obdurate and perverse," "useless," and "invincible," a fit emblem of both the Caliban to which Melissa succumbs and the Ariel to which Coverly aspires.

FALCONER

First published: 1977
Type of work: Novel

A man's attraction to the natural world and to spiritual light leads him out of the prison of self.

Hailed as "Cheever's Triumph," *Falconer* seemed to surprise many of its reviewers. They were surprised that a writer of short stories could, after three missteps, finally write a "real" novel, especially after the "broken-backed" performance of *Bullet Park* eight years before. They were also surprised that this "Chekhov of the exurbs," as one reviewer of *The World of Apples* (1973) put it, would set his latest fiction in a prison and, more shockingly, write so explicitly about fratricide and homosexuality. Their surprise points all too well not to any change in Cheever's writing but instead to the shortcomings on the part of Cheever's critics and reviewers. The prison setting, as Cheever would himself point out, functions much as St. Botolphs and fictional suburbs such as Proxmire Manor, Shady Hill, and Bullet Park (as well as Italy and Sutton Place apartment buildings) do as metaphors of the confinement that figures in virtually all of Cheever's fiction. *Falconer* is not a prison novel in any narrow sense, nor is it about Sing Sing, where Cheever taught in 1971 and 1972; although it draws on information supplied by his inmate/students, *Falconer* represents what Cheever called "the sum of my experience." Just as important, *Falconer* is not any more "novelistic" than *Bullet Park* or the Wapshot books, though it is certainly more narrowly and more intensively focused. Rather, all four employ the same parallel structure, which Cheever also uses in his short stories. Finally, the homosexual theme in *Falconer* represents more a culmination than a new direction in his work; what is different about Cheever's handling of homosexuality in *Falconer* is his forgoing the comedy which previously allowed him to defuse the subject's personal and thematic explosiveness. Begun during Cheever's darkest period (not later than 1974), it was completed in a single year-long stretch following his release from Smithers Rehabilitation Clinic and from his addictions to drugs and alcohol.

Falconer differs most from the earlier works in its intensity. Never before, for example, had the close, often strained, occasionally hostile relations between brothers actually ended in death. ("I killed you off in *Falconer*," Cheever could jokingly say to Fred a few weeks before the latter's death on May 30, 1976.) Never before was the contrast between light and dark, spirit and flesh, "the invincible potency of Nature" and one's deadened sensibility to that potency been so starkly portrayed. Never before was Cheever quite so clear or quite so determined about the need for spiritual redemption apart from all psychoanalytical explanations and excuses. Neither psychological nor sociological in its import, *Falconer* is an essentially religious work in which the criminals are "miscreants," the crime is "fratricide," and the meaning is "the mystery of imprisonment."

Falconer Prison is a world apart from affluent Indian Hill, Connecticut, and forty-eight-year-old Ezekiel Farragut's life there as husband, father, and professor; it is also the epitome of a life which has made addiction to heroin, to methadone, and ultimately to all forms of self-love and self-indulgence its center. Sentenced for up to ten years, Farragut must do more than serve his time; he must learn "to leach self-pity out of his emotional spectrum." It is a task made difficult not only by Farragut's self-pitying nature but also by the number of targets there are for him justifiably to blame for his condition: his narcissistic wife Marcia, the father who wanted his fetus aborted, the mother who would spare him none of her time, the brother who (Farragut believes) tried to kill him. Yet none of them serves as adequate answer to the question that soon becomes the novel's refrain, "Farragut, Farragut, why is you an addict?"

The men Farragut meets in *Falconer* are all grotesques: the sadistic deputy warden, Chisholm; the immensely fat guard, Tiny; the Prussian-looking Marshack; and the "freaks" of F-Block—Chicken Number Two, Bumpo, the Cuckold (with his stores of food with which to bribe the others into listening to his stories), Tennis—each in his own way a distorted mirror image of what Farragut has or will become. Farragut's homosexual love for the youthful-looking Jody serves as the novel's turning point. Unlike all the other prisoners, Jody is willing to speak truthfully about himself, to blame himself for who, what, and where he is, and to admit that he has no future. (Jody's escape from prison is not so much unbelievable as miraculous, proof that *Falconer* is more religious than realistic, closer to romance than to realism.) Farragut's love for Jody (as well as his doubts about that love) leads him out of the prison of self and eventually out of Falconer Prison as well. He takes his second step beyond self when he begins to build a contraband radio (another kind of bridge) to bring news of the riot at Amana Prison (modeled on the Attica riot of September, 1971) to Falconer's inmates and so, Farragut optimistically and mistakenly believes, to cause them to band together with their "brothers" at "the Wall." The idea is overly ambitious, bearing about as much relation to the reality of prison life, with each man in his own cell of self, as do Farragut's sexual fantasies. The "torpor" of the men, like the unchanging summer weather, proves as indomitable as it does perverse.

The riot is broken; the men stay as they were—torpid, selfish, and lonely—except for a change in the color of their clothing, from gray to a "noncommittal green." The change in Farragut is far more dramatic. Free of his addiction (though through no effort on his part), he attends to the dying Chicken Number Two and finally recalls the events leading up to his brother Eben's death. As the reader comes to understand, in killing Eben Farragut he was trying to kill a part of himself. Self-pity has become self-awareness. It becomes, too, a selflessness that paradoxically—or miraculously—restores Farragut to himself, to the need to take his rightful place in the world. Employing courage and cunning, he undergoes a metaphorical death and rebirth. He puts himself in Chicken Number Two's body bag and coffin, is carried out of the prison, and makes his escape, having lost his fear of falling "and all his other fears as well." The ending is (again) unrealistic but nevertheless entirely convincing, a quiet but liturgically intense affirmation of faith: "Rejoice, he thought, rejoice."

THE ENORMOUS RADIO

First published: 1947
Type of work: Short story

The Westcotts discover that evil lies within the heart, not out in the world.

What distinguishes "The Enormous Radio" from the Hemingway-like stories of his first collection, *The Way Some People Live*, is the unsettling mixture of realism and fantasy that characterizes the best of his later work. "The Enormous Radio" concerns the Westcotts, who live in a Sutton Place (New York) apartment building and who resemble other young (mid-thirties), college-educated, upwardly mobile couples of the immediately postwar period in all respects but one; their special fondness for classical music. When their old radio breaks down, Jim buys Irene a new, rather expensive one as a present. Larger and more powerful than its predecessor, the new radio becomes a disturbing presence in the Westcotts' (especially in Irene's) life. She does not like its ugly gumwood cabinet, confounding complexities, violent forces, "malevolent green light," and "mistaken sensitivity to discord."

This "aggressive intruder" invades and disrupts not only Irene's world but also that of her neighbors. Irene is appalled yet fascinated by what she hears—evidence of her neighbors' financial, social, and sexual anxieties—but also worried that her neighbors may be able to hear what she and Jim say in the privacy of their own apartment. Irene becomes apprehensive, and this in turn leads Jim to express his own long-suppressed financial worries and finally to broadcast his wife's secret sins: taking her mother's jewels before the will was probated, cheating her sister, making another woman's life miserable, and going to an abortionist. Like Nathaniel Hawthorne's Young Goodman Brown, Irene has entered the dark forest of moral ambiguity and emerged a different person—emerged, that is, as she truly is rather than as she would like to appear. The breakdown of the old radio prepared the way for the breakdown of the Westcotts' moral façade and for their and the reader's discovery that the "heart of darkness" lies not without, as Irene wished to believe, but within. The ultimate truth, however, may very well lie somewhere between the Westcotts' fondness for harmony and the radio's "mistaken sensitivity to discord."

GOODBYE, MY BROTHER

First published: 1951
Type of work: Short story

The conflict between two brothers centers on their different visions of the world and reflects the conflict raging within the narrator.

The theme of "Goodbye, My Brother," a story based on Cheever's relationship with his older brother, Fred, is one which preoccupied Cheever over the course of his entire career, from the early story "The Brothers" (1937) to the late novel *Falconer*. The story takes place on Laud's Head, on the New England coast, where the geographically distant but "close in spirit" Pommeroy clan (a widowed mother, one recently divorced daughter, and three brothers with wives and children) gathers at the family's summer house, built in the 1920's. The unnamed narrator, one of the brothers, is thirty-eight, a schoolteacher resigned to a future without much promise who, like the rest of his family (other than the youngest brother), believes that while the Pommeroys may not be distinguished, they are unique.

The late arrival of Lawrence, the youngest, a lawyer, is the return of the prodigal son, only in reverse. Known variously as Tifty (from the sound his slippers made when he was a child), Croaker, and Little Jesus, he has no enthusiasm—indeed, much contempt—for the activities in which the rest of the family take so much pleasure: drinking, talking, dancing, playing games, and above all, swimming, which during Lawrence's visit they seem to do more as a way to cleanse themselves of his doleful presence than as a form of physical exercise. "He could make a grievance out of everything," the narrator complains about a brother who sees moral as well as physical decay everywhere. Lawrence is not only "gloomy," however; he is also at least partly correct in his unwanted judgments: There is indeed a crack in the sea wall, the summer house was built to make it appear old even though it was not, the family members do delude themselves in various ways, as even the narrator seems to realize if not quite admit. It is as much Lawrence's willingness to articulate—or croak—these cracks in the Pommeroy dream as it is his failure to entertain that lyrical vision and sense of ceremony and decorum with which the other Pommeroys are so preoccupied that causes the narrator to strike him on the head. The ever complaining and ever departing, ever disappointed Lawrence deludes himself in thinking that he has important things to do—things which his frivolous and now murderous family have kept him from doing.

Lawrence, too, appears to be marked for failure, branded like Cain by the Cain-like brother who has just tried to kill him. The ending of the story compounds the ambiguity, for the richness of lyrical phrase and mythic allusion creates a sense of affirmation and illusion. The doubleness is crucial to Cheever's effect and to the reader's perception that the external conflict between the two brothers and their very different visions reflects the internal conflict raging within the narrator and, one suspects, within the author as well.

THE COUNTRY HUSBAND

First published: 1958
Type of work: Short story

The comic hero takes a rather absurd route in an effort to reclaim his self-esteem and rightful place in the world.

"The Country Husband" typifies Cheever's use of humor to underscore the absurd ways in which people, like its hero, Francis Weed, attempt to overcome their sense of having suddenly become displaced, socially or sexually. An emergency landing in a field while returning from a business trip precipitates Weed's crisis; he will soon run the risk of becoming as unwanted as his namesake in his suburban Garden of Eden, Shady Hill. Once returned, he can find no audience for his tale of near-extinction: His children turn the house into a battlefield, and his wife Julia prepares, serves, and eats the family dinner while pretending to ignore the chaos. Escaping into his backyard, Weed finds not the peace and understanding he craves but instead the proof of Shady Hill's essential triviality: old Mr. Nixon defending his bird feeder from the squirrels while another neighbor, Donald Goslin, plays (as he does every night) the "Moonlight Sonata" in "an outpouring of tearful petulance, lonesomeness, and self-pity—of everything it was Beethoven's greatness not to know."

Curiously, Weed's awareness of the self-pity of others does not prevent him from succumbing to it himself as he falls madly in love with the teenage babysitter whose very name—Anne Murchison—adds to the story's comic absurdity, as it effectively undermines Weed's exalted image of her and his mistaken belief in her power to restore him to his rightful place in the world. As Weed's romantic fantasy grows ever more adolescent, his wife grows more perturbed and more absurd. His cutting remark to one of the community's most important women costs her a party invitation, thus putting her closer to that "most natural dread of chaos and loneliness," against which her only weapon is a hyperactive social schedule. Worse or sillier still, Julia (ignorant of Weed's love for Anne) claims that he has been subconsciously expressing his hatred for her by leaving his dirty underwear around the house. Weed does eventually regain his place, if not his self-esteem. On the advice of a psychiatrist, he takes up woodworking and in this way channels his desires into a harmless pursuit, not unlike Donald Goslin's piano playing. The ending—"Then it is dark; it is a night where kings in golden suits ride elephants over the mountains"—is clearly lyrical, but perhaps duplicitously so, evoking both transcendental affirmation and ironic doubt.

THE DEATH OF JUSTINA

First published: 1960
Type of work: Short story

Adversity becomes absurdity as Moses discovers the fear of death upon which "the good life" is founded.

In "The Death of Justina" it is not merely a brush with death (as in "The Country Husband") but death itself which serves as catalyst not only for a change in the narrator-protagonist's life but for Cheever's comic genius as well. "So help me God it gets more and more preposterous, it corresponds less and less to what I remember and what I expect as if the force of life were centrifugal and threw one further and further away from one's purest memories and ambitions"; the speaker is a version of the figure Cheever imagined in 1959—the man in a quagmire looking up at a tear in the sky—but one whose predicament has somehow become funnier as well as more dire. If, as the narrator would like to believe, fiction is art, and if art is the triumph over chaos brought about by the exercise of choice, then how is the writer or authorial narrator to continue to effect that triumph in a world in which change occurs too rapidly and in which the basis for making aesthetic as well as moral choices appears to have disappeared? How is one to build Coverly Wapshot's bridge between "memories and ambitions"?

Aside from the setting (Proxmire Manor) and names (Moses and Justina), "The Death of Justina" exists independently of *The Wapshot Scandal* in all but two important respects—structure and theme, and specifically in Moses' wanting to know how, in the world's most prosperous land, there can be so many disappointed people. "The Death of Justina" provides a possible answer. When his wife's cousin dies in his home, Moses suddenly learns that his neighborhood and the suburban good life it represents are not zoned for death. As the mayor explains, "The importance of zoning just can't be overestimated," and Moses will simply have to wait a few days or weeks until an exemption can be issued. When Moses threatens to bury the corpse in his backyard, the mayor—acting illegally—relents. Matters do not end there, however, for that night Moses has a dream in which a thousand grotesquely garbed shoppers, desexed and penitential, wander around a brilliantly lit supermarket, its windows darkened, the contents of all packages unknown. At the checkout counter, large men tear open the packages, express their disgust, and then push the humiliated shoppers out the door into a sea of tormented souls.

This blackly humorous updating of Dante's *Inferno* (c. 1320) manages to create a certain sympathy for those it satirizes and for modern man's mistaken efforts to realize his deepest longings. Burying Justina in a cemetery which, like a dump, lies on the town's outskirts—out of sight, out of mind—leads Moses to ask, "How can a people who do not mean to understand death hope to understand love, and who will sound the alarm?" Apparently, Moses will. Told by his boss to rewrite a commercial for a product called Elixircol, he first composes a parody, "Only Elixircol can save you"; then, when threatened with a kind of death—being fired—he copies out the Twenty-Third Psalm. In the nightmare world of the supermarket of the soul, the words that Moses chooses, "the Lord is my shepherd, I shall not want," sound both sane and strangely convincing.

THE SWIMMER

First published: 1964
Type of work: Short story

An afternoon swim becomes a psychologically powerful fable of the fall of man and his expulsion from a modern Garden of Eden.

The comic absurdity and artful randomness of "The Death of Justina" differ sharply from the dark ambiguity and the tight, almost inexorable structure of "The Swimmer," another Cheever story concerning modern man's efforts to guard himself from every painful memory and every proof of his own mortality. "The Swimmer" begins on a summer day around the Westerhazy's pool when the youthful Neddy Merrill decides to "enlarge and celebrate" the day's beauty and his own good fortune—including his wife Lucinda and his "four beautiful daughters"—by swimming home to Bullet Park, eight miles (sixteen pools) away. Thinking of himself as a legendary figure, a pilgrim, an explorer, "a man with a destiny," Neddy seems childlike, even comically childish, yet nevertheless preferable to the others who sit around the pool complaining of having drunk too much the night before.

The first half of the story moves along rapidly from their chronic plaint to Neddy's chosen plan and the swimming of nine pools in one hour. Neddy's odyssey is not without some difficulties—a thorny hedge, gravel that cuts the feet, drinks proffered and politely drunk, a brief storm, a sudden coolness in the air, a drained pool, and an overgrown yard. There is also a small plane "circling around and around and around in the sky with something like the glee of a child in a swing," which, twice noticed, delights Neddy but also distracts him and perhaps serves to remind the reader of not only the joy but also the futility of Neddy's act, the inexorable closure of his destiny. In the story's first half, the disappointments and impediments are generally minor and cause neither Neddy nor the reader much inconvenience or delay. In the second half, however, the obstacles increase and the pace of both the swim and the reading slackens. It takes a page, for example, to cross the divided highway where Neddy suddenly seems vulnerable, even pitiful, unable to turn back and unsure when this bit of afternoon play turned serious. As the pace slackens, the evidence mounts that Neddy's ability to repress all unpleasantness has "damaged his sense of truth" until inevitably, yet (in terms of conventional realism) inexplicably, Neddy finally reaches the empty house that was once his home.

For the reader, Neddy's defeat is doubly troubling. Like Neddy, the reader must confront the emptiness at journey's end and all that this ironic reversal of Odysseus' homecoming suggests about Neddy and more generally about the precariousness of American upper-middle-class life. The reader must also face the fact that a story which began as more or less conventional, certainly comic, realism has transmogrified into a dark fantasy in which it is not only the day that has gone by but the seasons, indeed the years of a man's life, leaving him, like the narrator at the end of *The Wapshot Scandal*, with "nothing, nothing at all." While the specific cause of Neddy's downfall may be financial (as well as psychological), the power of this story (like Washington Irving's "Rip Van Winkle," which it resembles in certain ways) derives from some much deeper, less specific source whose terror, as Edgar Allan Poe said of his own Gothic tales, is "not of Germany"—or of the suburbs—but "of the soul."

Summary

John Cheever is one of the very few writers who have attained major status in both the novel and the short story, a form to which the retrospective collection *The Stories of John Cheever* (1978) brought renewed interest and a much greater measure of respect. Equally important, however, are the ways in which Cheever managed to combine so subtly and so successfully traditional storytelling with narrative innovation and conventional realism with lyrical fabulism, and to invest his middle-class characters and suburban settings with mythic resonance.

Bibliography

Bosha, Francis J. *John Cheever: A Reference Guide*. Boston: G. K. Hall, 1981.

Cheever, Susan. *Home Before Dark*. Boston: Houghton Mifflin, 1984.

Coale, Samuel. *John Cheever*. New York: Frederick Ungar, 1977.

Collins, Robert G., ed. *Critical Essays on John Cheever*. Boston: G. K. Hall, 1982.

Donaldson, Scott, ed. *Conversations with John Cheever*. Jackson: University Press of Mississippi, 1987.

_____. *John Cheever: A Biography*. New York: Random House, 1988.

Hunt, George. *John Cheever: The Hobgoblin Company of Love*. Grand Rapids, Mich.: Eerdmans, 1983.

O'Hara, James F. *John Cheever: A Study of the Short Fiction*. Boston: G. K. Hall, 1989.

Waldeland, Lynne. *John Cheever*. Boston: Twayne, 1979.

Robert A. Morace

KATE CHOPIN

Born: St. Louis, Missouri
February 8, 1851
Died: St. Louis, Missouri
August 22, 1904

Principal Literary Achievement

Renowned for her literary naturalism and feminism, Chopin's fiction forthrightly challenged traditional roles for women and addressed other controversial themes, such as interracial relationships and human sexuality.

Biography

Kate O'Flaherty Chopin was born into a wealthy Catholic family in St. Louis, Missouri, on February 8, 1851. Her mother, Eliza Faris, was from an aristocratic French-Creole family, and her father, Thomas O'Flaherty, was an Irish immigrant who became a prominent merchant in St. Louis. After her father died in 1855, Kate was reared in a home that included three generations of strong-willed and self-sufficient female relatives who undoubtedly influenced her attitudes about women.

On June 9, 1870, two years after she was graduated from a St. Louis convent school, Kate married Oscar Chopin, a French-Creole. After the marriage, Chopin moved with her husband to New Orleans, where he had a cotton-brokering business. In the first years of her marriage, Chopin's life revolved around the social obligations she bore as the wife of a notable New Orleans businessman and the rearing of a large family. In 1879, however, Chopin found herself once again relocating, because of the failure of her husband's business. This time the family, which now included six children, settled in Cloutierville, in central Louisiana, where the Chopins managed a plantation store and a small farm belonging to Oscar's family. Although these were difficult years, the region would become the locale for many of Chopin's best short stories and novels.

On December 10, 1882, Oscar died unexpectedly from a fever. Chopin and her six children were left with surprisingly little financial security. At the time, the only alternative seemed to be to remain on the plantation and assume its management. Within a few years, Chopin had regained her financial standing, and in 1884 she returned to her mother's home in St. Louis. As she had in New Orleans, she attempted to follow the life expected of a socially prominent St. Louis widow, but in 1889 she turned to the writing career that would sustain her for the remainder of her

life. Chopin became a prolific author of poems, short stories, novels, literary criticism, and drama. Within her first decade as an author, she had written three novels (one, destroyed by the author, was never published), twenty poems, several essays of literary criticism, and almost one hundred short stories.

While publishing short stories in local magazines, Chopin wrote her first novel, *At Fault* (1890). Using the Southern plantation locale that she knew so well, this novel was conventional in style and, unlike her later works, sentimental rather than realistic, although it did address divorce and alcoholism, two controversial issues for the time. In spite of these topics, the novel received virtually no critical response.

Chopin continued to publish her short stories, and two volumes of her collected works soon appeared: *Bayou Folk* (1894) and *A Night in Acadie* (1897). A third collection, tentatively titled "A Vocation and a Voice," was never published in book form. Several of the published stories address the theme of women's lack of personal fulfillment under society's restrictive rules for women, and they present women characters who, like the author, were beginning to challenge such traditions. Chopin soon gained a reputation as a gifted author of short stories, but it was with the publication in 1899 of her masterpiece, *The Awakening*, that she reached the culmination of her theme of women's oppressed lives. Because this novel dealt openly with female sexuality and adultery, however, and because it presented a woman who refused, at all costs, to adhere to social restrictions, it received widespread condemnation from critics. The response of outrage was so pervasive that Chopin was socially ostracized in her own hometown. The novel was pulled from circulation, and it quickly went out of print until 1969 when Per Seyersted issued, in two volumes, *The Complete Works of Kate Chopin*. On August 22, 1904, five years after the controversy that arose from the publication of *The Awakening*, Kate Chopin died.

Analysis

In the late nineteenth century, when Kate Chopin "came of age" as a writer, the prevailing attitude was still that woman's proper sphere was in the home and that her purpose in life should be to nurture and encourage her husband and her children. She was to be, as Chopin termed it in *The Awakening*, "a mother woman." Such definitions reveal the dependent, relational nature of woman's existence in nineteenth century America: With no individual identity, a woman was notable only in relation to another—a father, a husband, a child. These restrictions were not only socially condoned but also legally enforced, since women, in spite of suffrage movements, did not have the right to the vote and thus were allowed no effective voice in political or civic matters. Against this background of oppression, Chopin chose to air these issues in her fiction and to challenge the validity of such assumptions about "true womanhood."

Chopin understood that if a woman were always seen in the context of another, relationships became the central issue of her life and, consequently, of her self-identity. Thus Chopin's fiction consistently explores the interactions between men and women in their daily lives. Many authors of this period were exploring similar issues. In

McTeague (1899), for example, Frank Norris studied the consequences for a marriage when the possibility of great wealth is interjected between the wife and husband. Chopin's fiction, like Norris', is often described as realistic or naturalistic; however, she was interested not in the exceptional stituation but in the consequences of everyday interactions between spouses. Further, she extended her analysis of relationships to include the exchanges, intimate as well as public, between men and women who were not married and, perhaps most radically, to the interactions among women that enforced or negated woman's traditional role in society.

Chopin explored these themes of social conflict throughout her writing career, beginning with her earliest published short stories, such as "A Point at Issue" and "Wiser Than a God." Both stories, published in 1889, concern a woman's sense of stifled existence in a marriage relationship; the women were required to subordinate their lives to their husbands'. In the latter story, the protagonist decides to risk the insecurity of pursuing a career in music rather than opt for the social and financial security of marriage. She achieves success both in her artistry and in her personal life when she becomes a renowned pianist and develops a love relationship with her music instructor. As Chopin continued to explore the complexities of relationships between the sexes, however, she moved away from such romantic reconciliations and began to depict the incongruity for women of attaining public and private happiness in a culture that did not condone a woman's sense of individuality.

It would be erroneous to suggest that Chopin's themes related only to gender; she was equally concerned with racial relationships in the United States at the end of the century. In her regional fiction, she realistically portrayed the diversity of American peoples and integrated Creole and Cajun lives and dialects into her literature. Many of her short stories were set in the Louisiana bayou country in which she had lived for so many years; the stories' realistic details and vivid descriptive passages suggest the keenness of her observations of the people and customs of that region. These stories also acknowledge the class structures within groups as well as within American society as a whole: She depicts aristocratic Creoles and enslaved blacks, impoverished Acadians and upper-class Caucasians. As Chopin's stories spread far beyond the local periodicals in which she first published to magazines with national circulations, her readers were allowed to explore vicariously a seemingly alien region but at the same time were exposed to the universal human dilemmas that her characters confronted.

As Chopin recognized, the maltreatment of minority peoples and the disparate economic and legal status of many Americans, and all women, were political issues. Although women did not have the power to enact legislation or elect their representatives, they were not spared the consequences of political machinations. Chopin recognized that one way in which women could comment politically, however, was through art. Thus, many of her women characters seek careers in the arts—especially in music and painting—and, certainly, her own career as an artist stood as testament to women's ability to combine intellectual and artistic activism. In one of Chopin's most frequently anthologized short stories, "Désirée's Baby," she brings together many of her themes: miscegenation, women's restricted lives, the injustice of social codes. Désirée is happy in her married life; after the birth of her child, however, her husband suspects that she has hidden from him that fact that she has some "black blood" in her. The tragic consequences of miscegenation are rendered through Désirée's decision to drown herself and her child, an act that symbolizes the limited options for women who found themselves without male support (emotional as well as financial) and with no means to establish their own independence. As with many of her best short stories, this story's central, provocative concept would be brought to its culmination in the tragic conclusion to *The Awakening*.

Because of the controversial nature of Chopin's themes, especially as they culminated in the publication of *The Awakening*, her work was largely ignored for many years. She was relegated to the status of a "local color" short story writer, and she received limited critical consideration at best; however, when Per Seyersted published the two-volume *Complete Works of Kate Chopin* in 1969, a new era in Chopin scholarship began. Her works have been analyzed in terms of the influence of American and French writers, including Nathaniel Hawthorne, Walt Whitman, and Guy de Maupassant; her ability to work within numerous genres (essay, poetry, short story, and novel) and numerous literary modes (romanticism, realism, and naturalism) attest her original and influential artistry. With the advent in the 1970's of feminist critical interest in Chopin's writings, her work began to receive deserved attention for its feminist ideals and cultural critiques of patriarchal American society. She is recognized as a major literary artist whose psychological and sociopolitical insights have helped to reshape an understanding of her writings—and of the society within which they were created.

THE AWAKENING

First published: 1899
Type of work: Novel

In the repressive world of nineteenth century America, a woman awakens to a sense of herself but can find no socially acceptable means of self-fulfillment.

The Awakening begins with a seemingly insignificant event: Léonce Pontellier is disturbed while trying to read the newspaper. As Chopin reveals, however, this incident reflects the patriarchal structure of most late nineteenth century American marriages in which the entire family's activities are inordinately structured around the husband's wishes and moods, no matter how trivial.

The life-style of the Creole summer resort of Grand Isle is relaxed. It is this setting that allows Léonce's wife, Edna, to confront her dissatisfactions with her marriage and to explore first her awakened sexuality through the attentions of Robert LeBrun and then the subsequent desires for an alternative life-style that this awakening creates. While they are at Grand Isle, Léonce has no objections to Robert's flirtations; indeed, he seems indifferent to the developing intimacy between Edna and Robert. When the family returns to New Orleans, however, Léonce assumes that Edna will return to her duties of being a supportive wife.

Edna has awakened, however tentatively, to the excitement of personal liberty, and she discovers within herself a growing desire to control her own life. She has within her social circle two role models for women's lives: the beautiful Madame Ratignolle, "a faultless Madonna," who dedicates her life to her husband and children and who is, therefore, honored by everyone in the community; and Mademoiselle Reisz, a single woman who has dedicated her life to her music but who, therefore, is distinctly a social outcast and whose life seems stale and isolated. Not surprisingly, neither alternative appeals to Edna's growing excitement about the prospect of personal freedom.

Each woman counsels Edna on the decisions she is about to make: Madame Ratignolle asserts that Edna must place her children's needs before her own. Mademoiselle Reisz, though cautiously encouraging Edna, also notes that an artist must possess a courageous soul; she adds, "The bird that would soar above the level plain of tradition and prejudice must have strong wings." Each woman's advice represents societal truths. If Edna chooses to remain a traditional woman, her children and her husband must come before her own needs; if she seeks new avenues of self-fulfillment, however, she must recognize that she will be confronting tempest-like winds of controversy that will lead to social banishment.

At first, Edna believes that she can reject traditional wisdom and weather the brunt of conventional reactions. In spite of warnings, she becomes involved with the infamous Alcée Arobin, and she eventually moves into a home of her own. Yet, as the designation for her new residence—the pigeon house—suggests, Edna has not escaped the trappings of her marriage; she has only exchanged them for an illusion of freedom. Although she begins to paint and finds some success in selling her creations, Edna discovers that independence and art alone cannot fulfill her. Her sexuality has been awakened, and she does not want to confine herself to the sterility of an existence like Mademoiselle Reisz's.

If Edna's awareness of options for women has changed, society's perspective has not. Edna finds herself unable to escape the numerous demands and desires of her old and new lives: Though she is able to leave her husband, she cannot escape her maternal status, and her new independence is quickly separating her from old friends without affording her new support systems. She is unable to attain success as an artist and at the same time satisfy the sensual self that she has discovered. In the face of these irreconcilable realities, Edna returns to Grand Isle.

The conclusion of *The Awakening* has created interpretive controversies since its first publication and remains a point of debate among scholars. Some critics see Edna's final swim out into the ocean as one more instance of her capricious behavior; they believe that her death is an accident. Most critics, however, recognize Edna's act as a conscious recognition of the inescapable limitations of her life that continue to stifle her creative and sensual endeavors. That Chopin intended the ending to be ambiguous is indicated in the shifting allusions that surround Edna's final act: a broken-winged bird falls to the water, suggesting that Edna has been unable to withstand the social prejudices that Mademoiselle Reisz had warned her against. Yet as Edna contemplates her movement into the water, she removes all of her clothing, freeing herself of the symbols of society and suggesting that it is her awakened self that is preserved in this final act. By forcing the reader to consider these shifting perspectives, Chopin also forces the reader to confront the causes behind Edna's inability to find personal fulfillment; the oppressive nature of nineteenth century America is symbolized in the waves that wash over Edna as she enters the water. It is only by swimming far beyond the boundaries of the shore that she finally escapes and finds freedom. The tragedy is that this is the only kind of freedom a woman such as Edna could find in her society.

THE STORY OF AN HOUR

First published: 1894
Type of work: Short story

A woman with heart trouble dies not when she hears of her husband's death but when she discovers that he is still alive.

In "The Story of an Hour," the fact that Mrs. Mallard is "afflicted with a heart trouble" becomes an ironic reality, for Mrs. Mallard's "heart trouble" in the beginning of the story is that she feels emotionally thwarted in her marriage. When her husband is believed to have been killed in a train accident, her friends notify her cautiously, assuming she will be devastated. The news, however, brings her tears of release rather than of grief. She is enlivened by her new situation and symbolically insists that all the doors of the house be opened. When Brently Mallard suddenly returns home, however, Mrs. Mallard's death is both literal and symbolic—in one hour, her freedom has been won and lost. For Chopin, Mrs. Mallard represents the numerous women who silently bear the feelings of being trapped in unhappy marriages but whose escapes could be ephemeral at best.

THE STORM

First published: 1969
Type of work: Short story

Although a married woman spontaneously commits adultery, she responds not with shame but with joy at her sexual awakening and continued love for her husband.

Written only six months after the publication of *The Awakening*, "The Storm" continues Chopin's confrontation with the theme of women's sexuality and the complexities of the married state. In this five-part short story, the narrative structure allows Chopin to present varying perspectives on a single situation as a means of suggesting that "reality" is, at best, relative. The situation is simple enough: Calixta's husband, Bobinôt, and her son, Bibi, are in town when a storm hits; alone at home, Calixta is about to shut the windows and doors against the storm when her former lover, Alcée Laballière, rides into the yard seeking shelter. While the storm rages, Calixta and Alcée renew their passionate feelings for one another; their desire finally leads them into making love. When the storm abates, Alcée departs and Calixta welcomes her family back home. The story concludes, "So the storm passed and every one was happy."

Like all Chopin's best fiction, "The Storm" does not offer pat moral truisms; indeed, the shocking element of this story's conclusion is that the retribution one might expect for the act of adultery never comes. In section 2, the crucial love scene is played out against ironic allusions to Christian symbolism: the Assumption, an immaculate dove, a lily, and the passion. Chopin offers a moral tale in which a woman's sexual experience is not condemned but celebrated and in which she uses that experience not to abandon her family but to accept them with a renewed sense of commitment. Unlike *The Awakening*, "The Storm" allows a woman to gain personal fulfillment and to remain happily married. As in most naturalistic fiction, morality—like reality—is relative.

Summary

Kate Chopin revealed through her artistry the realities of many women's stifled lives and the oppression of often-overlooked minority groups such as the Creoles and Cajuns. Yet Chopin also depicted the beauty of these people's lifestyle in the Louisiana bayou region and the power of individuals to shape their own lives. Through lyrical depictions of natural settings, Chopin compared the powers of nature to the potential for human self-empowerment.

Bibliography

Bloom, Harold. *Kate Chopin.* New York: Chelsea House, 1987.

Ewell, Barbara. *Kate Chopin.* New York: Frederick Ungar, 1986.

Martin, Wendy. *New Essays on "The Awakening."* Cambridge, Mass.: Cambridge University Press, 1988.

Seyersted, Per. *Kate Chopin: A Critical Biography.* Baton Rouge: Louisiana State University Press, 1969.

Stein, Allen F. *After the Vows Were Spoken: Marriage in American Literary Realism.* Columbus: Ohio University Press, 1981.

Sharon M. Harris

JAMES FENIMORE COOPER

Born: Burlington, New Jersey
September 15, 1789
Died: Cooperstown, New York
September 14, 1851

Principal Literary Achievement

One of the nineteenth century's most popular storytellers, Cooper presented a simpler, idealized view of America's westward migration.

Biography

James Fenimore Cooper (the Fenimore was added to his name in 1826) was born on September 15, 1789, in Burlington, New Jersey. The twelfth of thirteen children born to William and Elizabeth (Fenimore) Cooper, James was only fourteen months old when his father moved the family to Cooperstown, a village he had founded on Otsego Lake, the source of the Susquehanna River and the model for Glimmerglass of the Leatherstocking Tales.

A descendant of English Quakers, William Cooper played a great part in the developing prosperity of the newly-settled area and enjoyed the fruits of his hard work. His popularity and wealth allowed James to enjoy many urban comforts during his childhood at Otsego Hall, a beautiful brick mansion. Elizabeth, who detested the frontier, introduced young James to cultural refinements that she had brought in from Albany, Philadelphia, and New York City. It was during these early years that James developed his lifelong love of the wilderness.

After a few years at a local academy, young James was sent in 1801 to a preparatory school in Albany run by the Reverend Thomas Ellison, an Episcopal clergyman. In 1803, thirteen-year-old James entered Yale College, only to be expelled two years later for playing pranks.

In 1806, Cooper's father sent him to sea as a common sailor, and later Cooper sailed the Mediterranean on a merchant ship. Two years later he was issued a midshipman's warrant in the U.S. Navy. His three years in the Navy made him an expert on naval warfare and provided the raw material for his sea novels.

His father was killed by a political opponent in 1809. Cooper inherited $50,000 and a portion of his father's $700,000 estate. In 1811, he resigned from the Navy

J. Fenimore Cooper

and married Susan Augusta De Lancey, the daughter of a wealthy and renowned family in Westchester County. After a few years of moving between Cooperstown and Westchester, the couple settled on De Lancey land in Scarsdale, where Cooper led the life of a gentleman farmer and pillar of the community. During this period, five daughters were born to the couple, but one of them died.

In 1819, Cooper became the head of the family after the death of the last of his five elder brothers. As a result of high living and speculation, most of the family fortune had been lost, and the estate taken charge of by Cooper was heavily in debt. On a dare from his wife he wrote *Precaution* (1820), a novel about English life that was very imitative of Jane Austen's work and not successful. It was published anonymously, a great deal of animosity having arisen between Cooper and the publisher over a rash of printer's errors.

In 1821 he published *The Spy*, a novel set in the revolutionary American colonies but endowed with the spirit of an English romance. The book went through three editions, was translated into several languages, and even adapted for the stage. Certainly Cooper was on his way to success. *The Spy* was quickly followed by *The Pioneers* (1823), the first of the Leatherstocking Tales. His fame was such that the novel sold three thousand copies on the first day. All was not well however; his son Fenimore died, and his household goods were seized to cover outstanding debts. Only his revenues from writing saved him from financial ruin.

A year later, again on a dare, he wrote *The Pilot* (1824), the first of eleven nautical tales he would produce over the next three decades. His experience in the Navy and with the whalers he had sailed on allowed him to challenge Sir Walter Scott's latest romance with a tale of the sea that was accurate (as Cooper claimed Scott's work was not) in its nautical detail. In 1826, he continued his explosion of writing with *The Last of The Mohicans* and, with his financial situation stabilized, sailed for Europe after a gala send-off by a host of celebrities and politicians, all eager to attest Cooper's talent. The trip to the Continent provided an education for the family, a chance for Cooper to improve his failing health, and an opportunity for the author to thwart the many pirated European editions of his works while ensuring that the authorized edition became more profitable. During the two years the family spent in Paris, Cooper was introduced into the high life of the international social set. He published *The Prairie* (1827) while there.

In 1828, the Cooper family left Paris for the grand tour of Europe, a trip that the prolific writer would chronicle in five books of European travels. Also in 1828, he published in London *Notions of the Americans*, a book intended to correct European views of the United States but found offensive by both British and American critics.

On his return to Paris in 1830, he became embroiled in French politics in an attempt to aid his old friend General Lafayette. In the following three years before he left Paris, he wrote three political novels about Europe. In addition, he published *A Letter of J. Fenimore Cooper to General Lafayette* (1831), a book on American finance that won for him disapproval at home for meddling in foreign affairs. Before returning to the United States he became embroiled in a transatlantic squabble with the New York press over a review of one of his novels that effectively damaged his reputation with the press, editors, and the public.

In 1833, Cooper returned to the United States and seclusion in Cooperstown. His reputation in decline, he yearned to live a life of privacy, but his next few years were spent in various controversies with neighbors over land and property rights. In 1838, he published *The American Democrat*, a defense of his political and social philosophy, and two novels, *Homeward Bound* and *Home as Found*. The next year he followed with the two-volume *The History of the Navy of the United States of America* (1839). His latest period of productivity saw him publish the last two novels in the Leatherstocking Tales, *The Pathfinder* (1840) and *The Deerslayer* (1841).

In 1842, he won judgments in two of the seemingly countless libel suits he filed against newspapers during the bitter later years of his career. The following year he edited *Ned Myers: Or, a Life Before the Mast*, the autobiography of a shipmate from his earlier merchant seaman days. Between 1845 and 1846 he published a fictional trilogy concerning the Anti-Rent Wars in New York State; in 1850 he published *The Ways of the Hour*, his last novel. James Fenimore Cooper died in Cooperstown on September 14, 1851.

Analysis

To appreciate Cooper's accomplishments, one must understand the literary and historical climate of the early nineteenth century United States. In the 1820's, American fiction was much scorned by the European literati. One British critic went so far as to ask sarcastically, "Who reads an American book?" Before Cooper's work, few people outside the United States had; after his widespread acceptance, many did.

A related and much-debated question often troubled early nineteenth century American writers: Was there sufficient material in the United States for a truly American book in terms of form and themes? Until Cooper, most American writers borrowed their subject matter and literary styles from Europe, especially the great English writers. Cooper proved that such imitation was not necessary. By utilizing American history—specifically the French and Indian War, the American Revolution, and the westward migration—he became a role model for the so-called Columbian Ideal. It might be said that in his thirty-two novels, he (along with Washington Irving) truly wrote the American literary declaration of independence. Moreover, by gaining international fame, Cooper proved that an American could make a living being a fulltime writer.

In 1850, for a new edition of the combined Natty Bumppo quintet, Cooper penned a preface to the Leatherstocking Tales that is absolutely indispensable in understanding his style and purpose. He labeled his five novels "romances," not realistic fiction. Since Mark Twain's stinging criticism in "Fenimore Cooper's Literary Offences," critics have pointed out that Natty Bumppo is as pure as a saint, his diction is often too poetic for a man not formally educated, and his adventures are marred by improbabilities and coincidences. Cooper, however, was self-admittedly writing romances, and in that form everything is subordinate to the book's didactic purpose.

As the author claims: "It is the privilege of all writers of fiction, more particularly when their works aspire to the elevation of romances, to present the *beau-idéal* of their characters to the reader." In other words, Natty Bumppo is not meant to be read as a mirror of any real person or persons, but instead as a moral paragon, a character who "possessed little of civilization but its highest principles."

In Natty Bumppo, Cooper also created a character whose life parallels the growth of the United States, a national hero in every sense of the term. The young Natty is a resourceful hunter living in the woods; just as the United States matured and cut its umbilical cord with its mother country, Natty must deal with the eighteenth century switchover to an agrarian economy, the westward expansion, and the creation of a civilized legal system. The five Leatherstocking Tales, then, constitute an elaborate initiation story, the favorite pattern in American literature. Natty begins in *The Deer-slayer* as a callow youth who must determine whether it is right under any circumstances to take another's life, and he dies in *The Prairie* having learned that justice and the march of civilization are inevitable. Along the way, he comes to an understanding of women and love in *The Pathfinder* and the necessity of the law in *The Pioneers*.

Of course, as a romancer, Cooper was primarily interested in Natty's code, his ethical system for living. Essentially, his hero embodies the spirit that formed America, a trait that would later be called rugged individualism. His code, though triangulated by the Christianity of the Moravian missionaries who reared him, the laws of civilization (as shown with their flaws and attributes in the characters of Judge Marmaduke Temple and Ishmael Bush), and Indian customs, is Natty's own creation. Natty is finally a rebel whose life is his own.

This is not to say that James Fenimore Cooper was wholly original. Although he did use the matter of America as his subject, his manner was often that of the English novelists, especially Sir Walter Scott. Admittedly, some of Cooper's novels justify his epithet "the American Scott" (in one novel, Cooper has the mounted Indians jousting like characters out of Scott's 1819 novel *Ivanhoe*). As Natty Bumppo journeys across the ever-expanding countryside, encountering America's heroic past with his faithful companion Chingachgook, Cooper's hero is not unlike Don Quixote and his squire; Cooper obviously read a great many historical, gothic, and sentimental romances.

Why were the Leatherstocking Tales so popular? As noted earlier, Cooper was able to adapt the popular English styles of the moment while tapping into America's archetypal character. He gave the American public what it desperately wanted—a national hero whose history was theirs. In his aforementioned preface, Cooper predicted that if anything of his would endure, it was "the series of the Leatherstocking Tales." Another reason Natty Bumppo came alive was that he kept popping up; he was America's first popular recurring character in fiction. Even Cooper's desultory writing for the series worked to his hero's popularity, for after his death in 1827 (in *The Prairie*), two more Natty Bumppo novels were published, suggesting a certain immortality to Leatherstocking. With his didactic purpose, Cooper mined that religious vein that ran deep throughout early American history. The majority of the colonies were founded for religious reasons, especially in the Northeast, the country's literary center during the early nineteenth century. Since its beginning, America had been described as the New Eden, an image pattern Cooper continued. As Natty Bumppo, for example, wrestled with the Christian ideal "Thou shalt not kill" in *The Deerslayer*, he was everyone in the United States trying to translate abstract Christianity into a practical moral system. Natty Bumppo became one of the first examples of the American Adam—the basically good man in American literature.

Even today, some of these reasons endure. If nothing else, Cooper knew how to tell an adventure story, with his clear-cut good guys fighting against obvious evil. Cooper provided a link in the popular writing chain that went from the Indian captivity narratives of writers such as John Smith through him to the dime novels and Western tales. In fact, Natty Bumppo—with his eye for detail, his ability to track friend or foe, his survival skills, and his refusal to follow the conventional mores of civilization blindly—is the prototype for that distinctly twentieth century American literary invention, the hardboiled private investigator.

Despite critics such as Twain, then, Natty Bumppo remains one of the true originals of American fiction. Paradoxically, he is simultaneously the antihero and the mythic representation of American national character. For readers today and for Cooper's contemporary audience, The Leatherstocking Tales presents a simpler version of American history, a nostalgic journey to a more innocent time where gray had not begun to shade good and evil, and a place where individual action is not only possible but is also rewarded.

THE DEERSLAYER

First published: 1841
Type of work: Novel

In his first warpath, a young man comes to terms with taking a life as well as with the corrupt values of civilization and the Indians.

The Deerslayer, a prequel (the last published but the first in the hero's chronology of The Leatherstocking Tales), introduces Cooper's youthful protagonist. Natty Bumppo, a young man in his twenties, has come to Glimmerglass (Otsego Lake) in upper New York state to help his blood brother, Chingachgook, rescue the Delaware chieftain's betrothed, Hist. In this idealized natural world of the 1740's, these two noble savages must formulate a practical morality somewhere between abstract Christianity, Indian savagery, and corrupt civilization's values.

The Deerslayer is a good example of a romance, that nineteenth century version of the novel. In order to ensure its didactic intent, the romance presents a simpler view of reality. Characters are clearly good or bad. Natty, Chingachgook, and Hist are basically heroic representatives of civilization and the Indian world, while Hurry

Harry, Tom Hutter, and Rivenoak are their evil counterparts. Similarly, the Delaware Indians are good; the Hurons, bad. Natty is the moral paragon, refusing, for example, to take scalps, as Hurry Harry and Tom Hutter do. Appropriate for a man caught between ethical codes. Natty is part white and part Indian as well as part Christian and part savage.

The highly episodic plot follows the popular novel pattern of pursuit, capture, and escape. There are no surprising reversals, and the ending is pure *deus ex machina*, complete with the King's troops arriving for a nick-of-time rescue. Good defeats evil, though the happy ending is partially diluted by Natty turning down the charms of the beautiful Judith Hutter. Cooper even foreshadows the familiar Western theme by suggesting that ultimate happiness is found in nature and that the male-male bond (Natty and Chingachgook) is often greater than that between a man and a woman. As with most romances, the setting is manipulated. Cooper conveniently narrows and deepens the river when it suits his needs, and the idyllic Glimmerglass, in reflecting the heavens, becomes the ultimate moral symbol in the book.

The human moral model is Natty himself, and the novel's focus is implied in its subtitle, *The First Warpath*. Known at the beginning of the story as the Deerslayer, Natty is given a morally symbolic sobriquet by the enemy. Natty is forced to kill a Huron/Mingo when he spots a rifle leveled at him, and as he gives water to his dying foe, the Indian nicknames him Hawkeye. It is this eye of the hawk that allows Natty to pierce the false philosophies of both civilization and savagery to see God's law applicable in the wilderness. The ultimate test of Natty's superior ethical code comes when Rivenoak, the Huron chieftain, grants Natty, after having captured him, a day's furlough to act as a go-between for the Indians and the white settlers. Though it means certain death, at the end of the twenty-four hours Deerslayer returns as promised to his captors.

Cooper's success in *The Deerslayer*, then, comes from his successful blending of several popular English novel types and setting the action in America. He borrowed some of the techniques of Sir Walter Scott and adapted the historical romance; Cooper also used elements of the Gothic novel. In the middle of Glimmerglass lies the Hutter castle as well as a damsel in distress. Hutter himself has a dark secret, a hidden crime (he was once a pirate). Realists, including Mark Twain, have criticized the book's language and the implausibility of some action (especially the Indian attack on the ark), but in truth it is the very simplicity of the tale, from its characters and plot to its moral stance, that has provided its lasting appeal.

THE LAST OF THE MOHICANS
First published: 1826
Type of work: Novel

For the United States to reach its potential, men of all races must work together and try to understand one another.

The Last of the Mohicans, both the second of the Leatherstocking Tales published and the second in the hero's chronology, picks up the story of Natty Bumppo and Chingachgook in 1757, some fourteen years later. In this, the most popular of the quintet, the scene has moved northward in New York state to Glen Falls and Lake George. The plot centers on a true historical event, the British surrender of Fort William Henry to the French and their massacre by Indians immediately following. Cooper explores the themes of miscegenation, the expansion of America, and the decline of the Indians' power and domain. Although the story is based on fact, Cooper fictionally realigns the Indians' true historical alliances to the French and English in order to suit his storytelling needs.

The Last of the Mohicans is first and foremost an adventure story in the tradition of the historical romance. The Delaware are the good Indians: the Huron/Mingoes, treacherous. While Natty, now known as Hawkeye, and Chingachgook remain the moral center of the book, Cooper offers two new creations in his good-evil dichotomy. Uncas, the son of Chingachgook and Hist (who has died), is a living example of physical and moral perfection. Ironically (and appropriately) Uncas' death occurs because he violates his noble instincts and rushes ahead of the rescue party to save Cora, the woman he loves. Like *The Deerslayer, The Last of the Mohicans* is a pursuit, capture, and escape story. Hawkeye spends most of the novel either trying to free Alice and Cora Munro from their Indian captors or trying to escape the evil Huron, Magua. Magua, probably Cooper's best-drawn villain, is portrayed as a once-noble savage whose life has been corrupted by civilization, especially its particular form of poison, alcohol. Magua is actually motivated in his pursuit of Cora Munro by his desire for revenge—he was whipped for showing up for work drunk, and he lost his natural honor. Cooper also borrows from the sentimental romance with the many disguises donned, the comic relief in the form of the crazy Yankee psalmodist (David Gamut), the courtship of Major Heyward and Alice Munro, and the pathos-filled ending, wherein the Indians suggest that the spirits of Cora and Uncas will be united in the afterlife.

Perhaps the main thrust of the novel is the usually overlooked national theme that is often hidden by the critics' overconcern for the more controversial miscegenation theme. Leslie Fiedler and D. H. Lawrence, in particular, have suggested that the secret theme of *The Last of the Mohicans* is interracial marriage. Indeed, the Indian Uncas and the mulatto Cora are undeniably attracted to each other, and even Hawkeye considers this match in the context of its naturalness. In a larger sense, though, the novel has a sociological purpose. Having represented the three main races in America at the time, Cooper seems to be asking whether the country as melting pot is a viable concept. By killing off both Uncas and Cora, Cooper perhaps indicates that the creation of a new race may be a utopian dream. Just as important, however, he states that the whites and Indians can live in harmony—shown by the prototypal relationship of Hawkeye and Chingachgook. Their friendship endures, foreshadowing future literary endeavors such as Herman Melville's *Moby-Dick* (1851) and Mark Twain's *The Adventures of Huckleberry Finn* (1884).

Ultimately, *The Last of the Mohicans* should be read as more than simply a boy's book or an adventure story. The novel is Cooper's prediction of the United States' future success and, just as important, the passing of the Indian. As Tamenund, the old chief, remarks at the conclusion, "The pale-faces are masters of the earth, and the time of the redmen has not yet come again."

THE PATHFINDER

First published: 1840
Type of work: Novel

There comes a time when a man must choose between conventional courses of action and his true calling.

The Pathfinder, the fourth of the Leatherstocking Tales published (the third in Deerslayer's chronology), is an often-overlooked part of the quintet; its protagonist seems to act more like a Sir Walter Scott hero than the famed frontiersman. Deerslayer, now called Pathfinder, is two years older than in *The Last of the Mohicans* and, with Chingachgook, has moved westward to Lake Ontario. This novel also has a historical backdrop, taking place during the French and Indian War. The focus of the novel, however, is not on the usual pursuit, capture, and escape plot, the westward migration, or even the simplistic moral view (good Indian against bad Indian, Deerslayer against bad white men), but on Deerslayer himself as a vulnerable human being.

With his interest in the person of Deerslayer, Cooper is content to reuse many elements from *The Last of the Mohicans*. Once again Cooper disregards fact and has the Iroquois (Mingoes, to Deerslayer), historically allied with the British, as the villains. Mabel Dunham, like the Munro sisters, is a woman traveling through the wilderness to visit her British military father at a fort. The Indian guide—Arrowhead, in this case—is, like Magua, a treacherous Iroquois leading the group into an ambush. Also like Magua, he falls for a white woman. This party also runs into Deerslayer and Chingachgook, who again save them. Instead of Uncas, a red paragon of natural virtue and strength, Cooper offers a white version, frontiersman and seaman Jasper Western, who emerges as second best to Deerslayer. Instead of multiple land battles with the Indians being the major action, Cooper draws on his sea background to show Jasper as a master mariner. There is also an element of espionage, as Lt. Muir turns out to be a French spy.

Some critics have labeled the Leatherstocking Tales fictional hagiography and referred to Deerslayer as a secular saint. The real strength of *The Pathfinder* is that it deeply humanizes Deerslayer to such a degree that Cooper could never decide whether he thought this novel or *The Pioneers* was his finest. *The Pathfinder* is constructed around the familiar love triangle of the sentimental romance. Deerslayer is attracted to Mabel Dunham, the daughter of an old friend (who wants Deerslayer to marry his daughter). Mabel is attracted to, respectful of, and honored by Deerslayer's eventual proposal, but she in turn truly loves Jasper. Jasper returns this love, but he is best friends with Deerslayer. Ultimately Deerslayer realizes all these relationships and, knowing that Jasper is younger and more educated (and that Mabel truly loves the young man), bows out. There is a saintliness about Deerslayer when Mabel kneels before him for his blessing, but more important, there is also a full-blooded human being, a man vulnerable from the fact that he has considered love, marriage, and all that such a relationship entails.

At the end of *The Pathfinder*, Deerslayer and Chingachgook set out westward once again. Though tempted by civilization and romantic love, Deerslayer remains true to his code, to his vocation. Jasper becomes a successful merchant, thus fulfilling the Horatio Alger aspect of the American Dream. Deerslayer, perhaps the last autonomous man, is less concerned with "things" and more with the original American Dream.

THE PIONEERS

First published: 1823
Type of work: Novel

In the clash between the communal agrarian economy and the individual freedom of the hunter, progress will be served.

The Pioneers, the first-published of the Leatherstocking Tales, but the fourth in Deerslayer's chronology, though containing some of the usual Scott influences, is essentially a mirror of American history. Deerslayer, now known as Leatherstocking, has advanced to his early seventies, and the action takes place in 1793 and 1794. The setting is Templeton, which Cooper identifies in his introduction to the novel as representing the customs and inhabitants of early Cooperstown. Although the plot concerns the Temple-Effingham feud (complete with Romeo and Juliet lovers, Oliver and Elizabeth), the novel's strength is its re-creation of daily scenes from late eighteenth century American life (such as lake fishing and a turkey shoot) and its central theme of economic change and the law.

Cooper's basic conflict is still between two differing ways of life, but this time they are not the Indian's and white man's. Templeton is a farming community that survives by cutting trees, planting crops, and turning hunting grounds into pastures. As such, it represents the new American agrarian economy. In order to prosper, it has to create a new system of laws, as, in a larger sense, the United States must. The living embodiment of this emerging system is Judge Marmaduke Temple (modeled upon Cooper's father), who, though fallible, tries to apply these laws equitably. Built into the system are its flaws, including political patronage and the sometime destruction of personal freedom for the greater good. Opposing this new system is that of Leatherstocking. As the hunter, he lives in a cabin on the outskirts of the community. He represents the old America whose day, at least in the East, is slowly fading. Cooper uses the time passage in the novel—from opening on Christmas Eve to closing in autumn—to suggest such change is both natural and inevitable.

The community conflicts with the hunter. Without the time to learn to kill game with a single ball, the farmers have resorted to mass slaughter and waste of the forest denizens. In April, the Templetonians shoot thousands of pigeons that are migrating in sky-darkening flocks. In counterpoint, Leatherstocking kills the one bird he needs and calls the townsfolk sinful for their waste. In chapters 23 and 24, the townspeople employ a huge seine to catch fish, also slaughtering more than they need. Leatherstocking spears only one fish. Ultimately Leatherstocking kills a deer, but the townspeople have created a new law that claims he is out of season. When they come to arrest him, he forcibly opposes them. Leatherstocking is convicted of assault and battery as well as resisting a search warrant. For this crime he is imprisoned and fined, but not before burning his long-standing home so that it cannot be entered against his will.

Another theme-reinforcing subplot involves Leatherstocking's oldest companion: Chingachgook has become Christianized by civilization and given the name John Mohegan. Civilization has also provided him with alcohol and turned him into a hopeless drunk. Finally, after donning his battle garb, the once-noble chief is killed by an exploding canister of gunpowder—another product of civilization. *The Pioneers*, then, concludes with the only possible resolution of the major conflict. Unable to triumph against inevitable progress, Leatherstocking heads westward to the new frontier; the future belongs to the Templetons and Judge Temple. *The Pioneers* has been called the first genuinely American novel.

THE PRAIRIE

First published: 1827
Type of work: Novel

As civilization and justice come to the frontier, the day of the hunter and pure individual freedom are over.

The Prairie, the third-published novel of the Leatherstocking Tales but the last in Deerslayer's chronology, depicts Leatherstocking, now known as the trapper or the old man, in his final days. The setting is the edge of the Great Plains, the time is 1805, and the hero is in his eighties—his maturation and movement have paralleled that of the United States. Although Cooper himself never traveled to his locale, he researched his subject well. Unfortunately, with the familiar good against bad Indians dichotomy (this time the Pawnee and Sioux, respectively), wise sayings that sound more like platitudes, and the stock romance pursuit, capture, and escape plot, Natty Bumppo's exit is not as memorable as his entrance.

The Prairie offers Natty one last chance to return to his glory. Reduced in his last days to mere trapping, he has the opportunity to be a scout once again with the arrival of the Bush party of squatters. By way of continuity, Cooper also has Natty run into Captain Duncan Uncas Middleton, the grandson of Duncan Heyward and Alice Munro Heyward of *The Last of the Mohicans*; moreover, the Captain's middle name is that of Chingachgook's son. Much of this novel, though, reads like a rehash. The evil Sioux chieftain, Mahtoree, is a lesser copy of Magua (from *The Last of the Mohicans*, which Cooper had written the year before). The narrative is laden with tricks, some improbable and some clichéd. Dr. Obed Bat (like David Gamut) exists only to provide comic relief; the scholarly naturalist uses Latin names for everything, but he knows less about the frontier than Natty (and probably Natty's dog).

One of the true strengths of the novel is the character of Ishmael Bush. As patriarch of the Bush family, he is in charge of moving them West. Ironically, for a man in conflict with the law, Bush, when all the chase is over, must preside over a makeshift frontier court. He rules on white and Indian cases, doling out justice fairly even when it means sentencing his wife's brother to die. As *The Pioneers* suggests, justice eventually comes to the frontier.

The final days of Natty Bumppo, then, are a return to his roots. In the new frontier of the West he goes to live among the Indians—with the Pawnee and Hard-Heart, his adopted son. Although he is offered quarters in civilization, he chooses the freedom of nature. The legend concludes as Natty, knowing his time has passed, dies among the tribe, facing the setting sun.

Summary

In the Leatherstocking Tales, Cooper created one of the earliest, one of the most representative, and one of the best American heroes. Natty Bumppo, like young America, is an orphan who must forge his destiny on the edge of civilization. A moral man, he sorts through his Christian background, the mores of civilization, and the laws of the Indians to create his individual code of behavior.

Cooper brought this vision not only to the United States but also to the world. At a time when American literature was devalued, he offered hope by weaving a tapestry of America's own past and presenting it in a popular form, the romance, for all to see.

Bibliography

Dekker, George. *James Fenimore Cooper the Novelist*. London: Routledge & Kegan Paul, 1967.

Walker, Warren. *James Fenimore Cooper: An Introduction and Interpretation*. New York: Barnes & Noble Books, 1962.

_____, ed. *Leatherstocking and the Critics*. Chicago: Scott Foresman, 1965.

_____. *Plots and Characters in the Fiction of James Fenimore Cooper*. Hamden, Conn.: Archon Books, 1978.

Hal Charles

ROBERT CORMIER

Born: Leominster, Massachusetts
January 17, 1925

Principal Literary Achievement
Robert Cormier has contributed several of the most important works to the "new realism" genre of young adult fiction.

Biography
For a writer who has dealt with a number of extreme subjects—including death, the occult, and terrorism—Robert Cormier has lived a rather quiet and unassuming life. Born in Leominster, Massachusetts, into a large French-Canadian family, Cormier still lives in that small town some thirty miles from Boston. After a year at Fitchburg State College, he began work at a radio station in nearby Worcester before joining a newspaper, first in Worcester and then in Fitchburg in 1955. He worked for Fitchburg newspapers as a reporter, editor, and columnist, until he left to write full time in 1978; during that period, he won several awards for his stories and columns. ("John Fitch IV" was his pseudonym as a newspaper columnist.)

Throughout his adult life, Cormier has also been producing fiction. His stories have appeared in *Redbook*, *McCalls*, and other popular publications, and he has published a short story collection, *Eight Plus One* (1980), as well as three adult novels—*Now and at the Hour* (1960), *A Little Raw on Monday Mornings* (1963), and *Take Me Where the Good Times Are* (1965). His literary career dramatically changed in 1974, when his agent convinced Cormier that *The Chocolate War* was really a "young adult" title. Pantheon agreed, and the novel was an instant success. Since that date, Robert Cormier has become known primarily as a writer for young people. During his career, Cormier and his wife have reared four children and have maintained as normal a life in Leominster as a writer can manage in the United States. They have lived for years at the same Main Street address, and Cormier even listed his phone number in one of his novels. He has always remained accessible to his readers, and young people call and write him regularly to ask about his novels and his career as a novelist.

In many ways, Cormier is a very autobiographical writer. The settings of his novels resemble the Massachusetts locales near where he lives in Leominster in a number of significant details, and the action of his fiction often has a personal origin. *The Chocolate War*, for example, began in an incident during his son Peter's paro-

404

chial school chocolate sale; *Fade* (1988) retells much of Cormier's own French-Canadian family history and Roman Catholic background. Yet Cormier's novels are not really as autobiographical as they appear, for once his settings and characters have been established, what takes place in his fiction has a terrifying life of its own that ranges far beyond the rather mundane details of his own quiet life in Leominster.

Analysis

In 1974, when Cormier agreed to allow Pantheon to market *The Chocolate War* as a young adult novel, a little-known journalist who had been writing adult fiction for several decades became almost instantly one of the most popular and respected writers in the young adult field. This novel about a teenager fighting almost alone against the evil at a Catholic boys' school—and apparently losing—caused an immediate sensation and controversy. Cormier's novels since *The Chocolate War* have only confirmed this reputation and continued the extreme, often violent subjects of his fiction. *I Am the Cheese* (1977) is a mystery thriller about a young boy trying to learn his family history before the killers pursuing his parents and himself catch them all. *After the First Death* (1979) is a violent novel about terrorists taking over a schoolbus full of children. *The Bumblebee Flies Anyway* (1983) is a bleak depiction of a young boy trying to find out why he is in a hospital with terminally ill children. *Beyond the Chocolate War* (1985) continues some of the same themes of Cormier's first young adult novel, but it focuses on different characters. *Fade* concerns several generations of a family tragically gifted with the power of invisibility. Cormier has produced some of the most vivid and compelling works in the young adult field, but his subjects are often grim and his treatment rarely sentimental. Every three years or so, Cormier has contributed another important if unsettling work to the canon of young adult fiction.

Cormier's novels are all set in the same general location, in various urban, suburban, or rural locales in northeastern Massachusetts where he himself has lived all of his life. They are also linked by a careful formal technique. The point of view in each novel, for example, is usually multiple or complex and aids in the suspense that builds throughout the work. The language of the novels is not difficult for younger readers, but it is usually recognizable for its metaphorical intent (the religious symbolism in *The Chocolate War*, for example). Characterization is facile and at times two-dimensional, but the tense structure of each work keeps readers moving quickly. Cormier's novels highlight his unique central protagonists in their struggles with forces more powerful than themselves.

Cormier's novels resemble one another most significantly in these themes. All of his young adult works focus on an individual struggling to survive in a society dominated by evil and defined by violence. The individual has few chances against the system or the institution he or she faces but usually manages to bring meaning to these struggles for survival. (Most of Cormier's heroes are male, but Kate Forrester, the schoolbus driver who dies trying to save the children from the terrorists who hold them, is the real heroine of *After the First Death.*) In spite of the similarity of his subjects, Cormier's novels are hardly formulaic, and each one has its own special appeal. If each is somehow bleak or depressing, each is also compelling in its own way.

Cormier's novels are not didactic; his protagonists face their situations without benefit of authorial moralizing. Yet his heroes often leave readers with a real sense of courage: Young people, in the face of almost overwhelming odds, somehow manage to carve meaning out of their desperate lives. In a culture in which young people are often seen as soft or cynical, it is an inspiring model.

Cormier himself has said that his focus is on the individual versus the system. The institutions which represent this "system" change from novel to novel—from the Catholic prep school in *The Chocolate War* to the corrupt government agencies in *I Am the Cheese* to the impersonal hospital in *The Bumblebee Flies Anyway*—but the focus remains on often innocent individuals struggling against these evil agencies. In one sense, then, Cormier is a very political writer, for he is concerned with the power relationships among individuals and institutions and with the ways that those institutions (and the people who run them) misuse their power. The villains in his novels are not faceless institutions but the authoritarian individuals acting in their name (Brother Leon in *The Chocolate War*, Dr. Lakendorp in *The Bumblebee Flies Anyway*) without regard for individual human need.

Like many political novelists—and many other Roman Catholic writers—Cormier is at heart a moralist. He applauds those individuals (such as Jerry Renault in *The Chocolate War*) who stand up against the system and are martyred in their battles with it. Cormier's connections to Henry David Thoreau, Mark Twain, Ken Kesey, and other American writers in this tradition of social protest are clear.

Cormier's success as a writer can best be gauged by the number of awards he has garnered over the length of his career, both as a newpaperman and as a writer for young people. Most important, when *The Chocolate War* was first published in 1974, the American Library Association's *Booklist* journal gave the novel a black-bordered review, indicating an obituary for naïve optimism. Prior to this work, even the most realistic young adult novel had left its protagonists on an upbeat note. After *The Chocolate War*, the young adult novel was capable of true tragedy. More than any other single writer, Robert Cormier is responsible for having broadened the possibilities of this emergent young adult genre.

THE CHOCOLATE WAR

First published: 1974
Type of work: Novel

Jerry Renault learns much during his freshman year at a Catholic boys' school, both about being true to himself and about the forces that stand opposed to him gaining his own identity.

The Chocolate War is an unrelentingly bleak account of life in a Catholic boys' school, from its opening line ("They murdered him.") to the closing defeat of its young protagonist and the reascendancy of the school's evil forces. Yet the novel is also an important example of the realistic quality of much young adult fiction, and it is certainly Cormier's strongest effort in this field.

Set in a small New England city, the novel could take place in any urban academic setting—at least in any school where the pressures of grades, conformity, and repressed sexuality create an unhealthy and competitive atmosphere. Trinity is a school where privacy is nonexistent, where teachers intimidate students, and where students brutalize one another. Cormier's view of Trinity is singularly gloomy, but few readers would argue that it is totally unrealistic.

The story in this short, fast-paced novel is neither complex nor difficult. Jerry Renault is in his first year at Trinity and is trying to become a quarterback on the football team. He needs this success badly, for his mother has died the previous spring, and Jerry is living in an apartment with his father, who sleepwalks through his days. Jerry wants desperately to fit in, but a contrary impulse also motivates him. In his school locker, Jerry has a poster that shows

> a wide expanse of beach, a sweep of sky with a lone star glittering far away. A man walked on the beach, a small solitary figure in all that immensity. At the bottom of the poster, these words appeared—*Do I dare disturb the universe?* By Eliot, who wrote the Waste Land thing they were studying in English. Jerry wasn't sure of the poster's meaning. But it had moved him mysteriously.

In the course of *The Chocolate War*, Jerry will discover the full import of the poster's message.

Jerry accepts an "assignment," or school stunt, from the powerful Vigils secret society, to refuse to sell chocolates in the annual Trinity sale, but when the ten days of his prank are up, Jerry continues his rebellion, in protest now against the authoritarian tactics of Brother Leon, the acting headmaster, and against Jerry's own isolation at the school. He gains a new identity through his rebellion: "I'm Jerry Renault and I'm not going to sell the chocolates," he declares to Brother Leon and his homeroom. The Vigils, enlisted by Brother Leon, however, whip up school support for the chocolate sale and ensure that every student has sold his fifty boxes— everyone except Jerry. Emile Janza, a school bully who badly wants to get into The Vigils, gathers a gang of younger kids to beat up Jerry, and when Archie, the true leader of The Vigils, arranges a boxing match in front of the whole student body between Jerry and Janza, Jerry accepts. The fight has been arranged so that Jerry cannot win, and in fact the young hero loses the very individuality he had earlier gained in his protest. In the end, Jerry is being treated for a possible broken jaw and internal injuries, he is advising his friend Goober not to "disturb the universe," and The Vigils and Brother Leon are even more firmly in control of Trinity.

The meaning of *The Chocolate War* is complex and, for many readers, depressing—the makers of the 1989 film of the novel created a more upbeat ending—but it is an important novel for young people. As with any work of this complexity, there are a number of subthemes: loss, violence in its many forms, and power—how it is maintained in human society and the hatred and brutality that its misuse breeds. *The Chocolate War* is a novel of initiation in which the young protagonist, like the reader, learns a number of crucial lessons about the adult world—most of them negative.

Like all Cormier's novels, the central theme of *The Chocolate War* is the relation of the individual to society and the price one pays for conformity or (the other side of this theme) the greater sacrifices one must make in order to achieve one's individuality. Jerry's protest is not an easy decision, but he gains a new identity through his actions. What this idea becomes in the novel is the concept of being true to oneself, and standing up to the evil that one perceives in the world. The only character who is true to himself in the novel is Jerry—but at a terrible price. Goober tries to emulate Jerry, but, in a crucial test, caves in: when The Vigils make sure that a "50" is posted after his name in the auditorium, Goober does not have the courage to challenge it and tell the truth. The situation raises all kinds of questions, in the novel as in society: Which is more important, loyalty to oneself or to the group? Which takes more courage? What are the real consequences of conformity? How can evil be stopped except by heroic individual human action?

In the end, Jerry did disturb the universe: He stood up against peer pressure and teacher intimidation to protest the evil he recognized in the world, and his example is a model of courage in the face of cowardice and conformity. He is, in the true sense of the word, a martyr, and, if he gives in at the end, that action only makes the novel more psychologically realistic and his earlier courage even greater. The evil at Trinity can only be defeated if more people speak up. The power of *The Chocolate War* is this social and psychological realism: The novel shows what happens to someone who stands up for his rights in a totalitarian system.

There are several stylistic elements that distinguish *The Chocolate War* from most young adult novels and that distinguish Robert Cormier himself as a writer. For one thing, the multiple point of view in the novel is much more complex than in most adolescent novels. The language in the book is not very difficult, but the honesty and maturity with which its subjects are treated may cause problems for some readers. The students here act like real teenagers—they swear and frequently think about sex. Irony plays a large part in the novel, and readers will notice the double meanings that pepper *The Chocolate War*. There is also a rich religious symbolism. On one level, Jerry is a Christ figure who tries to change the world but is metaphorically crucified in the attempt. Trinity is a religious school, but evil predominates there over any kind of Christian love or spirit. The complex religious symbolism in the novel underscores the themes that Cormier is raising: Must someone else be crucified before the evil is banished? Finally, as a powerful psychological novel, *The Chocolate War*'s characterization is realistic if unremittingly grim.

I AM THE CHEESE

First published: 1977
Type of work: Novel

In this mystery thriller, a young boy tries to determine his family's history and fate.

Cormier's next novel, *I Am the Cheese*, was a departure from his first success in a number of ways—except that the fear at the heart of *The Chocolate War* had only intensified in the three years between the two young adult books to become the terror here. The multiple points of view of the first novel had become, by the second, a mosaic of perspectives that challenge the reader and build the tension in the novel until its very last word.

Even the innocuous opening of the novel—"I am riding the bicycle and I am on Route 31 in Monument, Massachusetts, on my way to Rutterburg, Vermont, and I'm pedaling furiously . . . "—raises mysteries: Who, the reader wonders, is riding, and why? The second chapter only adds to reader confusion, for it starts with a transcript of what appears to be a counseling session between the boy and a psychiatrist. Is Adam Farmer trying to recall his own lost history, or is his interrogator trying to get information from him?

What is slowly revealed, as Adam uncovers his past for the reader and for the mysterious Brint, is that his father had been a reporter for a small New York state newspaper who discovered evidence of government corruption and testified in Washington about what he knew. When attempts were made on his life, Anthony Delmonte joined a witness protection program, and he and his wife and small son (Paul) were given new names and identities and moved to Monument, Massachusetts. The new identities do not work, however (Grey, the government contact responsible for the family, is apparently a double agent); they are forced to flee Monument, and Adam's parents are killed. In the stunning shock of the last chapter, it is revealed that Adam/Paul's "furious" bike ride has only been around the grounds of a hospital where he himself is a patient, and where some malevolent and mysterious government agency has confined him, after murdering his parents, until they can decide what is to be done with him or (as the last paragraph reveals) "until termination procedures are approved."

This is no simplistic young adult work; rather, it is a thriller in which the reader is left hanging until the very end—and beyond, in fact, for there are several loose ends intentionally not tied up. Similarly, it is no didactic novel: If there is a lesson here, it is the same one as in many adult thrillers, to trust no one, not even—or especially not—the government. Like *The Chocolate War*, however, there is also the theme of the young innocent trying to establish his identity in a violent world where the authorities (government agents here, school officials in the earlier novel) are doing everything they can to destroy the will of the young protagonist. The novel was chosen one of the best books of the year for young readers by both the *New York Times Book Review* and the Young Adult Services Division of the American Library Association.

As with all Cormier titles, literary technique is prominent, and it facilitates meaning and power. The point of view and plot are both structured so that the tension of the novel is increased until the very last page. (The film that was made of the novel in 1983 only turned the suspense into confusion.) As in *The Chocolate War*, the literary language and imagery reinforce meaning. The title comes from the children's song, "The Farmer in the Dell." Adam is himself the "farmer," at least in one of his identities, but in the end he does "stand alone" like the cheese of the last line of the song.

THE BUMBLEBEE FLIES ANYWAY

First published: 1983
Type of work: Novel

Young Barney Snow tries to discover why he is in a hospital with terminally ill young people.

The Bumblebee Flies Anyway has another institutional setting (a hospital, as in *I Am the Cheese*), but there is perhaps a larger glimmer of hope, for the focus of the novel is on the meaning that the individual can make of his own life, in spite of overwhelming odds—in this case, imminent death.

As in *I Am the Cheese*, the tension is almost unbearable. Barney Snow is in "the Complex," his name for a hospital for the incurably ill, but he does not know why he is there, for he is clearly not ill. All he knows for certain is that he is part of an experiment, as are the other young patients around him, and is being administered drugs under the careful supervision of the person he calls "the Handyman," Dr. Lakendorp. The story of the novel is Barney's attempt to piece together his past and with it the reasons why he is there.

His story is also tied up with the lives of the other terminally ill patients in his ward, such as Mazzo, Billy, and others. Barney falls in love with Mazzo's sister, who comes to visit her twin brother but who uses Barney for her own ends, and the relationship actually provides some relief from the clinical depression of the setting. Barney is also fascinated with "the bumblebee," a wooden mock-up of a sports car that sits in a lot next to the hospital. When Barney finally locates the truth—that he is just as ill as all the other patients there and is a victim of medical experiments to make him forget his past, including his earlier hospitalization—he gets the car to the roof of the hospital and makes elaborate plans to give Mazzo one last ride. Mazzo dies in Barney's arms, however, and Barney lets the bumblebee fly off the roof empty, in the dramatic high point of the novel and in a conclusion that gives readers some release from the gloom that has preceded it. The flight of the car becomes Barney's transcendence from this life and from the pain and suffering that surround him.

Although *The Bumblebee Flies Anyway* resembles *I Am the Cheese* and *The Chocolate War* most in its bleak setting and mood, it also resembles them in its theme, the struggle of the individual to stay alive and to beat the system in even the most dire circumstances. In an institution which (under the guise of scientific experimentation to lessen suffering) is actually playing callously with human life, Barney Snow frees himself and perhaps others; he cannot beat death (as no one can), but he helps his friend Mazzo, and his own end is clearly brightened by what he has been able to accomplish. Like Randle P. McMurphy in Ken Kesey's *One Flew Over the Cuckoo's Nest* (1962), another novel about men trapped in inhuman institutions, Barney Snow leaves a heroic echo for readers.

Cormier's gift is his ability to sustain the tension, and reader interest, amidst subjects so morbid and themes so heavy. There are problems with the novel—with characterization, for example; Cassie never really comes alive for readers as she so clearly does for Barney, and Dr. Lakendorp (although he says, "We are not monsters here. We are human beings.") remains a monster instead of a human being throughout the book. Most of the elements in the novel, however, help to reinforce the powerful and poignant story. Like the most significant of contemporary adult titles, *The Bumblebee Flies Anyway* forces the reader to confront a number of significant problems, not only the issue of death, for example, but also the whole question of medical ethics.

FADE

First published: 1988
Type of work: Novel

The gift of becoming physically invisible is a curse to several generations of a New England family, as Paul Moreaux discovers.

Fade is possibly the blackest of Cormier's realist young adult novels, and there is some question whether it is a young adult work at all. Cormier seems to be aspiring to the popular adult genre (popular with teenagers, as well) presided over by such writers as Stephen King and V. C. Andrews. The sex, the violence, and, more than anything, the tone of this supernatural story raise questions about its appropriateness for the teenage audience.

The "summary" printed on the publishing information page (a common practice in young adult novels) only hints at the violence of the novel: "Paul Moreaux, the thirteen-year-old son of French-Canadian immigrants, inherits the ability to become invisible, but this power soon leads to death and destruction." The novel itself is broken into five uneven parts. In the first, Paul Moreaux narrates the story of his realization in 1938, at the age of thirteen, of his fateful power. Paul discovers, from his Uncle Adelard, that every generation of this fated family produces a member with the supernatural power to become invisible. The nomadic Adelard has it; now he identifies it in his nephew Paul. The power seems to be a teenager's fantasy come true: to be able to go into houses unseen and spy on lives. What Paul witnesses while in "the fade," however, hardly brings him joy: He sees only the evil, including his own, of which humans are capable, especially behind closed doors. In particular, he witnesses two sexual acts (cunnilingus and incest) and spies on and lusts after his own Aunt Rosanna.

The power of the first half of the novel lies not only in Paul's story of his new-found invisibility but also in the broader background of Paul's history. In no earlier Cormier novel has there been such a rich historical setting: the French-Canadian family struggling to survive in late 1930's America, the labor struggles of a de-pressed New England factory town, and the violent strike that ends the struggle. Paul sees personal evil in the fade, but in his normal self he witnesses the evil that socio-economic conditions produce.

The second half of the novel is much choppier. In the next segment, and in pres-ent fictional time, a young female cousin of Paul works with his literary agent in New York trying to determine if the manuscript fragment that is the first half of *Fade* is really the work of the famous "Paul Roget," the novelist who died at age forty-two in 1967. The third and fourth sections continue the manuscript, as Paul dis-covers who has the "fade" in the next generation and tracks him down. This is where the "death and destruction" begin, for the thirteen-year-old Ozzie Slater, the abandoned son of Paul's sister Rose, has become a psychopathic killer who is ter-rorizing the small Maine town where he lives. In the novel's final violent scene, the older fader must kill his successor.

What bothers some critics and reviewers of young adult fiction about this Cormier novel is more than its sex and violence. The sexuality in the first part is certainly adult, and is sickening to the young Paul. In the second half of the novel, the sex disappears and is replaced by grisly violence, in a supernatural story that rivals those of Stephen King and other practitioners of this adult genre. What is most bother-some is that there is no serious theme to balance the sex and violence; rather, the focus of the novel is on the effects themselves, and the author's aim seems to be to startle and frighten the reader. Many of the elements in the novel are autobiographi-cal (Cormier himself grew up in the same town in a French-Canadian family in the 1930's), but Cormier seems to be unable to find the lessons from his story that have been the strengths of all his earlier works. The simplest contrast is to *I Am the Cheese*, since both novels are suspenseful thrillers with violent endings. In the earlier work, however, Adam Farmer seemed to be trying to make sense of his past and to resist the forces threatening him in the present. Paul Moreaux's life, on the contrary, has no such inherent meaning (except perhaps how to deal with the "fade"), and the juxtaposition of the secondary plot in the present time mitigates what meaning there may be in his story.

Summary

Robert Cormier has become the premier novelist of young adult "new realism" in a few short years, and his half dozen works challenge readers with their grim, often violent subjects. He also offers important messages about the ability of the individual to battle the system. Until *Fade*, at least, Cormier's novels are distinguished by depressing subjects but transcendent themes, and his writing is characterized by tense stories that are full of literary language and multiple points of view that intensify their suspense. Few young adult writers can match Cormier in his ability to keep younger readers entranced in a story with an important message.

Bibliography

Campbell, Patricia J. *Presenting Robert Cormier*. Boston: Twayne, 1985.

Donelson, Kenneth L., and Alleen Pace Nilsen. *Literature for Today's Young Adults*. 3d ed. Glenview, Ill.: Scott, Foresman, 1989.

Ishandert, Sylvia Patterson. "Readers, Realism, and Robert Cormier." *Children's Literature* 15 (1987): 7-18.

Rees, David. *The Marble in the Water: Essays on Contemporary Writers for Children and Young Adults*. Boston: Horn, 1980.

Veglahn, Nancy. "The Bland Face of Evil in the Novels of Robert Cormier." *The Lion and the Unicorn: A Critical Journal of Children's Literature* 2 (June 12, 1988): 12-18.

David Peck

MAGILL'S
SURVEY
OF
AMERICAN
LITERATURE

GLOSSARY

Absurdism: A philosophical attitude underlining the alienation that humans experience in what absurdists see as a universe devoid of meaning; literature of the absurd often purposely lacks logic, coherence, and intelligibility.

Act: One of the major divisions of a play or opera; the typical number of acts in a play ranges from one to four.

Agrarianism: A movement of the 1920's and 1930's in which John Crowe Ransom, Allen Tate, Robert Penn Warren, and other Southern writers championed the agrarian society of their region against the industrialized society of the North.

Allegory: A literary mode in which a second level of meaning (wherein characters, events, and settings represent abstractions) is encoded within the narrative.

Alliteration: The repetition of consonant sounds focused at the beginning of syllables, as in: "Large *m*annered *m*otions of his *m*ythy *m*ind."

Allusion: A reference to a historical event or to another literary text that adds dimension or meaning to a literary work.

Alter ego: A character's other self—sometimes a double, sometimes another side of the character's personality, sometimes a dear and constant companion.

Ambiguity: The capacity of language to sustain multiple meanings; ambiguity can add to both the richness and the concentration of literary language.

Angst: A pervasive feeling of anxiety and depression, often associated with the moral and spiritual uncertainties of the twentieth century.

Antagonist: The major character or force in opposition to the protagonist or hero.

Antihero: A fictional figure who tries to define himself and to establish his own codes, or a protagonist who simply lacks traditional heroic qualities.

Apostrophe: A poetic device in which the speaker addresses either someone not physically present or something not physically capable of hearing the words addressed.

Aside: A short passage generally spoken by one dramatic character in an undertone, or directed to the audience, so as not to be heard by the other characters onstage.

Assonance: A term for the association of words with identical vowel sounds but different consonants; "stars," "arms," and "park," for example, all contain identical "a" (and "ar") sounds.

Atmosphere: The general mood or tone of a work; it is often associated with setting, but can also be established by action or dialogue.

Autobiography: A form of nonfiction writing in which the author narrates events of his or her own life.

Avant-garde: A term describing works intended to expand the conventions of a genre through the experimental treatment of form and/or content.

Bardic voice: A passionate poetic voice modeled after that of a bard, or tribal poet/singer, who composed lyric or epic poetry to honor a chief or recite tribal history.

***Bildungsroman*:** Sometimes called the "novel of education," the *Bildungsroman* focuses on the growth of a young protagonist who is learning about the world and finding his place in life; typical examples are James Joyce's *A Portrait of the Artist as a Young Man* (1916) and Thomas Wolfe's *Look Homeward, Angel* (1929).

Biography: Nonfiction that details the events of a particular individual's life.

Black humor: A general term of modern origin that refers to a form of "sick humor" that is intended to produce laughter out of the morbid and the taboo.

Blank verse: Lines of unrhymed iambic pentameter; it is a poetic form that allows much flexibility, and it has been used since the Elizabethan era.

Caesura: A pause or break in a poem; it is most commonly indicated by a punctuation mark such as a comma, dash, semicolon, or period.

Canon: A generally accepted list of literary works; it may refer to works by a single author or works in a genre. The literary canon often refers to the texts that are thought to belong on university reading lists.

Catharsis: A term from Aristotle's *Poetics* referring to the purgation of the spectators' emotions of pity and fear as aroused by the actions of the tragic hero.

Character: A personage appearing in any literary or dramatic work.

Chorus: An individual or group sometimes used in drama to comment on the action; the chorus was used extensively in classical Greek drama.

Classicism: A literary stance or value system consciously based on classical Greek and Roman literature; it generally denotes a cluster of values including formal discipline, restrained expression, reverence for tradition, and an objective rather than a subjective orientation.

Climax: The moment in a work of fiction or drama at which the action reaches its highest intensity and is resolved.

Comedy: A lighter form of drama that aims chiefly to amuse and that ends happily; comedic forms range from physical (slapstick) humor to subtle intellectual humor.

Comedy of manners: A type of drama which treats humorously, and often satirically, the behavior within an artificial, highly sophisticated society.

Comic relief: A humorous incident or scene in an otherwise serious or tragic work intended to release the reader's or audience's tensions through laughter without detracting from the serious material.

Conceit: One type of metaphor, the conceit is used for comparisons which are highly intellectualized. When T. S. Eliot, for example, says that winding streets are like a tedious argument of insidious intent, there is no clear connection between the two, so the reader must apply abstract logic to fill in the missing links.

Confessional poetry: Autobiographical poetry in which personal revelation provides a basis for the intellectual or theoretical study of moral, religious, or aesthetic concerns.

Conflation: The fusion of variant readings of a text into a composite whole.

Conflict: The struggle that develops as a result of the opposition between the protagonist and another person, the natural world, society, or some force within the self.

Connotation: A type of meaning that depends on the associative meanings of a word beyond its formal definition. (*See also* Denotation.)

Conventions: All those devices of stylization, compression, and selection that constitute the necessary differences between art and life.

Counterplot: A secondary action coincident with the major action of a fictional or dramatic work. The counterplot is generally a reflection on or variation of the main action and is strongly integrated into the whole of the work.

Couplet: Any two succeeding lines of poetry that rhyme.

Cubism: In literature, a style of poetry, such as that of E. E. Cummings and Archibald MacLeish, which first fragments an experience, then rearranges its elements into some new artistic entity.

Dactyl: A metrical foot in which a stressed syllable is followed by two unstressed syllables; an example of a dactyllic line is "After the pangs of a desperate lover."

Deconstruction: An extremely influential contemporary school of criticism based on the works of the French philosopher Jacques Derrida. Deconstruction treats literary works as unconscious reflections of the myths of Western culture; the primary myth is that there is a meaningful world which language signifies or represents. The Deconstructionist critic is often concerned with showing how a literary text tacitly subverts the very assumptions or myths on which it ostensibly rests.

Denotation: The explicit, formal definition of a word, exclusive of its implications and emotional associations. (*See also* Connotation.)

Denouement: Originally French, this word literally means "unknotting" or "untying" and is another term for the catastrophe or resolution of a dramatic action, the solution or clarification of a plot.

Detective story: In the so-called "classic" detective story, the focus is on a crime solved by a detective through interpretation of evidence and clever reasoning. Many modern practitioners of the genre, however, have deemphasized the puzzle-like qualities, stressing instead characterization, theme, and other elements of mainstream fiction.

Determinism: The belief that a person's actions are essentially determined by biological and environmental factors, with free will playing a negligible role. (*See also* Naturalism.)

Deus ex machina: Latin, meaning "god out of a machine." In the Greek theater, it referred to the use of a god lowered by means of a mechanism onto the stage to untangle the plot or save the hero. It has come to signify any artificial device for the easy resolution of dramatic difficulties.

Dialogue: Speech exchanged between characters or even, in a looser sense, the thoughts of a single character.

Dime novel: A type of inexpensive book very popular in the late nineteenth century that told a formulaic tale of war, adventure, or romance.

Domestic tragedy: A serious and usually realistic play with lower-class or middle-class characters and milieu, typically dealing with personal or domestic concerns.

Donnée: From the French verb meaning "to give," the term refers to the premise or the given set of circumstances from which the plot will proceed.

Drama: Any work designed to be represented on a stage by actors. More specifically, the term has come to signify a play of a serious nature and intent which may end either happily (comedy) or unhappily (tragedy).

Dramatic irony: A form of irony that most typically occurs when the spoken lines of a character are perceived by the audience to have a double meaning or when the audience knows more about a situation than the character knows.

Dramatic monologue: A poem in which the narrator addresses a silent persona whose presence greatly influences what the narrator tells the reader.

Dramatis personae: The characters in a play; often it refers to a printed list defining the characters and their relationships.

Dramaturgy: The composition of plays; the term is occasionally used to refer to the performance or acting of plays.

Dream vision: A poem presented as a dream in which the poet-dreamer envisions people and events that frequently have allegorical overtones.

Dualism: A theory that the universe is explicable in terms of two basic, conflicting entities, such as good and evil, mind and matter, or the physical and the spiritual.

Elegy: The elegy and pastoral elegy are distinguishable by their subject matter, not their form. The elegy is usually a long, rhymed, strophic poem whose subject is meditation upon death or a lamentable theme; the pastoral elegy uses a pastoral scene to sing of death or love.

Elizabethan: Of or referring to the reign of Queen Elizabeth I of England, lasting from 1558 to 1603, a period of important artistic achievements; William Shakespeare was an Elizabethan playwright.

End-stop: When a punctuated pause occurs at the end of a line of poetry, the line is said to be end-stopped.

Enjambment: When a line of poetry is not end-stopped and instead carries over to the next line, the line is said to be enjambed.

Epic: This term usually refers to a long narrative poem which presents the exploits of a central figure of high position; it is also used to designate a long novel that has the style or structure usually associated with an epic.

Epilogue: A closing section or speech at the end of a play or other literary work that makes some reflection on the preceding action.

Episodic narrative: A work that is held together primarily by a loose connection of self-sufficient episodes. Picaresque novels often have an episodic structure.

Epithalamion: A bridal song or poem, a genre deriving from the poets of antiquity.

Essay: A nonfiction work, usually short, that analyzes or interprets a particular subject or idea; it is often written from a personal point of view.

Existentialism: A philosophical and literary term for a group of attitudes surrounding the idea that existence precedes essence; according to Jean-Paul Sartre, "man is nothing else but what he makes himself." Existential literature exhibits an awareness of the absurdity of the universe and is preoccupied with the single ethical choice that determines the meaning of a person's existence.

Expressionism: A movement in the arts, especially in German painting, dominant in the decade following World War I; external reality is consciously distorted in order to portray the world as it is "viewed emotionally."

Fabulation: The act of lying to invent or tell a fable, sometimes used to designate the fable itself.

Fantastic: The fantastic has been defined as a genre that lies between the "uncanny" and the "marvelous." All three genres embody the familiar world but present an event that cannot be explained by the laws of the familiar world.

Farce: A play that evokes laughter through such low-comedy devices as physical humor, rough wit, and ridiculous and improbable situations and characters.

First person: A point of view in which the narrator of a story or poem addresses the reader directly, often using the pronoun "I," thereby allowing the reader direct access to the narrator's thoughts.

Flashback: A scene in a fictional or dramatic work depicting events that occurred at an earlier time.

Foot: A rhythmic unit of poetry consisting of two or three syllables grouped together; the most common foot in English is the iamb, composed of one unstressed syllable attached to one stressed syllable.

Foreshadowing: A device used to create suspense or dramatic irony by indicating through suggestion what will take place in the future.

Formalism: A school of literary criticism which particularly emphasizes the form of the work of art—that is, the type or genre to which it belongs.

Frame story: A story that provides a framework for another story (or stories) told within it.

Free verse: A poem that does not conform to such traditional conventions as meter or rhyme, and that does not establish any pattern within itself, is said to be a "free verse" poem.

Genre: A type or category of literature, such as tragedy, novel, memoir, poem, or essay; a genre has a particular set of conventions and expectations.

Genre fiction: Categories of popular fiction such as the mystery, the romance, and the Western; although the term can be used in a neutral sense, "genre fiction" is often used dismissively to refer to fiction in which the writer is bound by more or less rigid conventions.

Gothic novel: A form of fiction developed in the eighteenth century that focuses on horror and the supernatural.

Grotesque: Characterized by a breakup of the everyday world by mysterious forces, the form differs from fantasy in that the reader is not sure whether to react with humor or with horror.

Half rhyme. *See* Slant rhyme.

Hamartia. *See* Tragic flaw.

Harlem Renaissance: A flowering of black American writing, in all literary genres, in the 1930's and 1940's.

Hero/Heroine: The most important character in a drama or other literary work. Popularly, the term has come to refer to a character who possesses extraordinary prowess or virtue, but as a technical term it simply indicates the central participant in a dramatic action. (*See also* Protagonist.)

Heroic couplet: A pair of rhyming iambic pentameter lines traditionally used in epic poetry; a heroic couplet often serves as a self-contained witticism or pithy observation.

Historical novel: A novel that depicts past events, usually public in nature, and that features real as well as fictional people; the relationship between fiction and history in the form varies greatly depending on the author.

Hubris: Excessive pride, the characteristic in tragic heroes such as Oedipus, Doctor Faustus, and Macbeth that leads them to transgress moral codes or ignore warnings. (*See also* Tragic flaw.)

Humanism: A man-centered rather than god-centered view of the universe that usually stresses reason, restraint, and human values; in the Renaissance, humanism devoted itself to the revival of the life, thought, language, and literature of ancient Greece and Rome.

Hyperbole: The use of gross exaggeration for rhetorical effect, based upon the assumption that the reader will not respond to the exaggeration literally.

Iamb: The basic metric foot of the English language, the iamb associates one unstressed syllable with one stressed syllable. The line "So long as men can breathe or eyes can see" is composed of five iambs (a form called iambic pentameter).

Imagery: The simulation of sensory perception through figurative language; imagery can be controlled to create emotional or intellectual effects.

Imagism: A school of poetry prominent in Great Britain and North America between 1909 and 1918. The objectives of Imagism were accurate description, objective presentation, concentration and economy, new rhythms, freedom of choice in subject matter, and suggestion rather than explanation.

Interior monologue: The speech of a character designed to introduce the reader directly to the character's internal life; it differs from other monologues in that it attempts to reproduce thought before logical organization is imposed upon it.

Irony: An effect that occurs when a writer's or a character's real meaning is different from (and frequently opposite to) his or her apparent meaning. (*See also* Dramatic irony.)

Jazz Age: The 1920's, a period of prosperity, sweeping social change, frequent excess, and youthful rebellion, for which F. Scott Fitzgerald is the acknowledged spokesman.

Künstlerroman: An apprenticeship novel in which the protagonist, a young artist, faces the conflicts of growing up and coming to understand the purpose of his life and art.

Leitmotif: The repetition in a work of literature of a word, phrase, or image which serves to establish the tone or otherwise unify the piece.

Line: A rhythmical unit within a poem between the foot and the poem's larger structural units; the words or feet in a line are usually in a single row.

Lyric poetry: Poetry that is generally short, adaptable to metrical variation, and personal in theme; it may explore deeply personal feelings about life.

Magical realism: Imaginary or fantastic scenes and occurrences presented in a meticulously realistic style.

Melodrama: A play in which characters are clearly either virtuous or evil and are pitted against one another in suspenseful, often sensational situations.

Memoir: A piece of autobiographical writing which emphasizes important events in which the author has participated and prominent people whom the author has known.

Metafiction: Fiction that manifests a reflexive tendency and shows a consciousness of itself as an artificial creation; such terms as "postmodernist fiction," "antifiction," and "surfiction" also refer to this type of fiction.

Metaphor: A figure of speech in which two different things are identified with each other, as in the T. S. Eliot line, "The whole earth is our hospital"; the term is also widely used to identify many kinds of analogies.

Metaphysical poetry: A type of poetry that stresses the intellectual over the emotional; it is marked by irony, paradox, and striking comparisons of dissimilar things, the latter frequently being farfetched to the point of eccentricity.

Meter: The rhythmic pattern of language when it is formed into lines of poetry; when the rhythm of language is organized and regulated so as to affect the meaning and emotional response to the words, the rhythm has been refined into meter.

Mise-en-scène: The staging of a drama, including scenery, costumes, movable furniture (properties), and, by extension, the positions (blocking) and gestures of the actors.

Mock-heroic style: A form of burlesque in which a trivial subject is absurdly elevated through use of the meter, diction, and familiar devices of the epic poem.

Modernism: An international movement in the arts which began in the early years of the twentieth century; modernism in general was characterized by its international idiom, by its interest in cultures distant in space or time, by its emphasis on formal experimentation, and by its sense of dislocation and radical change.

Monologue: An extended speech by one character in a drama. If the character is alone onstage, unheard by other characters, the monologue is more specifically referred to as a soliloquy.

Musical comedy: A theatrical form mingling song, dance, and spoken dialogue which was developed in the United States in the twentieth century; it was derived from vaudeville and operetta.

Myth: Anonymous traditional stories dealing with basic human concepts and fundamentally opposing principles; a myth is often constructed as a story that tells of supposedly historical events.

Narrator: The character who recounts the story in a work of fiction.

Naturalism: The application of the principles of scientific determinism to fiction. Although it usually refers more to the choice of subject matter than to technical conventions, conventions associated with the movement center on the author's attempt to be precise and objective in description and detail, regardless of whether the events described are sordid or shocking. (*See also* Determinism.)

Neoclassicism: The type of classicism that dominated English literature from the Restoration to the late eighteenth century. Modeling itself on the literature of ancient Greece and Rome, neoclassicism exalts the virtues of proportion, unity, harmony, grace, decorum, taste, manners, and restraint; it values realism and reason.

New Criticism: A reaction against the "old criticism" that either saw art as self-expression, applied extrinsic criteria of morality and value, or gave credence to the professed intentions of the author. The New Criticism regards a work of art as an autonomous object, a self-contained universe. It holds that a close reading of literary texts will reveal their meanings and the complexities of their verbal texture as well as the oppositions and tensions balanced in the text.

New journalism: Writing that largely abandons the traditional objectivity of journalism in order to express the subjective response of the observer.

Nonfiction novel: A novel such as Truman Capote's *In Cold Blood*, which, though taking actual people and events as its subject matter, uses fictional techniques to develop the narrative.

Novel: A long fictional form that is generally concerned with individual characterization and with presenting a social world and a detailed environment.

Novel of ideas: A novel in which the characters, plot, and dialogue serve to develop some controlling idea or to present the clash of ideas.

Novel of manners: The classic example of the form might be the novels of Jane Austen, wherein the customs and conventions of a social group of a particular time and place are realistically, and often satirically, portrayed.

Novella, novelle, nouvelle, novelette: These terms usually refer to that form of fiction which is said to be longer than a short story and shorter than a novel; "novella" is the term usually used to refer to American works in this genre.

Ode: A lyric poem that treats a unified subject with elevated emotion and seriousness of purpose, usually ending with a satisfactory resolution.

Old Criticism: Criticism predating the New Criticism and bringing extrinsic criteria to bear on the analysis of literature as authorial self-expression (Romanticism), critical self-expression (Impressionism), or work that is dependent upon moral or ethical absolutes (new humanism).

Omniscient narration: A godlike point of view from which the narrator sees all and knows everything there is to know about the story and its characters.

One-act play: A short, unified dramatic work, the one-act play is usually quite limited in number of characters and scene changes; the action often revolves around a single incident or event.

Opera: A complex combination of various art forms, opera is a form of dramatic entertainment consisting of a play set to music.

Original Sin: A concept of the innate depravity of man's nature resulting from Adam's sin and fall from grace.

Paradox: A statement that initially seems to be illogical or self-contradictory yet eventually proves to embody a complex truth.

Parataxis: The placing of clauses or phrases in a series without the use of coordinating or subordinating terms.

Pathos: The quality in a character that evokes pity or sorrow from the observer.

Pentameter: A line of poetry consisting of five recognizable rhythmic units called feet.

Picaresque novel: A form of fiction that involves a central rogue figure, or picaro, who usually tells his own story. The plot structure is normally episodic, and the episodes usually focus on how the picaro lives by his wits.

Plot: The sequence of the occurrence of events in a dramatic action. A plot may be unified around a single action, but it may also consist of a series of disconnected incidents; it is then referred to as "episodic."

Poem: A unified composition that uses the rhythms and sounds of language, as well as devices such as metaphor, to communicate emotions and experiences to the reader or hearer.

Point of view: The perspective from which a story is presented to the reader. In simplest terms, it refers to whether narration is first-person (directly addressed to the reader as if told by one involved in the narrative) or third-person (usually a more objective, distanced perspective).

Postmodernism: The term is loosely applied to various artistic movements which have followed so-called high modernism, represented by such giants as James Joyce and Pablo Picasso. The term is frequently applied to the works of writers (such as Thomas Pynchon and John Barth) who exhibit a self-conscious awareness of their predecessors as well as a reflexive treatment of fictional form.

Prose poem: A type of poem, usually less than a page in length, that appears on the page like prose; there is great stylistic and thematic variety within the genre.

Protagonist: Originally, in the Greek drama, the "first actor," who played the leading role. The term has come to signify the most important character in a drama or story. It is not unusual for there to be more than one protagonist in a work. (*See also* Hero/Heroine.)

Psychoanalytic theory: A tremendously influential theory of the unconscious developed by Sigmund Freud, it divides the human psyche into three components—the id, the ego, and the superego. In this theory, the psyche represses instinctual and sexual desires, and channels (sublimates) those desires into socially acceptable behavior.

Psychological novel: A form of fiction in which character, especially the inner life of characters, is the primary focus. The form has characterized much of the work of James Joyce, Virginia Woolf, and William Faulkner.

Psychological realism: A type of realism that tries to reproduce the complex psychological motivations behind human behavior; writers in the late nineteenth and early twentieth centuries were particularly influenced by Sigmund Freud's theories. (*See also* Psychoanalytic theory.)

Pun: A pun occurs when words which have similar pronunciations have entirely different meanings; a pun can establish a connection between two meanings or contexts that the reader would not ordinarily make. The result may be a striking connection or simply a humorously accidental connection.

Quatrain: Any four-line stanza is a quatrain; other than the couplet, the quatrain is the most common type of stanza.

Rationalism: A system of thought which seeks truth through the exercise of reason rather than by means of emotional response or revelation.

Realism: A literary technique in which the primary convention is to render an illusion of fidelity to external reality. Realism is often identified as the primary method of the novel form; the realist movement in the late nineteenth century coincided with the full development of the novel form.

Regional novel: Any novel in which the character of a given geographical region plays a decisive role; the Southern United States, for example, has fostered a strong regional tradition.

Representationalism: An approach to drama that seeks to create the illusion of reality onstage through realistic characters, situations, and settings.

Revue: A theatrical production, typically consisting of sketches, song, and dance, which often comments satirically upon personalities and events of the day; generally there is no plot involved.

Rhyme: A full rhyme comprises two or more words that have the same vowel sound and that end with the same consonant sound: "Hat" and "cat" is a full rhyme, as is "laughter" and "after." Rhyme is also used more broadly as a term for any correspondence in sound between syllables in poetry. (*See also* Slant rhyme.)

Rhyme scheme: Poems which establish a pattern of rhyme have a "rhyme scheme," designated by lowercase letters; the rhyme scheme of ottava rima, for example, is abababcc. Traditional stanza forms are categorized by their rhyme scheme and base meter.

Roman à clef: A fiction wherein actual persons, often celebrities of some sort, are thinly disguised.

Romance: The romance usually differs from the novel form in that the focus is on symbolic events and representational characters rather than on "as-if-real" characters and events. Character is often highly stylized, serving as a function of the plot.

Romantic comedy: A play in which love is the central motive of the dramatic action. The term often refers to plays of the Elizabethan period, such as William Shakespeare's *As You Like It* and *A Midsummer Night's Dream*, but it has also been applied to any modern work that contains similar features.

Romanticism: A widespread cultural movement in the late-eighteenth and early-nineteenth centuries, Romanticism is frequently contrasted with classicism. The term generally suggests primitivism, an interest in folklore, a reverence for nature, a fascination with the demoniac and the macabre, and an assertion of the preeminence of the imagination.

Satire: Satire employs the comedic devices of wit, irony, and exaggeration to expose and condemn human folly, vice, and stupidity.

Scene: In drama, a division of action within an act (some plays are divided only into scenes instead of acts). Sometimes scene division indicates a change of setting or locale; sometimes it simply indicates the entrances and exits of characters.

Science fiction: Fiction in which real or imagined scientific developments or certain givens (such as physical laws, psychological principles, or social conditions) form the basis of an imaginative projection, frequently into the future.

Sentimental novel: A form of fiction popular in the eighteenth century in which emotionalism and optimism are the primary characteristics. The best-known examples are Samuel Richardson's *Pamela* (1740-1741) and Oliver Goldsmith's *The Vicar of Wakefield* (1766).

Sentimentalism: A term used to describe any emotional response that is excessive and disproportionate to its impetus or occasion. It also refers to the eighteenth century idea that human beings are essentially benevolent, devoid of Original Sin and basic depravity.

Setting: The time and place in which the action of a literary work happens. The term also applies to the physical elements of a theatrical production, such as scenery and properties.

Short story: A concise work of fiction, shorter than a novella, that is usually more concerned with mood, effect, or a single event than with plot or extensive characterization.

Simile: Loosely defined, a simile is a type of metaphor which signals a comparison by the use of the words "like" or "as." Shakespeare's line, "My mistress' eyes are nothing like the sun," establishes a comparison between the woman's eyes and the sun, and is a simile.

Slant rhyme: A slant rhyme, or half rhyme, occurs when words with identical consonants but different vowel sounds are associated; "fall" and "well," and "table" and "bauble" are slant rhymes.

Slapstick: Low comedy in which physical action (such as a kick in the rear, tripping, and knocking over people or objects) evokes laughter.

Social realism: A type of realism in which the social and economic conditions in which characters live figure prominently in their situations, actions, and outlooks.

Soliloquy: An extended speech delivered by a character alone onstage, unheard by other characters. Soliloquy is a form of monologue, and it typically reveals the intimate thoughts and emotions of the speaker.

Sonnet: A traditional poetic form that is almost always composed of fourteen lines of rhymed iambic pentameter; a turning point usually divides the poem into two parts, with the first part presenting a situation and the second part reflecting on it.

Southern Gothic: A term applied to the scenes of decay, incest, madness, and violence often found in the fiction of William Faulkner, Erskine Caldwell, and other Southern writers.

Speaker: The voice which speaks the words of a poem—sometimes a fictional character in an invented situation, sometimes the author speaking directly to the reader, sometimes the author speaking from behind the disguise of a persona.

Stanza: When lines of poetry are meant to be taken as a unit, and the unit recurs throughout the poem, that unit is called a stanza; a four-line unit is one common stanza.

Stream of consciousness: The depiction of the thought processes of a character, insofar as this is possible, without any mediating structures. The metaphor of consciousness as a "stream" suggests a rush of thoughts and images governed by free association rather than by strictly rational development; the term is often used loosely as a synonym for interior monologue.

Stress: When more emphasis is placed on one syllable in a line of poetry than on another syllable, that syllable is said to be stressed.

Subplot: A secondary action coincident with the main action of a fictional or dramatic work. A subplot may be a reflection upon the main action, but it may also be largely unrelated. (*See also* Counterplot.)

Surrealism: An approach to literature and art that startlingly combines seemingly incompatible elements; surrealist writing usually has a bizarre, dreamlike, or nightmarish quality.

Symbol: A literary symbol is an image that stands for something else; it may evoke a cluster of meanings rather than a single specific meaning.

Symbolism: A literary movement encompassing the work of a group of French writers in the latter half of the nineteenth century, a group that included Charles Baudelaire, Stéphane Mallarmé, and Paul Verlaine. According to Symbolism, there is a mystical correspondence between the natural and spiritual worlds.

Syntax: A linguistic term used to describe the study of the ways in which words are arranged sequentially to produce grammatical units such as phrases, clauses, and sentences.

Tableau: A silent, stationary grouping of performers in a theatrical performance.

Terza rima: A rhyming three-line stanza form in which the middle line of one stanza rhymes with the first line of the following stanza.

Tetrameter: A line of poetry consisting of four recognizable rhythmic units called feet.

Theater of the absurd: The general name given to plays that express a basic belief that life is illogical, irrational, formless, and contradictory and that man is without meaning or purpose. This perspective often leads to the abandonment of traditional theatrical forms and coherent dialogue.

Theme: Loosely defined as what a literary work means. The theme of W. B. Yeats's poem "Sailing to Byzantium," for example, might be interpreted as the failure of man's attempt to isolate himself within the world of art.

Thespian: Another term for an actor; also, of or relating to the theater. The word derives from Thespis, by tradition the first actor of the Greek theater.

Third person: Third-person narration is related from a point of view more distant from the story than first-person narration; the narrator is not an identifiable "I" persona. A third-person point of view may be limited or omniscient ("all-knowing").

Three unities. *See* Unities.

Tone: Tone usually refers to the dominant mood of a work. (*See also* Atmosphere.)

Tragedy: A form of drama that is serious in action and intent and that involves disastrous events and death; classical Greek drama observed specific guidelines for tragedy, but the term is now sometimes applied to a range of dramatic or fictional situations.

Tragic flaw: Also known as hamartia, it is the weakness or error in judgment in a tragic hero or protagonist that causes the character's downfall; it may proceed from ignorance or a moral fault. Excessive pride (hubris) is one traditional tragic flaw.

Travel literature: Writing which emphasizes the author's subjective response to places visited, especially faraway, exotic, and culturally different locales.

Trimeter: A line of poetry consisting of three recognizable rhythmic units called feet.

Trochee: One of the most common feet in English poetry, the trochee associates one stressed syllable with one unstressed syllable, as in the line, "Double, double, toil and trouble."

Unities: A set of rules for proper dramatic construction formulated by European Renaissance drama critics and derived from classical Greek concepts: A play should have no scenes or subplots irrelevant to the central action, should not cover a period of more than twenty-four hours, and should not occur in more than one place.

Verisimilitude: The attempt to have the readers of a literary work believe that it conforms to reality rather than to its own laws.

Verse: A generic term for poetry; verse also refers in a narrower sense to poetry that is humorous or merely superficial, as in "greeting-card verse."

Verse paragraph: A division within a poem that is created by logic or syntax rather than by form; verse paragraphs are important for determining the movement of a poem and the logical association between ideas.

Victorian novel: Although the Victorian period extended from 1837 to 1901, the term "Victorian novel" does not include works from the later decades of Queen Victoria's reign. The term loosely refers to the sprawling works of novelists such as Charles Dickens and William Makepeace Thackeray, which are characterized by a broad social canvas.

Villanelle: The villanelle is a French verse form assimilated by English prosody. It is usually composed of nineteen lines divided into five tercets and a quatrain, rhyming aba, bba, aba, aba, abaa.

Well-made play: A type of play constructed according to a nineteenth century French formula; the plot often revolves around a secret (revealed at the end) known only to some of the characters. Misunderstanding, suspense, and coincidence are among the devices used.

Western novel: The Western novel is defined by a relatively predictable combination of conventions and recurring themes. These predictable elements, familiar from television and film Westerns, differentiate the Western from historical novels and other works which may be set in the Old West.

Worldview: Frequently rendered as the German *weltanschauung*, it is a comprehensive set of beliefs or assumptions by means of which one interprets what goes on in the world.

LIST OF AUTHORS

LIST OF AUTHORS